EZEKIEL

EZEKIEL

by
John M Riddle

40 Beansburn, Kilmarnock, Scotland

ISBN-13: 978 1 914273 15 5

Copyright © 2020 by John Ritchie Ltd.
40 Beansburn, Kilmarnock, Scotland

www.ritchiechristianmedia.co.uk

All rights reserved. No part of this publication may be reproduced, stored in a retrievable system, or transmitted in any form or by any other means – electronic, mechanical, photocopy, recording or otherwise – without prior permission of the copyright owner.

Typeset by John Ritchie Ltd., Kilmarnock
Printed by 4edge Ltd., Essex

Contents

Preface	7
An Outline of the Book	11
Chapter 1	21
Chapter 2	33
Chapter 3	42
Chapter 4	53
Chapter 5	64
Chapter 6	72
Chapter 7	82
Chapter 8	92
Chapter 9	106
Chapter 10	115
Chapter 11	125
Chapter 12	134
Chapter 13	143
Chapter 14	154
Chapter 15	164
Chapter 16	173
Chapter 17	187
Chapter 18	198
Chapter 19	208
Chapter 20:1-44	218
Chapter 20:45 to 21:32	231

EZEKIEL

Chapter 22	243
Chapter 23	254
Chapter 24	266
Chapter 25	278
Chapter 26	290
Chapter 27	300
Chapter 28:1-19	313
Chapter 28:20-26	325
Chapter 29	333
Chapter 30	344
Chapter 31	355
Chapter 32	366
Chapter 33	376
Chapter 34	389
Chapter 35	400
Chapter 36:1-15	409
Chapter 36:16-38	418
Chapter 37	427
Chapter 38	439
Chapter 39	451
Chapter 40:1-4	465
Chapter 40:5-16	473
Chapter 40:17-47	480
Chapter 40:48 to 41:26	488
Chapter 42	502
Chapter 43	510
Chapter 44	524
Chapter 45	535
Chapter 46	547
Chapter 47	556
Chapter 48	566

Dedication

TO DEREK BISHOP

of Belmont Hall, Harrow, who went to be with the Lord on 12th January 2016, and whose encouragement led, not only to the Monday evening Ministry Meetings there on Ezekiel's prophecy, but to this book.

John Riddle
Cheshunt, Hertfordshire
November 2021

EZEKIEL

Preface

Unlike most previous publications in this series, this book is not the product of Bible Class discussions at Mill Lane Chapel. The notes on which the book is based were originally distributed to members of the assembly which meets at Belmont Hall, Harrow, West London. The distribution took place in connection with Monday evening meetings held there between October 2011 and October 2016.

With this in mind, I must take the opportunity to express my deep appreciation of the warm welcome extended to me by the believers at Belmont Hall during these meetings, something, let it be said, that I have enjoyed over many years and on many occasions, and continue to do so.

It has been nicely said of the 'big three' prophetic books in the Old Testament, that 'while Isaiah was the poet, and Jeremiah the preacher, Ezekiel was the artist'. Ezekiel certainly paints pictures of glowing colour and graphic detail. He was, moreover, an actor as well as an artist, for he was not only commanded to state his God-given parables, but to act them out in the presence of the people. The same quotation (not surprisingly) is also to be found in the preface to *Living with the Glory of the Lord* – an excellent book dealing with Ezekiel's prophecy, written by Malcolm Davis, and published by John Ritchie Ltd. Both Malcolm Davis and the present writer also heartily endorse the title (not to mention the contents!) of Charles Lee Feinberg's work, *The Prophecy of Ezekiel: the Glory of the LORD*.

During the course of my visits to Belmont Hall, Harrow, I was frequently accompanied by Mr. Ken Lloyd, late of Cheshunt and now 'at home with the Lord'. Rather than complaining about the traffic during the homeward journey, we 'chewed the cud', after which, in the comfort of his home, brother Ken checked not a few of the 'Ezekiel manuscripts'. The "memory of the just is blessed" (Prov. 10: 7).

EZEKIEL

As always, the friends at John Ritchie Ltd have been most helpful, and Mr. Fraser Munro must have spent a lot of time putting things right. My thanks to the whole team.

John Riddle
Cheshunt, Hertfordshire
November 2021.

EZEKIEL

AN OUTLINE OF THE BOOK

What immediately follows is exactly that - an outline. It does not purport to be an introduction to the book. Brief details of the time and place in which the prophecy was delivered to Ezekiel, together with even briefer details of the man himself, are given at the commencement of the prophecy (1: 1-3), and we will address these in our study of Chapter 1.

The prophecy of Ezekiel may be divided into four sections: *(1)* the ruin of Judah and Jerusalem (chs.1-24); *(2)* the retribution on surrounding nations (chs.25-32); *(3)* the restoration of Israel (chs.33-39); *(4)* the return of the glory of the Lord (chs.40-48).

Alternatively, it could be said that the book divides as follows: *(1)* Predictions before the siege of Jerusalem (chs.1-23). The commencement of the siege is recorded in Chapter 24 verses 1-2. Compare 2 Kings 25 verse 1: both passages refer to the ninth year and tenth month of King Zedekiah's reign. *(2)* Predictions largely during the siege of Jerusalem (chs.24-32): these are directed against Israel's neighbours. *(3)* Predictions after the siege of Jerusalem (chs.33-48).

However, for the purpose of these studies we will adopt the first of these two suggestions, which brings us to:

1) THE RUIN OF JUDAH AND JERUSALEM, Chapters 1-24

The first section of the prophecy may be divided as follows: *(a)* the commissioning of Ezekiel (1: 1 - 3: 15); *(b)* the coming judgment (3: 16 - 7: 27); *(c)* the contributory causes of judgment (8: 1 - 19: 14); *(d)* the consistency of national sin (20: 1 - 23: 49); *(e)* the commencement of hostilities (24: 1-27).

EZEKIEL

a) The commissioning of Ezekiel, 1: 1 - 3: 15

In this section the prophet tells us what he saw (1: 1-28), what he heard (2: 1-10), and where he went (3: 1-15).

- *What he saw, 1: 1-28.* "As I was among the captives by the river of Chebar, that the heavens were opened, and I *saw* visions of God" (1: 1).

- *What he heard, 2: 1-10.* "And the spirit entered into me when he spake unto me, and set me upon my feet, that I heard him that *spake* unto me" (2: 2).

- *Where he went, 3: 1: 15.* "Go speak unto *the house of Israel* ... get thee unto *the house of Israel* ... get thee to *them of the captivity*" (3: 1, 4, 11).

b) The coming judgment, 3: 16 - 7: 27

In this section, Ezekiel acts as a watchman (3: 17-21), and warns the people, already in exile, of coming judgment on Judah and Jerusalem. He warns the people visually (3: 22 - 5: 17) and verbally (6: 1 - 7: 27).

- *The warning visually, 3: 22 - 5: 17.* This involved five signs, of which the first, the confinement of Ezekiel to his own house, was evidently a picture of the confinement of God's people during the siege of the city. This served to introduce four further signs depicting *(i)* the commencement of the siege (4: 1-3); *(ii)* the cause of the siege (4: 4-8); *(iii)* the conditions during the siege (4: 9-17); *(iv)* the conclusion of the siege (5: 1-17).

- *The warning verbally, 6: 1 - 7: 27.* The first message (6: 1-14) was directed against "the mountains of Israel" (v.1) and stressed the *inevitability* of divine judgment, whereas the second message (7: 1-27) announced the *imminence* of divine judgment.

The commissioning of Ezekiel and the commencement of his ministry (chs.1-7) all took place in "the *fifth year* of king Jehoiachin's captivity" (1: 2).

c) The contributory causes, 8: 1 - 19: 14

In this section, Ezekiel gives the further reasons for coming judgment. They are described visually (8: 1 - 11: 25) and verbally (12: 1 - 19: 14). Put another way, the contributory causes to the coming judgment are highlighted

OUTLINE

in the vision given to Ezekiel (chs.8-11) and in the verbal messages given by Ezekiel (chs. 12-19).

The second phase of his ministry (chs.8-19) commenced with a *vision* of degrading idolatry in the temple at Jerusalem (chs. 8-11), which the prophet then relates to the exiles at Tel-abib (11: 25), followed by a series of *verbal* messages (chs.12-19), each introduced by the words, "The word of the LORD came unto me, saying ..." (12: 1; 12: 8; 12: 17; 12: 26; 13: 1; 14: 2; 14: 12; 15: 1; 16: 1; 17: 1; 17: 11; 18: 1). It seems likely that these messages were "uttered at short intervals, allowing time for each to produce its impression upon the people" (*Ellicott's Commentary*).

- *The reasons described visually, 8: 1 - 11: 25*. In this passage, Ezekiel describes Israel's idolatry (8: 1-18) resulting in discriminatory judgment (9: 1-11), destruction from God (10: 1-22), and depopulation and scattering (11: 1-25). The solemn message of these chapters is conveyed by the *vision* given *to* Ezekiel (chs. 8-11), which ends with the withdrawal of the glory of the Lord from the temple (11: 22-23).

- *The result described visibly, 12: 1-28.* In these verses, the coming siege and deportation is depicted in an acted parables.

- *The reasons given verbally, 13: 1 - 19: 14.* The 'verbal messages' may be summarised as follows: **(i)** pictures of coming judgment (ch.12); **(ii)** reasons for coming judgment (chs.13-17); **(iii)** objections to coming judgment (ch.18); **(iv)** lamentation over coming judgment (ch.19). The section ends with a lamentation over the failed princes and the consequent end of national life.

The pictures of coming judgment (ch.12) comprise two acted parables and two answers to objections. **The reasons for coming judgment** (ch.13-17) can be summarised as follows: **(i)** the untruthful prophets (ch.13); **(ii)** the unseen idolatry (ch.14); **(iii)** the useless vine (ch.15); **(iv)** the unfaithful wife (ch.16); **(v)** the unreliable promises (ch.17). **The objections to coming judgment** (ch.18) are examined and rejected. **The lamentation over coming judgment** (ch.19) brings the section to an end. This chapter commences and concludes with the words "a lamentation" (vv.1, 14).

This phase of Ezekiel's ministry took place in "the *sixth year*" of King Jehoiachin's captivity (8: 1).

d) The consistency of national sin, 20: 1 - 23: 49

Chapters 20-23, which highlight the reasons for coming judgment by laying bare the sin of Judah and Jerusalem, commence and conclude with a description of their rebellion against the Lord. In the first case, their rebellion is described in actual historical terms (Ch.20) and in the second in parabolic terms (Ch.23). In both cases, the Lord traces the rebellion of His people from the earliest days of nationhood – in Egypt. (See 20: 5-9; 23: 3).

Ezekiel's ministry in these chapters was delivered in the "***seventh year*** (that is, of king Jehoiachin's captivity), in the fifth month, the tenth day of the month" (20: 1). They are the last prophecies in the book before the fall of Jerusalem. At the time, Nebuchadnezzar was either about to leave Babylonia, or had actually commenced the march (21:18-22). Divine judgment, to be executed by the king of Babylon, was imminent: Amongst other things, Ezekiel Chapter 21 describes his advance on Jerusalem (vv.19-23). The days of Zedekiah, the "profane, wicked prince of Israel", were numbered. His day "***is come***, when iniquity shall have an end" (21: 25), and the theme of imminent judgment continues in Chapter 22: "Thus saith the Lord God, The city sheddeth blood in the midst of it, ***that her time may come***, and maketh idols against herself to defile herself. Thou art become guilty in thy blood that thou hast shed; and hast defiled thyself in thine idols which thou hast made; and thou hast caused ***thy days to draw near, and art come even unto thy years***" (22: 3-4). Chapter 23 deals with the history of God's people under the figure of two sisters: Aholah, representing the northern kingdom of Israel, and Aholibah, representing the southern kingdom of Judah. The two kingdoms are identified by their capital cities: "Thus were their names; Samaria is Aholah, and Jerusalem Aholibah" (v.4). The words "whoredom", "whoredoms" or "whoring" occur seventeen times in the passage.

e) The commencement of hostilities, 24: 1-27

This oracle is dated "in the ***ninth year***" of King Jehoiachin's captivity (24: 1). "Son of man, write thee the name of the day, even of this same day: the king of Babylon set himself against Jerusalem this same day" (24: 2).

The hour has come. Judgment is about to fall. With this chapter, we come to the climax of all that Ezekiel has been saying in previous chapters. The passage may be divided as follows: ***(1)*** the parable of the boiling pot (vv.1-14): "Utter a parable ... Set on a pot ... make it boil well" (vv.3, 5); *(2)* the sign of the bereaved prophet (vv.15-24): "I take away from thee the desire of thine eyes with a stroke ... at even my wife died ... Thus Ezekiel is unto you a sign" (vv.16, 18, 24); *(3)* the sign of the fulfilled prophecy (vv.25-27): "thou shalt speak, and be no more dumb: and thou shalt be a sign unto them" (v.27).

2) *THE RETRIBUTION ON SURROUNDING NATIONS, Chapters 25-32*

Since all the oracles in these chapters were delivered during or shortly after the siege of Jerusalem, we can reasonably conclude that they occur at this point in the book in view of their immediate context, that is, Chapter 24, in which Ezekiel was told to expect the arrival of the news of the fall of Jerusalem, and Chapter 33, in which the news actually arrived.

As C.L.Feinberg (*The Prophecy of Israel – The Glory of the Lord*) points out, the oracles in Chapter 25, against Ammon, Moab, Edom, and Philistia, "are to be dated soon after 586 BC (which was 'the eleventh year' of the captivity') because they presuppose the fall of Jerusalem", something which evidently delighted these neighbouring nations, particularly the Ammonites (v.6). The oracle against Tyre, including Zidon, is dated "the eleventh year" of the captivity (26: 1). The oracles against Egypt are dated "the tenth year, in the tenth month" of the captivity (29: 1), the "eleventh year, in the first month" (30: 20), "the eleventh year, in the third month" (31: 1), and "the twelfth year, in the twelfth month" (32: 1, 17). The reference to "the seven and twentieth year" (29: 17) looks totally out of place, but it is nothing of the sort! Leaving aside, for the time being, the reason for its inclusion, it is quite clear that it points, as do other chronological references, to the deliberate arrangement of these oracles. They are not given in chronological sequence, but rather in national sequence.

In studying this section of the prophecy, we should bear in mind the following: *(a)* the significance of the oracles; *(b)* the structure of the oracles; *(c)* the sequence of the oracles.

a) *The significance of the oracles*

Their inclusion emphasises *(i)* the Lord's concern for His people, despite their waywardness and sinfulness; *(ii)* the Lord's cognisance of the affairs of all nations; *(iii)* the Lord's law of sowing and reaping.

*i) **The Lord's concern for His people.*** In this connection, it should be noted that in the first four cases, at least, the nations are held responsible for their treatment of God's people, reminding us that He had said, "I will bless them that bless thee, and curse him that curseth thee" (Gen. 12: 3), and that "he that toucheth you toucheth the apple of his eye" (Zech. 2: 8).

It has been pointed out that it is highly unlikely that these messages were actually delivered to the nations concerned, and that they are placed here for the benefit of Israel.

*ii) **The Lord's cognisance of the affairs of all nations.*** He is not a tribal deity. He is "the Judge of all the earth" (Gen. 18: 25). All men are accountable to Him. He will judge all nations. The seven cases surveyed in these chapters are therefore of relevant interest: they allow us to see something of God's dealings with the nations at all times. We are not to think that these are isolated cases, for He remains in perfect control of the international situation: no nation is permitted to exceed the allotted place in His purposes or to avoid payment for its wickedness.

In the case of Tyre, which rejoiced in the overthrow of Jerusalem although not personally involved in the event (26: 2), judgment is pronounced on the city in view of her godless commercial pride and complete self-sufficiency. The pride and self-sufficiency of Egypt are similarly condemned.

*iii) **The Lord's law of sowing and reaping.*** The section illustrates Galatians 6 verse 7: "Be not deceived; God is not mocked: for whatsoever a man soweth, that shall he also reap". In this connection, we should notice that God does not deal with the nations in a purely arbitrary fashion, but advances adequate reasons for the severity of His judgments upon them. He pronounces His sentences with a full explanation in each case.

b) The structure of the oracles

The heart of the section lies in 28 verses 24-26: "And there shall be no more a pricking briar unto the house of Israel ... Thus saith the Lord God; When I shall have gathered the house of Israel from the people among whom they are scattered, and shall be sanctified in them in the sight of the heathen, then shall they dwell in their land that I have given to my servant Jacob ..." C.J.H.Wright (*The Message of Ezekiel, The Bible Speaks Today*) points out that this passage is preceded by ninety-seven verses of predictions against Ammon, Moab, Edom, Philistia and Tyre (25: 1 - 28: 23), and succeeded by ninety-seven verses of predictions against Egypt (29: 1 - 32: 33). This speaks for itself. As always, Israel lies at the centre of God's purposes for the world.

c) The sequence of the oracles

In the words of John B.Taylor (*Ezekiel, Tyndale Old Testament Commentaries*), "A further sign of editorial planning is the geographical pattern of the oracles". They begin "with Ammon (25: 1-7) to the north-east of Jerusalem, swinging southwards through Moab (25: 8-11) to Edom in the south-east (25:12-14), then round to Philistia in the west (25: 15-17), and finally going farther afield in a northerly direction to Tyre and Sidon (26: 1 - 28: 24), before ending up with the distant major power, Egypt, in the south (29: 1 – 32: 32)".

The omission of Babylon calls for comment. Some see "Babylon as standing apart from the other nations, inasmuch as it was the instrument of God's punishment upon Israel", whilst others go further and regard "the Babylonian invaders as being the instruments of judgment upon all the nations mentioned here, as well as on Israel" (John B.Taylor).

3) THE RESTORATION OF ISRAEL, Chapters 33-39

With Chapter 33, having again contested the charge, "the way of the Lord is not equal" (vv.17, 20), news is brought to Ezekiel of Jerusalem's capture. The prophecy now reflects a distinct change of theme. Chapters 34-39 anticipate in glowing terms, the restoration of the nation. Chapter 36 verse 11 indicates the blessing of these coming days: "I ... will do better unto you than at your beginnings".

The third section of the book, dealing with the restoration of Israel, may be summarised as follows:

i) **The restoration of the monarchy, 34: 1 - 35: 15.** This section comprises *(i)* the past failure of the kings (34: 1-10); *(ii)* the prospective blessing for Israel (34: 11-31); *(iii)* the perpetual desolation of Edom (35: 1-15). Israel will enjoy the reign and care of a shepherd-king, and be totally free from the threat of occupation by her neighbours.

ii) **The restoration of the land, 36: 1-15.** "But ye, O mountains of Israel, ye shall shoot forth your branches, and yield your fruit to my people of Israel; for they are at hand to come" (36: 8).

iii) **The restoration of the people, 36: 16-38.** This section comprises *(i)* the restoration of the people to **the land** (vv.16-24); *(ii)* the regeneration of the people by **the Lord** (vv.25-38).

iv) **The restoration of national life, 37: 1-14.** "Behold, O my people, I will open your graves" (v. 12), "and bring you into the land of Israel. And ye shall know that I am the LORD, when I have opened your graves, O my people, and brought you up out of your graves, and shall put my Spirit in you, and ye shall live, and I shall place you in your own land: then shall ye know that I the LORD have spoken it, and performed it, saith the LORD" (37: 12-14).

v) **The restoration of national unity, 37: 15-28.** "Thus saith the Lord GOD; Behold, I will take the stick of Joseph, which is in the hand of Ephraim, and the tribes of Israel his fellows, and will put them with him, even with the stick of Judah, and make them one stick, and they shall be one in mine hand" (37: 19).

vii) **The restoration of national security, 38: 1 - 39: 29.** The book of Ezekiel commences with a successful invasion: God did not deliver His people from the Babylonian armies. But in these chapters, a colossal invasion from "the north parts" (38: 15; 39: 2) is summarily judged on "the mountains of Israel" (39: 4).

4) THE RETURN OF THE GLORY OF THE LORD, Chapters 40-48

The glory of the Lord, last seen standing "upon the mountain which is on the east side of the city" (11: 23), returns "from the way of the east ... came into the house by the way of the gate whose prospect is toward the east... and, behold, the glory of the LORD filled the house" (43: 1-5). The book closes with the words, "and the name of the city from that day shall be, The LORD is there" (48: 35).

These chapters deal with three aspects of the millennial kingdom: *(a)* the millennial temple (40: 1 - 42: 20); *(b)* the millennial worship (43: 1 - 46: 24); *(c)* the millennial land (47: 1 - 48: 35).

OUTLINE

a) The millennial temple, 40: 1 - 42: 20

This speaks for itself. Ezekiel was told, "Son of man, behold with thine eyes, and hear with thine ears, and set thine heart upon all that I shall shew thee; for to the intent that I might shew them unto thee art thou brought hither: declare all that thou seest to the house of Israel" (40: 4).

These chapters cover: *(i)* temple courts and entrances (40: 5-47); *(ii)* the temple and its buildings (40: 48 - 41: 1-26); *(iii)* the priests' quarters (42: 1-14); *(iv)* the encircling wall (42: 15-20).

b) The millennial worship; 43: 1 - 46: 24

Ezekiel, the artist, draws a magnificent picture: "Behold, the glory of the God of Israel came from the way of the east: and his voice was like a noise of many waters: and the earth shined with his glory ... And the glory of the LORD came into the house by the way of the gate whose prospect is toward the east" (43: 2, 4).

These chapters deal with the following: *(i)* the advent of the glory of the Lord (43: 1-12); *(ii)* the altar of worship (43: 13-27); *(iii)* the approach to God (44: 1-31); *(iv)* the allocation of land (45: 1-8); *(v)* the application at the time (45: 9-12); *(vi)* the appointed offerings (45: 13 - 46: 24).

c) The millennial land, 47: 1 - 48: 35

These chapters may be summarised as follows: *(i)* Israel's millennial river (47: 1-12); *(ii)* Israel's national borders (47: 13-23); *(iii)* Israel's northern sub-divisions (48: 1-7); *(iv)* Israel's holy central area (48: 8-22); *(v)* Israel's southern sub-divisions (48: 23-29); *(vi)* Israel's millennial city (48: 30-35).

Addendum

It will be of interest, and, hopefully, provoke further study, to note some contrasts between the earlier and later chapters.

i) The book **begins** with the glory of God (1: 28), and **ends** with the glory of God (43: 2-3, "And, behold, the glory of the God of Israel came from the way of the east ... and the visions were like the vision that I saw by the river

Chebar"). "The glory of the LORD" is a key phrase in the book. (Note ... the following references: 1: 28; 3: 12, 23; 8: 4; 9: 3; 10: 4, 18, 19; 11: 22, 23; 43: 2, 4, 5; 44: 4.)

This reminds us that "the Lord of glory" (1 Cor. 2: 8; James 2: 1) came into the world, but like the glory in Ezekiel 11 verse 23, He left the temple, saying as He did so, "Ye shall not see me henceforth, till ye shall say, Blessed is he that cometh in the name of the Lord" (Matt. 23: 39), and went to the Mount of Olives (Matt. 24 1-3). Ezekiel describes His return: "And, behold, the glory of the God of Israel came from the way of the east ... and, behold, the glory of the LORD filled the house" (Ezek. 43: 1-5). Israel **will** see Him again, with the language of Psalm 118 verse 26 on their lips: "Blessed be he that cometh in the name of the LORD".

ii) The book **begins** with the prediction of a successful invasion (chs. 4-5), and **ends** with the prediction of an unsuccessful invasion (chs. 38-39).

iii) The book **begins** with impurity in the house (see, for example, 8: 6-18: note the words, "behold every form of creeping things, and abominable beasts, and all the idols of the house of Israel, pourtrayed upon the wall round about") and **ends** with purity in the house (see, for example 42: 13-14 which refer to the "holy chambers ... the most holy things", also saying that "the place is holy" and that the priests' garments "are holy").

iv) The book **begins** with a river (1: 1, 3), and **ends** with a river (47: 1-12). The first, as noted, was evidently a man-made river: the last will be divinely-provided.

All is summed up in the final verse of the prophecy –

"THE LORD IS THERE"

God's purposes for Israel will be brought to absolute and complete fulfilment in the millennial age. He will dwell with His people in conditions of holiness and uncontaminated purity.

EZEKIEL CHAPTER 1

Unlike Isaiah and Jeremiah, who prophesied largely in Judah (part of Jeremiah's preaching took place in Egypt), Ezekiel preached in Babylonia to which he had been deported in approximately 600 BC, some eleven years before Jerusalem finally fell to Nebuchadnezzar. Although he was taken "in the visions of God" to Jerusalem (8: 3), he ministered for some twenty years to his fellow-exiles in the land of their captivity.

Ezekiel's contemporaries were Jeremiah and Daniel. Jeremiah's ministry began in the reign of Josiah, and he lived through the reigns of Jehoahaz, Jehoiakim, Jehoiachin and Zedekiah (and beyond). According to Daniel 9 verse 2, Daniel read the prophecy of Jeremiah. It is important to notice God's faithfulness to His people. He ensured that His Word reached them wherever they went. **Daniel** was involved in the first deportation in the days of Jehoiakim, **Ezekiel** with the second deportation in the days of Jehoiachin, and **Jeremiah** remained in Jerusalem throughout the entire period reminding us that God will not leave "himself without witness" (Acts 14: 17), not even in the darkest days at the end-time as Revelation 11 makes clear.

The opening chapter of the prophecy falls into two parts: **(1)** the introduction (vv.1-3), and **(2)** the vision (vv.4-28).

1) INTRODUCTION, vv.1-3

In these introductory verses we should consider: *(a)* the time; *(b)* the place; *(c)* the man.

a) The time, vv.1-2

"Now it came to pass in the thirtieth year, in the fourth month, in the fifth day of the month ... In the fifth day of the month, which was the fifth year of king Jehoiachin's captivity."

i) It was "in the thirtieth year" (v.1). This evidently refers to Ezekiel's thirtieth birthday, when he would have normally entered the priestly ministry. See Numbers 4 verse 3. It should be said that some refer this to the Passover kept in the reign of Josiah: see 2 Kings 23 verses 21-23. Lamar E. Cooper (*Ezekiel, The New American Commentary*) suggests that this refers to the thirtieth year after the discovery of the book of the law in the Temple and the beginning of Josiah's reforms. (2 Chron. 34: 14-33).

We cannot continue without noticing that the Lord Jesus "began to be about thirty years of age" (Luke 3: 23) when His public ministry began and, like Ezekiel some six hundred yeas before, He too was at a river (Luke 3: 21-22). Ezekiel saw "that the heavens were opened" (Ezek. 1: 1), and the same heavens were 'opened' to the Lord Jesus (Mark 1: 10). We may go further and add that following the vision given to Ezekiel, the prophet tells us that "the spirit ('Spirit', JND) entered into me", reminding us that following His baptism, the Spirit of God 'descended 'like a dove' and lighted upon the Lord Jesus (Mark 1: 10). To say that all this is 'interesting' would be a total understatement!

ii) It was in "the fifth year of king Jehoiachin's captivity" (v.2). See 2 Kings 24 verses 8-16. This reminds us that Ezekiel was called to serve at a time when the morale of God's people was at a very low ebb. What could be better than a vision of the glory of the Lord to revive flagging spirits!

b) The place, vv.1, 3

"As I was among the captives by the river of Chebar … the word of the LORD came expressly unto Ezekiel the priest… in the land of the Chaldeans by the river of Chebar." This evidently refers to a Jewish colony on the Chebar river in Chaldea. "Recent authorities generally identify it with the *Nahr Malcha,* or royal canal of Nebuchadnezzar, on the excavation of which it is supposed the Jewish captives were employed for a time. These were doubtless 'the rivers of Babylon' by whose side the Jewish exiles wept when they 'remembered Zion' (Psalm 137: 1)" (*Ellicott's Commentary*). C.L.Feinberg concurs in saying that "the river of Chebar" was "known among the Babylonians as the grand canal; it flowed southeast from the Euphrates at Babylon. Canals were vital to the irrigation of the land. Along this river the prophet made his home at Tel-abib" (3: 15).

c) The man, v.3

"The word of the LORD came expressly unto Ezekiel the priest, the son of

CHAPTER 1

Buzi ... and the hand of the LORD was there upon him." In this connection, we should notice the following:

i) **His name**. Ezekiel, meaning 'God will strengthen' or 'strength of God', was appropriately named. He certainly needed the strength of God to carry out his commission, which lasted for over twenty years, and strength was indeed imparted to him, "Behold, I have made thy face strong against their faces, and thy forehead strong against their foreheads" (3: 8). Believers today are "strengthened with all might, according to his glorious power" (Col. 1: 11). *We* are to be "strong in the Lord" (Eph. 6: 10).

We know nothing of his father, Buzi.

ii) **His occupation**. He was a priest (v.3). On the assumption that Ezekiel had not entered on his priestly duties prior to the captivity (which seems to be the case if we take the reference to the "thirtieth year" as reference to his birthday), his removal to the Jewish colony in Chebar must have seemed disastrous. "It seemed that all the elaborate training for the functions of a priest was in vain" (F.Cundick, *The Book of Ezekiel – a Precious Seed* publication). We shall see, however, that the Lord had priestly work for Ezekiel of a nature he could never have anticipated. How typical of God's purposes! What seems, initially, to be a terrible disappointment, becomes the occasion for profitable service to the glory of God. The priestly background of Ezekiel made him a most suitable recipient of those divine revelations concerning the temple which lie at the heart of this prophecy. This is clear from the words, "The word of the LORD came **expressly unto Ezekiel the priest**, the son of Buzi ... and the hand of the LORD was there upon him".

We must therefore next consider:

iii) **His calling**. "The word of the LORD came expressly unto Ezekiel ...and the hand of the LORD was there upon him" (v.3). There are seven references to "the hand of the LORD" upon the prophet. (See 1: 3; 3: 14 ("the hand of the LORD was strong upon me"); 3: 22 ("the hand of the LORD was there upon me"; 8: 1 ("the hand of the Lord GOD fell there upon me"); 33: 22; 37: 1; 40: 1.) This implies that the prophet was subject to divine authority and filled with divine power. It was this power that opened "his eyes to see the visions, his ears to hear the voice of God, and his heart to receive both" (Dennis Pierce, writing in *Precious Seed*, November 2015). This is so necessary for public preaching and personal witness. Luke describes the result: "And the hand of the Lord was with them: and a great number believed, and turned unto the Lord" (Acts 11: 21). Without this, nothing can be accomplished. We must pray that the Lord's hand will be upon *us.* Paul tells us that his preaching at Corinth was "not with enticing words of man's wisdom, but in demonstration of the Spirit and of power" (1 Cor. 2: 4)

The expression "the word of the LORD" (v.3) occurs over fifty times in the book, reminding us that it was Ezekiel's business to convey God's word to His people. A prophet had no other business apart from the proclamation of the word of God, and nothing has changed in this respect. The Lord Jesus commanded His disciples to "Go ... and teach all nations ('make disciples of all nations'), baptizing them in the name of the Father, and of the Son, and of the Holy Ghost: teaching them to observe all things whatsoever I have commanded you" (Matt. 28: 19-20), and they "went forth, and preached every where, the Lord working with them, and confirming the word with signs following" (Mark 16: 20). The early believers at Jerusalem "were all filled with the Holy Ghost, and they spake the word of God with boldness" (Acts 4: 31). There are at least twenty-four references to the declaration of "the word" in the book of Acts. It was fundamental to the proclamation of the message, and it is our business to use "the holy scriptures, which are able to make ... wise unto salvation through faith which is in Christ Jesus" (2 Tim. 3: 15). See also 2 Timothy 4 verse 2.

Ezekiel served with the "hand of the LORD" upon him, and faithfully declared the "word of the LORD" committed to him. He served in the power of the Lord, proclaiming the word of the Lord.

2) THE VISION, vv.4-28

It has been nicely said that Isaiah was the **poet**, Jeremiah the **preacher**, and Ezekiel the **artist**. Ezekiel certainly paints pictures of glowing colour and graphic detail. He was moreover an actor as well as an artist, for he was not only commanded to state his parables, but to act out many of them in the presence of the people. Hence, having dug through a wall at twilight with all his worldly goods on his back, he was commanded to say, "I am your sign: like as I have done, so shall it be done unto them: they shall remove and go into captivity" (12: 11). But before that, he was commanded to lie on his "left side" for "three hundred and ninety days" and then on his "right side" for "forty days" (4: 4-6). Just think of the 'pins and needles'! There is another example in Chapter 24 verses 15-27.

CHAPTER 1

Ezekiel's brightest painting is of the "glory of the LORD", and this lies on the threshold of the book. The vision concerns the chariot-throne of the Lord. It is a mobile throne. Its constituent parts are described in the vision. The throne of God is both "set" (immoveable) in heaven (Rev. 4: 2), and mobile!

The key words of the chapter are found in verse 28: "This was the appearance of the likeness of the glory of the LORD". The vision had an immediate effect upon Ezekiel: "And when I saw it, I fell upon my face, and I heard a voice of one that spake" (v.28).

These colourful verses may be divided, with acknowledgements to F.Cundick (*The Book of Ezekiel,* published by *Precious Seed*), as follows: *(a)* the direction of the chariot-throne (v.4); *(b)* the description of the chariot-throne (vv.4-26); *(c)* the director of the chariot-throne (vv.26-28).

A) THE DIRECTION OF THE CHARIOT-THRONE, v.4

The chariot-throne came from "the north". "And I looked, and, behold, a whirlwind ('stormy wind') came out of the **north**, a great cloud, and a fire infolding itself." This is indicative of judgment from that direction. Compare Jeremiah 1 verses 14-15, "Then the LORD said unto me, Out of the **north** an evil shall break forth unto all the inhabitants of the land. For, lo, I will call all the families of the kingdoms of the **north**, saith the LORD, and they shall come, and they shall set every one his throne at the entering of the gates of Jerusalem". The lesson is clear: the movements of armies and nations are under the control of the throne of God. Put another way, "the most High ruleth in the kingdom of men, and giveth it to whomsoever he will" (Dan. 4: 17).

B) THE DESCRIPTION OF THE CHARIOT-THRONE, vv.4-26

Associated with the wind is a cloud and a fire - a swirling fire. This is explained in verses 26-28. See also Chapter 8 verse 2. Compare Exodus 24 verse 17: "And the sight of the glory of the LORD was like devouring fire on the top of the mount in the eyes of the children of Israel". The wind, cloud, and fire (v.4) are all symbols of God's glory. See Psalm 18 verses 8-13. "The general appearance is that of a tremendous thunderstorm seen from afar, in which the great ominous cloud is lighted up repeatedly by flashes of lightning" (C.L.Feinberg). We should notice: *(a)* the body of the chariot (vv.5-14); *(b)* the wheels of the chariot (vv.15-21); *(c)* the seat in the chariot (vv.22-26).

a) The body of the chariot, vv.5-14

The body of the chariot comprises the four living creatures, elsewhere called "cherubim" fifteen times in Chapter 10, once in Chapter 11 and three times in Chapter 41. Compare Isaiah 6 and Revelation 4 where it appears that the same living creatures are the seraphim. Commentators distinguish the seraphim from the cherubim, but there does seem to be a correspondence with the "living creatures" in Ezekiel 1 verse 13: "their appearance was like burning coals of fire, and like the appearance of lamps". While it is true that the cherubim in Ezekiel's visions had four wings, the same "living creatures" have six wings when described in Revelation 4. This is not as confusing as it may seem. Four is the number of universality, and six is the number of man; these symbolic creatures are described in differing contexts, and take their symbolic significance from the particular setting at the time. It is particularly interesting and appropriate to notice that the word 'seraph' is used, not of burning as incense (as in Lev 1: 9; 2: 9; 3: 16), but of burning judicially, as in the sin and trespass offerings. These absorbing verses can be studied with reference to the repetition of the following words: ***"four ... man ... joined".***

i) The repetition of "four"

There are "four living creatures" (v.5). See also verse 10. The "living creatures" have "four faces, and... four wings" (v.6). See also verse 8. The numeral "four" also occurs in the next section in relation to the wheels of the chariot. See verses 16, 17 and 18. This is indicative of **universality**. "I saw four angels standing on the four corners of the earth" (Rev. 7: 1). This throne has world-wide dominion.

Each of the "four living creatures" has four faces: the face of a man (conveying dominion/intelligence), lion (conveying power), ox (conveying strength) and eagle (conveying vision/rapidity). "Thus were their faces" (vv.10-11). "These faces taken together are an expression of full life" (F.Cundick). According to C.L.Feinberg, the rabbis said of the living creatures, "Man is exalted among creatures; the eagle is exalted among birds; the ox is exalted among domestic animals, and lion is exalted among wild beasts; and all of them have received dominion, and greatness has been given them, yet are they stationed below the chariot of the Holy One (Midrash Rabbah Shemoth)". F.Cundick adds: "In man intelligence is at its highest level, in the lion strength at its greatest, in the ox service at its meekest, and in the eagle movement at its swiftest". Bearing in mind, as we shall see, that the cherubim moved in square formation, it seems likely that each side of the chariot displayed a complete range of faces.

The "four living creatures", or cherubim, are distinguished from angels (see Rev. 5: 11), and therefore belong to a different order. As noted above, they evidently display attributes of Deity (dominion, power, strength, vision). The four faces certainly suggest that they convey God's interests in creation and His authority over creation. In the words of F.Cundick, "Divine sovereign authority is expressed through them relative to earth. This, perhaps, is the reason for the constant association of the cherubim with man and creation. Small as the earth is in comparison with the known creation, it is the crown thereof, and the special sphere of the revelation of the glory of God".

C.L.Feinberg points out that "Cherubim, wherever found in Scripture, are related to the holiness of God. They do not represent the likeness of God, which was forbidden by commandment. They are instruments of His government". They convey the character of the divine Occupant of the throne (vv.26-28). It is therefore significant that the four 'living creatures' ("beasts", AV) "rest not day and night, saying, Holy, holy, holy, Lord God Almighty" (Rev. 4: 8), at which "the four and twenty elders" say "Thou art worthy, O Lord, to receive glory and honour and power: for thou hast created all things, and for thy pleasure they are and were created" (Rev.4: 9-11). The faces of the cherubim (the 'living creatures') exhibited God's creatorial power and authority. It will not escape notice that the four faces convey the character of the four Gospels: Matthew, the Gospel of the lion; Mark the Gospel of the ox; Luke the Gospel of the man, and John the Gospel of the eagle.

ii) The repetition of "man"

Each of the "living creatures" had "the likeness of a man (v.5). If the repetition of "four" indicates the interest of the throne in creation **generally**, then the repetition of "man" indicates the interests of the throne in man **particularly.** Note reference to "feet" (v.7) and "hands" (v.8). This indicates their connection with **humanity.** Man is "the crown of God's creative work (Gen.1: 26-28) and the central focus of His creation (Gen. 2: 8-25)" (Lamar E. Cooper).

- **Their feet**. "And their feet were straight feet (without bend); and the sole of their feet was like the sole of a calf's foot: and they sparkled like the colour of burnished brass" (v.7). Brass speaks of judgment. Compare Revelation 1 verse 15, "And his feet like unto fine brass, as if they burned in a furnace". See Micah 4 verse 13, "Arise and thresh, O daughter of Zion … and I will make thy hoofs brass". F.Cundick observes, "Threshing was done by the kine trampling the sheaves on the threshing floor; *firmness of purpose* is symbolised".

- Their hands. F.Cundick suggests that this indicates "full capacity and *aptitude for service*". Hands, in the Bible, suggest work: "No man having put his hand to the plough …" (Luke 9: 62).

iii) The repetition of "joined"

This is indicative of **harmony.** That is, harmony in movement. The picture seems to be of a square formation: "Their wings were joined one to another; they turned not when they went; they went every one **straight forward**" (v.9). See also verse 11: "and their wings were stretched upward; two wings of every one were joined together". See also verse 12: "And they went every one **straight forward**; whither the spirit was to go, they went; and they turned not when they went". As F.Cundick observes, "The undeviating course that they took left the prophet in no doubt as to the character of his own service. Similarly we are to keep a straight course in the execution of divine commands". We must note the following:

- The control. The harmony of movement is attributed to unseen control: "Whither the spirit was to go, they went" (v.12). See also verses 20-21. This reminds us that although there is variety of gift among the Lord's people, the gracious Holy Spirit is in control. God is not the "author of confusion" (1 Cor. 14: 33).

- The holiness. "Their appearance was like burning coals of fire, and like the appearance of lamps: it went up and down among the living creatures; and the fire was bright, and out of the fire went forth lightning" (v.13). There is a lesson for us here. "Our God is a consuming fire." The execution of His will demands purity on the part of the messengers.

- The rapidity. This harmony of movement was exhibited in the speed in which the demands of the throne (the demands of the Director) were executed: "and the living creatures ran and returned as the appearance of a flash of lightning" (v.14). There is another lesson for us here. The execution of God's will demands promptitude.

It is of interest to notice that later in the prophecy, the plural becomes the singular: "And the glory of the God of Israel was gone up from ***the cherub*** whereupon he was, to the threshold of the house" (9: 3). ***Not*** now the four cherubim which form the body of the chariot, ***but*** "the cherub". See Chapter 10 verses 2 and 4, "Go in between the wheels, even under ***the cherub*** ... Then the glory of the Lord went up from ***the cherub***, and stood over the threshold of the house". This seems to repeat Chapter 9 verse 3. The singular and the plural are found together in Chapter 10 verse 20.

Perhaps the explanation lies in the fact that since the four cherubim (the "living creatures", 1: 5) move together in perfect harmony (their wings joined etc), they are collectively called "the cherub". They move ***as one.*** Hence Psalm 18 verses 9-10: "He bowed the heavens also, and came down: and darkness was under his feet. And he rode upon ***a cherub,*** and did fly: yea, he did fly upon the wings of the wind". See also Ezekiel 10 verse 15, "This is the ***living creature*** (singular) that I saw by the river of Chebar". This brings us to:

b) The wheels of the chariot, vv.15-21

"Now as I beheld the living creatures, behold one ***wheel*** upon the earth by the living creatures (that is, beside each of the cherubim), with his four faces" (v.15). (Compare Daniel 7: 9: "his throne was like a fiery flame, and his wheels as burning fire"). "Wheels, it has been suggested, mean primarily and naturally the revolution of time. The wheels connect the chariot with the earth. Nothing is stationary in God's universe: all is in motion and progressing" (C.L.Feinberg). We should notice the following:

i) The wings are now associated with wheels. The former indicates heavenly movements, and the latter indicates earthly movements. So, "behold one wheel upon the earth" (v.15). This indicates that the will of heaven is executed on earth. The throne of God is relevant to earth.

ii) The wheels, like the faces of the cherubim, have a fourfold character. "The appearance of the wheels and their work was like unto the colour of a beryl (the meaning is uncertain, but probably chrysolite: a gold topaz): and they four had one likeness: and their appearance and their work was as it were a wheel in the middle of a wheel" (v.16). That is "set at right angles to each other like the equator and meridian on a globe of the earth" (F.Cundick). Hence, no turning in movement, "they went upon their four sides: and they turned not when they went" (v.17). This should evidently be translated "towards their four sides", that is "the four directions which the creatures faced, and not *upon their four sides* (as AV, RV)" (John P.Taylor). Like the "living creatures", the wheels pointed in all four directions, emphasising, once again, the universal sphere of God's chariot-throne.

iii) The wheels move with perfect knowledge. "As for their rings (rims), they were so high that they were dreadful; and their rings were full of eyes round about them four" (v.18). The knowledge of God is awe-inspiring and complete. The movements of the throne are dictated by perfect knowledge. Compare Proverbs 15 verse 3, "The eyes of the LORD are in every place, beholding the evil and the good". See also 2 Chronicles 16 verse 9 (addressed to Asa), "For the eyes of the LORD run to and fro throughout the whole earth". This conveys divine **omniscience.** The expression "full of eyes" means that everything is seen simultaneously. See also Revelation 4 verse 6, "and in the midst of the throne, and round about the throne, were four beasts full of eyes before (prophecy) and behind (history)"; Revelation 4 verse 8, "And the four beasts had each of them six wings about him; and they were full of eyes within". Daniel refers to the "decree of **the watchers**, and the demand by the word of the holy ones" (4: 17: see also 4: 23).

iv) The wheels move in perfect harmony with the cherubim. We should notice that the expression "whither the spirit was to go, they went; and they turned not when they went" (v.12) is repeated here: "Whithersoever the spirit was to go, they went" (v.20) and "they turned not when they went" (v.17). The movements of the throne whether in earthly or heavenly sphere, are marked by perfect harmony. All that is done on earth is in perfect accord with heaven. See verses 20-21. All is animated by one controlling spirit.

c) The seat in the chariot, vv.22-26

The seat is actually a throne! "And above the firmament that was over their heads as the likeness of a throne" (v.26). We should notice:

i) **The foundation of the throne**. "And the likeness of the firmament upon the heads of the living creatures was as the colour of the terrible crystal (or 'transparent as ice', Newberry margin), stretched forth over their heads above" (v.22). For "terrible crystal" see Revelation 4 verse 6, "And before the throne there was a sea of glass like unto crystal". We have already noted what follows: "and in the midst of the throne, and round about the throne, were four beasts ('living creatures') full of eyes before and behind". The throne rests on the basis of perfect righteousness and purity. "Justice and judgment are the habitation ('foundation', JND) of thy throne" (Psalm 89: 14).

ii) ***The response to the throne.*** We must notice the expressions "when they went" (v.24) and "when they stood" (vv.24-25).

iii) ***The movement of the living creatures***: "And when ***they went***, I heard the noise of their wings, like the noise of great waters, as the voice of the Almighty, the voice of speech, as the noise of an host" (v.24). Compare Revelation 1 verse 15, "And his voice as the sound of many waters". They convey the ***power*** of the throne. Notice that with one pair of wings "they ... covered their bodies", suggesting humility in service.

iv) ***The stillness of the living creatures***: "when ***they stood***, they let down their wings. And there was a voice from the firmament that was over their heads, when they stood, and had let down their wings" (vv.24-25). They listened to the voice from the throne. There are times when we must all 'let down our wings'.

v) ***The colour of the throne***. "And above the firmament that was over their heads was the likeness of a throne, as the appearance of a sapphire stone" (v. 26). We move now beyond the "living creatures". For "sapphire stone", see Exodus 24 verses 9-10. Blue is the colour of the heavenly throne.

C) THE DIRECTOR OF THE CHARIOT-THRONE, vv.26-28

Ezekiel now describes the Occupant of the chariot. It was an occupied throne. "And upon the likeness of the throne was the likeness as the appearance of ***a man*** above upon it." Nine times in this chapter the word "likeness" is mentioned. "We can only think of God by reasoning from what is highest in our thoughts of human greatness, entirely apart from their present limitations. Ezekiel did not see God himself (John 1: 18), but certain likenessess and appearances conveyed to him the character and attributes of the majestic and sovereign God" (C.L.Feinberg). We should notice:

i) The "***appearance*** of a man": 'the likeness ... of a man' (v.26). Compare Isaiah 6. There is ***now*** a man - not the "appearance of a man" - on the throne!

ii) The "*appearance* of fire" (v.27). This has been rendered, "What might have been brass glowing like fire in a furnace" (NEB). This emphasises His absolute holiness.

iii) The "*appearance* of the bow that is in the cloud in the day of rain, so was the appearance of the brightness round about" (v.28). Taking the second and third references to "appearance" together, we have judgment and mercy. "The bow shows that the God of all majesty and power is also the God of promise and grace who is ever mindful and faithful to His covenant regarding the earth" (C.L.Feinberg). This would have had a particular significance for the captives in Babylonia. God had not forsaken them. His promises would be fulfilled. He would not forget His covenant with the patriarchs, neither will He forget His covenant with *us*.

iv) The "*appearance* of the likeness of the glory of the LORD" (v.28). We learn, then, that "our God is a consuming fire".

Like Ezekiel, we should 'fall on our faces' (v.28) as we contemplate the glory of the Lord.

EZEKIEL CHAPTER 2

The ministry of Ezekiel began with the first of five visions given to him of "the glory of the LORD" (1: 28). Of the five, three are found in Chapter 3 verse 23, Chapter 8 verse 4 and Chapter 9 verse 3, and the remaining two in Chapters 10 – 11 and Chapter 43. As F.Cundick observes, "the description of the heavenly chariot is enough to convince us (let alone Ezekiel) of a power and authority that has control of all things. There is no part of the universe outside the range of God's government". The vision describes the "resistless divine activity, controlling alike the agencies of judgment and of mercy, directed to every corner of the earth, and requiring of all profoundest homage and veneration" (Ellicott's Commentary). This prepared Ezekiel for the coming fall of Jerusalem and assured him that although events seemed to prove otherwise, "The Lord God omnipotent reigneth" (Rev. 19: 6), and the prophet now embarks on his service with this confidence.

With the vision of "the glory of the LORD" before him, Ezekiel fell upon his face. See Chapter 1 verse 28 and Chapter 3: 23. Daniel (8: 17), Saul of Tarsus (Acts 9: 4) and John (Rev. 1: 17) did the same. Isaiah cried "Woe is me ... for mine eyes have seen the King, the LORD of hosts" (Isaiah 6: 5). The overpowering vision of the Lord's glory filled them with worship, adoration and godly fear. But the "glory of the LORD" was not intended to paralyse His servants and, like Saul of Tarsus who was told "rise, and stand upon thy feet" (Acts 26: 16), Ezekiel is commanded, "Son of man, stand upon thy feet, and I will speak unto thee" (2: 1).

Ezekiel 1 therefore concludes with the prophet 'upon his face' (v.28) in worship and adoration at the vision of the "glory of the LORD", and Ezekiel 2 commences with the prophet 'on his feet' in readiness for service. This brings us to the commissioning of Ezekiel, and we should note the following: **(1)** the readiness of the servant (v.1); **(2)** the power of the servant (v.2); **(3)** the authority of the servant (v.3); **(4)** the circumstances of the servant vv.3-4); **(5)** the message of the servant (v.4); **(6)** the effect of the servant (vv.5-7); **(7)** the separation of the servant (v.8); **(8)** the resources of the servant (2: 8 - 3: 3).

EZEKIEL

1) THE READINESS OF THE SERVANT, v.1

"And he said unto me, Son of man, stand upon thy feet, and I will speak unto thee." The expression "son of man" (literally 'child of man') is common enough throughout the Scriptures, meaning simply *man,* but it is never used as an address to a prophet, except to Ezekiel and Daniel. Daniel is addressed in this way once (Dan. 8: 17), while the phrase is used some ninety times with reference to Ezekiel. (See, for example, 2: 1, 3, 6, 8; 3: 1, 4, 10, 17, 25.) While it conveys the tenderness of God, it also emphasises the frailty of the servant and the necessity for humility. In context, the expression "son of man" stresses "his insignificance compared to the glory he has just seen, but it is in no way depreciatory, for man, in spite of his fall, is and remains the climax of God's creating" (H.L.Ellison, *Ezekiel, The Man and his Message*).

We should note that Paul was given "visions and revelations of the Lord", but he was also given "a thorn in the flesh ... lest I should be exalted above measure" (2 Cor. 12: 1, 7). God knows how to keep His people humble!

The words, "stand upon thy feet" describe readiness to move in the service of God. This was the case with Elijah: "As the LORD God of Israel liveth, before whom I **stand**" (1 Kings 17: 1) and with Gabriel: "I am Gabriel, that **stand** in the presence of God; and am sent to speak unto thee, and to shew thee these glad tidings" (Luke 1:19). Isaiah 'stood on his feet' in saying, "Here am I, send me" (Isaiah 6: 8), and it is noteworthy that the same passage describes the readiness of the seraphim: "Above it (the throne) **stood** the seraphims" (v2). Readiness to serve is described in 2 Timothy 2 verse 21, "If a man therefore purge himself from these, he shall be a vessel unto honour, sanctified, and meet for the master's use, and **prepared** unto every good work".

Centuries later another man, Saul of Tarsus, saw the glory of Christ, and was told "rise and stand upon thy feet: for I have appeared unto thee for this purpose, to make thee a minister and a witness both of these things which thou hast seen, and of those things in the which I will appear unto thee" (Acts 26: 16).

It follows that we are not likely to hear his voice ("I will speak unto thee") unless we are willing to be used in his service ("stand upon thy feet"). It has been pointed out (A.B.Davidson) that: "It is man erect, man in his manhood, with whom God will have fellowship and with whom He will speak". H.L.Ellison observes that "there are times and seasons, when the child of God will be found prostrate before the Lord, but when he is to be God's 'fellow-worker', he is to stand upon his feet".

(For further references to readiness, see Romans 1: 15; 2 Timothy 4: 6.)

2) THE POWER OF THE SERVANT, v.2

"And the spirit ('the Spirit', JND) entered into me when he spake unto me, and set me upon my feet, that I heard him that spake unto me." Compare Chapter 3 verse 24, "Then the spirit ('the Spirit', JND) entered into me, and set me upon my feet, and spake with me, and said unto me, Go, shut thyself within thine house". There can be no doubt that "'the spirit' is here the Spirit of God, and not merely the prophet's own human vigour and courage; and this is made still more plain in Chapter 3 verse 24" (*Elicott's Commentary*).

D.C.Hinton (writing in the *Believer's Magazine*) points out that "the Holy Spirit is mentioned more in connection with Ezekiel than with any other person in the Old Testament. More than that, he was given a revelation of the work of the Spirit that was only for him".

The Lord Jesus said, "Ye shall receive power, after that the Holy Ghost is come upon you: and ye shall be witnesses unto me ..." (Acts 1: 8). The fact that Ezekiel says, "the spirit entered into me when he spake to me", emphasises that divine commands are accompanied by divine power. God does not call His servants and then leave them to their own resources. The call of Gideon illustrates the point. "And the LORD looked upon him, and said, Go in this thy might, and thou shalt save Israel from the Midianites: have not I sent thee? And he said unto him, Oh my Lord, wherewith shall I save Israel? Behold, my family is poor in Manasseh, and I am the least in my father's house. And the LORD said unto him, Surely *I will be with thee* and thou shalt smite the Midianites as one man" (Judges 6: 14-16).

3) THE AUTHORITY OF THE SERVANT, v.3

"And he said unto me, Son of man, *I send thee* ..." Notice the relationship here. On the one hand we have Ezekiel, addressed as "son of man (*adam*)", with all his weakness. On the other we have the Lord ("*I* send thee") with all His divine strength and power.

This was Ezekiel's only authority. He was sent by **the Lord**. It will be this conviction that will enable us to persevere in the face of difficulty and discouragement. The ministry of Jeremiah, with all the opposition that he was to face, began with God-given assurance that he had been divinely called: "Before I formed thee in the belly I knew thee; and before thou camest forth out of the womb I sanctified thee; and I ordained thee a prophet unto the nations" (Jer. 1: 5). Paul evidently refers to this in saying, "God, who separated me from my mother's womb, and called me by his grace, to reveal his Son in me, that I might preach him among the nations" (Gal. 1: 15-16). Amos made it clear to Amaziah, the priest of Bethel, that his authority was God-given: "I was no prophet, neither was I a prophet's son ... and the LORD took me as I followed the flock, and the LORD said unto me, Go, prophesy unto my people Israel" (Amos 7: 14-15). John the Baptist put it like this, "He that sent me ... said unto me" (John 1: 33).

A few days before his death, F.S.Arnot wrote the following "The missionary, conscious of his call, can only 'go forward', irrespective of men and women, come life, come death". It is not a case of volunteering to serve the Lord, but "Pray ye therefore the Lord of the harvest, that *he* will send forth labourers into his harvest" (Matt. 9: 38).

We should notice that in Ezekiel's case, as in the case of most believers, he was "sent" to his own people: "Son of man, I send thee to the children of Israel". See also Chapter 3 verses 5-6, "Thou art not sent to a people of a strange speech and of an hard language, but to the house of Israel; not to many people of a strange speech and of an hard language, whose words thou canst not understand". More likely than not, he sends us to our own neighbourhood. In the inimitable words of Jack Hunter, 'We cannot expect to cross the oceans if we are not prepared to cross our own street in the service of God'. A sense of conviction is as necessary for the Lord's work in our own backyard as it is anywhere else.

4) THE CIRCUMSTANCES OF THE SERVANT, vv.3-4

"Son of man, I send thee to the children of Israel, to a rebellious nation that hath rebelled against me: they and their fathers have transgressed against me, even unto this very day. For they are impudent children and stiffhearted. I do send thee unto them." The words "rebellious nation" are actually 'rebellious nations', and Ellicott's Commentary says the following: "The word being the same as that commonly used distinctively for the heathen, so that the children of Israel are here spoken of as 'rebellious heathen'. There could be no epithet which would carry home more forcibly to the mind of an Israelite the state of antagonism in which he had placed himself against his God ... Yet still, the God from whom they had turned aside was even now sending to them His prophet, and seeking to win them back to love and obedience ..."

They are called "rebellious" five times: see verses 3, 5, 6, 7 and 8. They had forgotten to whom they belonged. They are also described as "impudent and stiffhearted". The word "impudent" here means 'sharp of face': in Chapter 3 verse 7 it means 'strong of forehead'. They had a history of rebellion: "they and their fathers have transgressed against me, even unto this very day". They were, in fact, a more difficult people than those of a "strange speech and of an hard language!" (3: 5). The Lord continues by saying, "Surely, had I sent thee to them, they would have hearkened unto thee. But the house of Israel will not hearken unto thee ..." (3: 6-7). This is certainly true today. In many overseas countries there is a far greater response to the gospel than in the U.K!

We also serve in adverse circumstances: amongst men and women with a history of rebellion against God. In the 'parable of the pounds' (Luke 19: 12-27) the ten servants are told "Occupy (trade) till I come" in a society which said of their Master, "We will not have this man to reign over us".

5) THE MESSAGE OF THE SERVANT, v.4

"And thou shalt say unto them, Thus saith the Lord GOD (Adonahy Jehovah)." We should notice that the Lord Jesus never said, "Thus saith the Lord": He said, "Verily, verily, I say unto you", emphasising that He *is* the Lord!

We have no authority to communicate anything other than the word of God. Our mandate is clear: "Go ye into all the world, and preach the gospel to every creature" (Mark 16: 15). In Paul's words, we are to "Preach the word; be instant in season, out of season ..." (2 Tim. 4: 2).

The assembly at Thessalonica furnishes us with an excellent example: "from you sounded out the word of the Lord not only in Macedonia and Achaia, but also in every place your faith to God-ward is spread abroad; so that we need not to speak any thing" (1 Thess. 1: 8). This statement can be understood in various ways, all of which are mutually complimentary:

i) **It is *"the word of the Lord"*** as to its ***origin***. It is His word. Hence the expressions, "the gospel of God", and "the gospel of Christ." It is not our property, and therefore we must not tamper with it. Jeremiah said, ***"Thy*** words were found, and I did eat them; and ***thy*** word was unto me the joy and rejoicing of mine heart" (Jer. 15: 16).

ii) **It is the *"word of the Lord"*** as to its ***subject***. Hence Paul wrote, "We preach not ourselves, but Christ Jesus the Lord; and ourselves your servants for Jesus' sake" (2 Cor. 4: 5). Hence Peter's words, "Preaching peace by Jesus Christ: (he is Lord of all)" (Acts 10: 36).

iii) **It is the *"word of the Lord"*** as to its ***authority***. This applies to the preachers. They have a duty to proclaim "the whole counsel of God". See, for example, Matthew 28 verses 19-20, "Go ye therefore, and teach (make disciples) all nations, baptizing them in the name of the Father, and of the Son, and of the Holy Ghost; teaching them to observe all things whatsoever I have commanded you". This also applies to the hearers. They have a responsibility to obey.

Very clearly, we have a duty to emulate the Thessalonians. They not only preached "the word of the Lord", but they preached ***nothing else*** but "the word of the Lord".

6) THE EFFECT OF THE SERVANT, v.5-7

"And they, whether they will hear, or whether they will forbear, (for they are a rebellious house) yet shall know that there hath been a prophet among them" (v.5). As D.C.Hinton observes, "Nothing is harder for the servant than not to see result for his labours. Yet this did not deter Ezekiel. How do we compare with him? Do we persevere in gospel testimony even though there is no visible result?"

The words, "yet shall know that there hath been a prophet among them" (see also 33: 33), must be emphasised. Ezekiel was not to concern himself with results. In fact, he is promised nothing! Only God can "give the increase". ***Our*** business is to "preach the word" (2 Tim. 4: 2). We are to do so "in season and out of season", and this seems strikingly similar to "whether they will hear, or whether they will forbear".

We should add that, irrespective of results, the gospel preacher and his ministry should be "unto God a sweet savour of Christ". Here is the complete passage, "For we are unto God a sweet savour of Christ, in them that are saved, and in them that perish: to the one we are the savour of death unto death; and to the other the savour of life unto life" (2 Cor. 2: 15-16).

It is worth remembering that "every man shall receive his own reward according to his own labour" (1 Cor. 3: 8). Not 'according to the blessing seen on his labour', but "according to his … labour". Nil results (apparently) do not necessarily mean nil reward! (Not that we work for reward: the "love of Christ" constrains us in our work for Him, 2 Cor. 5: 14.)

But Ezekiel could expect more than plain disinterest. He could expect active opposition. "And thou, son of man, be not afraid of them, neither be afraid of their words, though briers and thorns be with thee, and thou dost dwell among scorpions: be not afraid of their words, nor be dismayed at their looks, though they be a rebellious house. And thou shalt speak my words unto them, **whether they will hear, or whether they will forbear**: for they are most rebellious" (vv.6-7). He could expect scathing, scratching and stinging words! Compare Psalm 57 verse 4, "My soul is among lions; and I lie even among them that are set on fire, even the sons of men, whose teeth are spears and arrows, and their tongue a sharp sword".

The emphasis is not now so much on their rebellion against God alone, but on their hostility to God's servant. So: "be not afraid of their words, nor be dismayed at their looks". Compare Joshua 1 verse 8, "Have not I commanded thee? Be strong and of a good courage; be not afraid, neither be thou dismayed: for the LORD thy God is with thee whithersoever thou goest". Ezekiel's mandate is clear: "be not afraid of **their words**" (v.6): "thou shalt speak **my words**" (v.7).

It has to be said that some people have such a nice way of rejecting God's word: "Also, thou son of man, the children of thy people are still talking against thee by the walls and in the doors of the houses, and speak to one another, every one to his brother, saying, Come, I pray you, and hear what is the word that cometh forth from the LORD. And they come unto thee as the people cometh, and they sit before thee as my people, and they hear thy words, **but they will not do them**: for with their mouth they shew much love, but their heart goeth after their covetousness. And, lo, thou art unto them as a very lovely song of one that hath a pleasant voice, and can play well on an instrument, for they hear thy words, **but they do them not**" (Ezek 33: 30-32).

EZEKIEL

7) THE SEPARATION OF THE SERVANT, v.8

"But thou, son of man, hear what I say unto thee; Be not thou rebellious like that rebellious house ..." It is striking that Israel is called "that rebellious house", literally, 'a house of rebellion' (F. Gardiner, *Ellicott's Commentary*). Gardiner continues: "This phrase, used in Ezekiel about eleven times, seems to be more than a simple epithet; it is a significant substitution for the name in which they gloried. Instead of 'house of Israel, the prince of God', they had come to be "house of rebellion". Ezekiel was to be distinct in his obedience to the Lord. In New Testament language, he was not to be "conformed to this world" (Rom. 12: 2). He was not to compromise, and neither should we, even though "they think it strange that ye run not with them to the same excess of riot, speaking evil of you" (1 Pet. 4: 4).

Paul deals with this in 2 Corinthians 6 verses 14-16: "Be ye not unequally yoked together with unbelievers: for what fellowship hath righteousness with unrighteousness? And what communion hath light with darkness? And what concord hath Christ with Belial? Or what part hath he that believeth with an infidel? And what agreement hath the temple of God with idols? For ye are the temple of the living God ... Wherefore come out from among them, and be ye separate, saith the Lord ..." It has been pointed out (J. Boyd Nicholson) that these oft-quoted verses do not advocate no contact with evil, for that would be impossible, but no **contract** with evil.

8) THE RESOURCES OF THE SERVANT, 2: 8 - 3: 1-3

We should notice that Chapter 2 verse 8 to Chapter 3 verse 3 **lie at the centre of Ezekiel's commission**. The prophet's commission begins and ends with reference to the power of the Holy Spirit: "the spirit ('the Spirit', JND) entered into me when he spake unto me ... the spirit ('the Spirit', JND) lifted me up, and took me away" (2: 2; 3: 14). The commands "eat that I give thee ... eat this roll ... fill thy bowels with this roll" (2: 8; 3: 1-3) lie between almost parallel passages in Chapter 2 verses 3-8 and Chapter 3 verses 4-14. The servant of God must appropriate God's word. We should notice that there is no reference here to the inner bitterness experienced by the apostle John in Revelation 10 verses 9-10.

"Open thy mouth, and **eat** that I give thee. And when I looked, behold, an hand was sent unto me; and, lo, a roll of a book was therein; and he spread it before me; and it was written within and without: and there was written therein lamentations, and mournings, and woe. Moreover he said unto me, Son of man, *eat* that thou findest; eat this roll, and go speak unto the house of Israel. So I opened my mouth, and he caused me to *eat* that roll. And he said unto me, Son of man, cause thy belly to *eat*, and fill thy bowels with this roll that I give thee. Then did I *eat* it; and it was in my mouth as honey for sweetness" (2:8 - 3:1-3).

Jeremiah did the same: "Thy words were found, and I did *eat them*; and thy word was unto me the joy and rejoicing of my heart: for I am called by thy name, O LORD God of hosts" (Jer. 15: 16). See also Revelation 10 verses 2, 8-11. John took "the little book out of the angel's hand, and *ate* it up ... And he said unto me, Thou must prophesy again before many peoples, and nations, and tongues, and kings". He needed the contents of "the little book" in order to do this.

As H.L.Ellison points out, this "strikingly illustrates the union of the divine and human in the prophetic message. The message is clearly divine, from God, for the roll is already written, and that 'within and without', and there is, therefore, no room for any additions by the prophet himself. But the prophet does not merely take it with him to Tel-Abib and read it to the exiles. He has to eat it, to assimilate it, to make it a living part of himself; this is the human part of the message".

Ezekiel was to appropriate God's word. Although containing "lamentations, and mournings, and woe", he found it "as honey for sweetness" (3: 3). In view of the message which follows this seems rather strange! Perhaps this refers to the entire prophecy, which certainly ends on the sweetest of notes! We should note, however, that the "lamentations, and mournings, and woe" could account for his "bitterness and "heat of ... spirit" when he was taken to Tel-Abib (3: 14).

How much do we make the Word of God part of us? In the words of David Newell, "The Bible is not a 'dry-as-dust' text-book, but a hungry man's meal!"

EZEKIEL CHAPTER 3

It is often pointed out that the chapter division here is unfortunate (chapter divisions are not inspired!), and that we should read Chapter 2 verses 8-10 with Chapter 3 verses 1-3 without pausing for breath!

As we have already noted, Chapter 2 verse 8 to Chapter 3 verse 3 **lie at the centre of Ezekiel's commission**, which begins and ends with reference to the power of the Holy Spirit: "the spirit ('the Spirit', JND) entered into me when he spake unto me ... the spirit ('the Spirit', JND) lifted me up, and took me away" (2: 2; 3: 14). The commands "eat that I give thee ... eat this roll ... fill thy bowels with this roll" (2: 8; 3: 1-3) occur between almost parallel passages in Chapter 2 verses 3-8 and Chapter 3 verses 4-14. The lesson is clear: in order to serve the Lord effectively, His servants must personally appropriate and assimilate God's word.

It is worth repeating that this is exactly what Jeremiah did: "Thy words were found, and I did *eat them*; and thy word was unto me the joy and rejoicing of my heart: for I am called by thy name, O LORD God of hosts" (Jer. 15: 16). Every servant of God must do the same. Otherwise he (or she) will have nothing to say of spiritual value. C.L.Feinberg puts it nicely: "No true prophet ever chose his own message; he always followed a course of action given to him by God. The message had to be received and assimilated by the prophet, for he who gives forth the Word of the Lord must feed on it himself".

Having reiterated the lesson of the chapter's opening verses, the balance of the passage may be divided as follows: **(1) withstanding the pressure** (vv.4-14): "As an adamant harder than flint have I made thy forehead: fear them not" (v.9); **(2) warning the people** (vv.15-21): "I have made thee a watchman unto the house of Israel ... give them warning from me" (v.17); **(3) withholding the message** (vv.22-27): "thou shalt be dumb, and shalt not be to them a reprover (v.26). Amongst other lessons we learn that if people reject the word of God (v.7), it will be withheld from them (v.24). This is exactly

CHAPTER 3

what Amos predicted: "Behold the days come, saith the Lord GOD, that I will send a famine in the land, not a famine of bread, nor a thirst for water, but of hearing the words of the LORD: and they shall wander from sea to sea, and from the north even to the east, they shall run to and fro to seek the word of the LORD, and shall not find it" (Amos 8: 11-12). In the early days of Samuel, "the word of the LORD was precious ('rare') in those days; there was no open vision" (1 Sam. 3: 1). But, as we shall see, it appears that Ezekiel was not to be totally "dumb", but only when it came to a particular subject.

1) WITHSTANDING THE PRESSURE, vv.4-14

As we have noted, this section of the chapter completes the preparation of Ezekiel for his life's work. Having told us what he saw (1: 1-28), and what he heard (2: 1-10), he now tells us where he went (3: 1-15). (See vv.1, 4, 11.) He then joins the captives at Tel-abib where he "sat where they sat, and remained there astonished ('overwhelmed', NIV) among them seven days" (v.15). We should notice: *(a)* the people to whom he was sent (vv.4-11); *(b)* the power in which he was sent (vv.12-14).

a) The people to whom he was sent, vv.4-11

It has to be said that Ezekiel did not commence his service for God on an up-beat note. He was not promised years of fruitful service. He certainly did not arrive in Tel-abib (v.15) singing

> *Bringing in the sheaves!*
> *Bringing in the sheaves!*
> *We shall come rejoicing,*
> *Bringing in the sheaves!*

Just listen to this: "the house of Israel will not hearken unto thee; for they will not hearken unto me: for all the house of Israel are impudent and hardhearted" (v.7). The Lord Jesus told His disciples that the "harvest truly is plenteous, but the labourers are few; pray ye therefore the Lord of the harvest, that he will send forth labourers into his harvest" (Matt. 9: 37-38). But there was no such encouragement for Ezekiel. The going would be hard, very hard indeed. He wasn't promised a single soul! But that was not to be a deterrent. He was to say to them, "Thus saith the Lord GOD", and do so "whether they will hear, or whether they will forbear ('fail to listen', NIV)". In this connection we must notice the following:

i) The proclamation. "Son of man, go, get thee unto the house of Israel, and speak with my words unto them" (v.4). Do notice that the Lord does not say 'my word', but "my **words**". See also verse 10: "all my **words**". This is most important. Ezra was "a scribe of the **words** of the commandments of the LORD, and of his statutes to Israel" (Ezra 7: 11). Paul put it like this: "Which things also we speak, not in the **words** which man's wisdom teacheth, but which the Holy Ghost teacheth; comparing spiritual things with spiritual" (1 Cor. 2: 13).

ii) The people. "For thou art not sent to a people of strange speech (literally 'deep lipped') and of an hard language (literally, 'heavy tongued'), but to the house of Israel; not to many people of a strange speech and of an hard language, whose words thou canst not understand" (vv.5-6). While some servants of God are certainly sent to "people of a strange speech and of an hard language", the majority of us serve amongst our own neighbours and fellow-citizens. As we have already noted, we should never contemplate crossing the oceans to serve the Lord if we are not prepared to cross our own street to speak to someone about salvation (J.Hunter). Witnessing locally can be particularly difficult, and witnessing to our own family more so. Before Gideon took the battle to the Midianites, he had to demolish his father's altar to Baal and the "the grove that is by it" (Jud. 6: 25). That could not have been an easy task!

Had Ezekiel been sent to "people of a strange speech and of an hard language (or 'strange language and difficult speech, JND)" he would have had some success (v.6), but not here: "the house of Israel will not hearken unto thee; for they will not hearken unto me: for all the house of Israel are impudent and hardhearted ('hard of forehead and stiff of heart', JND)" (v.7). See also Chapter 2 verse 4 where the word **"impudent"** means 'sharp of face'. Perhaps Paul had verse 6 in mind when he said to the Jews at Rome, "Be it known therefore unto you, that the salvation of God is sent unto the Gentiles, and that they will hear it" (Acts 28: 28). As C.L.Feinberg observes. "Strange languages are more easily mastered than the spiritual hindrance of unbelieving hearts. This telling comparison reveals that God's people were more hardened in spirit than were their heathen neighbours". Compare Matthew 11 verses 21-24 and Luke 4 verses 24-29. The hearts of God's people when the Lord was here had not changed in the intervening centuries.

iii) The power. The circumstances were enough to break any preacher's heart, but Ezekiel would be equal to the circumstances: "Behold, I have made thy face strong against their faces, and thy forehead strong against their foreheads. As an adamant (or diamond, as the same word is rendered in Jeremiah 17: 1) harder than flint have I made thy forehead: fear them not, neither be dismayed at their looks, though they be a rebellious house" (vv.8-9). Compare Jeremiah 1 verses 17-19.

How does the Lord impart such strength and resolution to His servants? The answer follows: "Moreover he said unto me, Son of man, **all** my words that I shall speak unto thee **receive in thine heart, and hear with thine ears** (an unusual order)" (v.10). This evidently refers to the instructions, "eat that thou findest; eat this roll" (v.1). He would be strengthened by receiving and hearkening to the word of God. In Paul's words, he would be "strengthened with might by his Spirit in the inner man" (Eph. 3: 16). We should notice that the Lord specifically says, "**all** my words that I shall speak unto thee receive in thine heart, and hear with thine ears". Paul reminded the Ephesians elders that he had "kept back nothing that was profitable unto you" and continued, "I have not shunned to declare unto you **all** the counsel of God" (Acts 20: 20, 27).

iv) **The persistence**. He was to "go, get thee to them of the captivity, unto the children of thy people (**not** "my people), and speak unto them, and tell them, "Thus saith the Lord GOD; whether they will hear, or whether they will forbear ('fail to listen', NIV)" (v.11). Ezekiel was to convey God's message - "Thus saith the Lord GOD" - whatever the response. See also Chapter 2 verse 7. Giving up was not an option! It was a case of:

Watch and pray,
And plug away.

b) The power in which he is sent, vv.12-14

"Then the spirit ('the Spirit', JND) took me up ... So the spirit ('the Spirit', JND) lifted me up, and took me away" (vv.12, 14). It is often argued that this was a 'visionary experience' of the kind described in Chapter 8 verse 3, "And the spirit lifted me up between the earth and the heaven, and brought me in the visions of God to Jerusalem". But the fact that on arrival at Tel-abib he "sat where they sat, and remained there astonished among them seven days" (v.15) strongly suggests literal movement, rather than a 'visionary experience'. Similar language is used of Philip: "And when they were come up out of the water, the Spirit of the Lord caught away Philip, that the eunuch saw him no more" (Acts 8: 39), but, once again, it seems unlikely that something miraculous occurred here, and that Philip was carried through the air. It is more likely that the words "caught away" have the general idea of 'force suddenly exercised' by way of constraint. This was the case with Ezekiel: "the hand of the LORD was strong upon me" (v.14). The rather attractive suggestion that the description of the Holy Spirit's power on the day of Pentecost ("there came a sound from heaven as of a rushing mighty wind", Acts 2: 2) confirms that the words "a voice of a great rushing" (v.12) and the "noise of a great rushing" (v.13) refer to the Holy Spirit, cannot be easily sustained. There is no apparent affinity between the words used in Ezekiel 3 verses 12-13 and Acts 2 verse 2. We should notice:

i) **The praise expressed.** "I heard behind me a voice of a great rushing, saying, Blessed be the glory of the LORD from his place" (v.12). This is not easily explained. If the words, "a voice of a great rushing" refers to the movement of the chariot-throne (cf. 1: 24), then the words, "Blessed be the glory of the LORD from his place" might mean that the very movements of the throne, controlling world affairs, bring honour and glory to God. The speaker or speakers are not identified, but the cherubim are the most likely candidates. They *do* speak: see Revelation 4 verses 8-9

ii) **The presence of the chariot-throne.** "I heard also the noise of the wings of the living creatures that touched one another, and the noise of the wheels over against them, and a noise of a great rushing" (v.13). So the chariot-throne, with all its immense significance, including "the likeness as the appearance of a man above upon it" (1: 26), was present throughout Ezekiel's commissioning. He was commissioned before the throne of God! God spoke to Ezekiel from His throne!

iii) **The power of the Holy Spirit.** "So the spirit ('the Spirit', JND) lifted me up, and took me away, and I went in bitterness, in the heat of my spirit; but the hand of the LORD was strong upon me" (v.14). Bearing in mind that Ezekiel was promised a 'rough ride', to put it mildly (see 2: 6), without the promise of ultimate success, it is hardly surprising that he was not a 'happy chappy'. After all, he had been told that all he could look forward to was a difficult and unrewarding task. No wonder he was resentful. But the Holy Spirit completely overrode his feelings: "the hand of the LORD was strong upon me". There was no retreat for Ezekiel! Jeremiah knew all about this: "Then I said, I will not make mention of him, nor speak any more in his name". He had just been put in the stocks by Pashur the son of Immer, and he didn't like it one little bit: "I am in derision daily, every one mocketh me ... the word of the LORD was made a reproach unto me, and a derision daily". But it made no difference: "But his word was in mine heart as a burning fire shut up in my bones, and I was weary with forbearing, and could not stay" (Jer. 20: 7-9).

It is noteworthy that others in the Scriptures bear witness to the inward compulsion of God's word, including David: "My heart was hot within me, while I was musing the fire burned: then spake I with my tongue" (Psalm 39: 3); Amos: "The lion hath roared, who will not fear? the Lord GOD hath spoken, who can but prophesy?" (Amos 3: 8); Peter and John: "For we cannot but speak the things which we have seen and heard" (Acts 4: 20); Paul: "For though I preach the gospel, I have nothing to glory of: for necessity is laid upon me; yea, woe is unto me if I preach not the gospel!" (1 Cor. 9: 16). It was at Corinth that Paul was "pressed in the spirit ('constrained by the word', RV), and testified to the Jews that Jesus was Christ" (Acts 18: 5).

2) WARNING THE PEOPLE, vv.15-21

Having been commissioned, Ezekiel arrives at Tel-abib, meaning 'hill of ears' or 'mound of green ears': "Then I came to them of the captivity at Tel-abib, that dwelt by the river of Chebar, and I sat where they sat, and remained there astonished (overwhelmed) among them seven days" (v.15). (Job's three friends sat with him for "seven days and seven nights" (Job 2: 13).) It has been suggested that the "seven days" inactivity alludes to the seven-day consecration of the priests (Lev. 8: 33), but this seems unlikely. The explanation of Lamar E. Cooper is preferable: "As a prophet in the midst of the people, he was able to identify with their needs and feel the weight of impending judgment". The words "I sat where they sat" remind us that although we do not participate in the godless life-style of unbelievers, we are not to be isolationists. We must distinguish between separation and isolation. As C.L.Feinberg points out, "his ministry began not with speaking, but with silence".

These verses centre on the role of Ezekiel as a "watchman" (v.17) and we should notice the following: *(a)* his appointment (vv.16-17); *(b)* his accountability (vv.18-21). The words "warn", "warning" or "warned" occur in each of the verses (vv.17-21). Ezekiel's responsibilities as a watchman are detailed again in Chapter 33.

a) His appointment as a watchman, vv.16-17

"And it came to pass at the end of seven days, that the word of the LORD came unto me, saying, Son of man, I have made thee a watchman unto the house of Israel: therefore hear the word at my mouth, and give them warning from me." This is the first occurrence of the phrase, "the word of the LORD came unto me". It occurs on forty-one occasions in the book (Lamar E. Cooper). It has been said that "For no other prophet is there a record of such sustained contact with the divine word, the very essence of prophecy".

Lamar Cooper points out that "a watchman was a city employee appointed to be a look-out from some high vantage point such as a tower or the city wall. Such an office was extremely important because the safety of the entire population rested with the watchman. If a watchman failed in his duty to warn inhabitants of the town of impending attack, he was held personally responsible for any loss". For examples, see 2 Samuel 18 verses 24-27 and 2 Kings 9 verses 17-20.

Paul, as a true watchman, was "pure from the blood of all men", and his explanation follows: "For I have not shunned to declare unto you all the counsel of God" (Acts 20: 26-27). He made it clear to the Ephesian elders that part of their work was to act as watchmen: "For I know this, that after my departing shall grievous wolves enter in among you, not sparing the flock. Also of your own selves shall men arise, speaking perverse things, to draw away disciples after them. Therefore *watch*, and remember ..." (Acts 20: 29-31). Elders are men that "watch (*agrupneo*: to be sleepless) for your souls, as they that must give account" (Heb .13: 17).

At the same time, we are *all* to be watchmen. Hence the injunctions, "***Watch*** ye, stand fast in the faith, quit you like men, be strong" (1 Cor. 16: 13); "Therefore let us not sleep, as do others; but let us *watch* and be sober" (1 Thess. 5: 6.) (In each case, the word "watch" translates *gregoreo*). Sadly, the watchmen in Isaiah's day were "all dumb dogs, they cannot bark; sleeping, lying down, loving to slumber" (Is. 56: 10).

b) His accountability as a watchman, vv.18-21

The words, "his blood will I require at thine hand" and "thou hast delivered thy soul", are repeated twice (vv.18-19; 20-21). Ezekiel was to act as a watchmen to "the wicked" (vv.18-19) and to "the righteous" (vv.20-21).

i)   To "the wicked". "When I say unto the wicked, Thou shalt surely die; and thou givest him not warning, nor speakest to warn the wicked from his wicked way, to save his life; the same wicked man shall die in his iniquity; but his blood will I require at thine hand. Yet if thou warn the wicked, and he turn not from his wickedness, nor from his wicked way, he shall die in his iniquity; but thou hast delivered thy soul" (vv.18-19).

ii)   To "the righteous". "When a righteous man doth turn from his righteousness, and commit iniquity, and I lay a stumblingblock before him (not in the sense of deliberately intending to stumble him, but in the sense of something that **becomes** a stumblingblock: see Isaiah 8: 14; 1 Pet. 2: 7-8) he shall die: because thou hast not given him warning, he shall die in his sin, and his righteousness which he hath done shall not be remembered; but his blood will I require at thine hand. Nevertheless if thou warn the righteous man, that the righteous sin not, and he doth not sin, he shall surely live, because he is warned; also thou hast delivered thy soul" (vv.20-21).

Lamar Cooper points out that "the responsibility of a believer in Christ is no less awesome. Once the message of salvation is entrusted to us, we are responsible and accountable to share it with those that are lost". Paul recognised this: "I am debtor both to the Greeks, and to the Barbarians; both to the wise, and the unwise" (Rom.1:14). Paul had a deep sense of obligation. Proclaiming the Gospel to others was the discharge of a debt. He felt this deeply: "Necessity is laid upon me; yea, woe is unto me, if I preach not the gospel!" (1 Cor. 9: 16).

3) WITHHOLDING THE MESSAGE, vv.22-27

These verses mark the commencement of Ezekiel's ministry. C.L.Feinberg describes it as "Ezekiel's first prophetic act and announcement". The passage certainly describes the first in a series of signs which continues in Chapters 4-5: the sign of the tile (4: 1-3); the sign of the recumbent prophet (4: 4-8); the sign of the defiled food (4: 9-17); the sign of the shave and haircut (5: 1-17).

The details in the passage are absorbing. We should notice *(a)* the place appointed: "go forth into the plain" (v.22); *(b)* the presence of the throne: "behold the glory of the LORD stood there ... which I saw by the river of Chebar" (v.23); *(c)* the posture of the prophet: "I fell on my face ... set me upon my feet" (vv.23-24); *(d)* the prohibition from preaching (vv.24-27).

EZEKIEL

a) The place appointed, v.22

"And the hand of the LORD was there upon me; and he said unto me, Arise, go forth into the plain, and I will there talk with thee." For the third time we read that "the hand of the LORD" was upon Ezekiel (see 1: 3; 3: 14). As already noted, this implies that the prophet was subject to divine authority and filled with divine power.

Ezekiel was to leave the community of captives at Tel-abib (v.15) for the peace and quiet of "the plain" or 'valley' (JND). The word rendered "plain" means 'a cleft' or 'an opening', meaning an open valley surrounded by hills. "Like Paul after his call, Ezekiel was summoned to go into the desert to receive further instruction for his assignment (Gal. 1: 16-17)" (Lamar Cooper). How important it is for us all to get away from the hustle and bustle of everyday life in order to be alone with God.

b) The presence of the throne, v.23

"Then I arose, and went forth into the plain: and, behold, the glory of the LORD stood there, as the glory which I saw by the river of Chebar." It seems almost superfluous to say that Ezekiel did as he was told ("Arise, go forth into the plain ... I arose, and went forth into the plain"), but it is the simple lessons that we need most!

Ezekiel was not allowed to forget the glory of the Lord whom he served, nor His power and authority. Nothing had changed in this respect: it was "the glory which I saw by the river of Chebar". In the midst of the problems and difficulties which lay before him he was not to forget that God is unchanging and unchangeable.

c) The posture of the prophet, vv.23-24

"The glory of the LORD stood there, as the glory which I saw by the river of Chebar: and *I fell on my face*. Then the spirit entered into me, and *set me upon my feet*, and spake with me." He exhibited the same reverential awe (see 1: 28). Familiarity had not bred contempt! The same readiness to serve (see 2: 1). The same power of the Holy Spirit (see 2: 2). The same voice from the throne (see 2: 1). The Lord is still speaking!

CHAPTER 3

d) The prohibition from public preaching, vv.24-27

Over these verses it could be written, "a time to keep silence, and a time to speak" (Eccl. 3: 7). As C.L.Feinberg points out, it does seem "that the prophet's ministry was to be a private one, limited to those who would come to his house" (8: 1; 14: 1). We should note the following:

i) **The self-imposed prohibition.** "Go, shut thyself within thine house" (v.24); "thou shalt not go out among them" (v.25). The suggestion (by C.L.Feinberg and others) that the further restriction, "they shall put bands upon thee, and shall bind thee with them, and thou shalt not go out among them" (v.25), refers to moral rather than physical restraint, is appealing. That is, that the people would "bind him" figuratively by placing an embargo upon him. On the other hand, it would make good sense to take the binding quite literally. "Like the first restriction ('shut thyself within thine house') it was to be self-imposed, perhaps with the help of family and friends" (Lamar Cooper). Ezekiel was to confine himself to his house.

As noted above, this was first of a series of signs which continues in Chapters 4-5.

ii) **The divinely-imposed prohibition.** As a result of the self-imposed prohibition, Ezekiel became subject to a divinely-imposed prohibition: "And I will make thy tongue cleave to the roof of thy mouth, that thou shalt be dumb, and shalt not be to them a reprover: for they are a rebellious house" (v.26). Because God's people had become "a rebellious house", the Lord would cease to speak to them. So the watchman was tied up and tongue-tied!

While it could be said that although the voice of Ezekiel was silent, his very actions, whether self-imposed or imposed upon him, were louder than words, this is evidently *not* the explanation. Ezekiel was *not* completely dumb: see, for example Chapter 11 verses 16, 17. It is therefore better to understand the prophet's silence with reference to the command, "thou ... shalt *not* be to them as a *reprover*". The word "reprover" means, literally, 'a man of litigation' (C.J.H.Wright). He would not act as an arbitrator or a mediator: his ministry would be purely judicial, that is, until his mouth was opened in Chapter 24 verses 25-27 and Chapter 33 verses 21-22. This follows:

iii) **The prohibition was not permanent.** "But **when I speak with thee**, I will **open thy mouth, and thou shalt say unto them**, Thus saith the Lord

GOD; He that heareth, let him hear; and he that forbeareth, let him forbear: for they are a rebellious house" (v.27). Until then, that is, until the fall of Jerusalem, the prohibition on any conciliatory or consolatory preaching would remain. Further details of the fulfilment of the promise, "I will **open thy mouth**", are given, as noted above, in Chapter 24: "he that escapeth in that day shall come unto thee, to cause thee to hear it with thine ears … In that day shall thy mouth be opened to him that is escaped, and thou shalt speak, and be no more dumb" (vv.25-27). The actual fulfilment of the promise is recorded in Chapter 33 verses 21-22.

No such restraint is placed upon us today. Paul asked the assembly at Ephesus to pray that "utterance may be given unto me, that I may open my mouth boldly, to make known the mystery of the gospel, for which I am an ambassador in bonds: that therein I may speak boldly, as I ought to speak" (Eph. 6: 19-20).

EZEKIEL CHAPTER 4

In considering the previous chapter, we noted that verses 22-27 mark the commencement of Ezekiel's ministry, and that C.L.Feinberg describes the confinement of Ezekiel to his own house (3: 24-27) as his "first prophetic act and announcement". As noted, this is the first of a series of signs which continues in Chapters 4-5. These are: *(i)* the sign of the inscribed tile (4: 1-3); *(ii)* the sign of the recumbent prophet (4: 4-8); *(iii)* the sign of the defiled food (4: 9-17); *(iv)* the sign of the shaven head (5: 1-17). These verses (3: 24 - 5: 17) are a visual declaration of coming judgment, whereas Chapter 6 verse 1 to Chapter 7 verse 27 cover the same event verbally.

Chapter 4 therefore commences with Ezekiel confined to his house and silent so far as public preaching was concerned. Some suggest that this does not mean to say that he never left his house and that once Ezekiel had "performed his daily demonstration, he could release himself and do some of the other symbolic acts associated with the siege. Then, presumably, when no spectators were around, he could revert to a more normal manner of conduct within his house" (John B.Taylor). In the words of Thomas Constable (*Notes on Ezekiel, 2010 Edition),* "it appears that the prophet acted out his drama for only a few hours each day, and it was during this time that God enabled him to lie quietly". This may be correct, especially when it came to the long periods during which he was commanded to lie on his left and right sides! However, the reason for his confinement and silence when it came to conciliatory and consolatory preaching is given twice: "they are a rebellious house" (3: 26, 27). Ezekiel's confinement and silence was a sign of God's judgment upon His rebellious people. But although Ezekiel was silent, God was speaking!

Since all four signs are connected with the future siege of Jerusalem, we can go further and suggest that since Ezekiel did not open his mouth, at least publicly, until Jerusalem fell (24: 25-27), his confinement was a picture of the confinement of God's people during the siege of the city. With this in mind we should notice: *(i)* that the words "lay *siege* against it" are used in connection with the sign of the inscribed tile (vv.2, 3); *(ii)* that the words "thou shalt set thy face toward the *siege* of Jerusalem" and "till thou hast ended the days of thy *siege*", are used in connection with the sign of the recumbent prophet (vv.7, 8); *(iii)* that siege conditions are certainly described in the sign of the defiled food: "I will break the staff of bread in Jerusalem" (v.16); *(iv)* that reference is made to the siege of Jerusalem in the sign of the shaven head: "Thou shalt burn with fire a third part (of his hair) in the midst of the city, when the days of the *siege* are fulfilled" (5: 2).

The order in which the four signs above are given strongly suggests a chronological series of interconnected events: *(1) the commencement of the siege* is depicted in the sign of the inscribed tile (vv.1-3); *(2) the cause of the siege* is depicted in the sign of the recumbent prophet (vv.4-8); *(3) the conditions during the siege* are depicted by the defiled food (vv.9-17); *(4) the conclusion of the siege* is depicted in the sign of the shaven head (5: 1-17). We must remember that the siege in question had not yet commenced, and the signs therefore demonstrate that the Lord knows the end from the beginning. See Isaiah 41: 26; Acts 15: 18.) In fact, He *is* "the beginning and the ending" (Rev. 1: 8), meaning that He initiates and concludes all things.

1) THE COMMENCEMENT OF THE SIEGE, vv.1-3

The sign of the siege's commencement is in two parts: **(a)** the sign of the tile (vv.1-2); **(b)** the sign of the iron pan (v.3). The two signs depict different aspects of the siege. As John B.Taylor points out, "We must imagine that the strange actions which Ezekiel was now told to perform were carried out just inside his house or, more likely, on the open space in front of his doorway. The actions were pointless unless they could be watched by a large number of people, and we must suppose that it was not long before the word got around that Ezekiel was doing some unusual things near his home. In a close-knit community like that of the Tel-abib exiles, nothing could be kept secret for long".

a) The sign of the tile, vv1-2

"Take thee a tile, and lay it before thee, and pourtray upon it the city, even Jerusalem: and lay siege against it, and build a fort against it; set the camp also against it, and set battering rams against it round about." The word translated "tile" (*lebenah*) actually means 'brick', leading John B.Taylor to say that the "centrepiece of this silent charade was a large, rectangular, sun-baked brick ... on which he had drawn the easily recognisable outline of Jerusalem". Some commentators suggest that the "tile" could have been a soft clay tablet used by the Babylonians for a writing pad. The brick was then placed on the ground, in the sand, and surrounded by either models or markings in the sand depicting "siege-towers, mounds and military encampments" (J.P.Taylor).

No explanation is needed! The meaning of the 'acted parable' is perfectly clear. The tile was to depict the city surrounded by the machinery of war, including siege works. According to J.B.Taylor, the word translated "fort" (*dayeg*) is a collective noun, and its use in 2 Kings 25 verse 1 and Jeremiah 52 verse 4 suggests "a chain of offensive towers built around the besieged city".

b) The sign of the iron pan, v.3

"Moreover take thou unto thee an iron pan, and set it for a wall of iron between thee and the city: and set thy face against it, and it shall be besieged. And thou shalt lay siege against it. This shall be a sign to the house of Israel."

While there are other suggestions, the iron pan ('iron plate', JND) evidently represents the besieging enemy encamped around the city like a 'ring of steel'. Ezekiel was to station himself behind the iron pan which, presumably, was stood on end, and act out a siege. The 'iron plate', probably a griddle used for baking, was evidently employed to emphasise the strength of the siege. Since it lay between Ezekiel and the tile, or brick, depicting Jerusalem, we have some justification for concluding that in the acted parable, the prophet himself depicted, not so much the invader, but the Lord himself who had initiated the invasion.

The Lord was waging war against Jerusalem, and this is strikingly emphasised by the repetition of the word *"against"*. It occurs seven times in verses 2-3. Ezekiel's 'visual aid' depicted what **would happen** to Jerusalem, and when the city eventually fell, Jeremiah made it clear that the Lord had brought about its destruction. He had acted against His own people: "The Lord ... remembered not *his* footstool ... he hath destroyed *his* strong holds ... he hath ... taken away *his* tabernacle ... the Lord hath cast off *his* altar ... he hath abhorred *his* sanctuary" (Lam. 2: 1-7). He had fulfilled His own solemn promise: "But go ye now unto *my* place which was in Shiloh, where I set *my* name at the first, and see what I did to it for the wickedness of my people Israel ... therefore will I do unto ***this house***, which is called by ***my*** name, wherein ye trust, and unto ***the place*** which I gave to you and to your fathers, as I have done to Shiloh" (Jer 7: 12,14).

All this has a warning voice for God's people today. The Lord's letter to Ephesus (Rev. 2: 1-7) clearly proves that He continues to remove what He has established, if it fails to fulfil its original purpose: "I have somewhat against thee, because thou hast left thy first love. Remember therefore from whence thou art fallen, and repent, and do the first works; or else I will come unto thee quickly, and will remove thy candlestick out of his place, except thou repent" (Rev. 2: 4, 5). God does not bless His people 'for old time's sake'. Current blessing demands current spirituality. God is not duty bound to maintain something if His people have turned it into a farce.

2) THE CAUSE OF THE SIEGE, vv.4-8

"Lie thou also upon thy left side, and lay the iniquity of the house of Israel upon it; according to the number of the days that thou shalt lie upon it thou shalt bear their iniquity. For I have laid upon thee the years of their iniquity, according to the number of days, three hundred and ninety days: so shalt thou bear the iniquity of the house of Israel. And when thou hast accomplished them, lie again on thy right side, and thou shalt bear the iniquity of the house of Judah forty days: I have appointed thee each day for a year" (vv.4-6). As we shall see, this discloses the reason for the siege.

These verses raise four questions: **(a)** the significance of the prophet's position; **(b)** the significance of the 430 days; **(c)** the significance of the 430 years; **(d)** the significance of the prophet's actions: the set face and the uncovered arm (v.7).

a) The significance of the prophet's position

"**Lie** thou also upon thy left side ... **lie** again on thy right side." But it wasn't a case of lying down to relax, perhaps to enjoy a little sun-bathing! Ezekiel was to lie down under a burden: "Lie thou also upon thy left side, and **lay the iniquity of the house of Israel upon it** ... lie again on thy right side, and thou shalt **bear the iniquity of the house of Judah**". Ezekiel's discomfort as he lay prone on the ground (or floor) depicted the **coming** suffering of Israel and Judah because of their **past** iniquity. Their "iniquity" is mentioned five times in verses 4-6. Let it be said again that the **coming** siege of Jerusalem, when the nation would bear their iniquity, would be the result of their **past sin**. F.Gardiner (*Ellicott's Commentary*) puts it clearly: "The expression *to bear the iniquity of any one*, is common in Scripture to denote the suffering of punishment due to sin". See, again, Numbers 14 verse 34, "After the number of the days in which ye searched the land, even forty days, each day for a year, shall ye bear your iniquities".

In lying on the ground for a total of 430 days, Ezekiel was **not** saying that the coming siege and suffering of Jerusalem would last for that period of time, **but** that the siege would be entirely due to their own **past** wickedness over the number of years represented by the number of days. Quite obviously, the period did not coincide with the length of the coming siege since that lasted for approximately eighteen months (2 Kings 25: 1-4). It should also be said, contrary to the view adopted by some commentators, that the 430 days do **not** represent 430 years of **coming** suffering, commencing with the destruction of Jerusalem. To summarise, the 430 days represent:

- **Not** the length of the coming siege: that persisted for eighteen months: something like 540 days.

- **Not** the length they would have to suffer after the siege.

- **But** the length of their **past** iniquity.

Having noted the details, we must emphasise **the lesson**. This is clearly stated in the New Testament: "Be not deceived; God is not mocked: for whatsoever a man soweth, that shall he also reap. For he that soweth to his flesh shall of the flesh reap corruption; but he that soweth to the Spirit shall of the Spirit reap life everlasting" (Gal. 6: 7-8). God's judgment on sin is inevitable. He "requireth that which is past" (Eccl. 3: 15) In His longsuffering and unwillingness that any should perish, He may wait for years, but "the day of the Lord will come" (2 Pet. 3: 9-10).

b) The significance of the 430 days

While there is considerable difference of opinion when it comes to identifying the **years** in question, there can be no doubt, as already noted, that each **day** of Ezekiel's uncomfortable position **represented one year** of Israel's and Judah's past history: "I have laid upon thee the **years** of their iniquity, **according to the number of days**, three hundred and ninety days (v.5) ... I have appointed thee **each day for a year**" (v.6). (The calculation is reversed in Numbers 14: 34, "After the number of the days in which ye searched the land, even forty days, each day for a year shall ye bear your iniquities"). Ezekiel's discomfort as he lay prone on the ground (or floor) vividly illustrated that the coming suffering of God's people was the result of their "iniquity" over the past 390 years in the first case, and over the past 40 years in the second.

Although some commentators disagree, it does seem clear that the 40 days in respect of Judah must be added to the 390 days in respect of Israel, making a total period of 430 days. Although it is of minor importance, it might be interesting to ascertain, if possible, when the 430 days during which Ezekiel lay on the ground actually commenced, and when they concluded. A suggestion is made in the addendum.

Having noted the details in connection with the 430 days, we must emphasise the lesson: God's judgment on sin ("the years of their iniquity") is inevitable. The 430 days recalled "the years of their iniquity" (v.5). The passage of time did not mean that God had forgotten His people's sin. "God requireth that which is past" (Ecc. 3: 15). In His longsuffering and unwillingness "that any should perish", He may wait for years, but "the day of the Lord **will** come ..." (2 Pet. 3: 9-10).

We should also notice, that the Lord knew about every day of Ezekiel's testimony in this way. The same lesson is spelt out in the New Testament. At the end time He will be aware of every day (all 1,260 of them) of His faithful servants' testimony (Rev. 11: 3), and of His people's suffering (Rev. 12: 6).

c) The significance of the 430 years

We now have to ascertain, if possible, the identity of the 390 years of Israel's iniquity, and the 40 years of Judah's iniquity. This is easier said than done. There are difficulties attached to any explanation. The traditional Jewish interpretation (Kimchi: cited in the *Pulpit Commentary*) has considerable merit, and the following suggestions are made on that basis:

i) *The years of Israel's iniquity.* The 390 days cannot represent the duration of the northern kingdom (Israel), since that ran from 975 BC (the secession under Jeroboam) to 721 BC (the captivity by Assyria), that is, for 254 years. However, the period from the secession under Jeroboam in 975 BC to the destruction of Jerusalem in 585 BC is 390 years. This seems to be an attractive solution, but the passage does say "the iniquity of the house of Israel" (v.5), as opposed to the "iniquity of the house of Judah" (v.6). If the 390 years do represent the period between the secession under Jeroboam (who founded the northern kingdom of Israel, which was annexed by Assyria in 721 BC) and the destruction of Jerusalem, then both Israel and Judah must be included. In support of this suggestion, it can be argued that the expression, "the house of Israel", *does* refer to the whole nation (Israel and Judah) since the words: "This shall be a sign to the house of Israel" (v.3) must mean more than the northern kingdom (Israel). After all, the people at Tel-abib (Ch 3 v.15) were from Judah. The period of 390 days therefore represents Israel's sin over the 390 years from the secession under Jeroboam in 975 BC to the final destruction of Jerusalem in 585 BC,

ii) The years of Judah's iniquity. Whatever some commentators say, the 390 days and the 40 days do appear to be consecutive. It is possible, however, that they actually represent concurrent events, that is, that the period relating to Judah is part of the period relating to the nation at large. On this basis, although "the iniquity of the house of Judah" was part of "the iniquity of the house of Israel", **Judah's guilt was particularly emphasised** in the presence of the Judaean exiles in Tel-abib. On this assumption, the forty days could represent the period of approximately forty years between the commencement of Josiah's reforms in 625 BC and the destruction of Jerusalem in 585 BC. If this is the case, then "the iniquity of the house of Judah" was her resistance to Josiah's reforms and her rapid relapse into apostasy.

d) The significance of the prophet's movements

"Therefore thou shalt set thy face toward the siege of Jerusalem (probably referring to the "tile" or brick), and thine arm shall be uncovered, and thou shalt prophesy against it. And, behold, I will lay bands upon thee, and thou shalt not turn thee from one side to another (that is, not transfer from his left side to his right side), till thou hast ended the days of thy siege" (vv.7-8).

As F.Gardiner points out, "set thy face" is a common Scriptural expression for any steadfast purpose (see, for example, Lev. 17: 10; 20: 3, 5, 6; Isa. 50: 7). The uncovering of his arm signifies readiness for battle. See, for example, Isaiah 52 verse 10, "The LORD hath made bare his holy arm in the eyes of all the nations". One commentator calls this, 'the symbol of energetic action'. Finally, Ezekiel was not to deviate from his instructions: "thou shalt not turn thee from one side to another, *till* thou hast ended the days of thy siege" (v.8)

Having noted the details, we must emphasise *the lesson.* God's work requires ongoing application and discipline. Ezekiel had to 'keep going until the job was done'. We cannot minimise the cost to him in terms of inconvenience and discomfort. But the message he conveyed in this way demanded complete commitment on his part. It has been nicely said that "Preparing for a Sunday School class week after week, leading a Bible study year by year, visiting shut-ins steadily as time goes by, patiently shaping the behaviour of and caring for children as the years come and go ... Faithfulness involves sticking to tasks where the reward cannot necessarily be experienced right away. Loyal Christian servants may not see in this life the rewards of their steady labours, but we carry on because God's work is never done in vain, no matter how hard it may be (1 Cor. 15: 58)" (quoted by Thomas Constable, *Notes on Ezekiel, 2010 Edition).*

3) THE CONDITIONS DURING THE SIEGE, vv.9-17

Details of Ezekiel's diet during this period are given in order to illustrate the conditions in Jerusalem during the coming siege. We should notice *(i)* the ingredients (v.9); *(ii)* the amounts (vv.10-11); *(iii)* the preparation (vv.12, 14-15); *(iv)* the significance (vv.13, 16-17).

i) **The ingredients**. "Take thou also unto thee wheat, and barley, and beans, and lentils, and millet, and fitches, and put them in one vessel, and make thee bread thereof, according to the number of the days that thou shalt lie upon thy side, three hundred and ninety days shalt thou eat thereof" (v.9). Wheat and barley were the most important and widely used grains in the ancient Near East. Beans and lentils were also staple products, usually not mixed with grain or used for flour. Millet is mentioned only here in the Old Testament, but it was used in Mesopotamia. "Fitches" or 'spelt' was sometimes planted as a border to wheat and barley. The list of different grains strongly suggests that Ezekiel's meals would be made from whatever he could obtain in siege conditions. A meal made of scraps! We must note that of the two periods specified in verses 5-6, only the former is mentioned: "three hundred and ninety days shalt thou eat thereof". No explanation is offered for the omission of the forty-day period relating to Judah.

CHAPTER 4

ii) The amounts. "And thy meat which thou shalt eat shall be by weight, twenty shekels a day: from time to time shalt thou eat it. Thou shalt drink also water by measure, the sixth part of an hin: from time to time shalt thou drink" (vv.10-11). According to John.B.Taylor, on the basis that a shekel weighed about 11.4 grammes, Ezekiel would have eaten "almost exactly eight ounces of bread per day". The "sixth part of an hin" would have been "equal to a fraction over a pint, or 0.61 litres". J.B.Taylor continues: "this is not far short of starvation rations on any reckoning, and it seems incredible that Ezekiel could have lasted on it for over a year". No wonder the reduced quantities of food and water are called the "evil arrows of famine" (5: 16).

Perhaps, however, we should remember that this was a pubic demonstration, and that the prophet ate better meals behind the scenes! The twice-repeated expression "from time to time" evidently means, not just daily, but at the same time each day, or at set times each day.

iii) The preparation. "Thou shalt eat it as barley cakes, and thou shalt bake it with dung that cometh out of man, in their sight" (v.12). This rather nauseating instruction was quite deliberate since, presumably, this would actually happen in the coming siege. Human waste was considered defilement (Deut 23: 9-14). The priestly training of Ezekiel made this unsavoury manner of baking bread obnoxious to him (v.14), and the Lord therefore makes a concession: "Lo, I have given thee cow's dung for man's dung, and thou shalt prepare thy bread therewith" (v.15). The Lord is gracious to His children! "He knoweth our frame; he remembereth that we are dust" (Psalm 103: 14). Peter was similarly appalled at 'unclean food': see Acts 10 verses 9-16.

iv) The significance. "And the LORD said, Even thus shall the children of Israel eat their defiled bread among the Gentiles, whither I will drive them" (v.13). But their sufferings in this way would begin with the horrors of the siege: "Son of man, behold, I will break the staff of bread in Jerusalem: and they shall eat bread by weight, and with care: and they shall drink water by measure, and with astonishment ('silent, speechless, grief', Amplified Version): that they may want bread and water, and be astonied one with another, and consume away for their iniquity" (vv.16-17). Eating "bread by weight, and with care" and drinking "water by measure, and with astonishment" is clearly depicted in the appointed measure of Ezekiel's consumption of food and water.

There can be no doubt about the principle *lesson* of the passage. Sin will rob us of spiritual nourishment. Jeremiah describes the situation like this: "They that did feed delicately" were "desolate in the streets" (Lam. 4: 5). According to M.F.Unger, the words, "They that did feed delicately", mean that "they that used to feed on delicacies". Today, healthy eating is all the rage! But spiritual healthy eating is even more important, and Jeremiah himself is a prime example: "Thy words were found, and I did eat them; and thy word was unto me the joy and rejoicing of mine heart" (Jer. 15: 16). Like Timothy, the Lord's people need to be "nourished up in the words of faith and of good doctrine" (1 Tim 4. 6). Tragically, there are believers today who once feasted on the word of God, and frequented places where it was taught, but are now "desolate in the streets". The overall lesson of these passages must not be forgotten; sin and disobedience will bring reduced circumstances into the lives of God's people, and sin and disobedience will deprive the Lord's people today of their spiritual food. Alas, in such circumstances it can no longer be said, "thy soul prospereth" (3 John v.2)

4) THE CONCLUSION OF THE SIEGE, 5: 1-17

We will consider the fourth and final sign in our next study.

ADDENDUM

The significance of the days

We have to ask if it is possible to ascertain when the 430 days commenced and concluded. With this in mind, it should be noted that a new section of the prophecy commences with 8 verse 1, where we find Ezekiel sitting in his house, following which he is taken "in the visions of God to Jerusalem" (8. 3).

H.L.Ellison has pointed out that the difference in time between the dates mentioned in Chapter 1 verse 2 and Chapter 8 verse 1, which marks this new section of the prophecy, is exactly a year and two months. On the basis of the Jewish lunar year of 354 days (six months of 30 days alternating with six months of 29 days), this allows only a total of 413 days. However, by allowing that this was a leap year (which today occurs about twice in five years, and involves the insertion of an extra 29-day month), the total can

CHAPTER 4

be extended no further than 442 days. This just allows for the 430 days, bearing in mind that allowance must be made for the seven days of 3.15 and any other extra days that were needed for his preparations.

Quite clearly, it is impossible to be dogmatic, but this does seem a reasonable suggestion although, having said all this, H.L.Ellison himself opts for a different explanation!

EZEKIEL CHAPTER 5

We have already noted that after preparation and commissioning (2: 1 - 3: 23), Ezekiel's twenty-year ministry (1: 2; 40: 1) commenced with a series of signs. The first was the confinement of Ezekiel to his own house, when the prophet was told: "Thou shalt be dumb, and shalt not be to them a reprover ('a man of litigation'): for they are a rebellious house" (3: 26). As noted previously, according to C.J.H.Wright, the word "reprover" can have the meaning of an arbitrator or mediator, so that the prophet was dumb in the sense that he made no appeal to the people. His messages were purely judicial. He was not completely dumb: see, for example Chapter 11 verses 16, 17. This condition continued until the fall of Jerusalem (see: 3: 27; 24: 27; 33: 21-22), after which "his messages were of a more consolatory nature" (C.L.Feinberg).

But although in this sense Ezekiel was silent, God was speaking! According to the New Testament, God spoke "at sundry times and in *divers manners* ... by the prophets" (Heb. 1: 1). The "divers manners" includes the acted parables described this prophecy, and Ezekiel's confinement to his own house is the first of a succession of signs which continues in Chapters 4-5. The first sign (3: 24-27) introduces four others: *(i)* the sign of the inscribed tile (4: 1-3); *(ii)* the sign of the recumbent prophet (4: 4-8); *(iii)* the sign of the defiled food (4: 9-17); *(iv)* the sign of the shaven head (5: 1-17).

Having dealt in our previous study with the first three of these four signs, we are now given details of the fourth sign - the sign of the shaven head. If the first three signs depict the commencement of the coming siege (4: 1-3), the cause of the siege (4: 4-8) and the conditions during the siege (4: 9-17), then the fourth sign depicts the conclusion of the siege (5: 1-17). We must therefore now consider -

4) THE CONCLUSION OF THE SIEGE, 5: 1-17

As already noted, the fourth sign was to be given "when the days of the *siege*

CHAPTER 5

are fulfilled" (5: 2). We have called this 'the sign of the shaven head', but 'the sign of the divided hair' would do just as well! Either way, the chapter is easily summarised: *(a)* the demonstration of coming judgment (vv.1-4); *(b)* the justification for coming judgment (vv.5-11); *(c)* the amplification of coming judgment (vv.12-17).

a) The demonstration of coming judgment, vv.1-4

There are two parts to the demonstration: *(i)* shaving the head (v.1); *(ii)* dividing the hair (vv.2-4).

i) Shaving the head, v.1

"And thou, son of man, take thee a sharp knife, take thee a barber's rasor, and cause it to pass upon thine head and upon thy beard." According to the Authorised Version, Ezekiel was to take "a sharp knife" *and* "a barber's rasor", whereas the Revised Version makes them one and the same: "take thee a sharp sword, as a barber's razor shalt thou take it unto thee". The word rendered "knife" (*chereb*) is usually translated 'sword'. As Lamar E. Cooper points out, "the sword was an implement of warfare, which is just the point. He was to use the sword as a barber's razor to convey a specific message of judgment". It is not going too far to suggest that the removal of hair from head and face symbolised the removal of the population from Judah and Jerusalem, particularly the latter: see verse 2 ("the midst of the city"); verse 5 ("This is Jerusalem"). Shaving the head was a mark of mourning (Isa. 15: 2; Jer. 48: 37) or of disgrace and humiliation (2 Sam. 10: 4-5). Undoubtedly, the 'sword' here stands for the Babylonians in the same way that the razor stood for the Assyrians earlier. (See Isaiah 7: 20.)

ii) Dividing the hair, vv.2-4

"Then take thee balances to weigh, and divide the hair" (v.1). The hair was to be weighed before it was divided. Weighing was "a symbol of evaluation and impending judgment" (L.E.Cooper). See Daniel 5 verse 26; Proverbs 21 verse 2 ("the Lord weigheth the hearts", RV); 1 Samuel 2 verse 3. Ezekiel's hair was to be divided as follows:

i) "Thou shalt burn with fire a third part in the midst of the city, when the days of the siege are fulfilled" (v.2). This is later interpreted as follows: "A third part of thee shall die with the pestilence, and with famine shall they be consumed in the midst of thee" (v.12). We must say that the expression, "in the midst of the city" must refer to the tile representing the city (4: 1-2): after all, the actual city was a long way from Tel-abib! A third of the inhabitants would be destroyed within the city by famine and its aftermath. The "pestilence" and "famine" were judicial, hence the command to "burn with *fire*" a third part of the hair.

ii) "Thou shalt take a third part, and smite it about with a knife" (v.2). Once again the word "knife" (*chereb*) refers to a sword (see v.1): "thou shalt take a third part, and smite with the sword round about it" (RV). The words "round about it" evidently mean, 'round about the city', that is, the tile representing the city. So a further third of the population would die fighting without the city. This too is confirmed later: "a third part shall fall by the sword round about thee" (v.12).

iii) "A third part thou shalt scatter in the wind; and I will draw out a sword after them" (verse 12). This is virtually repeated in v.12 without further explanation, but J.B.Taylor must be correct in saying "a third would be scattered among the nations and would continue to be harried by hostile forces". This had been predicted by Moses: "I will scatter you among the heathen, and will draw out a sword (*chereb*) after you" (Lev. 26: 33). See also Jeremiah 9 verse 16.

iv) "Thou shalt also take thereof a few in number, and bind them in thy skirts. Then take them again, and cast them into the midst of the fire, and burn them in the fire" (vv.3-4). The "skirts" refers to "the lower extremities of the long ankle-length tunic, which could be gathered up and tucked into the girdle to form a pouch for carrying things" (J.B.Taylor). F.A.Tatford points out that "of those of Jerusalem who took flight but who were still threatened with danger, a small number were divinely preserved for the fulfilment of God's purposes. But even out of this small number, some were to be cast into the fire indicating that even some of the survivors would be consumed, reducing still further the number actually preserved". C.L.Feinberg concurs: "even the remnant was to undergo further trial and ordeal", and continues: "In Jeremiah 40-44 can be found their trials in the land which took place even after the destruction of the city and the sanctuary; in this category are the difficulties after the assassination of Gedaliah by Ishmael, and the descent into Egypt under Johanan".

The words, "for thereof shall a fire come forth into all the house of Israel" (v.4) or "from there a fire will come forth into all the house of Israel" (RV), are not easily explained, but F.A.Tatford is probably correct in suggesting that the fire of divine judgment which would consume the inhabitants of Jerusalem would spread to all the house of Israel, wherever they were to be found.

It has also been suggested that this part of the prophecy might well embrace events far distant at the time, including to events in AD 70 when judgment fell on Jerusalem at the hand of the Romans under Titus, and even further ahead, the fearful persecution through which the nation will pass at the end-time.

b) The justification for coming judgment, vv.5-11

It is for very good reason that C.L.Feinberg entitles this chapter 'Judgment on abused privilege'. We should note *(i)* Jerusalem's privilege (v.5); *(ii)* Jerusalem's perfidy (v.6); *(iii)* Jerusalem's punishment (vv.7-11).

i) Jerusalem's privilege, v.5

"Thus saith the Lord GOD (*Adonai Jehovah*); This is Jerusalem: I have set it in the midst of the nations and countries that are round about her." This is reiterated later in the prophecy: "And thou (the northern invader at the end-time) shalt say, "I will go up to the land of unwalled villages; I will go to them that are at rest ... that are gathered out of the nations, which have gotten cattle and goods, that dwell in the midst of the land ('earth', RV)" (Ezek. 38: 11-12). According to the RV margin here (Ezek. 38: 12), the word "middle" (AV 'midst') is literally, 'navel' (see also Judges 9: 37 margin), leading F.A.Tatford to say: "Many of the Rabbis referred to Jerusalem as geographically the navel of the world". While the words, "I have set it in the midst of the nations and countries that are round about her", are understood by some commentators with reference to "her place theologically as the centrepiece of God's favour in the world" (J.B.Taylor), it does seem more than likely that this is linked with her geographical position: "When the Most High divided to the nations their inheritance, when he separated the sons of Adam, he set the bounds of the people their habitation according to the number of the children of Israel" (Deut. 32: 8). It has been suggested that the words, "This is Jerusalem", refer to the inscribed tile (4: 1) which, presumably, still lay on the ground outside Ezekiel's house, but this seems a little imaginative. The expression, "the nations and the countries that are round about her", re-occurs, with variations, in subsequent verses: see verses 6, 7, 14 and 15.

This reminds us of our privileged position. The Lord Jesus said, "Ye shall receive power, after that the Holy Ghost is come upon you: and ye shall be witnesses unto me both in Jerusalem, and in all Judaea, and in Samaria, and unto the uttermost part of the earth" (Acts 1: 8).

b) Jerusalem's perfidy, v.6

"She hath changed my judgments into wickedness more than the nations, and my statutes more than the countries that are round about her: for they have refused my judgments and my statutes, they have not walked in them." Instead of being an example to the surrounding nations, Jerusalem had exceeded them in wickedness. This made her guilt immeasurably greater than that of her heathen neighbours because, unlike the heathen, she was thoroughly aware of God's statutes and judgments. Great privilege carries great responsibility. In the words of the Lord Jesus, "For unto whomsoever much is given, of him shall be much required" (Luke 12: 48). See also Matthew 11 verses 20-24.

F.A.Tatford has some very searching things to say in this connection: "The culpability of those who know the truth and reject it is always greater than those who are ignorant of it. The Christian today has greater responsibilities and a fuller accountability than the unbeliever who has no personal relationship with Christ. He is the witness to God in the midst of unbelievers; his failure is far more reprehensible than that of others".

Jerusalem's culpability in this way is now further emphasised in describing her punishment.

c) Jerusalem's punishment, vv.7-11

In view of Jerusalem's wickedness, divine judgment is pronounced: "Therefore (v.7) ... Therefore (v.8) ... Therefore (v.10) ... Wherefore (v.11) ... therefore (v.11)". Amongst other things we should notice the following:

i) **"Therefore ... I ... am against thee."** "Therefore thus saith the Lord GOD; Because ye multiplied ('because ye are turbulent' or 'more unruly') more than the nations that are round about you, and have not walked in my statutes; neither have kept my judgments, neither have done according to the judgments of the nations that are round about you; **therefore** thus saith the Lord GOD; Behold, I, even I, am against thee, and will execute judgments in the midst of thee in the sight of the nations. And I will do in thee that which I have not done, and whereunto I will not do any more the like, because of thine abominations" (vv.7-9).

The word "multiplied" (AV), meaning 'turbulent' (RV/JND), is only found here. It is evidently associated with a verb meaning 'to make a noise' or 'to rage', leading C.L.Feinberg to say, "Israel, endowed with position and privilege, became turbulent; they raged in their opposition against God". The statement that God's people had not even (see JND) matched the standards of the surrounding nations can be illustrated from the preaching of Jeremiah: "Hath a nation changed their gods, which are yet no gods? *But my people* have changed their glory for that which doth not profit" (Jer. 2: 11). Earlier still, Amos invited the Philistines and the Egyptians to "Assemble ... upon the mountains of Samaria, and *behold* the great tumults in the midst thereof, and the oppression in the midst thereof" (Amos 3: 9). Lamar E. Cooper puts it succinctly: "Since the people of God refused to be an example of righteousness and godliness (v.5), they would be an example of chastening. Because of their abominations and idolatry, God pledged to do what He had not done before nor would ever do again (v.9). He promised the severest forms of judgment. Abominations that are unprecedented call for extraordinary judgment".

ii) ***"Therefore ... the whole remnant of thee will I scatter into all the winds."*** "Therefore the fathers shall eat the sons in the midst of thee, and the sons shall eat their fathers; and I will execute judgments in thee, and the whole remnant of thee will I scatter into all the winds" (v.10). We have only to read the book of Lamentations for confirmation that cannibalism was practised during the siege of Jerusalem. See Lamentations 4 verse 10. The threats uttered by Moses (Lev. 26: 29; Deut. 28: 53), and reiterated by Jeremiah (Jer. 19: 9), were all fulfilled (Lam. 2: 20). We are horrified at the very thought of cannibalism, but are we horrified at the thought of spiritual cannibalism? See Galatians 5 verse 15,

The statement, "the whole remnant will I scatter into all the winds" (v.10) should be compared with Matthew 24 verse 31, "And he shall send his angels with a great sound of a trumpet, and they shall gather together his elect from the four winds, from one end of heaven to the other". Dispersion will ultimately give place to regathering.

iii) ***"Therefore will I also diminish thee."*** "Wherefore, as I live, saith the Lord GOD; Surely, because thou hast defiled my sanctuary with all thy detestable things, and with all thine abominations, therefore will I also diminish thee; neither shall mine eye spare, neither will I have any pity" (v.11). The way in which they had "defiled" God's sanctuary is made clear later. See Ezekiel 8 verses 5-18. The "detestable things" were "their rites and images borrowed from foreign cults" (C.L.Feinberg). Since they had 'diminished' (*gara*) the word of God (cf. Deut. 4: 2; 12: 32), God would "diminish" (*gara*) them". According to Gesenius, the word "diminish" means 'to take away'. The New Testament reads similarly: "Know ye not that ye are the temple of God ... If any man defile (*phtheiro*, 'mar') the temple of God, him shall God destroy (*phtheiro*, mar); for the temple of God is holy, which temple ye are" (1 Cor. 3: 16-17).

The certainty of divine judgment in this way is vested in the very existence of God. The expression, "as I live, saith the Lord GOD" occurs fourteen times in the book, more often than in any other prophecy. See 5: 11; 14: 16, 18, 20; 16: 48; 17: 16, 19; 18: 3; 20: 3, 8, 31, 33; 33: 11; 34: 8; 35: 6.)

3) *The amplification of coming judgment, vv.12-17*

Since the symbolism of the divided hair (v.2) has already been explained with reference to verse 12, no further comment is needed. Here is the text of the explanation: "A third part of thee shall die with the pestilence, and with famine shall they be consumed in the midst of thee: and a third part shall fall by the sword round about thee; and I will scatter a third part into all the winds, and I will draw out a sword after them". It should be noted that the "few hairs" bound in Ezekiel's skirts and then burned in the fire is not explained here. The three forms of judgment ("pestilence...famine...sword") are repeated in Chapter 6 verse 12. However, the explanation of the divided hair is expanded in the following verses (vv.13-17) with the thrice-repeated, "I the Lord have spoken it" (vv.13, 15, 17). The following should be noticed:

i) *"I will be comforted", v.13.* "Thus (referring to the threefold judgment described in v.12) shall mine anger be accomplished, and I will cause my fury to rest upon them (or, 'I will quieten my fury' in the sense of 'appease' or 'assuage'), and I will be comforted: and they shall know (so they would recognise His anger) that I the LORD have spoken it in my zeal, when I have accomplished my fury in them" (v.13). According to C.L.Feinberg, "the verb 'comforted' is used either of the feeling of compassion, or of consoling oneself by taking vengeance (Isa 1: 24), probably the latter here". The context strongly suggests that this is correct.

ii) **"I will make thee waste", v.14.** "Moreover I will make thee waste (a desolation or a ruin), and a reproach among the nations that are round about thee, in the sight of all that pass by. So it shall be a reproach and a taunt, an instruction and an astonishment unto the nations that are round about thee, when I shall execute judgments in thee in anger and in fury and in furious rebukes. I the LORD have spoken it" (vv.14-15). As C.L.Feinberg observes, "God's honour, flouted by the people in the sight of the nations, had to be vindicated before the eyes of those very nations". It would be "an instruction … unto the nations that are round about thee". They would learn that no nation can 'play fast and loose' with the laws of God, and remain unscathed.

The words, "So it shall be a reproach and a taunt" to the surrounding nations, illustrate the teaching of the Lord Jesus, "Ye are the salt of the earth: but if the salt have lost his savour, wherewith shall it be salted? It is thenceforth good for nothing, but to be cast out, and to be trodden under foot of ***men***" (Matt. 5: 13). See also John 15 verse 6, "***men*** gather them (the fruitless vine-branches), and cast them into the fire". An example of the "taunt" occurs in Lamentations 2 verse 15, "All that pass by clap their hands at thee; they hiss and wag their head at the daughter of Jerusalem, saying, Is this the city that men call The perfection of beauty, The joy of the whole earth?"

iii) **"I will send to destroy you", v.16.** "When I shall send upon them the evil arrows of famine, which shall be for their destruction, and which I will send to destroy you: and I will increase the famine upon you, and will break your staff of bread: so will I send upon you famine and evil beasts, and they shall bereave thee; and pestilence and blood shall pass through thee; and I will bring the sword upon thee. I the LORD have spoken it" (vv.16-17). These are later called God's "four sore judgments … the sword, and the famine, and the noisome beast ('evil beast', JND), and the pestilence" (Ezek. 14: 21). The entire world will be similarly afflicted at the end time: "And power was given unto them ('him', JND: that is, "Death") over the fourth part of the earth, to kill with sword, and with hunger, and with death (probably in the sense of 'pestilence' or 'plague'), and with the beasts of the earth" (Rev. 6: 8).

It has been said that "the more indifferent men are to God's laws, the louder He has to speak" (J.B.Taylor). We do well to remember this when disasters hit the news. God is not a disinterested bystander. Each earthquake, flood or 'natural disaster' is nothing less than the voice of God. Oh that men might come to realise that "I the LORD have spoken it", and turn to Him in repentance and faith.

EZEKIEL CHAPTER 6

Thus far in our studies, we have noted: *(a)* the commissioning of Ezekiel; *(b)* the commencement of Ezekiel's service.

a) The commissioning of Ezekiel

In this connection, we noticed *(i) what he saw* (1: 1-28): "I saw visions of God" (1: 1); *(ii) what he heard* (2: 1-10): "I heard him that spake unto me" (2: 2); *(iii) where he went* (3: 1-15): "I came to them of the captivity of Tel-abib" (3: 15).

b) The commencement of Ezekiel's service

Having been called and commissioned, Ezekiel then tells us that "it came to pass at the end of seven days, that the word of the LORD came unto me" (3: 16). This marked the first phase of Ezekiel's service which continued until the conclusion of Chapter 7. It is worth mentioning at this juncture that the second date in the prophecy introduces the second phase of Ezekiel's ministry (8: 1 - 11: 25). This section commences with the words: "And it came to pass in the sixth year, in the sixth month, in the fifth day of the month" (8: 1). The first and second phases of his ministry were therefore separated by a period of exactly fourteen months (1: 1-2; 8: 1).

Bearing in mind his task to act as a watchman, and warn "the house of Israel" (3: 17-22), the prophet was instructed to convey the warning **visually** (3: 22 - 5: 17) and **verbally** (6: 1 - 7: 27). In both cases, the prophet was equipped with the "word of the LORD" (3: 16; 6: 1; 7: 1).

This brings us to the beginning of Chapter 6 and to the first of two messages that Ezekiel was commanded to deliver verbally. Both are introduced with the words, "the word of the LORD came unto me (6: 1; 7: 1). *The Expositor's Bible Commentary* calls these chapters "pendants to the theme which is dealt with in this opening section of the book of Ezekiel". The first message

CHAPTER 6

(6: 1-14) was directed against "the mountains of Israel" (v.2) and stressed the *inevitability* of divine judgment, whereas the second message (7: 1-27) announced the *imminence* of divine judgment. See, for example, "the end is come" (v.2); "an evil ... is come" (v.5); "the time is come" (v.12). The first message describes the conditions which necessitated divine judgment, and the second declared that it was about to fall. The "mountains of Israel" were defiled by idolatry, which was practised "upon every high hill, in all the tops of the mountains, and under every green tree, and under every thick oak" (6: 13). As a result, the Lord says, "I will recompense thee according to thy ways and thine abominations that are in the midst of thee" (7: 9).

It is worth asking why Ezekiel was told to convey God's word in this way to the Jewish exiles by "the river Chebar". After all, they were already in captivity, and Judah and Jerusalem were hundreds of miles away. Amongst other things, Ezekiel's ministry was intended to counter the pronouncement of the false prophets among the Judaean exiles in Babylonia. See Jeremiah 29 verses 8-9; 15-23. These men evidently followed the teaching of Hananiah in Jerusalem, who proclaimed that within two years the captives would all be safely back home, together with Jehoiachin (Jeconiah) and the temple vessels. See Jeremiah 28 verses 1-17. These predictions were false, and the exiles were not to be 'buoyed up' with empty promises. Jerusalem and Judah would fall. The exiles would have nowhere to go.

Chapter 6, the first of the two chapters in which Ezekiel declares "the word of the LORD" verbally, may be divided with reference to the expressions, "ye shall know that I am the LORD" or "they shall know that I am the LORD" (vv.7, 10, 13, 14). H. L. Ellison observes that the expression, "Thou shalt (or 'ye shall ... they shall') know that I am the LORD" is "the most characteristic expression of Ezekiel. It occurs in this simple form no less than 54 times and with some expansion another 18 times. This knowledge is always connected either with the judgments of God or with His acts of grace; it is probably only due to the greatly predominating stress on God's judgment in Ezekiel that the majority of the passages fall into the former category". In the present passage, the expression is used to emphasise that God's people will be made acutely aware that He is alone the true, eternal and self-sufficient God, and that the gods they worshipped on "the mountains of Israel" were nothing more than lifeless "images" (v.4). The expression emphasises, not so much the existence of Jehovah, but His identity. Ultimately, all men will have no other option but to acknowledge that He is "the LORD".

The current chapter may be divided as follows: *(1)* the destruction of the shrines (vv.1-7); *(2)* the preservation of a remnant (vv.8-10); *(3)* the execution of divine wrath (vv.11-14). As noted above, each section concludes with, "and ye shall know (or "they shall know") that I am the LORD" (vv.7, 10, 14).

1) THE DESTRUCTION OF THE SHRINES, vv.1-7

The message is addressed to "the mountains of Israel" (v.2) and H.L.Ellison rightly observes that this "explains that the sin that was bringing destruction on Jerusalem was above all a religious one". While F.Gardiner (*Ellicott's Commentary*) states: "It is not uncommon to address prophetic utterances to inanimate objects as a poetic way of representing the people", he does continue by saying, "The mountains are especially mentioned as being the chosen places of idolatrous worship. See Deuterony 12 verse 2; 2 Kings 17 verses 10-11; Jeremiah 2 verse 20; Jeremiah 3 verse 6; Hosea 4 verse 13. Baal, the sun-god (see vv.4, 6 margin, 'sun images'), was the idol especially worshipped upon the hills". The section continues by referring to "the rivers, and to the valleys" (v.3), leading F.Gardiner to continue: "Such places were also favourite places for idolatrous rites (see 2 Kings 23: 10; Isa. 57: 5-6; Jer. 7: 31; Jer. 32: 35), especially for the worship of the Phoenician Astaroth, the female deity worshipped in conjunction with Baal".

These verses contain important lessons for us all: *(a)* the incidence of idolatry (v.3); *(b)* the impotence of idolatry (vv.3-5; *(c)* the influence of idolatry (vv.6-7).

a) The incidence of idolatry, v.3

It was everywhere: on "the mountains", on "the hills", by "the rivers", and in "the valleys". See also verse 13, "upon every high hill, in all the tops of the mountains, and under every green tree, and under every thick oak". The Canaanite nations "served their gods, upon the high mountains, and upon the hills, and under every green tree" (Deut. 12: 2), so there is no doubt that in spite of warnings, God's people followed suit.

Idolatry is an ever-present danger. Idolatrous Corinth necessitated Paul to say, "Wherefore, my dearly beloved, flee from idolatry ... Ye cannot drink the cup of the Lord, and the cup of devils (demons): ye cannot be partakers of the Lord's table, and the table of devils (demons)" (1 Cor. 10: 14-21). But idolatry takes other forms. Paul refers to "covetousness, which is idolatry"

(Col. 3: 5) or "unbridled desire which is idolatry" (JND). The context here, together with the context of Ephesians 5 verse 5, which refers to a "covetous man, who is an idolator", suggests sensuality, as opposed to covetousness in its normal meaning. The desire of David for Bath-sheba is a sad example of transgressing the tenth commandment: "Thou shalt not covet ... thy neighbour's wife" (Exodus 20: 17). Sensuality can become the be-all and end-all, and therefore constitute idolatry. There can be no doubt, however, that the concluding words of 1 John are all-embracing: "Little children, keep yourselves from idols" (1 John 5: 21). At first glance, this seems like an anti-climax, but the context proves otherwise. Having spoken about the "true God" ("He is the true God", JND v.20), John makes it clear that anything that takes His place in our hearts and lives is a false god.

> *Jesus calls us from the worship*
> *Of the vain world's golden store;*
> *From each idol that would keep us,*
> *Saying, "Christian, love Me more!"*

b) The impotence of idolatry, vv.3-5

"Behold, I, even I, will bring a sword upon you, and I will destroy your high places. And your altars shall be desolate, and your images ('sun images', JND) shall be broken: and I will cast down your slain men before your idols. And I will lay the dead carcases of the children of Israel before their idols; and I will scatter your bones round about your altars." As F.Gardiner (*Ellicott's Commentary*) observes: "The Israelites had defiled the land with idols: now the idols themselves should be defiled by their dead bodies". However, the principal point here is that idols have no power to deliver their devotees from death. Isaiah makes the same point. Having said that "their land also is full of idols; they worship the work of their own hands, that which their own fingers have made", he continues, "In that day a man shall cast his idols of silver, and his idols of gold, which they made each one for himself to worship, to the moles and to the bats; to go into the clefts of the rocks, and into the tops of the ragged rocks, for fear of the LORD, and for the glory of his majesty, when he ariseth to shake terribly the earth" (Isaiah 2: 8, 20-21). Isaiah emphasises the impotence of idols and idolatry again: "they have no knowledge that set up the wood of their graven image, and pray unto a god that cannot save" (Isa. 45: 20).

The "vain world's golden store", whatever form it may take, will give no refuge or joy in the crises of life. The believer, devoted to the Lord, can sing:

'Tis what I know of Thee, my Lord and God,
That fills my soul with peace, my lips with song;
Thou art my health, my joy, my staff and rod;
Leaning on Thee, in weakness I am strong."

c) The influence of idolatry, vv.6-7

It would bring divine judgment on national life in its entirety. The "dwellingplaces" and "cities" would be "laid waste" as well as "the high places" with their altars and images: "In all your dwellingplaces the cities shall be laid waste, and the high places shall be desolate; that your altars may be laid waste and made desolate, and your idols may be broken and cease, and your images may be cut down, and your works may be abolished. And the slain shall fall in the midst of you, and ye shall know that I am the LORD".

The homes and cities of the people would be "laid waste" as the result of idolatry. Attendance at the altars in "the high places" would ultimately affect every part of life, reminding us that when our devotion to the Lord is either impaired or destroyed, it will not be long before the result is seen in our lives. When things go wrong in our relationship with God, they go wrong everywhere, and the lives of many of the Lord's people have been "laid waste" for this very reason.

The book of Ezekiel assures us that idolatry will not have the last word so far as "the mountains of Israel" are concerned. Those same mountains will ultimately be places of divine blessing. See Ezekiel 36 verses 1-12. Note, in particular, verses 8-11: "But ye, O mountains of Israel, ye shall shoot forth your branches, and yield your fruit to my people of Israel; for they are at hand to come. For, behold, I am for you, and I will turn unto you, and ye shall be tilled and sown ... And I will multiply upon you man and beast: and they shall increase and bring fruit: and I will settle you after your old estates, and will do better unto you than at your beginnings: and ye shall know that I am the LORD".

2) THE PRESERVATION OF A REMNANT, vv.8-10

The remnant answers to the "few" hairs which Ezekiel was to "bind" in his "skirts" (5: 3). We should notice the following: *(a)* the scattering of the remnant (v.8); *(b)* their sorrow for sin (v.9); *(c)* the strength of God's word (v.10).

CHAPTER 6

a) The scattering of the remnant, v.8

"Yet will I leave a remnant, that ye may have some that shall escape the sword among the nations, when ye shall be scattered through the countries." The Lord would not make "a full end" of His people (Jer. 30: 11; 46: 28). But this did not mean that the "remnant" would be unscathed. This had been made clear when Ezekiel was commanded to take a few hairs, and "bind them in thy skirts. Then take of them again, and cast them into the midst of the fire, and burn them in the fire" (5: 3-4). In the language of Jeremiah: "I will not make a full end of thee: but I will correct thee in measure, and will not leave thee altogether unpunished" (Jer. 30: 11). Jeremiah gives us a glimpse of at least part of this remnant: after the fall of Jerusalem, "Johanan the son of Kareah, and all the captains of the forces, took all the remnant of Judah, that were returned from all nations whither they had been driven, to dwell in the land of Judah … so they came into the land of Egypt" (Jer. 43: 5-7). Zechariah gives us a more enlarged picture: "I will sow them among the people ('peoples' JND): and they shall remember me in far countries: and they shall live with their children, and turn again" (Zech. 10: 9). God's people will be ultimately regathered, and the promises made to the patriarchs will be completely fulfilled: "I will plant them upon their land, and they shall no more be pulled up out of their land which I have given them, saith the LORD thy God" (Amos 9: 15).

b) Their sorrow for sin, v.9

They would be convicted of their sin in turning from the Lord: "And they that escape of you shall remember me among the nations whither they shall be carried captives, because I am broken with their whorish heart (or 'when I shall have broken their whorish heart', JND), which hath departed from me, and with their eyes, which go a whoring after their idols: and they shall loathe (some AV's have 'lothe') themselves for the evils which they have committed in all their abominations".

The sin of idolatry had invaded every part of their lives. Reference is made to the following:

- Their *thoughts* were defiled: "their whorish heart".

- Their *sight* was defiled: "their eyes … go a whoring after their idols".

- Their *actions* were defiled: "the evils which they have committed".

The expression "whorish heart" emphasises their unfaithfulness to the Lord who had said, "Turn, O backsliding children, saith the LORD; for I am married unto you" (Jer. 3: 14). This explains the previous statement: "through the lightness of her whoredom ... she defiled the land, and committed adultery with stones and with stocks" (Jer. 3: 9). The New Testament makes the same point: "Ye adulterers and adulteresses, know ye not that the friendship of the world is enmity with God?" (James 4: 4). The word "idols" (*gillulim*) "is a favourite with Ezekiel, occurring no less than thirty-eight times, as against nine times in the rest of the Old Testament" (J.B.Taylor). (There are other words translated "idol" or "idols".) According to C.L.Feinberg the word here means 'dung-gods', and according to J.B.Taylor, the word comes from a noun whose consonants mean 'a pellet of dung'. No wonder he adds, "The final combination carries about as much disdain and revulsion as any word could do".

The words "loathe themselves" (see also 20: 43; 36: 31) indicate true repentance. The remnant would recognise that the destruction of their homeland and their subsequent exile were nothing less than divine judgment. The utter folly, not to say wickedness, of idolatry would become apparent to them as never before, and they would "loathe themselves for the evils which they have committed in all their abominations". It would be "godly sorrow" working "repentance to salvation not to be repented of" (2 Cor. 7: 10). Their sorrow for sin is mentioned again in Chapter 7 verse 16, "But they that escape of them shall escape, and shall be on the mountains like doves of the valleys, all of them mourning, every one for his iniquity". It has been said that men 'grieve over the evil that sin brings, but not over the sin that brings evil'. However, this does not appear to be the case here.

Hosea sets out the result of divine chastening: "the children of Israel shall abide many days "without a king, and without a prince, and without a sacrifice, and without an image, and without an ephod, and without teraphim" (Hos. 3: 4). The nation would be purged of idolatry.

c) *The strength of God's word, v.10*

"And they shall know that I am the LORD, and that I have not said in vain that I would do this evil unto them." It was a case of "my word ... shall not return unto me void" (Isaiah 55: 11). While, in context, these oft-quoted words emphasise the certainty of God's word in connection with the restoration and blessing of His people, we should remember that His word will not 'return unto Him void' in other ways as well. Zechariah gives us an example: "my words and my statutes, which I commanded my servants the prophets, did they not take hold of (overtake) your fathers? and they returned and said, Like as the LORD of hosts thought to do unto us, according to our ways, and according to our doings, so hath he dealt with us" (Zech. 1: 6).

Whether in blessing or, as here, in judgment, God will always honour His promises. There are some things that God cannot do, and here is one of them: "God, that cannot lie ..." (Titus 1: 2). If we reject His word, the consequences are inevitable. The "fathers" (Zech. 1: 6) were obliged to acknowledge that God was faithful to His own word. The "fathers" here includes the very people to whom Ezekiel refers in this chapter: "And they shall know that I am the LORD, and that I have not said in vain that I would do this evil unto them".

3) THE EXECUTION OF DIVINE WRATH, vv.11-14

The third section of this chapter commences with another piece of drama. Having done various things with his hair (5: 1-4), he is now told to "Smite with thine hand, and stamp with thy foot, and say, Alas for all the evil abominations of the house of Israel!" (v.11). The Jews at Tel-abib must have wondered whatever he would get up to next! We should notice the following: *(a)* judgment would be inevitable (v.11); *(b)* judgment would be inescapable (vv.11-12); *(c)* judgment would be informative (v.13); *(d)* judgment would be inclusive (v.14).

a) Judgment would be inevitable, v.11

While, according to C.L.Feinberg, "there has been a wide divergence of opinion as to the meaning of these gestures", Ellicott's Commentary seems correct in saying that "To clap the hands and stamp the feet, either singly (Num. 24: 10; Ezek. 21: 14, 17; 22: 13) or together (Ezek. 25: 6), is a gesture of strong emotion or earnestness of purpose. The prophet is here directed to use it as indicating God's unchangeable determination united to a sense of grievous wrong". At least one commentator suggests that "clapping the hand and stamping the foot were gestures of scornful delight" and that the words "say, Alas" should be rendered 'say, Hurrah' (John B. Taylor). While this might have been true in the case of the Ammonites (25: 6), it could hardly be true here. H.L.Ellison suggests that "Ezekiel is called on to rejoice that the accumulated evil of centuries is to be swept away". This seems rather unlikely.

b) Judgment would be inescapable, vv.11-12

The comprehensive nature of coming judgment on Judah (v.14) is emphasised. Having said, "they shall fall by the sword, by the famine, and by the pestilence (plague)" (v.11), the Lord continues: "He that is far off shall die of the pestilence (plague); and he that is near shall fall by the sword; and he that remaineth and is besieged shall die by the famine: thus will I accomplish my fury upon them". The three forms of judgment here are repeated from Chapter 5 verse 12. Jeremiah also predicted that the Lord would send upon them (the "vile figs") the sword, the famine, and the pestilence" (Jer. 29: 17). It has been suggested that the words "he that is far off" and "he that is near" are "a typical Hebrew comprehensive term ... meaning all without distinction" (J.B.Taylor). Examples occur in Ezekiel 22 verse 5; Jeremiah 25 verse 26; Daniel 9 verse 7. Alternatively, "he that is far off" may refer to those remote from Jerusalem, "he that is near" to those in close proximity to Jerusalem, and "he that remaineth and is besieged", obviously, to those in Jerusalem. Perhaps we could go further and trace the progress of the invasion: entering the land, nearing Jerusalem, besieging Jerusalem.

c) Judgment would be informative, v.13

"Then shall ye know that I am the LORD, when their slain men shall be among their idols round about their altars, upon every high hill, in all the tops of the mountains, and under every green tree, and under every thick oak, the place where they did offer sweet savour to all their idols."

The carnage throughout the land would vividly remind them that Jehovah was the living and eternal God who always implemented His word, as opposed to their powerless and lifeless idols which could accomplish nothing. The frequently-repeated expression, "Then shall ye know that I am the LORD", has been described as "the holy and royal monogram. When this seal is attached, God Himself vouches for the truth of what has been declared" (C.L.Feinberg).

d) Judgment would be inclusive, v.14

"So will I stretch out my hand upon them, and make the land desolate, yea, more desolate than the wilderness toward Diblath, in all their habitations: and they shall know that I am the LORD." We should notice reference, not just to Jerusalem, or to the hills and mountains (vv.2-3), but to "the

CHAPTER 6

land", and then to "all their habitations". H.L.Ellison should be read with great caution here: "In verse 14 we have probably a case of one of the commonest of all scribal errors in the Old Testament, the confounding of D and R". Ellison continues by stating that it should be rendered "'from the wilderness to Riblah' (RSV), i.e. from South to North (cf. Num. 34: 11)". F.Gardiner (Ellicott's Commentary) has a different view: "The name *Diblath* does not occur elsewhere; but *Diblathaim*, the dual form, is mentioned in Numbers 33 verses 46-47, Jeremiah 48 verse 22, as a double city on the eastern border of Moab, beyond which lay the great desert which stretches thence eastward, nearly to the Euphrates. It was customary to call any wilderness by the name of the nearest town". Ellicott is preferable to Ellison! C.L.Feinberg notes that "most modern commentators favour this revision (i.e. Riblah instead of Diblah), and adds, significantly, that "none of the old versions supports it".

EZEKIEL CHAPTER 7

Having been commissioned by the Lord (1: 1 - 3: 15), Ezekiel's service commenced with instructions to act as a watchman, and warn "the house of Israel" of coming judgment (3: 16-22). As we have seen, the prophet was told to convey the warning **visually** (3: 22 - 5: 17) and **verbally** (6: 1 - 7: 27), and in both cases he was equipped with the "word of the LORD" (3: 16; 6: 1; 7: 1). If Chapter 6 emphasises the *inevitability* of divine judgment, then Chapter 7 emphasises the *imminence* of divine judgment. In the words of F.Gardiner (*Ellicott's Commentary*), "The prophecy of this chapter is occupied with the nearness and completeness of the judgment already foretold. It takes the form, to some extent, of a song of lamentation; and is more thoroughly poetic in its structure than anything which has gone before".

We must remember that although Ezekiel's ministry is addressed to the exiles at Tel-abib in Babylonia, it describes, at this point, the coming judgment of Jerusalem which lay, at a rough guess, approximately one thousand miles away. It took Ezra and his party four months to make the journey (Ezra 7: 9), although there can be no doubt that a mounted messenger could cover the distance in a much shorter time. Ezekiel deals with coming events in Judah in order to disabuse the exiles in Babylonia of the idea that they would only be there for a short time. The false prophets had predicted that "friends, relatives, and leaders taken hostage to Babylon would be coming home soon" (Lamar E. Cooper). See Jeremiah 28 verses 1-4. This would not be the case.

It is worth noting that the expression "ye shall know that I am the LORD" or "they shall know that I am the LORD", which occurs four times in Chapter 6 (vv.7, 10, 13, 14), also occurs three times in Chapter 7 (vv.4, 9, 27). God's people would not be allowed to forget that the Lord (Jehovah) was the living and eternal God who always implemented His word. While He certainly implements His word in blessing, He does so equally in judgment: the words "I will ... judge thee according to thy ways" (vv.3, 8) and "I will recompence

CHAPTER 7

thee according thy ways" (v.9) are closely connected with the words, "and ye shall know that I am the LORD" (v.4) or "and ye shall know that I am the LORD that smiteth" (v.9). Similarly, the warning, "I will do unto them after their way, and according to their deserts will I judge them", is followed by the words, "and they shall know that I am the LORD" (v.27)

More particularly however, Chapter 7 is punctuated by references to the imminence of God's wrath: "An end, the end is *come*" (v.2); "Now is the end *come* upon thee" (v.3); "An evil, an only evil, behold, is *come*" (v.5); "An end is *come*, the end is *come*: it watcheth for thee; behold it is *come*" (v.6); "The morning ('doom', RV) is *come* unto thee ... the time is *come*, the day of trouble is *near*" (v.7); "Now will I *shortly* pour out my fury upon thee" (v.8); "Behold the day, behold, it is *come*" (v.10); "The time is *come*, the day *draweth near*" (v.12). The judgment anticipated in these verses fell within four to five years with the commencement of the eighteen month siege of Jerusalem by the Chaldeans. See 2 Kings 25 verses 1-5.

The chapter presents expositors with several problems, and commentators hold different views in interpreting some verses. Bearing this in mind, and without any claim to superior judgment, we tentatively suggest the following summary: *(1)* the imminence of judgment (vv.1-9); *(2)* the iniquity at its height (vv.10-11); *(3)* the inclusiveness of judgment (vv.12-16); *(4)* the impotence of wealth (vv.17-19); *(5)* the impurity of the temple (vv.20-22); *(6)* the ineffectiveness of the leadership (vv.23-27).

1) THE IMMINENCE OF JUDGMENT, vv.1-9

We have already noticed the repetition of the word "come": it occurs eight times in these verses. The message of impending doom is twice-repeated in these verses (vv.2-4; vv.5-9), evidently for emphasis: "The frequent repetitions of this chapter are designed, and give great force to the denunciation of woe" (F.Gardiner, *Ellicott's Commentary*). C.L.Feinberg concurs: "It is remarkable how soon even threatening messages are forgotten by the hearers. There was a need to enforce and reinforce the heart of the message so that when the blow did fall, they would realise that the Lord is a God of judgment, and that the visitation had proceeded from Him".

a) The first message, vv.2-4

"Thus saith the Lord GOD unto the land of Israel; An end, the end is come upon the four corners of the land. Now is the end come upon thee, and I will send mine anger upon thee, and will judge thee according to thy ways, and will recompense upon thee all thine abominations. And mine eye shall not spare thee, neither will I have pity: but I will recompense thy ways upon thee, and thine abominations shall be in the midst of thee (meaning that their evil in departing from the Lord would then be clear to them): and ye shall know that I am the LORD."

The expression, "the end is come" first occurs in the preaching of Amos: "Thus hath the Lord GOD shewed unto me: and behold a basket of summer fruit ... Then said the LORD unto me, The end is come upon my people of Israel: I will not again pass by them any more" (Amos 8: 1-2). Normally, "a basket of summer fruit" would have been a pleasant sight, but on this occasion Amos was told that it was a picture of Israel. The "basket of summer fruit" was ready for eating, and Israel was ripe for judgment.

Returning now to Ezekiel's preaching, two hundred years later, we must note that divine judgment would be:

i) **Unavoidable.** It would fall "upon the four corners of the land" (v.2). No city would be spared, confirming the earlier prediction that "In all your dwellingplaces the cities shall be laid waste" (6: 6). This should remind *us* that "*every man's* work shall be made manifest: for the day shall declare it, because it shall be revealed by fire ... If any man's work shall be burned, he shall suffer loss: but he himself shall be saved; yet so as by fire" (1 Cor. 3: 13-15).

ii) **Unquestionable**: "I ... will judge thee according to thy ways, and will recompence upon thee all thine abominations" (v.3). This should remind *us* that "God is not mocked: for whatsoever a man soweth, that shall he also reap" (Gal. 6: 7). We must never labour under the delusion that because we are God's children, the objects of His infinite love, that He will therefore never punish us for wrongdoing. He is a God of holiness as well as a God of love.

iii) **Unsparing**: "And mine eye shall not spare thee, neither will I have pity" (v.4). This should remind *us* that we should be unsparing in *self-judgment*: "Mortify therefore your members which are upon the earth; fornication, uncleanness, inordinate affection, evil concupiscence, and covetousness which is idolatry" (Col. 3: 5).

CHAPTER 7

b) The second message, vv.5-9

This message is more emphatic: "Thus saith the Lord GOD: An evil, an only evil, behold, is come. An end ('the end', JND) is come, the end is come: it watcheth for thee ('it awakeneth against thee', JND); behold it is come. The morning ('doom', JND) is come unto thee, O thou that dwellest in the land: the time is come, the day of trouble is near, and not the sounding again ('joyous cry', JND) of the mountains" (vv.5-7).

According to F.Gardiner, the words "an only evil" (v.5), literally, 'an evil which is one', indicate "an evil so all-embracing as to be complete in itself, and needing no repetition. Compare the same thought in Nahum 1 verse 9, 'Affliction shall not rise up the second time'". The word translated "morning" (*tsephirah*, v.7) is unusual. According, again, to F.Gardiner, "the most probable sense is *circuit*" leading to the translation "the circuit of thy sins is finished, and the end is come upon thee". The word is used again in verse 10: "the morning is gone forth". The word "sounding" (*hed*) is only found here (v.7). "The day would be one of terror and tumult, far removed from the joyous cry of the vintage (Is. 16: 10; Jer. 25: 10)" (C.L.Feinberg).

The following two verses (vv.8-9) virtually repeat verses 3-4: "Now will I shortly pour out my fury upon thee, and accomplish mine anger upon thee, and I will judge thee according to thy ways, and will recompense thee for all thine abominations. And mine eye shall not spare, neither will I have pity: I will recompense thee according to thy ways and thine abominations that are in the midst of thee; and ye shall know that I am the LORD that smiteth". Once again, the judgment would be:

i)   Unavoidable. It is addressed not only to the citizens of Jerusalem, but to "thou that dwellest in the land" (v.7).

ii)   Unquestionable. "I will judge thee according to thy ways, and will recompense thee for all thine abominations" (v.8) and, more particularly, "I will recompense thee according to thy ways and thine abominations that are in the midst of thee" (v.9). There was no dispute about their guilt. As F.A.Tatford (*Dead Bones Live*) points out, "His sentence would be executed while they were still actually engaging in idolatrous worship ... They would be in no better plight than the thief or murderer caught red-handed". F.A.Tatford continues: "The message might well be conned over by the Christian who does despite to divine grace, and who imagines that he may indulge his sinful habits or desires without restraint since he will never be discovered".

iii) **Unsparing.** "And mine eye shall not spare, neither will I have pity." Note the additional words here, "and ye shall know that I am the LORD that smiteth" (v.9). As John B. Taylor observes, "the description of God as 'I am the LORD that smiteth' cries out for emendation by those who fail to see the grim irony in so much prophetic writing". It should be said at this juncture, that differences in *translation* are often understandable and acceptable, but *meddling with the original text* is totally unacceptable.

2) THE INIQUITY AT ITS HEIGHT, vv.10-11

"Behold the day, behold, it is come: the morning (see v.7) is gone forth; the rod hath blossomed, pride hath budded. Violence is risen up into a rod of wickedness." Some commentators suggest that the "rod" here refers to the Babylonian invader as the agent of divine visitation upon Israel, in the same way that Assyria is called "the rod of mine anger" (Isa. 10: 5), and support for this is found in the words "I am the LORD that smiteth" (v.9). It is suggested, however, that the clear allusion here to "Aaron's rod that budded" (Heb. 9: 4; Num. 17: 8), points to God's people themselves: "There the rod of Aaron was made to bud and blossom by divine power in evidence of his having been chosen of God: here the rod representing the tribe at Jerusalem in its self-will and pride has budded and blossomed to its destruction" (F.Gardiner). The budding and blossoming is explained here: "violence is risen up into a rod of wickedness" (v.11). The rod, representing the tribe of Judah, had blossomed into a wicked people. They had become "a rod of wickedness", and in consequence "none of them shall remain, nor of their multitude, nor of any of theirs: neither shall there be wailing for them" or "nothing of them [shall remain] nor of their multitude, nor of their wealth, nor of the magnificence in the midst of them" (JND). Neither people nor wealth would remain, and since, according to C.L.Feinberg, 'lamentation' or 'wailing' is a better translation than 'magnificence' or 'eminency' (RV), "no one would survive to lament the dead". This brings us to:

3) THE INCLUSIVENESS OF JUDGMENT, vv.12-16

These verses, like the preceding sections, are introduced by the words "is come" (cf. vv.2, 10). Attention is drawn to the repeated phrase, "wrath is upon **all the multitude** thereof ... the vision is touching **the whole multitude**

CHAPTER 7

thereof ... my wrath is upon **all the multitude** thereof" (vv.12, 13, 14). As the result of this:

i)   *Trade would be lost.* "Let not the buyer rejoice, nor the seller mourn: for wrath is upon all the multitude thereof" (v.12). Their disobedience and departure from the Lord would bring an end to their commercial activity. As John B. Taylor observes, "Once this doom falls, commercial transactions will be of no consequence, and the smile of the buyer who thinks he has made a good bargain, and the long face of the seller who pretends he has been worsted, will be a thing of the past". For *ourselves*, disobedience will have the same result. It will no longer be a case of "always abounding in the work of the Lord, forasmuch as ye know that your labour is not in vain in the Lord" (1 Cor. 15: 58), and there will be no fulfilment of the Saviour's command, "Occupy (trade) till I come" (Luke 19: 13). Sin in our lives will destroy our service. C.L.Feinberg makes the interesting observation that Paul seemed to have this passage in mind in 1 Corinthians 7 verses 29-31.

It should be said that Israel's commercial activity will be resumed with national restoration. See Jeremiah 32 verses 15, 37 and 43. It does appear, however, that the Lord refers here to a particular transaction, and this follows:

ii)   *Inheritance would be lost.* "For the seller shall not return to that which is sold, although they were yet alive: for the vision is touching the whole multitude thereof, which shall not return" (v.13). This evidently refers to the 'year of jubilee' in which, by law, all land must revert to its possession by inheritance. See Leviticus 25 verses 10-16. But not now! "Buyers would not remain long in the possession of their purchase ... The seller, who convinced himself that he would one day return to his property, was living in a fool's paradise" (F.A.Tatford). He continues: "He would not return as long as he and the buyer lived. The coming calamity would obliterate all entitlements, and also the very concept of jubilee". The words, "Neither shall any strengthen himself in the iniquity of his life", mean that because of their iniquities they had forfeited all right to live. For *ourselves*, disobedience will have the same result. We will lose the joy of our present inheritance, of which Paul writes in Ephesians 1 verses 3-14. The Lord has an inheritance in us (Eph. 1: 11, RV) and we have an inheritance in Him (Eph. 1: 14).

iii)   *Strength would be lost.* "They have blown the trumpet, even to make all ready; but none goeth to the battle: for my wrath is upon all the multitude thereof" (v.14). There would be neither power nor courage to withstand the enemy. For *ourselves*, disobedience will rob us of spiritual strength. We will no longer be "strong in the Lord, and in the power of his might" and there will be no question of putting on "the whole armour of God, that ye may be able to stand against the wiles of the devil (Eph. 6: 10-11).

iv) Life would be lost. "The sword is without, and the pestilence and the famine within: he that is in the field shall die with the sword; and he that is in the city, famine and pestilence shall devour him" (v.15). This is quite self-explanatory. Nowhere would be safe, either without or within the city. Disobedience meant loss of life. For *ourselves*, disobedience means loss of spiritual life. Not loss of salvation, but loss of spiritual vitality. Since "the field is the world" (Matt. 13: 38), we could say that disobedience will imperil our witness in the world and, further, that our assembly life, where there should be peace and security, will also be imperilled by the spiritual ills of "famine and pestilence". Lack of spiritual food in the assembly is inevitably accompanied by life-sapping spiritual ailments.

v) Joy would be lost. "But they that escape of them shall escape, and shall be on the mountains like doves of the valleys, all of them mourning, every one for his iniquity" (v.16). Amongst other things, doves are a symbol of mourning: see Isaiah 38 verse 14 and Isaiah 59 verse 11. As F.A.Tatford observes, "They would naturally seek refuge in the mountains and there they would bemoan their helpless condition". For *ourselves*, disobedience can only cause deep regret and sorrow. Peter reminds us that believers can rejoice even in trials: "Wherein ye greatly rejoice, though now for a season, if need be, ye are in heaviness through manifold temptations", adding "that the trial of your faith ... might be found unto praise and honour and glory at the appearing of Jesus Christ: whom having not seen, ye love; in whom, though now ye see him not, yet believing, ye rejoice with joy unspeakable and full of glory" (1 Pet. 1: 6-8). Sin in our lives can rob us of this joy, and there must be many believers who mourn "every one for his iniquity".

4) THE IMPOTENCE OF WEALTH, vv.17-19

"All hands shall be feeble, and all knees shall be weak as water. They shall also gird themselves with sackcloth, and horror shall cover them; and shame shall be upon all faces, and baldness upon all their heads" (vv.17-18). While these verses could extend the description of the escapees mourning on the mountains (v.16), it seems more likely that they refer to the plight of the besieged inhabitants of Jerusalem. F.A.Tatford concurs: "Turning from the fugitives, the prophecy reverted to those left in Jerusalem". (Now we know the origin of the expression "as weak as water!": see also 21: 7.) The city of Nineveh repented at the preaching of Jonah. Having heard his message, "Yet forty days, and Nineveh shall be overthrown", the Ninevites "believed God, and proclaimed a fast, and put on sackcloth from the greatest of them (including the king) even to the least of them", and "God repented of the evil, that he had said that he would do unto them, and he did it not" (Jonah 3: 4-10). But for Jerusalem it was too late. They had consistently rejected the word of God, and their sackcloth would avail nothing. The expression, "baldness upon all their heads" was evidently a sign of mourning. See Micah 1 verse 16: "Make thee bald, and poll thee for thy delicate children; enlarge thy baldness as the eagle; for they are gone into captivity from thee". However, this was expressly forbidden: "Ye are the children of the Lord your God: ye shall not cut yourselves, nor make any baldness between your eyes for the dead" (Deut. 14: 1). M.F.Unger quotes B.A.Copass and E.L.Carson *(The Prophet Micah)*: "Perhaps Micah indicated here that Jerusalem is gone so far into heathen practice that even her mourning follows that pattern". All semblance of godliness had gone!

In their deep distress they would recognise the uselessness of the things in which they trusted: "They shall cast their silver in the streets, and their gold shall be removed ('shall be as an impurity', JND): their silver and their gold shall not be able to deliver them in the day of the wrath of the LORD (see also Prov. 11: 4): they shall not satisfy their souls, neither fill their bowels: because it is the stumblingblock of their iniquity" (v.19). While it is usually said that the people of Jerusalem would have no further use for their wealth since it could not buy them food, H.L.Ellison suggests that silver and gold here refers to their silver and golden idols which were not able to "deliver them". This does seem to be confirmed by the balance of the verse: "because it is the stumblingblock of their iniquity". The "stumblingblock" refers unquestionably to their idols. See Chapter 14 verses 3-4. However, since "silver and gold" can become an idol in another sense, we do well to listen to F.A.Tatford here: "It was a vivid and tragic picture, but not entirely inappropriate to the present day. Christ presents to the believer the acquisition of heavenly treasures as the supreme object of life, but how many spend their time in the acquisition of material treasures, the value of which can be liquidated overnight". The Lord Jesus said, "Lay not up for yourselves treasures upon earth, where moth and rust doth corrupt, and where thieves break through and steal: but lay up for yourselves treasures in heaven ..." (Matt. 6: 19-20). In gratefully acknowledging their gift to him, Paul told the Philippians that it was "fruit" that would "abound to their account" (Phil. 4: 17).

5) THE IMPURITY OF THE TEMPLE, vv.20-22

"As for the beauty of his ornament, he set it in majesty: but they made the images of their abominations and of their detestable things therein: therefore have I set it far from them ('therefore have I made it an impurity unto them', JND: that is, by allowing it be defiled by the Chaldeans)" (v.20). While this verse has been variously interpreted, C.L.Feinberg clearly adopts the view, confirmed by the passage itself, that Ezekiel refers here to the temple in Jerusalem: "One position takes the ornament to mean the silver and the gold of the people of which they had made their idols, as just noted. The other and better view understands Ezekiel to be speaking of the temple of the Lord. The very place God meant to be beautified, they had polluted with multiplied abominations which are described in Chapter 8 verses 3-17. Since Israel had already profaned the temple of God, He saw no further purpose in keeping it from the desecration of the enemy. Thus the temple with all its sacred appointments was given over to the invading army". The context demands this explanation. Hence we read further: "And I will give it into the hands of the strangers for a prey, and to the wicked of the earth for a spoil; and they shall pollute it. My face will I turn also from them, and they shall pollute my secret place: for the robbers shall enter into it, and defile it" (vv.21-22). It should be noted that that the enemy could only enter the precincts of the temple and penetrate "the holy of holies" ("my secret place"), because the Lord had deliberately removed His protection. See the removal of "the glory of God" from the temple (8: 4; 9: 3; 10: 4; 10: 18-19; 11: 22-23).

This should lead us all to think seriously about our assembly life. We quote, sometimes all too glibly, the Lord's words, "Where two or three are gathered together in my name, there am I in the midst of them" (Matt. 18: 20). Leaving aside the context of these oft-quoted words, are we right in claiming His promise at all times and in every circumstance? Is it possible that our disobedience has deprived us of His presence? Unless, that is, that He is present in judgment. We must listen again to C.L.Feinberg: "God has no desire to keep mere outward worship in operation as long as such worship is accompanied with and encrusted over by idolatries that profane the very essence of that worship".

6) THE INEFFECTIVENESS OF THE LEADERSHIP, vv.23-27

The pollution of the temple ("they made the images of their abominations

CHAPTER 7

and of their detestable things therein", v.20) was accompanied by "the land ... full of bloody crimes (crimes meriting the death-penalty), and the city ... full of violence" (v.23). This is not surprising: when things go wrong at the centre, they go wrong everywhere. Hence, divine judgment was coming: captivity was imminent: "Make a *chain* ... I will bring the worst of the heathen, and they shall possess their houses: I will also make the pomp of the strong to cease; and their holy places (perhaps referring to places of idolatrous worship) shall be defiled. Destruction cometh; and they shall seek peace, and there shall be none" (vv.23-25). The expression, "the worst of the heathen", refers to the Chaldeans, described by Habakkuk as "that bitter and hasty nation ... They are terrible and dreadful ... They shall come all for violence: their faces shall sup up as the east wind, and they shall gather the captivity as the sand ..." (Hab. 1: 6-10).

Ezekiel continues: "Mischief shall come upon mischief, and rumour shall be upon rumour; then shall they seek a vision of the prophet; but the law shall perish from the priest, and counsel from the ancients. The king shall mourn, and the prince shall be clothed with desolation, and the hands of the people of the land shall be troubled ('shall tremble', JND). I will do unto them after their way, and according to their deserts will I judge them; and they shall know that I am the LORD". The prophet would have no vision (v.26); the priests, who should teach the law, would have nothing to say (v.26); the elders ("the ancients"), to whom the nation looked in civil matters, would be silent (v.26); the royal house would, and could, do nothing but mourn (v.27), and the people would tremble (v.27, JND). It was nothing short of disastrous that the trembling people would find no help or guidance from the leadership. All classes were completely helpless. Let every assembly elder beware. Woe to the assembly without spiritual leadership. Woe to the elder unable to give guidance to the flock of God.

God had forsaken the people who had rejected Him: "I will do unto them after their way, and according to their deserts will I judge them; and they shall know that I am the Lord" (v.27).

This concludes the first phase of Ezekiel's ministry. The next phase of His ministry is covered by Chapters 8-11. These chapters describe the "images of their abominations and of their detestable things" in the temple (7: 20), together with the withdrawal of the presence of God. They prove that coming wrath is fully justified.

EZEKIEL CHAPTER 8

With this chapter we come to the second phase of Ezekiel's ministry. This began "in the sixth year, in the sixth month, in the fifth day of the month" (8: 1) and continued for a period of eleven months and five days, until the third phase of his ministry, which commenced in "the seventh year, in the fifth month, the tenth day of the month" (20: 1). Chapters 1-19 may be summarised as follows: *(A)* the commissioning of Ezekiel (1: 1 - 3: 15); *(B)* the coming judgment (3: 16 - 7: 27); *(C)* the contributory causes (8: 1 - 19: 14).

A) THE COMMISSIONING OF EZEKIEL, 1: 1 - 3: 15

In this connection, we noticed *(i) what he saw* (1: 1-28): "I saw visions of God" (1: 1); *(ii) what he heard* (2: 1-10): "I heard him that spake unto me" (2: 2); *(iii) where he went* (3: 1-15): "I came to them of the captivity at Tel-abib" (3: 15).

B) THE COMING JUDGMENT, 3: 16 - 7: 27

Bearing in mind his task to act as a watchman, and warn "the house of Israel" (3: 17-22), we noted that the prophet was instructed to convey the warning *visually* with a series of signs (3: 22 - 5: 17), and *verbally* with two messages (6: 1 - 7: 27). In both cases, the prophet was equipped with the "word of the LORD" (3: 16; 6: 1; 7: 1). This brings us to:

C) THE CONTRIBUTORY CAUSES, 8: 1 - 19: 14

The second phase of his ministry (chs.8-19) commences with a ***vision*** of degrading idolatry in the temple at Jerusalem (chs. 8-11), which the prophet then relates to the exiles at Tel-abib (11: 25), followed by a series of ***verbal*** messages (chs.12-19), each introduced by the words, "The word of the LORD came unto me, saying …" (12: 1, 8, 17, 21, 26; 13: 1; 14: 2, 12; 15:

CHAPTER 8

1; 16: 1; 17: 1, 11; 18: 1). It seems likely that these messages were "uttered at short intervals, allowing time for each to produce its impression upon the people" (F.Gardiner, *Ellicott's Commentary*). To summarise, this section of the book can be divided between *(a)* the vision given *to* Ezekiel (chs. 8-11); *(b)* the verbal messages given *by* Ezekiel (chs.12-19). We must now give particular attention to the first of these.

As our titles suggest, the coming judgment upon Judah and Jerusalem (chs. 4-7), and the contributory causes (chs.8-19), are not disconnected. In particular, Chapters 8-11 expand the earlier statement, "As for the beauty of his ornament (referring to the temple in Jerusalem), he set it in majesty: but they made the images of their abominations and of their detestable things therein" (7: 20). Hence we now read of "the image of jealousy ... great abominations ... wicked abominations ... greater abominations ... greater abominations ... the abominations" (8: 3, 6, 9, 13, 15, 17). As F.Gardiner observes, "the extreme sinfulness of the people remaining there is pointed out" so that "the exiles might understand the reason, and therefore the certainty of the impending judgment upon Jerusalem".

The four chapters describing Ezekiel's vision (chs.8-11) commence and conclude in the same way: "and the *spirit* ('the Spirit', JND) *lifted me up* ... and brought me in the visions of God to Jerusalem" (8: 3); "Afterwards *the spirit* ('the Spirit', JND) *took me up*, and brought me in a vision by the Spirit of God into Chaldea, to them of the captivity. So the vision that I had seen went up from me" (11: 24). Ezekiel then "spake unto them of the captivity all the things that the Lord had shewed me" (11: 25). We must also notice that the passage commences with "the *glory of the God of Israel* ... there (Jerusalem)" (8: 4)., and concludes with "the *glory of the LORD*" going up "from the midst of the city" and standing "upon the mountain which is on the east side of the city" (11: 22-23).

It is suggested that these four chapters may be entitled: *(1) degrading idolatry* (ch.8): the temple had become defiled by four forms of idolatry (vv.6, 10, 15, 17), each called an 'abomination'; *(2) discriminatory judgment* (ch.9): the godly were preserved (v.4), but the idolaters were destroyed (vv.5-6); *(3) destruction from God* (ch.10): fire was scattered over the city (v.2); *(4) depopulation and scattering* (ch.11): "I will bring you out of the midst thereof, and deliver you into the hands of strangers" (v.9), but the nation would be regathered and purified (vv.17-20).

EZEKIEL

1) DEGRADING IDOLATRY, 8: 1-18

Chapter 8 may be divided as follows: *(A)* the attendance of the elders (v.1); *(B)* the appearance of the Man on the throne (vv.2-4); *(C)* the abominations in the temple (vv.5-16); *(D)* the announcement of judgment (vv.17-18).

A) The attendance of the elders, v.1

"And it came to pass in the sixth year, in the sixth month, in the fifth day of the month, as I sat in mine house, and the elders of Judah sat before me, that the hand of the Lord GOD fell there upon me." These introductory words should be read in conjunction with Jeremiah 29 verses 1-10 where the exiles are encouraged to settle down in Babylonia for the next seventy years, and ignore the false prophets who predicted an imminent return to Judaea. The message was addressed to all the exiles, including the elders (Jer. 29: 1). Ezekiel had evidently heeded the message: he lived in his own house! It is generally agreed that the presence of the elders here indicates that Ezekiel was now recognised as a prophet. We are not told why the elders were in attendance, but the vision that follows makes it seem more than likely that they were enquiring about the possibility of returning to Judah and Jerusalem. While H.L.Ellison suggests that "Ezekiel had become a highly respected member of his community", it should be noted that the same elders sat in Ezekiel's presence on two other occasions (14: 1; 20: 1) when it appears that he was nothing like "a highly respected member of his community"! On this occasion (in the current chapter), they were about to hear some most unpleasant things as the result of Ezekiel's visionary visit to Jerusalem.

It is worth pointing out, whatever we may think of these particular elders, that New Testament elders should always have a healthy appetite for the Word of God. It should be their consuming desire to be acquainted with the Scriptures, and to implement them. See, for example, Titus 1 verse 9. We should also notice that, for the fourth time, "the hand of the LORD" was upon Ezekiel (see 1: 3; 3: 14, 22). As already noted, this implies that the prophet was subject to divine authority and filled with divine power, and this serves to remind us that the New Testament teacher must "speak as the oracles of God" (1 Pet. 4: 11). This is more than correct theology. It is God-given ability to speak to the hearts and consciences of His people.

CHAPTER 8

B) The appearance of the Man on the throne, vv.2-4

We should notice at least three things in these verses: *(a)* the identity of the Man (vv.2-3); *(b)* the impetus of the Spirit (v.3); *(c)* the image of jealousy (vv.3-4).

a) The identity of the Man, vv.2-3

While Ezekiel was yet to see, for the third time, the chariot-throne of Jehovah (cf. 1: 4-28; 3: 22-23; 8: 4), he is touched here by the **occupant** of the throne: "Then I beheld, and lo a likeness as the appearance of fire: from the appearance of his loins even downwards, fire; and from his loins even upward, as the appearance of brightness, as the colour of amber (the word refers to some form of bright metal perhaps glowing in its molten state). And he put forth the form of an hand, and took me by a lock of mine head (an action without parallel in the Old Testament)" (vv.2-3). Compare Chapter 1 verses 26-28: "and upon the likeness of the throne was the likeness as the appearance of a man above upon it. And I saw as the colour of amber, as the appearance of fire round about within it, from the appearance of his loins even upward, and from the appearance of his loins even downward, I saw as it were the appearance of fire, and it had brightness round about … This was the appearance of the likeness of the glory of the LORD". Who did Ezekiel actually see in Chapter 1? Who actually touched Ezekiel in Chapter 8? It was the same Person in both cases. It was, surely, the Lord Jesus in His pre-incarnate glory! Our privilege is even greater: "If a man love me, he will keep my words: and my Father will love him, and **we** will come unto him, and make **our** abode **with him**" (John 14: 23).

b) The impetus of the Spirit, v.3

We know from the New Testament that the Lord Jesus always acted in the power of the Holy Spirit, and this is also the case here: "And he put forth the form of an hand, and took me by a lock of mine head; and the spirit ('the Spirit', JND) lifted me up between the earth and the heaven, and brought me in the visions of God to Jerusalem" (v.3). This should be compared with Chapter 2 verses 1-2, "Son of man, stand upon thy feet, and I will speak unto thee. And the spirit ('the Spirit', JND) entered into me when he spake unto me". See also 3: 14; 43: 5.)

The prophet was taken "in the visions of God to Jerusalem": not, of course, literally, in the body, but as stated, in a vision. Ezekiel did not physically leave Chaldea at all: see Chapter 11 verse 24, "Afterwards the spirit ('the Spirit', JND) took me up, and brought me in a vision by the Spirit of God into Chaldea, to them of the captivity. So the vision that I had seen went up from me".

It has to be asked why, in the vision, Ezekiel's transportation to Jerusalem was accomplished in conjunction with the glory of the Lord and the power of the Holy Spirit. Why was the prophet not simply given an immediate vision of the debauched conduct in the temple? The answer may well be that it was to impress on him that the glory of the Lord who had touched him was being totally set aside in Jerusalem, and that those responsible were doing "despite unto the Spirit of grace" (Heb. 10: 29).

c) *The image of jealousy, vv.3-4*

A horrifying spectacle greeted the prophet. In this connection we should note the vivid contrast between the spectacle which greeted Ezekiel after the Spirit had lifted him up on this occasion (see v.5), and the spectacle after the Spirit had lifted him up in Chapter 43 verse 5! We should also note the contrast between the sight given to Ezekiel in the vision here, and the sight given the Paul in his vision: see 2 Corinthians 12 verses 1-4. Ezekiel is confronted with two irreconcilable things: *(i)* "the image of jealousy" (v.3); *(ii)* "the glory of the God of Israel" (v.4).

i) **"The image of jealousy, v.3.** "The spirit ... brought me ... to the door of the inner gate that looketh toward the north; where was the seat of the image of jealousy, which provoketh to jealousy". F.A.Tatford points out that "Ezekiel was deposited in spirit at the entrance of the northern gate of the inner court". He continues, "Solomon's temple did not have the court of the Gentiles provided later in Herod's temple, so that the inner court would have been the court of the priests, into which, of course, Ezekiel as a priest was entitled to enter. In the trance, he evidently stood at the porch of the gate, and did not attempt to enter into the building itself".

The description, "the image of jealousy", is immediately explained: "which provoketh to jealousy". The description does not imply a proper name - the name of any particular heathen divinity - but rather an image which aroused divine indignation. We need go no further than the book of Exodus for an explanation: "Thou shalt not bow down thyself to them ("any graven image"), nor serve them: for I the LORD thy God am a jealous God" (Ex. 20: 5); "For

CHAPTER 8

thou shalt worship no other god: for the LORD, whose name is Jealous, is a jealous God" (Ex. 34: 14). According to F.Gardiner, it has been thought that the term "the image of jealousy" is "not meant to indicate any particular idol, but is only a picture to set forth the prevailing idolatry". Gardiner continues by saying that "It is, however, altogether probable that at this time there actually were heathen idols set up in the temple, and nothing could give a more vivid picture of the corruption of priests and people alike than the mention of their presence ... Ahaz, under the influence of the Assyrian king, had placed an idolatrous altar in the temple itself, removing the brazen altar to make room (2 Kings 16: 10-18), and Manasseh afterwards did the same (2 Kings 21: 4). All the subsequent kings of Judah, except Josiah, were wicked men, and although this particular sin is not distinctly recorded of Zedekiah, yet it seems altogether likely that he too made use of the temple for idolatrous worship, and that Ezekiel in vision now saw his idols standing in the court".

We must never forget that God is jealous for His glory: "I am the LORD: that is my name: and my glory will I not give to another, neither my praise to graven mages" (Is. 42: 8). He will brook no rivals in our lives. In New Testament language, "Little children, keep yourselves from idols" (1 John 5: 21). Otherwise we are in peril of "the fire of his jealousy" (Zeph. 1: 18).

ii) *"The glory of the God of Israel", v.4.* "And, behold, the glory of the God (Elohim) of Israel was there, according to the vision that I saw in the plain." This was, in turn, the vision that he had seen "by the river of Chebar" (3: 23; 10: 15, 22). The words, "the God of Israel", are emphatic. It was the glory of the God who had loved and chosen Israel, and whom Israel should have served, in contrast with the idol which they had placed in His temple. As John B.Taylor observes, "It was as if he wanted to throw into sharp relief the difference between the God who belonged there and the deviations which were practised there, so making the crimes all the more heinous". Taylor adds that perhaps the presence of God here also indicates that He "would stay with His people until the very last moment of their rejection of Him". As these chapters demonstrate, the Lord will not share His glory with idols. He therefore leaves His temple and His people, with devastating results. Let us all be warned. If we allow rivals, whatever shape or form they may take, in our lives, we will lose His presence and power.

C) The abominations in the temple, vv.5-16

There are four 'abominations' portraying *(a)* sensuality worship (vv.5-

6); *(b)* animal worship (vv.7-13); *(c)* nature worship (vv.14-15); *(d)* sun worship (v.16). F.A.Tatford, apparently quoting H.L.Ellison, states that "It is difficult to imagine that the temple authorities - however far from God they were at heart - would have permitted such observances, in fact, in the temple, and it is probably wiser to regard the abominations as symbolical". It must be said that it is far easier to accept that Ezekiel is telling us exactly what he saw in the temple, and that F.A.Tatford is far nearer the truth in saying: "If the priests had actually apostatised so completely as to countenance such idolatry on the sacred site, there had been what one writer terms 'a complete disintegration of the national religion' (H.L.Ellison)". Precisely!

a) Sensuality worship, vv.5-6

"Son of man, lift up thine eyes now the way toward the north. So I lifted up mine eyes the way toward the north, and behold northward at the gate of the altar this image of jealousy in the entry. He said furthermore unto me, Son of man, seest thou what they do? Even the great **abominations** that the house of Israel committeth here, that I should go far off from my sanctuary?"

"The way toward the north" (v.5) indicates that Ezekiel in his vision was within the court of the priests, as otherwise he could not have looked *toward* the north to see the idol in the north gate. He had already seen this; but now his attention is directed to it particularly. The gate in question is called "the gate of the altar" because the sacrifices were killed on the north side of the altar (Lev. 1: 11). This is in itself most significant. We also have to ask if the idol barred the way to the altar.

Without being dogmatic, it seems nevertheless most likely that the "image of jealousy" depicted "Asherah or the queen of heaven and goddess of love and sex (2 Kings 21: 7, 2 Chron. 33: 7, 15)" (F.A.Tatford). John B.Taylor concurs: after referring to 2 Kings 21 verse 7 and 2 Chronicles 33 verse 15, he adds that "although Manasseh subsequently removed it, it must have reappeared, because Josiah had it taken out and burnt at the brook Kidron (2 Kings 23: 6). From Ezekiel's words it looks as if one of Josiah's successors had made another and set it up by the northern gate". It should be explained that "the groves (Asherim)", so often mentioned in the Old Testament, were devoted to the worship of Ashteroth, alias the Babylonian goddess Ishtar, the Aphrodite of the Greeks, and the Roman Venus. The worship of sensuality is all too present in modern society.

CHAPTER 8

Notice the words, "that I should go far off from my sanctuary" (v.6). That is exactly what happens in this section of the book. But not for ever! While in the original text, this is simply an infinitive, without any subject expressed ("for the removing far off"), there can be little doubt that the meaning is correctly given in the Authorised Version: it accords with the whole teaching of the vision. F.Gardiner makes the point that "There was a strong feeling among the people that they were safe at Jerusalem; God, whom they still regarded, notwithstanding their idolatries, as a powerful national God, would certainly protect His temple". Gardiner continues, "It is the office of the prophet to show that the transgressions of the people led, as their natural consequence, to His giving over the city to desolation".

But this was not the end: still worse is in store: "But turn thee yet again, and thou shalt see *greater abominations*" (v.6). These follow.

b) Animal worship, vv.7-13

We may simply divide these verses as follows: *(i)* the worship (vv.7-10); *(ii)* the worshippers (vv.11-12).

i) The worship, vv.7-10

"And he brought me to the door of the court; and when I looked, behold a hole in the wall (perhaps referring to a window, too small for entrance) ... and when I had digged in the wall, behold a door. And he said unto me, Go in, and behold the wicked *abominations* that they do here. So I went in and saw; and behold every form of creeping things and *abominable* beasts, and all the idols of the house of Israel, pourtrayed ('incised' or 'carved in relief') upon the wall round about" (vv.7-10).

The fact that the exact locality of the "door of the court ... the wall ... door" and chamber in which this idolatry was practised cannot be determined, emphasises that the detail is unimportant. F.Gardiner helpfully draws attention to the fact that "The object of this part of the vision is to show the extreme *secrecy* of what he is now to see - a secrecy made necessary by the connection of this idolatry with Egypt, the foe of Chaldaea".

The prophet is confronted by "every form of creeping things, and abominable beasts" (v.10). John B. Taylor notes that the reference to "creeping things", which includes serpents, could point to "The serpent-deities known from

Egyptian, Canaanite and Babylonian religions", and therefore provides ground for supposing that this incident reflects the widespread influence of foreign cults on Israelite worship, cultivated no doubt from political, more than purely religious, motives". This view is espoused by H.L.Ellison, whereas other commentators, including F.A.Tatford, opt particularly for Egyptian deities. C.L.Feinberg observes that "There is no question that such practices were carried on by more than one nation in antiquity, but the consensus of interpreters is that these were the animal cults of Egypt ... In Egypt such worship had perhaps its highest and most extensive development in ancient times". Moreover, the political relations of the time also point strongly in the same direction. "From a political point of view, the Jew would turn to Egypt for any hope of deliverance from the Babylonian oppressor, and it was natural, therefore, that he should address his supplications to Egypt's gods" (F.A.Tatford). However, as if this were not enough, "all the idols of the house of Israel" (v.10), gathered from every quarter, were also portrayed upon the walls.

ii) The worshippers, vv.11-12

"And there stood before them seventy men of the ancients of Israel, and in the midst of them stood Jaazaniah the son of Shaphan, with every man his censer in his hand; and a thick cloud of incense went up. Then said he unto me, Son of man, hast thou seen what the ancients of the house of Israel do in the dark, every man in the chamber of his imagery? For they say, the Lord seeth us not; the Lord hath forsaken the earth."

It has been pointed out that the seventy elders ("the ancients of Israel") were not the Sanhedrin, which was not constituted until after the return from Babylon, and the number is probably modelled on "the seventy chosen to enjoy with Moses the theophany of Exodus 24 verses 9-10, and the other seventy selected to share with him in the gifts of the Spirit (Num. 11: 16). In contrast with those selected for especial nearness to God, these seventy are engaged in abominations most abhorrent to Him" (F.Gardiner). The words, "with every man his censer in his hand" (v.11), remind us that the burning of incense was the exclusive function of the priesthood (Num. 16; 2 Chron. 26: 16-18); and therefore when the seventy elders offered incense to the idols they claimed to be the priests of those idols.

On the basis that Jaazaniah, the son of Shaphan (v.11) might have actually been the grandson of Shaphan (following the frequent use of "son" in that

CHAPTER 8

way), he may have been the same as "Jaazaniah, the son of Azur" (11: 1), one of the wicked princes of the people, against whom Ezekiel was directed to prophesy. It is hardly probable that two persons of the same character and the same (not very common) name should have been among the leaders of the people at the same time. If this is the case, then it was his grandfather who found the book of the law in the temple during the refurbishment ordered by Josiah (2 Kings 22: 10). Moreover Jaazaniah's brothers, Gemariah and Ahikam (Jer. 36: 10; 39: 14), were evidently pious Israelites. All this emphasises that godliness does not 'run in the blood'. Samuel would certainly agree with this conclusion! So would Eli! Jaazaniah was evidently a totally different character from the rest of his family.

This idolatry was practised "in the dark, every man in the chambers of his imagery" (v.12). A reason for this secrecy has already been suggested - to conceal their disposition towards Egypt – but, additionally, it might have been "to throw over it the charm of mystery, as was so common among the heathen" (F.Gardiner). Whichever way, it remains that 'men love ('loved' AV) darkness rather than light, because their deeds are evil'. Truth and godliness never need concealment.

The words, "every man in the chambers of his imagery" (v.12) are understood in different ways. Some, including C.L.Feinberg, suggest that this refers to "acts taking place in the homes of the people. They had carried the idolatry of the temple into their private homes". Others, including F.A.Tatford, suggest that "the chambers of his imagery" refers to their hearts and minds which "treasured these filthy idols and the unclean rites associated with them ... It was only natural that he should wish to indulge in the actual practices when he dwelt upon them in the darkness of his imagination". F.A.Tatford continues: "how many professing Christians there are who in public are ready to condemn what is generally acknowledged to be wrong. But in private, in the imaginations of their heart, they often surreptitiously dwell with desire upon the forbidden thing". We all do well to sing:

> *Throw light into the darkened cells*
> *Where passion reigns within;*
> *Quicken my conscience till it feels*
> *The loathsomeness of sin.*

These people stifled the voice of conscience, as in every age, by saying "The LORD seeth us not": compare, for example Psalm 10 verse 11 and Psalm

94 verses 5-7. Besides this, they argued, doubtless from the calamities that had already fallen upon their country, that "the LORD hath forsaken the earth ('the land', JND)", and therefore they must have recourse to other help. In the succinct words of John B. Taylor, they were "confident that there was no Jehovah around either to see or to care". They failed to remember the Psalmist's words: "If we have forgotten the name of our God, or stretched out our hands to a strange god; shall not God search this out? For he knoweth the secrets of the heart" (Psalm 44: 20-21). C.J.H.Wright makes the telling observation that in principle the actions of these men "is endemic to the people of God in every era. We proclaim our covenant loyalty to the living God. We put our lives under His protection and affirm His sovereign power. We sing songs about His great faithfulness and our eternal security. And yet so often in real life we act as though we had no confidence in God at all for our future. Instead, we expend enormous amounts of material and emotional resources on fixing things up for ourselves. It is well worth regularly checking where we have drawn the line between the wisdom that makes prudent provision for the future for ourselves and our families, and the idolatry that builds all our hope and security on the modern equivalents of the gods and armies of Egypt". These are weighty words indeed.

But even this was not the end: still worse is in store: "He said also unto me, Turn thee yet again, and thou shalt see **greater abominations** that they do" (v.13). These follow.

c) Nature worship, vv.14-15

"Then he brought me to the door of the gate of the Lord's house which was toward the north; and, behold, there sat women weeping for Tammuz" (v.14). It is thought that in the vision, Ezekiel was now right outside the sacred precincts of the temple, where he saw a new and exceedingly corrupt form of idolatry.

According to C.L.Feinberg, "the worship of Tammuz came from Babylon through the Phoenicians (Canaanites) and then the Greeks. Tammuz, mentioned nowhere else in the Scriptures, was the Babylonian Dumuzi, beloved of Ishtar, and is to be identified with the Greek Adonis". F.A.Tatford takes up the story: "In the heat of summer the vegetation withered and the rivers and streams dried up, and his devotees said that Tammuz, the god of vegetation and floods, had died. The female worshippers of the god, therefore gathered together in June and July (our months) to weep and wail over his death. Subsequently his sister, Ishtar, allegedly descended into the underworld to deliver him. His resurrection and marriage to her were the assumed cause of the coming of the rains and of the growth of vegetation in the spring. Fertility rites celebrated these events and, in theory, ensured the fruitfulness of the land". The annual feast of Adonis (alias Tammuz) "was accompanied by great abominations and licentiousness" (F.Gardiner). Very clearly, this myth was closely associated with the worship of nature. Tammuz worship was therefore a refusal to recognise that "the gifts of nature were derived from the Lord alone". The linkage between the mourning rites and the fertility rites was "an appalling disregard of His inherent holiness and purity" (F.A.Tatford).

Paul told his audience at Lystra that God "left not himself without witness, in that he did good, and gave us rain from heaven, and fruitful seasons, filling our hearts with food and gladness" (Acts 14: 17). James reminds us that "Every good gift and every perfect gift is from above, and cometh down from the Father of lights, with whom is no variableness, neither shadow of turning" (James 1: 17). This is far removed from the worship of Tammuz.

But even this was not the end: still worse is in store: "Then he said unto me, Hast thou seen this, O Son of man? Turn thee yet again, and thou shalt see **greater abominations** than these" (v.15). These follow. It should be noted that there is "a continual degression in sin, just as there are advance and growth upward under the Spirit of God in the things of grace and sanctification of the redeemed spirit" (C.L.Feinberg). See 2 Peter 3 verse 18.

d) Sun worship, v.16

Thus far, the prophet has seen in the different courts of the Temple the general image worship of the people, then the creature worship of their elders, and now the corrupt and debasing rites of their women. He now returns to the court of the priests: "And he brought me into the inner court of the LORD'S house, and, behold, at the door of the temple of the LORD, between the porch and the altar, were about five and twenty men, with their backs toward the temple of the LORD, and their faces toward the east; and they worshipped the sun toward the east". According to F.Gardiner, Ezekiel saw, not *about*, but *as it were* (referring to the nature of the vision) "twenty-five men". It is generally thought that these were the high priest and the heads of the twenty-four courses (1 Chron. 24: 1-19), representing the whole body of the priests. They were standing between the altar and the temple, therefore in the most sacred part of the court, and there, turning their backs (according to C.J.H.Wright, the word "can be used of the hindquarters of cattle": Gesenius agrees: he uses the words, 'rear' and 'end': we need say no more) upon the temple of the Lord, worshipped the sun. The adoration of the sun, probably the earliest form of false religion, was the especial worship of Persia, but had been long since practised by the kings and people of Judah (2 Kings 23: 5, 11). Thus all classes of the nation were involved in common sin; and the priests particularly were found practising "as complete a repudiation of the Lord as possible (see 2 Chron 29: 6). The cup of their iniquity had been filled to the brim" (C.L.Feinberg). According to the chronicler, "*all* the chief of the priests, and the people, transgressed very much after all the abominations of the heathen; and polluted the house of the LORD which he had hallowed in Jerusalem" (2 Chron. 36: 14)

4) The announcement of judgment, vv.17-18

"Then he said unto me, Hast thou seen this, O son of man? Is it a light thing to the house of Judah that they commit the abominations which they commit here? for they have filled the land with violence, and have returned to provoke me to anger" (v.17). "Corruption in religion here, as always, bore its proper fruit in moral deterioration. A people who go astray from their duty to God are always found to neglect also their duty to man. Israel had before fallen into great and grievous sins" (F.Gardiner). He adds, "Within the memory of those still living, the good king Josiah, supported by the prophet Jeremiah and many others, had made great effort at reformation, and had purged the Temple of its abominations; hence God says the people 'have *returned* to provoke me to anger'".

The words, "they put the branch to their nose" (v.17) tax the ability of all commentators. They are evidently an allusion to some custom well known at the time, but now lost. There is no satisfactory explanation as yet. Whatever its exact significance, it does seem to be a gesture of contempt toward God, leading to the translation 'they are as mockers' (Septuagint). Perhaps (just perhaps) our equivalent would be 'they fingered their noses at God'. It is just possible that Paul refers to this in saying, "Be not deceived; God is not mocked (from *mukter*, the nose)" (Gal. 6: 7). In other words, 'you cannot turn up your nose at God without incurring the direst consequences'. Men may fool themselves, but they cannot fool God. God is not to be sneered at.

CHAPTER 8

Judgment on this account is announced: "Therefore will I also deal in fury: mine eye shall not spare, neither will I have pity: and though they cry in mine ears with a loud voice, yet will I not hear them". Compare Chapter 5 verse 11 ("neither shall mine eye spare, neither will I have any pity"); Chapter 7 verse 4 (ditto); Chapter 7 verse 9 (ditto). The time for prayer was past. They had rejected God, and when His wrath came upon them it would be too late to turn to Him. (Compare Proverbs 1: 24-28; Matthew 7: 22-23.) It has been said that "the possibility of sinning beyond the term of the day of grace is one of the most important lessons of this chapter" (F.Gardiner).

Jeremiah was shown two baskets of figs. One contained "very good figs" and the other "very naughty figs, which could not be eaten, they were so bad" (Jer. 24: 1-2) The basket of "evil figs, which cannot be eaten, they are so evil", represented "Zedekiah ... and his princes, and the residue of Jerusalem, that *remain in this land*, and them that dwell in the land of Egypt" (Jer. 24: 8). In a similar passage, the people remaining in Jerusalem are told: "Behold I will send upon them the sword, the famine, and the pestilence, and will make them like *vile figs, that cannot be eaten, they are so evil*" (Jer. 29: 15-17). Having read Ezekiel Chapter 8 we now know why they are described as "vile figs, that cannot be eaten, they are so evil".

EZEKIEL CHAPTER 9

In introducing this section of the book, we suggested that the four chapters (8-11) may be entitled: *(1) degrading idolatry* (ch.8); *(2) discriminatory judgment* (ch.9); *(3) destruction from God* (ch.10); *(4) depopulation and scattering* (ch.11).

1) DEGRADING IDOLATRY, 8: 1-18

The depravity in the temple is portrayed in four ways, each progressively being called a 'greater abomination': *(a)* sensuality worship (vv.5-6); *(b)* animal worship (vv.7-13); *(c)* nature worship (vv.14-15); *(d)* sun worship (v.16). This now brings us to:

2) DISCRIMINATORY JUDGMENT, 9: 1-11

As C.L.Feinberg observes, "Such abominations in Jerusalem as described by Ezekiel in Chapter 8 call loudly for the visitation of God". Divine judgment would be both thorough and selective. It would be *thorough*: "let not your eye spare, neither have ye pity: slay utterly old and young, both maids, and little children, and women" (v.v.5-6). It would be *selective*: "but come not near any man upon whom is the mark" (v.6).

We must bear in mind that at this point, Ezekiel is "in the visions of God" at Jerusalem (8: 3). As H.L.Ellison rightly points out, the vision here is "*symbolically predictive*, for Zedekiah's rebellion against Nebuchadnezzar had not even broken out yet". It is a vision of what would happen when the Chaldeans sacked Jerusalem. But the overthrow of Jerusalem, with the attendant slaughter of its inhabitants, would be far more than 'a quirk of fate' or 'the fortunes of war'. The Chaldeans would be the agents of divine judgment. They would be constrained by angelic powers, and accomplish *God's* will. Like the Assyrian before them, the Chaldeans would be "the rod of mine anger, and the staff in their hand is mine indignation" (Isaiah 10: 5). There can be little doubt that the six men who "came from the way of the

CHAPTER 9

higher gate, which lieth toward the north" (v.2) were angels. This may not be the case with the "man among them ... clothed with linen, with a writer's inkhorn by his side" (v.2).

This illustrates God's forward-planning. Some six or seven years were to elapse before Jerusalem fell to the invader, but the arrangements had already been determined. There was no question of 'emergency measures'. God carries out His judgments in order and with precision. In the words of Habakkuk, God "stood, and measured the earth, and drove asunder the nations" (Hab. 3: 6). "Known unto God are all his works from the beginning of the world" (Acts 15: 18). Everything in this chaotic world is under divine control.

The chapter can be divided into four sections: *(A)* the channels of judgment (vv.1-2); *(B)* the course of judgment (vv.3-7); *(C)* the cry for mercy (vv.8-10); *(D)* the completion of deliverance (v.11).

The chapter begins: "He (the "Lord GOD", described in Chapter 8 verse 2, who had brought him in the vision to Jerusalem) cried also in mine ears with a loud voice". This gives "emphasis to what is said; it is the natural expression of the fierceness of the divine indignation and wrath" (F.Gardiner, *Ellicott's Commentary*). The sun-worshippers cried "with a loud voice" (8: 18), and now the time had come for the Lord to respond with "a loud voice" (9: 1).

A) THE CHANNELS OF JUDGMENT, vv.1-2

These verses describe the arrival of: *(a)* six men with their weapons of destruction (vv.1-2a); *(b)* one man with a writer's inkhorn (v.2b).

a) The men with weapons of destruction, vv.1-2a

"He cried also in mine ears with a loud voice, saying, Cause them that have charge over the city to draw near, even every man with his destroying weapon in his hand." And, behold, six men came from the way of the higher gate, which lieth toward the north, and every man a slaughter weapon in his hand". As F.Gardiner observes, "They are not earthly officers, but those to whom God has especially entrusted the execution of His will concerning Jerusalem". Their work is to execute God's wrath against the idolatrous city. Each carries "his destroying weapon in his hand ... every man a slaughter weapon in his hand". Angels are frequently called men because of their outward appearance. See, for example, Genesis 19 verses 1, 5, 10 and 12.

b) The man with the writer's inkhorn, v.2b

The seventh man was attired differently. He was "clothed with linen, with a writer's inkhorn by his side". According to C.L.Feinberg, the "inkhorn" was a small case for pens, ink and a knife - all the instruments of the Oriental scribe". Their use is made clear: "Go through the midst of the city ... and set a mark upon the foreheads of them that sigh and cry for all the abominations that be done in the midst thereof" (v.4).

This man is clearly superior to the other men (after all, 'the pen is mightier than the sword', Edward Lytton), and since they were evidently angels, it is not unlikely that he too was an angel of exalted rank. It is tempting to think that this angel was none other than the 'Angel of the Lord'. The fact that he was "clothed in linen" reminds us that Daniel saw "a certain man clothed in linen (see also Dan. 12: 6), whose loins were girded with fine gold of Uphaz" (Dan. 10: 5), and the description leaves little doubt that Daniel saw the Lord Jesus. There does seem to be a correspondence between the two passages (Ezek. 9: 2; Dan. 10: 5) and the vision of John who saw "one like unto the Son of man, clothed with a garment down to the foot" (Rev. 1: 13). It was a priestly garment, and priests wore linen. On the other hand, the occupant of the 'sapphire throne' (with the "likeness as the appearance of a man above upon it", Ezek. 1: 26: surely the Lord Jesus) "**spoke unto the man clothed with linen**, and said, Go in between the wheels, even under the cherub, and fill thine hand with coals of fire from between the cherubims, and scatter them over the city" (Ezek. 10: 1-2).

Having attempted to identify the six men with their 'destroying weapons', and the seventh man with writer's inkhorn by his side" (v.2), we should now notice:

i) **The direction from which they came**. "And, behold, six men came from the way of the higher gate, which lieth toward the north." This gate was built by Jotham (2 Kings 15: 35). It was evidently called "the high gate of Benjamin (Jer. 20: 2) or "the new gate" (Jer. 26: 10; 36: 10). As the text suggests, the gate was toward the north of the city. While the idolaters faced north (see 8: 5, 14), it is more likely that the detail is given to emphasise the direction from which the Chaldeans would come. Judgment would come from the north. Compare Jeremiah 1 verses 14-15, "Then the LORD said unto me, Out of the **north** an evil shall break forth upon all the inhabitants of the land. For, lo, I will call all the families of the kingdoms of the *north*, saith the LORD, and they shall come, and they shall set every one his throne at the entering of the gates of Jerusalem". (See also Jeremiah 4: 6; 6: 1.)

ii)   The place where they halted. "They went in, and stood beside the brazen altar." This was "the central point at once of the true worship of Israel, and of the present profanation of that worship" (F.Gardiner, *Ellicott's Commentary*). As F.A.Tatford points out, "The brazen altar was the one at which the sacrifices were presented: here sin was atoned for and the transgressor's guilt was pretermitted; here too the sweet savour offerings were burnt as part of the offerer's worship of God. It was, therefore, fitting that the small group should stand there to receive their instructions from Him".

B) THE COURSE OF JUDGMENT, vv.3-7

The section begins with the words, "And the glory of the God of Israel was gone up from the cherub, whereupon he was, to the threshold of the house" (v.3).

It has to be said that it is not always easy to avoid confusion between the cherubim above the mercy seat, and the cherubim associated with the chariot-throne. Most commentators suggest that the word "cherub" here is used collectively of the two cherubim on the mercy seat. It seems more consistent, however, to adopt the alternative view that the word "cherub is used collectively of the *four cherubim* (or "living creatures", 1: 5 *et al)* which form the body the chariot-throne. When Ezekiel was first taken in the vision to the temple in Jerusalem, with all its idolatry, he said: "behold, the glory of the God of Israel was there, according to the vision that I saw in the plain (referring to 3: 22-23)" (8: 4). We now learn that the chariot-throne had not moved (better, had not *yet* moved) from the temple precincts. However, at this point, "the glory of the God of Israel" left the chariot and rested at "the threshold of the house".

Support for the above suggestion that the word "cherub" is used collectively of the four cherubim is found in Chapter 10 verses 1-5: "Then I looked, and, behold, in the firmament that was above the heads of the *cherubim* there appeared over them as it were a sapphire stone, as the appearance of the likeness of a throne (clearly the throne seen by Ezekiel by the river Chebar). And he spoke unto the man clothed with linen, and said, Go in between the wheels, even under the *cherub*, and fill thine hand with coals of fire from between the *cherubims* ... Now the *cherubims* stood on the right side of the house, when the man went in; and the cloud filled the inner court. Then the glory of the LORD went up from the *cherub*, and stood over the threshold of the house ... and the sound of the *cherubims'* wings was heard even to the outer court".

It therefore seems relatively clear that since the four cherubim (the "living creatures", 1: 5) move together in perfect harmony, they are frequently called, collectively, "the cherub". Confirmation is found in Chapter 10: verse 15: "And the *cherubims* were lifted up. This is the *living creature* (singular) that I saw by the river of Chebar". See also Chapter 10 verses 16-20 where the "cherubims" are mentioned five times with the statement: "this is *the living creature* (singular) that I saw under the God of Israel by the river of Chebar" (v.20). Hence Psalm 18 verses 9-10: "He bowed the heavens also, and came down: and darkness was under his feet. And he rode upon *a cherub* and did fly: yea, he did fly upon the wings of the wind".

We must now notice *(a)* the preservation of the godly (vv.3-4); *(b)* the destruction of the ungodly (vv.5-7)

a) The preservation of the godly, vv.3-4

"And the Lord said unto him (the man with the inkhorn), Go through the midst of the city, through the midst of Jerusalem, and set a mark upon the foreheads of the men that sigh and cry for all the abominations that be done in the midst thereof" (v.4). It is gratifying to know that there was at least a remnant in society which abhorred idolatry. Over these verses we could write, "The Lord knoweth them that are his" (2 Tim. 2: 19). We should notice:

i) **The mark**. According to the scholars, the word translated "mark" (*tau*) is the last letter of the Hebrew alphabet (see Psalm 119: 169-176) and takes the form of a cross. At first glance, the Hebrew letter does not look like a cross at all, but C.L.Feinberg explains that it did in "the earlier script", all of which suggests that it would be rather unwise to read too much into this! The symbolism is taken from Genesis 4 verse 15, "And the LORD set a mark upon Cain, lest any finding him should kill him". See also Exodus 12 verse 13, "And the blood shall be to you for a token upon the houses where ye are: and when I see the blood, I will pass over you, and the plague shall not be upon you to destroy you, when I smite the land of Egypt". It also reminds us of the way in which the household of Rahab was marked for preservation by the 'scarlet cord' in the window of her house on the wall of Jericho (Joshua 2: 18-21). It is worth reading 2 Peter 2 verses 4-9 at this juncture, noting Peter's conclusion that in view of the examples given it is clear that "The Lord knoweth how to deliver the godly out of temptations, and to reserve the unjust unto the day of judgment to be punished" (2 Pet. 2: 9). Arising from this, it is relevant to notice the Lord's words to Lot: "Haste thee, escape thither; for I cannot do anything till thou be come thither (to Zoar)" (Gen. 19: 22). Similarly, judgment would not fall on Jerusalem until the godly remnant had been marked for preservation.

At the end-time, the true Jehovah's Witnesses will be "sealed ... in their foreheads" (Rev. 7: 3) which evidently means immunity from death (Rev. 9: 4). Every one of them will be preserved and take their place with the Lamb on mount Zion (Rev.14: 1).

Those at the end-time who have "the mark of the beast" (Rev. 13: 16-18; 14: 9, 11; 16: 2; 19: 20) will be eternally doomed.

ii) **The men.** They "sigh and cry for all the abominations that be done in the midst thereof". That is, those "abominations" described in Chapter 8. These men grieved and lamented over the detestable things done in the temple. We often 'huff and puff' over the "abominations" practised in society today, particularly when they are sanctioned and practised by religious leaders and their followers. But how *deeply* are we moved by such flagrant rejection of God's holy laws? Amos touches the subject in saying that the ruling classes of his day "chant to the sound of the viol, and invent to themselves instruments of musick, like David; that drink wine in bowls, and anoint themselves with the chief ointments: but they are not grieved for the affliction of Joseph" (Amos 6: 5-6).

In another connection, Zephaniah refers to those "that are sorrowful for the solemn assembly, who are of thee, to whom the reproach of it was a burden" (Zeph. 3: 18). This refers to the exiles who were unable to celebrate the 'feasts unto the Lord' at Jerusalem. They deeply regretted their absence. But God noted their concern and knew that they had His interests at heart. Does absence from assembly gatherings grieve *us*? We are not to forsake "the assembling of ourselves together, as the manner of some is" (Heb. 10: 25). Can *we* say, with the Psalmist, "My soul longeth, yea, even fainteth for the courts of the LORD?" (Psalm 84: 2).

b) The destruction of the ungodly, vv.5-7

"And to the others (the six men with their weapons of destruction) he said in mine hearing (emphasising that Ezekiel was not left to draw his own conclusions), Go ye after him through the city, and smite ..." (v.5). We should notice:

i) **The source of the judgment.** As noted above, Ezekiel was let in no doubt that the Lord would initiate the destruction described here.

ii) **The severity of the judgment, v.5.** "Let not your eye spare, neither have ye pity." See also verse 10. (Similar words are found in 5: 11; 7: 4; 7: 9; 8: 18.)

iii) **The scope of the judgment, v.6.** "Slay utterly old and young, both maids and little children, and women." As Lamar E. Cooper observes, "Judgment of the guilty was indiscriminate. God plays no favourites and gives no exemptions".

iv) **The salvation from judgment, v.6.** "But come not near any man on whom is the mark." Compare Revelation 9 verse 4: "And it was commanded them (the locusts) that they should not hurt the grass of the earth, neither any green thing, neither any tree; but only those men which have not the seal of God in their foreheads".

v) **The start of the judgment, v.6.** "Begin at my sanctuary." That is, the temple. It was "to begin at the sanctuary, where the gross sin of the people had culminated" (F.Gardiner). They "began at the ancient men which were before the house", evidently referring to the "seventy men of the ancients of the house of Israel ... with every man his censer in his hand" (8: 11). They were foremost in the apostasy, and therefore divine retribution would begin with them.

Divine judgment was executed in accordance with the divine principle that "judgment must begin at the house of God" (1 Pet. 4: 17). As C.L.Feinberg points out, "Privilege brings responsibility in every age of man's history. Where the greatest privilege and responsibility rest, there the judgment alights. In the sanctuary God should have been most honoured, but there He was most dishonoured and provoked, and there His holiness would be most fully and certainly vindicated".

vi) The slaughter in the judgment, v.7. "Defile the house, and fill the courts with the slain: go ye forth. And they went forth and slew in the city." The significance of this is explained by F.Gardiner: "The utmost possible pollution under the Mosaic economy was the touch of a dead body. See Numumbers 19 verse 11. It might be thought that the temple would be spared this defilement ... but in this case the very defilement itself was part of the judgment, since God was about to forsake His sanctuary, and give over even this to the destruction of the heathen". In the words of C.L.Feinberg, "The house of the Lord was to be defiled by their dead bodies, as they had already defiled it by their idolatry".

The words, "go ye forth", indicate that having completed the slaughter in the sanctuary, the six executioners left the temple precincts to continue their work in the city itself: "And they went forth and slew in the city". We must remember, of course, that while this terrible work would actually be carried out by the Chaldeans, they would be acting under angelic constraint.

C) THE CRY FOR MERCY, vv.8-10

The work of the "six men ... every man with a slaughter weapon in his hand" (v.2) proceeded with such thoroughness that Ezekiel cried out in horror, "wilt thou destroy all the residue of Israel in thy pouring out of thy fury upon Jerusalem?" We should notice *(a)* Ezekiel's plea (v.8); *(b)* God's reply (vv.9-10).

a) Ezekiel's plea, v.8

"And it came to pass, while they were slaying them, and I was left, that I fell on my face, and cried, and said, Ah Lord God! wilt thou destroy all the residue of Israel in thy pouring out of thy fury upon Jerusalem?"

According to F.Gardiner, Ezekiel's "words ('I was left') imply *left alone*. The prophet had just before seen the courts of the sanctuary thronged with idolaters in the full glory of their heaven-defying sin. Now it is a city of the dead, and he is left standing alone in the midst of the dead". While H.L.Ellison suggests that "all the residue of Israel" refers to Judah, "the only part of 'all Israel' left after the destruction of Samaria", it seems more likely that Ezekiel is referring to those left in Jerusalem who had survived the deportation that took place in the reign of Jehoiachin (2 Chron. 36: 8-10). This deportation included Ezekiel himself.

Ezekiel was no "merciless religious bigot" (C.L.Feinberg). He was a compassionate man and the wholesale destruction of his people caused him deep distress, reminding us of Abraham's intercession, "Wilt thou also destroy the righteous with the wicked?" (Gen. 18: 23-33). It reminds us too, of the intercession of Moses. (See Exodus 32: 11-14, 30-35; 34: 8-9.)

b) God's answer, vv.9-10

"The iniquity of the house of Israel and Judah is exceeding great, and the land is full of blood, and the city full of perverseness: for they say, The LORD hath forsaken the earth, and the LORD seeth not (see also 8: 12). And as for me also, mine eye shall not spare, neither will I have pity, but I will recompense their way upon their head." As H.L.Ellison observes, "Ezekiel's efforts to intercede (v.8) were of no avail, for evil had gone too far. This is a note frequently struck at this time. (See Ezekiel 11:13; 14: 14; Jeremiah 7: 16; 11: 14; 14: 11; 15: 1)". Attention is also drawn to Amos 7 verses 1-9, where, having twice heeded the prophet's call for mercy (vv.2-3, 5-6), the Lord says, "I will not again pass by them any more" (vv.8-9).

In the first place, the land had been filled with the blood of innocent victims and society had made no attempt to implement justice. In the second place, they had gone even further by concluding that God was neither interested in them nor even noticed their behaviour. They could not have been more deceived. The Lord repeatedly said that His "**eye** would not spare" (5: 11; 7: 4; 7: 9; 8: 18; 9: 5, 10), but they said, "the LORD **seeth** not".

D) THE COMPLETION OF DELIVERANCE, v.11

"And, behold, the man clothed with linen, which had the inkhorn by his side, reported the matter, saying, I have done as thou hast commanded me." This does not refer to the completion of judgment upon Jerusalem, but to the marking of the godly remnant for preservation. "In the midst of widespread judgment, God had not forgotten the godly remnant nor His promised grace to them" (C.L.Feinberg). This solemn chapter therefore ends on a note of hope for the future, and more is said about this in Chapter 11 verses 14-21.

EZEKIEL CHAPTER 10

As we have already noted, Chapters 8-19 deal with the causes contributing to the coming judgment upon God's people. This section of the prophecy reveals that the Lord would no longer dwell amongst His people, together with the reasons. The solemn message of these chapters is conveyed by the *vision* given *to* Ezekiel (chs. 8-11) and by the *verbal messages* given *by* Ezekiel (chs.12-19).

Chapters 8-11 are therefore a unit in themselves and, at the same time, form part of a larger unit (Chapters 8-19). With this in mind, we noticed that these four chapters may be entitled: *(1) degrading idolatry* (ch.8); *(2) discriminatory judgment* (ch.9); *(3) destruction from God* (ch.10); *(4) depopulation and scattering* (ch.11).

In summary, Chapters 8-10 may be presented in the following way:

- *Chapter 8* brings before us the *exposure* of sin, and anticipates the consequential removal of the glory of God: "Seest thou what they do? Even the great abominations that the house of Israel committeth here, that I should *go far off from my sanctuary?*" (8: 6). Having seen these "abominations", Ezekiel is told that judgement is imminent: "Therefore will I also deal in fury ..." (8: 18).

- *Chapter 9* brings before us the *judgment* of idolaters: "Defile the house, and fill the courts with the slain: go ye forth. And they went forth, and slew in the city" (9: 7).

- *Chapter 10* brings before us the *destruction* of the city. The people in Jerusalem are slain in Chapter 9. The city itself is destroyed by fire in Chapter 10. "Fill the hand with coals of fire from between the cherubims, and scatter them over the city" (10: 2). This was fulfilled by Nebuzar-adan who "burnt the house of the LORD, and the king's house, and all the houses of Jerusalem, and every great man's house burnt he with fire" (2 Kings 25: 8-9).

EZEKIEL

We come therefore to

3) DESTRUCTION FROM GOD, 10: 1-22

While the Chaldeans actually slaughtered the inhabitants of Jerusalem and destroyed the city, they were, unknowingly, the Lord's servants. He had decreed the destruction of the city and the death of its inhabitants. This is clearly emphasised. In the case of the inhabitants, the angelic executioners are commanded by the Lord (9: 5-7) and in the case of Jerusalem itself, the fire 'scattered over the city' came from "between the wheels, from between the cherubims", who form the body of His chariot- throne (10: 2, 6-7). (See our remarks on 1: 5-14.)

Chapter 10 may be divided as follows: *(A)* the destruction by fire (vv.1-7); *(B)* the description of the chariot (vv.8-17); *(C)* the departure of the glory (vv.18-22). The reason for the detailed description of the Lord's chariot-throne at this point in the prophecy is to emphasise that He is in absolute control of events, including the judgment of His own people.

A) The destruction by fire, vv.1-7

These verses may be summarised as follows *(a)* the instructions from the throne (vv.1-2); *(b)* the location of the throne (vv.3-4); *(c)* the sound of the wings (v.5); *(d)* the implementation of judgment (vv.6-7).

a) The instructions from the throne, vv.1-2

It does seem that these verses are introductory, and serve as a preface to verses 3-7. We are told what the Lord said to "the man clothed with linen" before the Lord actually "stood over the threshold of the house" to address him (vv.4-6).

i) **The throne.** "Then I looked, and, behold, in the firmament that was above the head of the cherubims there appeared over them as it were a sapphire stone, as the appearance of the likeness of a throne" (v.1). As already noted, when Ezekiel was first taken in the vision to the temple in Jerusalem, with all its idolatry, "behold, the glory of the God of Israel was there, according to the vision that I saw in the plain (referring to 3: 22-23)" (8: 4). Ezekiel first saw the same vision by the river Chebar (see 1: 4-28), and now, in this chapter, he gives a further detailed description: see verses 8-22.

CHAPTER 10

ii) The instructions. "And he spake unto the man clothed with linen, and said, Go in between the wheels (*galgal,* 'whirling wheels', RV: 'a rolling thing', Young's Concordance), even under the cherub, and fill thine hand with coals of fire from between the cherubim, and scatter them over the city. And he went in my sight" (v.2). This is certainly thought-provoking:

- *A new role for "the man clothed in linen".* In the first place, his work was to mark the godly remnant for preservation (9: 4, 6). Now he is to execute judgment. As C.L.Feinberg points out, "Whereas his activity in Chapter 9 was one of grace and mercy toward the godly, here it is a ministry of judgment upon the ungodly ... Like Sodom and Gomorrah of old, the city was to be destroyed by fire ... In Isaiah 6 the coals were for the purification of the prophet; here they were for the destruction of the wicked".

Reference is made to his linen garment, perhaps to emphasise his purity, but no reference is now made to his "inkhorn" (9: 2). While dogmatism is to be avoided, it is at least interesting to notice that only the Lord Jesus had the moral right to "open the book, and to loose the seven seals thereof", thus initiating the judgments of the coming "day of the Lord (Rev. 5: 1-5).

It is also worthy of note that "the man clothed with linen" was commanded to fill his "*hand* with coals of fire from between the cherubim, and scatter them over the city". No mention is made of "tongs": compare Isaiah 6 verse 6. This *might* infer that "the man clothed in linen" was exempt from divine judgment. However, having said this, we have already suggested (see our comments in connection with 9: 2) that since it is the Occupant of the 'sapphire throne' (with the "likeness as the appearance of a man above upon it", Ezek. 1: 26: surely the Lord Jesus) who "*spoke unto the man clothed with linen* ..." (10: 1-2), it is more likely that "the man" in question is another angel.

- *A new name for "the living creatures"* (1: 5, 13-15 *et al).* This is the first time, leaving aside Chapter 9 verse 3, that the word "cherubim" occurs in the prophecy. Previously, these created beings are called "living creatures" (1: 5). The fact that both expressions refer to the same beings is confirmed in Chapter 10 verse 20. This raises the question, 'Why is it not until now that Ezekiel uses the word "cherubims?"'. There appears to be no clear answer unless Ezekiel only realised that the "living creatures" were actually the cherubim when, in the vision, he saw their likeness "carved on the inside walls of the Temple (1 Kings 6: 29), and on the double-doors (1 Kings 6: 35), and on the Temple furnishings (1 Kings 7: 29)" (John B.

Taylor). While we cannot improve on this suggestion, it does not seem entirely satisfactory. It is, of course, quite possible that the Lord revealed the identity of "the living creatures" to Ezekiel.

The cherubim, with their four faces, evidently conveyed the attributes of the Lord, and exhibited His creatorial power and authority. As already noted, "In man intelligence is at its highest level, in the lion strength at its greatest, in the ox service at its meekest, and in the eagle movement at its swiftest" (F.Cundick).

We should notice the use of the singular and plural here: "And he spake unto the man clothed with linen, and said, Go in between the wheels, even under the **cherub**, and fill thine hand ('the hollow of thy hands', JND; 'both thine hands', RV)) with coals of fire from between the **cherubim**, and scatter them over the city". As already suggested, it appears that since the four cherubim (the "living creatures", 1: 5) move together in perfect harmony, they are sometimes collectively called "the cherub". This is evidently the case here (v.2) and in v.15, "This is the *living creature* (singular) that I saw by the river of Chebar". Compare Psalm 18 verses 9-10.

The reference to "the wheels" and "the cherubim" in connection with the "coals of fire" is significant. In the first place, "wheels" evidently convey the connection between the throne of God and earth. It is a universally mobile throne, and none are outside the range of judgment. In the second place, the appearance of the "living creatures" (*alias* "the cherubim") "was like burning coals of fire" (Ezek. 1: 13). The cherubim therefore convey the utter righteousness of God: "our God is a consuming fire" (Heb. 12: 29).

b) The location of the throne, vv.3-4

The location is most precise: "Now the cherubims stood on the right side of the house, when the man went in; and the cloud filled the inner court. Then the glory of the LORD went up from the cherub, and stood over the threshold of the house: and the house was filled with the cloud, and the court was full of the brightness of the LORD'S glory". This seems to suggest that while the chariot-throne "stood on the right side of the house" the divine Occupant of the throne had dismounted and was standing "over the threshold of the house". According to C.L.Feinberg, the location, "the right side of the house", indicates that the cherubim were "stationed on the southern side of the sanctuary", and this is perhaps significant since "the idolatries which

Ezekiel had seen were all being practised on the north side of the temple (8: 14)" (F.A.Tatford).

This was the second occasion on which this had happened. In the first case, the Lord had **dismounted** from His chariot-throne ("the glory of the God of Israel was **gone up** from the cherub") and stationed Himself at "the threshold of the house" in order to address the "man clothed with linen, which had the writer's inkhorn by his side" (9: 3). Now He **dismounts** from His chariot-throne for the second time ("the glory of the LORD went up from the cherub", 10: 4) in order to address the "man clothed in linen" again (10: 6). We know that the Lord then **remounted** His throne and "mounted up from the earth" (vv.18-19). (See also 11: 22-23.)

We should notice that "the house was filled with the cloud, and the court was full of the brightness of the Lord's glory". It is "***the*** cloud, rather than "***a*** cloud". In the Old Testament, the cloud was the symbol of the Lord's presence. See, for example, Exodus 19 verse 9, "And the LORD said unto Moses, I come unto thee in a thick cloud"; Exodus 40 verses 34-38, "Then a cloud covered the tent of the congregation, and the glory of the LORD filled the tabernacle … the cloud of the LORD was upon the tabernacle by day, and fire was on it by night". We can now understand why the three disciples "fell on their face, and were sore afraid" (Matt. 17: 6) and why, in Luke's words, they "feared as they entered into the cloud" (Luke 9: 34). Although not a Biblical expression, it is often called the 'Shekinah cloud', meaning 'God dwelling'.

It has been nicely pointed out that "the presence of the Lord was as glorious in His departure as it was in His entrance" (Ex 40: 34-35; 1 Kings 8: 10-11)" (C.L.Feinberg).

c) The sound of the wings, v.5

"And the sound of the cherubims' wings was heard even to the outer court, as the voice of the Almighty God (*El Shadday*, Newberry) when he speaketh." Notice the three graphic expressions: "like the noise of many waters (compare Rev. 1: 15), as the voice of the Almighty, the voice of speech, as the noise of an host". Compare Chapter 1 verses 24-25. John P. Taylor must be right in saying, "they are graphic similes and convey well the idea of God's awfulness, heard with the ear as well as seen by the eye". Perhaps the reference to sound here indicates that the chariot was ready to move. The "voice of the Almighty God" suggests infinite power.

d) The implementation of judgment, vv.6-7

The "man clothed with linen" does as he is told (v.2) and "one cherub stretched forth his hand from between the cherubims unto the fire that was between the cherubims, and took thereof, and put it into the hands of him that was clothed with linen: who took it, and went out". The references to the cherub's "hand" and "the hands of him that was clothed with linen" might indicate that the coming judgment would be implemented by human hands, even though the Chaldean invaders would not have the slightest suspicion that they were being used by heavenly powers. Perhaps this is what Patrick Fairbairn (*An Exposition of Ezekiel*) means in saying that "human agents should not be wanting, at the proper time, to carry into effect the judgment written".

It is, perhaps worth noting that two words are used here for the wheels: "Take fire from between the wheels (*galgal,* meaning 'a rolling thing') ... then he went in, and stood beside the wheels (*ophan,* meaning what it says – 'wheels)" (v.6).

It is also worth noting that the man clothed in linen is "strangely anonymous", and his "appearance of anonymity is only increased by the fact that we are never allowed to see him at work. We only know that his first task was completed because of the laconic report in Chapter 9 verse 11, and of the second all that is explicitly stated is that he took the burning coals from the hands of a cherub and *went out*" (John P.Taylor).

B) The description of the chariot, vv.8-17

This closely follows the description given in Chapter 1. Reference is made to the following:

i) **The hands of the cherubim.** "And there appeared in the cherubims the form of a man's hand under their wings" (v.8). In the original vision, the reference to the hands of the "living creatures" occurs in a section beginning, "they had the likeness of a man" (1: 5), indicating the interests of the throne in man. The "feet" and "hands" ("they had the hands of a man under their wings") are then mentioned.

ii) **The wheels by the cherubim.** "And when I looked, behold the four wheels (*ophan*) by the cherubims, one wheel by one cherub, and another

CHAPTER 10

wheel (*ophan*) by another cherub: and the appearance of the wheels was as the colour of a beryl stone." (The same original word - *ophan* – is used by Ezekiel thereafter, unless indicated.) As for their appearances, they four had one likeness, as if a wheel had been in the midst of a wheel. When they went, they went on their four sides: they turned not as they went, but to the place whither the head looked they followed it; they turned not as they went" (vv.9-11). Compare Chapter 1 verses 15-17 where, according to John P. Taylor, the words "a wheel in the middle of a wheel" are best understood as "two wheels, probably solid discs, which bisected each other at right angles, thus allowing movement in any of four directions without being turned". Taylor also suggests that the words, "upon their four sides" (1: 17 AV) are better translated "towards their four sides", that is, the four directions which the creatures faced. The perfect harmony between the direction ("the head") and movements ("wheels") of the chariot in relation to earth is emphasised in verse 11.

iii) **The eyes of the cherubim.** "And their whole body, and their backs, and their hands, and their wings, and the wheels, were full of eyes round about, even the wheels that they four had. As for the wheels, it was cried unto them in my hearing, O wheel (*galgal*)" (vv.12-13). The RSV has, "And their rims, and their spokes, and the wheels were full of eyes round about". According to H.L.Ellison, this is "quite possible", but his observation occurs in the context of remarks about "considerable textual error" with the observation, "it is likely that the text has been disordered". But this rendering does not seem to be sufficiently supported. Admittedly only the "rings" (rims) are said to be "full of eyes" in Chapter 1 verse 18, but this does not preclude further information. C.L.Feinberg, who observes that "the mention of the four wheels indicates that more details were added as Ezekiel got a closer view", is preferable: "Characteristic of all the cherubim and the wheels was the fulness of eyes, speaking of the omniscience of God (Gen.16: 13; Zech. 4: 10; Rev. 4: 6)." The "four beasts" ('four living creatures') are full of eyes before and behind" (Rev. 4: 6). Divine judgment rests upon perfect knowledge. As L.E.Cooper observes, "One day every individual will stand before a holy and righteous God who sees and knows all things".

According to H.L.Ellison, "Verse 14 is the immediate sequel to verse 12" and "verse 13, referring to the wheels, is out of place - perhaps a scribe's eye was caught by the mention of the wheels at the end of verse 12". But this seems to be a rearrangement of the text to suit the expositor! It is best to leave the text as it is. Verse 13 is simply extending verse 12 before verse 14 resumes the main direction. The words "O wheel" (v.13) can be taken as a command. The wheels were to be set in motion. The chariot was about to move. As we have noticed, the wings were evidently in motion (v.5).

iv) ***The faces of the cherubim.*** "And every one had four faces: the first face was the face of a cherub, and the second face was the face of a man, and the third the face of a lion, and the fourth the face of an eagle" (v.14). Compare Chapter 1 verse 10, "As for the likeness of their faces, they four had the face of a man, and the face of a lion, on the right side: and they four had the face of an ox on the left side: they four also had the face of an eagle". There is therefore a difference between the two passages, namely, that the face of the ox (1: 10) is now said to be the face of a cherub (10: 14). In spite of the fact that "all available manuscripts apparently agree" (F.A.Tatford), H.L.Ellison finds refuge in what he calls an "obvious ... careless scribal error", and John P.Taylor thinks similarly. F.Gardiner (*Ellicott's Commentary*) suggests that "the most natural solution of the difficulty in the text as it stands is that a cherub was ordinarily represented with the face of an ox", but he continues by saying, "But there is no evidence of this, and it is not impossible that a slight error may have been introduced into the text". His first explanation is preferable! There is no doubt, however, that Ezekiel is describing the same creatures. See verse 22, "And the likeness of their faces was the same faces which I saw by the river of Chebar, their appearances and themselves: they went every one straight forward". In any case, C.L.Feinberg has some good advice in saying, "Reverent Bible students will do well to treat difficulties in the text as problems rather than errors, and continue to search for meaningful solutions".

v) ***The movements of the cherubim.*** "And the cherubims were lifted up. This is the living creature that I saw by the river of Chebar. And when the cherubims went, the wheels went by them: and when the cherubims lifted up their wings to mount up from the earth, the same wheels also turned not from beside them. When they stood, these stood : and when they were lifted up, these lifted up themselves also: for the spirit of the living creatures was in them" (vv.15-17) Compare Chapter 1 verses 19-21. In a word, there was absolute harmony between wings and wheels. There is no discordant note about the throne of God. The earthly movements are directed by the heavenly. There can be no question of failure in God's purposes for earth, for "the spirit of the living creature (singular) was in them (the wheels)" (v.17).

C) The departure of the glory, vv.18-22

"Then the glory of the LORD departed from off the threshold of the house,

CHAPTER 10

and stood over the cherubims. And the cherubims lifted up their wings, and mounted up from the earth in my sight: when they went out, the wheels also were beside them, and (every one) stood at the door of the east gate of the LORD'S house; and the glory of the God of Israel was over them above" (vv.18-19). As noted earlier, very clearly the Lord had remounted His throne. As F.Gardiner points out, "In verse 3 the cherubim stood by the "right side of the house", and in verse 18 "the glory of the Lord left the threshold, and resumed its place above the waiting cherubim; now the whole mount up from the earth, and go "to the east gate of the Lord's house" - that is, to the main entrance of the outermost court". He also points out that "the words 'every one' (v.19) are not in the original text (they are italicised in the AV), and should be omitted. 'They stood', or 'it stood', would be better, the vision being regarded as a whole".

In His departure, the Lord fulfilled the warning uttered by Moses: "Then my anger shall be kindled against them in that day, and I will forsake them, and I will hide my face from them, and they shall be devoured, and many evils and troubles shall befall them; so that they shall say in that day, Are not these evils come upon us, because our God is not among us?" (Deut. 31: 17). Having left "the threshold of the house" (v.18) and lingered "at the door of the east gate of the LORD'S house" (v.19), "the glory of the LORD went up from the midst of the city, and stood upon the mountain which is on the east side of the city" (11: 22-23). But He will return! Ezekiel saw this too: "And, behold, the glory of the God of Israel came from the way of the east: his voice was like the voice of many waters: and the earth shined with his glory" (43: 2). "Ichabod ('the glory has departed') is not for ever!

We should remember, of course, that "God's presence had never been confined to the temple. Rather, the temple was where He made himself known in blessing, and received the worship of His people (see 1 Kings 8: 27-53)" (L.E.Cooper).

The prophet is at pains to stress that the vision of the Lord's throne accorded with the original vision given to him "by the river of Chebar" (vv.15, 20, 22). Notice particularly the words "This is the living creature that I saw **under the God of Israel** by the river of Chebar; and I knew that they were the cherubims" (v.20).

C.L.Feinberg has a most interesting explanatory note: "As a priest Ezekiel could have learned about the cherubim from the high priest or from the

Mosaic instructions for the tabernacle. The prophet's people were to live for a long time without benefit of the temple and its service, so he repeated the different features of the faces and wings, that they might know and recollect the glory and majesty that once dwelt among them".

We must not leave the chapter without take careful note of its outstanding lesson. In the words of L.E.Cooper, "God withdraws from unholy worship. We cannot come before the Lord any time and any way we choose. God demands holiness of those who would approach Him (Lev. 10: 1-7; 20: 1-7; Psalm 15: 1-5). God is long-suffering with us, as He was with Israel, but He ultimately withdraws when His call for righteousness is ignored (Ezek. 11: 4-12)".

EZEKIEL CHAPTER 11

As we have noticed, Chapters 8-11 comprise the first part of the section of the prophecy detailing the contributory causes of coming judgment upon Judah and Jerusalem. These first three of these chapters bring before us *the exposure of sin* (ch. 8), *the judgment on idolaters* (ch. 9) and *the destruction of the city* (ch.10). The fourth and final chapter in this section of the prophecy draws our attention to *depopulation and scattering* (ch.11).

Alternatively, as we have seen, the four chapters may be entitled: *(A) degrading idolatry* (ch.8), *(B) discriminatory judgment* (ch.9), *(C) destruction from God* (ch.10) and, as above, *(D) depopulation and scattering* (ch.11).

We now come, therefore, to

D) DEPOPULATION AND SCATTERING, 11: 1-25

The people who thought that they would remain in safety in the city would be brought "forth out of the midst of it" (v.7), delivered "into the hands of strangers" (v.9) and judged "in the border of Israel" (vv.10-11). But restoration to the land is predicted (vv.17-21). As C.J.H.Wright points out, "there is irony in the very structure of Chapter 11. In its first half, the leading citizens will be dragged out of the city for judgment and destruction (vv.7-11). In the second half, the exiles who have already been dragged out of the city in judgment will conversely eventually be gathered for restoration (vv.16-17)".

The chapter may be divided as follows: *(1)* the result of God's judgment (vv.1-13); *(2)* the return of God's people (vv.14-21); *(3)* the removal of God's glory (vv.22-23); *(4)* the report of God's servant (vv.24-25).

1) THE RESULT OF GOD'S JUDGMENT, vv.1-13

We should notice the following: *(a)* the cause of coming judgment (vv.1-3);

(b) the course of coming judgment (vv.4-12); *(c)* the evidence of coming judgment (v.13).

a) The cause of coming judgment, vv.1-3

The departing cherubim (forming the body of the Lord's chariot) paused at "the door of the east gate of the LORD'S house; and the glory of the God of Israel was over them above" (10: 19). The situation in the east gate is now described in verses 1-3. Quite clearly, the Lord could not allow His glory to remain there. Conditions in the temple and its courts have already been described (see 8: 1-18), and consequently "the glory of the LORD departed from off the threshold of the house" (10: 18) and "stood at the door of the east gate of the LORD'S house" (10: 19). But this location did not present a better picture: "Moreover the spirit lifted me up, and brought me unto the east gate of the LORD'S house, which looketh eastward: and behold at the door of the gate five and twenty men … that devise mischief, and give wicked counsel in this city" (vv.1-2). The "wicked counsel" was rejection of the very idea that the city would fall: "which say, It is not near; let us build houses: this city is the caldron and we be the flesh" (v.3).

i) **The men, v.1.** The twenty-five men included "Jaazaniah (meaning, 'Jehovah hears') the son of Azur ('the helper'), and Pelatiah ('Jehovah rescues') the son of Benaiah ('Jehovah builds'), princes of the people". Although some commentators think otherwise, there seem to be no serious grounds for doubting that these are the same twenty-five sun-worshippers described in Chapter 8 verse 16. These men are said to have "filled the land with violence" (8: 17), which is substantially repeated here: "Ye have multiplied your slain in this city, and ye have filled the streets thereof with the slain" (v.6). As H.L.Ellison observes, "Their activity in verse 2 suits their position as leading priests, while their blatant idolatry (8: 16) matches their cynicism". As a matter of interest, "recent archeological discoveries in the excavations of the city of David have yielded over two hundred and fifty clay seals used on official documents from the period just before the fall of Jerusalem. They were preserved because they were burned (perhaps he means 'buried') when the building in which they were housed was destroyed, probably in the destruction of 586 BC. Both the names Jaazaniah and Pelatiah appeared in this archive of seals of royal officials" (Lamar E. Cooper).

The name Jaazaniah occurs in Chapter 8 verse 11, where he is called "Jaazaniah the son of Shaphan" which may mean that he might have actually

CHAPTER 11

been the grandson of Shaphan (following the frequent use of "son" in that way), and therefore the same as "Jaazaniah, the son of Azur" (11: 1). As F.Gardiner (*Ellicott's Commentary*) points out (we noted this in considering 8: 11), "It is hardly probable that two persons of the same character and the same (not very common) name should have been among the leaders of the people at the same time. If this is the case, then it was his grandfather who found the book of the law in the temple during the refurbishment ordered by Josiah (2 Kings 22: 10). Moreover Jaazaniah's brothers, Gemariah and Ahikam (Jer. 36: 10; 39: 14), were evidently pious Israelites". All this emphasises that godliness does not 'run in the blood'.

F.Gardiner considers that the names are significant: "Names of this sort were common enough (*sic*) among the Jews, but they seem here intended to bring out the false hopes with which the people beguiled themselves; and in view of this the sudden death of Pelatiah (v.13) was particularly impressive".

ii) Their message, vv.2-3. "These are the men that devise mischief, and give wicked counsel in this city: which say, It is not near; let us build houses: this city is the caldron, and we be the flesh." This is nothing less than a scornful rejection of Ezekiel's proclamation of coming judgment. But if "the men that devise mischief" said in effect that predicted judgment "is not near; let us build houses (literally, 'not near to build houses')", Ezekiel points out that it is *very* near. (It should be pointed out, however, that the wording of verse 3 in the Hebrew text is not easily understood, and has been "the subject of different interpretations" (C.L.Feinberg). It has to be said, however, that the AV rendering is perfectly intelligible, although this is not likely to impress the linguists!)

Staying with the A.V. wording, the reason for ignoring predictions of imminent judgment, and encouraging the house-building industry, was the supposed security of the city. They believed "that the city defences would be impregnable: the defenders would be as safe from the fires of war as meat in the cauldron that protects it from the flames" (John B.Taylor). In their own words, "this city is the caldron, and we be the flesh". They regarded themselves as "the prime cuts of the meat" (C.J.H.Wright). Taylor continues: "Such an attitude would readily be seen by Ezekiel to be sheer folly and deserving the strongest condemnation. It not only ignored the explicit warnings of Jeremiah that resistance to Babylon would bring greater disaster than submission (Jer. 21: 8-10), but it also reeked of the sublime self-confidence which was to be Jerusalem's undoing". These people totally ignored Solomon's good advice: "Trust in the LORD with all thine heart; and lean not unto thine own understanding. In all thy ways acknowledge Him, and He shall direct thy paths. Be not wise in thine own eyes: fear the LORD, and depart from evil" (Prov. 3: 5-7).

Both H.L.Ellison and John B. Taylor say that "for them ('the men that devise mischief') the exiles under Jehoiachin were the offal thrown out on the dung-heap of Babylonia" while "they themselves were the good flesh preserved by God in Jerusalem".

b) *The course of coming judgment, vv.4-12*

This is set out in vverses 8-11. "First, the sword should come upon them (v.8); then they should be driven out of the city in which they trusted and delivered into the hands of strangers (v.9); and then, finally - what was most terrible to a Jew - they were to be arraigned and punished 'in the border', i.e. at the extremity or outside the land of Israel (v.10)" (F.Gardiner).

Wicked men had spoken (v.3), but now the Lord speaks! "Therefore prophesy against them, prophesy, O son of man. And the Spirit of the LORD fell upon me, and said unto me, Speak; Thus saith the LORD ..." (vv.4-5). As Lamar E. Cooper observes, this is "one of the most explicit statements of Ezekiel's divine inspiration", reminding us that "the prophecy came not in old time by the will of man: but holy men of God spake as they were moved by the Holy Ghost" (2 Pet. 1: 21). We should notice:

i) **The Lord's omniscience, v5.** "Thus have ye said, O house of Israel for I know the things that come into your mind, every one of them." He knew what they were thinking, let alone what they were saying! This will not surprise us since "all things are naked and opened unto the eyes of him with whom we have to do" (Heb. 4: 13).

ii) **The Lord's appraisal, vv.6-7.** "Ye have multiplied your slain in this city, and ye have filled the streets thereof with the slain. Therefore thus saith the Lord GOD; Your slain whom ye have laid in the midst of it, **they** are the flesh, and this city is the caldron." John B.Taylor uses rather graphic language in saying that "Ezekiel retorts that the real men of worth in Jerusalem were the many innocent men who had been slain, either by political purges or more likely in the fighting which was the result of these evil policies. He was virtually saying, 'The only good Jerusalemite is a dead Jerusalemite'. H.L.Ellison puts it like this: "God's favourites would be those whose deaths they had caused (vv.6-7). They would not even have the privilege of dying in Jerusalem (vv.7-10)". This leads to:

iii) **The Lord's judgment, vv.7-11.** The very people who claimed that the city walls would protect them would be brought "forth out of the midst of it" (v.7). Ezekiel continues, "Ye have feared the sword; and I will bring a sword upon you, saith the Lord GOD. And I will bring you out of the midst thereof, and deliver you into the hands of strangers, and I will execute judgments upon you. Ye shall fall by the sword; I will judge you in the border of Israel; and ye shall know that I am the LORD. This city shall not be your caldron, neither shall ye be the flesh in the midst thereof; but I will judge you in the border of Israel" (vv.8-11). They would be hauled out of their "caldron" and meet their doom "in the border of Israel" which, as H.L.Ellison observes, predicts "the execution of some of the leaders of the people at Riblah (2 Kings 25: 18-21)".

iv) **The Lord's explanation, v.12.** "And ye shall know that I am the LORD: for ye have not walked in my statutes, neither executed my judgments, but have done *after the manner of the heathen that are round about you.*" This verse reminds us that we are not to be "conformed to this world: but ... transformed by the renewing of your mind, that ye may prove what is that good, and acceptable, and perfect, will of God" (Rom. 12: 2).

c) The evidence of coming judgment, v.13

At this, Palatiah dies, and his death can be taken as the precursor of coming judgment. We must remember that Ezekiel is "in the visions of God" (8: 3; 11: 24) but although, therefore, "Pelatiah did not hear Ezekiel's message, there is no ground for considering his death as merely visionary or symbolic" (H.L.Ellison). The death of Pelatiah had such an effect on the prophet that he intercedes for the nation: "Then fell I down upon my face, and cried with a loud voice, and said, Ah Lord GOD! Wilt thou make a full end of the remnant of Israel?" Compare Chapter 9 verse 8. Ezekiel has a kindred spirit in Paul who wrote, "Brethren, my heart's desire and prayer to God for Israel is, that they might be saved" (Rom. 10: 1).

How deeply are we concerned about the spiritual welfare of unsaved men and women, let alone the welfare of our fellow-believers?

EZEKIEL

The answer to his petition follows in the next part of the chapter, reminding us of the Lord's words, "Fear thou not, O Jacob my servant, saith the LORD: for I am with thee; for I will make a full end of all the nations whither I have driven thee; but I will not make a full end of thee, but correct thee in measure; yet will I not leave thee wholly unpunished" (Jer. 46: 28).

2) THE RETURN OF GOD'S PEOPLE, vv.14-21

In answer to Ezekiel's entreaty, God announces His protection for the exiles, and their ultimate regathering to the land of Israel.

This is introduced with reference to the alleged superiority of the inhabitants of Jerusalem over the captives in Babylonia: "Son of man, thy brethren, even thy brethren, the men of thy kindred, (i.e 'men of thy exile') and all the house of Israel wholly, are they unto whom the inhabitants of Jerusalem have said, Get you far from the LORD: unto us is this land given in possession" (v.15). "The scornful 'Get you far from the LORD' (AV, RV) is reminiscent of David's lament in 1 Samuel 26 verse 19, 'They have driven me out this day that I should have no share in the heritage of the LORD, saying, Go, serve other gods'" (John B.Taylor). In the words of H.L.Ellison, "The exiles were looked on as far from Jehovah, because far from His land, while those living near the temple were thought to be basking in the smile of His favour".

We should note that the words, "men of thy kindred", are, literally, 'men of my redemption'. According to F.A.Tatford, "the word used is related to that for 'redeemer' (*goel*) and consequently implies that the exiles were not permanently lost to Jehovah, but would one day be repurchased and restored ... The exiles could not be regarded as disinherited (as implied by the people in Jerusalem, see v.15): redemption would one day be effected". John B. Taylor points out that "Ezekiel's fellow-captives ('thy brethren, even thy brethren, the men of thy kindred') now represented **the whole house of Israel**, adding **all of them** (AV 'wholly') as if to complete the identification. Far from being the outcasts of Israel, the exiles had become the true Israel".

In the verses that follow we should note *(a)* their preservation in exile (v.16); *(b)* their restoration to the land (vv.17-21).

a) Their preservation in exile, v.16

"Therefore say, Thus saith the Lord GOD; Although I have cast them far off among the heathen, and although I have scattered them among the countries, yet I will be to them as a little sanctuary in the countries where they shall come." Whilst H.L.Ellison may be right in saying, "We are not dealing with a gracious promise, but with the spiritual loss felt by the exiles by their separation from the temple ... the exile was punishment", nevertheless God had not abandoned them. F.Gardiner renders "a little sanctuary" as 'a sanctuary for a little' and suggests that this means 'a sanctuary for a little time'. As C.L.Feinberg points out, the words "little sanctuary" could never be true of God. He would watch over the remnant. F.Gardiner continues, "For a little while, during the term of their captivity, God's presence with them spiritually would be instead of the outward symbolical presence in His temple. The contrast is striking. God has already said that He would abandon the temple, and give up Jerusalem to destruction, and cast out its people; but now to the exiles, scattered among the heathen, He would Himself be for a sanctuary". The Lord's people today can rightly use Old Testament language in saying, "A glorious high throne from the beginning is the place of our sanctuary" (Jer. 17: 12). We can "come boldly unto the throne of grace, that we may obtain mercy, and find grace to help in time of need" (Heb. 4: 16).

b) Their restoration to the land, vv.17-21

"Therefore say, Thus saith the Lord GOD; I will even gather you from the people ('peoples', JND), and assemble you out of the countries where ye have been scattered, and I will give you the land of Israel ... And I will give them one heart (evidently referring to the reunion of the northern and southern kingdoms), and I will put a new spirit within you; and I will take the stony heart out of their flesh, and I will give them an heart of flesh: that they may walk in my statutes, and keep mine ordinances, and do them: and they shall be my people, and I will be their God" (vv.17-20). Notice the seven occurrences of *"I will"* in these verses. Compare Ezekiel 36 verses 24-27 and Jeremiah 31 verses 31-34. H.L.Ellison is worth quoting here: "Though Ezekiel stresses the sovereignty of God, he is no determinest. Salvation is God's work, but man has to prepare the way for it by repentance. God brings the people back to their land (v.17), but before the transformation of character (v.19), which is also God's work, there is the removal of all traces of idolatry by the people (v.18), the outward sign of their change of heart".

The regathering and regeneration here is still future, and will take place when men see "the Son of man coming in the clouds of heaven with power and great glory. And he shall send his angels with a great sound of a trumpet, and they shall gather together his elect from the four winds, from one end of heaven to the other" (Matt. 24: 30-31).

Regathered and regenerate Israel will "walk in my statutes" and enjoy divine blessing: "they shall be my people, and I will be their God" (v.20). But what of those whose "heart walketh after the heart of their detestable things and their abominations?". The answer follows: "I will recompense their way upon their own heads, saith the Lord GOD" (v.21). As H.L.Ellison observes, "The judgment on those left in Jerusalem is nothing arbitrary, the result of an unexplained divine decree ... These are in the first place the men of Jerusalem, as the vision of Chapter 8 had shown, and their destruction would be the punishment of their impenitent idolatry. But the threat holds good for the exiles too, if they cling to their old idols or turn to the idols of Babylon (cf. 14: 2-6)".

3) THE REMOVAL OF GOD'S GLORY, vv.22-23

The glory of the Lord is now withdrawn from the city. "Then did the cherubim lift up their wings, and the wheels beside them; and the glory of the God of Israel was over them above. And the glory of the LORD went up from the midst of the city, and stood upon the mountain which is on the east side of the city (the Mount of Olives)."

As F.A.Tatford observes, "The glory of Jehovah had left the temple but had remained temporarily poised at or over the eastern gate of the outer court of the temple. Now it was to withdraw still further ... The *shekinah* rose from the middle of the city and paused above the Mount of Olives on the east side of Jerusalem". He continues: "According to the Jewish rabbis (although on what basis is not clear), the glory remained on Olivet for three and a half years in the hope that Israel would repent and, only when it was clear that there was no probability of repentance, did the glory depart. From one stage to another, the glory had withdrawn slowly and deliberately, as though Jehovah was reluctant to leave the city and the people, without affording them every opportunity of returning in heart to Him. Such is ever the Divine long-suffering". From this point on, the temple was only an empty shell, and the offerings brought there were nothing but mere outward show. The same can happen to an assembly. It did at Laodicea (Rev. 3: 14-22).

CHAPTER 11

The departure of "the glory of the LORD" reminds us that "the Lord of glory" (1 Cor. 2: 8; James 2: 1) came into the world, but like the glory in Ezekiel 11 verse 23, He left the temple, saying "Ye shall not see me henceforth until the time that ye say, Blessed is He that cometh in the name of the Lord" (Matt. 23: 39), and went to the Mount of Olives (Matt. 24: 1-3). Ezekiel describes His return: "And, behold, the glory of the God of Israel came from the way of the east ... and, behold, the glory of the LORD filled the house" (Ezek. 43: 1-5). Israel *will* see Him again, with the language of Psalm 118 verse 26 on their lips: "Blessed be he that cometh in the name of the LORD".

4) THE REPORT OF GOD'S SERVANT, vv.24-25

The Spirit which had taken Ezekiel from Chaldea to Jerusalem (8: 3) brings him back: "Afterwards the spirit ('the Spirit', JND) took me up, and brought me in a vision by the Spirit of God into Chaldea, to them of the captivity. So the vision that I had seen went up from me. Then I spake unto them of the captivity all the things that the LORD had shewed me". There can be no doubt that he 'diminished not a word' (Jer. 26: 2).

As C.J.H.Wright points out, "For these men it must have been an uncomfortably nasty account to have to listen to ... To the extent that they recognised the truth of the report Ezekiel gave, they were then faced with a sharp choice. Either they must accept Ezekiel as a true prophet (since he had reported what they knew to be true), and then be moved to grief and repentance for their past actions. (We should remember that some of them could have been engaged in these practices themselves before their exile.) Or they could brazenly deny the truth, mock the messenger, and harden their hearts against God still further in their rebellion ... Such was the choice that now confronted the silent, stony faces in front of Ezekiel himself in that hot little room on 17th September 592 BC".

How do we react when the Word of God reveals sin in *our* lives?

EZEKIEL CHAPTER 12

In outlining the prophecy of Ezekiel (see the Introduction) we suggested that its first section ('The Ruin of Judah and Jerusalem, chs. 1-24') may be divided as follows: *(a)* the commissioning of Ezekiel (1: 1 - 3: 15); *(b)* the coming judgment (3: 16 - 7: 27); *(c)* the causes of judgment (8: 1 - 19: 14); *(d)* the consistency of national sin (20: 1 - 23: 49); *(e)* the commencement of hostilities (24: 1-27).

Further to the above, we suggested that the causes of judgment (8: 1 – 18: 14) are highlighted in the *vision* given *to* Ezekiel (chs. 8-11), which ends with the withdrawal of the glory of the Lord from the temple (11: 22-23), and the *visible* and *verbal messages* delivered *by* Ezekiel (chs.12-19). The verbal messages (Chs.13-19) are preceded by two acted parables (Ch.12). This phase of Ezekiel's ministry took place in "the *sixth year*" of King Jehoiachin's captivity (8: 1).

Having dealt with the vision given *to* Ezekiel (chs. 8-11), we therefore now come to the visible signs (acted parables) given *by* Ezekiel (ch.12), to be followed by the causes of coming judgment (chs.13-17), the objections to coming judgment (ch.18) and the lamentation over coming judgment (ch.19).

We come then to:

PICTURES OF COMING JUDGMENT, 12: 1-28

As C.L.Feinberg points out, "Chapters 4-11 have repeatedly shown the certainty of Jerusalem's destruction; chapters 12-19 present the necessity for it. The emphasis in the chapters is the moral cause of the exile ... Ezekiel's main purpose was to reveal how baseless was the people's confidence that the kingdom and its capital would be spared, and to arouse the remnant to repentance". In this connection we must remember that Ezekiel was *not in Jerusalem* but amongst the exiles *in Babylonia*. The two acted parables were therefore a sign to them that any cherished hope they entertained of returning to Judah and Jerusalem was illusory. He therefore acts as if he were leaving Jerusalem *en route* to exile.

Ezekiel 12 may be divided into two major sections: *(1)* Ezekiel acts two parables (vv.1-20); *(2)* Ezekiel answers two objections (vv.21-28). The four resulting paragraphs each commence with the words, "The word of the Lord came unto me saying" (vv.1, 17, 21, 26).

1) TWO ACTED PARABLES, vv.1-20

"The word of the LORD also came unto me, saying, Son of man, thou dwellest in the midst of a rebellious house, which have eyes to see, and see not; they have ears to hear, and hear not: for they are a rebellious house" (vv.1-2). H.L.Ellison suggests that the repeated "rebellious house" applies to the exiles who "were obviously still hoping for an early return to Jerusalem, so that they had no eyes for Ezekiel's vision of destruction".

Ezekiel already knew that God regarded His people as a "rebellious house" (see 2: 5, 6, 8), but it all started long before Ezekiel's era. Moses knew all about it: "And Moses called unto all Israel, and said unto them, Ye have seen all that the LORD did before your eyes in the land of Egypt", referring to their natural vision. So the people had seen all that the Lord had done but, at the same time, they had failed to learn lessons from the events which they had witnessed: "Yet the Lord hath not given you an heart to perceive, and eyes to see (referring to their spiritual vision), and ears to hear, unto this day" (Deut. 29: 2-4). It was for this very same reason that the Lord Jesus spoke to the people in parables: "In them is fulfilled the prophecy of Esaias, which saith, By hearing ye shall hear, and shall not understand; and seeing ye shall see, and shall not perceive" (Matt. 13: 13-15). We should remember that Paul distinguished between natural vision and spiritual perception in saying, "Moreover, brethren, I would not that ye should be ignorant ..." (1 Cor. 10: 1). He refers here, not to ignorance of the facts of Israel's history, but to ignorance of the lessons conveyed by their history, reminding us that we should read the Old Testament, including the historical sections, in view of the fact that "whatsoever things were written aforetime were written for our learning" (Rom. 15: 4). Bible history is far more than history! We need "eyes to see, and ears to hear" what God has to say to us in it all, and we must take steps to avoid becoming "a rebellious house".

Nevertheless, God persisted with His people: "Therefore, thou son of man, prepare thy stuff for removing, and remove by day in their sight; and thou shalt remove from thy place to another place in their sight: it may be that they will consider, though they be a rebellious house" (v.3). As John B. Taylor observes, The Lord's "use of the parabolic method of teaching is further indication of the principle that in God's service the preacher's knowledge that his words will be ignored is never to be used as an excuse for not uttering the words. Ezekiel ... had to be reminded that it was always possible that some would understand, and in this he may be regarded as the exemplar for all Christian workers in seemingly impossible situations or in singularly unfruitful spheres of service. There must always be the element of *perhaps they will* in such ministry". C.L.Feinberg puts it nicely: "They were indeed 'a rebellious house' (2: 8), but the God of grace was eager to give the heedless ones multiplied opportunities to obey His word".

The two parables describe *(a)* the fate of the prince (vv.1-16); *(b)* the fear of the people (vv.17-20).

a) The fate of the prince, vv.1-16

We should notice here *(i)* the acted message (vv.3-7); *(ii)* the interpreted message (vv.8-16).

i) The acted message, vv.3-7. "Therefore, thou son of man, prepare thee stuff for removing (literally 'baggage for exile'), and remove by day in their sight; and thou shalt remove from thy place to another place in their sight: it may be they will consider, though they be a rebellious house. Then shalt thou bring forth thy stuff by day in their sight, as stuff for removing: and thou shalt go forth in their sight, as **they that go forth into captivity**. Dig thou through the wall in their sight, and carry out thereby. In their sight shalt thou bear it upon thy shoulders, and carry it forth in the twilight: thou shalt cover thy face, that thou see not the ground (an indication of total dejection): for I have set thee for a sign unto the house of Israel" (vv.3-6).

We should notice the repeated words "in their sight" and "I have set thee for a sign unto the house of Israel". (See 4: 3; 24: 24). It has been pointed out that "the wall" is the wall of a house (*qir*) as opposed to a city-wall (*homa*). Ezekiel's house in Babylonia would have been made of sun-dried bricks. As John P. Taylor observes, "The essence of this action is that it is to be done in full view of Ezekiel's inquisitive compatriots. As earlier they gathered to watch the daily ritual of lying on the ground with hands tied (4: 4-8) and the weighing out of the prophet's meagre rations (4: 10), so now he is commanded to play the part of an exile for all to see". He continues, "The action consisted of two parts: by day he collected up the bare essentials for the long journey of going into exile; then as evening drew on he dug through the wall of his house, as though making a surreptitious getaway, and went out into the night carrying his bundle on his shoulder. As he did this he was to cover his eyes, according to verse 6, though this is omitted from the description of the following verse". The 'baggage for exile' (see above) would "include only the barest essentials - a skin for water, a mat for sleeping, and a bowl for food" (Lamar E. Cooper). C.L.Feinberg expands this a little: "staff, wallet, provisions and vessels needed for the way".

We must note Ezekiel's simple compliance with the word of God, even though, possibly, he did not at that time understand the significance of what he was doing. "And I did so as I was commanded: I brought forth my stuff by day, as stuff for captivity, and in the even I digged through the wall with mine hand; I brought it forth in the twilight (meaning 'in the dark'), and I bare it upon my shoulder in their sight" (v.7). His words, "I did so as I was commanded", provide ample opportunity for expansion! The words, "Whatsoever he saith unto you, do it" (John 2: 5), must surely be included in our sermon preparation!

ii) The interpreted message, vv.8-16. "And in the morning came the word of the LORD unto me, saying, Son of man, hath not the house of Israel, the rebellious house, said unto thee, What doest thou?" (vv.8-9). The exiles in Tel-abib (3: 15) certainly merited the above description – 'Ezekiel's inquisitive compatriots!' - and the prophet was told to say: "Thus saith the Lord GOD: This burden concerneth the prince **in Jerusalem**, and all the house of Israel that are among **them.** Say, I am your sign: like as I have done, so shall it be done unto **them**: **they** shall remove and go into captivity" (vv.10-11). Very clearly, the coming captivity and exile of God's people remaining in Jerusalem was intended to sound the death-knell of all hopes of a return to Judah by the community in Babylonia. This had been fuelled, doubtless, by the prophecy of Hananiah in Jerusalem two years before. See Jeremiah 28 verses 1-17.

The "prince" is Zedekiah, the last king of Judah. It is noticeable that Ezekiel always calls Zedekiah "prince" (*nasi*), never "king" (*melek*). Jehoiachin was regarded as the true king (Ezek. 17: 13).

As H.L.Ellison observes, "His prophecy about Zedekiah is especially interesting for the enigmatic way in which his fate is foretold, but how literally his actions and words were fulfilled!" Ezekiel was to continue his explanation: "And the prince that is among them shall bear upon his shoulder in the twilight, and shall go forth: they shall dig through the wall to carry out thereby: he shall cover his face, that he see not the ground with his eyes" (v.12). It has been suggested that in the first place, this was to avoid recognition by the Chaldeans, but more is implied: "***My*** net also will *I* spread upon him, and he shall be taken in *my* snare: and *I* will bring him to Babylon to the land of the Chaldeans; yet shall he not see it, though he shall die there" (v.13).

A full description of the fulfilment of this prophecy is given in 2 Kings 25 verses 1-7: "And it came to pass in the ninth year of his reign (the reign of Zedekiah) … that Nebuchadnezzar king of Babylon came, he, and all his host, against Jerusalem, and pitched against it … And the city was broken up, and all the men of war fled **by night** (see Ezek. 12: 7) by the way of the gate between two walls, which is by the king's garden … and the king went the way towards the plain. And the army of the Chaldeans pursued after the king, and overtook him in the plains of Jericho … So they took the king and brought him up to the king of Babylon to Riblah; and they gave judgment upon him. And they slew the sons of Zedekiah before his eyes, and put out the eyes of Zedekiah, and bound him with fetters of brass, and carried him to Babylon". See also Jeremiah 39 verses 4-7. For the death of Zedekiah in Babylon, see Jeremiah 52 verse 11. God's word, as ever, was fulfilled with pin-point accuracy. The words, "And I will **scatter** toward every wind all that are about him to help him, and all his bands; and I will draw out the sword after them" (v.14) were similarly fulfilled: see 2 Kings 25 verse 5, "And the army of the Chaldeans pursued after the king, and overtook him in the plains of Jericho, and all his army were **scattered from him"**. See also 2 Kings 25 verses 18-21.

Although the Chaldean army was responsible, the Lord made it clear that Zedekiah would be caught in "***my*** net" (a snare used to hunt fowl) and "***my*** snare". After all, Nebuchadnezzar was God's servant (Jer. 43: 10). Although the word "net" here (*resheth*) does not refer to a fishing net (see also 17: 20), the Chaldeans were certainly fishermen. "They take up all of them with the angle, they catch them in their net (*cherem*), and gather them in their drag (*mikmereth*)" (Hab. 1: 14-17).

CHAPTER 12

The scattering of Zedekiah's army (v.14) gives place to the scattering of the nation: "And they shall know that I am the LORD, when *I* shall scatter them among the nations, and disperse them in the countries. But I will leave a few men of them from the sword, from the famine, and from the pestilence; that they may declare ('confess', RSV; 'acknowledge', NIV) all their abominations among the heathen whither they come, and they shall know that I am the LORD" (vv.15-16).

John B.Taylor comments most appropriately here: "Their experiences will teach them what otherwise they would never have learnt, namely *that I am the Lord* (v.15). What men fail to learn in prosperity, they will occasionally learn through adversity. God will let a few of them escape so that they can testify to His truth and vindicate His honour (v.16). Only as they confess their people's sins among the nations will it be seen that Israel's God is both holy and powerful: without such admissions He would simply be regarded as incapable of protecting His own people against the enemy". C.L.Feinberg concurs: "A few would be left to show the nations that the calamity of Israel was not due to God's lack of power to help them, but because He brought it upon them to vindicate His holiness".

We have already noted the expression, "and they shall know that I am the Lord", See, for example 6: 14; 7: 27; 12: 20.) It occurs four times in this chapter: see verses 15, 16, 20, 25. It might be appropriate to quote H.L.Ellison again: "'Thou shalt (ye shall, they shall) know that I am the Lord' is the most characteristic expression of Ezekiel. It occurs in this simple form no less than 54 times and with some expansion another 18 times. This knowledge is always connected either with the judgments of God or with His acts of grace; it is probably only due to the greatly predominating stress on God's judgment in Ezekiel that the majority of the passages fall into the former category". He continues: "It is not the existence of Jehovah that is being stressed, but the identity ... of Jehovah".

b) The fear of the people, vv.17-20

These verses evidently refer, prophetically, to the terror of the inhabitants of Jerusalem and Israel (Judah) at the time of the Chaldean invasion. For the second time, we should notice *(i)* the acted message (vv.17-18); *(ii)* the interpreted message (vv.19-20).

i) The acted message, vv.17-18. "Moreover the word of the LORD came to me, saying, Son of man, eat thy bread with quaking, and drink thy water with trembling and with carefulness ('anxiety', JND)." In the words of Lamar E. Cooper, "Ezekiel performed a second dramatic action. He trembled while eating as a sign of fear and anxiety over the exile. The people would be forced to eat meagre rations in fear, not knowing if there would be another meal". (We should note the similarity here to 4: 9-12).

ii) The interpreted message, vv.19-20. "And say unto the people (*am hares*, the peasant population of Judah, as distinct from the ruling classes) of the land, Thus saith the Lord GOD of the inhabitants of Jerusalem, and of the land of Israel; They shall eat their bread with carefulness, and drink their water with astonishment, that her land may be desolate from all that is therein, because of the violence of all them that dwell therein. And the cities that are inhabited shall be laid waste, and the land shall be desolate; and ye shall know that I am the Lord", or "They shall eat their bread with fearfulness, and drink water in dismay, because their land will be stripped of all it contains" (RSV). According to F.Gardiner (*Ellicott's Commentary*) "The margin, which is the literal rendering, explains this: 'The land shall be stripped of its richness and excellence, of all that makes it desirable'".

C.L.Feinberg sums it up as follows: "Here are underscored the privations of the invasion of Nebuchadnezzar. The people would learn that the punishment for violence was to be violence. Desolation was decreed upon the whole land; there would be no turning back the stroke". In the words of John B.Taylor: "All this will come about on *account of the violence of those who dwell in it* (the land). The sufferings that the population will have to undergo are attributed directly to the sufferings which they have inflicted upon others" J.B.Taylor continues: "Violence breeds violence. If anyone dares to question his fate, the answer will be found within himself. Human perversity often imagines that, given reasonable luck, it is possible to sin with impunity. Ezekiel declares that in this instance oppression will get its due reward. In so doing God will show Himself righteous, and the sinner will at last realise that *I am the Lord* (v.20)".

2) TWO ANSWERED OBJECTIONS, vv.21-28

This section of the chapter details two reasons why the people at Tel-abib disbelieved the preaching of Ezekiel. In the first case they believed his preaching was time-barred (vv.21-25), and in the second that his preaching was time-distant (vv.26-28).

CHAPTER 12

a) His ministry was time-barred, vv.21-25

Their objection is stated in verses 21-22, and the Lord's answer through Ezekiel is given in verses 23-25.

i) The objection, vv.21-22. "And the word of the LORD came unto me, saying, Son of man, what is that proverb that ye have in the land of Israel, saying, The days are prolonged, and every vision faileth?" Quite possibly the people were appealing to the test of a prophet's ministry set out in Deuteronomy 18 verses 20-22. The complacency into which Israel had fallen, although confronted with signs of coming judgment, is expressed in their proverb, "The days are prolonged, and every vision faileth". "It was assumed that because past prophecies of doom had not gone into fulfilment, they had been annulled, not merely suspended" (H.L.Ellison). (Compare Zephaniah 1: 12.)

There is something strikingly familiar about this: Peter wrote to the believers of his day to remind them of "the words which were spoken before by the holy prophets, and of the commandment of us the apostles of the Lord and Saviour: knowing this first, that there shall come in the last days scoffers, walking after their own lusts, and saying, Where is the promise of his coming? For since the fathers fell asleep, all things continue as they were from the beginning of the creation" (2 Pet. 3: 1-4).

ii) The answer, vv23-25. "Tell them therefore, Thus saith the Lord GOD; I will make this proverb to cease, and they shall no more use it as a proverb in Israel; but say unto them, the days are at hand, and the effect ('accomplishment', JND: 'fulfilment', RSV) of every vision. For there shall be no more any vain vision nor flattering divination within the house of Israel. For I am the LORD: I will speak, and the word that I speak shall come to pass; it shall no more be prolonged: for in your days, O rebellious house, will I say the word, and will perform it, saith the Lord GOD." The fulfilment of God's word would be the death of "false prophecy which produced 'smooth' or *flattering* messages by doubtful means" (John B.Taylor). Far from being "prolonged", the word of God would shortly be performed - in the lifetime of the "scoffers" (to use Peter's adjective).

b) His ministry is time-distant, vv.26-28

Their objection is stated in verses 26-27, and the Lord's answer through Ezekiel is given in verse 28.

i)   The objection, vv.26-27. "Son of man, behold, they of the house of Israel say, The vision that he seeth is for many days to come, and he prophesieth of the times that are **far off**." Possibly, this was their reaction to Ezekiel's account of the vision given to him in Chapters 9-11, which concludes with the words, "Then I spake unto them of the captivity all the things that the LORD hath shewed me" (11: 25).

It does seem that "the second obstacle was one that Ezekiel personally met in the presumably more receptive section of the exiles ... Their experience had been such as to make them willing to believe his message, but whatever the reason they considered (perhaps hoped) that he was speaking of a future outside their own life-span" (H.L.Ellison). Compare Amos 6 verse 3.

ii) The answer, v.28. The fallacy of the assertion is made clear: "Therefore say unto them, thus saith the Lord GOD: There shall none of my words be prolonged any more, but the word which I have spoken shall be done, saith the Lord GOD". See Isaiah 55 verse 11.

Both objections are answered in the same way. Divine intervention was imminent. Having referred to the objections of the "scoffers", Peter continues, "But the day of the Lord will come as a thief in the night ..." (2 Pet. 3: 10). As Lamar E. Cooper rightly says, "These verses demonstrate that there are many ways to despise God's word, whether by outright denial or by diverting its message to other times and applications. Again God's response was simple and direct. As someone has said, God does not necessarily pay at the end of each week: nevertheless, He pays".

We can say of the Lord's return, "now is our salvation nearer than when we believed. The night is far spent, the day is at hand ..." (Rom. 13: 11-12). We can also say, "For yet a little while, and he that shall come will come, and will not tarry" (Heb. 10: 37).

EZEKIEL CHAPTER 13

As already noted, the causes for the coming judgment are highlighted in the vision given *to* Ezekiel (chs.8-11) and in the visible/verbal messages given *by* Ezekiel (ch.12 and chs.13-17), followed by the answer to objections to coming judgment (ch.18) and a lamentation over coming judgment (ch.19).

We come now to –

REASONS FOR COMING JUDGMENT

These may be summarised as follows: *(1)* the untruthful prophets (ch.13); *(2)* the unseen idolatry (ch.14); *(3)* the useless vine (ch.15); *(4)* the unfaithful wife (ch.16); *(5)* the unreliable promises (ch.17).

1) The untruthful prophets, Ch.13

The connection between Chapters 12 & 13 is spelt out nicely by John B.Taylor: "After dealing in Chapter 12 with the mistaken views of the people, Ezekiel addresses himself to the false prophets who have misled them. While not denying them their title of prophets, he denounces them scathingly for the deleterious effect their empty-headed pronouncements are having and have had upon Israelite life. They have undermined the stability of the nation at a time when it needed to be built up (v.5), and they have given their blessing to the crumbling edifice of state when it should have been condemned and reconstructed afresh (v.10)". Patrick Fairbairn puts it succinctly: "A very close connection exists between the subject of this chapter and the one immediately preceding. The former had denounced the false expectations of the people respecting the safety of Jerusalem; this denounces the persons who were the chief instruments in feeding those expectations".

We noted in connection with Chapter 12 that its four paragraphs each commence with the words, "The word of the Lord came unto me saying (vv.1, 17, 21, 26). Ezekiel was in receipt of divine revelation. But Chapter 13 deals with those who prophesy "out of their own hearts", including prophets (v.2) and prophetesses (v.17).

The chapter clearly divides into two sections: *(a)* an oracle against Israel's prophets (vv.1-16); *(b)* an oracle against Israel's prophetesses (vv.17-23). As noted above, they both "prophesy out of their own hearts". To the former the Lord says, *"Woe* unto the foolish prophets (v.3), and to the latter He says, *"Woe* to the women that sew pillows" (v.18).

a) Against Israel's prophets, vv.1-16

"And the word of the LORD came unto me saying, Son of man, prophesy against the prophets of Israel that prophesy, and say unto them that prophesy out of their own hearts, Hear ye the word of the LORD; Thus saith the Lord GOD; Woe unto the foolish prophets, that follow their own spirit, and have seen nothing!" (vv.1-3).

The parties involved were: *(i)* Ezekiel, who was to prophesy with divine authority: "Hear ye the word of the LORD" (v.2); *(ii)* the prophets of Israel "that prophesy out of their own hearts" and "that follow their own spirit, and have seen nothing!" (vv.2-3). So it was a case of one prophet confronting other prophets, but they were not prophets in the same category! Micaiah the son of Imla was in the same position as Ezekiel. He had to contend with four hundred false prophets (2 Chron. Ch.18).

It must be said that believers today are also in the same position. We must listen now to Peter: "But there were false prophets also among the people, even as there shall be false teachers *among you,* who privily shall bring in damnable heresies, even denying the Lord that bought them and bring upon themselves swift destruction" (2 Pet. 2: 1) Paul taught the same thing: "Also of *your own selves* shall men arise, speaking perverse things to draw away disciples after them" (Acts 20: 30).

The false prophets in Israel are described as "foolish prophets, that follow their own spirit, and have seen nothing". While, as H.L.Ellison observes, "There is no sin in using one's reason; to do so, instead of listening to God, when one is one of God's spokesmen, shows, however, extreme spiritual obtuseness ... They followed their own spirit (v.3). Spirit (*ruach*) in such a context is something powerful and dominating. Instead of letting themselves be dominated by the Spirit of God, they were dominated by their own desires and motives". C.L.Feinberg concurs: "Their sin was that they followed their own human, fallible spirit instead of the divine, infallible Holy Spirit, but this availed them nothing, because they saw nothing".

The word "foolish" (*nabal*) is the strongest word to describe folly. It covers much more than mere stupidity. "The fool was spiritually and morally insensitive; he was inclined to blasphemy ('Remember this, that the enemy hath reproached, O LORD, and that the foolish people have blasphemed thy name', Psalm 74: 18), and atheism ('The fool hath said in his heart, There is no God', Psalm 14: 1); he was churlish and arrogant, like his namesake Nabal of Carmel (1 Sam. 25: 25); he was capable of gross immorality ('And I, whither shall I cause my shame to go? And as for thee, thou shalt be as one of the fools in Israel': Tamar to Amnon, 2 Sam. 13: 13). He was in fact the very antithesis of all that the wise man stood for in terms of spiritual perception, self-discipline, restraint, godly fear and humility" (John B.Taylor).

The oracle against the prophets is in two parts:

- What they had not done (vv.4-9): "Ye have not gone up into the gaps, neither made up the hedges for the house of Israel, to stand in the battle in the day of the Lord" (v.5);

- What they had done (vv.10-16): "they have seduced my people, saying, Peace, and there was no peace; and one built up a wall, and, lo, others daubed it with untempered mortar" (v.10). Put another way, they were like: *(i)* destructive foxes (vv.4-9); *(ii)* a daubed wall (vv.10-16).

i)   *Destructive foxes, vv.4-9*

We should notice: their activities (vv.4-5); their emptiness (vv.6-7); their judgment (vv.8-9).

- ***Their activities, vv.4-5.*** "O Israel, thy prophets are like the foxes in the deserts." This has been rendered "foxes among ruins" and the word "deserts" is used in the sense of deserted habitations. Some commentators opt for 'jackals' rather than foxes, but the word "deserts" (*chorbah*) can certainly mean 'a desolation, a place laid waste, ruins' (Gesenius), and the translation "foxes among ruins" seems appropriate. Different words are normally used in connection with 'deserts' in the usual sense of the word. John B.Taylor puts it like this: The "picture suggests that the prophets have no real concern for the people among whom they live. They burrow among the foundations without any regard for the welfare of the place, intent only on making dens for themselves or, to change the metaphor, on feathering their own nests". He continues: "Far from being undermined, what Israel needed was to be buttressed in her hour of crisis ... what was broken down needed defending and restoring, and the false prophets had failed right there". In Ezekiel's words, "Ye have not gone up into the gaps, neither made up the hedges for the house of Israel, to stand in the battle in the day of the LORD" (v.5).

Very clearly, these verses do not refer to literal defences, although that might well be in the background, but to "the moral and spiritual defence of the people which was needed for the coming catastrophe" (C.L.Feinberg). Solomon tells us that "righteousness exalteth a nation: but sin is a reproach to any people" (Prov. 14: 34), but these defences had been breached by sin and idolatry. Men were needed to "make up the hedge, and stand in the gap before me for the land, that I should not destroy it: but I found none" (Ezek. 22: 30). The so-called prophets were not in the business of bringing the nation to repentance. They were not 'repairers of the breach' (Isaiah 58: 12).

The coming crisis, for which the people were completely unprepared, is called "the battle in the day of the LORD" (v.5). The expression, "the day of the LORD", usually refers to coming judgment at the end-time, but the term is used at times in the Old Testament with reference to imminent trouble, and in this case it evidently refers to the coming fall of Jerusalem.

New Testament prophets were quite unlike these Old Testament namesakes: "he that prophesieth speaketh unto men to **edification** (to build up), and **exhortation** (to stir up,) and **comfort** (to cheer up)" (1 Cor. 14: 3). Notice the order: "**edification**"; referring to doctrine; "**exhortation**"; referring to the practice of the doctrine; "**comfort**"; referring to the strength that doctrine imparts. We should remember that this verse is equally applicable to the New Testament teacher, whose ministry has superseded that of the New Testament prophet.

- ***Their emptiness, vv.6-7.*** "They have seen vanity and lying divination, saying, The LORD saith: and the LORD hath not sent them: and they have made others to hope that they would confirm the word ('and they make [them] to hope that the word will be fulfilled', JND). Have ye not seen a vain vision, and have ye not spoken a lying divination, whereas ye say, The LORD saith it; albeit I have not spoken?".

The use of "vanity ... vain" should be noticed: "They have seen vanity (v.6) ... Have ye not seen a vain vision (v.7) ... Because ye have spoken vanity (v.8) ... And my hand shall be upon the prophets that see vanity (v.9)". These verses emphasise the great care that must be used by all who speak in the name of the Lord. It is no light thing to take His name upon our lips! In New Testament language, "If any man speak, let him speak as the oracles of God" (1 Pet. 4: 11). This emphasises the great responsibility on the man who speaks publicly. He is to do so "as the oracles of God". W.E.Vine points out that the word "oracles" (*logion*), "a diminutive of *logos*, a word, narrative, statement", denotes "a divine response or utterance", and that in the Old Testament "divine oracles were given by means of the breastplate of the high priest". It has been nicely said that it was 'the word of God from the heart of God'.

When a man speaks in the assembly, he must address the Lord's people with the voice of God, rather like Jeremiah who spoke "from the mouth of the LORD" (2 Chron. 36: 12). The preacher or teacher has good cause to 'tremble at God's word' (Isaiah 66: 2). When a brother stands up in the assembly to teach, his ministry must come from the sanctuary. It has been said that "If a man does not know what he is going to say when he stands up, no one will know what he has said when he sits down!" (J.B.Watson). When a brother preaches the Gospel, the message must be written on his heart by the Spirit of God. The standard for the Bible Class leader or the Sunday School teacher cannot be less.

The object of speaking "as the oracles of God" and serving "as of the ability which God giveth" is "that God in all things might be glorified through Jesus Christ, to whom be praise and dominion for ever and ever. Amen" (1 Pet. 4: 11). He will not be glorified if men do not speak "as the oracles of God". He will not be glorified if men do not serve "as of the ability which God giveth". It would be tragic if it had to be said of *us*: "they prophesy out of their own hearts" (v.2); or, they "follow their own spirit, and have seen nothing!" (v.3); or, they say "The LORD saith; and the LORD hath not sent them" (v.6); or, they say, "The LORD saith it; albeit I have not spoken" (v.7).

- *Their judgment, vv.8-9.* "Therefore thus saith the Lord GOD, Because ye have spoken vanity, and seen lies, therefore, behold, I am against you, saith the Lord GOD. And mine hand shall be upon the prophets that see vanity, and that divine lies: they shall not be in the assembly of my people, neither shall they be written in the writing of the house of Israel, neither shall they enter into the land of Israel; and ye shall know that I am the Lord GOD." F.A.Tatford explains: "In the first instance, they would lose the privilege of participation in the council. Hitherto they had been regarded as leading citizens; their prophetic influence had established them as counsellors in the community, and others had sought their advice and guidance ... Secondly, they would lose their place in the national register or citizen's roll. Their names had rightly been inscribed there and possibly an indication had been entered later that they were deserving of special honour. But now the greater tragedy was to befall them: their names were to be expunged from the register in the same way as those of common criminals who had brought dishonour on the name of their nation. They were no longer regarded as members of the nation. Thirdly, the great hope entertained by all the exiles of one day returning to the promised land, was to be denied them ..."

ii) Daubed wall, vv.10-16

The preaching of the false prophets, which did nothing more than encourage a sense of false security, is likened to an unsubstantial or unsafe wall daubed with "untempered mortar". It looked substantial, but was nothing of the sort. The two 'bookends' of the section make this clear:

- "They have seduced my people, saying, Peace; and there was no peace; and one built up a wall, and, lo, others daubed it with untempered mortar" (v.10).

- "I will accomplish my wrath upon the wall, and on them that have daubed it with untempered mortar, and will say unto you, The wall is no more, neither they that daubed it; to wit, the prophets of Israel which prophesy concerning Jerusalem, and which see visions of peace for her, and there is no peace, saith the Lord GOD" (vv.15-16).

"The *wall* which the people build is a flimsy party-wall. (The Hebrew word, *hayis*, is found only here and described by Kimchi as 'an inferior partition'.) It stands for the empty hopes which they are erecting for themselves and which the false prophets are blandly endorsing" (John B.Taylor). Taylor is correct in saying that it is the false prophets who are 'daubing' the wall'. See

CHAPTER 13

verses 15-16: "The wall is no more, neither they that daubed it, the prophets of Israel who prophesy concerning Jerusalem and who see a vision of peace for her, and there is no peace, saith the Lord Jehovah" (JND). It may well be, however, that F.Gardiner is correct in saying: "One of the false prophets would build a wall, set up of his own device - some vision as a defence against the warnings of calamity; and his fellows would join in his deceit by covering this wall "'with untempered mortar'". He continues: "The word is not the usual one for plaster, and indeed is used in this sense only in these verses and in Ezekiel 22: 28". Gardiner's piece on the subject (in *Ellicott's Commentary*) is worth reading in full. According to John B.Taylor, the words "untempered mortar" are based on an incorrect identification with a root meaning 'unseasoned', and the word is better rendered 'whitewash'. Gesenius has 'lime, with which a wall is covered'. We might say 'lime-washed'.

As C.L.Feinberg points out, "The false prophets were compared to those who built an unsafe wall and cover up its defects ... Smooth words of false messengers hid from the people the actual seriousness of their spiritual condition". John B.Taylor is so right in saying, "So the people's futile hopes are encouraged by the prophets' lying lullabies of peace. It is a common failing for preachers to want to speak pleasing and appeasing words to their people, but if they are to be true to their calling they must be sure to receive and to impart nothing but God's clear word, irrespective of the consequences. When church leaders encourage their people in sub-Christian standards or unbiblical ways, they make themselves doubly guilty". These are wise words. See 2 Timothy 4 verses 3-4, "For the time will come when they will not endure sound doctrine; but after their own lusts shall they heap to themselves teachers, having itching ears; and they shall turn away their ears from the truth, and shall be turned unto fables". As F.A.Tatford observes, "It is tragic that people are always prepared to listen to the teacher who states what they wish to hear".

H.L.Ellison puts it like this: "The prophets are pictured as saying, 'All is well' - the implication of 'Peace' - and pictured as whitewashing (RSV) the jerrybuilt wall the people have put up. The very approval (whitewashing) by the prophets prevented the people seeing how flimsy was their structure, until the storm of judgment came and swept it all away". John B.Taylor is evidently correct in saying. "At this stage (referring to vv.15-16) the figure of the wall, which began by representing popular optimism, comes to be identified with the city of Jerusalem, on whose impregnability their empty hopes had centred".

When the wall fell, the disaster would destroy the prophets themselves: "So will I break down the wall that ye have daubed with untempered mortar, and bring it down to the ground, so that the foundation thereof shall be discovered, and it shall fall, and *ye shall be consumed in the midst thereof*: and ye shall know that I am the LORD" (v.14). The false prophets would be buried in the ruins of the city they said would not fall!

How glad we are that God's promises are totally reliable, and therefore completely different to the predictions of the false prophets. "For all the promises of God in him (Christ) are yea, and in him Amen" (2 Cor. 1: 20). The Lord Jesus said, "If I go and prepare a place for you, I will come again, and receive you unto myself: that where I am, there ye may be also" (John 14: 3). Believers today stand with Abraham who was "fully persuaded that, what he (God) had promised, he was able also to perform" (Rom. 4: 21). Promises are only as good as the people who make them. In our case they are made by God "that cannot lie" (Titus 1: 2): in the case of Judah, they were made by "foolish prophets, that follow their own spirit, and have seen nothing!" (v.3).

b) AGAINST ISRAEL'S PROPHETESSES, vv17-23

"Likewise, thou son of man, set thy face against the daughters of thy people, which prophesy out of their own heart; and prophesy thou against them" (v.17).

The only other prophetesses in the Old Testament known to us are Miriam (Exodus 15: 20), Deborah (Judges 4: 4), Huldah (2 Kings 22: 14) and Noadiah (Neh. 6: 14). Jezebel is described as a false prophetess in Revelation 2 verse 20.

This section of the chapter may be divided as follows: *(i)* their profession (v.17); *(ii)* their practices (v.18); *(iii)* their profanity (v.19); *(iv)* their punishment (vv.20-23).

i)   Their profession, v.17

"Set thy face against the daughters of thy people, which prophesy out of their own heart; and prophesy thou against them." The women described by Ezekiel "would be termed sorceresses rather than prophetesses today" (H.L.Ellison). C.L.Feinberg is bold enough to state that in the Old Testament "sorcery was practised mainly by women". See Exodus 22 verse 18, "thou shalt not suffer a witch to live". John B.Taylor is right in saying, "In times of national decay and crisis such quacks are often thrown up and they prey upon credulous and anxious minds. No doubt the successful encroachment of Babylonian influence, where divination and necromancy abounded, added further encouragement to their work".

ii) Their practices, v.18

Their witchcraft is described: "Woe to the women that sew pillows to all armholes ('elbows', AV margin), and make kerchiefs ('veils', JND) upon the head of every stature to hunt souls". The precise practices of these sorceresses are difficult to determine. F.Gardiner notes that bearing in mind the uncertainty of some words, the words, "Woe to the women that sew pillows to all armholes, and make kerchiefs upon the head of every stature to hunt souls", could be rendered: 'Woe to those who fasten charms (or amulets) on every finger joint, that place kerchiefs on heads of every height to snare souls'. Some suggest that the word "pillows" refers to wrist-bands ('wrists', JND), which the sorceress allegedly sewed upon people's wrists, possibly symbolising the power of the occult over them (M.F.Unger). It does seem that the sorceresses themselves also wore them (v.20). How 'pillows' can become 'wristbands' is not easily explained! We can only find refuge in C.L.Feinberg's observation that "some words in the passage are difficult because they occur nowhere else in the Old Testament". According to John B.Taylor, the word "kerchiefs" means "a long drape which reached to the ground, shrouding the whole body, and these apparently came in all sizes *for the heads of persons of every stature!*" The words, "hunt the souls" (v.18), make it evident that "these women were trying to possess and dominate those who come under their influence, and like so many witch-doctors they held the power of life and death over them" (J.B.Taylor). It seems that the "kerchiefs" (veils) enabled the sorceresses to dominate their clients by depriving them of the ability to see and hear (F.A.Tatford). The word "souls" has the meaning of the total person rather than a disembodied spirit.

iii) Their profanity, v.19

"And will ye pollute me among my people for handfuls of barley and for pieces of bread ...?" This could be understood with reference to payment in kind by the clients, but it seems more likely that these were used in divination "as auguries to be examined to see whether a sick client would live or die"

(J.B.Taylor). The words, "will ye **pollute me** among my people for handfuls of barley, and for pieces of bread", mean that the Lord's name "was 'polluted' by attaching His name and authority to that which was not true, and that would not come to pass, thus 'making him a liar' like themselves" (F.Gardiner). By pronouncing, in the Lord's name, the **death** of "***souls that should not die***", and the ***survival*** of those "***that should not live***" (v.19*)*, they brought His name into disrepute. It was the exact opposite of divine righteousness.

iv) *Their punishment, vv.20-23*

The words, "Behold, I am against your pillows (or wrist-bands, if this is the correct rendering), wherewith ye hunt the souls to make them fly; and I will tear them from your arms, and will let the souls go, even the souls that ye hunt to make them fly" (v20), are elsewhere rendered, "Behold, I am against your pillows, that the souls which ye catch by their means may fly away; and I will tear them from your arms, and will let the souls go, the souls that ye catch, that they may fly away" (JND). This does make the text a little clearer! It is worth quoting C.L.Feinberg here: "The thought in this portion is not that the sorceresses made their victims to fly as birds, but rather to fly into their nets to ensnare them as fowlers catch birds". This would come to an end: "Your kerchiefs also will I tear, and deliver my people out of your hand, and they shall be no more in your hand to be hunted; and ye shall know that I am the LORD" (v.21).

The crowning crime of the sorceresses, their pollution of the Lord's name (v.19), is restated in verses 22-23: "Because with lies ye have made the heart of the righteous sad, whom I have not made sad; and strengthened the hands of the wicked, that he should not return from his wicked way, by promising him life: therefore ye shall see no more vanity, nor divine divinations: for I will deliver my people out of your hand: and ye shall know that I am the LORD". As F.Gardiner observes, "As so often the judgment is expressed in the same form with the sin. These false prophetesses had sinned by their lying visions, and they should see them no more, because the event should soon expose their utter falsity to the eyes of all. The result would be the deliverance of God's people, whom they sought to ensnare, and their own conviction, not in penitence, but under judgment, that He is the Lord".

In connection with these verses, Brian Russell (*Choice Gleanings*, 30.07.2011) helpfully observes that "The Lord loves to give us joy in life. How terrible it is, therefore, when as believers, we dishearten the saints with gossip and unwarranted accusations. Never let us be found doing the work of the enemy, but rather endorse the work of our Father. Encourage someone today!"

F.A.Tatford brings his exposition of the chapter to a conclusion with timely words: "The need for the implicit warning of the chapter was never more necessary than in our twentieth century (he wrote this in 1977), when belief in magic, astrology and spiritism has spread to an unprecedented extent. The gift of 'discernment of spirits' (1 Cor. 12: 10) was never more essential. It cannot be too strongly emphasised that the full revelation of God has been made in His Word, and that all extra-biblical and extraneous teaching must be brought to the test of the inspired Scriptures".

EZEKIEL CHAPTER 14

Ezekiel 14 is the second of five chapters (chs.13-17), in which the prophet verbally addresses the reasons for coming judgment on Judah and Jerusalem. These chapters follow Chapter 12, in which we have two pictures of coming judgment, which in turn follow Chapters 8-11, in which the reasons for coming judgment are made clear in the prophet's God-given vision of the idolatry practised in the temple at Jerusalem.

As already noted, the five chapters above (ch.13-17) may be summarised as follows: *(1)* the untruthful prophets (ch.13); *(2)* the unseen idolatry (ch.14); *(3)* the useless vine (ch.15); *(4)* the unfaithful wife (ch.16); *(5)* the unreliable promises (ch.17).

Having already dealt with the 'untruthful prophets' (see Chapter 13), we come now to:

2) *The unseen idolatry, Chapter 14*

As a result of listening to Ezekiel's condemnation of Israel's prophets (13: 1-16) and prophetesses (13: 17-23), the elders at Tel-abib evidently decide to come to him, rather than other so-called prophets, for advice and guidance. Ezekiel was apparently recognised as a man who, like Jeremiah, spoke "from the mouth of the LORD" (2 Chron. 36: 12). We find the elders sitting before him on at least two other occasions. (See Ezekiel 8: 1; 20: 1.) As noted in our preceding study, men who address the Lord's people should "speak as the oracles of God" (1 Pet. 4: 11). As David E.West points out, "It is not simply that what is said *must* by Scriptural, this must always be the case, but the individual should be sure that what he says are the very words that God would have him say on that particular occasion" (*Believer's Magazine*, November 2012). But it is not too much to say that *all* believers should be known as people who are in touch with God.

CHAPTER 14

While we are not told why these elders came, it seems reasonable to suggest that they hoped to hear "some oracle about the length of their exile or giving news of affairs at home in Jerusalem" (J.P.Taylor). It is quite possible that they had come to realise that the smooth messages of the prophets were worthless, and that the Babylonians were not to be turned back from their attack on Jerusalem. They did not go unanswered. God certainly spoke to them through Ezekiel, but it was not what they expected! They were confronted by two facts:

- The futility of expecting God to speak to them whilst they persist in idolatry (vv.1-11). We should notice the repeated words, "idols in their heart ... idols in his heart ..." (vv.3, 4, 7), together with the words, "That I may take the house of Israel in their own heart, because they are all estranged from me through their idols" (v.5).

- The futility of expecting God to save them whilst they persist in iniquity (vv.12-23). Even, if it were possible, the presence of Noah, Daniel and Job ("these three men") could not save them from coming judgment (vv.14, 16, 18, 20).

Both messages are introduced by the words, "And the word of the LORD came unto me saying" (vv.1, 12). They can be summarised as follows: *(a)* idolatry in the heart (vv.1-11); *(b)* inescapable judgment (vv.12-23)

a) Idolatry in the heart, vv.1-11

In this section we should notice *(i)* deceitful enquirers (vv.1-8); *(ii)* deluded prophets (vv.9-11).

i)   Deceitful enquirers, vv.1-8

"Then came certain of the elders of Israel unto me, and sat before me. And the word of the LORD came unto me, saying, Son of man, these men have set up their idols in their heart ... should I be inquired of at all by them?" (vv.1-3). As noted above, the prominent lesson in these verses is conveyed by the repeated expression, "idols in their heart" or "idols in his heart" (vv.3, 4, 7). The expression, "the stumblingblock of their iniquity (or 'his iniquity)" is "peculiar to Ezekiel (7: 19; 14: 3, 4, 7; 18: 30; 44: 12), and usually refers to idols which the prophet recognised as being supremely 'the occasion of sin' for his people" (J.B.Taylor). The people were not practising open idolatry, but were idolatrous none the less. If idolatry was a "stumblingblock" to God's people, then faithfulness to His word would have preserved them: "My son, let not them (the laws of God) depart from thine eyes: keep sound wisdom and discretion: so shall they be life unto thy soul, and grace to thy neck. Then shalt thou walk in thy way safely, and thy foot shall not stumble" (Prov. 3: 21-23). The words, "these men have ... put the stumblingblock of their iniquity before their face", do not necessarily mean that they were blatantly idolatrous, but that they still longed privately for their past practices. The Lord Jesus said, prophetically, "I have set the LORD always before me" (Psalm 16: 8). We should now notice, amongst other things, the following:

- **The hypocrisy of the elders, vv.1-3.** It could be said of these men, as it was said earlier in the Old Testament, "This people draw near me with their mouth, and with their lips do honour me, but have removed their heart far from me" (Isaiah 29: 13). (See also Ezekiel 33: 31.) The Lord Jesus quoted the Isaiah passage in Matthew 15 verses 8-9. Jeremiah had to contend with a similar situation: "ye *dissembled in your hearts*, when ye sent me unto the LORD your God, saying, Pray for us unto the LORD our God" (Jer. 42: 20). Their request was purely cosmetic: they had already made up their minds to enter Egypt.

As already noted above, we must not miss the solemn words, "these men have set up their idols *in their heart*". This is a salutary reminder that "the LORD looketh on the heart" (1 Sam. 16: 7) and that He (strictly speaking, "the word of God") is "a discerner of the thoughts and intents of the heart" (Heb. 4: 12). He is omniscient. As J.B.Taylor observes, "The Lord demands an exclusive allegiance, inwardly as well as outwardly, from His people, and those who consult Him or pray to Him when they cherish other gods in their hearts, will not be heard". The Psalmist said, "If I regard iniquity in my heart, the Lord will not hear me", but he does continue by saying, "But verily God hath heard me: he hath attended to the voice of my prayer" (Psalm 66: 18-19). The Lord Jesus said, "Father, I thank thee that thou hast heard me. And I knew that thou hearest me always ..." (John 11: 41-42). Needless to say, there was no iniquity in His heart!

- **The answer of the Lord, vv.4-5.** "Thus saith the Lord GOD; Every man of the house of Israel that setteth up his idols in his heart, and putteth the stumblingblock of his iniquity before his face, and cometh to the prophet, I the LORD will answer him that cometh *according to the multitude of his idols*; that I may take the house of Israel in their own heart, because they are all estranged from me through their idols." He would answer them, *not* on the basis of appearances, *but* on the basis of their true condition: "according to the multitude of his idols" and according to "their own heart". In spite of appearances, they were estranged from Him. The words, "I the LORD will answer him", are ominous. They are enlarged in verses 7-8: "For every one of the house of Israel, or of the stranger that sojourneth in Israel, which separateth himself from me, and setteth up his idols in his heart, and putteth the stumblingblock of his iniquity before his face, and cometh to a prophet to inquire of him concerning me (which the elders were doing here); I the LORD will answer him by myself. And I will set my face against that man, and will make him a sign and a proverb, and I will cut him off from the midst of my people; and ye shall know that I am the LORD".

- *The appeal for repentance, v.6.* "Yet", as Patrick Fairbairn observes, "this is not what the Lord properly wished". "Thus saith the Lord GOD, *Repent, and turn* yourselves from your idols; and turn away your faces from all your abominations." Even here, the Lord exhibits longsuffering. Recovery was possible. He is "longsuffering to us-ward, not willing that any should perish, but that all should come to repentance" (2 Pet. 3: 9). Perhaps His word to *us* is, "Remember therefore from whence thou art fallen, and *repent*, and do the first works; or else I will come unto thee quickly, and will remove thy candlestick out of his place, except thou repent" (Rev. 2: 5).

ii) Deluded prophets, vv.9-11

"And if the prophet be enticed (deceived, AV) and shall speak a word, I Jehovah have enticed (deceived, AV) that prophet" (v.9, JND). This is exactly what happened when Ahab sought the guidance of four hundred prophets in connection with his expedition against Ramoth-Gilead. They told him what he wanted to hear, but only because, in Micaiah's words, "the LORD hath put a lying spirit in the mouth of these thy prophets, and the LORD hath spoken evil against thee" (2 Chron. 18: 18-22). In the words of the New Testament, "Evil men and seducers shall wax worse and worse, deceiving and being deceived" (2 Tim. 3: 13).

As Patrick Fairbairn observes, the chief point here is "the connection between the *self-deceived people* (vv.1-8) and the *deceiving prophet* (vv.9-11) … If the people were sincere in their desire to know the mind of God, for the purpose of obeying His will, the path was plain. They had but to forsake their idolatries, and the Lord was willing to meet them with direction and blessing.

But if, on the other hand, they were bent on playing the hypocrite, professing to inquire concerning Him while their hearts in reality were cleaving to corruption, punishment was sure to overtake them, and that too, in the first instance, after the form of their own iniquity. God would chastise their sin with a corresponding sin; and as they had rejected the safe direction of the true light, he would send the pernicious delusion of a false one". (See also 2 Thess. 2: 9-11.) In New Testament language: "Be not deceived; God is not mocked: for whatsoever a man soweth, that shall he also reap" (Gal. 6: 7). Three things should be noted here:

- **The part played by the prophet, v.9**. "And if the prophet be deceived when he hath spoken a thing, *I the LORD* have deceived that prophet." As J.B.Taylor rightly observes, "This does not mean that the prophet who acts wrongly is not a free agent and bears no responsibility. He is deceived because he has lost his spiritual perception (if he ever had any). He fails to detect the insincerity of his enquirer (or chooses to ignore it) and works up some answer, as the false prophets of Chapter 13 did, without true divine inspiration ... In the deepest sense, it was the Lord who was responsible for the chain reaction which showed itself in such behaviour. They had succumbed to spiritual blindness, and so the lies they uttered were all part of God's judgment upon them". H.L.Ellison concurs: "All unknown to him ... God would be behind the answer, using it to the destruction of both the enquirer and the prophet. The false prophet does not create a generation that does not know God, but is created by it, and he is one of God's instruments of judgment on that generation".

- **The punishment of the prophet, vv.9-10**. Moreover, because of his wickedness in the first place, the false prophet would be judged: "and I will destroy him from the midst of my people Israel" (v.9). The words, "And they shall bear the punishment of their iniquity", notice the change from "him (v.9) to "them" (v.10), appear to refer either to the people or, perhaps, better, to both prophet and people: hence "the punishment of the prophet shall be even as the punishment of him that seeketh unto him".

- **The purpose of the judgment, v.11**. "That the house of Israel may go no more astray from me, neither be polluted any more with all their transgressions; but that they may be my people, and I may be their God, saith the Lord GOD." This is an amazing statement. God determined to use the wickedness of His people, in this case both people and prophet, to effect their cleansing from pollution. Isaiah tells us that the Lord will wash away "the filth of the daughters of Zion ... by the spirit of judgment, and by the spirit of burning" (Isaiah 4: 4). This brings us to:

b) Inescapable judgement, vv.12-23

"The word of the LORD came again to me, saying, Son of man, when the land ('a land', JND) sinneth against me by trespassing grievously, then will I stretch out mine hand upon it, and will break the staff of the bread thereof, and will send famine upon it, and will cut off man and beast from it" (vv.12-13). J.B.Taylor suggests that "These verses are an answer to the objection of those who say that God will not be as ruthless in His judgment as prophets like Jeremiah and Ezekiel were saying He would be, because He cannot afford to ignore the righteousness of some of His godly people". It is worth mentioning that Israel (or Judah) is not mentioned specifically here, although there can be no doubt that this is particularly the "land" in question. However, the phraseology suggests that there is a general principle here. What is said is applicable to any "land". There are two prominent points in the argument:

- Firstly, that God's wrath cannot be diverted, and even if Noah, Daniel and Job ("these three") were present, they would only deliver themselves (vv.13-21).

- Secondly, that God's wrath will fall on Jerusalem, with "a remnant that shall be brought forth" (v.22). But it is a rather different kind of remnant to Noah, Daniel and Job, and for different reasons (vv.22-23).

In summary, we could say that these verses describe two remnants: *(i)* a righteous remnant (vv.13-21); *(i)* a wicked remnant (vv.22-23)

i) **The presence of a righteous remnant, vv.13-21**

"Though **these three men, Noah, Daniel and Job**, were in it, they should deliver but their own souls by their righteousness, saith the Lord GOD" (v.14). Not even the families of these men would have been be saved by proxy (vv.16, 18, 20).

The passage should be compared with Jeremiah 15 verse 1, "Though Moses and Samuel stood before me, yet my mind could not be toward this people: cast them out of my sight, and let them go forth". Both passages should be considered in light of Genesis 18 verses 23-33. The Lord would have been willing to spare Sodom and Gomorrah if there had been righteous people there, but not Judah and Jerusalem. This, surely, stresses the enormity of their sin. It might also emphasise that privilege determines responsibility. The selection of "these three" is well justified:

- **Noah.** He "was a just man, and perfect in his generations, and Noah walked with God" (Gen. 6: 9). He "became heir of the righteousness which is by faith" (Heb. 11: 7). Noah and his family, a godly remnant when "the wickedness of man was great in the earth" (Gen. 6: 5), were delivered from the overflowing judgment of the Flood.

- **Daniel.** In the days of Nebuchadnezzar, Daniel "purposed in his heart that he would not defile himself with the portion of the king's meat" (Dan. 1: 8), and in the days of Darius, he refused to obey the edict that none should "ask a petition of any God or man for thirty days, save of thee, O king" (Dan. 6: 7, 10). Daniel and his friends were a remnant, true to God, in a heathen court.

- **Job.** He was "perfect and upright, and one that feared God, and eschewed evil" (Job 1: 1), so much so that God was able to say to Satan who had been "going to and fro" and "walking up and down" in the earth, "Hast thou considered my servant Job, that there is none like him in the earth, a perfect and an upright man, one that feareth God, and escheweth evil?" (Job 1: 6-8). Quite clearly, Job stood out from all other men in his righteousness and godliness. Later, God said to Eliphaz, "Ye have not spoken of me the thing that is right, as my servant Job hath" (Job 42: 7).

It has been suggested (Harry Bell) that Noah overcame the *world*: "he prepared an ark to the saving of his house; by the which he condemned the world" (Heb. 11: 7); that Daniel overcame the *flesh*: "he purposed in his heart that he would not defile himself with the portion of the king's meat, nor with the wine that he drank" (Dan. 1: 8); that Job overcame the *devil*. It has also been suggested that Job is mentioned last because whereas Noah had his family and Daniel had his friends, Job was stripped "even of his family and household" (Patrick Fairbairn).

We should note the feeble arguments of H.L.Ellison and J.B.Taylor in connection with the identity of Daniel. To quote Ellison: "Furthermore, it must be looked on as extremely doubtful whether the well-known Daniel is intended at all. His name, as indeed that of the other two Daniels of Scripture

(1 Chron 3: 1; Ezra 8: 2/Neh. 10: 6), was spelled *Daniyy'l*, but Ezekiel spells it *Dani'el*, or more likely *Dan'el*. He would seem to be referring to a figure of hoar antiquity probably mentioned in tablets discovered at Ras Shamra dating before 1400 B.C. A scribal error on Ezekiel's part is most unlikely. If so, we know too little to form any opinion as to why he was mentioned". Can we imagine the Jews accepting such a suggestion?

F.Gardiner (Ellicott's Commentary) is undoubtedly correct in saying, "The mention of Daniel ... need occasion no surprise ... Daniel had now been for about twelve years in important office at the royal court, and possessed of the very highest rank. There is, therefore, no occasion for the strange supposition that the reference is to some older Daniel, of such eminence as to be spoken of in the way he is here and in Chapter 28 verse 3, and yet whose name has otherwise completely faded out from history. But besides all this, there was a special propriety, and even necessity for the purpose in hand, that Daniel should be mentioned. He was not only in high office, but was the trusted counsellor of Nebuchadnezzar by whom Jerusalem was to be destroyed. He was also a very holy man, and most patriotic Israelite. The Jews, therefore, might well have thought that his influence would avail to avert the threatened calamity, and by placing his name in the list, their last hope was to be dashed as it could be by nothing else".

The presence of "these three men", had that been possible, would not have secured the deliverance of any but themselves should God bring upon the land his "four sore judgments" (v.21). His "four sore judgements are "the sword, and the famine, and the noisome beast, and the pestilence" (v.21). These are all mentioned in verses 13-19:

- **Famine, vv.13-14**. "Son of man, when the land sinneth against me by trespassing grievously ('working unfaithfulness', JND; 'acting treacherously', J.B.Taylor: it is used of the sin of Achan), then will I stretch out my hand upon it, and will break the staff of the bread thereof, and will send **famine** upon it, and will cut off man and beast from it: though **these three men, Noah, Daniel and Job**, were in it, they should deliver but their own souls by their righteousness, saith the Lord GOD." (See Leviticus 26: 26.)

- **Wild beasts, vv.15-16.** "If I cause **noisome beasts** ('evil beasts', JND) to pass through the land, and they spoil it, so that it be desolate, that no man may pass through because of the beasts: though **these three men** were in it, as I live, saith the Lord GOD, they shall deliver neither sons nor daughters, they only shall be delivered, but the land shall be desolate.") See Leviticus 26: 22.)

- **The sword, vv.17-18**. "Or if I bring a sword upon that land, and say, Sword, go through the land; so that I cut off man and beast from it: though **these three men** were in it, as I live, saith the Lord GOD, they shall deliver neither sons nor daughters, but they shall only be delivered themselves." (See Leviticus 26: 25.)

- **Pestilence, vv.19-20.** "Or if I send a pestilence into that land, and pour out my fury upon it in blood, to cut off from it man and beast: though **Noah, Daniel, and Job**, were in, as I live, saith the Lord GOD, they shall deliver neither son nor daughter; they shall deliver but their own souls by their righteousness." (See Leviticus 26: 25.)

But Noah, Daniel and Job were *not* there, and so the Lord continues: **"How much more** (in the absence of "these three") when I send my four sore judgments upon Jerusalem, the sword, and the famine, and the noisome beast, and the pestilence, to cut off from it man and beast?" (v.21).

God's "four sore judgments", though not identical, are mentioned in the New Testament: "and power was given unto them ("Death and Hell") over the fourth part of the earth, to kill with sword, and with hunger, and with death, and with the beasts of the earth" (Rev. 6: 8).

b) The deliverance of a wicked remnant, vv.22-23

"Yet, behold, therein shall be left a remnant that shall be brought forth, both sons and daughters; behold, they shall come forth unto you, and ye shall see their way and their doings: and ye shall be comforted concerning the evil that I have brought upon Jerusalem, even all that I have brought upon Jerusalem, even concerning all that I have brought upon it. And they shall comfort you, when ye see their ways and their doings: and ye shall know that I have not done without cause all that I have done in it, saith the Lord GOD."

At first glance, this might seem to mean that there would be a godly remnant after all in Jerusalem, and that this would bring some comfort to the exiles in Babylonia. However, the concluding words - "and ye shall know that I have not done without cause all that I have done in it, saith the Lord GOD" - point us in another direction.

CHAPTER 14

F.Gardiner puts it as follows: "In this (v.22) and the following verse it is promised that a remnant shall be brought from Jerusalem; and it is clearly implied that they shall come to Babylonia. There the present exiles shall see them, and thus be comforted. But in what sense comforted? The connection absolutely decides this: 'when ye see their ways and their doings, ye shall know that I have not done without cause all that I have done in it'. That is, when you see the wickedness of His remnant, you will cease to mourn over the judgment, for you cannot but perceive that it was a righteous act of God". F.Gardiner points out that the words "they shall comfort you" (v.23) are explained by what is said in verse 22, which does not mean 'they shall administer comfort', but 'they shall be cause of comfort' by showing the exiles in Babylonia their exceeding wickedness. In Calvin's words, "Ye shall see the men to be so wicked, that ye shall be forced to confess the city was deserving of destruction, and the men themselves worthy of death". They will acknowledge that "the Judge of all the earth" (Gen. 18: 25) was right in all that He did. His ways are righteousness and truth.

EZEKIEL CHAPTER 15

Ezekiel 15 continues the section of the book (8: 1 - 19: 14) detailing the contributory causes of coming judgment on Judah and Jerusalem. As we have noted, the solemn message of these chapters is conveyed by the *vision* given *to* Ezekiel (chs. 8-11), which ends with the withdrawal of the glory of the Lord from the temple (11: 22-23), and by *the visible and verbal messages* given *by* Ezekiel (chs.12-19).

Chapter 15 details the third of five reasons for pending judgment on Judah and Jerusalem. The five reasons (chs.13-17) are *(1)* the untruthful prophets (ch.13); *(2)* the unseen idolatry (ch.14); *(3)* the useless vine (ch.15); *(4)* the unfaithful wife (ch.16); *(5)* the unreliable promises (ch.17),

Having already dealt with the 'untruthful prophets' (see Chapter 13) and the 'unseen idolatry' (see Chapter 14), we come now to:

3) The useless vine, Chapter 15

After considering the connection with preceding chapters, we must notice the way in which the passage illustrates Judah's condition, and the way in which it applies to coming judgment.

A) The connection

While the absence of fruit is certainly implied, this is not actually stated. Judah is not even described here as a cultivated vine. It is simply portrayed as a forest plant (vv.2, 6), whose wood is only fit for fuel. The previous two chapters explain why God's people, having been planted "a noble vine, wholly a right seed", had become "the degenerate plant of a strange vine unto me" (Jer. 2: 21).

- In Chapter 13, God's people had become useless (or unfruitful) because of the way in which both prophets and prophetesses had misrepresented

Him. He had been misrepresented by the predictions of the prophets (13: 1-16), and by the practices of the prophetesses (13: 17-23):

- *The prophet* had attributed *their predictions* to the Lord. "They have seen vanity and lying divination, saying, the LORD saith: and the LORD hath not sent them ... Have ye not seen a vain vision, and have ye not spoken a lying divination, whereas ye say, The LORD saith it; albeit I have not spoken?" (13: 6-7).

- *The prophetesses* had attributed *their practices* to the Lord. "Will ye pollute me among my people for handfuls of barley and for pieces of bread, to slay the souls (of them) that should not die, and to save the souls alive that should not live, by your lying to my people that hear your lies" (13: 19). These women were 'polluting' the Lord by "attaching His name and authority to that which was not true, and that would not come to pass, thus 'making Him a liar' like themselves" (F.Gardiner). By pronouncing, in the Lord's name, the *death* of "*souls that should not die*", and the *survival* of those "*that should not live*", they brought His name into disrepute. It was the exact opposite of divine righteousness.

In both cases, to use New Testament language, "their folly shall be manifest unto all men" (2 Tim. 3: 9). In the case of the prophets, their "wall ... daubed with untempered mortar", referring to their false predictions of deliverance from the Babylonian invader and return from captivity, would come crashing down (13: 10-16). In the case of the prophetesses, they would "see no more vanity, nor divine divinations: for I will deliver my people out of your hand: and ye shall know that I am the LORD" (13: 23).

- *In Chapter 14*, God's people had become useless (or unfruitful) because of their deceit (vv.1-11) and their depravity (vv.12-23). In the first case, "certain of the elders" had attempted to secure the Lord's help and guidance without abandoning their idolatrous inclinations: "these men have set up their idols in their heart, and put the stumblingblock of their iniquity before their face" (14: 3). In the second case, God's people had become so far removed from Him that even the presence, if it had been possible, of a godly remnant comprising Noah, Daniel and Job ("these three") could not have saved them.

B) The illustration, vv.1-5

All this is now summed up by the figure of a useless vine. As we have already observed, it is not so much an 'unfruitful vine', although this is implied, but a 'useless vine'. John P. Taylor puts it clearly: "In this poem, Ezekiel likens Israel to a vine, a comparison which has a long history in Hebrew tradition going back at least as far as the blessing of Jacob (Gen. 49: 22). Usually the force of the simile is to be found in the fruit-bearing properties of the vine which make it so highly esteemed among men, but are all too rarely evident in the life of Israel as a nation (see Deut. 32: 32; Isaiah 5: 1- 7; Jer. 2: 21; Hos. 10: 1). Ezekiel, however, ignores the fruit, as if to imply that there is no question of Israel producing anything good, and instead draws a picture of *a wild vine of the forest* (v.2), whose only point of comparison is the quality of its wood. This is notoriously useless, not being firm enough even for making a peg to hang a pot from, and it is of even less value when it has been charred in a fire". This vine would certainly be consigned to the fire. In Chapter 14, the Lord had served notice on Jerusalem that He would send His "four sore judgments" on the city - "the sword, and the famine, and the noisome beast, and the pestilence, to cut off from it man and beast" (14: 21).

There are two parts to the illustration: *(a)* the uselessness of the wood of the vine **before** its destruction (vv.2-3); *(b)* the uselessness of the wood of the vine **after** its destruction (vv.4-5).

a) The uselessness of the vine-wood before its destruction, vv.2-3

"And the word of the LORD came unto me, saying, Son of man, What is the vine tree more than any tree, or than a branch which is among the trees of the forest?" Shall wood be taken thereof to do any work? Or will men take a pin of it to hang any vessel thereon?"

According to John B.Taylor, "The phrase, *the vine branch which is among the trees of the forest* (v.2, RV, RSV), is in apposition to (it explains and defines) *the vine* of the first half of the verse, but in view of the comparison it is almost impossible to translate it idiomatically. The sense is clear: How much better is the wood of the vine than any other wood? Answer, it is no better. How much better is the branch of the vine (than any other branch) among the trees of the forest? Answer, not at all. The word *vine branch* (the same as is found in Ezek. 8: 17) is a twig that is trimmed off at pruning-time, and its use by Ezekiel serves to underline Israel's relative insignificance as a nation". We should notice two things in these verses:

CHAPTER 15

i) There was no distinctiveness, v.2

It was simply "among the trees of the forest", without further distinction. This was not always the case. We have only to think of the glory and influence of Israel under Solomon. Patrick Fairbairn puts it as follows: "In respect of those things which constitute the natural greatness of kingdoms, - antiquity of origin, extent of territory, abundance of resources, attainments in art and science - what could they boast of, in comparison of Egypt, Ethiopia, Babylon, and the greater kingdoms of the earth?". Fairbairn continues, significantly, "whenever they lost their distinction as a nation that kept the truth of God, and wrought righteousness in the earth, they were no longer capable of holding a place of power and influence in the destinies of the world. On the contrary, like salt that had lost its savour, they had become fit only to be cast out, or committed as a piece of vine-wood to the fire".

The absence of Israel's distinctiveness in this way should make us ask questions about *our* distinctiveness as children of God. We can become like the salt that has lost its "savour" and is "trodden under foot of *men"* (Matt. 5: 13), and like the withered vine branches which "*men* gather ... and cast ... into the fire" (John 15: 6).

ii) There was no usefulness, v.3

"Shall wood be taken thereof to do any work? Or will men take a pin of it to hang any vessel thereon?" We can justifiably press this a little further:

- ***It was useless for work***. The wood of the vine could not be used as timber in any kind of construction or craftsmanship. The wood is "soft and brittle" (Patrick Fairbairn) and therefore incapable of being made into a useful tool or, for that matter, into *anything* useful.

- ***It was useless for weight-bearing***. "The *pin* (Hebrew *yathed*) is the common word for a tent-peg, but it can also be used, as here, for a wooden *peg* fixed in a wall. It developed the meaning of someone who could be relied upon, as in Isaiah 22 verses 23-24, 'I will fasten him as a nail in a sure place ... and they shall hang upon him all the glory of his father's house'; Zechariah 10 verse 4, 'Out of him came forth the corner, out of him the nail, out of him the battle bow ...'); see also Ezra 9 verse 8" (John B. Taylor).

The lesson is clear, Israel was neither useful nor dependable. God could

EZEKIEL

not *employ* them in His service (v.3a), and He could not *entrust* them with responsibility (v.3b).

The absence of Israel's usefulness in this way should make us ask questions about *our* usefulnesss as children of God. Are *we* like that? Vine-wood could not be turned into "a vessel unto honour ... meet for the master's use, and prepared unto every good work" (2 Tim. 2: 21), but can *we* be used in this way? It would be nothing less than tragic if all we were fit for was the fire! We cannot lose our salvation, but we could lose everything by bad-workmanship. See 1 Corinthians 3 verse 15. This brings us to:

b) The uselessess of the vine-wood after its destruction, vv.4-5

The lesson is clear. If the vine-wood had no enduring use when it was growing, then it certainly had no enduring use after it had been consigned to the fire. "Behold, it is cast into the fire for fuel; the fire devoureth (*akal*) both the ends of it, and the midst of it is burned (*charar*, to be hot, heated). Is it meet for any work? Behold, when it was whole, it was meet for no work: how much less shall it be meet yet for any work, when the fire hath devoured (*akal*) it, and it is burned (*charar*)?" As John B. Taylor observes, "no part of Israel is unaffected by the searing experiences she has gone through". It is quite possible that the two ends refer to the ten tribes already carried away by Assyria, and to Judah, though rebellious, already subject to Babylon (2 Kings 24: 1), with the middle referring to the inhabitants of Jerusalem on the brink of ruin with the fire raging around them. But burnt, or charred, wood has no use.

All this makes solemn reading, particularly when we compare what God had intended for Israel (and still intends for Israel), and what she had become. He had intended her to resemble a cultivated vine, but she had become a wild vine. Reading the passage should create renewed desire in our hearts and lives not to follow suit, but to bring pleasure to the Lord. In Paul's words, "Wherefore we make it our aim (margin, 'are ambitious') whether at home or absent, to be well-pleasing unto him" (2 Cor. 5: 9, RV).

The subject is expanded in the Addendum.

C) THE APPLICATION, vv.6-8

"Therefore thus saith the Lord GOD; As the vine tree among the trees of the

CHAPTER 15

forest, which I have given to the fire for fuel (so God had man's warmth in mind in creating the wild vine), so will I give ('so have I given', RV: referring to the first Babylonian invasions in the reigns of Jehoiakim and Jehoiachin) the inhabitants of Jerusalem. And I will set my face against them; they shall go out from one fire, and another fire shall devour them" (vv.6-7), or, "they have gone forth from the fire, but the fire shall (still) devour them" (RV margin).

Jerusalem was just a piece of charred vine-wood. It had already been through the fire. It was not worthy to be compared with the surrounding nations and cities (just as the wild vine was insignificant among the forest trees), and had been "charred in the fires of enemy invasion in the days of Jehoiachin", though "spared from total destruction" (see 2 Kings 24: 8-16), but "fit for nothing more than to be thrown back into the fire to be utterly consumed", referring to the outcome of the siege of Jerusalem being conducted at the time by Nebuchadnezzar. (John B.Taylor). The "fire" was waiting to devour them.

As John B. Taylor rightly concludes, "Implicit in the parable is the prophet's response to those who imagined that Israel, as the vine of the Lord's planting, was indestructible. Cut down she might be, they thought, but it was only a temporary setback: before long the stock would shoot again and Israel would flourish as she had done in days gone by. Such naive optimism was the object of Ezekiel's incessant condemnation. Israel and Jerusalem were finished". We must add, 'But only for the time being!' The "stock" *will* shoot again. See Isaiah 11 verse 1.

The chapter concludes with the oft-repeated words, "and *ye shall know that I am the LORD*, when I set my face against them" (v.7). As we have noted before, these and similar words occur "no less than fifty-four times in the book and with some expansion another eighteen times ... It is the most characteristic expression of Ezekiel ... it is *not* the existence of Jehovah that is being stressed, *but* the identity ... of Jehovah" (H.L.Ellison). It conveys, not so much *who* He is, but *what* He is. In the words quoted by F. Cundick, they show that "God is the Ruler of history, and history is the vindication of His character". This is confirmed in the closing words: "And I will make the land desolate, because they have committed a trespass, saith the Lord GOD" (v.8), or "because they have wrought unfaithfulness, saith the Lord Jehovah" (JND). Judah and Jerusalem would be made painfully aware of His character. They had acted treacherously or faithlessly, and they would prove that "the face of the LORD is against them that do evil" (Psalm 34: 16).

The face can convey either favour and blessing, or disfavour and anger. For the former, see Numbers 6 verses 24-26, "The LORD bless thee, and keep thee: The LORD make his *face* to shine upon thee, and be gracious unto thee: The LORD lift up his countenance upon thee, and give thee peace". For the latter, see Revelation 6 verses 15-16 where men cry "to the mountains and rocks, Fall on us, and hide us from the *face* of him that sitteth on the throne, and from the wrath of the Lamb".

We do well to make our daily prayers include, "Make thy face to shine upon thy servant" (Psalm 119: 135).

Addendum

The cultivated vine and the wild vine

i) The cultivated vine

In the words of Asaph, "Thou hast brought a vine out of Egypt: thou hast cast out the heathen, and planted it. Thou preparedst room before it, and didst cause it to take deep root, and it filled the land. The hills were covered with the shadow of it, and the boughs thereof were like the goodly cedars. She sent out her boughs unto the sea, and her branches unto the river" (Psalm 80: 8-11). The Psalmist continues by referring to Israel as "the vineyard which thy right hand hath planted, and the branch that thou madest strong for thyself", but, alas, "It is burned with fire, it is cut down" (vv.15-16).

Isaiah takes up the subject: "Now I will sing to my well-beloved a song of my beloved touching his vineyard. My beloved hath a vineyard in a very fruitful hill" (Isaiah 5: 1-7). There is no doubt about the meaning of the passage: "For the vineyard of the LORD of hosts is **the house of Israel**" (v.7). The entire chapter should be read carefully. The "wild grapes" (literally 'stinking grapes') are identified in verse 8 ("Woe unto them that join house to house ... till there be no place, that they may be placed alone in the midst of the earth!"; verse 11 ("Woe unto them that rise up early in the morning, that they may follow strong drink"); verse 18 ("Woe unto them that draw iniquity with cords of vanity"); verse 20 ("Woe unto them that call evil good, and good evil"); verse 21 ("Woe unto them that are wise in their own eyes"); verse 22 ("Woe unto them that are mighty to drink wine, and men of strength to mingle strong drink").

Isaiah later returns to the subject: "In that day the LORD with his sore and great and strong sword shall punish leviathan that piercing serpent, even leviathan that crooked serpent: and he shall slay the dragon that is in the sea. In that day sing ye unto her, A vineyard of red wine. I the LORD do keep it: I will water it every moment: lest any hurt it, I will keep it night and day ... Israel shall blossom and bud, and fill the face of the world with fruit" (Isaiah 27: 1, 2, 3, 6). This will only take place after God has cleansed and purged the nation: notice the expressions, "By this, therefore, shall the iniquity of Jacob be *purged*" (v.9); "When the boughs thereof are withered, they shall be broken off: the women come and *set them on fire*" (v.11). John15 is now compulsory reading: especially verses 2 and 6.

These Old Testament passages give us the key to the New Testament parable of the vineyard (Matt. 21: 33-46; Mark 12: 1-12; Luke 20: 9-19). There is, of course, one reason, and one reason only, for planting a vineyard. "He looked that it should *bring forth grapes*" (Isaiah 5: 2). The parable of Jotham (Judges 9: 7-21) emphasises the point: "Then said the trees unto the vine, Come thou, and reign over us. And the vine said unto them, *Should I leave my wine*, which cheereth God and man, and go to be promoted over the trees?" (vv.12-13). There can, therefore, be no doubt about the reason for Israel's national existence. God intended His people to be a fruitful vineyard, that is, to bring Him joy and satisfaction. Micah sums it up like this: "What doth the LORD require of thee, but to do justly, and to love mercy, and to walk humbly with thy God" (Micah 6: 8). But God had to say, "Israel is an empty vine, he bringeth forth fruit unto himself" (Hosea 10: 1). There was nothing for Him.

All this should provoke serious thought. We are here for precisely the same reason as Israel. We must listen to the True Vine: "Ye have not chosen me, but I have chosen you, and ordained you, that ye should go and *bring forth fruit*" (John 15: 16). Each assembly should also be like a fruitful vineyard. See Galatians 5 verses 22-23: "But the fruit of the Spirit is love, joy, peace, longsuffering, gentleness, goodness, faith, meekness, temperance". All this is to mark the Lord's people corporately: the words "one another" (Gal. 5: vv.13, 15, 26) form the context of "the fruit of the Spirit".

How much pleasure do *we*, as *individuals*, bring to God? How much pleasure does the *assembly* with which we are associated, bring to God?

ii) The wild vine

Israel had become a wild vine, and this is stressed in Ezekiel 15. "Son of man, What is the vine tree more than any tree, or than a branch which is *among the trees of the forest*' (v.2), or "Son of man, what is the wood of the vine more than any wood, the vine-branch, which is among the trees of the forest' (JND); "As the vine tree *among the trees of the forest,* which I have given to the fire for fuel, so will I give the inhabitants of Jerusalem" (v.6).

It has been suggested that God's people had allowed 'the trees of the forest' to grow in His vineyard, reducing them to an inferior position – just as a cultivated area can be overrun by weeds and saplings (Ken Lloyd, late of Cheshunt).

Israel had originally brought some pleasure to God: "I found Israel like grapes in the wilderness" (Hos. 9: 10). But this had changed, and God had to say, as already noted, "Israel is an empty vine, he bringeth forth fruit unto himself" (Hos. 10: 1). But Ezekiel's picture is even worse: Israel had become nothing more than a "vine tree among the trees of the forest". As C.L.Feinberg observes, "The people of God in every age are like the vine – most valuable when bearing fruit for God, but worthless when barren and sterile". (Compare Mark 11: 12-14; Luke 13: 6-9.)

EZEKIEL CHAPTER 16

Ezekiel 16 continues the section of the book (8: 1 - 19: 14) detailing the contributory causes of coming judgment on Judah and Jerusalem. As we have noted, the solemn message of these chapters is conveyed by the *vision* given *to* Ezekiel (chs. 8-11), which ends with the withdrawal of the glory of the Lord from the temple (11: 22-23), and by *the visible and verbal messages* given *by* Ezekiel (chs.12-19).

Chapter 16 details the fourth of five reasons for pending judgment on Judah and Jerusalem. The five reasons (vv.13-18) are *(1)* the untruthful prophets (ch.13); *(2)* the unseen idolatry (ch.14); *(3)* the useless vine (ch.15); *(4)* the unfaithful wife (ch.16); *(5)* the unreliable promises (ch.17).

Having already dealt with the first three of the above, we come now to:

4) The unfaithful wife, Chapter 16

In introducing Chapter 16, F.Gardiner (*Ellicott's Commentary*) rightly observes: "In the magnificent allegory which occupies this chapter, the sin and consequent rejection of Israel (better, Jerusalem) is set forth in still stronger terms than in anything that has gone before". This rightly establishes the connection between the chapter and its predecessors. This series of chapters in the prophecy sets out in various ways the reasons for divine judgment on the nation. The message of the chapter is addressed to Jerusalem ("Son of man, cause Jerusalem to know her abominations", vv.1-2) in its representative role as the national capital. It had become the centre of national idolatry.

F.Gardiner continues: "The extreme aggravation of the sin is shown from the fact that Israel (better, Jerusalem) had no original claim upon God's favour, nor anything to make her attractive - she was merely an exposed and repulsive foundling (vv.3-5) when God took pity upon, and saved, and cared for her (vv.6-7). Then, when she had come of age, He entered into a covenant with, and greatly blessed, her (vv.8-14); but she proved utterly unfaithful to her covenant – an unfaithful wife; wanton beyond all precedent (vv.15-34). Hence her punishment". J.B.Taylor puts it like this: "Ezekiel in this chapter gives a survey of Israel's (better, Jerusalem's) spiritual history from her earliest origins up to his own day ... At the same time, Ezekiel sees beyond the immediate catastrophe of judgment, to God's ultimate purpose of restoration and forgiveness".

With this in mind, the chapter may be divided in the following way: *(1)* God's caring love (vv.1-14); *(2)* Jerusalem's commitment to idolatry (vv.15-34); *(3)* Jerusalem's coming judgment (vv.35-52): her judgment is described (vv.35-43) and deserved (vv.44-52); *(4)* God's covenant blessing (vv.53-63).

1) GOD'S CARING LOVE, vv.1-14

"Again the word of the LORD came unto me, saying, Son of man, cause Jerusalem to know her abominations" (vv.1-2). The depths of "her abominations" is contrasted with the heights to which divine grace had taken the nation. Her rich blessings in this way are described in these verses. The section can be divided into two parts: *(a)* her state before God blessed her (vv.3-6); *(b)* her state after God had blessed her (vv.7-14).

a) Her state before God blessed her, vv.3-6

i) **Her parentage, v.3.** "Thy birth and thy nativity is of the land of Canaan; thy father was an Amorite, and thy mother a Hittite." This evidently refers to the **original foundation of Jerusalem**. It was a Canaanite city. (See, for example, Joshua 10: 1, 3, 5.) J.B.Taylor suggests that the "statement is heavy with sarcasm ... for the term 'Canaanite' was a by-word for moral decadence". The words could hardly be applied to Israel as a nation. Compare Deuteronomy 26 verse 5 ("A Syrian ready to perish was my father"). Exodus 13 verse 5 refers to Canaan as follows: "And it shall be, when the LORD shall bring thee into the land of the **Canaanites**, and the **Hittites**, and the **Amorites**, and the **Hivites**, and the **Jebusites** (the people who dwelt in Jerusalem, see 1 Chron. 11: 4), which he sware to thy fathers to give thee ..." This verse is the best commentary on Ezekiel 16 verse 3! The Hittites were a brother nation to the Amorites. See Genesis 10 verses 15-19. Abraham negotiated with "the children of Heth", and in particular with "Ephron the Hittite", in connection with a burying place for Sarah. See Genesis 23 verses 1-20.

ii) Her birth, vv.4-5. "And as for thy nativity, in the day thou wast born, thy navel was not cut, neither wast thou washed in water to supple (an unidentified word: thought to mean 'wash') thee: thou wast not salted at all, nor swaddled at all. None eye pitied thee, to do any of these unto thee, to have compassion upon thee; but thou wast cast out into the open field, to the lothing of thy person, in the day that thou wast born." To quote F.Gardiner again, she "had no original claim upon God's favour, nor anything to make her attractive: she was merely an exposed and repulsive foundling when God took pity upon, and saved, and cared for her (vv.6-7)". Jerusalem, lying in Canaanite territory, as we have noted, was therefore, with the rest of Canaan, without any commendable features. It was a loathsome place: "thou wast cast out into the open field, to the lothing of thy person, in the day that thou wast born". Yet this was the very place where, ultimately, the Lord placed His name!

iii) Her salvation, v.6. "And when I passed by thee, and saw thee polluted in thine own blood, I said unto thee when thou wast in thy blood, Live; yea, I said unto thee, when thou wast in thy blood, Live." As noted above, Jerusalem became 'the place of the name'. It has an unrivalled future.

b) Her state after God blessed her, vv.7-14

"I have caused thee to multiply as the bud of the field, and thou hast increased and waxen great, and thou art come to excellent ornaments ('fulness of beauty', JND: 'arrived at full maidenhood', RSV): thy breasts are fashioned, and thine hair is grown, whereas thou wast naked and bare" (v.7). Whilst the words, "I have caused thee to multiply" could refer to the enlargement of the nation (although this would require the passage to refer to Israel generally, rather than to Jerusalem specifically, as stated in vv.2-3), it does seem that these verses refers to the growth and situation of the city.

It is described as "the place which the LORD your God shall choose out of all the tribes to put his name there … his habitation" (Deut. 12: 5). Initially, the 'place of the name' was Shiloh (Jer. 7: 12), but at the dedication of the temple God said, "I have hallowed this house which thou hast built, to put my name there for ever; and mine eyes and mine heart shall be there perpetually" (1 Kings 9: 3). No wonder that "the LORD loveth the gates of Zion more than all the dwellings of Jacob!" (Ps. 87: 2), and no wonder that it is a beautiful place: "Beautiful for situation, the joy of the whole earth, is mount Zion …" (Ps. 48: 2).

The way in which God speaks of His dealings with Jerusalem is most instructive. We should notice that the beauty (v.13) and renown (v.14) of the city were the direct result of God's love for her. Hence, "Now when I passed by thee, and looked upon thee, behold, thy time was the time of *love* ..." (v.8). Hence, as above, "the LORD loveth the gates of Zion more than all the dwellings of Jacob!" (Ps. 87: 2).

The words, "I spread my skirt over thee" (v.8) recall Ruth 3 verse 9. In saying, "spread therefore thine skirt over thine handmaid", Ruth was claiming his love. The word "skirt" is, literally, 'wing'. See Ruth 2 verse 12. Compare, for example, Psalm 17 verse 8; Psalm 36 verse 7 and Psalm 57 verse 1. Ruth was therefore claiming his protection. Mary and Martha appealed to the love of the Lord Jesus: "Lord, behold, he whom thou lovest is sick" (John 11: 3). We too are "beloved of the Lord" (2 Thess. 2: 13). The words, "yea, I sware unto thee, and entered into a covenant with thee, saith the Lord GOD, and thou becamest mine" (v.8), refer to a covenant of marriage. Jerusalem is regarded here as the wife of Jehovah. As we have seen, the Lord has put His name there "for ever". This will be demonstrated in the millennium: "Thou (Zion) shalt no more be termed Forsaken: neither shall thy land any more be termed Desolate; but thou shalt be called Hephzi-bah, and thy land Beulah: for the LORD delighteth in thee, and thy land shall be married. For as a young man marrieth a virgin, so shall thy (Zion's) sons marry thee: and as the bridegroom rejoiceth over the bride, so shall thy God rejoice over thee" (Isaiah 62: 4-5).

The glory of Jerusalem, with special reference to the reigns of David and Solomon, is described in magnificent language: "Then washed I thee with water: yea, I throughly washed away thy blood from thee (cleansed her from idolatry and wickedness), and I *anointed* thee with oil. I *clothed* thee also with broidered work, and *shod* thee with badgers' skin, and *girded* thee about with fine linen, and *covered* thee with silk. I *decked* thee also with ornaments, and put bracelets upon thy hands, and a chain on thy neck. And I put a jewel on thy forehead, and earrings in thine ears, and a beautiful crown upon thine head. Thus wast thou *decked* with gold and silver; and thy *raiment* was of fine linen, and silk, and broidered work: thou didst *eat* fine flour, and honey and oil: and thou wast exceeding beautiful, and thou didst prosper into a kingdom (which it did in the days of David: he was anointed king over all Israel)" (vv.9-13).

The result follows: "And thy renown went forth among the heathen for thy beauty: for it was perfect through my comeliness (magnificence, JND), which I had put upon thee, saith the Lord GOD" (v.14).

It should be carefully noted, again in the words of F.Gardiner, "that Israel (better, Jerusalem) had no original claim upon God's favour, nor anything to make her attractive". He took the *initiative* in her blessing, and all that she became was *solely due to His grace and provision*. He did it all! "*I* anointed thee ... *I* clothed thee ... *I* decked thee ..." We are reminded of Paul's words, "by the grace of God I am what I am" (1 Cor. 15: 10).

But the picture now darkens:

2) JERUSALEM'S COMMITMENT TO IDOLATRY, vv.15-34

Over these verses the following could be written:

> *God made me for Himself, to serve Him here,*
> *With love's pure service and in filial fear;*
> *To show His praise, for Him to labour now;*
> *Then see His glory where the angels bow.*

> *And I, poor sinner, cast it all away;*
> *Lived for the toil or pleasure of each day;*
> *As if no Christ had shed His precious blood,*
> *As if I owed no homage to my God.*

This section can be divided as follows: *(a)* her infidelity, vv.15-25; *(b)* her insatiability (vv.26-29); *(c)* her initiative (vv.30-34).

a) Her infidelity, vv.15-25

The description of Jerusalem's infidelity is introduced by the words "thou ... playedst the harlot" (vv.15-16). It began with pride and self-esteem. "But thou didst trust in thine own beauty, and playest the harlot because of thy renown" (v.15). (Compare Uzziah, 2 Chron. 26: 16). Her idolatry (thou ... deckest thy high places with divers colours, and playedst the harlot thereupon") was without parallel: "[the like] hath not come to pass, and shall be no more" (v.16, JND). The details follow:

i) **She devoted her resources to idolatry, vv.17-19.** "Thou hast also taken thy fair jewels of my gold and of my silver, which I had given thee, and **madest to thyself images** of men, and didst commit whoredom with them; and tookest thy broidered garments, and **coveredst them** (the images): and thou hast set mine oil and mine incense **before them**. My meat also which I gave thee, fine flour, and oil, and honey, wherewith I fed thee, thou hast even set it **before them** for a sweet savour: and thus it was, saith the Lord GOD."

Her resources were God-given: hence: "*my* gold ... *my* silver ... *mine* oil and *mine* incense ... *my* meat". We need to remember that:

> *Naught that I have my own I call,*
> *I hold it for the Giver:*
> *My heart, my strength, my life, my all,*
> *Are His, and His for ever.*

ii) **She devoted her children to idolatry, vv.20-21**. "Moreover thou hast taken thy sons and thy daughters, whom thou hast borne unto **me**, and these hast thou sacrificed **unto them** (the idols) to be devoured. Is this of thy whoredoms a small matter, that thou hast slain **my** children, and delivered them to cause them to pass through the fire **for them** (the idols)?" These verses explain that the child was first slain, and then its body was burnt as a sacrifice to the god.

At this point, God charges her with reverting to her original condition: "And in all thine abominations and thy whoredoms thou hast **not remembered** the days of thy youth, when thou wast naked and bare, and wast polluted in thy blood" (v.22).

iii) **She devoted her buildings to idolatry, vv.23-25.** "And it came to pass, after all thy wickedness (woe, woe unto thee! saith the Lord GOD), that thou hast also built unto thee an eminent place ('a place of debauchery', JND; 'arched place', JND margin), and hast made thee a high place in every street. Thou hast built thy high place at every head of the way, and hast made thy beauty to be abhorred, and hast opened thy feet to every one that passed by, and multiplied thy whoredoms."   J.B.Taylor comments as follows: "From the sin of idolatry at high places (v.16 *et al*), Ezekiel turns to the practice of heathen cults in the city of Jerusalem. The language suggests that shrines were set up at street corners, but in view of terms like 'eminent place' ('vaulted chamber', RSV) and 'high place' or 'lofty place' (vv.24-25), it may be that these were roof-top shrines which were situated at strategic and commanding positions at the intersections of city streets. They would be used for fertility rites in connection with Canaanite religion, rather than simply as places for commercial prostitution. The phrase 'opened thy feet' (v.25) is a euphemism for self-exposure".

b) Her insatiability, vv.26-29

Note the expressions, "thou wast unsatiable" (v.28); "couldest not be satisfied" (v.28); "thou wast not satisfied herewith" (v.29). The section deals with her desire, not only for foreign idols, but foreign alliances. As J.B.Taylor points out "in any such alliance between a lesser and a greater power, it was normal for the weaker party to take into its religious system the gods and the worship of the stranger as a sign that they were accepting his patronage". The section reminds us forcibly of James 4 verse 4, "Adulteresses, know ye not that friendship with the world is enmity with God? Whoever therefore is minded to be [the] friend of the world is constituted enemy of God" (JND). We notice therefore:

i) Friendship with Egypt, vv.26-27. "Thou hast also committed fornication with the Egyptians thy neighbours, great of flesh; and hast increased thy whoredoms, to provoke me to anger" (v.26). The expression "great of flesh" shows "partly Ezekiel's deep repugnance for all things Egyptian, partly the bitter lesson that Israel was so slow to learn from experience, that the apparent strength of Egypt was only flabby fat" (H.L.Ellison). Ellison also explains that "the only effect of turning to Egypt in the time of Hezekiah had been the cutting short of Judean territory by Sennacherib, who handed over many of the cities he had captured to the Philistine kings who had remained loyal to him". See verse 27. The expression, "which (the Philistines) are ashamed of thy lewd way", indicates the depths to which Jerusalem had descended.

ii) Friendship with Assyria, v.28. "Thou hast played the whore also with the Assyrians, because thou wast unsatiable; yea, thou hast played the harlot with them, and yet couldest not be satisfied." Alliances with Assyria are well-documented. See, for example, Isaiah 7 verse 20.

iii) Friendship with Chaldea, v.29. "Thou hast, moreover, multiplied thy fornication in the land of Canaan unto Chaldea, and yet thou wast not satisfied herewith."

c) Her initiative, vv.30-34

"How weak is thy heart, saith the Lord Jehovah, seeing thou doest all these [things], the work of whorish woman, under no restraint in that thou buildest thy place of debauchery at the head of every way, and makest thy high place in every street! And thou hast not been as a harlot, in that thou scornest reward, O adulterous wife, that taketh strangers instead of her husband" (vv.30-32, JND). "Indeed, Ezekiel goes for far as to say that no-one solicited her, but that she did the soliciting and actually bribed men to come to her (vv.33-34)" (J.B.Taylor). He continues: "Ellison well comments: 'The adulteress may by some be excused by the strength of passion and blind love, but for a harlot there is no excuse except that of stark necessity. But for Israel there is not even this excuse. She has not been paid by her lovers, but has paid those that have taken their pleasure of her' (cf. Hosea 8: 9)".

3) JERUSALEM'S COMING JUDGMENT, vv.35-52

This section of the oracle is in two parts: *(a)* her judgment is described (vv.35-43); *(b)* her judgment is deserved (vv.44-52).

a) Her judgment described, vv.35-43

The nations (vv.26-29) with whom Israel had committed spiritual immorality - and others (v.27) - would be used by God to execute judgment on Jerusalem, not to extinguish her, but to purge her of idolatry. We must therefore notice: *(i)* the execution of coming judgment (vv.35-41); *(ii)* the result of coming judgment (vv.41-43).

i) **The execution of coming judgment, vv.35-41.** These verses speak for themselves. "Wherefore, O harlot, hear the word of the LORD: Thus saith the Lord GOD, Because thy filthiness was poured out, and thy nakedness discovered through thy whoredoms with thy lovers, and with all the idols of thy abominations, and by the blood of thy children, which thou didst give unto them; Behold, therefore, *I will gather* all thy lovers, with whom thou hast taken pleasure, and all of them that thou hast loved, with all them that thou hast hated: *I will even gather them* round about against thee, and will discover thy nakedness unto them, that they may see all thy nakedness. And I will judge thee, as women that break wedlock, and shed blood, are judged: and I will give thee blood in fury and jealousy. And I will also give thee into their hand, and they shall throw down thy eminent place, and shall break down thy high places: they shall strip thee also of thy clothes, and shall take thy fair jewels, and leave thee naked and bare. They shall also bring up a company against thee, and they shall stone thee with stones, and thrust thee through with their swords. And they shall burn thy houses with fire, and execute judgments upon thee in the sight of many women." J.B.Taylor comments on the above, as follows: "Because Israel had courted the favours of heathen kingdoms and bribed them for support in times of national emergency and because she was sold on every kind of pagan practice and willingly absorbed foreign cults as the whim took her, God pronounces His unmistakable word of judgment upon her. Maintaining the language of the allegory, He promises that Israel's own lovers will be the agents of her devastation. They will surround her and expose her publicly (v.37) and inflict upon her the punishment due to adulteresses and infanticides (v.38). This applies well to the ravages of Babylonian armies under Nebuchadnezzar, but Ezekiel 25 castigates the Ammonites, the Moabites, the Edomites, and the Philistines also for their part in the total overthrow, so the words 'all thy lovers' (v.37) are truer than would first appear".

ii) The result of coming judgment, vv.41-43. The purpose of the predicted judgment is her cleansing from idolatry. We know from later chapters (see, for example, 36: 16-38) that divine judgment - for God must judge sin - is preparatory for divine blessing, not because Israel deserves it, but because God will vindicate His own name (36: 21-22). The Lord now says: "I will cause thee *to cease* from playing the harlot, and thou also shalt give *no hire any more.* So will I make *my fury toward thee to rest,* and my *jealousy shall depart from thee, and I will be quiet, and will no more be angry.* Because thou hast *not remembered the days of thy youth,* but hast fretted me ('raged against me', JND) in all these things; behold, therefore, I will also recompense thy way upon thine head, saith the Lord God; and thou *shalt not commit* this lewdness above (besides, JND) all thine abominations".

b) Her judgment deserved, vv.44-52

J.B.Taylor and H.L.Ellison refer to these verses as a 'new allegory'. The section is introduced with the proverb, "As is the mother, so is her daughter" (v.44). The following verse is not easily understood: "Thou (Jerusalem) art thy mother's daughter, that lotheth her husband and her children; and thou art the sister of thy sisters, which lothed their husbands and their children: your mother was an Hittite, and your father an Amorite (see v.3 with explanation)" (v.45).

The expression, "that lotheth her husband and her children" is understandable in relation to Jerusalem. As J.B.Taylor observes, in this case "the husband was Jehovah (Taylor uses the name *Yahweh*), see also Hosea. 2 verse 16, whom they had rejected by their proud and idolatrous ways, and the children were those whom they had sacrificed at heathen altars". In this, Jerusalem had followed the example of her Hittite mother (verses 44-45) and of her two sisters, Samaria and Sodom with their daughters, referring – it seems – to the surrounding villages. All three women had 'lothed' ('loathed' in modern English) their husbands. If, in the case of Jerusalem, the husband was Jehovah, then He must also be the husband in connection with the other three women. But in what sense? If married women owe allegiance to their husbands then these women, "notwithstanding their heathenism and long course of idolatry, are still regarded as having gone astray from primeval revelation, and proved false to the only true God whom they once had known" (F.Gardiner). See Romans 1 verses 18-23.

John B.Taylor quotes Theodoret here, "He shows by this, that He is not the God of the Jews only, but of Gentiles also; for God once gave oracles to them, before they chose the abominations of idolatry" – something with which F.Gardiner is evidently in full agreement! In summary, Jerusalem, with all her blessings and privileges, alas, was following her mother and her sisters in idolatry.

We then have to ascertain what is meant by, "And thine elder sister is Samaria, she and thy daughters that dwell at thy left hand: and thy younger sister, that dwelleth at thy right hand, is Sodom and her daughters" (v.46). F.Gardiner comes to our rescue again: "The words *elder* and *younger* mean, literally, *greater* and *smaller*. They thus come, like the Latin *major* and *minor*, to be used for *older* and *younger*; but still their original and most common meaning, which should be retained here, is greater and smaller. Chronologically, Sodom was not younger than Jerusalem, nor is there evidence that Samaria was older. The terms are to be understood of Samaria as the capital of the far larger northern kingdom, and of Sodom as a single city of no great population. The orientals, in describing geographic positions, considered themselves as facing the east, and hence Samaria at the north as on the left, and Sodom on the right. Sodom is spoken of poetically as if still in existence. They were both the spiritual sisters of Jerusalem, just as all alike were daughters of the Amorite and Hittite".

The balance of the section is devastating clear (for Jerusalem): even

CHAPTER 16

though Jerusalem's sisters "were in their day a byword for complacent prosperity and pride (Sodom, vv.49-50), and religious abominations of every kind (Samaria, v.51), Judah's sins have outstripped theirs both in number and intensity (v.52). In so doing Judah is said to have *justified* her sisters (v.52; AV, RV), or better, made your sisters appear righteous (RSV)" (J.B.Taylor). Here is the whole passage: "Yet hast thou not walked after their ways, nor done after their abominations; but, as if that were a very little thing, thou wast corrupted *more than they* in all thy ways. As I live, saith the Lord GOD, Sodom thy sister hath not done, she nor her daughters (probably referring to the surrounding villages), as thou hast done, thou and thy daughters (ditto). Behold, this was the iniquity of thy sister Sodom, pride, fullness of bread, and abundance of idleness, was in her and in her daughters, neither did she strengthen the hand of the poor and needy. And they were haughty, and committed abomination before me: therefore I took them away as I saw good. Neither hath Samaria committed half thy sins; but thou hast multiplied thine abominations more than they, and hast justified thy sisters in all thine abominations which thou hast done. Thou also, which hast judged thy sisters, bear thine own shame for thy sins that thou hast committed more abominable than they: they are more righteous than thou; yea, be thou confounded also, and bear thy shame, in that thou hast justified thy sisters" (vv.47-52).

In this connection we should compare the Lord's condemnation of Capernaum: "And thou, Capernaum, which art exalted to heaven, shalt be brought down to hell: for if the mighty works which have been done in thee had been done in Sodom, it would have remained unto this day. But I say unto you, That it shall be more tolerable for the land of Sodom on the day of judgment, than for thee" (Matt. 11: 23-24).

G.H.Lang (*The Histories and Prophecies of Daniel*) has the following to say about Sodom (vv.49-50): "Deep in the valley of the Jordan, 1,300 feet below sea-level, 4,000 feet lower than the flanking mountains of Moab and Judah, the Sodomites lived in the most tropical climate that men inhabit. The deep cleft conserved the rays and heat, the waters of the river and the springs made growth luxuriant and supplies abundant; cultivation was at the minimum; leisure at the maximum; the devil found mischief enough for these idle hands, and 'the men of Sodom were wicked and sinners against the LORD exceedingly' (Gen. 13: 10-13, RV)".

But now we come to an amazing change in the chapter:

EZEKIEL

4) GOD'S COVENANT BLESSING, vv.53-63

These are remarkable verses! They not only speak of a termination in Jerusalem's coming captivity, but also of the end of the captivities of Sodom and Samaria! All three cities are to "return to their former estate" (v.55). This expression, "return to their former estate", explains the meaning of "bring again their captivity". According to J.B.Taylor, "Turn again their captivity" (v.53, RV) should be translated throughout the Old Testament, with RSV, 'restore their fortunes'". The word "captivity" does not necessarily refer to bondage to a foreign power: it has the sense of the reversal of misfortune or disaster. See, for example, Job 42 verse 10, "And the Lord turned again the *captivity* of Job". We should notice:

a) Restoration after disaster, vv.53-57

i)   Jerusalem was unworthy of restoration, vv.53-54. The section commences, not with the restoration of Jerusalem, but of Sodom and Samaria. So: "And I will bring again their captivity, the captivity of Sodom and her daughters, the captivity of Samaria and her daughters, and the captivity of thy captives in the midst of them' (v.53, JND). This is evidently to emphasise how unworthy she was of divine restoration: "that thou mayest bear thy confusion, and mayest be confounded *for all that thou hast done*, in that thou comfortest them" (v.54, JND), that is, made them feel 'more comfortable' in view of Jerusalem's greater sin.

The promised restoration of Sodom certainly has no parallel in Scripture. F.Gardiner suggests that these verses are not actually predicting restoration, but that they emphasise the impossibility of restoration. He continues by stating that so far as Sodom was concerned, a "return to the former estate, that is, a state of happiness and prosperity ... was manifestly impossible; and even in the case of Samaria it would, if accomplished, lack any historical identification". It is difficult, however, to square Gardiner's argument with the actual passage, and C.L.Feinberg's suggestion is far more acceptable: "The passage does not refer to those sinners who will endure eternal fire (Jude 7); it is not treating the restitution of the wicked dead. Ezekiel was speaking of national restoration and the rebuilding of these cites in the millennium ... the restoration of Sodom will pose no difficulty for the omnipotence of God".

ii)   Jerusalem would be completely restored, v.55. "When thy sisters, Sodom and her daughters, shall return to their former estate, and Samaria and her daughters shall return to their former estate, then thou and thy daughters shall return to your former estate." Once again, Sodom and Samaria are placed before Jerusalem in order of mention. This is not without significance. See comments above.

iii) Jerusalem had ignored the lesson of Sodom, vv.56-57. "For thy sister Sodom was not mentioned by thy mouth ('not a lesson in thy mouth', JND margin) in the day of thy pride, before thy wickedness was discovered …". The sense of "thy wickedness was discovered" is evidently the revealing of her wickedness "at the time of thy reproach of the daughters of Syria, and all that are round about her, the daughters of the Philistines, which despise thee round about".

b) Renewal of the covenant, vv.58-63

As J.B.Taylor points out, these verses "presuppose the fall of Jerusalem". Hence, "Thou hast born thy lewdness and thine abominations" (v.58). But this does ***not*** mean, according to H.L.Ellison, that the section was written ***after*** that event. J.B.Taylor is right in saying, "We have already seen that many oracles of doom contained a clear ray of hope and there is surely no inconsistency in allowing a similar gleam here".

i) They had broken the covenant, vv.58-59. "Thou hast born thy lewdness and thine abominations, saith the LORD. For thus saith the Lord GOD, I will even deal with thee as thou hast done, which despised the oath in breaking the covenant." Her unfaithfulness would incur judgment.

ii) He would renew the covenant, vv.60-63. "Nevertheless, I will remember my covenant with thee in the days of thy youth, and will establish unto thee an everlasting covenant … and I will establish my covenant with thee; and thou shalt know that I am the LORD" (vv.60, 62).

At that future time, the fact that her restoration would be accompanied by the restoration of her "sisters", would remind her of past "ways" (see v.47). She would not be allowed to forget her shameful past. Whilst she would be given supremacy over her "sisters, thine elder and thy younger" (v.61), this would not be "by virtue of thy covenant" (JND). It would be "an act of God's goodness in no way depending on former relations" (A.B.Davidson).

They would never be allowed to forget this: "That thou mayest remember, and be confounded, and never open thy mouth any more because of thy shame ..." (v.63). As J.B.Taylor observes, "Not even the justified sinner should forget that he has a past of which he is right to be ashamed".

iii) ***The basis of the covenant, v.63***. This is most significant. "When I forgive thee (footnote: 'Literally, make atonement for') all that thou hast done, saith the Lord Jehovah" (JND). ***This is always the basis of God's dealings with His people.***

EZEKIEL CHAPTER 17

This chapter gives yet another reason for the imminent judgment on Judah and Jerusalem. As we have repeatedly noted, Ezekiel 13-17 deal extensively with the reasons for coming judgment as follows: *(1) untruthful prophets (ch.13)*: they had "spoken a lying divination" (v.7); *(2) unseen idolatry (ch.14)*: "these men have set up their idols in their heart" (v.3); *(3) the useless vine (ch.15)*: "Shall wood be taken thereof to do any work? or will men take a pin of it to hang any vessel thereon?" (v.3); *(4) the unfaithful wife (ch.16)*: "thou (Jerusalem) didst trust in thine own beauty, and playedst the harlot because of thy renown" (v.15); *(5) unreliable promises (ch.17)*: "As I live, surely mine oath that he hath despised, and my covenant that he hath broken, even it will I recompense upon his own head" (v.19).

Having already dealt with the first four of the above, we come now to:

5) The unreliable promises, Chapter 17

Each of these chapters (chs.13-18) commences in the same way: "And the word of the LORD came unto me, saying ..." (13: 1; 14: 2; 15: 1; 16: 1; 17: 1; 18: 1). This cannot be over-emphasised. Our mandate today is to "preach the word; be instant in season, out of season" (2 Tim. 4: 2). Unlike the prophets in Old and New Testaments, through whom God spoke directly (for the latter, see 1 Corinthians 14: 29-30), our business today is to draw attention to what God says in His Word. It is a case of, "what saith the scripture?" (Rom. 4: 3), and our authority is no less than that of the men who said, "The word of the LORD came unto me saying ..."

The reason for coming judgment given in this chapter is quite different from those already given. We are so thankful that the scriptures are self-interpreting (one passage throws light upon another), and the information we need in order to understand Ezekiel 17 is found in 2 Chronicles 36. The last king of Judah was Zedekiah. Judah was already under the heel of Nebuchadnezzar, and Zedekiah, having sworn loyalty to Nebuchadnezzar, reneged on his promise: "Zedekiah ... rebelled against king Nebuchadnezzar, who had made him swear by God: but he stiffened his neck, and hardened his heart from turning unto the LORD God of Israel", and turned to Egypt (2 Chron. 36: 11-13). The rebellion in question was undoubtedly the appeal by Zedekiah to Egypt for help cited by Ezekiel; "But he (Zedekiah, called 'the king's seed', v.13) rebelled against him ('the king of Babylon' v.12) in sending his ambassadors into Egypt, that they might give him horses and much people" (Ezek. 17: 15). H.L.Ellison calls this, 'The treacherous folly of Zedekiah'.

The chronicler (possibly Ezra) carefully states that Nebuchadnezzar made Zedekiah "**swear by God**" (2 Chron. 36: 13) and Ezekiel now refers to this: "Seeing he despised the oath by breaking the covenant, when, lo, he had given his hand, and hath done all these things, he shall not escape. Therefore thus saith the Lord GOD; As I live, surely **mine** oath, that he hath despised, and **my** covenant that he hath broken, even it will I recompense upon his own head" (vv.18-19).

There was, therefore, an aspect of Zedekiah's conduct even more serious than rebellion against Nebuchadnezzar. In citing the name of the Lord when swearing allegiance to the king of Babylon, Zedekiah had broken the third commandment: "Thou shalt not take the name of the LORD thy God in vain; for the LORD will not hold him guiltless that taketh his name in vain" (Exodus 20: 7). All this stands in direct contrast to the way in which God commends the patriarchs and others: "These all died in faith ... wherefore God is not ashamed to be called their God: for he hath prepared for them a city" (Heb. 11: 13-16).

Zedekiah was not 'a man of his word', reminding us that our pledges and promises should reflect the character of God himself. Paul puts it like this: "But **as God is true**, our word toward you was not yea and nay (that is, marked by uncertainty), for the Son of God, Jesus Christ, who was preached among you by us ... was **not** yea and nay, **but** in him was yea (absolute certainty). For **all the promises of God in him are yea, and in him Amen**, unto the glory of God by us" (2 Cor. 1: 18-20). Paul's promises and Paul's preaching had the character of God whom he served, and the character of the word of God that he preached.

Perhaps we should take this further. Whilst vows are not specifically required of us - they are voluntary in Scripture - none the less we **do** make promises to God. Who among us has not sung, "O Jesus, I have **promised** to serve

Thee to the end"? We must be people of our word - Godward as well as manward. Solomon addresses this as follows: "When thou vowest a vow unto God, defer not to pay it; for he hath no pleasure in fools: pay that which thou hast vowed. Better is it that thou shouldest not vow (Jephthah must have wished he hadn't vowed: see Judges 11: 30-31, 34-35), than that thou shouldest vow and not pay. Suffer not thy mouth to cause thy flesh to sin; neither say thou before the angel, that it was an error: wherefore should God be angry at thy voice, and destroy the work of thy hands?" (Eccl. 5: 4-6). We ought to act honourably before God, and before men. Not like some modern salesmen who evidently make promises that they know cannot possibly be fulfilled. It is dishonouring to God to make promises that we cannot fulfil. "In the multitude of words there wanteth not sin: but he that refraineth his lips is wise" (Prov. 10: 19). How tragic if we have to say when called to account, "It was an error". As an aside, "the angel" (Eccl. 5: 6), literally 'messenger', is either a messenger from the temple, or more likely, the priest himself. See Malachi 2 verse 7, "he (the priest) is the *messenger* of the LORD of hosts".

The chapter clearly divides into two major sections: *(1)* the parable of the eagles (vv.1-21); *(2)* the parable of the cedar (vv.22-24). The first concerns the end of the monarchy: it deals with the last kings of Judah. The second concerns the re-establishing of the monarchy, with the advent of Israel's Messiah.

1) THE PARABLE OF THE EAGLES, vv.1-21

The end of the monarchy

"And the word of the LORD came unto me, saying, Son of man, put forth a riddle, and speak a parable unto the house of Israel" (vv.1, 2). According to J.B.Taylor, a "riddle" means "anything put enigmatically and requiring explanation, and an allegory (AV 'parable') is the same word translated 'proverb' in Ezekiel 12 verse 22". This section of the chapter clearly divides into two sections *(a)* the parable itself (vv.1-10); *(b)* the parable interpreted (vv.11-21). Both sections are introduced by the words: "The word of the LORD came unto me, saying ..." (vv.1, 11).

a) The parable itself, vv.1-10

The parable describes two eagles as follows: *(i)* "a great eagle" (vv.3-6); *(ii)* "another great eagle" (vv.7-10).

- *"A great eagle", vv.3-6.* In view of the fact that the explanation follows, we will quote the text, without comment. It has been said that some people read commentaries without turning to their Bibles and reading the references. These notes are deliberately written with the text included. It really is most important to have the **Word of God before us** when we read Christian magazines and commentaries. Here is the text: "Thus saith the Lord GOD, A great eagle with great wings, long-winged, full of feathers, which had divers colours, came unto Lebanon, and took the highest branch of the cedar: he cropped off the top of his young twigs, and carried it into a land of traffic; he set it in a city of merchants. He took also of the seed of the land, and planted it in a fruitful field; he placed it by great waters, and set it as a willow tree. And it grew and became a spreading vine of low stature, whose branches turned towards him. And the roots thereof were under him: so it became a vine, and brought forth branches, and shot forth sprigs".

- *"Another great eagle", vv.7-10.* Once again, and for the same reason, here is the text: "There was also another great eagle with great wings and many feathers; and, behold, this vine did bend her roots toward him, and shot forth her branches toward him, that he might water it by the furrows of her plantation. It was planted in a good soil by great waters, that it might bring forth branches, and that it might bear fruit, that it might be a goodly vine" (vv.7-8).

But expectations were *not* fulfilled. The "vine" bent her roots toward him, and shot forth her branches toward him" *in vain.* "Say thou, Thus saith the Lord GOD, Shall it prosper? Shall he not pull up the roots thereof, and cut off the fruit thereof, that it wither? it shall wither in all the leaves of her spring, even without great power, or many people to pluck it up by the roots thereof. Yea, behold, being planted, shall it prosper? shall it not utterly wither, when the east wind toucheth it? it shall wither in the furrows where it grew" (vv.9-10).

b) The parable interpreted, vv.11-21

"Moreover, the word of the LORD came unto me, saying, Say now to the rebellious house, Know ye not what these things mean? Tell them ..." (vv.11-12). The explanation identifies first eagle (vv.3-6) as Nebuchadnezzar (vv.12-15), and the second eagle (vv.7-10) as Egypt (vv.15-21).

CHAPTER 17

i) The first eagle, vv.12-15

We should notice the following:

- The **"great eagle with great wings"** (v.3) is Nebuchadnezzar: "Tell them, Behold, the **king of Babylon** is come to Jerusalem" (v.12). Compare Daniel 7 verse 4, "The first (that is, the first of the four beasts described in the chapter) was like a lion, and had eagle's wings". H.L.Ellison points out that likening Nebuchnezzar to an eagle is "symbolic of the speed of the conqueror (Jeremiah 48 verse 40 and 49 verse 22)". F.Gardiner (*Ellicott's Commentary*) refers to the same passages in saying, "Nebuchadnezzar is compared to an eagle also in Jer. 48: 40; 49: 22; and Cyrus to a bird of prey in Isaiah 46 verse 11. He has great and long wings, because he has already flown victoriously over wide-spread lands; and he is 'full of feathers which had divers colours' (v.3) because he had embraced in his empire a variety of nations differing in languages, manners, and customs".

The words "A great eagle ... came unto Lebanon" (v.3) refer to Nebuchadnezzar's siege of Jerusalem: "Behold, the king of Babylon is come to Jerusalem" (v.12). "Jerusalem is called Lebanon, as in Jeremiah 22 verse 23, because Lebanon is the home of the cedar, and the royal palace in Jerusalem was so rich in cedar as to be called 'the house of the forest of Lebanon' (1 Kings 7: 2)" (F.Gardiner).

- The **"highest branch of the cedar"** (v.4) and **"the top of his young twigs"** (v.5) refer to the king and the nobility of the country (the "cedar" represents either Jerusalem or Judah respectively, or both): "the king of Babylon ... hath taken the king thereof, and the princes thereof, and led them with him to Babylon" (v.12). The details are given in 2 Kings 24 verses 11-14, "And Nebuchadnezzar king of Babylon came against the city, and his servants did besiege it. And Jehoiachin the king of Judah went out to the king of Babylon ... and the king of Babylon took him in the eighth year of his (Nebuchadnezzar's) reign ... And he carried away all Jerusalem, and all the princes, and all the mighty men of valour, even ten thousand captives, and all the craftsmen and smiths". **The "land of traffick"** and the **"city of merchants"** (v.4) are therefore Chaldea and Babylon respectively. Compare Revelation 18 verses 10-19. The words "land of traffic" are, literally, 'a land of Canaan' (referring to merchants or merchandise). Babylon is called "the land of merchants" (Ezek. 16: 29, JND).

- ***The "seed of the land"*** (v.5) is probably a reference to the royal house and to Zedekiah, Jehoiachin's uncle, in particular; "And hath taken of the king's seed, and made covenant with him, and hath taken an oath of him: he hath also taken the mighty of the land" (v.13). This is explained in 2 Kings 24 verses 15-17, "And he (Nebuchadnezzar) carried away Jehoiachin ("the highest branch of the cedar", v.3) to Babylon ... And the king of Babylon made Mattaniah his (Jehoiakim's) brother king in his stead, and changed his name to Zedekiah". The "mighty of the land" (v.13) are "the top of his young twigs" (v.4). Do notice why Nebuchadnezzar took "the mighty of the land": it was that "the kingdom might be base, that it might not lift itself up ..." (vv.13-14), or, in the words of C.L.Feinberg, "the mighty of the land were taken away as hostages, a precautionary measure against a possible revolt." This follows:

- ***The "spreading vine of low stature"*** (vv.5-6) is explained as follows: "And hath taken of the king's seed, and made a covenant with him, and hath taken an oath of him: he hath also taken the mighty of the land that the kingdom might be ***base,*** that it ***might not lift itself up***, but that by keeping of his covenant it might stand" (vv.13-14). The result of removing "the mighty of the land" is given in 2 Kings 24 verse 14: "none remained, save the poorest sort of the people of the land". This was Nebuchadnezzar's objective: reduce Judah to nothing more than a subservient province in the Babylonian empire.

The change from a "cedar" to a "spreading vine of low stature" (see ch.15) is a striking change of metaphor. We move from the stately cedar to a low-growing vine. (The change from a cedar to a willow is equally startling!: see v.5.) Since both figures are usually used of nations rather than individuals, it seems likely that this refers to Judah as a whole. However, the fortunes of Judah were bound up with their king, and J.B.Taylor makes the point that the "spreading vine of low stature" (Zedekiah) had only "limited powers and influence" and was "always dependent on his Babylonian master, and with his *branches turned* in subservience *toward him*". F.Gardiner observes that "This was Nebuchadnezzar's object – to make of Israel a flourishing kingdom, which should yet be entirely dependent upon himself and helpful to him in his great struggle with the power of Egypt; and hence his especial rage when his politic (Gardiner's word) arrangements were frustrated by Zedekiah's treachery and folly". The "good soil by great waters" (v.8) evidently refers to Zedekiah's homeland "in the watered fertile lands of Palestine, the 'land of brooks of water' (Deut. 8: 7; 11: 11), where he was able to grow up in dependence upon Babylon". (J.B.Taylor). This emphasises how unnecessary and unwise it was of him to court the favour of Egypt. But in it all, he was never anything more than a 'low spreading vine'.

ii) The second eagle, vv.15-21

What follows, with Zedekiah 'changing horses in mid-stream', illustrates the New Testament statement that "a double minded man is unstable in all his ways" (James 1: 8).

We should notice the following:

- *The second "great eagle"* (v.7) is Egypt: "But he (Zedekiah) rebelled against him (Nebuchadnezzar, to whom as the 'low spreading vine', Zedekiah had turned in subservience) in sending his ambassadors into Egypt, that they might give him horses and much people" (v.15). Once again, further details are given elsewhere, and in this case Jeremiah 37 verses 1-10 becomes compulsory reading. "Then Pharaoh's army was come forth out of Egypt: and when the Chaldeans that besieged Jerusalem heard tidings of them, they departed from Jerusalem" (Jer. 37: 5). We gather that "an Egyptian force was apparently sent in the direction of Jerusalem, probably in the summer of 588 BC, in response to Zedekiah's overtures, and that the approach of this army caused a temporary lifting of the siege of Jerusalem, which a Babylonian punitive force had already begun in January of the same year (2 Kings 25: 1; Jer. 52: 4). We know nothing of the fate of the Egyptians but we can presume that their efforts were unsuccessful, and possibly only half-hearted as well, because the Chaldean siege was soon renewed for a further year until Jerusalem finally fell in July 587 BC" (J.B.Taylor).

- *The redirection of the " roots"* (v.7) refers to anticipated help from Egypt. With this in mind, the parable becomes clear. The "spreading vine of low stature" which had formerly bent her roots towards Babylon (v.6) now bends her roots towards Egypt (v.7).

This is the time to ask ourselves about the direction of our "roots". It is through its roots that a plant or tree obtains its water and nourishment, and it is through their spiritual roots of communion and fellowship with God that believers gain spiritual nourishment. See Ephesians 3 verse 17 ("being rooted and grounded in love"); Colossians 2 verse 7 ("rooted and built up in him").

Having looked to Babylon for sustenance, Zedekiah turned to Egypt: "this vine did bend her roots toward him, and shot forth her branches toward him, that he might water it by the furrows of her plantation" (v.7). But to no avail. More than that, it proved utterly disastrous. This follows:

- **The destruction of the vine** (vv.9-10) was the result of courting Egypt. The vine would "wither away and be uprooted by the king of Babylon with the greatest ease" (J.B.Taylor). Nebuchadnezzar had planted it "in good soil by great waters, that it might bring forth branches, and that it might bear fruit, that it might be a goodly vine" (v.8), but as a result of Zedekiah's defection, the question is asked. "Shall it prosper? Shall he (Nebuchadnezzar) not pull up its roots, and cut off its fruit thereof, that it may wither? All its fresh sprouting leaves shall wither, even without a great arm and many people to pluck it up by its roots. And behold, being planted, shall it prosper? Shall it not utterly wither when the east wind toucheth it? It shall wither in the beds where it grew" (vv.9-10, JND). Hence we now read, "Shall he prosper? shall he escape that doeth such things? or shall he break the covenant, and be delivered?" (v.15).

The withering and uprooting of the vine, and the reason for this, is set out in verses 16-21: "As I live saith the Lord GOD, surely the place where the king dwelleth that made him king ('verily in the place of the king - Nebuchadnezzar - that made him - Zedekiah - king', JND), whose oath he despised, and whose covenant he brake, even with him, in the midst of Babylon he shall die. Neither shall Pharaoh, with his mighty army and great company, make for him ('do anything for him', JND) in the war, by casting up mounts, and building forts, to cut off many persons: seeing he despised the oath by breaking the covenant, when, lo, he had given his hand, and hath done all these things, he shall not escape. Therefore thus saith the Lord GOD, As I live, surely mine oath that he hath despised, and my covenant that he hath broken, even it will *I* recompense upon his own head. And *I* will spread *my net* upon him, and he shall be taken in *my snare* and *I* will bring him to Babylon, and will plead with him there for his trespass that he hath trespassed against me. And all his fugitives with all his bands shall fall by the sword, and they that remain shall be scattered toward all winds; and ye shall know that *I* the LORD have spoken it". This was duly fulfilled: see 2 Kings 25 verses 1-7.

So far as this chapter is concerned, the most notable feature of the explanation of Zedekiah's downfall is his disregard for a solemn covenant. J.B.Taylor comments as follows: "The implications of this attitude are far-reaching. It indicates that agreements entered into and obligations incurred by worshippers of God are as binding as if they had been made with God in person. What applied in the elemental code of international politics among the small states of the Middle East in the sixth century BC, must surely apply with equal force to international agreements in today's enlightened (Taylor rightly queries his own word here!) world. And what applies to nations must presumably be binding for social and personal relationships as well. The breaking of a treaty, a contract, a promise or any other kind of covenant, involves God as well as the person who is thus aggrieved".

2) THE PARABLE OF THE CEDAR, vv.22-24

The re-establishing of the monarchy

The change of direction in these verses is clearly charted by F.Gardiner: "With verse 21 the explanation of the parable ends. What follows is a distinct Messianic prophecy, which, although couched in the same figurative language, has nothing corresponding to it either in the parable or in its explanation". The hope of Israel was not be found in its deposed king (Jehoiachin) who had been carried off to Babylon (v.4) or in its present king (Zedekiah), who would shortly follow suit, but in even greater humiliating circumstances (v.20). God calls Zedekiah a "profane wicked prince" and continues, "Remove the diadem, and take off the crown ... I will overturn, overturn, overturn it: and it shall be no more, until he come whose right it is; and I will give it to him" (Ezek. 21: 25-27).

As king, Jehoichin was "the highest branch of the cedar" (v.3), but this designation is now given to the future King: "I will also take of the highest branch of the high cedar, and will set it; I will crop off from the top of his (the cedar's) young twigs a tender one, and will plant it upon an high mountain and eminent: in the mountain of the height of Israel will I plant it; and it shall bring forth boughs and bear fruit, and be a goodly cedar" (vv.22-23). As H.L.Ellison observes, "It was not the transplanted cedar twig (v.4) that was to be replanted in 'the mountain of the height of Israel' (Zion), but another twig altogether, not taken from the twig growing in exile, but from the parent tree".

It has been nicely said that "This time it is the Lord God who takes action. After the failure of the two great eagles to make a success of establishing the state of Israel under their extensive and powerful patronage, God says, *I myself* (emphatic) *will plant it* upon a high mountain where it will grow and be conspicuous and attract the birds of the air to shelter under its protection"

(J.B.Taylor). F.Gardiner concurs: "Now God Himself directly interposes, and takes a scion of the same 'high cedar', the royal house of David. In accordance with the allegory, this can only be a historical personage, and from the description that follows, this person can only be the Messiah". He is described as "a tender one", and "this epithet is used of the Messiah in reference to His immediate human origin and condition" (F.Gardiner). Compare Isaiah 11 verse 1, "And there shall come forth a rod out of the stem of Jesse, and a Branch shall grow out of his roots" or, "And there shall come forth a shoot out of the stock of Jesse, and a branch out of his roots shall bear fruit" (RV); Isaiah 53 verse 2, "he shall grow up before him as a tender plant, and as a root out of dry ground".

We should notice the complete reversal of Israel's position in the world when God's king sits on His "holy hill of Zion" (Psalm 2: 6). His people will no longer be subject to such powerful nations like Babylon and Egypt ("the high tree ... the green tree", v.24). They will all be "brought down" and "dried up" (v.24). To the contrary, the "low tree ... the dry tree" (Israel) will flourish. It will be universal in extent, and the nations of the world will benefit:

"Under it shall dwell all fowl of every wing; in the shadow of the branches shall they dwell. And all the trees of the field shall know that I the LORD have brought down the high tree, have exalted the low tree, have dried up the green tree, and have made the dry tree to flourish: I the LORD have spoken, and have done it" (vv.23-24). Then Psalm 96 verses 12-13 will be fulfilled: "Let the field be joyful, and all that is therein: then shall all the trees of the wood rejoice before the LORD: for he cometh, for he cometh to judge the earth: he shall judge the world in righteousness, and his people with truth".

Once Babylon had the distinction of being a tree with world-wide influence (see Daniel 4: 20-22) but only as long as God allowed, and Nebuchadnezzar had to learn that "God resisteth the proud, and giveth grace to the humble" (1 Pet. 5: 5). The Lord Jesus "humbled himself, and became obedient unto death, even the death of the cross", in consequence of which "God also hath highly exalted him, and given him a name which is above every name: that at the name of Jesus, **every knee** should bow, of things in heaven, and things in earth, and things under the earth; and that **every tongue** should confess that Jesus Christ is Lord, to the glory of God the Father" (Phil. 2: 8-11). Nebuchadnezzar's kingdom will be totally eclipsed by Christ's kingdom, as will all kingdoms of this world.

CHAPTER 17

Addendum

H.L.Ellison has a thought-provoking 'sting in the tail' in his comments on this chapter. "If the passage is Messianic (hopefully he means the 'if' of argument, not of doubt), then the ... birds must represent the nations of the world that come to the Messianic king (cf. Isaiah 2: 2ff). This being so, we do well not to accept without due thought the interpretation of the parable of the mustard seed (Mark 4: 30-32) which demands that the birds that come and lodge in the branches of the mustard plant must of necessity be symbols of something evil". He adds, "This view has recently found eloquent re-affirmation in Lang (he refers to G.H.Lang): *'Pictures and Parables'*, pp 87-92".

However, if we are to be consistent with other references in the parables of the kingdom, "the fowls of the air" (see, for example, Mark 4: 4, 15) point in another direction. They refer to "Satan" or "the wicked one" (Matt.13: 19). As W.Graham Scroggie *(A Guide to the Gospels)* rightly observes, "it may be laid down as a principle of interpretation that figures of speech are used consistently in discourse". We rest our case.

EZEKIEL CHAPTER 18

Ezekiel 8-19 deal with the reasons for the imminent judgment on Judah and Jerusalem. The justice of pending judgment is made perfectly clear in the **vision** given **to** Ezekiel (chs. 8-11), which ends with the withdrawal of the glory of the Lord from the temple (11: 22-23), and in the **visible** (ch.12) and **verbal** (ch.13-19) messages given **by** Ezekiel.The visible and verbal messages may be summarised as follows: *(i)* pictures of coming judgment (ch.12); *(ii)* reasons for coming judgment (chs.13-17); *(iii)* objections to coming judgment (ch.18); *(iv)* lamentation over coming judgment (ch.19).

Chapter 18 is rather different from preceding chapters. It deals, as noted above, with objections to coming judgment:

- "*What mean ye*, that ye use this proverb concerning the land of Israel, saying, The fathers have eaten sour grapes, and the children's teeth are set on edge ('blunted', C.L.Feinberg)?" (v.2).

- "*Yet say ye, Why?* doth not the son bear the iniquity of the father?" (v.19).

- "*Yet ye say*, The way of the LORD is not equal" (v.25);

- "*Yet saith the house of Israel*, The way of the LORD is not equal" (v.29).

The chapter falls into three major sections:

- *God's judgment is perfectly righteousness. (vv.1-20)*: "If a man be just, and do that which is lawful and right ... he shall surely live, saith the Lord GOD" (vv.5-9); "If he beget a son that is a robber, a shedder of blood ... He shall surely die; his blood shall be upon him" (vv.10-13); "Now, lo, if he beget a son, that seeth all his father's sins which he hath done, and considereth, and doeth not such like ... he shall not die for the iniquity of his father, he shall surely live" (vv.14-18).

CHAPTER 18

- *God takes into account changed lives (vv.21-29)*: "But if the wicked will turn from all his sins that he hath committed, and keep all my statutes ... he shall surely live, he shall not die" (vv.21-23); "But when the righteous turneth away from his righteousness, and committeth iniquity, and doeth according to all the abominations that the wicked man doeth, shall he live? ... in them shall he die" (v.24).

- *God appeals for repentance (vv.30-32)*: "Repent ... cast away from you all your transgressions ... turn yourselves, and live ye".

1) GOD'S JUDGMENT IS PERFECTLY RIGHTEOUS, vv.1-20

Attention is drawn to *(a)* the objection (v.2); *(b)* the answer (vv.3-20) with the conclusion, "The soul that sinneth, it shall die. The son shall not bear the iniquity of the father, neither shall the father bear the iniquity of the son" (v.20).

a) The objection, v.2

"The word of the LORD came unto me again, saying, What mean ye, that ye use this proverb concerning the land of Israel, saying, The fathers have eaten sour grapes, and the children's teeth are set on edge" (vv.1-2). This is not the only place in the Bible where the proverb is quoted: see Jeremiah 31 verses 29-30, "In those days they shall say no more, The fathers have eaten a sour grape, and the children's teeth are set on edge. But every one shall die for his own iniquity: every man that eateth the sour grape, his teeth shall be set on edge". The principal difference between the two passages is that Jeremiah anticipates what *will* happen ("in those days") whereas Ezekiel insists that the proverb should not be used forthwith. The proverb was a complaint that the current generation of Israelites, believing themselves to be innocent, were reaping the misdeeds of their forefathers, and that this was totally unjust.

The people's objection is difficult to understand in view of the principle clearly enunciated by Moses, "The fathers shall *not* be put to death for the children, neither shall the children be put to death for the fathers: every man shall be put to death for his own sin" (Deut. 24: 16), and it has been suggested that this misunderstanding arose from a wrong interpretation of Exodus 20 verses 5-6, "I the LORD thy God am a jealous God, visiting the iniquity of the fathers upon the children unto the third and fourth generations of them that hate me ..." This refers to cumulative guilt: those who practise the sins of past generations face divine judgment, not only because of their own guilt, but because that in doing so they ignore the guilt of their predecessors. God will visit "the iniquity of the fathers upon the children unto the third and fourth generations of them *that hate me*". The children are doubly guilty – guilty because of their own sin, and guilty because they have ignored the sins of their fathers. (See also 2 Kings 21: 10-14.) But in Ezekiel 18, the Lord emphasises the personal guilt of the people, leading F.A.Tatford to entitle the chapter 'Personal Responsibility'.

Perhaps we should say at this juncture that we are all personally responsible to God. We can all too easily blame other people, or blame our circumstances, when things go wrong. Sometimes, things start to deteriorate in assembly life, and good men, forgetting their responsibility to "earnestly contend for the faith" (Jude v.3), stay silent. Sometimes, the testimony weakens, and we forget our own responsibility to "strengthen the things which remain, that are ready to die" (Rev. 3: 2).

b) *The answer, vv.3-20*

Having quoted their proverb, the Lord answers their objection by saying, "As I live, saith the Lord GOD, ye shall not have occasion any more to use this proverb in Israel. Behold, all souls are mine; as the soul of the father, so also the soul of the son is mine: *the soul that sinneth it shall die*" (vv.3-4). He then illustrates this in verses 5-19, and concludes by restating their objection (turning from the proverbial to the factual), "Yet ye say ... doth not the son bear the iniquity of the father?" (v.19), and continues, "***The soul that sinneth, it shall die***. The son shall not bear the iniquity of the father, neither shall the father bear the iniquity of the son: the righteousness of the righteous shall be upon him, and the wickedness of the wicked shall be upon him" (v.20). The intervening verses (vv.5-19) establish beyond question that He deals righteously with His people. We should notice:

i) **That the Lord deals with men and women individually**. "Behold, all souls (meaning 'lives') are mine; as the soul of the father, so also the soul of the son is mine" (v.4). In the words of John B.Taylor: "In God's eyes people are individuals and He treats them as such. Every man is a matter of concern to Him".

This does not mean that the nation corporately was *not* coming under divine judgment because of its "accumulating acts of disobedience". While, as we

CHAPTER 18

have noted, there was certainly a sense in which the current generation *was* suffering because of the sins of the fathers, this did not exonerate the current generation from blame. As J.B.Taylor rightly observes, "far from their having cause to blame their sinful forebears for the present sufferings, the exiles were more guilty than their fathers because they had sinned more and their idolatries were greater (see Chapter 8)". This is made very clear in Jeremiah 16 verses 11-12: "your fathers have forsaken me ... and ye have done worse than your fathers". But in our current verses, God refers to His dealings with men and women individually. The chapter concludes on a similar note: "I will judge you, O house of Israel, *every man according to his ways*, saith the Lord GOD" (v.30).

ii) *That this is now illustrated by instancing three generations.* It has been suggested that the Lord has in mind *(a)* Hezekiah (vv.5-9), *(b)* Manasseh his son (vv.10-13), and *(c)* Josiah his great grandson (vv.14-18). For the purpose of our study, we will assume that this suggestion is correct. So:

- **Hezekiah, vv.5-9.** We will call him 'the first generation'. "But if a man be just, and do that which is lawful and right, and hath not eaten upon the mountains, neither hath lifted up his eyes to the idols of the house of Israel, neither hath defiled his neighbour's wife, neither hath come near to a menstruous women, and hath not oppressed any, but hath restored to the debtor his pledge, hath spoiled none by violence, hath given his bread to the hungry, and hath covered the naked with a garment; he that hath not given forth upon usury, neither hath taken any increase, that hath withdrawn his hand from iniquity, hath executed true judgment between man and man, hath walked in my statutes, and hath kept my judgments, to deal truly; he is just, he shall surely live, saith the Lord GOD." There is no need to expand these verses: they are quite self-explanatory.

It is said of Hezekiah that he "wrought that which was good and right and truth before the LORD his God. And in every work that he began in the service of the house of God, and in the law, and in the commandments to seek his God, he did with all his heart, and prospered" (2 Chron. 31: 20-21). Even if Ezekiel is *not* referring specifically to Hezekiah, the fact remains that he certainly provides a good example of the point in these verses!

The words, "he shall surely live" (v.9) together with "he shall surely die" (v.13) evidently refer to "what will take place in the judgment which is imminent"

(J.B.Taylor). This chapter cannot be used to support the suggestion that a person can be saved and then lost. It has particular reference to the coming judgment on Jerusalem and Judah. "The judgment will fall upon each man as it finds him" (J.B.Taylor). As C.L.Feinberg points out, "The judgments ... here are temporal judgments, and the death dealt with is physical death ... Ezekiel was doubtless speaking of suffering punishment, which is experiencing the wrath of God by being deprived of physical life. Life is used to mean continuance in the world, and death means removal from it". Lamar E. Cooper makes the thought-provoking statement that Ezekiel is "not discussing the issue of being lost or saved, but how all people, lost and saved alike, can avert the judgment of God for sin".

- **Manasseh, v.10-13.** We will call him 'the second generation'. "If he beget a son that is a robber, a shedder of blood, and that doeth the like to any one of these things, and that doeth not any of these duties, but even hath eaten upon the mountains, and defiled his neighbour's wife, hath oppressed the poor and needy, hath spoiled by violence, and not restored the pledge, and hath lifted up his eyes to the idols, hath committed abomination, hath given forth upon usury, and hath taken increase: shall he then live? He shall not live: he hath done all these abominations; he shall surely die; his blood shall be upon him."

It is said of Manasseh that he "did that which is evil in the sight of the LORD, like unto the abominations of the heathen, whom the LORD has cast out before the children of Israel" (2 Chron. 33: 2). However, we do have to say that he did turn to God from his wickedness, and became a splendid example of verses 21-23 and verses 27-28! Leaving this aside, it is very clear from Manasseh's early days that he could not "possibly claim the merits of his father's godly life" (C.L.Feinberg). Feinberg continues: "God is surely impartial: He will not lay to the charge of children the misdeeds of parents: but conversely He will not lay to their credit the godly conduct of parents when they themselves scorn every righteous precept of the Lord".

- **Josiah, vv.14-18.** We will call him 'the third generation'. "Now, lo, if he beget a son, that seeth all his father's sins which he hath done, and considereth, and doeth not such like, that hath not eaten upon the mountains, neither hath lifted up his eyes to the idols of the house of Israel, hath not defiled his neighbour's wife, neither hath oppressed any, hath not withholden the pledge, neither hath spoiled by violence, but hath given his bread to the hungry, and hath covered the naked with a garment, that hath taken off his hand from the poor, that hath not received usury nor increase, hath executed my judgments, hath walked in my statutes; he shall not die for the iniquity of his father, lo, he shall surely live" (vv.14-17).

To emphasise the point - that each individual is personally responsible to God for their actions - Ezekiel adds: "As for his father, because he cruelly oppressed, spoiled his brother by violence, and did that which is not good among his people, lo, even he shall die in his iniquity" (v.18).

Josiah was certainly not like his father. Amon "did that which was evil in the sight of the LORD" (2 Chron. 33: 22). But of Josiah it is said, "he did that which was right in the sight of the LORD, and walked in the ways of David his father, and declined neither to the right hand, nor to the left" (2 Chron. 34: 2).

These three cases combine to give substance to the conclusion in verses 19-20: "Yet say ye, Why? doth not the son bear the iniquity of the father?", to which God replies, "When the son hath done that which is lawful and right, and hath kept all my statutes, and hath done them, *he shall surely live*. The soul that sinneth, *it shall die*. The son shall not bear the iniquity of the father, neither shall the father bear the iniquity of the son: the righteousness of the righteous shall be upon him, and the wickedness of the wicked shall be upon him". In other words, the use of the proverb, "The fathers have eaten sour grapes, and the children's teeth are set on edge", could not be supported.

All this reminds us that "we must *all* appear before the judgment seat of Christ; that *every one* may receive ('receive back') the things done in his body, according to that he hath done, whether it be good or bad" (2 Cor. 5: 10), and "every one of us shall give account (not just '*an* account' but a *full* account) of himself to God" (Rom. 14: 12).

2) GOD TAKES INTO ACCOUNT CHANGED LIVES, vv.21-29

In this section of the chapter, God advances on what He has already said. He is not only just, but merciful. He now rebuts a second charge, similar to the first, against Him: "The way of the Lord is not equal" (vv.25, 29). Since He has no "pleasure at all that the wicked should die" (vv.23, 32), He not only pardons those who turn from their wickedness, but urges them to do so (vv.23,30-32). Conversely, since He is righteous, those who turn from righteousness to wickedness will die. "The reference is not to a temporary lapse, but to a persistent choice of evil which changes the course of a man's life" (J.B.Taylor).

The Lord's answer to the charge that His dealings with Israel are "not equal" is given twice (vv.21-25; 26-29). His reference to the "wicked" and the "righteous" (vv.21, 24) is reversed in verses 26 and 27). In both cases, He concludes with the questions, "Is not my way equal? Are not your ways unequal?" (vv.25, 29).

a) The "wicked" and the "righteous, vv.21-25

i) *"If the wicked will turn from all his sins", vv.21-23.* "But if the wicked will turn from all his sins that he hath committed, and keep all my statutes, and do that which is lawful and right, he shall surely live, he shall not die. All his transgressions that he hath committed, they shall not be mentioned unto him: in his righteousness that he hath done he shall live" (vv.21-22).

To which God adds: "Have I any pleasure at all that the wicked should die? Saith the Lord GOD; and not that he should return from his ways, and live?" (v.23). He is "longsuffering ... not willing that any should perish, but that all should come to repentance" (2 Pet. 3: 9).

As we have noted, Manasseh illustrates this: "And when he was in affliction, he besought the LORD his God, and humbled himself greatly before the God of his fathers, and prayed unto him: and he was intreated of him, and heard his supplication, and brought him again to Jerusalem into his kingdom. Then Manasseh knew that the LORD he was God. Now after this he built a wall without the city of David ... And he took away the strange gods ... and all the altars that he had built ... And he repaired the altar of the Lord" (2 Chron. 33: 11-16). It is worth noting that all the good kings in Judah built something, and this applies to Manasseh as well after his restoration.

ii) *"When the righteous turneth away from his righteousness", v.24.*
"But when the righteous turneth away from his righteousness, and committeth iniquity, and doeth according to all the abominations that the wicked man doeth, shall he live? All his righteousness that he hath done shall not be mentioned: in his trespass that he hath trespassed, and in his sin that he sinned, in them he shall die."

In this connection we may think of Joash who turned away from God after the death of Jehoiada (2 Chron. 24: 17-18), and Uzziah who "was marvellously helped, till he was strong. But when he was strong, his heart was lifted up to his destruction: for he transgressed against the LORD his God" (2 Chron. 26: 15-16).

The conclusion follows: "Yet ye say, the way of the Lord is not equal. Hear now, O house of Israel; Is not my way equal? are not your ways unequal?" (v.25). God's mercy towards the repentant sinner, and judgment upon those who turned from righteousness, proclaimed His righteousness and equity. It disproved their accusation, "The way of the Lord is not equal". He was both righteous and merciful: they were totally unrighteous: their ways were "unequal".

This is now repeated (vv.26-29) for emphasis, but in the reverse order. God's judgment on the man who lapses is followed by His mercy towards the man who repents. So:

b) The "righteous" and the "wicked", vv.26-29

i) "When a righteous man turneth away from his righteousness, v.26.
All we need to do is to quote the verse: "When a righteous man turneth away from his righteousness, and committeth iniquity, and dieth in them; for his iniquity that he hath done shall he die". See again, for example, Joash and Uzziah above.

ii) "When the wicked man turneth away from his wickedness, vv.27-28.
"Again, when the wicked man turneth away from his wickedness that he hath committed, and doeth that which is lawful and right, he shall save his soul alive. Because he considereth, and turneth away from all his transgressions that he hath committed, he shall surely live, he shall not die." See again, for example, Manasseh above.

The conclusion follows: "Yet saith the house of Israel, The way of the Lord is not equal. O house of Israel, are not my ways equal? are not your ways unequal?" (v.29.) God's judgment upon those who turned from righteousness, and mercy towards the repentant sinner, proclaimed His righteousness and equity. It disproved their accusation, "The way of the Lord is not equal". He was both righteous and merciful: they were totally unrighteous: their ways were "unequal".

We must remember, in a different connection, that at the judgment seat of Christ, we will all appear before "the righteous judge". Here is the full quotation: "I have fought a good fight, I have finished my course, I have kept the faith: henceforth there is laid up for me a crown of righteousness (a rightly-adjusted crown of reward), which the Lord, the righteous judge, shall give me at that day" (2 Tim. 4: 7-8).

Speaking about the "judgment seat of Christ" (2 Cor. 5: 10), it is worth noticing that the words "judgment seat" (*bema*) denote a raised place or platform from which tribunals were conducted. The word is used of: **Pilate's** judgment seat (Matt. 27: 19); **Herod's** throne (Acts 12: 21); **Gallio's** judgment seat (Acts 18: 12, 16, 17); **Festus'** judgment seat (Acts 25: 6, 17); **Caesar's** judgment seat (Acts 25: 10). In four out of the five cases, judgment was perverted. But this cannot possibly be said about the "judgment seat of Christ": He will be, as noted above, "the *righteous judge"* (2 Tim. 4: 8).

3) GOD APPEALS FOR REPENTANCE, vv.30-32

The chapter concludes with an appeal by God, based upon His willingness to save those who are prepared to turn from their wickedness. We must notice:

i) **His announcement of judgment.** "Therefore I will judge you, O house of Israel, every one according to his ways, saith the Lord GOD" (v.30)

ii) **His appeal for repentance**. "Repent, and turn yourselves from all your transgressions: so iniquity shall not be your ruin. Cast away from you all your transgressions, whereby ye have transgressed; and make you a new heart and a new spirit: for why will ye die, O house of Israel? For I have no pleasure in the death of him that dieth, saith the Lord GOD: wherefore turn yourselves, and live ye" (vv.30-32). Judgment is God's "strange work" (Isaiah 28: 21).

While this provides good material for the gospel preacher who will declare the necessity for "repentance toward God, and faith toward our Lord Jesus Christ" (Acts 20: 21), it also reminds us that Christians sometimes need to repent. For example, the church at Ephesus was urged by the Lord Jesus to "remember therefore from whence thou art fallen, and repent, and do the first works; or else I will come unto thee quickly, and will remove thy candlestick out of his place, except thou repent" (Rev. 2: 5).

Thinking now in terms of gospel preaching, J.B.Taylor rightly reminds us

CHAPTER 18

that "It is the Lord's longing and will and purpose that men should be saved. Such a longing should be shared by every preacher who ventures to speak about the judgment of God".

What God urges His people Israel to do here, "make you a new heart and a new spirit" (v.31), which in the current context refers to a new attitude towards sin, He will do for them in the fullest sense in the future. See Ezekiel 11 verse 19 and 36 verse 26, "A new heart also will I give you, and a new spirit will I put within you..." The believer today already enjoys these blessings.

EZEKIEL CHAPTER 19

With this chapter we come to the end of the second phase of Ezekiel's ministry. This began "in the sixth year, in the sixth month, in the fifth day of the month" (8: 1) and continued for a period of eleven months and five days, until the third phase of his ministry, which commenced in "the seventh year, in the fifth month, the tenth day of the month" (20: 1). As we have noted in past studies, Chapters 1-19 may be summarised as follows: *(i)* the commissioning of Ezekiel (1: 1 - 3: 15); *(ii)* the coming judgment (3: 16 - 7: 27); *(iii)* the contributory causes (8: 1 - 19: 14).

The prophecy of Ezekiel is punctuated by 'time-markers'. The first occurs on the threshold of the book: "Now it came to pass in the thirtieth year" (1: 1), which evidently refers to Ezekiel's age, with the additional information: "which was the fifth year of king Jehoiachin's captivity" (1: 2). The next two 'time-makers' are noted above (8: 1; 20: 1), to be followed by ten more: (See 24: 1; 26: 1; 29: 1; 29: 17; 30: 20; 31: 1; 32: 1; 32: 17; 33: 21; 40: 1.) However, these 'time-markers' do not necessarily divide the book, although it would be very convenient if they did! For example, the 'foreign nations' section of the prophecy (25: 1- 32) commences with the words, "The word of the Lord came again unto me, saying ..." (25: 1), with no reference to any particular year.

Whatever we may conclude about the structure of the book, it does seem clear that Ezekiel 8-19 are a unit in which the Lord gives reasons for the imminent judgment on Judah and Jerusalem. In this connection, we have noted that the Lord deals with this in the *vision* given *to* Ezekiel (chs. 8-11), which ends with the withdrawal of the glory of the Lord from the temple (11: 22-23), and the *visible* (ch.12) and *verbal* (chs.13-19) messages given *by* Ezekiel. These may be summarised as follows: *(i)* pictures of coming judgment (ch.12); *(ii)* reasons for coming judgment (chs.13-17); *(iii)* objections to coming judgment (ch.18); *(iv)* lamentation over coming judgment (ch.19).

CHAPTER 19

The unit therefore closes with "a lamentation" (ch.19), where the first and last verses describe the chapter in this way: "Moreover take thou up a lamentation ... This is a lamentation, and shall be for a lamentation" (vv.1, 14). In particular, it is a lamentation for the royal house. The opening verse intimates this: "Moreover take thou up a lamentation for the **princes of Israel**". It is noteworthy that Ezekiel avoids the word "king" (*melek*) in favour of the more general word "princes" (*nasi*).

John B.Taylor observes that Ezekiel's "zeal for the Davidic covenant ... did not allow him to see three of its inheritors disappear into exile without profound sorrow and emotion. This was no taunt-song. The judgment of the Lord could be very grievous, and Ezekiel felt it keenly". Solomon said, "Rejoice not when thine enemy falleth, and let not thine heart be glad when he stumbleth" (Prov. 24: 17). How much more when God's people stumble and fall! It has been said that "this chapter forms the close of this long series of prophecies, and consists of a lament over the fall of the royal family of Israel, and over the utter desolation of the nation itself. It fitly closes the series of warnings, and takes away any lingering hope of escape from the divine judgments" (F.Gardiner, *Ellicott's Commentary*).

The chapter may clearly be divided into two sections: *(1)* the captivity of the monarchy (vv.2-9); *(2)* the cessation of the monarchy (vv.10-14). In connection with the former, Ezekiel uses the figure of a lioness and her whelps: in connection with the latter, he uses the figure of a vine and its rods. As might be expected, the chapter has been variously interpreted, but it does seem best to see Jehoahaz and Jehoichin in the two "whelps" (vv.2-9), and the demise of the nation under Zedekiah in the destruction and removal of the vine (vv.10-14).

All this is a far cry from the glorious days of Solomon when "Judah and Israel dwelt safely, every man under his vine and under his fig tree, from Dan even to Beer-sheba" (1 Kings 4: 25), and a far cry from even greater glories in the future when, again, "they shall sit every man under his vine and under his fig tree: and none shall make them afraid: for the mouth of the LORD hath spoken it" (Micah 4: 4). Israel will not then be "planted in the wilderness, in a dry and thirsty ground" (v.13), neither will she then be bereft of a king. The last king of Judah, Zedekiah, was a "profane wicked prince of Israel, whose day is come", of whom the Lord said, "Remove the diadem, and take off the crown ... I will overturn, overturn, overturn it: and it shall be no more, *until he come* whose right it is; and I will give it him"

(Ezek. 21: 25-27). The Lord Jesus will sit "upon the throne of David and upon his kingdom, to order it, and to establish it with judgment and with justice from henceforth even for ever" (Isa. 9: 7). (See also Luke 1: 32-33.)

1) THE CAPTIVITY OF THE MONARCHY, vv.2-9

This section is in three parts: *(a)* "she nourished her whelps (v.2); *(b)* "she brought up one of her whelps" (vv.3-4); *(c)* "she took another of her whelps" (vv.5-9). The word "whelps" (*gur*) is self-explanatory. Gesenius puts it rather quaintly: a lion "still sojourning under the care of its mother".

a) The mother of the whelps, v.2

"Moreover, take thou up a lamentation for the princes of Israel, and say, What is thy mother? A lioness: she lay down among lions, she nourished her whelps among young lions." In the first case, Ezekiel uses a word (*aryeh*) which describes "a lion, as if, plucking, tearing abroad ... an image both of strength and of fierceness and cruelty" (Gesenius). In the second, he uses a word (*kephir*) which describes "a young lion already weaned and having begun to ravin" (Gesenius). C.L.Feinberg explains the verse most satisfactorily: "Judah took her place majestically and securely among the nations". F.A.Tatford adds to this: "Judah dwelt fearlessly and securely among the other lions (or nations) as long as they retained their loyalty to Jehovah", and C.L.Feinberg continues: "The whelps were the descendants of the house of David who were exposed to the corrupting influences of the surrounding heathen kings by whom they were nurtured".

The lioness is not Hamutal, the wife of Josiah and mother of Jehoahaz and Zedekiah (2 Kings 23: 31; 24: 18), but **the nation** which mothered these kings. The figure of a lion is used to depict **Judah** nationally in the following passages: "Judah is a lion's (*aryeh*) whelp ... he stooped down, he couched as a lion (*aryeh*), and as an old lion (*labi*); who shall rouse him up?" (Gen. 49: 9); "And the remnant of Jacob shall be among the Gentiles in the midst of many people as a lion (*aryeh*) among the beasts of the forest, as a young lion (*kephir*) among the flocks of sheep" (Mic. 5: 8). See also Numbers 23 verse 24: "Behold the people shall rise up as a great lion (*labi*), and lift up himself as a young lion (*aryeh*)"; Numbers 24 verse 9: "He couched, he lay down as a lion (*aryeh*), and as a great lion (*labi*): who shall stir him up?" In the words of F.Gardiner: "Mother stands for the whole national community, the theocracy, as is plain from verse 10 ("Thy mother is like a vine in thy blood, planted by the waters"). This was represented, since the captivity of the ten tribes, by Judah; and her 'princes', of the line of David, were the legitimate kings of the whole nation".

We must pause to say that the Lord Jesus is "the Lion of the tribe of Judah, the Root of David" (Rev. 5: 5). The last "princes of Israel" prevailed over nothing, but the Lion of the tribe of Judah "prevailed to open the book, and to loose the seven seals thereof". Judah's last princes were overcome, but the Lord Jesus overcame (*nikao*, to conquer, prevail). He prevailed as the Lamb of God (Rev. 5: 6). The book of Revelation makes it clear that He will be known for His death as the Lamb, rather than His power as the Lion! As the "Lion of the tribe of Juda" we have His coming character. As the 'Lamb slain', we see His past triumph, though eternally remembered, and this is His title to act as the Executor of the throne.

b) The first whelp, vv.3-4

"And she brought forth one of her whelps: it became a young lion (*kephir*), and it learned to catch the prey; it devoured men. The nations also heard of him; he was taken in their pit, and they brought him with chains (*chach*: literally 'nose-rings') unto the land of Egypt."

This refers to the captivity of **Jehoahaz**, which had already taken place. See 2 Kings 23 verses 31-34: "Jehoahaz was twenty and three years old when he began to reign; and he reigned three months in Jerusalem ... And he did that which was evil in the sight of the LORD, according to all that his fathers had done. And Pharaoh-nechoh put him in bands at Riblah in the land of Hamath, that he might not reign in Jerusalem ... And Pharaoh-Necho made Eliakim the son of Josiah king in the room of Josiah his father, and turned his name to Jehoiakim, and took Jehoahaz away: and he came to Egypt, and died there". (See also 2 Chron. 36: 1-4.) Jehoahaz is elsewhere known as Shallum (Jer. 22: 10-12).

In view of his age and short-lived reign it might seem a little unexpected to read of his feats: this 'young lion' "learned to catch the prey: it devoured men". However, quite clearly, he quickly demonstrated his wicked nature, and there seems no need to suggest that since he "reigned for only three months ... the description of his renown must be regarded as a poetic transference to express the glory of the Davidic line which Jehoahaz represented" (John B.Taylor). Far younger people have caused mayhem. We should add that

Jehoahaz was evidently a threat to the neighbouring nations (v.4). In New Testament terms, he did not "walk in wisdom toward them that are without" (Col. 4: 5) and did not have "a good report of them which are without" (1 Tim. 3: 7). The lessons for ourselves are clear.

Jehoahaz's successor, Jehoiakim, is not mentioned here by Ezekiel. C.L.Feinberg suggests that he is omitted "because his judgment was not so conspicuous as that of the others (2 Kings 24: 6). He died peacefully". However, he died unlamented, and Jeremiah tells us that he would be "buried with the burial of an ass, drawn and cast forth beyond the gates of Jerusalem" (Jer. 22: 18-19). In other words, he would not be buried at all. This brings us to:

c) *The second whelp, vv.5-9*

"Now when she saw that she had waited, and her hope was lost, then she took another of her whelps, and made him a young lion (*kephir*). And he went up and down among the lions (*aryeh*), he became a young lion (*kephir*), and learned to catch the prey, and devoured men. And he knew their desolate palaces, and he laid waste their cities; and the land was desolate, and the fulness thereof, by the noise of his roaring. Then the nations set against him on every side from the provinces, and spread their net over him: he was taken in their pit. And they put him in ward in chains (*chach,* nose-rings), and brought him to the king of Babylon: they brought him into holds, that his voice should no more be heard upon the mountains of Israel." Like "the whelp" before him, this "young lion" used his youthful energies to bad effect. The description of his destructive powers is somewhat startling! In writing to Timothy, Paul said: "Let no man despise thy youth; but be thou an example of the believers, in word, in conversation, in charity, in spirit, in faith, in purity" (1 Tim .4: 12). This "young lion" certainly did not meet these requirements.

These verses refer, ***not*** to the captivity of Jehoiakim, who was certainly put in chains (2 Chron. 36: 6) but who died in Jerusalem and "slept with his fathers" (2 Kings 24: 6, which does not necessarily mean that he was buried), but to the captivity of his son, **Jehoiachin**. See 2 Kings 24 verses 8-16, "Jehoiachin was eighteen years old when he began to reign, and he reigned in Jerusalem three months ('three months and ten days', 2 Chron. 36: 9) ... And he did that which was evil in the sight of the LORD, according to all that his father (Jehoiakim) had done ... And Nebuchadnezzar king

CHAPTER 19

of Babylon came against the city, and his servants did besiege it. And Jehoiachin the king of Judah went out to the king of Babylon, he, and his mother, and his servants, and his princes, and his officers: and the king of Babylon took him in the eighth year of his (Nebuchadnezzar's) reign ... and he carried away Jehoiachin to Babylon". Jehoiachin is elsewhere known as Coniah and Jeconiah (Jer. 22: 24-30).

It is to be hoped that some of the statements in this section of the chapter will become more comprehensible as a result of the following:

i) The words, *"Now when she saw that she had waited, and her hope was lost" (v.5)*, evidently refer to Judah's hope that Jehoahaz might return from Egypt, something that Jeremiah attempted to dispel: "Weep ye not for the dead, neither bemoan him: but weep sore for him that goeth away: for he shall return no more, nor see his native country. For thus saith the LORD touching Shallum (Jehoahaz) the son of Josiah king of Judah, which reigned instead of Josiah his father, which went forth out of his place: He shall not return thither any more: but he shall die in the place whither they have led him captive, and shall see this land no more" (Jer. 22: 10-12). The permanence of Jehoahaz's exile is emphasised three times by Jeremiah: "he shall return no more, nor see his native country" (v.10); he "went forth out of this place; He shall not return thither any more" (v.11); "he shall die in the place whither they have led him captive, and shall see this land no more" (v.12). Jehoahaz means 'the Lord will help', but there would be no help for him. It is not known for how long he survived in Egypt. "There is no trace of him being alive when the prophet is dragged by his countrymen to Egypt (Jer. 43: 6,7)" (Ellicott's Commentary).

ii) The words, *"he knew their desolate places" (v.7)*, have been rendered 'he knew their widows' (RV margin; JND margin), which C.L.Feinberg calls "another reading", and suggests that this "would indicate to what lengths the cruel king went", adding, "However, Ezekiel was probably speaking of widowed palaces or places". J.B.Taylor refers to what he calls "the incredible RV margin" and points out that "the Hebrew for 'widows' and 'citadels' is very similar, and that "the RSV quite rightly renders he 'ravaged their strongholds', which makes perfect parallelism with the phase that follows it". Put another way, the AV has it quite accurately!

iii) The words, *"then the nations (plural) set against him on every side from the provinces" (v.8)*, probably refer to a repetition of the situation at

213

the end of his father's reign when the Lord sent the "bands of the Chaldees ... of the Syrians ... of the Moabites ... of the children of Ammon" against Jehoiakim (2 Kings 24: 2).

iv) The word, *"ward" (v.9)* means 'cage' (*sugar*), and refers to "either an animal's cage, or a neck-band with which lines of prisoners were roped together. The word in modern Hebrew means a dog-collar!" (J.B.Taylor). When eighteen year-old Jehoichin came to the throne, Jerusalem was evidently already under attack because of Jehoiakim's refusal to pay tribute to Nebuchadrezzar. Jehoiachin's reign was "brief and pathetic, and his exile in Babylon long and wearisome" (J.B.Taylor). After thirty-seven years in captivity, "Evil-merodach king of Babylon ... did lift up the head of Jehoiachin king of Judah out of prison" (2 Kings 25: 27-30). (See also Jer. 52: 31-34.) As H.L.Ellison observes, "when he was finally released ... it was as a broken man of fifty-five with no hope of restoration to his throne and with the right of succession for his descendants denied by God (Jer. 22: 29; cf. 1 Chron. 3: 17)". He was so unlike the apostle Paul: see 2 Timothy 4 verses 7-8.

2) THE CESSATION OF THE MONARCHY, vv.10-14

The second section describes the cessation of rule in Israel, and therefore refers to Zedekiah. As Zedekiah "had not yet rebelled and succumbed to Babylonian might, some ... therefore regard vv.10-14 as a later edition, and this may be true ... Alternatively, the reference to Zedekiah's disastrous end could be prophetic, and the poem could then be regarded as a unity" (John B.Taylor). Taylor's second suggestion is much to be preferred!

Instead of being described as "a lioness" (v.2), Israel (Judah) is now described as "a vine" (v.10). Both figures are used of Judah in Genesis 49 verses 9-11, "Judah is a *lion's whelp*: from the prey, my son, thou art gone up: he stooped down, he couched as a lion, and as an old lion; who shall rouse him up? The sceptre shall not depart from Judah, nor a lawgiver from between his feet, until Shiloh come; and unto him shall the gathering of the people be. Binding his foal unto *the vine*, and his ass's colt unto *the choice vine*; he washed his garments in wine, and his clothes in the blood of grapes". The vine is the familiar Old Testament figure for Judah (Psalm 80: 8-11; Isaiah 5: 1-7; Ezek. 15: 1-6; 17: 5-10).

We must notice *(a)* the dominance of the nation in the past (v.10-11); *(b)* the devastation of the nation in the present (vv.12-14).

CHAPTER 19

a) The dominance of the nation in the past, vv.10-11

"Thy mother is like a vine in thy blood, planted by the waters: she was fruitful and full of branches by reason of many waters. And she had strong rods for the sceptres of them that bare rule, and her stature was exalted among the thick branches ('clouds', RV margin: 'it may be "amidst the clouds", and so in 31: 3, 10, 14', JND), and she appeared in her height with the multitude of her branches." The "strong rods for the sceptres of them that bare rule" must refer, in the first case, to David and Solomon, although C.L.Feinberg is right in saying that "there is no need to limit the reference to them". The "strong rods" represent the nation's succession of rulers. The reign of Solomon certainly saw the nation "exalted among the thick branches" (perhaps 'clouds': see above), and appearing "in her height with the multitude of her branches".

The words, "Thy mother is like a vine in thy blood", are not easily understood. F.Gardiner suggests that if the text is taken as it stands (i.e. without emendation), the meaning could well be: "Thy mother is like a vine living in the blood (i.e. in the life) of her children". F.Gardiner continues, with justification, "This would then be a statement amplified in the following words, 'fruitful and full of branches'".

b) The devastation of the nation in the present, vv.12-14

"But she was plucked up in fury, she was cast down to the ground, and the east wind dried up her fruit: her strong rods were broken and withered; the fire consumed them. And now she is planted in the wilderness, in a dry and thirsty ground. And fire is gone out of a rod of her branches, which devoured her fruit, so that she hath no strong rod to be a sceptre to rule."

The vine, once "planted by the waters" (v.10), would now be "planted in the wilderness, in a dry and thirsty ground" (v.13). Once it produced "strong rods for the sceptres of them that bare rule" (v.11), but there would now be "no strong rod to be a sceptre to rule" (v.14). The disaster that overtook Judah (or, was to overtake Judah) was nothing less than national deportation. As F.A.Tatford points out, the nation's fate was inextricably linked with the fate of Zedekiah.

i) **The fate of the nation, vv.12-13.** F.A.Tatford continues: "The vine was plucked up in wrath and cast to the ground. From its lofty height the nation spectacularly fell, its days as a kingdom finished, its separate identity gone. It was, of course, divine wrath that fell upon it to uproot it and cast it down". The "east wind" was an apt symbol of the invading Babylonian army. National life died. There was no more fruit. There were no more kings: "her strong rods were broken and withered; the fire consumed them". "The vine was transplanted from the well-watered land to a dry and thirsty land, a clear reference to the deportation of the people to the barren soil of Babylon where national life could scarcely thrive" (F.A.Tatford). No wonder the exiles exclaimed, "How shall we sing the LORD'S song in a strange land?" (Psalm 137: 4). Judah was in captivity.

ii) ***The fate of Zedekiah, v.14.*** The fate of the nation is attributed to misdeeds of Zedekiah, who is described as "a rod of her branches (Judah's branches)". It was Zedekiah whose sin finally destroyed the nation. National judgment was directly due to the wickedness of the ungodly kings, especially Zedekiah, of whom Jeremiah said, "thou ... shalt be taken by the hand of the king of Babylon: and thou shalt cause this city to be burned with fire" (Jer. 38: 23). His rebellion against Nebuchadnezzar, to whom he had sworn allegiance, brought disaster. See Ezekiel 17 verses 11-21. The words, "fire is gone out of a rod of her branches, which devoured her fruit" indicate that Zedekiah, the last Judaean king, was the cause of the nation's ultimate collapse. With his removal, Judah had "no strong rod to be a sceptre to rule",

F.Gardiner sums up well: "The rods, as shown in verse 11, are the royal sceptres of her kings. It was by the sin and folly of these kings, together with the sins and follies of the whole people, that judgment was drawn down upon them. Many of them did their full share of the evil work; but 'a rod' is here spoken of in the singular, with especial reference to the last king, Zedekiah, who finally brought on the utter ruin of both himself and his people".

The emphasis here on the failure of the leadership reminds us of the heavy responsibilities of assembly elders whose work it is to "feed (tend) the church of God" (Acts 20: 28). It has been said that an assembly seldom, if ever, rises above the spiritual calibre of its elders. Those who "take care of the church of God" (1 Tim. 3: 5) have a most responsible position, and should be given unstinting prayerful support.

The chapter ends as it begins: "Moreover take thou up a lamentation ... This is a lamentation, and shall be for a lamentation" (vv.1, 14). F.Gardiner explains the closing words as follows: "It is a lamentation now in the half accomplished desolation: it shall remain for a lamentation when all shall be fulfilled". Ezekiel was not a party to the downfall of king and country, but he was evidently deeply touched by their demise. The sad condition of God's people should be regarded, not with disdain, and certainly not with self-congratulation, but with godly sorrow.

We must note, however, that Genesis 49: 10 ("The sceptre shall not depart from Judah, nor a lawgiver from between his feet, until Shiloh come; and unto him shall the gathering of the people be") has not been rescinded or proved to be without effect. The sceptre remains with Judah, though not exercised at present. Ezekiel is yet to show us that God has not reneged on His promises.

EZEKIEL CHAPTER 20: 1 - 44

With Chapters 20-23, we come to a new section of the prophecy (strictly speaking, a new *sub-section* of the prophecy).

Thus far, under the general title, 'The ruin of Judah and Jerusalem (1: 1 – 24: 27)', we have considered: *the commissioning of Ezekiel* (1: 1 - 3: 15), *the coming judgment* (3: 16 - 7: 27) and *the contributory causes* (8: 1 - 19: 14).

This brings us to *the consistency of national sin* (20: 1 - 23: 49) and, finally to *the commencement of hostilities* (24: 1-27).

Throughout this period of Ezekiel's ministry, the Lord regularly and consistently spoke to His rebellious people through the prophet:

- Both the commissioning of Ezekiel and the commencement of his ministry (chs.1-7) took place in "the *fifth year* of king Jehoiachin's captivity" (1: 2).

- The messages detailing the reasons for coming judgment were preached in "the *sixth year*" of king Jehoiachin's captivity (8: 1).

- The messages emphasising the consistency of national sin (20: 1 - 23: 49), something particularly highlighted by the historical reviews in Chapters 20 & 23, were delivered in "the *seventh year*" of king Jehoiachin's captivity (20: 1).

- The commencement of hostilities (24: 1-27) is dated "the *ninth year*" of king Jehoiachin's captivity (24: 1). "Son of man, write thee the name of the day, even of this same day: the king of Babylon set himself against Jerusalem this same day" (24: 2). (Compare 24: 1 with 2 Kings 25: 1-2.)

Returning now to Chapters 20-23, whilst H.L.Ellison is right in saying that "while traversing much of the ground again, he goes deeper and seeks to lay bare the deeper reasons for Jerusalem's sin", we have to determine

CHAPTER 20:1-44

why this is emphasised at this particular time. The answer may lie in the fact that Nebuchadnezzar was on his way. (See 21: 18-22.) Perhaps, therefore, we could say that Chapters 4-23, which we have said may be entitled 'Predictions before the Siege of Jerusalem', can be re-described as 'Predictions before the siege of Jerusalem' (Chapters 4-19) and 'Predictions *immediately* before the siege of Jerusalem' (Chapters 20-23).

Chapter 20 clearly divides into two main sections with reference to the *expressed* and *unexpressed* desires of "the elders" of Israel": *(1)* what they intimated (vv.1-31): "Certain of the elders of Israel came to inquire of the LORD, and sat before me" (v.1); *(2)* what they intended (vv.32-44): "And that which cometh into your mind shall not be at all, that ye say, We will be as the heathen ... to serve wood and stone" (v.32).

We should notice that the concluding verses of the chapter (vv.45-49) are part of the message in chapter 21. "The Chapter division is unfortunate, for this (20: 45 - 21: 32) is one section, as is duly recognized in the Hebrew" (H.L.Ellison). J.B.Taylor concurs: "The unity of this section (20: 45 - 21: 32) is made more plain in the Hebrew text, where Chapter 21 begins at Chapter 20 verse 45 (EVV) and goes on for thirty-seven verses".

J.B.Taylor points out that "Unlike the illustration of the foundling child (Chapter 16) and the parable of Oholah and Oholibah (Chapter 23), we have here a description of Israel's past history of continuing rebellion against the Lord, expressed in actual historical terms without the aid of metaphor and allegory".

1) WHAT THE ELDERS INTIMATED, vv.1-31

The passage may be divided as follows *(a)* the request by the elders (v.1); *(b)* the refusal by the Lord (vv.2-3); *(c)* the rebellion of the fathers (vv.4-29); *(d)* the reason for refusal (vv.30-31).

a) The request of the elders, v.1

"And it came to pass in the seventh year, in the fifth month, the tenth day of the month, that certain of the elders of Israel came to enquire of the LORD, and sat before me." (Compare 8: 1; 14: 1.) The commentary on the people who said amongst themselves, "Come, I pray you, and hear what is the word that cometh forth from the LORD" (Ezek. 33: 30-33) is certainly applicable here! So is Isaiah 29 verse 13: "This people draw near me with their mouth, and with their lips do honour me, but have removed their heart far from me". Let us all be warned.

In passing, and in a totally different context, assembly elders ought always to "enquire of the LORD". After all, they are charged with the care of His flock (1 Pet. 5: 2).

b) The refusal by the Lord, vv.2-3

The Lord's response to their enquiry is akin to His response on the previous occasion (14: 1-3): "Are ye come to enquire of me? As I live, saith the Lord GOD, I will not be enquired of by you" (v.3). Having reviewed the history of the fathers (vv.4-29) and indicated that the current generation were no better than they were (vv.30-31), the Lord restates His refusal: "As I live, saith the Lord GOD, I will not be inquired of by you" (v.31). They had totally forgotten the words of the Psalmist, "If I regard iniquity in my heart, the LORD will not hear me" (Psalm 66: 18). Again, let us all be warned.

c) The rebellion of the fathers, vv.4-29

This section of the chapter is introduced by the words, "cause them to know the abominations of their fathers" (v.4). J.B. Taylor is right in saying, "To interpret this as an accusation against the elders on the grounds of their forefather's sins would involve a denial of much that Ezekiel has been arguing in relation to individual responsibility". See Chapter 18, with its reference to the proverb in current use: "The fathers have eaten sour grapes, and the children's teeth are set on edge" (v.2). This was not the case here: the sins of the fathers were being perpetuated by the current generation. According to J.B. Taylor, the words: "Wilt thou judge them, son of man, wilt thou judge them?" have the imperative meaning, 'set out the case against them'. This is confirmed by the words which follow: "cause them to know the abominations of their fathers".

Ezekiel proceeds to do this by pointing out that Israel had a history of rebellion: *(i)* in Egypt (vv.5-9); *(ii)* in the wilderness (vv.10-26); *(iii)* in the land (vv.27-29).

i) Rebellion in Egypt, vv.5-9

Notice the references to Egypt (vv.5, 6, 7, 8, 9), and the words: "But they

CHAPTER 20:1-44

rebelled against me, and would not hearken unto me" (v.8). The section may be divided as follows:

- **Their relationship with God, v.5.** "Thus saith the Lord GOD; in the day when I chose Israel, and lifted up my hand unto the seed of the house of Jacob, and made myself known unto them in the land of Egypt, when I lifted up mine hand unto them, saying, I am the LORD your God." This refers to the commencement of Israel's relationship with God *nationally.* As J.B.Taylor observes, "Israel's history begins therefore, not with Abraham, but with Moses and the burning bush and the name of Jehovah, revealed as the definitive name of Israel's covenant God".

The expression "lifted up my hand" occurs in verses 5, 6, 15, 23, 28, 42. It means 'to swear', and "illustrates the abundance of God's grace in so binding Himself to His covenant mercies to Israel" (J.B.Taylor). (See also 47: 14. Compare Rev. 10: 5-6.)

- **Their redemption by God, v.6.** "In the day that I lifted up mine hand unto them, to bring them forth out of the land of Egypt into a land that I espied for them, flowing with milk and honey, which is the glory of all lands." We must note the words "a land that I espied for them" and "which is the glory ('ornament', JND) of all lands". See also verse 15. The Lord both redeemed them and provided a good inheritance for them. We should now read 1 Peter 1 verses 1-5, noting the words "sprinkling of the blood of Jesus Christ", and "an inheritance incorruptible, and undefiled, and that fadeth not away, reserved in heaven for you". *Our* inheritance must be 'the glory of the universe!'

- **Their requirement by God, v.7.** "Then said I unto them, Cast ye away every man the abominations of his eyes, and defile not yourselves with the idols of Egypt: I am the LORD your God." A redeemed people with such an inheritance should be a holy people. If God has blessed us with redemption and provided us with such an inheritance, then surely He must reign in our hearts without rival. (See 1 John 5: 21.)

- **Their rebellion against God, v.8.** "But they rebelled against me, and would not hearken unto me: they did not every man cast away the abominations of their eyes, neither did they forsake the idols of Egypt: then I said, I will pour out my fury upon them, to accomplish my anger against them in the midst of the land of Egypt."

Verses 7-8 give us information not available in the Exodus record, that is, Israel's idolatry, and their refusal to forsake it. But the Lord withheld judgment upon them in Egypt. This follows:

- *The reason for the mercy of God, v.9.* "But I wrought for my name's sake, that it should not be polluted before the heathen, among whom they were, in whose sight I made myself known unto them, in bringing them forth out of the land of Egypt." Judgment was withheld, not because Israel deserved it, but because the Lord had in mind His own honour in the sight of men. This will be so in the future: see, for example, Ezekiel 20 verse 44 and 36 verse 22.

ii) Rebellion in the wilderness, vv.10-26

We should notice the references to the wilderness (vv.10, 13, 15, 17, 18, 21, 23), and the words "the house of Israel rebelled against me" (v.13); "the children rebelled against me" (v.21).

This section of the chapter is in two parts: the first generation in the wilderness (vv.10-17) and the second generation in the wilderness (vv.18-26). The former commences with the words, "Wherefore I caused them to go forth out of the land of Egypt, and brought them into the wilderness" (v.10); the latter commences with, "But I said unto their children in the wilderness, Walk ye not in the statutes of your fathers, neither observe their judgments, nor defile yourselves with their idols" (v.18).

The first generation, vv.10-17

We should notice here: their redemption by God (v.10); the requirements of God (vv.11-12); the rebellion against God (v.13); the reason for the mercy of God (v.14); the retribution of God (vv.15-16); the restraint of God (v.17).

- **Their redemption by God, v.10.** "Wherefore (that is, because of His "name's sake", v.9) I caused them to go forth out of the land of Egypt, and brought them into the wilderness." Not 'they went forth out of the land of Egypt', but "*I caused* them to go forth out of the land of Egypt". Their redemption was divinely initiated and divinely accomplished.

- **The requirements of God, vv.11-12.** "And I gave them my statutes, and shewed them my judgments, which if a man do, he shall even live in them. Moreover also I gave them my sabbaths, to be a sign between me and them, that they might know that I am the LORD that sanctify them." J.B.Taylor interprets the words "he shall even live in them" as 'prosper' and adds, 'both materially and spiritually'. Israel was privileged to have the law. See Romans 3 verses 1-2. H.L.Ellison makes the significant observation that "We are so accustomed to a weekly day of rest that probably only those that have lived in pagan lands can grasp what life without it means, or what an immense innovation it represented. In spite of strong arguments to the contrary, it seems conclusive from this chapter and from Nehemiah 9 verse 14, that the Sabbath is part of the Sinai revelation and does not date from Eden. Certainly all efforts to find a trace of weekly rest-day elsewhere in the ancient world have conspicuously failed". Ellison continues, "It is easy enough to keep the Sabbath in a legalistic way, but once it is correctly understood, it becomes a very real test of man's faith". He refers here, presumably to the words: "that they might know that I am the LORD that sanctify them".

- **Their rebellion against God, v.13.** "But the house of Israel rebelled against me in the wilderness (as they did in Egypt, v.8): they walked not in my statutes, and they despised my judgments, which if a man do, he shall even live in them; and my sabbaths they greatly polluted: then I said, I would pour out my fury upon them in the wilderness, to consume them (as He had said in connection with their rebellion in Egypt, v.8)."

- **The reason for the mercy of God, v.14.** As in Egypt (v.9): "But I wrought for my name's sake, that it should not be polluted before the heathen, in whose sight I brought them out". Notice that Moses and Joshua used the same argument: see Exodus 32 verse 12, Numbers 14 verses 13-16, Joshua 7 verse 9. Judgment, on account of further rebellion (v.13) is again withheld: "then I said, I would pour out my fury ... But I wrought for my name's sake, that it should not be polluted before the heathen, in whose sight I brought them out".

- **The retribution of God, vv.15-16.** "Yet also I lifted up my hand unto them in the wilderness, that I would not bring them into the land which I had given them, flowing with milk and honey, which is the glory of all lands; because they despised my judgments, and walked not in my statutes, but polluted my sabbaths: for their heart went after their idols." As H.L.Ellison observes, "Of Israelite idolatry in the wilderness we know little. Joshua 24 verse 14 is evidence enough that it must have been widespread enough, even if secret, and Leviticus 17 verse 7 shows one form it took - the placating of the desert demons". See also Acts 7 verses 42-43, although the latter verse evidently refers to the prophet's (Amos) own time.

- **The restraint of God, v.17.** "Nevertheless mine eye spared them from destroying them, neither did I make an end of them in the wilderness." Like Jeremiah, we all have to exclaim, "It is of the LORD'S mercies that we are not consumed, because his compassions fail not ..." (Lam. 3: 22-23). How glad we are that "the LORD is merciful and gracious, slow to anger, and plenteous in mercy ... He hath not dealt with us after our sins; nor rewarded us according to our iniquities" (Psalm 103: 8-10).

The second generation, vv.18-26

The new generation in the wilderness is reviewed in these verses. The same sequence occurs: the requirements of God (vv.18-20); the rebellion against God (v.21); the reason for the mercy of God (v.22); the retribution of God (vv.23-26).

- **The requirements of God, vv.18-20.** "But I said unto their children in the wilderness, Walk ye not in the statutes of your fathers, neither observe their judgments, nor defile yourselves with their idols: I am the LORD your God; walk in my statutes, and keep my judgments, and do them; and hallow my sabbaths; and they shall be a sign between me and you, that ye may know that I am the LORD your God."

- **The rebellion against God, v.21.** "Notwithstanding the children rebelled against me: they walked not in my statutes, neither kept my judgments to do them, which if a man do, he shall even live in them; they polluted my sabbaths: then I said, I would pour out my fury upon them, to accomplish my anger against them in the wilderness."

- **The reason for the mercy of God, v.22.** "Nevertheless I withdrew mine hand, and wrought for my name's sake, that it should not be polluted in the sight of the heathen, in whose sight I brought them forth."

- **The retribution of God, vv.23-26.** J.B.Taylor is most helpful here: "This time, although once again God refrains from pouring out His wrath, He does leave Israel with two unhappy legacies, namely the threat of dispersion from Canaan among foreign peoples (vv.23-24), and the harmful ordinance of the offering of the firstborn (vv.25-26)".

As to the former: "I lifted up mine hand unto them also in the wilderness, that I would scatter them among the heathen, and disperse them through the countries; because they had not executed my judgments, but had despised my statutes, and had polluted my sabbaths, and their eyes were after their fathers' idols" (vv.23-24). He warned them in this way, for example, in Deuteronomy. 28 verses 15-68. See, particularly, verse 64.

As to the latter: "Wherefore I gave them also statutes that were not good, and judgments whereby they should not live; and I polluted them in their own gifts, in that they caused to pass through the fire all that opened the womb, that I might make them desolate, to the end that they might know that I am the Lord" (vv.25-26).

These seemingly difficult verses are clearly explained by F.Gardiner. "The statutes of the Mosaic law are not intended here at all (v.25), as is plain from the particular instance of the consecration of children to Moloch in the next verse (v.26). These evil statutes and judgments were those adopted from the heathen whom they had suffered to dwell among them, and from the surrounding nations. But how can the Lord say that *He* gave these to them? In the same way that it is said in Isaiah 63 verse 17, 'O LORD, why hast thou made us to err from thy ways, and hardened our heart from thy fear?'. So also Paul says of the heathen (Rom. 1: 21-28) that God 'gave them up to uncleanness ... unto vile affections ... to a reprobate mind' ... And Stephen says of these very Israelites at this very time, 'God gave them up to worship the host of heaven' (Acts 7: 42). It is part of that universal moral government of the world, to which Ezekiel so frequently refers, that the effect of disobedience and neglect of grace is to lead the sinner on to greater sin. The Israelites rebelled against the divine government, and neglected the grace given to them; the natural consequence was that they fell under the influence of the heathen". H.L.Ellison makes the valid comment that "Ezekiel does not say that human sacrifice marked Israel's religion down through its history, but rather that it was the natural climax of its downward path".

iii) Rebellion in the land, vv.27-29

"Therefore, son of man, speak unto the house of Israel, and say unto them, Thus saith the Lord GOD; Yet in this your fathers have blasphemed me, in that they have committed a trespass against me. For when I had brought them into *the land*, for the which I lifted up mine hand to give it to them, then they saw every high hill, and all the thick trees, and they offered *there* their sacrifices, and *there* they presented the provocation of their offering:

there also they made their sweet savour, and poured out ***there*** their drink-offerings." As J.B.Taylor observes, "The crowning rebellion of Israel's history was that when finally, in the mercy of God, they entered into the land of promise, they promptly took over the heathen Canaanite hill-top shrines as their own places of sacrifice, and offerings which should have proved acceptable to God were nothing less than an 'irritation' (v.28) to Him".

The words, "What is the high place whereunto ye go? And the name is called Bamah unto this day" (v.29), have been variously explained. It seems that Bamah, deriving from *ma* (what) and *ba* (go), means - from its own etymology - the place of human choice: not a place of divine choice. We would call it a pun: a play on words. This brings us to:

d) The reason for refusal, vv.30-31

That is, God's refusal to respond to their enquiry (vv.2-3). "Wherefore say unto the house of Israel, Thus saith the Lord GOD, Are ***ye*** polluted after the manner of your fathers? And commit ***ye*** whoredom after their abominations? For when ***ye*** offer your gifts, when ***ye*** make your sons to pass through the fire, ***ye*** pollute yourselves with all your idols, even unto this day; and shall I be inquired of by you, O house of Israel? As I live, saith the Lord GOD, ***I will not be enquired of you.***" This repeats, now with the reason (see vv.4-29), what the Lord had said to the elders in verse 3. They had not learnt from the sins of their fathers. They were as idolatrous as their fathers had been. This brings us to the second major section of the passage:

2) WHAT THE ELDERS INTENDED, vv.32-44

The section clearly has two parts: ***(a)*** their intention (v.32); ***(b)*** God's intention (vv.33-44). God would not allow their intentions to proceed. He would intervene.

a) Their intention, v.32

"And that which cometh into your mind shall not be at all, that ye say, We will be as the heathen, as the families of the countries, to serve wood and stone." This is an incredible statement! Their exile was entirely due to their idolatry, yet they were determined to persist in their sin. As F.Gardiner points out, "The desire to be 'like the nations that are round about' had long been a ruling ambition with the Israelites, as shown in their original desire for a king (1 Sam. 8: 5, 20), and this desire, as shown in the text, had been one chief reason for their tendency to idolatry".

b) God's intention, vv.33-44

He makes this abundantly clear: "As I live, saith the Lord GOD, surely with a mighty hand, and with a stretched out arm, and with fury poured out will I rule over you" (v.33). He would not allow them to be like the nations and "serve wood and stone" (v.32). He would rule over them in judgment (vv.33-39) and in blessing (vv.40-44).

i) He will rule over them in judgment, vv.33-39

These verses refer to regathering (vv.33-34), chastening (vv.35-37) and cleansing (vv.38-39).

- Regathering, vv.33-34. The Lord would not allow His people to be absorbed by the nations amongst whom they had been dispersed. "As I live, saith the Lord God, surely with a mighty hand, and with a stretched out arm, and with *fury poured out*, will I rule over you. And I will bring you out from the people ('peoples', JND), and will gather you out of the countries wherein ye are scattered, with a mighty hand, and with a stretched out arm, and with *fury poured out*." We know that the Lord will "gather together his *elect* from the four winds, from one end of heaven to the other" (Matt. 24: 31), but Ezekiel evidently refers here to a rather different aspect of Israel's regathering. We know that the nation will pass through "the time of Jacob's trouble" (Jer. 30: 7), *alias* the judgment of the great tribulation, which will certainly be "fury poured out", but the current passage evidently refers to the time when "the Son of man shall send forth his angels, and they shall gather out of his kingdom all things that offend, and them which do iniquity; and shall cast them into a furnace of fire: there shall be wailing and gnashing of teeth" (Matt. 13: 41-42). Previously, as we have noted, God had said "I will (or would) *pour out my fury*", but He had withheld that judgment (vv8-9, 13-14, 21-22), but now that "fury" *is* "poured out".

These verses therefore describe a coming day in which Israel will be subject to God's fury. The object of this regathering for judgment is not the elimination of the nation, but the chastening and purging of the nation, which brings us to:

- **Chastening, vv.35-37**. "And I will bring you into the wilderness of the people, and there will I plead with you face to face. Like as I pleaded with your fathers in the wilderness of the land of Egypt, so will I plead with you, saith the Lord GOD. And I will cause you to pass under the rod, and I will bring you under the bond of the covenant." Compare Hosea 2 verses 14-15: "Therefore, behold, I will allure her, and bring her into the wilderness, and speak comfortably unto her. And I will give her vineyards from thence, and the valley of Achor for a door of hope: and she shall sing there, as in the days of her youth, and as in the day when she came up out of the land of Egypt". This describes the result of the chastening. Notice the reference to "the valley of Achor": it was there that Israel's guilt was purged (Joshua 7: 26).

While C.I.Scofield calls the wilderness here "the old wilderness of the wanderings", this is by no means certain, and C.L.Feinberg makes the point that Ezekiel likens the coming judgment to God's dealings with their rebellious ancestors in the wilderness after their deliverance from Egypt. However Scofield rightly continues, "The issue of this judgment determines who of Israel in that day shall enter the land for kingdom blessing". The "wilderness of the people", if it is an actual geographical location, remains unidentified, unless it refers to the wilderness described in Revelation 12 verse 14: "And to the woman were given two wings of a great eagle, that she might fly into **the wilderness**, into her place, where she is nourished for a time, and times, and half a time, from the face of the serpent". But this seems unlikely.

The words "there will I plead ... like as I pleaded with your fathers in the wilderness" recall Numbers 14 verses 21-23 and 28-29. The expression "pass under the rod" refers to 'the shepherd's way of counting and examining his flock' (Lev. 27: 32; Jer. 33: 13; Micah 7: 14). "The bond of the covenant" ("I will bring you into the bond of the covenant") evidently refers to God's unswerving purpose to bring His people into the good of His intentions for them. See verse 42: "And ye shall know that I am the LORD, when I shall bring you into the land of Israel, into the country for the which **I lifted up mine hand** to give it to your fathers". **He** would implement the covenant. (See Jer. 31: 31-34.) This would involve:

- **Cleansing, vv.38-39.** "And I will purge out from among you the rebels, and them that transgress against me: I will bring them forth out of the country where they sojourn, and they shall not enter into the land of Israel; and ye shall know that I am the LORD" (v.38). The "rebels" at the end-time will be the successors of those who "rebelled" in the past (vv.8, 13, 21). Rebellious Jews will *not* enter the land, only those acceptable to the Lord. See verse 40.

It does seem that verse 39 refers to the time *then present* (i.e. to Ezekiel's day): "As for you, O house of Israel, thus saith the Lord GOD; Go ye, serve ye every one his idols, and hereafter also ('Go ye, serve every one his idols henceforth also ...', JND), if ye will not hearken unto me: but pollute ye my holy name no more with your gifts, and with your idols" (v.39). It is quite unthinkable that this should be said to anyone when the Lord returns! It is a case here of, "He that is unjust, let him be unjust still: and he which is filthy, let him be filthy still ..." (Rev. 22: 11). As F.A.Tatford observes, "Such a consistent repudiation of Him would be preferable to their present vacillation, and could put an end to their profanation of His holy name by their attempted compromise".

ii)   He will rule over them in blessing, vv.40-44

God's people *at the time* were not to "pollute" God's "holy name" by endeavouring to combine orthodoxy with idolatry (syncretism). There will be no such thing as idolatry *in His coming kingdom.* Features of His coming rule follow:

- *Holiness, v.40.* "For in mine *holy mountain*, in the mountain of the height of Israel, saith the Lord GOD, there shall all the house of Israel ... serve me." It will indeed be "mine holy mountain" then. There will be no idol-pollution. This reminds us of 1 Corinthians 3 verses 16-17.

- *Unity, v.40.* "There shall all the house of Israel, *all* of them in the land, serve me", reminding us of Philippians 1 verse 27. The expression "all of them in the land" evidently refers to those Jews acceptable to the Lord. Every one of them will be there. Compare verse 38. See Ezekiel 39 verse 28.

- *Priesthood, v.40.* "There shall all the house of Israel, all of them in the land, *serve* me." According to C.L.Feinberg, the word "serve" translates "the technical term for priestly ministry", reminding us of 1 Peter 2 verse 5.

- *Acceptance, vv.40-41.* "There will I accept them, and there will I require your offerings, and the firstfruits of your oblations, with all your holy things. I will accept you with your sweet savour (unlike Isaiah 1: 11-15), when I bring you out from the people ('peoples', JND: referring to the Gentiles), and gather you out of the countries wherein ye have been scattered; and I will be sanctified in you before the heathen." Compare verses 9, 14, 22. This reminds us again of 1 Peter 2 verse 5.

- **Recognition, v.42-43**. They will recognise God's faithfulness to His promise. "And ye shall know that I am the LORD, when I shall bring you into the land of Israel, into the country for the which I lifted up mine hand to give it to your fathers." God will fulfil His promise made at the time of the exodus when "I lifted up mine hand unto them, to bring them ... into a land that I had espied for them" (v.6). They will then fully recognise their own sinfulness: "And there shall ye remember your ways, and all your doings, wherein ye have been defiled; and ye shall lothe yourselves in your own sight, for all your evils that ye have committed".

All this will take place on the basis of God's grace: "And ye shall know that I am the LORD, when I have wrought with you for my name's sake, not according to your wicked ways, nor according to your corrupt doings, O ye house of Israel, saith the Lord GOD" (v.44). The words, "when I have wrought with you for my name's sake" occur earlier in the passage (vv.9, 14, 22). God always has the glory of His name before Him, whether in withholding judgment or in executing judgment. We too should always have the honour of His name before us. "Whatsoever ye do, do all to the glory of God" (1 Cor. 10: 31).

EZEKIEL CHAPTER 20: 45 – 21: 32

As we have already noted, Ezekiel 20-24 bring us to events culminating with the fall of Jerusalem. The overthrow of Jerusalem is not actually recorded until Chapter 33 verse 21, but these chapters (chs.20-24) refer, amongst other things, to the commencement of Nebuchadnezzar's advance on the city (21: 18-22), and to the commencement of the siege (24: 1-2). The Lord had, indeed, drawn His "sword out of his sheath" (21: 5).

As we have often noted, divine judgment is never arbitrary: it is always accompanied with cogent reasons (see, particularly, Amos 1-2), and both events above are accompanied by explanations. This serves to remind us that believers today will appear before "the *righteous* judge" (2 Tim. 4: 8).

We have also noted that the concluding verses of Chapter 20 (vv.45-49) are part of the message in Chapter 21. As J.B.Taylor points out "The unity of this section (Chapter 20 verse 45 - 21: 32) is made more plain in the Hebrew text, where Chapter 21 begins at 20: 45 (EVV) and goes on for thirty-seven verses". (EVV stands for 'the English Versions'.)

It is quite clear:

- That a new message commences with Chapter 20 verses 45-49, "Moreover *the word of the LORD came unto me,* saying ..." (v.45).

- That the above verses (20: 45-49) are linked with the opening verses of Chapter 21. We should notice the common language: "Moreover the word of the LORD came unto me, saying, Son of man, *set thy face* toward the south, and *drop thy word* toward the south, and prophesy against the forest of the south field; and say to the forest of the south (20: 46-47) ... And the word of the LORD came unto me, saying, Son of man, *set thy face* toward Jerusalem, and *drop thy word* toward the holy places, and prophesy against the land of Israel, and say to the land of Israel ..." (21: 1-3). Notice too: "And *all flesh* shall see that *I the LORD* have kindled it: *it shall not* be quenched (20: 48) ... That **all flesh** may know that **I the LORD** have drawn forth my sword out of his sheath: **it shall not** return any more" (21: 5).

The passage (20: 45 - 21: 32) may be divided as follows: **(1)** the prophecy against the south (20: 45-49); **(2)** the prophecy against Jerusalem (21: 1-27); **(3)** the prophecy against Ammon (21: 28-32).

- The prophecy against the south predicts judgment by **fire**: "I will kindle a fire in thee ... the flaming flame shall not be quenched, and all faces from the south to the north shall be burned therein" (20: 47).

- The prophecy against Jerusalem predicts judgment by **the sword**: "I ... will draw forth my sword out of his sheath ... therefore shall my sword go forth out of his sheath ... that all flesh may know that I the LORD have drawn forth my sword out of his sheath ... Say, A sword, a sword is sharpened, and also furbished ..." (21: 3-4; 9-11). (See also vv.12-15; 19-20.)

- The prophecy against Ammon refers to both **sword** (21: 28-30) and **fire** (21: 31-32).

1) THE PROPHECY AGAINST THE SOUTH, 20: 45-49

That is, against the south of Judah, although this may well refer to Judah generally. We should notice: **(a)** judgment predicted (vv.45-47); **(b)** judgment recognised (v.48); **(c)** judgment ridiculed (v.49).

a) Judgment predicted, vv.45-47

"Moreover the word of the LORD came unto me, saying, Son of man, set thy face toward the south, and drop thy word toward the south, and prophesy against the forest of the south field; and say to the forest of the south, Hear the word of the LORD, Thus saith the Lord GOD, Behold, I will kindle a fire in thee, and it shall devour every green tree in thee, and every dry tree: the flaming fire shall not be quenched, and all faces from the south to the north shall be burned therein."

Three different words here are translated "south" in these verses: *temana* ("set thy face toward the south", v.46); *darom* ("drop thy word toward the south", v.46); *negeb* ("prophesy against the forest of the south field; and say to the forest of the south ... all faces from the south to the north shall be burned therein", vv.46-47). According to J.B.Taylor, "the first two words are general poetic words to describe the southerly direction, whereas the third refers to a named geographical area, called in modern Israel the Negev, which lay to the south of the Judean hills". Taylor continues: "Today this is waterless desert, except where agricultural settlements have irrigated it into a state of cultivation, but we know that in Old Testament times there was greater afforestation throughout Palestine, and so a reference to the *forest of the Negeb* (RSV) does not have to be regarded as completely figurative". Perhaps the specific reference to this area of Judah emphasises that the coming invasion would extend to the southernmost part of the land. Alternatively, it might be a figurative reference to the nation (the forest) and its people (the trees). In this case, the *forest of the Negeb* ("the forest of the south", AV) stands for the whole land.

Having noted this, there can be little doubt from what follows in Chapter 21, where the figure of fire is replaced by the figure of a sword, that in these verses (vv.45-48) we have "a very figurative description of the coming destruction of Jerusalem under the picture of a forest fire" (H.L.Ellison). It is worth remembering that although "Judah lay to the west of Tel-abib, Ezekiel has been transported in spirit to the Chaldean army, which was marching south from Carchemish and the Euphrates" (H.L.Ellison).

b) Judgment recognised, v.48

"And all flesh shall see that I the LORD have kindled it: it shall not be quenched." Men in general would realise that the coming destruction had been sent by the Lord as an act of judgment. Such recognition is mentioned elsewhere in the Old Testament. See, for example, Joshua 2 verses 9-11. The ancient world had a greater understanding of God than the modern world with all its so-called enlightenment. How much do *we* recognise the hand of God in our own lives, and in the world?

c) Judgment ridiculed, v.49

"Then said I, Ah Lord GOD! they say of me, Doth he not speak in parables?" This presupposes that Ezekiel had conveyed the message, and had been "ridiculed by his hearers as a *speaker of parables* (RV), or, to retain the cognate form of the Hebrew, a 'riddler of riddles'" (J.B.Taylor). As H.L.Ellison observes, "While Ezekiel's fellow-exiles might well not understand the details of such an oracle, the general intention must have been obvious. But they showed a trait we are all familiar with today. As now so then, because something in the Word was obscure, it is taken as an excuse for ignoring the whole message".

2) THE PROPHECY AGAINST JERUSALEM, 21: 1-27

We can call this passage 'the message of the drawn sword': see verses 3, 9, 28. These verses may be divided in the following way: *(a)* the sword drawn (vv.1-7); *(b)* the sword sharpened (vv.8-17); *(c)* the sword identified (vv.18-32). So far as the last is concerned, the sword is wielded against Judah and Jerusalem (vv.21-27), and against Ammon and Rabbath (vv.28-32).

a) The sword drawn, vv.1-7

As we have noted above, this section amplifies verses 45-49 of the previous chapter. The connection is clear. See, for example, the expression "from the south to the north" (20: 47; 21: 4), and the result of divine judgment: "all flesh shall see" (20: 48); "and all flesh shall know" (21: 5). J.B.Taylor puts it succinctly: 'The phraseology of verses 2-5 is designed to match that of Chapter 20 verses 46-48. The south becomes first *Jerusalem*, then the *sanctuaries*, and finally *the land of Israel* (v.2). The forest fire becomes a *sword*, which will slay *both righteous and wicked* (v.3), that is the "green tree" and the "dry tree (20: 47), and all flesh will recognise that it is the Lord who had done this (v.5)".

We should notice *(i) the sword* (vv.2-5): the Lord's sword is drawn against Jerusalem; *(ii) the sigh* (vv.6-7): Ezekiel was to sigh "with breaking heart and with bitterness" (v.6, Amp.V), and then to explain why: "For the tidings; because it cometh ... behold it cometh, and shall be brought to pass, saith the Lord GOD" (v.7). (Compare Amos 7: 2, 5; Jer. 4: 19, 31: 26.)

i) The sword, vv.2-5. "Son of man, set thy face toward Jerusalem, and drop thy word toward the holy places, and prophesy against the land of Israel, and say to the land of Israel, Thus saith the LORD, behold I am against thee, and will draw forth *my sword* out of his sheath, and will cut off from thee the righteous and the wicked. Seeing then that I will cut off from thee the righteous and the wicked, therefore shall *my sword* go forth out of his sheath against all flesh from the south to the north; that all flesh may know that I the LORD have drawn *my sword* out of his sheath: it shall not return any more."

It has been rightly said that the theme of the sword can be traced back to Joshua's encounter, on the banks of the Jordan, with "the captain of the host of the LORD with "his sword drawn in his hand" (Joshua 5: 13-15). "There He was fighting for His people ... in other passages, especially in the prophets, God wields His sword against Israel's enemies (Deut. 32: 41; Isaiah 31: 8, 34: 5-8; 66: 16; Jer. 25: 31, 50: 35ff; Zeph. 2: 12) ... Ezekiel, however, uses the figure of the sword here in referring to God's punishment upon Israel". He puts His sword into the hands of Israel's enemies and through them He accomplishes His purpose. This is clear from this chapter (vv.19-20) See also Ezekiel 30 verse 24, 32 verses 11-15. It is well worth remembering that God *still acts* against His own people. (See, for example, 1 Cor.11: 29-31; Rev. 2: 4-5.)

ii) The sigh, vv.6-7. "*Sigh*, therefore, thou son of man, with the breaking of thy loins; and with bitterness *sigh* before their eyes. And it shall be, when they say unto thee, Wherefore *sighest* thou? that thou shalt answer, For the tidings, because it cometh: and every heart shall melt, and all hands shall be feeble, and every spirit shall faint, and all knees shall be as weak as water: behold it cometh, and shall be brought to pass, saith the Lord GOD."

"Ezekiel's distress is yet another symbol of the overwhelming dismay that will come upon Israel in their moment of judgment ... he speaks his message with the symbolism, not of actions, but of emotions. *With the breaking of thy loins* (AV, RV), for which the RSV gives *with breaking heart*, is a phrase expressing deep emotional distress. The loins were regarded as the seat of strength, and so this represents complete nervous and physical collapse (cf. Ezek. 29: 7, Psalm, 69: 23, Nahum 2: 10). The same sense of panic and emotional paralysis will afflict the people when they hear 'the tidings', or 'the news': 'It's coming!'" (J.B.Taylor).

How does the imminence of divine judgment affect *us?* We have been delivered from "the wrath to come", but does the prospect of coming judgment upon others cause *us* distress?

b) The sword sharpened, vv.8-17

"Again, the word of the LORD came unto me, saying ..." (v.8). Commentators call these verses, 'The song of the sword'. The imminence of divine judgment is emphasised here. We should notice, again, frequent references to the "sword". These verses describe *(i)* the sword (vv.9-11); *(ii)* the smiting (vv.12-17).

EZEKIEL

i) The sword, vv.9-11

"Son of man, prophesy, and say, Thus saith the LORD; Say, **A sword, a sword** is sharpened, and also furbished (polished): it is sharpened to make a sore slaughter: it is furbished (polished) that it may glitter (compare Deut. 32: 41): should we then make mirth? It contemneth the rod of my son, as every tree. And he hath given it to be furbished (polished), that it may be handled: *this sword* is sharpened, and it is furbished (polished), to give it into the hand of the slayer." The "slayer" (v.11) is not identified here, but he will soon be named. See verse 19, where the "sword" of these verses lies in the hand of "the king of Babylon".

The words "should we then make mirth? *It contemneth the rod of my son as every tree*" ('It despiseth the rod of my son as [all] wood', JND margin), are not easily understood. According to J.B.Taylor, the MT (Masoretic Text) is "impossible to understand". He continues by pointing out that 'the RSV emends the pointing slightly to give, *You have despised the rod, my son, with everything of wood'* and continues, 'Taken this way, the prophet is rebuking his hearers for inattention ('do you think that I am joking?'), and accusing them of scorning all former instruments of punishment. The rod suggests Isaiah's description of the Assyrians as "the rod of my anger" (Isaiah 10: 5)'. H.L.Ellison agrees: "'Or do we make mirth?' - i.e. is the warning a mere joke – 'You have despised the rod, my son, with everything of wood' - i.e. all lesser chastisement has been despised". Perhaps the words, "It contemneth the rod of my son as every tree" might mean, 'It (the nation) contemneth (hath contempt for or hath despised) the rod (of divine judgment) of my son (laid upon my son) as every tree (as on all other occasions)'.

These verses (vv.9-10), whatever their exact meaning, remind *us* that we should be 'deadly serious' in communicating God's word and, at the same time, equally serious in listening to God's word. The message of coming judgment is *not* a matter for humour.

ii) The smiting, vv.12-17

Ezekiel was to "smite" his thigh (v.12) and to "smite ... hands" (v.14). The latter reflects the fact that the Lord would "smite" His "hands together" (v.17).

- **Smiting his thigh.** "Cry and howl, son of man; for it shall be upon my people, it shall be upon all the princes of Israel: terrors by reason of the sword shall be upon my people: smite therefore upon thy thigh" (v.12). F.Gardiner rightly understands this to be "a mark of extreme grief", and cites Jeremiah 31 verse 19: "After that I was instructed, I smote upon my thigh: I was ashamed, yea, even confounded, because I did bear the reproach of my youth". The context ("Cry and howl, son of man") strongly suggests that F.Gardiner is correct. Compare verse 6, "sigh, therefore, thou son of man, with the breaking of thy loins; and with bitterness sigh before their eyes".

- Smiting his hands. The reason for the sighing (see vv.6-7) is the reason for the smiting: "Because it is a trial, and what if the sword contemn the rod? It shall be no more, saith the Lord GOD ('For the trial [is made]; and what if the contemning sceptre shall be no [more]? saith the Lord Jehovah', JND)" (v.13). F.Gardiner offers the following explanation: "The words for 'rod' and 'contemn' are the same as in verse 10, and must be taken in the same sense. The most satisfactory translation is this: 'For it (the sword) has been proved (viz. on others), and what if this contemning rod shall be no more?' i.e., the power of the sword of Babylon had already been proved; and the sceptre of Judah, which despises it, shall be clean swept away".

Bearing therefore in mind that the sceptre of Judah would be 'clean swept away' (see above), Ezekiel is told, "Thou, therefore, son of man, prophesy, and smite thine hands together ..." (v.14). Both J.B.Taylor and H.L.Ellison suggest that smiting "thine hands together" indicates exultation, but F.Gardiner maintains that this too is "a gesture of strong emotion" and refers to Ezekiel 6 verse 11 ("Thus saith the Lord GOD, Smite with thine hand, and stamp with thy foot, and say, Alas for all the evil abominations of the house of Israel!"), to Ezekiel 22 verse 13 ("Behold, therefore, I have smitten mine hand at thy dishonest gain which thou hast made, and at thy blood which hath been shed in the midst of thee"); and to Numbers 24 verse 10 ("And Balak's anger was kindled against Balaam, and he smote his hands together ..."). This explanation is to be preferred.

The prophet's strong emotion, expressed in this way, was fully justified. We must notice the severity of coming judgment: "and let the sword be doubled the third time (RSV 'let the sword come down twice, yea thrice')" (v.14). While the exact meaning of the original text is uncertain, the general meaning is plain enough: "the activity of the sword is to be intensified to the utmost" (F.Gardiner). The sword in question is described as "the sword of the slain: it is the sword of the great men that are slain ('Literally, the sword of the overthrown [plural], it is the sword of the overthrow [singular] of the great one ... with especial reference to the king', F.Gardiner), which entereth into their privy chambers" (v.14). The words "which entereth into their privy chambers" or "which encompasses them privily" (JND) are helpfully rendered *"which begirts them round about"*, with the explanation "so that none can escape" (F.Gardiner).

The passage continues: "I have set the point of the sword ('the threatening sword', JND) against all their gates, that their heart may faint, and their ruins be multiplied ('and the stumblingblocks be multiplied', JND)" (v.15). According to F.Gardiner, this means that "in the coming desolation trouble shall be on every side and, in their perplexity, occasions for ill-advised action shall arise all round". The imminence of divine judgment is stressed: "Ah! It is made bright ('glittering', JND), it is wrapped up ('whetted', JND, or 'drawn') for the slaughter. Go thee (addressing the sword) one way or other, either on the right hand, or on the left, whithersoever thy face is set" (v.16). The sword was under divine control. Divine judgment is never indiscriminate. In this case, the reference to "the right hand, or on the left" could be explained by verses 18-22.

The section concludes: "I will also smite my hands together, and I will cause my fury to rest: I the LORD have said it" (v.17). In smiting his hands, Ezekiel was displaying the Lord's strong emotion over His people's sin, but divine fury would cease, "because it has accomplished its purpose and has nothing more to do" (F.Gardiner). Compare Ezekiel 5 verse 13; and 24 verse 13, where the words "till I have caused my fury to rest upon thee" means "till I have satisfied my fury upon thee" (JND).

c) *The sword identified, vv.18-32*

The sword in the previous verses is most certainly a divine sword, but it is wielded by the king of Babylon: "The word of the LORD came unto me again, saying, Also, thou son of man, appoint thee ('set before thee') two ways, that **the sword of the king of Babylon** may come: both twain shall come forth out of one land; and choose thou a place, choose it at the head of the way to the city" (vv.18-19). F.Gardiner gives a helpful explanation here: "The prophet is directed to represent Nebuchadnezzar as about to go forth with his armies, and hesitating whether he should take first the road to Jerusalem or to the capital of the Ammonites. His choice of the former is determined, as he supposes, by his divinations, but really by the overruling hand of the Lord, who thus shows beforehand what it shall be". So we read: "Appoint a way,

CHAPTER 20:45 - 21:32

that the sword may come to Rabbath of the Ammonites (modern Amman), and to Judah in Jerusalem the defenced. For the king of Babylon stood at the parting of the way (the point where the road forks), at the heads of the two ways, to use divination: he made his arrows bright ('he shaketh [his] arrows', JND), he consulted with images, he looked in the liver" (vv.20-21).

According to J.B.Taylor, "Three methods of divination are described. The first is shaking the *arrows,* or belomancy. In this, arrows were marked with names of people or places, shaken up in a quiver, and one was drawn out, as in drawing lots. The second is consultation of the *teraphim*: these were small images of household or ancestral gods, the possession of which played an important part in matters of legal inheritance (cf. Gen. 31: 19ff). They were sometimes used idolatrously or for necromancy, and were among the abominations removed by Josiah (2 Kings 23: 24) ... The third is hepatoscopy, examination of the *liver* or entrails of a sacrificed victim ... The interpretation of the markings on such organs was one of the skills in which Ancient Near Eastern soothsayers were instructed ..." How glad **we** should be that we have the **Word of God** to guide and direct us!

Both Jerusalem (vv.22-27) and Rabbath (vv.28-32) would fall to the Babylonians, and in that order. Notice the words "whose day is come" in relation to the king of Judah (v.25) and in relation to Ammon (v.29).

The divination for Jerusalem: "At his right hand was the divination (or '*into his right hand came* the divination' (F.Gardiner), or "In his right hand is the lot of Jerusalem to appoint battering rams ('captains', AV, but see margin), to open the mouth for bloodshed, to lift up the voice with shouting, to appoint battering-rams against the gates, to cast mounds, to build siege-towers" (vv.22-23, JND).

The reaction of the people of Jerusalem follows: "And it shall be to them as a false divination in their sight, to them that have sworn oaths: but he will call to remembrance their iniquity, that they may be taken. Therefore thus saith the Lord GOD, because ye have made your iniquity to be remembered, in that your transgressions are discovered, so that in all your doing your sins do appear; because I say, that ye are come to remembrance, ye shall be taken with the hand" (vv.23-24). As J.B.Taylor observes, "It will be no use the people of Jerusalem shrugging off these warnings and regarding them as *false divination:* Nebuchadnezzar will come and will bring their guilt home to them". The reference to "oaths", and to "their iniquity" and "transgressions", must be understood in the light of Ezekiel 17 verses 12-21. Judah had reneged on its oath of allegiance to Nebuchadnezzar, and he was on his way to exact vengeance.

Let *us* be warned: "we *must all* appear before the judgment seat of Christ; that every man may receive the things done in his body, whether it be good or bad" (2 Cor. 5: 10). This cannot be shrugged off either. We must remember, of course, that the "judgment seat of Christ" (the *bema*) is not a place of vengeance, but of reward. Even so, a "man's work" may "be burned", in which case "he shall suffer loss (of reward); but he himself shall be saved; yet so as by fire" (1 Cor. 3: 15).

Zedekiah would not escape: "and thou, profane wicked prince (not *melek*, king, but *nasi*, prince, 'a word without Messianic overtones', J.B.Taylor) of Israel, whose day is come, when iniquity shall have an end ('at the time of the iniquity of the end', JND), Thus saith the Lord God. Remove the diadem (or 'mitre', the turban worn by the high priest: here a symbol of royalty: or, as F.Gardiner suggests, 'not only was the royal but **also the high-priestly office** to be overthrown in the approaching desolation'), and take off the crown; this shall not be the same ('what is shall be no [more]', JND): exalt him that is low, and abase him that is high. I will overturn, overturn, overturn it; and it shall be no more, until he come whose right it is ('to whom justice belongs', JND margin); and I will give it him" (vv.25-27). He will be **both king and priest** (Zech. 6: 13).

Two monarchs are in view. The first is called "thou, profane, wicked prince of Israel, whose day is come ... remove the diadem, take off the crown". This is Zedekiah. No further monarch is to be expected until the second Monarch in this prophecy appears: "Until he come, whose right it is; and I will give it him". It was said of Him, "He shall be great, and shall be called the Son of the Highest: and the Lord God shall give unto him the throne of his father David: and he shall rule over the house of Jacob for ever; and of his kingdom there shall be no end" (Luke 1: 32-33). Zedekiah was Israel's last monarch: Christ is the next! Between the two lie the "times of the Gentiles" which commenced with Nebuchadnezzar, king of Babylon.

J.B.Taylor has a very nice piece here: "The triple repetition of a word is the strongest superlative the Hebrew language can give ... So Ezekiel spells out the overthrow of the kingly line, and he concludes with a cryptic reference back to Genesis 49 verse 10 with its distant prospect of the one who had always been expected and to whom the right of kingship genuinely belonged. When He eventually appears, the crown and diadem will be given to Him, for He will be the culmination of everything to which the Davidic house and the Messianic kingship in Israel have always pointed". Excellent! Genesis 49 verse 10 reads as follows: "The sceptre shall not depart from Judah, nor a lawgiver from between his feet, until Shiloh come; and unto him shall the gathering of the people be". We learn therefore that the sword of Babylon would not extinguish Israel for ever. God uses human agencies in preparation for the fulfilment of His ultimate purposes.

3) THE PROPHECY AGAINST AMMON, 21: 28-32

As we have already noticed, the king of Babylon had two objectives in view: the destruction of Jerusalem and the destruction of Rabbath (v.20), the capital city of Ammon.

F.Gardiner is most helpful: "At the opening of this prophecy (vv.19-20) the king of Babylon was represented as hesitating whether to attack Jerusalem or Rabbah, and as being led to the determination of attacking the former. This would leave the inference that the Ammonites might escape altogether; and from the destruction of God's peculiar people, along with the immunity of their ancient enemies, the heathen would be likely to draw conclusions inconsistent with the power and majesty of God. Hence this prophecy is added to show that His judgment shall certainly fall upon them also, and in this case the ruin foretold is final and hopeless, and without the promise given to Israel in v.27 ... As a matter of history, the Ammonites were conquered, and their country desolated, by Nebuchadnezzar a few years after the desolation of Jerusalem, and they gradually dwindled away until their name and place among the nations finally disappeared".

The coming conquest and destruction of Jerusalem has been described. As noted above, there would be no escape either for Rabbath. Divine judgment on Ammon would involve "the sword" (vv.28-30,) and "the fire" (vv.31-32):

a) The sword, vv.28-30

"And thou, son of man, prophesy, and say, Thus saith the Lord GOD concerning the Ammonites, and concerning their reproach (their exultation in the desolation of Israel: see, for example, Ezekiel 25: 3; Zephaniah 2: 8); even say thou, **The sword, the sword is drawn**; for the slaughter it is furbished (polished), to consume because of the glittering ('that it may glitter', JND)" (v.28). The deceit of Ammon's false prophets would be exposed: "whiles they see (referring to their false 'visions') vanity unto thee, whiles they divine a lie unto thee, to bring thee upon the necks of them that are slain, of the wicked". According to F.Gardiner, this means that "Judah is to fall first, then Ammon immediately after, as it were, upon the necks of those already slain. The figure is taken from the battle, in which one warrior falls upon the body of him who fell before him". There would be no delay: "whose day is come, when their iniquity shall have an end" (v.29), not meaning that the nation would repent, but because iniquity "ceases of necessity with the death of the sinner" (F.Gardiner). The sword would then be returned to its sheath: "Restore [it] to its sheath" (v.30, JND). Coming judgment could not be averted There would be no escape: "I will judge thee in the place where thou wast created, in the land of thy nativity" (v.30).

b) *The fire, vv.31-32*

"And I will pour out mine indignation upon thee; I will blow against thee in the fire of my wrath ('as fire is turned by the wind upon a forest to its destruction', F.Gardiner), and deliver thee into the hand of brutish men, and skilful to destroy. Thou shalt be for fuel to the fire; thy blood shall be in the midst of the land; thou shalt be no more remembered; for I the LORD have spoken it." See also Jeremiah 49 verses 1-6.

Ammon would suffer at the hands of "brutish men, and skiful to destroy" (v.31). While some suggest that this refers to "the men of the east" (25: 4), the savage tribesmen of the desert, F.Gardiner points out that "the men of the east ... are described as its possessors, not its conquerors". It therefore appears that the "brutish men, and skiful to destroy" are the Babylonians, and that the "men of the east" occupy the territory later. J.P.Taylor points out that the ultimate fate of the Ammonites would be "worse than Israel's, and worse even than Egypt's, for they will be *no more remembered.* To the Semitic mind nothing could be more terrible: no prospect of restoration, no continuance in succeeding generations, no memorial, not even a memory. Oblivion". To which we add: "but he that doeth the will of God abideth for ever" (1 John 2: 17).

EZEKIEL CHAPTER 22

As we noted in our two previous studies, Ezekiel 20-24 bring us to events culminating with the fall of Jerusalem, and while the overthrow of Jerusalem is not actually recorded until Chapter 33 verse 21, these chapters refer to Nebuchadnezzar's advance on the city (21: 18-22), the nearness of his arrival (22: 3-4) and the commencement of the siege (24: 1-2).

The judgment anticipated in Chapters 1-19 was now imminent. The invasion had commenced. The days of Zedekiah, the "profane, wicked prince of Israel", were numbered. His day "is come, when iniquity shall have an end" (21: 25). Hence we read, "Thus saith the Lord GOD, The city sheddeth blood in the midst of it, *that her time may come*, and maketh idols against herself to defile herself. Thou art become guilty in thy blood that thou hast shed; and hast defiled thyself in thine idols which thou hast made; and thou hast caused *thy days to draw near, and art come even unto thy years*". Details are given in Chapter 23: "The Babylonians, and all the Chaldeans, Pekod, and Shoa, and Koa, and all the Assyrians with them ... shall come against thee with chariots, wagons, and wheels, and with an assembly of people, which shall set against thee buckler and shield and helmet round about" (vv.23-24).

Chapter 22 divides into three clear sections, each commencing with the words, "the word of the LORD came unto me, saying" (vv.1, 17, 23). These sections may be entitled: *(1)* the causes of judgment (vv.1-16); *(2)* the crucible of judgment (vv.17-22); *(3)* the classes for judgment (vv.23-31).

1) THE CAUSES OF JUDGMENT, vv.1-16

This part of the chapter is introduced with the words, "Moreover the word of the LORD came unto me, saying, Now, thou son of man, wilt thou judge, wilt thou judge the bloody city? yea, thou shalt shew her all her abominations" (vv.1-2). According to J.B.Taylor the phrase, "wilt thou judge", means "much more than simply acting as an arbiter. It involves the prophet in the job which today is done partly by the prosecutor, and partly by the judge when he passes sentence on a man already pronounced guilty by a jury. So Ezekiel's 'judging' consists of showing to the guilty city of Jerusalem both the extent of her crimes, and also the consequences that are about to be inflicted upon her".

There are numerous references to blood in these verses (see vv.2, 3, 4, 6, 9, 12, 13), and numerous occurrences of the expression "in thee" or "in the midst of thee" (see vv.6, 7, 9, 10, 12, 13), leading H.L.Ellison to say that "One gets the impression that in the vision accompanying the words, Ezekiel saw the city he knew so well through a shimmer of blood". Ellison continues with a helpful piece on the sanctity of the blood: "God is the giver of life, which is outside man's power to bestow. For that reason the taking of life, symbolically expressed by 'the shedding of blood', except by God's permission or command, was supremely an insult to Him". We must now notice the following: *(a)* the charge (vv.3-12); *(b)* the sentence (vv.13-16).

a) The charge, vv.3-12

As noted above, the charge against Jerusalem is punctuated by references to blood: *(i)* the city was guilty of shedding blood (vv.3-5); *(ii)* the princes had power to shed blood (vv.6-8); *(iii)* there were men carrying tales to shed blood (vv.9-11); *(iv)* they had taken gifts to shed blood (v.12).

i) The city was guilty of shedding blood, vv.3-5

Blood-shedding and idolatry are associated here: "Thus saith the Lord GOD, The city **sheddeth blood** in the midst of it, that her time may come, and **maketh idols** against herself to defile herself. Thou art become guilty in **thy blood that thou hast shed**; and hast defiled thyself in **thine idols** which thou hast made; and thou hast caused thy days to draw near, and art come even unto thy years" (vv.3-4). J.B.Taylor points out that "the combination of bloodshed and idolatry in verse 3 is a reminder that the worship of idols did involve bloodshed in the form of child sacrifice ('making your sons to pass through the fire to Molech'; cf. 16: 21; 20: 26, 31; 23: 37) ... as well as ... any act of violence which incurred blood-guiltiness". It was Jerusalem's sin in this way that brought judgment upon her at the hands of Nebuchadnezzar and the Babylonian armies.

As noted above, the extent of idolatry is frightening: idol worship was accompanied by the shedding of blood, all of which solemnly reminds us that to ignore the injunction, "Little children, keep yourselves from idols" (1 John 5: 21), could lead to serious consequences in our lives. For example, if we worship what the hymn-writer calls "the vain world's golden store", we become exposed to what Paul calls "temptation and a snare, and ... many foolish and hurtful lusts, which drown men in destruction and perdition" (1 Tim. 6: 9).

As always, sin brings reproach, and the coming destruction of Jerusalem would make her "a reproach to the nations, and a mocking to all the countries. Those who are near and those who are far from you will mock you, you infamous one, full of tumult" (vv.4-5, Amplified Version). Compare Lamentations 2 verse 15. See Deuteronomy 28 verse 37: "And thou shalt become an astonishment, a proverb, and a byword, among all nations whither the LORD shall lead thee". (Compare 1 Kings 9: 7-9; Jer. 42: 18; Ezek. 36: 20-22.) There is no question here of having "a good report of them which are without" (1 Tim. 3: 7). The assembly at Thessalonica had an enviable testimony, not only in Macedonia and Achaia, but "in every place" their faith in God was "spread abroad" (1 Thess. 1: 8-10). It is nothing short of disastrous when an assembly loses its good standing in the community.

ii) The princes had power to shed blood, vv.6-8

"Behold, the princes of Israel, every one were in thee to their power to shed blood ('the princes of Israel have been in thee to shed blood, each according to his power', JND)" (v.6). H.L.Ellison calls this "judicial murder, doubtless for allegedly high purposes of state", and suggests that while the "princes" (*nasi*) may be the heads of the great families, the use of the word in Ezekiel 12 verse 12 (evidently referring to Zedekiah) makes it more likely that Ezekiel refers here to what Ellison calls "the corrupter kings". Manasseh was a case in point: see 2 Kings 21 verse 16 and 24 verse 4. "The rulers, who should have preserved order and administered justice, were foremost in deeds of violence" (F.Gardiner).

This reminds us that assembly elders are to "take care of the church of God" (1 Tim. 3: 5). They are not to be "lords over God's heritage, but ... ensamples to the flock" (1 Pet. 5: 3), or "not as lording it over your possessions, but being models for the flock" (JND).

Other sins are associated with murder: "In thee have they set light by ('made light of', JND) father and mother; in the midst of thee have they dealt by oppression with the stranger: in thee have they vexed the fatherless and the widow. Thou hast despised mine holy things, and hast profaned my sabbaths" (vv.7-8). H.L.Ellison refers to "the list of sins with which Jerusalem is charged in this section" and observes that "they lead to an inevitable collapse of society".

iii) There were men carrying tales to shed blood, vv.9-11

We should note Leviticus 19 verse 16 in this connection: "Thou shalt not go up and down as a talebearer among thy people: neither shalt thou stand against the blood of thy neighbour". For an example, see the successful attempt to discredit and then murder Naboth (1 Kings 21: 1-16). The 'inevitable collapse of society' (see above) is hastened by the practices named in these verses: "In thee are men that carry tales to shed blood: and in thee they eat upon the mountains: in the midst of thee they commit lewdness. In thee have they discovered their fathers' nakedness: in thee have they humbled her that was set apart for pollution. And one hath committed abomination with his neighbour's wife; and another hath lewdly defiled his daughter in law; and another in thee hath humbled his sister, his father's daughter". According to H.L.Ellison, 'eating upon the mountains' (v.9) refers to "the orgiastic feasts in the semi-Canaanised high places in which sexual promiscuity played a large part", adding that "sexual promiscuity is always a tremendous evil", and that we should not be surprised that "today, when adultery finds many an apologist, unnatural vice is steadily increasing".

iv) They had taken gifts to shed blood, v.12

"In thee have they taken gifts to shed blood; thou hast taken usury and increase, and thou hast greedily gained of thy neighbours by extortion, and hast forgotten me, saith the Lord GOD." As J.B.Taylor observes, "The over-all picture of extortion, bloodshed, immorality, incest and irreligion is a terrifying description of any nation whose appointed time is drawing near. Political commentators please note". The passage describes the complete transgression of the ten commandments:

- Thou shalt have no other gods before me. See verses 3-4: "maketh idols ... defiled thyself in thine idols".

- Thou shalt not make unto thee any graven image. See, again verses 3-4.

- Thou shalt not take the name of the LORD thy God in vain. See verse 28 in this connection.

- Remember the sabbath day to keep it holy. See verse 8.

- Honour thy father and thy mother. See verse 7.

- Thou shalt not kill. See verses 3, 6.

- Thou shalt not commit adultery. See verse 11.

- Thou shalt not steal. See verse 12 ("extortion"); verse 13 ("dishonest gain").

- Thou shalt not bear false witness. See verse 9.

- Thou shalt not covet. See verse 12 ("usury and increase ... greedily gained of thy neighbours").

b) *The sentence, vv.13-16*

The flagrant transgression of God's law can only result in divine judgment. Hence "I shall deal with thee. I the LORD have spoken it, and will do it" (v.14). We should notice *(i)* the smitten hand (vv.13-14); *(ii)* the scattered nation (vv.15-16).

i) God smites His hand, vv.13-14

"Behold, therefore I have smitten mine hand at thy dishonest gain which thou hast made, and at thy blood which hath been in the midst of thee. Can thine heart endure, or can thine hands be strong, in the days that I shall deal with thee? I the LORD have spoken it, and will do it."

As noted in connection with Chapter 21 verse 14, the smiting of hands is 'a gesture of strong emotion' (F.Gardiner). See Ezekiel 6 verse 11 ("Thus saith the Lord GOD, Smite with thine hand, and stamp with thy foot, and say, Alas for all the evil abominations of the house of Israel!"); Ezekiel 22 verse 13 ("Behold, therefore, I have smitten mine hand at thy dishonest gain which thou hast made, and at thy blood which hath been 'shed' in the midst of thee"); Numbers 24 verse 10 ("And Balak's anger was kindled against Balaam, and he smote his hands together ..."). See also Chapter 21 verse 17, "I will also smite my hands together, and I will cause my fury to rest: I the LORD have said it". This should be compared with Chapter 20 verses 5-6, 28 and 42, where God's hand is lifted up in blessing, but it is lifted up in judgment too: see Chapter 20 verses 15, 23. The Lord has a strong hand, but the hands of Jerusalem would not be strong under judgment: "Can thine heart endure, or can thine hands be strong, in the days that I shall deal with thee?"

ii) God scatters the nation, vv.15-16

"And I will scatter thee among the heathen, and disperse thee in the countries, and will consume thy filthiness out of thee. And thou shalt take thine inheritance in thyself in the sight of the heathen, and thou shalt know that I am the LORD." Compare Chapter 20 verse 23. The words "will consume thy filthiness out of thee" lead to the second oracle in the chapter (vv.17-22) where Jerusalem is placed "in the midst of the furnace" (vv.18, 20).

The words, "And thou shalt take thine inheritance in thyself in the sight of the heathen" have given commentators palpitations. The Revised Version reads as follows: "And thou shalt be profaned in thyself in the sight of the nations". Compare, verse 5: "Those that be near, and those that be far from thee, shall mock thee, which art infamous and much vexed". According to F.Gardiner, "The meaning is that through their own misconduct they forfeit the privileges of a holy nation, and become profaned or dishonoured in the sight of the heathen".

2) THE CRUCIBLE OF JUDGMENT, vv.17-22

"Jerusalem is represented as the refining pot into which the people were to be cast, because this was at once their national centre, and also the centre of the war by which they were carried into captivity" (F.Gardiner, *Ellicott's Commentary*).

"And the word of the LORD came unto me saying, Son of man, the house of Israel is to me become dross: all they are brass and tin, and iron, and lead, in the midst of the furnace; they are even the dross of silver" (vv.17-18). While the figure of refining precious metal is frequently found in the Old Testament (see Isaiah 1: 22, 25; 48: 10; Jer. 6: 27-30; 9: 7; Zech. 13: 9; Mal. 3: 2-4), on this occasion the figure is used to show Israel is nothing but worthless dross. Silver is mentioned in verses 18, 20, 22, but only in connection with the actual process on which the metaphor is based. As

J.B.Taylor points out, in this case "Israel has no silver in her: she is utterly worthless, all dross", and H.L.Ellison goes further in saying, "This gives the true meaning to the threat in verse 15 ('I ... will consume thy filthiness out of thee). Such a purification meant the blotting out of the survivors, for there was *only filthiness in them*". In this connection, we should note the references to God's "fury" (vv.20, 22). (See also 20: 8, 13, 21, 34.)

The New Testament emphasises that believers are often found in the crucible, not as base metal ("brass ... tin ... iron ... lead") but as precious metal. The Lord's people are "kept by the power of God through faith unto salvation ready to be revealed in the last time. Wherein ye greatly rejoice, though now for a season, if need be, ye are in heaviness through manifold temptations (trials): that the trial of your faith, being much more precious than of gold that perisheth, though it be tried with fire, might be found unto praise and honour and glory at the appearing of Jesus Christ" (1 Pet. 1: 5-7).

3) THE CLASSES FOR JUDGMENT, vv.23-31

"And the word of the LORD came unto me, saying, Son of man, say unto her, Thou art the land that is not cleansed, nor rained upon in the day of indignation" (vv.23-24). As in verses 17-22, this evidently refers to verse 15, "I ... will consume thy filthiness out of thee". The words "nor rained upon" indicate the withdrawal of divine favour (compare Deut. 28: 23-24; 1 Kings 17: 1). H.L.Ellison suggests that "the day of indignation" began with the death of Josiah at Megiddo.

All sections of the community are examined in relation to the uncleanness of God's people: *(a)* the prophets (v.25); *(b)* the priests (v.26); *(c)* the princes (vv.27-28); *(d)* the people (v.29).

a) The prophets, v.25

"There is a conspiracy of her prophets in the midst thereof, like a roaring lion ravening the prey: they have devoured souls; they have taken the treasure and precious things; they have made her many widows in the midst thereof." It should be said that some commentators feel that the Hebrew word here, *nebi'im*, should read *nesi'im*, meaning 'princes'. J.N.Darby notes this: "Others read 'princes', as the LXX. It is a change of one letter in the Hebrew". But he retains "her prophets" in his translation!

Zephaniah describes these prophets as "light and treacherous persons" (Zeph. 3: 4). They deceived people with false hopes. There was no honesty about their preaching. The false prophets were known for their self-initiated ministry. See Jeremiah 23 verse 16, "They speak a vision of **their own heart,** and not out of the mouth of the Lord". This reminds us that the servants of God must speak as "the oracles of God" (1 Pet. 4: 11). There is all the difference in the world between a message and an address! False prophets were motivated by financial gain. See Micah 3 verse 11, "The heads thereof judge for reward, and the priests thereof teach for hire, and **the prophets thereof divine for money**". This reminds us that servants of God must not be influenced by either financial gain or prestige. The apostle Paul had the purest of motives in serving God: "For we are not as many, which corrupt (make a trade of) the word of God: but as of sincerity, but as of God, in the sight of God speak we in Christ" (2 Cor. 2: 17).

b) The priests, v.26

"Her priests have violated my law, and have profaned mine holy things: they have put no difference between the holy and the profane, neither have they shewed difference between the unclean and the clean, and have hid their eyes from my sabbaths, and I am profaned among them." The priests who were "entrusted with God's law (*tora*) ... had done violence to it, and to the holiness which they were intended to preserve. All had been reduced to a common level of uncleanness, whether it was holiness of worship or of foods or of times and seasons. Their failure to maintain the distinctive quality of the things of God meant that God too was disregarded and treated with contempt" (J.B.Taylor). Compare Romans 2 verses 23-24: "Thou that makest thy boast of the law, through breaking the law dishonourest thou God? For the name of God is blasphemed among the Gentiles through you".

c) The princes, vv.27-28

The word "princes" (*sarim*) means 'nobles' and refers to the leaders or chiefs of the people. "Her princes in the midst thereof are like wolves ravening the prey, to shed blood, and to destroy souls, to get dishonest gain." Zephaniah describes the princes in similar language: "Her princes within her are roaring lions" (Zeph. 3: 3). Compare Micah 3 verses 1-3, where the "princes of the house of Israel" were acting like cannibals: "who also eat the flesh of my people, and flay their skin from off them; they break their bones, and chop them in pieces, as for the pot, and as flesh

CHAPTER 22

within the cauldron". They should have been shepherds. But they were feeding themselves.

As already noted, Peter warns God's shepherds against acting in a similar way: "Neither as lords over God's heritage" or 'Not as lording it over your possessions' (JND)' (1 Pet. 5: 3). Spiritual leaders can easily forget that they are only 'under-shepherds', and begin to feed, for example, on power and love of position. Here is the passage in full: "The elders which are among you I exhort ... Feed the flock of God which is among you, taking the oversight thereof, not by **constraint** (not marked by love of ease, and not as a slave), but willingly; not for **filthy lucre** (not marked by love of money, and not as a hireling), but of a ready mind; neither as being **lords over God's heritage** (not marked by love of power, and not as a master), but being ensamples to the flock". The word, "feed" means 'shepherd', and involves more than giving food. It involves general care. God's shepherds must be proactive. Prevention is better than cure. Caring for "the flock of God" includes regular visitation. The shepherd must know the sheep. Overseership is a **work,** not a seat at the monthly overseers' meeting!

It is not surprising that in this the princes were **supported by the prophets** (of whom similar things are said in v.25): "And her prophets have daubed them with untempered mortar, seeing vanity, and divining lies unto them, saying, Thus saith the Lord GOD, when the LORD hath not spoken".

For "untempered mortar", see Chapter 13 verse 10 where we noted that "the word is not the usual one for plaster, and indeed is used in this sense only in these verses (Chapter 13 verses 10-16) and in Chapter 22 verse 28" (F.Gardiner). (His piece on the subject, in *Ellicott's Commentary*, is worth reading in full.) According to J.B.Taylor, the words "untempered mortar" are based on an incorrect identification with a root meaning 'unseasoned', and the word is bettered rendered 'whitewash'". Gesenius has "lime, with which a wall is covered". We might say 'lime-washed'. J.B.Taylor states that the word is closely akin to a root meaning 'to plaster over' and cites Job 13 verse 4, "As for you, you whitewash with lies" (RSV), although this does not appear to be supported by Gesenius. However, Taylor is correct in saying, "So the people's futile hopes are encouraged by the prophets' lying lullabies of peace. It is a common failing for preachers to want to speak pleasing and appeasing words to their people, but if they are to be true to their calling they must be sure to receive and to impart nothing but God's clear word, irrespective of the consequences. When church leaders encourage their people in sub-Christian standards or unbiblical ways, they make themselves doubly guilty". We add that the expressions here "seeing vanity" and "divining lies" (v.28) describe "pretended and false visions" (F.Gardiner). See Chapter 13 verses 7 and 9.

d) The people, v.29

"The people of the land have used oppression, and exercised robbery, and have vexed the poor and needy; yea, they have oppressed the stranger wrongfully." According to J.B.Taylor (supported by Ellison), "The *am hares* were the common people; not obviously the poorest of the peasantry, but all those who possessed full citizen rights. They were thus able to find some people less privileged than themselves whom they could tyrannize". The Lord's people today are to be so different: "be ye kind one to another, tenderhearted, forgiving one another, even as God for Christ's sake hath forgiven you" (Eph. 4: 32).

The oracle concludes on the saddest of notes: "And I sought for a man among them, that should make up the hedge and stand in the gap before me for the land, that I should not destroy it; but I found none. Therefore have I poured out mine indignation upon them; I have consumed them with the fire of my wrath: their own way have I recompensed upon their heads, saith the Lord GOD" (vv.30-31). Compare Ezekiel 13 verses 3-5: "Woe unto the foolish prophets, that follow their own spirit, and have seen nothing! O Israel, thy prophets are like the foxes in the deserts. Ye have not gone up into the gaps, neither made up the hedge for the house of Israel, to stand in the battle in the day of the LORD". According to F.Gardiner, this does not mean "that there was not a single godly man, but not one of such a pure, strong, and commanding character that his intercession might avert the threatened doom". There was no Abraham on this occasion! See Genesis 18 verses 23-33. The reference could be to a prophet of indomitable character, but it does seem more likely that the absence of a godly king is lamented here. There was no Hezekiah or Josiah. "With this degree of universal corruption, God looks in vain for just one man who will try to interpose himself to stop the national ruin. But there was no-one with the moral courage to stem the tide: the leaders were ungodly and those who should have been godly had compromised their position. Presumably Jeremiah was an exception to Ezekiel's general condemnation, but he had no kingly status and few listened to his words. Any nation which lacks godly leadership, as Israel did at that time, must surely be on the way out. Compare Isaiah 59 verse

CHAPTER 22

16 and 63 verse 5, where by contrast the continuing absence of a 'man to intervene' leads the Lord to gain the victory with His own right hand. For Ezekiel, however, this state of affairs was but the prelude to the imminent and final act of judgment on the citizens of Jerusalem, when their own way would be recompensed upon their own heads" (J.B.Taylor). His footnote (page 170) is worth reading and noting.

Paul writes: "God for Christ's sake hath forgiven you" (Eph. 4: 32). But here there was no intercessor, and nothing which provided grounds for withholding judgment. How different our position! "There is one God, and one mediator between God and man, the man Christ Jesus" (1 Tim. 2: 5).

EZEKIEL CHAPTER 23

Chapters 20-24 record the last prophecies in the book before the fall of Jerusalem. At the time, Nebuchadnezzar was either about to leave Babylonia, or had actually commenced the march (21: 18-22). Divine judgment, to be executed by the king of Babylon, was imminent: The days of Zedekiah, the "profane, wicked prince of Israel", were numbered. His day "*is come*, when iniquity shall have an end" (21: 25), and the theme of imminent judgment continues, as already noted, in Chapter 22: "Thus saith the Lord God, The city sheddeth blood in the midst of it, *that her time may come*, and maketh idols against herself to defile herself. Thou art become guilty in thy blood that thou hast shed; and hast defiled thyself in thine idols which thou hast made; and thou hast caused *thy days to draw near, and art come even unto thy years*" (vv.3-4).

Chapters 20-23, which highlight the reasons for coming judgment by laying bare the sin of Judah and Jerusalem, commence and conclude with a description of their rebellion against the Lord. In the first case, their rebellion is described in actual historical terms (Ch.20) and in the second in parabolic terms (Ch.23). In both cases, the Lord traces the rebellion of His people from the earliest days of nationhood – in Egypt. (See 20: 5-9; 23: 3.)

Chapter 23 deals with the history of God's people under the figure of two sisters: Aholah, representing the northern kingdom of Israel, and Aholibah representing the southern kingdom of Judah. The two kingdoms are identified by their capital cities: "Thus were their names; Samaria is Aholah, and Jerusalem Aholibah" (v.4). Bearing in mind that the words "whoredom", "whoredoms" or "whoring", occur seventeen times in the passage, the chapter may be divided as follows: *(1)* the whoredom of Aholah and Ahilobah in Egypt (vv.1-4); *(2)* the whoredom of Aholah with the Assyrians (vv.5-10); *(3)* the whoredom of Aholibah with the Chaldeans (vv.11-35); *(4)* the whoredom of Aholah and Aholibah restated (vv.36-49).

The chapter therefore commences and concludes with the two 'sisters', and deals with them individually in the intervening verses, noting that both of them had turned to Egypt for help. It will be noted that three of the above sections may be divided into: *(a)* the pollution; *(b)* the punishment.

The four sections indicated above may be summarised as follows:

- ***Initiation, vv.1-4.*** Idolatry began in Egypt - in the nation's infancy: in early life when habits are formed.

- ***Infatuation, vv.5-10.*** First of all with **people**: the "Assyrians ... clothed with blue, captains and rulers, all of them desirable young men, horsemen riding upon horses" (v.6).

- ***Infatuation, vv.11-35.*** Secondly with **pictures of people:** "the images of the Chaldeans pourtrayed (on walls) with vermilion" (v.14). People today are certainly infatuated with pictures of people – moving pictures. In fact, they are sometimes called 'movies' *et al.*

- ***Integration, vv.36-49.*** "For when the had slain their children to their idols, then they came the same day into my sanctuary to profane it. And lo, thus have they done in the midst of my house" (v.39).

1) THE WHOREDOM OF AHOLAH AND AHOLIBAH IN EGYPT, vv.1-4

"The word of the LORD came again unto me, saying, Son of man, there were two women, the daughters of one mother; and they committed whoredoms in Egypt; they committed whoredoms in their youth ... And the names of them were Aholah the elder, and Aholibah her sister: and they were mine, and they bare sons and daughters. Thus were their names; Samaria is Aholah, and Jerusalem Aholibah."

Israel's history of idolatry began in the nation's infancy in Egypt: "they committed whoredoms in their youth" (v.3). Bearing in mind that Aholah and Aholibah represent Israel and Judah respectively, the "one mother" represents their common ancestry. Some suggest that the "one mother" was Sarah, but identification in this way is not necessary. The two daughters in the passage are designated sisters in Jeremiah 3 verse 7.

"Although the division of the kingdom did not take place until later (although the seeds of division were present: see Judges 8: 1; 12: 1; 2 Sam. 19: 43), both sisters are pictured as residing in Egypt, and it is stated that they played the harlot in that country; they were prostitutes in their youth" (F.A.Tatford). The passage, with its allusions to sexual impurity, refers to the idolatry of God's people. See Chapter 20 verses 7-8, "Then said I unto them ... defile not yourselves with the idols of Egypt". What happened in the infancy of the nations never left them: see verse 8 (Aholah: Samaria) and verses 19, 21 (Aholibah: Jerusalem). In this case, the two 'sisters' were both adulteresses and prostitutes: the Lord says, "they were mine" (v.4). Idolatry is often described as adultery in the scriptures. See, for example, verse 37.

It has been pointed out that the results of idolatry in Egypt were seen at Sinai: "the golden calf episode reveals that they were both touched by the idolatry practised about them (Ezek. 16: 26; 20: 7-8), and the comment of Joshua was both interesting and determining in the matter (Joshua 24: 14)" (C.L.Feinberg).

The names are significant. Both derive from *'ohel*, meaning 'tent', but Aholah means "her tent" and Aholibah means "my tent is in her" (C.L.Feinberg). In the first case, the name probably refers to the pagan tent-shrines of the northern kingdom, whereas in the second, reference is evidently made to "the selection of Jerusalem as the place for God's 'tent' (2 Sam. 6: 17; Psalm 48: 1-14) or place of worship" (Lamar E.Cooper). Samaria (Aholah) is called "the elder" perhaps because "she preceded Judah both in defection and captivity", or possibly because "the northern kingdom was the more populous of the two" (C.L.Feinberg).

2) THE WHOREDOM OF AHOLAH WITH THE ASSYRIANS, vv.5-10

The Assyrians are mentioned three times in this section of the chapter (vv.5, 7, 9). As noted above, these verses may be further divided into: *(a)* her pollution (vv.5-8); *(b)* her punishment (vv.9-10). (Or **doting** on the Assyrians ... **destroyed** by the Assyrians: see also vv.12, 16. 20).

a) Her pollution, vv.5-8

"And Aholah played the harlot when she was mine; and she doted on her lovers, on the Assyrians her neighbours ... Thus she committed her whoredoms with them, with all them that were the chosen men of Assyria, and with all on whom she doted: with all her idols she defiled herself" (vv.5, 7). The word "doted" (meaning 'infatuated') occurs in verses 5, 7 and 9.

CHAPTER 23

Leaving aside archeological evidence of Samaria's appeals to Assyria, and payment of tribute, in the reigns of Omri, Jehoash and Jehu (John B.Taylor), the Old Testament describes the payment of tribute to Assyria by Menahem and Hoshea (2 Kings 15: 19; 17: 3). According to Hosea, "Israel is swallowed up … For they are gone up to Assyria, a wild ass alone by himself: Ephraim hath hired lovers" (Hos. 8: 8-9). (See also Hosea 5: 13; 7: 11; 12: 1.) Samaria was evidently dazzled by Assyria: "the Assyrians … were clothed with blue, captains and rulers, all of them desirable young men, horsemen riding upon horses" (v.6). C.L.Feinberg has a telling piece here: "Aholah doted on the Assyrians because of their striking apparel, their high offices, and their costly means of travel. The appeal, then as now, was to youth, strength, position, wealth and self-gratification: that is, the world with all its dazzle and attractiveness".

Political liaisons led to religious liaisons: "Thus she committed her whoredoms with them, with all them that were the chosen men of Assyria, and with all on whom she doted: with all their idols she defiled herself" (v.7). Practices in Egypt were repeated with the Assyrians (v.8). As John B.Taylor observes, "she was merely perpetuating the patterns of behaviour she had learnt in Egypt".

b) Her punishment, vv.9-10

"Wherefore I have delivered her into the hand of her lovers, into the hand of the Assyrians, upon whom she doted" (v.9). The statement of verse 10 ("These discovered her nakedness: they took her sons and her daughters, and slew her with the sword") must be read in conjunction with 2 Kings 17 verses 3-6. Samaria's lovers became her destroyers, to the extent that "She became a byword among women, and punishment was inflicted on her" (v.10, NIV). The words, "these discovered her nakedness", refer to the despoliation and denuding of the land.

We might have expected the southern kingdom, Judah, to have learnt from her sister's terrible mistakes, but, alas, this was not the case. We come now to:

3) THE WHOREDOM OF AHOLIBAH WITH THE CHALDEANS, vv.11-35

As noted above, this section may be further divided into *(a)* her pollution (vv.11-21); *(b)* her punishment (vv.22-35). (Or *doting* on the Chaldeans … *destroyed* by the Chaldeans. The word "doted" occurs in verses 12, 16 and 20.

a) Her pollution, vv.11-21

"And when her sister Aholibah saw this, she was more corrupt in her inordinate love than she, and in her whoredoms more than her sister in her whoredoms" (v.11). Compare Jeremiah 3 verses 6-11, "And I said after she (Israel) had done all these things, Turn thou unto me. But she returned not. And her treacherous sister Judah saw it, And I saw, when for all the causes whereby backsliding Israel committed adultery I had put her away, and given her a bill of divorcement; yet her treacherous sister Judah feared not, but went and played the harlot also" (vv.7-8).). C.L.Feinberg explains this clearly: "One needs only to consider the long and abominable reign of Manasseh (2 Kings 21: 1-16; 2 Chron. 33: 1-9). She had the example of the northern kingdom clearly before her, both as to the gravity of her transgressions and the severity of the punishment for them, but no impression was made upon the heart to turn to God".

Like Israel (Aholah), Judah (Aholibah) "doted upon the Assyrians her neighbours, captains and rulers clothed most gorgeously, horsemen riding upon hoses, all of them desirable young men" (v.12). Ahaz placed the southern kingdom under the protection of Tiglath-pileser III (2 Kings 16: 7-10), a political manoeuvre denounced by Isaiah (Isa. 7: 3-17)" (C.L.Feinberg).

But worse was to follow: "Then I saw that she was defiled, that they took both one way ('they both took the same way', RSV) and that she increased her whoredoms: for when she saw men pourtrayed upon the wall, the images of the Chaldeans pourtrayed with vermilion, girded with girdles upon their loins, exceeding in dyed attire upon their heads, all of them princes to look to, after the manner of the Babylonians of Chaldea, the land of their nativity: and as soon as she saw them with her eyes, she doted upon them, and sent messengers unto them into Chaldea" (vv.13-16). According to Lamar E. Cooper, "The Assyrians and the Babylonians were noted for decorating walls with carved bas-reliefs ('a carving in low relief'), some ten to twelve feet high, depicting the glories and conquests of the empire".

While precise details of Judah's infatuation with Chaldea are not given, we do know that good relations were formed during the reign of Hezekiah (see Isaiah 39: 1-8), and these evidently continued. "Enamoured by foreign nobility, Judah sent ambassadors to Chaldea to form alliances or establish good relations" (C.L.Feinberg). With the demise of Assyria, Judah evidently turned to Babylonia, and became subject to her influence. As C.L.Feinberg observes, "Political alliances again gave place to religious defection". In Bible language, "And the Babylonians came to her into the bed of love, and they defiled her with their whoredom, and she was polluted with them" (v.17). It seems distinctly possible the worship of "the queen of heaven" was one aspect of this defilement and pollution. "Seest thou not what they do in the cities of Judah and in the streets of Jerusalem? The children gather wood, and the fathers kindle the fire, and the women knead their dough, to make cakes to the queen of heaven, and to pour out drink-offerings unto other gods, that they may provoke me to anger?" (Jer. 7: 17-18). According to T.Laetsch (*Jeremiah*), "The Queen of Heaven is evidently to be identified with Astarte (Ashtarte), or Ashtoreth, a Semitic goddess, the Ishtar of the Balylonian-Assyrian cult". C.L.Feinberg states "the fact is that Ishtar was known by the Babylonian title *sharrat shame* ('Queen of Heaven'), goddess of the planet Venus".

But infatuation with the Chaldeans did not last: "her mind was alienated from them". As C.L.Feinberg points out, "verses 17-19 indicate Judah's vacillating policy in turning from one great political power to another in order to gain the greatest political benefit from her alliances". John B. Taylor calls this "the pendulum-like swing from a pro-Babylonian policy to an anti-Babylonian policy that marked Judah's political history during the last hundred years before the exile". "So she discovered ('flaunted', RSV) her whoredoms, and discovered her nakedness: then my mind was alienated from her, like as my mind was alienated from her sister" (v.18), reminding us that "the friendship of the world is enmity with God ... whosoever therefore will be the friend of the world is the enemy of God" (James 4: 4).

The references to Egypt in this connection (vv.19-21) may possibly refer to what J.B.Taylor calls "contemporary pro-Egyptian intrigues (cf. Jer. 37: 5)", but continues by saying that "it is not necessary that it should be so interpreted, The dominant thought is the influence of Judah's Egyptian upbringing". "Yet she multiplied her whoredoms, in calling to remembrance the days of her youth, wherein she played the harlot in the land of Egypt. For she doted upon their paramours ... Thus thou calledst to remembrance the lewdness of thy youth, in bruising thy teats by the Egyptians for the paps of thy youth." The influence of former days persisted.

b) Her punishment, vv.22-35

Judgment is now pronounced on Aholibah (Jerusalem). Just as Aholah

(Samaria) had been ultimately destroyed by her lover, Assyria, so Aholibah would be destrioyed by her lovers, the Babylonians and Chaldeans *et al* (v.23). The punishment of Aholibah is described in four oracles, each commencing with the words, "thus saith the Lord GOD" (vv.22, 28, 32, 35).

i) ***The first oracle describes the invasion, vv.22-27***. "Behold, I will raise up thy lovers against thee, from whom thy mind is alienated, and I will bring them against thee on every side; the Babylonians, and all the Chaldeans, Pekod and Shoa, and Koa, and all the Assyrians with them: all of them desirable young men, captains and rulers, great lords and renowned, all of them riding upon horses. And they shall come against thee with chariots, wagons, and wheels, and with an assembly of people, which shall set against thee buckler (a small round shield) and shield (a large body shield) and helmet round about: and I will set judgment before them, and they shall judge thee according to their judgments" (vv.22-24). We should notice that the Chaldean armies execute the judgment of God: "***I will*** set judgment before them".

The people called "Pekod and Shoa, and Koa" were "all groups in the eastern part of the Babylonian empire", although some commentators understand them differently. The "Assyrians" are those who fought with Nebuchadnezzar's armies: Assyria was by this time part of the Babylonian empire. As C.L.Feinberg observes, the "same qualities which attracted her at first (v.6) were those which accomplished her undoing and destruction". The lesson here cannot be mistaken!

The purpose of the invasion is clearly stated. It demonstrates the jealousy of God: "And I will set my jealousy against thee" (v.25), reminding us that His name is "Jealous" (Ex. 34: 14). The cutting off of nose and ears (v.25) is said to be "the punishment of an adulteress" (C.L.Feinberg). By such stern measures, the Lord would purge His people from the idolatry dating back to their sojourn in Egypt: "Thus will I make thy lewdness to cease from thee, and thy whoredom brought from the land of Egypt: so that thou shalt not lift up thine eyes unto them, nor remember Egypt any more" (v.27). "Following the Babylonian exile, idolatry was never again a problem" (Lamar E. Cooper).

ii) ***The second oracle gives the explanation, vv.28-31***. "For thus saith the Lord God; Behold, I will deliver thee into the hand of them whom thou hatest, into the hand of them from whom thy mind is alienated (see v.17): and they shall deal with thee hatefully, and shall take away all thy labour, and shall leave thee naked and bare: and the nakedness of thy whoredoms shall be discovered, both thy lewdness and thy whoredoms. I will do these things unto thee, because thou hast gone a whoring after the heathen, and because thou art polluted with their idols. Thou hast walked in the way of thy sister; therefore will I give her cup into thy hand."

As John B.Taylor points out, unlike the first oracle, "no atrocities are described, but the results of a hostile invasion are indicted by the removal of "all thy labour", i.e. the wealth which was the fruit of their labour, and by their being "naked and bare", as if after the destruction of their armies or their fortifications". The words "therefore will I give her cup into thy hand" (v.31) lead to the third oracle.

iii) ***The third oracle emphasises the intensity of suffering, vv.32-34.***
"Thus saith the Lord GOD; Thou shalt drink of thy sister's cup deep and large: thou shalt be laughed to scorn and had in derision; it containeth much. Thou shalt be filled with drunkenness and sorrow, with the cup of astonishment and desolation, with the cup of thy sister Samaria. Thou shalt even drink it and suck it out, and thou shalt break the sherds thereof, and pluck off thine own breasts: for I have spoken it, saith the Lord GOD."

C.L.Feinberg is worth quoting here *in extenso*: "The figure of the cup is employed in Scripture in two diametrically opposed senses. In certain cases it refers to the blessing of God poured out in abundant measure (Psalm 23: 5). At other times it points to the wrath of God for sinners (Psalm 75: 8; Isaiah 51: 17-22; Jer. 25: 15-29; Hab. 2: 16). In the highest sense it is used of the death of Christ for sinners when He drank the cup of God's wrath for us (see Matt. 20: 22 and parallel passages). Judah would not only drink to the full the cup of God's wrath, but would even gnaw the sherds of the cup. Ezekiel vividly portrayed the utter despair of the outcast who would drink herself to madness, tearing at her breasts."

The solemn fact is that Jerusalem had failed to learn the lesson of Samaria, and would therefore "drink of thy sister's cup deep and large: thou shalt be laughed to scorn and had in derision; it containeth much".

iv) ***The fourth oracle emphasises the reason for her suffering, v.35***.
"Therefore thus saith the Lord GOD; because thou hast forgotten me, and cast me behind thy back, therefore bear thou also thy lewdness and thy whoredoms." Nothing more needs to be said.

4) THE WHOREDOM OF AHOLAH AND AHOLIBAH RESTATED, vv.36-49

The final section of the chapter addresses Aholah and Aholibah together. "The LORD said moreover unto me, Son of man wilt thou judge (in the sense of 'judge' or 'make known') Aholah and Aholibah? Yea, declare unto them their abominations" (v.36). This section may be divided as follows: *(a)* the detailed indictment (vv.36-44); *(b)* the declaration of punishment (vv.45-49). In verses 36-44 Ezekiel 'declares unto them their abominations', and in verses 45-49 he declares the judgment of Aholah and Aholibah.

a) The detailed indictment, vv.36-44

Both are described in the clearest terms as harlots: "Yet they went in unto her, as they go unto a woman that playeth the harlot: so went they in unto Aholah and Aholibah, the lewd women" (v.44). Both are described as adulteresses (v.45). Such are God's terms for compromise and identification on the part of His people with heathen nations. As we have seen, the New Testament is equally clear. See James 4 verses 3-4. The charges against the 'sisters' are set out in verses 37-44.

i)   Idolatry, v.37

"They have committed adultery, and blood is in their hands, and with their idols have they committed adultery." The connection between adultery and idolatry is spelt out through Jeremiah: "she defiled the land, and committed adultery with stones and with stocks" (Jer. 3: 9).

ii)   Child sacrifice, v.37

The connection between idolatry and child sacrifice is clear from the words, "They have committed adultery, and blood is in their hands". The verse continues: "and have also caused their sons, whom they bare unto me, to pass for them through the fire, to devour them". Note the expression, "their sons, whom they bare **unto me**". As F.A.Tatford explains, "Jehovah referred to their descendants as those borne to Him, since He had parabolically portrayed Himself as the sisters' spouse".

iii) Defilement of the sanctuary, vv.38-39

"Moreover this they have done unto me: they have defiled my sanctuary in the *same day*, and have profaned my sabbaths. For when they had slain their children to their idols, then they came the *same day* into my sanctuary to profane it: and, lo, thus have they done in the midst of mine house." "With a complete disregard for the holiness of Jehovah and His temple, they associated His worship with that of the idols of the heathen – an intolerable situation" (F.A.Tatford). The lesson must be noted: do we have double standards – a 'best of both worlds' attitude – servants of sin on the one hand, and professed servants of God on the other?

It should be noted that *both* sisters are charged with the defilement of the sanctuary at Jerusalem. John B.Taylor suggests that "the separation of Israel from Jerusalem was still regarded with bitterness, unless this refers to the successors of the Israelites, (later called Samaritans) who still travelled south to worship Jehovah at Jerusalem (cf. Jer. 41: 5)". However, representatives of the ten tribes do appear to have come to Jerusalem in Josiah's day (2 Chron. 35: 18), and some may well have come at other times with blood in their hands.

iv) *Compromise with the nations, vv.40-44*

While the language of the entire passage is couched in terms of prostitution, the "significance was, of course, still the improper alliances made by Israel and Judah with pagan nations for political reasons" (F.A.Tatford). With this in mind, noting that "the two women took the initiative in seeking paramours from a distance" (F.A.Tatford), we read: "And furthermore, that ye have sent for men to come from far, unto whom a messenger was sent; and, lo, they came: for whom thou didst wash thyself, paintedst thy eyes, and deckedst thyself with ornaments, and satest upon a stately bed, and a table prepared before it, whereupon thou hast set mine incense and mine oil. And a voice of a multitude being at ease was with her: and with the men of the common sort were brought Sabeans (or 'drunkards': JND margin) from the wilderness (perhaps, according to C.L.Feinberg, Arabs, Edomites, Moabites), which put bracelets upon their hands, and beautiful crowns upon their heads. Then said I unto her that was old in adulteries (evidently referring to Judah), Will they now commit whoredoms with her, and she with them? Yet they went in unto her, as they go unto a woman that playeth the harlot: so went they in unto Aholah and Aholibah, the lewd women".

b) *The declaration of judgment, vv.45-49*

Attention is drawn *(i)* to the judges themselves (v.45); *(ii)* to the justice of their actions (v.45); *(iii)* to the judgment described (vv.46-47); *(iv)* to the judgment's result vv.48-49).

i) The judges themselves, v.45

"And the righteous men, they shall judge them ..." While John B.Taylor states that "the 'righteous men' can hardly be the lovers of verses 22-24", he does have to continue by adding, "even though the nations will eventually be the instruments of God's judgment", and further, "It must mean that those who judge the two sisters will judge them righteously. The stress is on the way the judging will be done, not on who will do the judging". Lamar E. Cooper suggests that the description of the judges probably means "that heathen paramours were more righteous by comparison, than the two sisters".

ii) The justice of their actions, v.45

"And the righteous men, they shall judge them after the manner of adulteresses, and after the manner of women that shed blood; because they are adulteresses, and blood is on their hands."

iii) The judgment described, vv.46-47

"For thus saith the Lord GOD; I will bring up a company upon them, and will give them to be removed and spoiled. And the company shall stone them with stones, and dispatch them with their swords; and they shall slay their sons and their daughters, and burn up their houses with fire." Quite clearly, their punishment will be the common penalty for all adulteresses (Lev. 20: 10). John B.Taylor is surely right in saying "that the similarity of this penalty with the state of siege of a city bombarded with sling-stones and incendiary missiles can scarcely have been coincidence. The shame of the guilty person's end under Mosaic law will be exactly matched by the fate of Samaria and Jerusalem".

iv) The judgment's result, vv.48-49

"Thus will I cause lewdness to cease out of the land, that all women may be taught not to do after your lewdness. And they shall recompense your lewdness upon you, and ye shall bear the sins of your idols: and ye shall know that I am the Lord GOD."

CHAPTER 23

"By such drastic means would the women's lewdness be ended, or the land be purged of idolatrous practices. It would also serve as an example to others that they should be warned against following a similar course. Retribution would be meet, and would be exacted to the full. The two nations would bear the penalty for their sinful idolatry. Adonai Jehovah would make Himself known by His righteous judgment, and the guilty nations would, in that day, acknowledge Him" (F.A.Tatford).

As Lamar E.Cooper points out, Chapter 23 concludes with "additional statements about the sins and judgment of the two harlot sisters ... The verdict was reached in Chapters 23 verses 46-49, and in Chapter 24, Nebuchadnezzar arrived to carry out the sentence.

EZEKIEL CHAPTER 24

Ezekiel 24 brings us to the end of the first major section of the prophecy (Chs. 1-24), which we entitled 'The Ruin of Judah and Jerusalem', and subdivided as follows: *(a)* the commissioning of Ezekiel (1: 1 - 3: 15); *(b)* the coming judgment (3: 16 - 7: 27); *(c)* the causes of judgment (8: 1 - 19: 14); *(d)* the consistency of national sin (20: 1 - 23: 49); *(e)* the commencement of hostilities (24: 1-27).

The hour has now come. Judgment is about to fall. In this chapter, we come to the climax of all that Ezekiel has been saying in previous chapters.

The passage may be divided as follows: *(1)* the parable of the boiling pot (vv.1-14): "utter a parable ... Set on a pot ... make it boil well" (vv.3, 5); *(2)* the sign of the bereaved prophet (vv.15-24): "I take away from thee the desire of thine eyes with a stroke ... at even my wife died ... Thus Ezekiel is unto you a sign" (vv.16, 18, 24); *(3)* the sign of the fulfilled prophecy (vv.25-27): "thou shalt speak, and be no more dumb: and thou shalt be a sign unto them" (v.27).

1) THE PARABLE OF THE BOILING POT, vv.1-14

These verses fall into two distinct sections *(a)* the date of the message (vv.1-2); *(b)* the details of the parable (vv.3-14).

a) The date of the message, vv.1-2

"Again in the ninth year, in the tenth month, in the tenth day of the month, the word of the LORD came unto me, saying, Son of man, write thee the name of the day, even of this same day: the king of Babylon set himself against Jerusalem this same day." This was the "day" of Nebuchadnezzar's arrival: Ezekiel also tells us about the "day" of his success (v.26).

According to John B.Taylor, the date is "normally given as 15th January

588 BC". It is the date mentioned in 2 Kings 25 verse 1 and Jeremiah 52 verse 4. We also know from Zechariah 8 verse 19, "the fast of the tenth (month)", that this date became the occasion of a fast for the exiles in commemorating one of the critical days in the fall of Jerusalem. Some commentators cannot understand how Ezekiel could possibly have been aware of such an event at such a distance from Jerusalem, and conclude that the prophet must have been in the locality at the time. The problem disappears when we remember that "holy men of God spake as they were moved by the Holy Ghost" (2 Pet. 1: 21). God is conversant with all that is happening everywhere ("The eyes of the LORD are in every place, beholding the evil and the good", Prov. 15: 3) and able to communicate His knowledge to His servants. This applies not only to current events, but to future events. See, for example, Isaiah's reference to Cyrus: "That saith of Cyrus, He is my shepherd, and shall perform all my pleasure: even saying to Jerusalem, Thou shalt be built; and to the temple, Thy foundation shall be laid" (Isa. 44: 28). This was fulfilled in 536 BC, approximately one hundred and seventy-five years after the prophecy was made. See Ezra 1 verses 1-3. It has to be said, sadly, of commentators belonging to the 'liberal' school that:

> *Blind unbelief is sure to err*
> *And scan God's work in vain.*
> *God is His own interpreter,*
> *And He will make it plain.*

b) The details of the parable, vv.3-14

Since these verses were probably cast in metrical form, they have been called 'The song of the cauldron' (J.B.Taylor). Similar language is used, though in a different connection, in connection with the wicked princes (see 11: 3, 7, 11). The words "caldron" here, and "pot" (24: 3, 6) translate the same Hebrew word (*sir*). While in the past, Ezekiel had been instructed to convey God's word by 'acted parables' (see, for example 4: 1 - 5: 4; 12: 4-16), this does not appear to be the case here. Ezekiel is told to use a familiar picture from every-day life to illustrate the coming siege and overthrow of Jerusalem. In the words of F.A.Tatford, "Once more the parabolic form of message was employed. The allegory was to convey to the exiles the full character of the coming disaster, although its meaning was not evident until it was interpreted". The parable is addressed to "the rebellious house" (cf. 2: 5, 6, 8; 3: 9).

The details of the parable illustrate *(i)* the siege of Jerusalem (vv.3-9); *(ii)* the destruction of Jerusalem (vv.10-14).

i) ***The siege of Jerusalem illustrated, vv.3-9***

"Thus saith the Lord GOD; Set on a pot, set it on, and also pour water into it: gather the pieces thereof into it, even every good piece, the thigh, and the shoulder; fill it with the choice bones, Take the choice of the flock, and burn ('pile', RV) also the bones under it ('and also [put] a pile of wood under it, for the bones', JND), and make it boil well, let them seethe the bones of it therein" (vv.3-5).

The explanatory verses which follow (vv.6-9) make it clear that the cauldron (the "pot") represents Jerusalem, its contents represent her inhabitants, and the fire is the siege. "Make it boil well", or "bring it to a boil" (NIV), alludes to the ferocity of the Babylonian onslaught against Jerusalem. It has been said (S.Fisch) that "Boiling bones is an allusion to the barbarism of the Babylonians". It has been suggested that the "good and choice pieces and the bones refer to "the leaders of the nation" (C.L.Feinberg).

- ***The character of the cauldron***. This describes Jerusalem as "the bloody city, like a the pot whose scum ('rust', RV/JND) is therein, and whose scum (ditto) is not gone out of it!" (v.6). Lamar E. Cooper puts it most succinctly: "This pot was encrusted with residue and could not be cleansed. The terminology describes an unclean, filthy cooking pot that could not be cleaned and was therefore unusable (v.6; cf. vv.12-13)". The word rendered "scum" (*chelah*) occurs only here in the Old Testament, and "its meaning must be drawn mainly from its context" (J.B.Taylor). In all probability, the word refers to the corrosion of the pot, and J.B.Taylor puts it rather neatly in referring to "a rusty scum" and "this reddish mess".

In New Testament terms, Jerusalem was a vessel "to dishonour", and it is worth saying at this juncture that we should strive to be vessels "unto honour, sanctified, and meet for the master's use, and prepared unto every good work" (2 Tim. 2: 20-21). We are all liable to harbour "scum" in our lives, but provision has been made for cleansing: "If we confess our sins, he is faithful and just to forgive us our sins, and to cleanse us from all unrighteousness" (1 John 1: 9).

- ***The contents of the cauldron.*** This describes evil inhabitants of

Jerusalem. "Bring it out piece by piece; let no lot fall upon it. For her blood is in the midst of her; she set it upon the top of a rock; she poured it not upon the ground, to cover it with dust; that it might cause fury to come up to take vengeance; I have set her blood upon the top of a rock, that it should not be covered" (vv.6-8).

The words, "Bring it out piece by piece; let no lot fall upon it (or 'without making a choice')" (v.6) evidently mean that there would be no lot cast in order to spare any of the population" (C.L.Feinberg). Status would mean nothing. The reason for unsparing judgment follows: "For her blood is in the midst of her; she set it upon the top of a rock; she poured it not upon the ground, to cover it with dust; that it might cause fury to come up to take vengeance" (vv.7-8). The law required that the blood of the sacrifices (see, for example, Lev.4: 7; 16: 15) and of animals slain for food (see, for example, Deut.12: 16) must be poured upon the ground, that it might be absorbed and covered out of sight. These instructions emphasise the sanctity of the blood. But Jerusalem callously disregarded the sanctity of *human* life. She made no attempt to cover her violent crimes. This lack of concern for the victims of bloodshed was "further evidence of the cruelty and heartlessness of the people" (L.A.Cooper), and provoked divine anger: judgment was inevitable. Jerusalem had made no attempt to observe the sanctity of human life: "For her blood is in the midst of her; she set it upon the top of a rock" (v.7), and the Lord determined that their guilt in this way should remain: "I have set her blood upon the top of a rock, that it should not be covered" (v.8). J.B.Taylor makes the insightful observation that "The dispersion of the Jew has not provided a solution to this greater issue of the nation's guilt".

Centuries later, Judas Iscariot exclaimed, "I have sinned in that I have betrayed the innocent blood", to which the Jewish leaders replied "What is that to us? see thou to that" (Matt. 27: 4). Later, the people of Jerusalem cried, "His blood be on us, and on our children" (Matt. 27: 25). The nation is yet to pay a dreadful price for rejecting her Messiah.

- **The fire under the cauldron**. This describes the Babylonian siege. "Therefore thus saith the Lord GOD; Woe to the bloody city! I will even make the pile for fire great" (v.9).

ii) *The destruction of Jerusalem illustrated, vv.10-14*

Having said, "I will even make the pile for fire great" (v.9), the parable proceeds further: "Heap on wood, kindle the fire, consume the flesh, and spice it well, and let the bones be burned. Then set it empty upon the coals thereof, that the brass of it may be hot, and may burn, and that the filthiness of it may be molten in it, that the scum (as in v.6) of it may be consumed" (vv.10-11). This describes, in parabolic language, the destruction of the city's inhabitants (v.10); the destruction of the city itself, and the reasons (v.11-14).

- ***The destruction of the city's inhabitants, v.10.*** F.Gardiner (*Ellicott's Commentary*) calls this "great energy of description" and suggests that the disputed words "spice it well" (sometimes translated 'empty out the broth', but without manuscript authority) refer to the thoroughness of the work (as in the preparation of a meal). F.Gardiner continues: "The process is to be continued until the water in the cauldron is all evaporated (see v.3), the flesh consumed, and even the bones burned". This refers to the people of Jerusalem.

- ***The destruction of the city itself, v.11-14.*** "Then set it empty upon the coals thereof, that the brass of it may be hot, and may burn, and that the filthiness of it may be molten in it, that the scum (as in v.6) of it may be consumed." C.L.Feinberg speaks for other commentators in saying, "The caldron itself was to remain on the fire until it also melted, thus doing away with the rust. That it had been emptied signified that a full captivity would depopulate the land. Moreover it was not sufficient that the people only be destroyed. The city itself had to be demolished (see the injunctions for the treatment of leprosy in a house in Lev. 14: 34-45). There was no mistaking the intention of God; in order to purge the city, He would have to destroy it completely".

The reason follows. As C.L.Feinberg observes, "In concluding this theme, Ezekiel passed from the figure into the realm of fact.". "She hath wearied herself with lies, and her great scum (as before) went not forth out of her: her scum (ditto) shall be in the fire. In thy filthiness is lewdness: because I have purged thee, and thou wast not purged, thou shalt not be purged from thy filthiness any more, till I have caused my fury to rest upon thee ... I the LORD have spoken it: it shall come to pass, and I will do it; I will not go back, neither will I spare, neither will I repent; according to thy ways, and according to thy doings, shall they judge thee, saith the Lord GOD" (vv.12-14). "The Lord had sought to purge them through the ministry of prophets, providential dealings and calamities, but nothing procured the desired result. They were now left to the dire consequences of their evil deeds" (C.L.Feinberg).

CHAPTER 24

The agency by which this would be accomplished was "the king of Babylon" (v.2). There was no possibility of alteration: "I the LORD have spoken it: it shall come to pass, and I will do it; I will not go back, neither will I spare, neither will I repent". Three times He avers that judgment is coming, and three times He avers that there would be no reversal. In connection with cleansing by fire, note Isaiah 4 verses 3-4, which refers to the final cleansing of Jerusalem at the beginning of the millennium: "And it shall come to pass, that he that is left in Zion ... shall be called holy ... when the Lord shall have washed away the filth of the daughters of Zion, and shall have purged the blood of Jerusalem from the midst thereof by the spirit of judgment, and by the spirit of burning".

We should remember that "our God is a consuming fire" (Heb. 12: 29) and that amongst other things, the reservation of "the heavens and the earth ... unto fire" should constantly remind us of the necessity for holiness and godliness. In view of the dissolution of creation, "what manner of persons ought ye to be in all holy conversation and godliness...?" (2 Pet. 3: 10-11).

2) THE SIGN OF THE BEREAVED PROPHET, vv.15-24

The second section of the chapter relates yet another instance in which the prophet himself is made a sign to Jerusalem. On this occasion the sign relates to the bereavement of Ezekiel: "behold, I take away from thee the desire of thine eyes with a stroke ... and at even my wife died" (vv.16-18). We should notice *(a)* the death of his wife (vv.15-17); *(b)* the dedication of the prophet (v.18); *(c)* the declaration of the meaning (vv.19-24).

a) The death of his wife, vv.15-17

"Son of man, behold, I take away from thee the desire of thine eyes with a stroke: yet neither shalt thou mourn or weep, neither shall thy tears run down. Forbear to cry, make no mourning for the dead, bind the tire of thine head upon thee, and put on thy shoes upon thy feet, and cover not thy lips, and eat not the bread of men." The death of Mrs. Ezekiel was evidently forecast the morning of the day that it happened, and there is no reason to suppose that it was not very close to the date mentioned at the beginning of the chapter. Indeed, the context might well demand that this was the case. We should notice:

i) What she meant to him.

She is called "the desire of thine eyes" (v.16). He had eyes for her alone. The

Lord knew that Ezekiel was not a man who had "eyes full of adultery" who "cannot cease from sin" (2 Pet. 2: 14). H.L.Ellison dedicated his commentary on Ezekiel to:

> THE DESIRE OF MY EYES
> who is yet with me
> (24: 16)

J.B.Taylor has a nice piece here: "In these verses we catch a glimpse of the inner Ezekiel which rarely appears through his apparently harsh and unyielding exterior. His austerity and rigid self-discipline, his passion for truth and for the honour of God's holy name, very nearly conceal the tender heart that lies within". J.B.Taylor quotes another commentator (E.L.Allen): "men who are called by God often have to pay a heavy price for their concern with human needs and their identification with God's purpose. They are called again and again to surrender their private lives to the requirements of their public responsibility ... Behind the laconic phrase in verse 18, 'And on the next morning I did as I was commanded' (RSV), there must have been long hours of sleeplessness and spiritual anguish".

ii) *How he mourned for her*

The prophet is instructed not to exhibit the customary evidences of mourning: "yet neither shalt thou mourn nor weep, neither shall thy tears run down. Forbear to cry ('sigh in silence', JND), make no mourning for the dead, bind the tire (turban) of thine head upon thee, and put on thy shoes upon thy feet, and cover not thy lips, and eat not the bread of men". Ezekiel was not forbidden to sorrow, for, as C.L.Feinberg points out, "even our Lord wept at the grave of Lazerus", but he was prohibited from displaying the usual signs of mourning. He was to wear his usual headgear instead of covering his head with dust and ashes (see, for example, Joshua 7: 6; 1 Sam. 4: 12; Job 2: 12). He was to put on his sandals instead of taking them off (see, for example, 2 Sam. 15: 30). He was not to cover his lips (see Micah 3: 7, although this does refer to rather different circumstances). He was not to eat the usual funeral meal. The expression "the bread of men" evidently means the ordinary mourners' funeral meal. Compare Jeremiah 16 verses 7-8.

Ezekiel sorrowed over the death of his wife, but he was not to do so in the accepted way, reminding us that we "sorrow not, even as others which have no hope" (1 Thess. 4: 13)

CHAPTER 24

b) The dedication of the prophet, v.18

"So I spoke to the people in the morning: and at even my wife died; and I did in the morning as I was commanded." We should notice:

i) His service in the morning

That is, the morning of his wife's death. "So I spoke to the people in the morning." C.L.Feinberg says it all: "In spite of the fact that he knew his wife's hours were numbered, he went about the ministry committed to him. What an example of obedience!" For Ezekiel, it was 'business as usual'. Perhaps he was reiterating the warning of the coming catastrophe on Jerusalem, but this is purely speculative.

ii) His sorrow in the evening

"And at even my wife died." This simple statement of fact, shorn of any emotion or grief, is in keeping with his God-given instructions for mourning. Thankfully, we can say so much more: "absent from the body … present (at home) with the Lord" (2 Cor. 5: 8); "to be with Christ; which is far better" (Phil. 1: 23).

iii) His obedience the following morning

"And I did in the morning as I was commanded." "Despite the fountain of tears welling up within him, the prophet did as he had been directed" (F.A.Tatford). Obedience often has a price-tag.

c) The declaration of the meaning, vv.19-24

Knowing Ezekiel as they did, the people immediately realised that the prophet's unusual behaviour in the circumstances must have some significance for them, and we should notice *(i)* the people's question (v.19); *(ii)* the prophet's answer (vv.20-24).

i) The people's question

"Wilt thou not tell us what these things are *to us*, that thou doest so?" (v.19). J.B.Taylor puts it like this: "it is to his credit and to that of his fellow-exiles that they immediately suspected that it had some special significance". Most believers worthy of the name, will have fielded similar questions! After all, the behaviour of the Lord's people should be quite distinct, and set people thinking. In quite different circumstances, it is quite true of many of the Lord's people that friends and acquaintances "think it strange that ye run not with them to the same excess of riot (the same sink of corruption', JND), speaking evil of you" (1 Pet. 4: 4).

ii) The prophet's answer

He tells them that "The word of the LORD came unto me, saying, Speak unto the house of Israel, Thus saith the Lord GOD; Behold, I will profane my sanctuary, the excellency of your strength, the desire of your eyes, and that which your soul pitieth ('the pride of your strength, the desire of your eyes, and your soul's longing', JND); and your sons and your daughters whom ye have left shall fall by the sword. And ye shall do as I have done: ye shall not cover your lips, nor eat the bread of men. And your tires shall be upon your heads, and your shoes upon your feet: ye shall not mourn nor weep; but ye shall pine away for ('in', JND) your iniquities, and mourn one toward another. Thus Ezekiel is unto you a sign: according to all that he hath done shall ye do: and when this cometh, ye shall know that I am the Lord GOD" (vv.20-24).

While this is quite self-explanatory, we must not miss the fact that Ezekiel simply repeated what God had told him to say: "The word of the LORD came unto me, saying, Speak unto the house of Israel, Thus saith the Lord GOD; Behold I will profane my sanctuary ..." Our business is to do the same, and emulate John the Baptist: "he that sent me ... said unto me ..." (John 1: 33).

To summarise Ezekiel's answer, the nation was about to lose **her** dearest object ("my sanctuary, the excellency of your strength, the **desire of your eyes**") in the same way that he had lost **his** dearest object ("the **desire of thine eyes**", v.16). The 'desire of **their** eyes' was the temple: the 'desire of **his** eyes' was his wife. But that was not all. Additionally, they would lose their families: "and your sons and your daughters whom ye have left shall die by the sword". In consequence, they would react in the same way as Ezekiel: "And ye shall do as I have done: ye shall not cover your lips, nor eat the bread of men. And your tires shall be upon your heads, and your shoes upon your feet: ye shall not mourn nor weep; but ye shall pine away for your iniquities, and mourn one toward another. Thus Ezekiel is unto you a sign: according to all that he hath done shall ye do".

CHAPTER 24

Perhaps J.B.Taylor is correct in saying that "Ezekiel had not wept, and Israel would not weep either: because in both cases the tragedy was too deep and stunning for any expression of grief to prove adequate". This is supported by C.L.Feinberg: "Because of the widespread nature of the calamity and the vast issues involved for God and for His people, no mourning would be able to do the occasion justice. Grief would be paralysed; they would at the most mourn privately". On the other hand there is some mileage in the suggestion that they would be unable to mourn because they would be immediately taken away as captives to Babylon. F.Gardiner espouses this view: "In the tumult, distress and captivity of the approaching judgment there would be no opportunity for the outward display of grief; but all the more should it press upon them inwardly ..." Compare Leviticus 26 verse 39.

The section concludes with the familiar words, "when this cometh, ye shall know that I am the Lord GOD". He is as good as His word.

Since the temple is called "the pride of your strength, the desire of your eyes, and your soul's longing" (v.21 JND), we might well examine our attitude towards the local assembly. After all, that too is a temple: "Know ye not that ye are the temple of God, and that the Spirit of God dwelleth in you?" (1 Cor. 3: 16). How much do *we* value the assembly to which we belong?

3) THE SIGN OF THE FULFILLED PROPHECY, vv.25-27

The final section of the chapter describes the impact of the destruction of Jerusalem on Ezekiel. For the second time in the chapter (cf. v.24) he would become a sign to the people (v.27), and on this occasion it would mark a turning-point in his life's work. This is how J.B.Taylor puts it: "his message would be vindicated and for the first time he would have ready hearers. More particularly, the ritual dumbness, which was imposed upon him at the time of his call, would be taken from his mouth, and he would be able to speak freely (cf. 3: 26; 33: 22)".

The destruction of Jerusalem would fulfil the prophecy contained in the parable of the boiling pot, and the destruction of the temple would fulfil the clear predictions made through Ezekiel in connection with his wife's death: Ezekiel had lost 'the desire of his eyes' (v.16) and the nation would lose 'the desire of their eyes' (v.21). In the day that Ezekiel received the news, his mouth would be opened (v.27).

Here is the whole quotation: "Also, thou son of man, shall it not be *in the day* when I take from them their strength, the joy of their glory, the desire of their eyes (cf. vv.16, 21), and that whereupon they set their minds, their sons and their daughters, *that he that is escaped in that day shall come unto thee*, to cause thee to hear it with thine ears? In that day (that is, the day that the escapee arrived with the news) shall thy mouth be opened to him which is escaped, and thou shalt speak, and be no more dumb and thou shalt be a sign unto them; and they shall know that I am the LORD". Although commentators appear to think otherwise, it does seem that on the day of Jerusalem's fall (v.25) a man would escape (v.26) and come with news to Ezekiel, whereupon, on the day of his arrival (v.27), his mouth would be opened.

This does, however, raise a problem. Jerusalem fell in the eleventh year of Zedekiah's reign "on the ninth day of the fourth month" but according to Ezekiel 33 verses 21-22 the fugitive arrived "in the twelfth year of our captivity, in the tenth month, and the fifth day of the month". The means that it took the man something like eighteen months to get from Jerusalem to Tel-abib. However, according to C.L.Feinberg, "the Syriac version and some Hebrew manuscripts read eleventh instead of twelfth year, which would allow six months rather than a year and a half for the news of Jerusalem's fall to reach the exiles, and many accept this date". Explanations of this type are not completely satisfactory, and F.Gardiner reasons that approximately a year and half could well have passed before Ezekiel received "full and circumstantial details", not from a man who has 'escaped to tell the tale' in the usual sense, but from one of the men who had arrived as a captive from Jerusalem in the group of slow-moving exiles described in Jeremiah 52 verse 15. There we must leave it.

The words, "thou shalt speak, and be no more dumb: and thou shalt be a sign unto them" (v.27), take us back to the silence imposed upon him at his commission: "And I will make thy tongue cleave to the roof of thy mouth, and thou shalt be dumb, and shalt not be to them a reprover ... But when I speak with thee, I will open thy mouth, and thou shalt say unto them, Thus saith the Lord GOD ..." (3: 26-27). As noted above, this took place "in the twelfth year of our captivity, in the tenth month, in the fifth day of the month" (33: 21). It may be significant in this connection that with the mention of this sign, Ezekiel's ministry to Israel ceases until Chapter 33, the chapter which records the destruction of Jerusalem.

It will be noticed that Ezekiel's dumbness is mentioned in Chapter 3 verses

CHAPTER 24

26-27; 24 verse 27; 29 verse 21 and 33 verse 22, but in other passages he is shown as speaking normally. (See, for example 14: 4; 17: 2, 12; 20: 3.) As H.L.Ellison observes, "It could be urged that in all these cases God had suspended the dumbness as promised in Chapter 3 verse 27. But in fact there is never any hint that this was the case ... It seems probable that Ezekiel's dumbness was not actual inability to speak, but a refusal to speak on ordinary matters with those who had refused to hear him as God's messenger." As we noted in connection with the silence imposed upon Ezekiel at his commissioning, the prophet was told, "thou ... shalt *not* be to them as a *reprover*", where the word "reprover" means, literally, 'a man of litigation' (C.J.H.Wright). He would not act as an arbitrator or a mediator: his ministry would be purely judicial, that is, until his mouth was opened. That day had now come.

We could therefore say that, thus far, Ezekiel's ministry had concerned the fall of the city to the exclusion of all else. But when the city fell, his preaching in this way would be needed no longer, and the restriction on his speaking of other subjects would be removed. In the words of J.B.Taylor, "Then at last Ezekiel will be free. His prophecies of doom will no longer need to be uttered. He will be able to act as a shepherd and a watchman to his people. He will be free to work constructively towards the building up of a new community, a new Israel". As C.L.Feinberg observes, "Interestingly enough, from the time the word of the calamity arrived, Ezekiel's messages were of a more consolatory nature". Lamar E. Cooper makes the same point: "From that point, when the prophet's message changed from primarily judgment to restoration and hope, he would be free to move among the people and to relate his messages".

With Chapter 25 we come to the second major section of the prophecy (Chs.25-32), which we entitled, 'The Retribution on Surrounding Nations'.

EZEKIEL CHAPTER 25

Introduction

As we have noticed, the prophecy of Ezekiel may be divided into four sections: *(1)* the ruin of Judah and Jerusalem (chs.1-24); *(2)* the retribution on surrounding nations (chs.25-32); *(3)* the restoration of Israel (chs.33-39); *(4)* the return of the glory of the Lord (chs.40-48).

1) THE RUIN OF JUDAH AND JERUSALEM, Chapters 1-24

These chapters are largely devoted to predictions in connection with the siege and fall of Jerusalem. They were given over a period of 4½ years, commencing with the fourth month of the fifth year of Jehoiachin's captivity (1: 1-2) and concluding with the tenth month of the ninth year of his captivity (24: 1), the date on which Nebuchadnezzar "came, he and all his host, against Jerusalem, and pitched against it" (2 Kings 25: 1). Ezekiel 24 concludes with the Lord's prediction that a survivor would bring the prophet news of the fall of Jerusalem, at which point his mouth would be opened: "In that day shall thy mouth be opened to him that is escaped, and thou shalt speak, and be no more dumb: and thou shalt be a sign unto them; and they shall know that I am the LORD" (24: 27). Up to this point, Ezekiel's ministry had been purely judicial: "Thou shalt *not* be unto them as a *reprover*", meaning a 'man of litigation' (3: 26). He was not to act as an arbiter or mediator, but only to announce coming judgment. This period of his ministry was now ending.

The city fell some eighteen months later in the fourth month of "the eleventh year of Zedekiah (which could be expressed as 'the eleventh year of our captivity')" (Jer. 52: 5-6), although the news did not reach Ezekiel until the tenth month of "the twelfth year of our captivity" (33: 21). The news therefore took some eighteen months to reach Ezekiel in Tel-abib, and we considered the possible reasons for this long delay in our last study.

CHAPTER 25

As Christopher J. H. Wright *(The Message of Ezekiel)* observes. "After the intense and tragic narrative of chapter 24, with its concluding prediction that a messenger would come with news of the fall of the city, we would like to read on to hear of his arrival and the reaction to the news itself. But instead, like the exiles themselves, we must sit and wait". And while we wait, the Lord gives us a series of oracles "aimed in a very different direction from all that has gone before". This brings us to:

2) THE RETRIBUTION ON SURROUNDING NATIONS, Chapters 25-32

Since all the oracles in these Chapters 25-32, with one exception, were delivered during or shortly after the siege of Jerusalem, we can reasonably conclude that they occur at this point in the book in view of their immediate context, that is, Chapter 24, in which Ezekiel was told to expect the arrival of the news of the fall of Jerusalem, and Chapter 33, in which the news actually arrived.

As C.L.Feinberg points out, the oracles in Chapter 25, against Ammon, Moab, Edom, and Philistia, "are to be dated soon after 586 BC (which was 'the eleventh year' of the captivity) because they presuppose the fall of Jerusalem. The occasion appears to be the delight these neighbouring nations had when Jerusalem was made captive in that fateful year". The oracle against Tyre, including Zidon, is dated "the eleventh year" of the captivity (26: 1). The oracles against Egypt are dated "the tenth year, in the tenth month" of the captivity (29: 1), the "eleventh year, in the first month" (30: 20), "the eleventh year, in the third month" (31: 1), and "the twelfth year, in the twelfth month" (32: 1, 17). The reference to "the seven and twentieth year" (29: 17) looks totally out of place, but it is nothing of the sort! Leaving aside, for the time being, the reason for its inclusion, it is quite clear that it points, as do other chronological references, to the deliberate arrangement of these oracles. They are not given in chronological sequence, but rather in national sequence.

Bearing in mind the context of this 'foreign nations' section, the reason for its inclusion at this point in the prophecy is not difficult to ascertain. We must therefore briefly consider the significance, structure, and sequence of these oracles. (Prophecies regarding other nations follow in Chapters 35 and 38-39).

a) The significance of the oracles

Their inclusion emphasises *(i)* the Lord's concern for His people, despite their waywardness and sinfulness; *(ii)* the Lord's cognisance of the affairs of all nations; *(iii)* the Lord's law of sowing and reaping.

i) **The Lord's concern for His people.** In this connection, it should be noted that in the first four cases, at least, the nations are held responsible for their treatment of God's people, reminding us that He had said: "I will bless them that bless thee, and curse him that curseth thee" (Gen. 12: 3), and that "he that toucheth you toucheth the apple of his eye" (Zech. 2: 8).

It has been pointed out that it is highly unlikely that these messages were actually delivered to the nations concerned, and that they are placed here for the benefit of Israel.

ii) **The Lord's cognisance of the affairs of all nations.** He is not a tribal deity. He is "the Judge of all the earth" (Gen. 18: 25). All men are accountable to Him. He will judge all nations. The seven cases surveyed in these chapters are therefore of relevant interest: they allow us to see something of God's dealings with the nations at all times. We are not to think that these are isolated cases, for He remains in perfect control of the international situation: no nation is permitted to exceed the allotted place in His purposes or to avoid payment for its wickedness.

In the case of Tyre, which rejoiced in the overthrow of Jerusalem although not personally involved in the event (26: 2), judgment is pronounced on the city in view of her godless commercial pride and complete self-sufficiency. The pride and self-sufficiency of Egypt are similarly condemned.

iii) **The Lord's law of sowing and reaping.** The section illustrates Galatians 6: 7: "Be not deceived; God is not mocked: for whatsoever a man soweth, that shall he also reap". In this connection, we should notice that God does not deal with the nations in a purely arbitrary fashion, but advances adequate reasons for the severity of His judgments upon them. He pronounces His sentences with a full explanation in each case.

b) The structure of the oracles

The heart of the section lies in Chapter 28 verses 24-26: "And there shall be no more a pricking brier unto the house of Israel ... Thus saith the Lord GOD: When I shall have gathered the house of Israel from the people among whom they are scattered, and shall be sanctified in them in the sight of the heathen, then shall they dwell in their land that I have given to my servant Jacob ..." C.J.H. Wright points out that this passage is preceded by ninety-seven verses of predictions against Ammon, Moab, Edom, Philistia and Tyre (25: 1 - 28: 23), and succeeded by ninety-seven verses of predictions against Egypt (29: 1 - 32: 32). This speaks for itself. As always, Israel lies at the centre of God's purposes for the world.

It has also been pointed out that the whole section is dominated by 'sevens'. Here is C.J.H.Wright again: "Thus we have oracles against seven nations, and the two major oracles, against Tyre and against Egypt, each break up into seven internal sections that are clearly demarcated in the text". (For Tyre, see 26: 1-6; 26: 7-14; 26: 15-18; 26: 19-21; 27: 1-36; 28: 1-10; 28: 11-19. For Egypt, see 29: 1-16; 29: 17-21; 30: 1-19; 30: 20-26; 31: 1-18; 32: 1-16; 32: 17-32.)

c) The sequence of the oracles

In the words of John B.Taylor, "A further sign of editorial planning is the geographical pattern of the oracles". They begin "with Ammon (25: 1-7) to the north-east of Jerusalem, swinging southwards through Moab (25: 8-11) to Edom in the south-east (25:12-14), then round to Philistia in the west (25: 15-17), and finally going farther afield in a northerly direction to Tyre and Sidon (26: 1 - 28: 24), before ending up with the distant major power, Egypt, in the south (29: 1 – 32: 32)".

The omission of Babylon calls for comment. Some see "Babylon as standing apart from the other nations, inasmuch as it was the instrument of God's punishment upon Israel", whilst others go further and regard "the Babylonian invaders as being the instruments of judgment upon all the nations mentioned here, as well as on Israel" (J.B.Taylor).

As J.B.Taylor points out, the section dealing with Israel's neighbours "marks a clear hiatus between Ezekiel's ministry and message before 587 BC, and his quite different treatment of the exiles once the disaster had vindicated his words and created the atmosphere of stunned repentance, in which he could begin to restore the nation's confidence in the good purposes of God".

We must now give attention to Chapter 25 which deals with Ammon, Moab, Edom, and Philistia. The first three nations are all linked with Israel by heredity and, together with the Philistines, were all in the immediate vicinity of Israel. It is said that "all four countries could be seen by the naked eye on a clear day from a vantage point in Jerusalem itself" (C.J.H.Wright). They all took pleasure in the misfortune of Israel, something, alas, to which even believers can be prone, especially when those concerned seem more favoured materially and spiritually than themselves.

All four oracles are similarly constructed. Each nation is accused of either malicious gloating over Judah's misfortune, or of actual revenge "in which old hatreds and ancient enmities were fully vented, and old scores violently settled" (C.J.H.Wright). Judgment is then pronounced on them.

1) THE AMMONITES, vv: 1-7

"The word of the LORD came again unto me, saying, Son of man, set thy face against the Ammonites, and prophesy against them" (vv.1-2).

The children of Ammon were the descendants of Lot, who was both their father and grandfather. They lived on the edge of the desert east of the Jordan and north of the land of Moab. Their territory was located between the Arnon and Jabbok rivers. Their capital was Rabbah, now known as Amman. They had allied themselves with Babylon against Judah about 600 B.C. (2 Kings 24: 2). Later, in 594 B.C., together with Edom, Moab, Tyre and Sidon, they attempted to enlist Judah's help in an alliance against Babylon (Jer. 27: 1-11). According to Ezekiel 21 verses 18-20, Nebuchadnezzar had started out against Judah and Ammon 593 B.C. and, but as there is no record of an attack on the Ammonites, it can be concluded that they had capitulated and turned against Judah (Jer.21: 27). We must now notice *(a)* the charges (vv.3, 6); *(b)* the condemnation (vv.4-5; 7).

a) The first charge, v.3

"Hear the word of the Lord GOD; Thus saith the Lord GOD; because thou saidst, Aha, **against** my sanctuary, when it was profaned; and **against** the land of Israel, when it was desolate; and **against** the house of Judah, when they went into captivity ..." C.L.Feinberg points out that Ezekiel evidently had in mind Ammon's seizure of Gad's territory (Jer. 29: 1) when referring to "the land of Israel, when it was desolate".

Notice the words, "because thou **saidst**, Aha, against my sanctuary, when it was profaned ..." (According to Young's Concordance, "Aha" is an expression of 'malicious joy': see also Ezek. 26: 2; 36: 2; Ps. 35: 21; 40: 15; 70: 3, Is. 44: 16.) They did not take up the sword against God's people, but they took a malicious delight in the downfall of God's people, especially in the destruction of the temple. We must never forget that the Lord is thoroughly cognisant of what we say as well as with what we do. It is refreshingly different to hear Malachi say, "Then they that feared the LORD spake often one to another: and the LORD **hearkened** and **heard** it" (Mal. 3: 16).

The Ammonites had obviously never read the book of Proverbs: "Rejoice not when thine enemy falleth, and let not thine heart be glad when he stumbleth: lest the LORD see it, and it displease him, and he turn away his wrath from him" (Prov. 24: 17-18). We must not forget the New Testament injunction: "Let all bitterness, and wrath, and anger, and clamour, and evil speaking, be put away from you, with all malice: and be ye kind one to another, tenderhearted, forgiving one another, even as God for Christ's sake hath forgiven you" (Eph. 4: 31-32).

b) The divine condemnation, vv.4-5

"Behold, therefore I will deliver thee to the men of the east for a possession, and they shall set their palaces in thee, and make their dwellings in thee: they shall eat thy fruit, and they shall drink thy milk. And I will make Rabbah a stable ('pasture', JND) for camels, and the Ammonites a couchingplace for flocks: and ye shall know that I am the LORD." The word "couchingplace" is explained by Zephaiah 2 verse 15, "a place for beasts to lie down in".

Ammon was to be occupied by the "men of the east" who would consume the produce of their country. According to C.L.Feinberg, "Opinions vary as to the identity of the "children of the east:" some take them to be the Bedouin, the nomadic tribes beyond the Jordan (Judges 6: 3); others feel they are Ishmaelites; and yet others think they are doubtless the Babylonians. Although no group mentioned is automatically ruled out, usage would appear to favour the nomadic tribes of Transjordan". C.L.Feinberg continues: "So complete would be the subjugation of Ammon by their enemies that their land would be freely used by the invaders". The capital, Rabbah, would be overgrown, and its streets would provide pasturage for camels.

There can be little doubt that Ammon was overthrown by Nebuchadnezzar. According to Josephus, Nebuchadnezzar defeated Ammon in the fifth year after the destruction of Jerusalem (cited by C.L.Feinberg), and it is suggested that having been weakened in this way, their territory was occupied by the "men of the east". They are "described as its possessors, not its conquerors" (F.Gardiner).

c) The second charge, v.6

"Because thou hast clapped thine hands, and stamped with the feet, and rejoiced in heart with all thy despite against the land of Israel ..." It gets worse. The Ammonites were totally consumed by their malicious joy. It knew no bounds. Hands, feet, and heart were given over to "unseemly and unfeeling glee" (C.L.Feinberg).

d) The divine condemnation, v.7

"Behold, therefore will I stretch out mine hand upon thee, and will deliver thee for a spoil to the heathen; and I will cut thee off from the people, and I will cause thee to perish out of the countries: I will destroy thee; and thou shalt know that I am the LORD."

The words, "hast clapped thine hands" (v.6) are matched by "I will stretch out mine hand" (v.7). Divine determination to destroy Ammon is expressed by the repeated "I will". They had rejoiced in the despoliation of the temple (v.3): they would become "a spoil to the heathen". They had rejoiced when Judah "went into captivity" (v.3): they would be "cut ... off from the people ('peoples', JND)". As F.A.Tatford observes, "Not only would they be helpless prey to these nations, but they would be completely destroyed as a distinct nation ... They would cease to be recognised as a separate race. The judgment was to be utterly devastating. Ammon was to be destroyed".

Having described the desolation of Ammon, Jeremiah adds, "And afterward I will bring again the captivity of the children of Ammon, saith the LORD" (Jer. 49: 6). This possibly refers to the country of Jordan (F.A.Tatford). Compare Daniel 11 verse 41. The oracle concludes with, "and thou shalt know that I am the LORD". See also verses 11 and 17. We have already observed that this frequently-repeated statement emphasises the Lord's identity rather than His existence. He is utterly distinct from man-made gods. His ability to implement His word bears eloquent testimony to His identity as the eternal, self-sufficient God. F.Gardiner puts it like this: "It refers not to a penitent recognition of the Lord, but to an experience of His wrath so plain that they can no longer refuse to acknowledge His power".

2) THE MOABITES, vv.8-11

The children of Ammon were also the descendants of Lot in the same way as the children of Moab. Their territory lay south of the Arnon river along the lower region of the Dead Sea. Once again, we must notice *(a)* the charge (v.8); *(b)* the condemnation (vv.9-11). In his book, (*Living with the Glory of God*), Malcolm C. Davis notes that many Bible students consider that Ammon and Moab represent fallen human nature: "Ammon represents active fleshly activity, hostility towards God and His interests, while Moab represents lazy or indolent flesh, which is self-indulgent and seductive towards God's people, as their women were in the matter of Baal-Peor".

a) The charge, v.8

"Thus saith the Lord GOD, because that Moab and Seir do say, Behold, the house of Judah is like unto all the heathen ..." The overthrow of Judah and Jerusalem had led Moab to the conclusion that the unique position and privileges of God's people were illusory: the nation had fallen to Babylon in the same way as others, and therefore the God of Israel was no better than the gods of the heathen nations. "Israel's fall seemed to point to a failure of the Lord's purpose in her, thus reflecting on the power and honour of the Lord Himself" (C.L.Feinberg). "The purpose of their taunts was to contradict Judah's claim that they were God's chosen people" (L.E.Cooper).

Some commentators would like to omit the reference to Seir, but it has proven textual authority! F.Gardiner states the obvious: "The two nations, here mentioned together, are afterwards treated separately: Moab (vv.9-11) and Edom (vv12-14)". They are mentioned together for the obvious reason that they both said the same thing!

This solemnly reminds us that our bad conduct could bring the Lord's name into disrepute. Paul had to say of the Jews, "the name of God is blasphemed among the Gentiles through you" (Rom. 2 verse 24). The added words in Romans 2: 24, "as it is written", refer to Ezekiel 36 verses 20 and 23: "And when they entered unto the heathen, whither they went, they profaned my holy name .... I will sanctify my great name, which was profaned among the heathen which ye have profaned in the midst of them". Compare 2 Samuel

12 verse 14: "thou hast given great occasion to the enemies of the LORD to blaspheme".

b) The condemnation, vv.9-11

"Therefore, behold, I will open the side of Moab from the cities, from his cities which are his frontiers, the glory of the country, Beth-jeshimoth, Baal-meon, and Kiriathaim, unto the men of the east with the Ammonites, and will give them in possession, that the Ammonites may not be remembered among the nations. And I will execute judgments upon Moab; and they shall know that I am the LORD" (v.9), or "I will open the side of Moab from the cities, from his cities even unto the last of them, the glory of the country, Beth-jeshimoth, Baal-meon, and Kiriathaim" (JND).

The words, "I will open the side of Moab (literally 'the shoulder of Moab')" mean 'lay it open to the enemy' (F.Gardiner), and the words "from his cities which are his frontiers" mean 'in every quarter' (C.L.Feinberg) or 'even to the last of them' (JND). The cities of Beth-jeshimoth, Baal-meon and Kiriathaim were located *north* of the river Arnon in territory captured by Moab from the Reubenites. They were evidently fortress towns, and "if the enemy could capture and destroy the Moabite fortresses, the land would obviously be open to him" (F.A.Tatford). Travelling from north to south, the three cities lay beneath one another in the order given. They evidently lay in the mountains of Moab which may well have been the 'shoulder of Moab'.

The Lord would do to Moab as He would do to Ammon: He would "open the side of Moab ... unto the men of the east with (along with) the Ammonites, and give (it) them ("the men of the east") that the Ammonites (as predicted in v.7) may not be remembered among the nations. And I will execute judgment upon Moab; and they shall know that I am the LORD" (vv.10-11). Moab eventually ceased to have an independent existence as a nation. As with Ammon, Nebuchadnezzar destroyed Moab in the fifth year after the destruction of Jerusalem. Both were absorbed by the Arabs.

3) THE EDOMITES, vv.12-14

Edom (or Seir) was related more closely to Israel than with Ammon or Moab (Gen. 25: 23; Deut. 23: 7). They settled the territory south of Moab from the Dead Sea to the Gulf of Aqaba. For the third time, we must notice *(a)* the charge (v.12); *(b)* the condemnation (vv.13-14).

CHAPTER 25

a) The charge, v.12

"Because that Edom hath dealt against the house of Judah by taking vengeance, and hath greatly offended, and revenged himself upon them ..."

This is a case of 'getting his own back': of settling old grudges. The "vengeance" of Edom was rooted in bitter hatred for God's people. The Psalmist refers to this: "Remember, O LORD, the children of Edom in the day of Jerusalem; who said, Rase it, rase it, even to the foundation thereof" (Psalm 137: 7). Obadiah verses 10-14 refer to this in more detail: "For thy violence against *thy brother* Jacob, shame shall cover thee, and thou shalt be cut off for ever" (v.10). Their burning hatred and bitter animosity over the years, culminated in the atrocities committed at the destruction of Jerusalem. Israel was expressly forbidden to act towards Edom in this way: "Thou shalt not abhor an Edomite; for he is *thy brother:* thou shalt not abhor an Egyptian; because thou wast a stranger in his land" (Deut. 23: 7). The whole history of Edom as it touched Israel is summed up in Amos 1 verses 11-12: "Thus saith the Lord; For three transgressions, and for four, I will not turn away the punishment thereof; because he did pursue *his brother* with the sword, and did cast off all pity, and his anger did tear perpetually, and he kept his wrath for ever".

The exact opposite must mark God's people: see Colossians 3 verses 12-14, "Put on therefore, as the elect of God, holy and beloved, bowels of mercies, kindness, humbleness of mind, meekness, longsuffering, forebearing one another, and forgiving one another, if any man have a quarrel against any: even as Christ forgave you, even so do ye". The New Testament describes "violence against thy brother": see, for example, Galatians 5 verses 13-15. "But if ye bite and devour one another, take heed that ye be not consumed one of another". See also, again, Ephesians 4: 31. We are to "love as brethren, be pitiful, be courteous" (1 Pet. 3: 8). We must never forget the Lord's teaching in John 13 verses 34-35.

b) The condemnation, vv.13-14

"Therefore thus saith the Lord GOD; I will also stretch out mine hand upon Edom, and will cut off man and beast from it: and I will make it desolate from Teman; and they of Dedan shall fall by the sword. And I will lay my vengeance upon Edom by the hand of my people Israel: and they shall do in Edom according to mine anger and according to my fury; and they shall know my vengeance, saith the Lord GOD." It is a case of "whatsoever a man soweth, that shall he also reap": Edom had taken "vengeance" against Judah (v.12) and the Lord would lay His "vengeance" upon Edom by the hand of His people Israel" (v.14).

Teman and Dedan cannot now be pinpointed with accuracy. According to H.L.Ellison (C.L.Feinberg does not seem to be quite so sure) the prophecy of Edom's downfall was "fulfilled n the time of John Hyrcanus (134-104 BC); he conquered the Edomites and gave them the choice of Judaism or the sword. Though many of the Edomites, or Idumeans, remembered their origin, they became fanatical Jews in religion (according to Josephus). This was how Herod could become king of the Jews". C.L.Feinberg adds "Now all three nations (Ammon, Moab and Edom) are known by the general name of Arabs. For the time, as Ezekiel foretold, they have faded from history as recognisable entities". More is said about Edom in Chapter 35.

4) THE PHILISTINES, vv.15-17

As C.L.Feinberg rightly says, "Among the enemies of Israel the Philistines were more often referred to in the Old Testament than any other nation. They gave their name to the entire land (Palestine) although they were able to subjugate to their rule only a small portion on the coast". For the fourth time we must notice *(i)* the charge (v.15); *(ii)* the condemnation vv.16-17).

i) The charge, v.15

"Because the Philistines have dealt by revenge, and have taken vengeance with a despiteful heart, to destroy it for the old hatred ..." Since the three preceding oracles concerned nations which had expressed their vindictive jealousy and hatred for God's people, particularly at the overthrow of Jerusalem, it seems likely that the Philistines were involved in the same way, and this is confirmed by Joel: "Yea, and what have ye to do with me, O Tyre and Zidon, and all the coasts of Palestine ('all the districts of Philistia', JND)? ... ye have taken my silver and my gold, and have carried into your temples my goodly pleasant things: the children also of Judah and the children of Jerusalem have ye sold unto the Grecians, that ye might remove them far from their border" (Joel 3: 4-6). Interestingly enough, the next two oracles concern Tyre (26: 1 - 28: 19 and Zidon (28: 20-24). The expressions, "dealt by revenge ... taken vengeance with a despiteful heart ... the old hatred" are chilling.

The New Testament warns against nursing 'old hatred': "Dearly beloved, avenge not yourselves, but rather give place unto wrath: for it written, Vengeance is mine; I will repay, saith the Lord" (Rom. 12: 19); "But if ye have bitter envying and strife in your hearts, glory not, and lie not against the truth. This wisdom descendeth not from above, but is earthly, sensual, devilish. For where envying and strife is, there is confusion and every evil work" (James 3: 14-16). The Lord's people must not 'gun' for one another.

ii) The condemnation, vv.16-17

"Therefore thus saith the Lord GOD; Behold, I will stretch out mine hand upon the Philistines, and I will cut off the Cherethites, and destroy the remnant of the sea coast. And I will execute great vengeance upon them with furious rebukes; and they shall know that I am the LORD, when I shall lay my vengeance upon them." According to F.A.Tatford, "the Cherethites were the Philistines who lived along the coast (Zeph. 2: 5), and the Septuagint refers to them as Cretans in indication of their origin". See Jeremiah 47 verse 4 and Amos 9 verse 7. (Caphtor is the ancient name for Crete). No other nation is mentioned here as the agent for the destruction of Philistia, but we do know that while Pharaoh smote Gaza, Philistia would be inundated by "an overflowing flood" "out of the north" (Jer. 47: 1-2). The expression "out of the north" is frequently used in the book of Jeremiah with reference to Babylon, and occurs first in connection with the commissioning of the prophet: "Out of the north an evil shall break forth upon all the inhabitants of the land" (Jer. 1.14). The Philistines would be completely obliterated (Amos 1: 8), and "they did actually disappear from sight as a nation" (F.A.Tatford).

Only then would the Philistines recognise that the God of Israel was a true and living God: "and they shall know that I am the LORD, when I shall lay my vengeance upon them".

EZEKIEL CHAPTER 26

Following the four short oracles concerning, Ammon, Moab, Edom and Philistia (25: 1-17), almost three chapters (26: 1 - 28: 19) are devoted to the downfall of Tyre. After the introduction, "And it came to pass in the eleventh year, in the first day of the month (which is not given), that the word of the LORD came unto me, saying, Son of man, because that Tyrus hath said against Jerusalem, Aha, she is broken that was the gates of the people: she is turned unto me: I shall be replenished, now she is laid waste" (vv.1-2), the section comprises seven oracles: *(i)* Chapter 26 verses 3-6; *(ii)* Chapter 26 verses 7-14; *(iii)* Chapter 26 verses 15-18; *(iv)* Chapter 26 verses 19-21; *(v)* Chapter 27 verses 1-35; *(vi)* Chapter 28 verses 1-10; *(vii)* Chapter 28 verses 11-19. Each oracle is introduced by the words, "thus saith the Lord GOD" (26. 3, 7, 15, 19) or "the word of the LORD came ... unto me, saying" (27: 1; 28: 1; 28: 11).

Before embarking on our studies in these most interesting chapters, it might be helpful to notice the following: *(i)* her commercial importance; *(ii)* her relationship with Israel; *(iii)* her geographical location; *(iv)* her later history.

i) *Her commercial importance*

The first mention of Tyre in the Bible occurs in Joshua 19 verse 29 where it is called "the strong city Tyre". It was an ancient Phoenician city. According to C.L.Feinberg, it was "the wealthy capital of Phoenicia which had held a supremacy among the Phoenician cities since the thirteenth century B.C". F.A.Tatford provides further information: "She established her own colonies all round the Mediterranean - in Cyprus, North Africa, Spain and even farther afield in the Scilly Isles - and her mariners travelled beyond the Pillars of Hercules (known to us as the Straits of Gibraltar), and even as far as the Canary Islands". Tyre was predominantly a seafaring city and became extremely prosperous through her trade with all parts of the then known world. She was the commercial centre of the Mediterranean world: "a mart of nations" (Isa. 23: 3). At the time of Ezekiel she was still at the zenith of her commercial prosperity and international importance. F.Gardiner (*Ellicott's Commentary*) expands: "It must be remembered how numerous the colonies of Phoenicia were. They had been established in Cyprus, Rhodes, Malta, Spain, Sicily, Sardinia, the Balearic Islands, and Africa. In some of these there were several colonies, as Utica and Carthage in Africa, Gades (Cadiz), Kalpe (Gibraltar) and Malaka (Malaga) in Spain. All these looked up to Tyre as their mother city, and received from her their high priests".

ii) Her relationship with Israel

As C.L.Feinberg points out, "During the reigns of David and Solomon, Tyre exercised a great influence on the commercial and political and even the religious life of Israel. Hiram, king of Tyre, was a devoted friend of David (2 Sam. 5: 11), who helped him and Solomon in their building operations (see 1 Kings 5: 1-2; 1 Chron. 14: 1; 2 Chron. 2: 3, 11-12)". We are told that "Hiram sent in the navy (Solomon's Navy) shipmen that had knowledge of the sea, with the servants of Solomon" (1 Kings 9: 26-28). Feinberg continues: "Though Tyre and Israel were friendly in the reigns of David and Solomon, they drifted apart later. Tyrians sold Jews as slaves to the Greeks and Edomites (Joel 3: 4-8; Amos 1: 9-10)".

iii) Her geographical location

Tyre had what C.L.Feinberg calls a "strong natural location, situated as she was on the mainland, and on a row of islands not far from the shore". F.A.Tatford confirms this and adds further detail. "The original city, Palae-Tyrus ... was built on the mainland. There was a small island lying half a mile from the shore which was little more than two rocky ledges, partly submerged, and seemingly quite unsuitable as a site for a city. King Hiram, however, decided on a massive building operation. The canal between the two rocks was filled in and thousands of men were employed for many years in the construction. The temples, palaces and principal buildings, the market-place where business was transacted, and the two excellent harbours (the inner, or Sidonian, and the outer or Egyptian) for which Tyre was famed, were all located on the island (others say that the harbours were located on the island and on the mainland respectively). The city's name is said to have derived from the Hebrew *tsur* (rock) but this is by no means established". However, other commentators seem very certain about this!

iv) Her later history

Before Ezekiel's time, the Assyrians made, it seems, more than one attempt to conquer Tyre. We are told that Shalmaneser attempted for five years (726-721 BC) to capture the rock fortress (F.A.Tatford), and that (according to C.L.Feinberg) Sennacherib took part of the city on the mainland but did not capture Tyre itself, which resisted the Assyrian invader for five years (701-696 BC). Additionally (according to F.A.Tatford), Ashurbanipal made a further and equally unsuccessful attempt to conquer the city in 664 BC.

After the fall of Jerusalem (586 BC), Nebuchadnezzar and the Babylonians marched against Tyre and laid siege to the city for thirteen years (586-573 BC). The length of the siege was due to the fact that the Tyrians obtained their supplies by sea. Despite contrary views, Nebuchadnezzar evidently took the mainland fortress (this is clear from Ezekiel 29: 18) as predicted in our current chapter (see vv.7-11), only to find that 'the cupboard was bare' and that after thirteen years hard graft there was no booty. But God always pays His workmen, and Nebuchadnezzar received the wealth of Egypt in lieu of the expected wealth of Tyre (Ezek. 29: 19-21).

But even though island Tyre did not fall to Nebuchadnezzar, even after a thirteen-year siege, trade undoubtedly ceased, and did so, according to Isaiah 23 verse 17, for seventy years, after which Tyre was restored, and resumed her old life-style: "after the end of seventy years shall Tyre sing as an harlot ... And it shall come to pass, after the end of seventy years, that the Lord will visit Tyre, and she shall return to her hire, and shall commit fornication with all the kingdoms of the world upon the face of the earth" (Isaiah 23: 15,17). And so, 240 years after the Babylonians left for Egypt, another invader arrived in the form of Alexander the Great. He demolished all the buildings of the old mainland city and built a causeway with them to the island, and captured the city in 332 BC after only seven months, fulfilling the prophecy in Zechariah 9 verses 3-4. It was then that the prophecy was fulfilled: "And they shall destroy the walls of Tyrus, and break down her towers: I will also scrape her dust from her, and make her like the top of a rock. It shall be a place for the spreading of nets in the midst of the sea" (Ezek. 26: 4-5). According to Christopher Wright, "Alexander's causeway remains beneath the peninsular that has silted up over it in the centuries since". As C.L.Feinberg observes, "Commentators have long noticed the change of pronoun in Ezekiel 26 from the "he" of the previous verses to the "they" of verse 12. It is rightly understood that Ezekiel was carrying the picture beyond Nebuchadnezzar to other invaders as well, who would complete what he began. Especially this would be true of Alexander".

In the words of Morrish's Bible Dictionary, "*God* was known in all the palaces of Jerusalem (cf. Psalm 48: 3), but the god of this world in Tyre: there could be gratified the lust of the eyes, the lust of the flesh, and the pride of life". Howbeit, the Lord Jesus said, "Woe unto thee Chorazin! Woe unto thee, Bethsaida! For if the mighty works, which were done in you, had been done in Tyre and Sidon, they would have repented long ago in sackcloth and ashes. But I say unto you, It shall be more tolerable for Tyre and Sidon at the day of judgment, than for you" (Matt. 11: 21-22).

The three chapters may be entitled *(1)* the ruin of Tyre (26: 1-21); *(2)* the renown of Tyre (27: 1-35); *(3)* the rulers of Tyre (28: 1-19).

1) THE RUIN OF TYRE, 26: 1-21

The following should be noted; *(a)* the cause of her downfall (vv.1-6); *(b)* the conqueror at her downfall (vv.7-14); *(c)* the consternation at her downfall (vv.15-18); *(d)* the consequence of her downfall (vv.19-21).

a) The cause of her downfall, vv.1-6

In the opening section of the chapter, we should notice the reason (v.2) and the result (vv.3-6) of her downfall:

i) **The reason, v.2.** As in the four cases in Chapter 25, the reason for Tyre's destruction is given: "Son of man, because that Tyrus hath said against Jerusalem, Aha, she is broken that was the gates of the people: she is turned unto me: I shall be replenished, now she is laid waste". As John B.Taylor observes, "The offence of Tyre is that she rejoices over the fall of Jerusalem, and congratulates herself that she has lost a serious commercial competitor". F.A.Tatford explains that "because her country lay across the great trade routes from the south, Judah had been able to impose tolls on merchants who passed through to Tyre". C.L.Feinberg writes similarly: "Tyre's exclamation at the fall of Jerusalem manifested unfeeling exultation over the calamity of Israel, as she looked for self-enrichment through the fall of God's people as a commercial rival (see Prov. 17: 5). Tyre rejoiced over Jerusalem's ruin because free passage for her caravans would mean greater prosperity in trade. Taxes were doubtless levied by the Jews, here called 'the gate of the peoples' (JND) from the north to the south (Egypt). When Judah was strong and subjugated Edom, she controlled the caravan routes to the Red Sea., thus hindering the Phoenicians from gaining all the profit they had hoped for".

Tyre's rejoicing in the elimination of a commercial rival is comparable with those of whom Paul said, "Some indeed preach Christ even of **envy** (displeasure over the advantage or prosperity of others) **and strife** (the expression of enmity)", and did so out of "**contention** ('faction', RV, or a 'party spirit'), not sincerely (*hagnos*, not with pure motives) supposing to add affliction to my bonds". (Phil. 1: 15-16). So they were brethren with ulterior motives. People like that always cause difficulties. They were not the false teachers of the day, but "Christians who were jealous of Paul, and who sought to undermine his influence" (S. Maxwell). The whole thing smacks of rivalry. How dreadful: rivalry amongst Christians! We can almost hear their conversation: 'Paul has had the limelight for too long: now it's our turn. We'll show him that he's not the only pebble on the beach. We'll show him that we can preach too!' It was a golden opportunity for them. Paul was "in bonds", and they were free! They took the opportunity to 'kick a man when he's down', although, strictly speaking, Paul wasn't 'down' at all!

Unlike Tyre, believers should "esteem other better than themselves" and "look not every man on his own things (his own interests), but every man also on the things (the interests) of others" (Phil. 2: 3-4).

ii) The result, vv.3-6. The judgment of Tyre is very clearly stated: "Behold, I am against thee, O Tyrus, and will cause **many nations** to come up against thee, as the sea causeth his waves to come up. And **they** shall destroy the walls of Tyrus, and break down her towers: I will also scrape her dust from her, and make her like the top of a rock. It shall be a place for the spreading of nets in the midst of the sea: for I have spoken it, saith the Lord GOD: and it shall become a spoil to the nations" (vv.3-5). See also verse 14. In New Testament language, "they that will be rich fall into temptation and a snare, and into many foolish and hurtful lusts, which drown men in destruction and perdition. For the love of money (this is a good description of Tyre) is the root of all evil: which while some coveted after, they have erred from the faith, and pierced themselves through with many sorrows" (1 Tim. 6: 9-10). Tyre would prove that Solomon was correct in saying, "Labour not to be rich: cease from thine own wisdom, Wilt thou set thine eyes upon that which is not? For riches certainly make themselves wings; they fly away as an eagle toward heaven" (Prov, 23: 4-5). This can be called "the deceitfulness of riches" (Matt. 13: 22).

Ezekiel predicts the punishment of Tyre in language suited to her maritime location. "Wave after wave of invaders were to beat against her to bring about her doom. The prophet could well have had in mind the successive invaders of the city through the coming centuries until it fell at the hands of the Saracens in the fourteenth century A.D. Walls and towers were to be destroyed, as in the invasion of Nebuchadnezzar. Then the dust from her ruined walls, homes, temples and palaces was to be scraped from her, leaving her as a bare rock. This Alexander did when he built the road to the island. Rubble from the mainland city served him well when he built the causeway. Spreading of nets was for the purpose of drying them. Such has been the main use of Tyre for centuries" (C.L.Feinberg).

The "daughters" of Tyre (v.6) are her suburbs or dependencies on the mainland together with her colonies. They would suffer the fate of the mother city. They are mentioned again in verse 8: "He shall slay with the sword thy daughters in the field."

b) *The conqueror at her downfall, vv.7-14*

This prophecy was fulfilled to the very detail. "To prevent Nebuchadnezzar (Ezekiel calls him Nebuchadrezzar, the Babylonian form of his name) from getting her valuables, Tyre transported herself to an island a half mile out in the sea. The conqueror destroyed the city and left. But more than two centuries later, Alexander the Great took the ruins of the old city, even scraping up the dust, end made a causeway to the island, thus fulfilling the prophecy exactly" (Amplified Version footnote).

We should notice that Nebuchadnezzar is described as "a king of kings" (v.7). The Babylonian monarch is "a king of kings" because he had made many rulers subject to him, and more important, because God had delegated to him universal rule: "Thou, O king, art a king of kings: for the God of heaven hath given thee a kingdom, power, and strength, and glory ... Thou art this head of gold" (Dan. 2: 37-38). The Lord Jesus is not "a king of kings": He is "KING OF KINGS, AND LORD OF LORDS" (Rev. 19: 16).

The details of the coming siege are given: "Behold, I will bring upon Tyrus Nebuchadrezzar king of Babylon, a king of kings, from the north. With horses, and with chariots, and with horsemen, and companies, and much people. *He* shall slay with the sword thy daughters in the field: and *he* shall make a fort against thee, and cast a mount against thee, and lift up the buckler against thee. And *he* shall set engines of war against thy walls, and with his axes shall *he* break down thy towers. By reason of the abundance of *his* horses their dust shall cover thee: thy walls shall shake at the noise of the horsemen, and of the wheels, and of the chariots, when *he* shall enter into thy gates, as men enter into a city wherein is made a breach. With the hooves of his horses shall *he* tread down all thy streets: *he* shall slay thy people by the sword, and thy strong garrisons ('pillars or columns of thy strength', JND) shall go down to the ground" (vv.8-11). According to C.L.Feinberg, "the buckler" (v.8) refers to "the roof of shields ... used to protect against missiles thrown from the walls", and the 'pillars' (v.11, JND) were actually obelisks, and were probably those mentioned by the historian Herodotus as erected in the temple of Heracles at Tyre. One was of gold and the other of emerald, which shone brilliantly at night, and were dedicated to Melkarth god of Tyre. These impressive pillars would be demolished by the invader". The Latin word for the 'roof of shields' above is, very appropriately, *testudo,* meaning, 'tortoise'

Very clearly, this is a land-based siege. A "mount ... engines of war ... horses ... wheels ... chariots" could not be used against an island!

As already pointed out, the pronoun "he" is used throughout these verses, but now the pronoun "they" is employed, suggesting that what Nebuchadnezzar began, others would complete: "And *they* shall make a spoil of thy riches, and make a prey of thy merchandise: and *they* shall break down thy walls, and destroy thy pleasant houses: and *they* shall lay thy stones and thy timber and thy dust in the midst of the water" (v.12). The prophecy has moved on from Nebuchadnezzar's invasion to Alexander's invasion, and perhaps even beyond that. Zechariah, who prophesied after the era of Nebuchadnezzar and predicted the fall of the city at the hand of Alexander the Great, wrote: "And Tyrus did build herself a strong hold, and heaped up silver as the dust, and fine gold as the mire of the streets. Behold, the Lord will cast her out, and he will smite her power in the sea; and she shall be devoured with fire" (Zech. 9: 3-4).

But that is not all. If Nebuchadnezzar is the destroyer in verses 7-12, and Alexander, with others, is the destroyer in verse 12, then the Lord Himself is the destroyer in verses 13-14: "And *I* will cause the noise of thy songs to cease; and the sound of thy harps shall be no more heard. And *I* will make thee like the top of a rock: and thou shalt be a place to spread nets upon; thou shalt be built no more: for *I* the LORD have spoken it, saith the Lord GOD" (vv.13-14).

c) The consternation at her downfall, vv.15-18

These verses describe the wider repercussions of Tyre's downfall. The maritime influence of the city is clearly stressed: "Shall not the isles shake at the sound of thy fall, when the wounded cry, when the slaughter is made in the midst of thee? Then all the princes of the sea shall come down from their thrones (in accordance with the customs of Oriental mourning, see Jonah 3: 6), and lay away their robes, and put off their broidered garments: they shall clothe themselves with trembling; they shall sit upon the ground, and shall tremble at every moment, and be astonished at thee. And they shall take up a lamentation for thee, and say to thee, How art thou destroyed, that wast inhabited of seafaring men, the renowned city, which wast strong in the sea, she and her inhabitants, which cause their terror to be on all that haunt it! Now shall the isles tremble in the day of thy fall; yea, the isles that are in the sea shall be troubled at thy departure".

As John B.Taylor observes, "Not the least result of Tyre's crashing fall will be the dismay felt by the rulers of neighbouring principalities, dependent on Tyrian trade for their prosperity, and appalled at the destruction of such a powerful overlord. The "isles" are really *coastlands* (RSV), i.e. the small city-states of the Mediterranean seaboard". C.L.Feinberg suggests, as we have already noted from Ellicott's Commentary, that the passage probably has in view "the heads of the Phoenician colonies in the Mediterranean" which were "in Cyprus, Rhodes, Malta, Spain, Sicily, Sardinia, the Balearic Islands and Africa, with all looking to Tyre as their headquarters, and sending annual gifts to the Tyrian Heracles". C.L.Feinberg adds that, "Interestingly, the commercial activities of Tyre were not represented as oppressive". Revelation 18 describes, similarly, the downfall of another commercial power of vast influence.

d) The consequence of her downfall, vv.19-21

Having listened to the funeral dirge (vv.17-18), we now observe the burial of Tyre: "For thus saith the Lord GOD; When I shall make thee a desolate city, like the cities that are not inhabited; when I shall bring up the deep upon thee, and great waters shall cover thee; when I shall bring thee down with them that descend into the pit, with the people of old time, and shall set thee in the low parts of the earth, in places desolate of old, with them that go down to the pit, that thou be not inhabited; and I shall set glory in the land of the living; I will make thee a terror, and thou shalt be no more: though thou be sought for, yet shalt thou never be found again, saith the Lord GOD".

F.A. Tatford helpfully explains the language here. "The words in themselves were not strictly appropriate to a literal city, but Tyre was assumed to possess a personality and, in that imagery, when she had been buried under the sea, she went down to the abode of the dead to join those who had died long ago". Very clearly, the destruction of Tyre would be so complete that she would be comparable to an uninhabited city. The references to "the deep" and "great waters" can only mean that the ruins of the city would be submerged. The meaning of "the pit" here (*bor*, meaning 'pit' or 'well') is clear from its use elsewhere in the Old Testament. See, for example, Isaiah 14 verse 15, "Yet thou (Lucifer) shalt be brought down to hell, to the sides of the pit". The "people of old time" refers, not evidently as some suggest, to those of Noah's day, but to former generations in general.

Proud Tyre could not escape the lot of all men. The words, "I shall bring thee down with them that descend into the pit ... and I shall set glory in *the land of the living*" (v.20) "does not refer to Judah, as some suggest, but to the whole earth in contrast to the realm of the dead just under consideration" (C.L. Feinberg). The Amplified Version, following the Greek Septuagint text, renders the verse as follows: "Then I will thrust you down with those who descend into the pit, to the people of olden times, and will make you, Tyre, to dwell in the lower world, like the places that were desolate of old, with those who go down to the pit (realm of the dead), *that you be not inhabited or shed forth your glory and renown in the land of the living"*. Tyre would totally disappear: "I will make thee a terror, and thou shalt be no more: though thou be sought for, yet shalt thou never be found again, saith the Lord GOD" (v.21). The words, "I will make thee a terror", appear to mean that the destruction of Tyre would be the cause of terror to others. "While the existence of Tyre produced fear of reprisal in all opponents (v.17), the absence of Tyre would produce the fear of dismay and uncertainty (v.21)" (Lamar E. Cooper).

As F.A. Tatford observes, "Tyre had hoped to profit by the fall of Jerusalem, but instead she had reached her end from which there could be no revival ... the

CHAPTER 26

very city was swept from the face of the earth. What Ezekiel predicted was literally fulfilled". As noted above, "they that will be rich fall into temptation, and a snare, and into many foolish and hurtful lusts, which drown men in destruction and perdition" (1 Tim. 6: 9). Materialism can destroy us spiritually. In Paul's words, "be not conformed to this world: but ye transformed by the renewing of your mind, that ye may prove what is that good, and acceptable, and perfect, will of God" (Rom. 12: 2). Else, like Tyre, we will lose our testimony and be "trodden under foot of men" (Matt. 5: 13).

EZEKIEL CHAPTER 27

We have already noted that the three chapters dealing with the downfall of Tyre may be entitled *(1)* the ruin of Tyre (26: 1-21); *(2)* the renown of Tyre (27: 1-35); *(3)* the rulers of Tyre (28: 1-19).

1) THE RUIN OF TYRE, 26: 1-21

We have noted: *(a)* the cause of her downfall (vv.1-6); *(b)* the conqueror at her downfall (vv.7-14); *(c)* the consternation at her downfall (vv.15-18); *(d)* the consequence of her downfall (vv.19-21). This brings us to:

2) THE RENOWN OF TYRE, 27: 1-35

In Bible language, this chapter can be called "a lamentation for Tyrus". Here is the full quotation: "The word of the LORD came again unto me, saying, Now, thou son of man, take up a lamentation for Tyrus" (vv.1-2). The linguistic experts tell us that this is, largely, the second funeral dirge relating to the destruction of Tyre. The first is found in Chapter 26 verses 17-18. Both are set in special poetic meter for which the technical word is *qinah*. We are told that the chapter commences with a prose introduction (vv.1-3a), followed by the first part of the 'funeral song' (vv.3b-9), a prose interlude (vv.10-24), and the second part of the funeral song (vv.25-36).

C.L.Feinberg is well-worth quoting *in extenso*: "This chapter is a lamentation over the loss of Tyre's earthly splendour, written in the *kinah* (lamentation) measure. The passage dwells on the world-wide trade, commerce and material wealth of Tyre. Throughout this chapter Tyre is likened to a ship, well-outfitted, wrongly piloted and ultimately shipwrecked. Ezekiel's description is considered a classic on the nature, scope and variety of the commerce of the ancient world, together with an invaluable geographic list of the chief cities concerned. It has been claimed that, judging from a literary viewpoint alone, Chapters 27-28 are among the most beautiful in the entire prophecy. Many feel that the vividness of detail of this chapter places it practically without parallel in the history of literature". But with it all, it is a clear denunciation of human pride. "Thus saith the Lord GOD; O Tyrus, thou hast said, I am of perfect beauty" (v.3). Bearing in mind that New Testament injunction, "Let him that thinketh he standeth take heed lest he fall" (1 Cor. 10: 12), this chapter may well be entitled, 'The fame and fall of Tyre'.

The lamentation over Tyre assumes that its doom and destruction has already taken place, emphasising the certainty of the prophecy. The city is described as "situate at the entry (entries, JND) of the sea ... a merchant of the people for many isles" (v.3). The words 'entries of the sea' (JND) can be rendered 'gateways to the sea', and refer to Tyre's two harbours, the Sidonian to the north and the Egyptian to the south. According to F.Gardiner, the Sidonian harbour also had "an outer harbour or roadstead, formed by a ledge off the north-west extremity of the island". The city is said to be "a merchant of the people for many isles (coastlands)" (v.3), and this is expanded with great detail in later verses in the chapter (vv.12-25). Notice the repetition of "merchant" in these verses (vv.12, 13, 15, 16, 17, 18, 20, 22, 23, 24).

As already noted, Tyre is described here as a proud ship, and after the introduction (vv.1-3), the chapter may be divided as follows: *(a)* the ship's construction (vv.4-7); *(b)* the ship's crew (vv.8-11); *(c)* the ship's cargo (vv.12-25); *(d)* the ship's catastrophe (vv.26-36).

a) The ship's construction, vv.4-7

Strictly speaking, the words "Thus saith the Lord GOD; O Tyrus, thou hast said, I am of perfect beauty" (v.3b) mark the beginning of the section "written in the *kinah* (lamentation) measure" (C.L.Feinberg). Tyre's proud boast echoed the pride of its ruler: "Son of man, say unto the prince of Tyrus, Thus saith the Lord GOD; Because thine heart is lifted up, and thou hast said, I am a God, I sit in the seat of God, in the midst of the seas; yet thou art a man, and not God, though thou set thine heart as the heart of God" (28: 2). Centuries later another city (Laodicea) was equally self-complacent: "I am rich, and increased with goods, and have need of nothing" (Rev. 3: 17).

The beauty of Tyre is likened to a splendid ship, and her "builders" (v.4) are therefore likened, not to stone-masons or brick-layers, but to ship-builders. The "builders" are, of course, her rulers. Since the good ship Tyre is at her moorings, ("thy borders are in the midst of the seas" is sometimes rendered 'thy moorings are in the heart of the seas'), we have the opportunity to notice her "ship boards (v.5) ... masts (v.5) ... oars (v.6) ... benches (v.6) ... sail" (v.7). The details here, like the details of the ships crew and the cargo which follow, are informative and absorbing:

i) Her planking. "They have made all thy shipboards ('planks', RV) of fir trees of Senir" (v.5). According to J.N.Darby, they were "double boards of cypress trees of Senir". The word rendered "shipboards" is in "the dual, with reference to its two sides" (F.Gardiner). Senir is another name for Hermon: "which Hermon the Sidonians call Sirion; and the Amorites call it Shenir" (Deut. 3: 9). The same timber, supplied by Hiram king of Tyre (1 Kings 5: 8-10) was used for the floor of the temple (1 Kings 6: 15).

ii) Her masts. "They have taken cedars from Lebanon to make masts for thee" (v.5). Centuries before, Hiram, king of Tyre, "gave Solomon cedar trees and fir trees according to all his desire" (1 Kings 5: 10), in preparation for the building of the temple.

iii) Her oars. "Of the oaks of Bashan have they made thine oars" (v.6). Bashan, to the east of the Sea of Galilee, was renowned for its oak forests. Interestingly enough, the "cedars of Lebanon" and the "oaks of Bashan" are used as symbols of human pride: "For the day of the LORD of hosts shall be upon every one that is proud and lofty, and upon every one that is lifted up; and he shall be brought low: and upon all the cedars of Lebanon, that are high and lifted up, and upon all the oaks of Bashan" (Isa. 2: 12-13).

iv) Her deck. "The company of the Ashurites have made thy benches of ivory, brought out of the isles of Chittim" (v.6) or, omitting "the company of the Ashurites", "they made thy benches ('deck', JND/RV margin) of 'ivory, inlaid in box-wood', out of the isles of Chittim" (RV/JND). According to C.L.Feinberg, "The use of ivory for ships and homes was developed to a high degree in Tyre (cf. Ahab's ivory palace after his marriage to a Sidonian queen, 1 Kings 22: 39). According to Pliny, the best boxwood came from Cyprus. Kittim (or Chittim v.6) in this instance may have included not only Cyprus but other areas as well (Dan. 11: 30)". It seems, however, the name Chittim was used in a more widespread sense after Ezekiel's time, although F.Gardiner's explanation is noteworthy: "the isles of Chittim (as in Jer. 2: 10) stands for the islands and coasts whose fleets, in coming to the East, made their rendezvous at Cyprus".

v) Her sails. "Fine linen, with broidered work from Egypt, was that which thou spreadest forth to be thy sail" (v.7) or "Byssus with broidered work from Egypt was thy sail, to serve thee for a banner" (JND). Egypt was famous for its linen (byssus). F.Gardiner observes that to "a modern sailor, 'fine linen' may seem both an extravagant and an insufficient material for a ship's sails, but the State ships of antiquity were often fitted out in this way, and the sails embroidered in colours in place of a pennon".

vi) Her awning. "Blue and purple from the isles of Elishah was that which covered thee ('was thine awning', JND/RV)" (v.7). The "isles (coasts) of Elishah" are unidentified. Since Elishah was one of the sons of Javan (Gen. 10: 4), known to us as Greece, it seems likely that Elishah was somewhere on the Mediterranean coast. (The "king of Grecia", Dan. 8: 21, is 'king of Javan' in Hebrew. See also Dan. 10: 20; 11: 2; Zech. 9: 13). Javan evidently founded the maritime nations.

Like the *Titanic* and, one hundred years later, the *Costa Concordia*, the good ship *Tyre* looked marvellously impressive, but it would eventually sink. It was built of the very best materials that earth could provide. But that was all. The ark looked laughable by comparison, but God was on board. See Genesis 7 verse 1 and 8 verse 16.

b) The ship's crew, vv.8-11

Having inspected the ship itself, we must now inspect her crew. Reference is made to her "mariners...pilots...calkers", and to her "marines" (!), that is, to her military strength (vv.10-11).

i) Her rowers. "The inhabitants of Zidon and Arvad were thy mariners 'rowers', JND/RV)" (v.8). Sidon lay to the north of Tyre, and was evidently the oldest city in Phoenicia (Gen. 10: 15). According to C.L.Feinberg, Arvad is now called Ruad, and was situated on an island north of modern Tripoli.

ii) Her pilots. "Thy wise men, O Tyrus, that were in thee, were thy pilots" (v.8). While Tyre used crewmen of different nationalities, the overall control and direction of the good ship Tyre was determined by Tyreans themselves.

iii) Her calkers. "The ancients of Gebal (meaning the prominent men of the city), and the wise men thereof, were in thee thy calkers" (v.9) or "The elders of Gebal and the wise men thereof were in thee repairing thy leaks (margin, literally 'making fast thy chinks')" (JND). Calkers repaired leaks and fissures. They dealt with cracks in the seams. We would probably call them 'shipwrights' today. According to Morrish's *Bible Dictionary*, Gebal was a maritime city of Phoenicia identified with Jebiel (modern Jubayl) and known in the Greek world as Byblos. It lay just north of Beirut. Its inhabitants are called Giblites (Joshua 13: 5). Some of them were stone-masons and assisted in the construction of the temple (1 Kings 5: 18, JND: the RV calls them 'Gebalites').

At this point in the description of Tyre, "the figure of a ship gives place for a time to plain language, the better to set forth the military resources and power of this great city" (F.Gardiner), although John B. Taylor suggests that "the picture of a ship is still maintained, with the shields of its occupants hung up in array on either side". The Viking ships were adorned in this way. We should notice:

i) Her customers. "All the ships of the sea with their mariners were in thee to occupy thy merchandise ('to barter with thee', JND: to exchange thy merchandise', RV)" (v.9). As C.L.Feinberg observes, "Not one land that carried on commercial and maritime activity failed to deal with Tyre".

ii) Her soldiery. "They of Persia (the first mention of Persia in the Old Testament), and of Lud (Lydia), and of Phut, were in thine army, thy men of war: they hanged the shield and helmet in thee; they set forth thy comeliness ('they gave splendour to thee', JND). The men of Arvad, with thine army, were upon thy walls roundabout, and the Gammadims were in thy towers: they hanged their shields upon thy walls round about: they have made thy beauty perfect" (vv.10-11). We would call these people 'mercenaries'. Lud evidently refers to Lydia in Asia Minor, although some opt for a location further east. According to F.A.Tatford, Phut probably refers to Cyrenaicia, but he points out that others opt for western Egypt or Libya. The word Gammadims could simply mean 'fighting men (JND margin) or 'valorous men' (RV margin). The walls of Tyre would be destroyed and her towers demolished (26: 4), and all the mercenaries in the world would not be able to prevent it happening.

While it could be said in passing that every assembly needs rowers, pilots, calkers, and fighting men, that really isn't the point here. The good ship Tyre had the best possible crewmen on board, but it still sank. A strong and united labour force (the rowers), a clever and innovative board of directors (the pilots), first class tradesmen (the calkers), tremendous commercial enterprise, and a world-class army will never save humanity from disaster.

The chapter commences with two references to Tyre's pride: "thou hast said, I am of perfect beauty ... thy builders have perfected thy beauty" (vv.3, 4) and now, after examining the ship's construction and the ship's crew, we read of the mercenaries, "they have made thy beauty perfect" (v.11). "Tyre thus laid claim on many sources to enhance her beauty, fortify her city and spread her influence. Precisely the same spirit pervades the nations of the world today, but it is without thought or concern for God. Thus their doom is sure, and they only await God's hour" (C.L.Feinberg).

c) The ship's cargo, vv.12-25

While nautical terms are absent in these verses, and the emphasis shifts to "merchants" and "fairs", it will not be long before the ship goes again to sea, and to disaster (v.26). Tyre, with its "riches ... fairs ... merchandise ... pilots ... calkers ... occupiers of thy merchandise ('they that barter with thee', JND) ... men of war" sinks "in the midst of the seas" (v.27).

The commercial activity of Tyre is dealt with at length in these verses. The merchants and their commodities are of great interest. Tyre was obviously of immense influence as the centre of Middle East trade, and beyond. John P. Taylor (who calls these verses 'the trade directory'), and others, point out that "the list of cities who traded with Tyre is given in geographical order, beginning with Tarshish in the west (v.12) to Rhodes (thought to be Dedan, v.15, although this is by no means certain) in the eastern Mediterranean, and then travelling from Edom (Syria, AV: again, the suggested change is by no means certain) northwards to Damascus (vv.16-18), with Arabia and Mesopotamia (vv.21-22) put last".

i) Tarshish. "Tarshish was thy merchant by reason of the multitude of all kind of riches: with silver, iron, tin and lead, they traded in thy fairs ('they furnished thy markets', JND)" (v.12). Tarshish is usually identified with Tartessus in Spain, but there are other suggestions. It was a Phoenician colony noted, amongst other things, for its silver (Jer. 10: 9). According to C.L.Feinberg, her "ships were the larger merchant vessels for distant traffic". F.A.Tatford states that "Spanish Tartessus was a port and also a mining district". It seems that the Tarshish fleet traded over a wide area. See 1 Kings 10 verse 22.

ii) Javan, Tubal, and Meshech. "Javan, Tubal, and Meshech, they were thy merchants: they traded in the persons of men and vessels of brass in thy market" (v.13). What a combination! Commerce can be absolutely heartless. Anything to make money. Javan, Tubal, and Meshech were descendants of Japheth (Gen. 10: 2; 1 Chron. 1: 5). Javan refers to the Ionians or Greeks (see our remarks at v.7), and Tubal and Meshech refer to peoples who evidently lived between the Black and Caspian Seas. The Assyrian cuneiform records called them the Tabali and the Mushki, and Herodotus called them the Tibareni and the Moschi. As F.A.Tatford observes, "Joel disclosed that Tyre was engaged in slave traffic and condemned the Tyrians for selling the people of Judah to Javan (Joel 3: 4-6)".

iii) Togarmah. "They of the house of Togarmah traded in thy fairs ('furnished thy markets', JND) with horses, and horsemen, and mules ('horses and war horses and mules', RV)" (v.14). Togarmah was one of the sons of Gomer (brother of Javan, Tubal and Meshech, Gen. 10: 3; 1 Chron. 1: 6) and Beth-Togarmah ("the house of Togarmah") are generally thought to be "the Til-garimmu of the Assyrians or the Armenia of the present day" (F.A.Tatford). The historians Xenophon, Strabo and Herodotus all point out that the Armenians were a people in the Taurus country noted for horses and mules (C.L.Feinberg). It is worth pointing out that in Bible times, horses were used in warfare, not labour.

iv) Dedan. "The men of Dedan were thy merchants; many isles were the merchandise of thy hand: they brought thee for a present ('rendered in payment', JND) horns of ivory and ebony" (v.15). There are differences of opinion in attempting to identify Dedan. The name occurs again in verse 20 where it evidently refers to a different place. The current reference associates Dedan with the coastlands and islands ("many isles were the mart of thy hand", JND), without specifying the area. Some suggest Rhodes, where there were certainly Phoenician colonies, and others opt for islands in either the Persian Gulf or Red Sea. *Prima facie,* it seems unlikely that ivory tusks and ebony would have been native products of Rhodes, but it is possible that a trade in these commodities existed with other areas. The Amplified Version boldly states "The men of Dedan (in Arabia) traded with you ..."

v) Syria. "Syria was thy merchant by reason of the multitude of the wares of thy making; they occupied in thy fairs ('they traded in thy markets', JND) with emeralds ('carbuncle's, JND), purple, and broidered work, and fine linen, and coral (possibly 'pearls' (JND), and agate ('rubies', JND)" (v.16). Some scholars assert that the Hebrew word *Aram* should read *Adam,* turning Syria into Edom, but changes like this, often on the basis that the amendment makes easier reading, should be regarded with caution, if not suspicion. Differences in **translating** words are allowable, particularly with lesser-used Hebrew words, but **altering** words in the so-called interests of better understanding is an entirely different matter. Tyre certainly had a big trade in luxury goods!

vi) Judah and Israel. "Judah, and the land of Israel, they were thy merchants; they traded in thy market wheat of Minnith, and Pannag ('sweet cakes', JND), and honey, and oil, and balm" (v.17). Minnith was an Amorite town (Judges 11: 33) evidently in a wheat-growing area, whereas Pannag refers, not to a place, but, it is said, to a sweetmeat made from honey. The RV margin has 'perhaps a kind of confection'. The Amplified Version is quite different: it says 'olives or early figs'.

vii) Damascus. "Damascus was thy merchant in the multitude of the wares of thy making, for the multitude of all riches; in the wine of Helbon, and white wool" (v.18). According to C.L.Feinberg, wine was the chief export of Damascus. Helbon (or Aleppo) was a vine-growing region northeast of Damascus. According to F.A.Tatford, "Its choice wine was mentioned by Nebuchadnezzar and also in Assyrian inscriptions, and Persian kings drank no other wine".

viii) Vedan and Javan. "Dan also and Javan going to and fro, occupied in thy fairs ('traded in thy markets', JND): bright iron, cassia, and calamus, were in thy market ('traffic, JND: literally, 'barter', JND margin)" (v.19). The words, "Dan also and Javan going to and fro" pose problems. In the first place, the text begins with 'Vedan' rather than 'Dan'. In any case, Dan (the tribe) had been deported years before. Since this verse is followed by references to the Arabian area, scholars do seem justified in suggesting that Vedan may well refer to Aden, and Javan, not to Greece itself (see our comments at v.13), but to a Greek colony in Arabia. Moreover, the words "going to and fro" could be rendered 'with yarn for thy wares' (RV) with a marginal note 'from Uzal'. J.N.Darby is bolder still: "Vedan and Javan of Uzal traded in thy markets", with a marginal note: 'probably Saana, the capital of Yemen'. The bright iron, or wrought iron, may well refer to sword blades for which, we are told, Yemen was famous. Cassia and calamus were ingredients in the holy anointing oil (Exodus 30: 23-24).

ix) Dedan. "Dedan was thy merchant in precious clothes for chariots ('precious riding-cloths', JND)" (v.20). Once again, luxury goods. Dedan here is to be distinguished from the place of the same name mentioned in verse 15. We appear to be in Arabia in verse 20

x) Arabia. "Arabia, and all the princes of Kedar, they occupied with thee in lambs and rams and goats; in these were they thy merchants" (v.21). Kedar was a nomadic tribe whose people were descended from Ishmael (Gen. 25: 13). They were evidently well-known for their flocks of sheep, and will be in the future (Isaiah 60: 7).

xi) Sheba and Raamah. "The merchants of Seba and Raamah, they were thy merchants: they occupied in thy fairs ('they furnished thy markets', JND) with chief of all spices, and with all precious stones, and gold" (v.22). According to F.A.Tatford, "Sheba (Job 6: 19; 1 Kings 10: 1) was the ancient kingdom of the Sabeans in southern Arabia, and was well-known for its gold, precious stones and aromatics (1 Kings 10: 10; Psalm 72: 10, 15; Is. 60: 6; Jer. 6: 20). Raamah, like Sheba, was descended from Cush, (Gen. 10: 7; 1 Chron. 1: 9) and the territory probably lay on the Persian Gulf".

xii) Haran, Canneh, and Eden. "Haran, and Canneh, and Eden, the merchants of Sheba, Asshur, and Chilmad, were thy merchants. These were thy merchants in all sorts of things ('excellent things', RV margin: 'sumptuous clothes', JND), in blue clothes ('in wrappings, or bales, of blue', RV), and broidered work, and in chests of rich apparel, bound with cords, and made of cedar, among thy merchandise" (vv.23-24). Haran, Canneh (Calneh) and Eden were all Mesopotamian cities. Haran was the birthplace of Abraham. It lay "at the junction of two great caravan routes, the one along the Tigris, the other along the Euphrates" (F.Gardiner). Calneh was an important commercial city on the Tigris, and was later known as Ctesiphon. Eden is unidentified These cities evidently operated as 'middle-men' for Sheba, Asshur (not Assyria, but the commercial city of Sura, on the banks of the Euphrates), and Chilmad.

As C.L.Feinberg observes, "The description of materials and wares is so precise and detailed throughout this section of the prophecy that the impression is given that Ezekiel had seen the merchants with their merchandise. With the mention of the ships of Tarshish, the great deep-sea ships which sailed to the remotest parts, Ezekiel's sketch of the commerce of Tyre was brought to a conclusion, and there was a resumption of the figure of the ship begun in verse 4. "The ships of Tarshish did sing of thee in thy market; and thou wast replenished, and made very glorious in the midst of the seas" (v.25).

C.L.Feinberg continues: "What an array of merchandise, what a variety of wares, what a range of places, and all of it for self and pride. ***God was in none of it***". F.Cundick has telling comments here: "When this spirit engrosses the whole mind of man, making all other thoughts secondary and subservient, then the throne of God in the heart is usurped. Man has yet to listen to the words of Christ, 'What is a man profited, if he shall gain the whole world, and lose his own soul? Or what shall a man give in exchange for his soul?'" (Matt. 16: 26).

d) The ship's catastrophe, vv.26-36

You can almost hear the Lutine Bell ringing in Lloyd's Building in London. (For the uninitiated, the Lutine Bell is rung when a ship sinks.) On this occasion, the fully-laden cargo ship 'Tyre' has sunk in the Mediterranean. Here is the story: "Thy rowers have brought thee into great waters: the east wind hath broken thee in the midst of the seas. Thy riches, and thy fairs, thy merchandise, thy mariners, and thy pilots, thy calkers, and the occupiers of thy merchandise ('they that barter with thee', JND), and all thy men of war, that are in thee, and in all thy company which is in the midst of thee, shall fall into the midst of the seas in the day of thy ruin" (vv.26-27). These verses emphasise the thorough destruction of Tyre. F.A.Tatford calls Tyre "an overloaded ship ... steered by its pilots into the open sea and into dangerous waters"

The passage assigns the cause of Tyre's downfall to her "rowers", but the preceding chapter emphasises that it was God who was her ultimate judge: "Behold, I am against thee, O Tyrus, and will cause many nations to come up against thee, as the sea causeth his waves to come up" (26: 3); "I will cause the noise of thy songs to cease ... I will make thee like the top of a rock ... I will make thee a terror, and thou shalt be no more" (26: 13, 14, 21). The "east wind" could possibly refer to Nebuchadnezzar (26: 7) rather than Alexander who was responsible for the final destruction of Tyre and came from West to attack the city in the fourth century B.C. On the other hand, the "east wind", with its violent gusts, may be used here to describe the destructive power of the invader. The Tarshish sailors were well aware of the power of the east wind. See Psalm 48 verse 7. The "east wind" is often used as a symbol of divine judgment: (See Ex. 10: 13; 14: 21; Job 27: 21; Is. 27: 8; Jer. 18: 17; Hosea 13: 15.)

The fall of Tyre is matched in the New Testament by the fall of Babylon (Rev. 18: 1-24) Here again stands an eminently successful commercial city over which "the kings of the earth" and "the merchants of earth" (vv.9, 11) stand grieving. No longer is there trade in "gold, and silver, and precious stones, and of pearls, and fine linen, and purple, and silk, and scarlet, and all thyine wood, and all manner of vessels of ivory, and all manner of vessels of most precious wood, and of brass, and iron, and marble, and cinnamon, and odours, and ointments, and frankincense, and wine, and oil, and fine flour, and wheat, and beasts, and sheep, and horses, and chariots, and slaves, and souls of men" (vv.12-13). The "merchants of these things, which were made rich by her, shall stand afar off for fear of her torment, weeping and wailing ... And every shipmaster, and all the company in ships, and sailors, and as many as trade by sea stood afar off, and cried when they saw the smoke of her burning, saying, What city is like unto this great city" (vv.15, 17-18). The two cities with the grief at their downfall are remarkably similar!

Bearing in mind the extent of her trade and influence (vv.12-25), the downfall of Tyre would be an event of tremendous consequence. It would be a maritime and commercial disaster to nations far beyond its own borders. Her end would cause untold grief: "The suburbs shall shake at the sound of the cry of thy pilots. And all that handle the oar, the mariners, and all the pilots of the sea, shall come down from their ships, they shall stand upon the land; and shall cause their voices to be heard against thee ('over thee', JND), and shall cry bitterly, and shall cast up dust upon their heads, and they shall wallow themselves in ashes. And they shall make themselves utterly bald for thee, and gird them with sackcloth, and they shall weep for thee with bitterness of heart and bitter wailing" (vv.28-31). Compare Chapter 26 verse 16. Whilst attempts have been made to substitute the word "waves" (AV margin) for "suburbs" ('open places', JND) in view of the fact that island Tyre had no suburbs, the word evidently refers to open places on the mainland belonging to Tyre (C.L.Feinberg).

The lamentation of Tyre's former beneficiaries follows: "And in their wailing they shall take up a lamentation for thee, and lament over thee, saying, What city is like Tyrus, like the destroyed in the midst of the sea?" (v.32). As Christopher Wright observes, "The cry, 'Who is like Tyre' would once have been uttered in adulation, matching the boast of verse 3. Now it echoes that boast only in the terrible negation of a city sunk and silenced for ever".

i) They would recount the past glories of Tyre: "When thy wares went forth out of the seas, thou filledst many people; thou didst enrich the kings of the earth with the multitude of thy riches and of thy merchandise!" (v.33).

ii) They would mourn the present destruction of Tyre: "In the time when thou shalt be broken by the sea in the depths of the waters, thy merchandise, and all thy company in the midst of thee, shall fall. All the inhabitants of the isles shall be astonished at thee, and their kings shall be sore afraid, they shall be troubled in their countenance" (vv.34-35).

iii) They would recognise the permanent ruin of Tyre: "The merchants among the people shall hiss at thee; thou shalt be a terror, and never shall be any more" (v.36). According to C.L.Feinberg, the hiss of the merchants represents "elements of scorn, dismay at the calamity, and even malicious joy". However, it seems much more likely that John B.Taylor is correct in saying that the word "hiss" does not mean 'to deride', but to let out the air through the teeth to express any vivid emotion, usually of astonishment (cf. 1 Kings 9: 8). The words, "thou shalt be a terror", refer to the effect that Tyre's downfall would have on her trading partners: they would be terrified. Compare Chapter 26 verse 21.

And it all came to pass: the Amplified Version comments in connection with verses 34-36 as follows: "Down to the thirteenth century AD the grandeur of the ancient city of Tyre was still visible. But God's word does not fail. Soon Tyre had become an almost uninhabited pile of ruins. A large part of the western section of the "island" became covered by the sea, and early travellers told of seeing "houses, towers and streets far down in the deep". In modern times the population of Tyre, made up largely of fishermen who spread their nets on its beaches, has increased to around. 6000, but the city as such has never been revived, and the original site has long since become obliterated".

C.L.Feinberg's 'postscript' is well worth reproducing in full: "The record of Tyre has a peculiar relevance for our day, for those areas in which she excelled and was the envy of the entire ancient world are precisely the fields in which every modern nation seeks superiority. But Tyre has a message for our age, and it is that riches without God are unable to satisfy the heart of man, and often keep many from dependence upon God. Has not this spirit invaded the church, and does it not pervade the lives of too many Christians?" 1 Timothy 6 verses 9-10 now become compulsory reading. The passage also illustrates the oft-quoted (and sometimes misquoted) verse: "Pride goeth before destruction, and an haughty spirit before a fall" (Prov. 16: 18). To this we must add Christopher Wright's 'postscript': "Ultimately, however, Ezekiel's purpose is not to educate us about Tyre's economy, but to reinforce the message that all her wealth and power would be useless against the sovereignty of Jehovah. In human terms it was true just as much in ancient times as today, that 'she who controls the economy rules the world, and accumulates vast quantities of wealth'. But in Jehovah's sovereign rule over the rise and fall of nations, history, as the sea is to shipwrecks, becomes the graveyard of successive economic empires".

The fall of Tyre also reminds us that "When the storm of judgment comes, those who do not rest safely in God will be removed. Those who build their lives on the solid foundation of His word will stand (Is. 40: 8; Matt. 7: 24-28)" (Lamar E. Cooper).

EZEKIEL CHAPTER 28: 1-19

We have already noted that the three chapters dealing with the downfall of Tyre may be entitled *(1)* the ruin of Tyre (26: 1-21); *(2)* the renown of Tyre (27: 1-35); *(3)* the rulers of Tyre (28: 1-19).

The latter part of Chapter 28 (vv.20-26) is devoted to an oracle concerning Zidon (vv.20-24), and a brief reference to the regathering and resettlement of Israel (vv.25-26).

1) THE RUIN OF TYRE, 26: 1-21

We have noted: *(a)* the cause of her downfall (vv.1-6); *(b)* the conqueror at her downfall (vv.7-14); *(c)* the consternation at her downfall (vv.15-18); *(d)* the consequence of her downfall (vv.19-21).

2) THE RENOWN OF TYRE, 27: 1-35

We have noted that Tyre is described here as a proud ship, and that after the introduction (vv.1-3), the chapter may be divided as follows: *(a)* the ship's construction (vv.4-7); *(b)* the ship's crew (vv.8-11); *(c)* the ship's cargo (vv.12-25); *(d)* the ship's catastrophe (vv.26-36). This brings us to:

3) THE RULERS OF TYRE, 28: 1-19

The messages in this section of the chapter are addressed to two personalities connected with the city of Tyre: "***the prince of Tyrus***" (vv.1-10) and "***the king of Tyrus***" (vv.11-19). It should be said that there is considerable divergence among commentators over their identity. According to C.L.Feinberg, some suggest that the "prince" and the "king" are the same person, while others find two separate individuals. He adds, "Some identify the first person with the Antichrist of prophetic times, and the second as Satan". H.L.Ellison espouses the view that the passage refers to one person only, and studiously rejects any suggestion that "the king of Tyrus" is Satan. C.L.Feinberg, F.A.Tatford, and L.E.Cooper do not agree at all with H.L.Ellison on this point.

While firmly espousing the view that we must distinguish between the "prince of Tyrus" and the "king of Tyrus", F.A.Tatford suggests that the passage refers to the "prince of Tyrus" (v.2) "as figurative of the people", and that "it would be a mistake to conclude that the description given by Ezekiel was appropriate to him personally". John B.Taylor inclines towards this view. C.L.Feinberg demurs and suggests rather "that at this point the main figure was the actual ruler of Tyre at the time". (History tells us that this was Ithobal II, also known as Ethbaal II.) C.W.J.Wright agrees: "A city, and indeed a whole empire, can be metaphorically portrayed as a ship. But the reality is, of course, that all empires are built by people and ruled over by people. God's judgments in history are not directed impersonally at abstractions or structures, but at the human beings who run them and benefit from them. So here, Ezekiel turns his attention from Tyre itself to the man who ruled over it at the time - Ethbaal II". L.E.Cooper agrees. It should also be said, however, that C.W.J.Wright is another commentator who believes that the "prince" and the "king" are one and the same!

Quite clearly any expositor must make up his own mind when diverse views are expressed, and after careful reflection, these notes have been written on the basis that the passage refers to two individuals, the first being the human ruler of Tyre, and the second being his unseen master, Satan, whose character he clearly reflects.

A) The prince of Tyre, vv.1-10

We should notice *(a)* his pride (vv.2-5): "thine heart is lifted *up*" (vv.2, 5); *(b)* his punishment (vv.6-10): "they shall bring thee *down* to the pit" (v.8).

a) His pride, vv.2-5

The expression "thine heart is lifted up" forms the 'book-ends' of the passage. It is all about his massive pride. In fact, his pride was on a par with that of Nebuchadnezzar: "Is not this great Babylon, that I have built for the house of the kingdom by the might of my power, and for the honour of my majesty?" (Dan. 4: 30). The "prince of Tyrus" was: *(i)* proud of his status (v.2); *(ii)* proud of his wisdom (v.3); *(iii)* and proud of his riches (vv.4-5).

CHAPTER 28:1-19

i) ***He was proud of his status***. "Because thine heart is lifted up, and thou hast said I am a God, I sit in the seat of God, in the midst of the seas; yet thou art a man, and not God though thou set thine heart as the heart of God" (v.2). His riches and power had fed his pride to the extent that he claimed to be divine. As C.L.Feinberg observes, "Self-deification was his greatest sin". Herod's head was turned in the same way (Acts 12: 20-23). Significantly enough it was "the inhabitants of Tyre and Sidon" who shouted, "It is the voice of a god, and not a man", following which "the angel of the Lord smote him, because he gave not God the glory" (Acts 12: 20-23).

Bible students have long pointed to similar sentiments in the case of Lucifer. He too is guilty of blasphemous pride: "For thou hast said in thine heart, *I will* ascend into heaven, *I will* exalt my throne above the stars of God: *I will* sit also upon the mount of the congregation, in the sides of the north: *I will* ascend above the heights of the clouds; *I will* be like the most High" (Isa. 14: 13-14). Paul describes the same blasphemer (not Satan, but the last great Gentile ruler, "the beast") as follows: "who opposeth and exalteth himself above all that is called God, or that is worshipped; so that he as God sitteth in the temple of God, shewing himself that he is God" (2 Thess. 2: 4). In this he mirrors the aspirations of his dark master who said, "All these things will I give thee, if thou wilt fall down and worship me" (Matt 4:9), and who is called "the god of this world" (2 Cor. 4: 4).

The "prince of Tyrus" was "behaving as if he had divine power and authority. He had delusions of grandeur, invincibility, omnipotence and world sovereignty. Nations bowed to his supremacy. The destiny of so many peoples seemed to hang on economic decisions made by his government. And, as it must have seemed to him, it had all come about by the appliance of science, the skilful use of technology and economic theory, and the amassing of capital and wealth through advantageous domination of world trade (vv.3-5). What is being described in these verses may have been an ancient empire, but it has all the factors found in the western economic hegemony of late modernity: claims to intellectual and economic superiority coupled with massive arrogance and complacency" (C.J.H.Wright). The Bible is certainly 'more up to date than tomorrow's newspaper' (E.T.Riddle).

We cannot afford to ignore the warning note for ourselves here. The Lord Jesus taught that "whosoever exalteth himself shall be abased; and he that humbleth himself shall be exalted" (Luke 14: 11, cp. Luke

18: 14). See also 1 Peter 5 verse 5, "Yea, all of you be subject one to another, and be clothed with humility: for God resisteth the proud, and giveth grace to the humble".

ii) **He was proud of his wisdom.** "Behold, thou art wiser than Daniel: there is no secret that they can hide from thee" (v.3). It has been pointed out that by the time Tyre was besieged by Nebuchadnezzar, Daniel had been in his court for about twenty-five years. Quite obviously his fame had spread far and wide. While Ezekiel might have been speaking ironically in comparing the prince of Tyre with Daniel, there is every possibility that the prince of Tyre seriously thought that he really was wiser than Daniel. The prince of Tyre might have had a vast store of *economic* wisdom, but Daniel was full of *spiritual* wisdom! The "wisdom of men" and the "wisdom of this world" are one thing, but "the wisdom of God" is another! See 1 Corinthians 2 verses 5-7. But even believers must take steps to ensure that they do not become 'wise in their own conceits' (Rom. 12: 16). We must not become proud of our Bible knowledge.

This isn't the first time that Ezekiel has mentioned Daniel: see Chapter 14 verses 14 and 20. Since H.L.Ellison and J.B.Taylor refer to their previous remarks at this point in their commentaries, we will do the same. This is what we said: "We should note the feeble arguments of H.L.Ellison and J.B.Taylor in connection with the identity of Daniel. To quote Ellison: 'Furthermore, it must be looked on as extremely doubtful whether the well-known Daniel is intended at all. His name, as indeed that of the other two Daniels of Scripture (1 Chron 3: 1; Ezra 8: 2/Neh. 10: 6), was spelled *Daniyye'l*, but Ezekiel spells it *Dani'el*, or more likely *Dan'el*. He would seem to be referring to a figure of hoar antiquity probably mentioned in tablets discovered at Ras Shamra dating before 1400 B.C. A scribal error on Ezekiel's part is most unlikely. If so, we know too little to form any opinion as to why he was mentioned". Can we imagine the Jews accepting such a suggestion?

F.Gardiner (Ellicott's Commentary) is undoubtedly correct in saying, "The mention of Daniel ... need occasion no surprise ... Daniel had now been for about twelve years in important office at the royal court (that is, at the time of Ezekiel's prophecy in Tel-abib), and possessed of the very highest rank. There is, therefore, no occasion for the strange supposition that the reference is to some older Daniel, of such eminence as to be spoken of in this way he is here (14: 14 ,20) and in Chapter 28 verse 3, and yet whose name has otherwise completely faded out from history"

iii)** **He was proud of his riches. "With thy wisdom and with thine understanding thou hast gotten thee riches, and hast gotten gold and silver into thy treasuries. By thy great wisdom and by thy traffick hast thou increased thy riches, and thine heart is lifted up because of thy riches" (vv.4-5). We are reminded of another man who said to himself, "Soul, thou hast much goods laid up for many years", only to lose it all within hours: "But God said unto him, Thou fool, this night thy soul shall be required of thee" (Luke 12: 16-21). When the day of reckoning came for Ithobal II (the prince of Tyre), it became clear that "Riches profit not in the day of wrath" (Prov. 11: 4). Paul urged Timothy to "Charge them that are rich in this world, that they be not high-minded, nor trust in uncertain riches, but in the living God who giveth us richly all things to enjoy" (1 Tim. 6: 17). The Lord Jesus said, "Lay not up for yourselves treasures upon earth, where moth and rust doth corrupt, and where thieves break through and steal: but lay up for yourselves treasures in heaven …" (Matt. 6: 19-20). In view of the looming crisis, when Jerusalem would fall to the Babylonians, the Lord said through Jeremiah: "but let him that glorieth glory in this, that he understandeth and knoweth me, that I am the LORD which exercise lovingkindness, judgment, and righteousness, in the earth: for in these things I delight, saith the LORD" (Jer. 9: 23-24). We must be "rich toward God" (Luke 12: 21), not forgetting the injunction, "Let the word of Christ dwell in you richly in all wisdom" (Col. 3: 16).

b) His punishment, vv.6-10

Impiety of this character cannot remain unpunished, and Ezekiel announces the destruction of "the prince of Tyrus": "Therefore thus saith the Lord GOD; Because thou hast set thine heart as the heart of God; behold, therefore I will bring strangers upon thee, the terrible of the nations: and they shall draw their swords against the beauty of thy wisdom, and they shall defile thy brightness. They shall bring thee down to the pit, and thou shalt die the deaths of them that are slain in the midst of the seas" (vv.6-8). The expression, "the beauty of thy wisdom" evidently refers to the beauty produced by Tyre's wisdom, and the word "brightness" to its splendour.

Commentators seem fairly well united in saying that the "strangers … the terrible of the nations" are the Babylonians" who "swept through the countries, ruthlessly liquidating all adversaries, seizing loot and property and showing a complete lack of mercy and compassion" (F.A.Tatford). However, it was not Nebuchadnezzar and his armies who finally destroyed Tyre, when the city died "the deaths (intensive plural, emphasising the violence involved) of them that are slain in the midst of the sea". The ultimate downfall of Tyre was accomplished by the Macedonian armies under Alexander the Great. It is therefore better to say that the words "strangers ... the terrible of the nations" describe both invaders. Although mainland Tyre fell to Nebuchadnezzar, island Tyre did not, and after thirteen years, the king of Babylon went away empty-handed. Alexander, 240 years later, was successful in capturing and destroying the city.

In view of coming destruction, the question is asked, "Wilt thou yet say before him that slayeth thee I am God? But thou shalt be a man, and no God, in the hand of him that slayeth thee. Thou shalt die the deaths of the uncircumcised by the hand of strangers: for I have spoken it, saith the Lord GOD" (vv.9-10). While there are other explanations, "the deaths of the uncircumcised" (which some suggest was a term of contempt for those whose corpses were treated with disrespect and left unburied) more likely describes those outside the covenant with God. (Compare 1 Samuel 17: 36; 31: 4.) The Tyreans had no hope for the future.

The certainty of coming judgment upon Tyre is emphasised by the concluding words: "I have spoken it, saith the Lord GOD" (v.10). This brings us to:

B) *The king of Tyre, vv.11-19*

The second message is addressed to "the king of Tyrus", and it is immediately apparent that a person of different origin is in view, doubtless wielding his power and exerting his influence through the "prince of Tyrus". The following will underscore the point: "Thou sealest up the sum, full of wisdom, and perfect in beauty, Thou hast been in Eden the garden of God ... Thou art the anointed cherub that covereth; and I have set thee so: Thou wast upon the holy mountain of God; Thou hast walked up and down in the midst of the stones of fire. Thou wast perfect in thy ways from the day that thou wast created, till iniquity was found in thee". The language can hardly describe "the prince of Tyrus", as some suggest. While, as C.L.Feinberg rightly observes, "the description utilises highly figurative language", he continues by rightly saying that "the importation into the chapter of a foreign mythology or pagan legends must be resisted".

The usually conservative John B.Taylor has a rather shocking piece here: Having referred to verses 13-16, he writes: "So the imagery is dependent on more than just the Genesis story, from which it diverges significantly, and

CHAPTER 28:1-19

rather than suppose that another version of the Eden tradition (his words) was in circulation, it seems more likely that Ezekiel's *imagination wandered freely* and drew on a wide variety of symbolic background all interwoven with his message of the fall of Tyre". F.A.Tatford points out, with disapproval, that "Taylor and others insist that the king was a picture of the perfect primeval man, or Adam". F.A.Tatford also notes that the "several allusions to the earthly Paradise of Eden" are "dismissed by most commentators as incidental and merely indicative of the sin of pride alleged to have been common to both Adam and Tyre".

H.L.Ellison (who believed that the "prince" and the "king" were one and the same person) is hardly better: "In our justifiable rejection of the modern view that the early stories of Genesis are merely pagan myths purified of their polytheism, we tend to forget the far truer view of our fathers that the pagan myths represent a polytheistic corruption of the truths of the Bible". So far so good. Ellison continues: "We do not know enough about the Canaanite myth to be certain what form their corruption of the Eden story may have taken, but it is *more than probable that we have it reflected here*". While Ellison admits that "Many will find it distasteful to find it suggested that we may have a heathen myth in the Bible", he covers himself by saying that "we have here a mocking funeral dirge over a heathen king, in which a mocking use of the king's own beliefs is to be expected". The passage is certainly a funeral dirge ("a lament", v.11), but to say that the case against the 'king of Tyre' is taken from ancient mythology cannot be right.

As already noted, these notes are written on the basis that the description and history of "the king of Tyrus" can only refer to "some great spiritual being" (F.A.Tatford), namely Satan. This will become increasing clear as consideration is given to the passage (vv.11-19). The "prince of Tyrus" was under the mastery of "the king of Tyrus", and reflected his character.

However, further clarification is necessary in view of the fact that the "lamentation upon the king of Tyrus" (undoubtedly Satan) ends with, "I will cast thee to the ground, I will lay thee before kings, that they may behold thee ... I will bring thee to ashes upon the earth in the sight of all them that behold thee. All they that know thee among the people shall be astonished at thee: thou shalt be a terror, and never shalt thou be any more" (vv.17-19). This can hardly refer directly to Satan, but is a most appropriate reference to Tyre itself, represented by her "prince". Ezekiel still has in mind the character and conduct of "the prince of Tyrus", but the Lord now enables him to discern "the motivating force and personality who was impelling him in his opposition to God. In short, he saw the work and activity of Satan, whom the prince of Tyre was emulating in so many ways" (C.L.Feinberg). A comparable passage is found in the New Testament: "Then Peter took him (the Lord Jesus), and began to rebuke him saying, Be it far from thee, Lord: this shall not be unto thee. But he turned, and said unto Peter, Get thee behind me, Satan ..." (Matt. 16: 22-23). As C.L.Feinberg points out, "No sterner words were spoken to anyone in Christ's earthly ministry. But He did not mean that Peter had somehow become Satan himself. He was indicating that the motivation behind Peter's opposition to His going to Calvary was none other than the prince of the demons. This appears to be a similar situation".

To summarise "the "prince of Tyrus" was motivated by "the king of Tyrus". The prince of Tyre followed the king of Tyre in his opulence, beauty and pride, and would follow him in his destruction. These verses (vv.11-19) evidently describe *(a)* the exaltation of "the king of Tyrus" (vv.12-15); *(b)* the eviction of the "the king of Tyrus" (vv.16-19).

a) His exaltation, vv.12-15

"Moreover the word of the LORD came unto me, saying Son of man, take up a lamentation upon the king of Tyrus, and say unto him, Thus saith the Lord GOD ..." (vv.11-12). On the basis that Ezekiel refers here to Satan, the dark master of "the prince of Tyrus", we must now notice:

i) **His original perfection**. "Thou sealest up the sum, full of wisdom, and perfect in beauty" (v.12). The words, "Thou sealest up the sum", evidently mean, 'Thou sealest up the measure of perfection' (JND). "To seal mean simply to close up or fasten ... The individual addressed was, therefore, the acme of perfection" (F.A.Tatford): "Thou who sealest up the measure of perfection, full of wisdom and perfect in beauty ..." (JND). While this may not directly refer to Satan's appearance in the garden Eden, C.I.Scofield is worth quoting here: "The serpent, in his *Edenic* form, is not to be thought of as a writhing reptile. That is the effect of the curse (Gen. 3: 14). The creature which lent itself to Satan may have been the most beautiful as it was the most 'subtle' of creatures less than man ... In the serpent, Satan first appeared 'as an angel of light' (2 Cor. 11: 14)".

ii) **His original location**. "Thou hast been in Eden the garden of God" (v.13). As F.A.Tatford observes, "The prophet did not indicate whether he referred to the earthly Eden, or to the heavenly paradise". The passage may well indicate that it is to the latter that Ezekiel refers. "Thou, who sealest up the measure of perfection, full of wisdom and perfect in beauty, thou wast in Eden, the garden of God. Every precious stone was thy covering ... The workmanship of thy tambours and of thy pipes was in thee: in the day that thou wast created were they prepared" (v.13, JND). While it is interesting that nine precious stones are mentioned, as opposed to the twelve on the high priest's breastplate (Exodus 28: 17-20), C.L.Feinberg rightly says that "Parallels of this nature need not be pressed for some hidden meaning. The stones evidently signified the beauties and glories that were bestowed upon him, just as the stones mentioned in Revelation 21 have such a connotation". C.L.Feinberg continues with the question, "What is meant by the tabrets and the pipes?", and answers, "One view holds that he was charged with the music and praises of the heavenly hosts". The words, "The workmanship of thy tambours and of thy pipes was in thee: *in the day that thou wast created* were they prepared" (v.13, JND), are hardly applicable to "the prince of Tyrus", but when "taken to refer ultimately to Satan, they are eminently intelligible and in place" (C.L.Feinberg). Perhaps it should be said that Satan, along with all the "principalities and powers" was evidently created during the 'six days' of creation: see Genesis 2 verse 1.

iii)   His original position. "Thou art the anointed cherub that covereth; and I have set thee so: thou wast upon the holy mountain of God; thou hast walked up and down in the midst of the stones of fire" (v.14). It should be noted that "the king of Tyrus" is described as having been originally anointed 'covering cherub' by Jehovah Himself, whereas whilst the cherubim in Ezekiel's original vision were associated with the throne, they did not cover it. The throne was above their heads (Ezek. 1: 26). It should also be noted that "in the case of the ark of the covenant in the tabernacle and in the temple, a cherub at each end of the mercy seat extended its wings to cover the mercy-seat on which the glory of God rested (Ex. 25: 18-20)" (F.A.Tatford). Quite clearly, the words, "Thou art the anointed cherub that covereth", could never be said of "the prince of Tyrus", the human ruler of the city.

The expression, "the holy mountain of God", is "frequently used to denote the abode of the Almighty (Isaiah 14: 13)" (F.A.Tatford). The words, "thou hast walked up and down in the midst of the stones of fire", evidently refer to Satan's original "continuous and unhindered access to the glorious presence of God" (C.L.Feinberg). "Fire is a well-known symbol of God Himself (Heb. 12: 29), and the manifestation of His glory is represented under the figure of beautiful stones (Exodus 24: 10, 17)" (C.L.Feinberg). F.A.Tatford interprets "the stones of fire" as "a feature of the court of approach to the throne of God". We can only conclude that "the anointed cherub" occupied a place of special prominence.

iv) His original conduct. "Thou wast perfect in all thy ways from the day that thou wast created, till iniquity was found in thee" (v.15). As C.L.Feinberg observes, "By what stretch of the imagination could the words of verse 15 be applied to any earthly king? They must be taken to mean prosperity without defect". F.A.Tatford concurs: "It is perhaps significant that both verses 13 and 15 refer to the king being created: if a human being was the object of the description, the natural term would have been 'born' rather than 'created'. When this one was created, he was blameless and continued so until, for some unstated reason, iniquity was found in him. It could hardly be said of any man that his life and walk were unblemished, and the pagan king of Tyre could have been no exception to the general rule. Here again there seems to be an indication that the prophet was speaking of a created being who was other than man". While, as F.A.Tatford observes, Ezekiel attributes his "iniquity" to 'some unstated reason', the New Testament indicates that his sin was pride. See 1 Timothy 3 verse 6.

b) His eviction, vv.16-19

These verses are not easily explained. Difficulties of identification arise from a seeming shift of focus between the human ruler of Tyre ("the prince of Tyrus") and his dark master ("the king of Tyrus").

- On the one hand, the Lord is clearly addressing the dark master of the "prince of Tyrus". Having said, "Thou sealest up the sum, full of wisdom, and perfect in beauty" (v.12), and "Thou art the anointed cherub that covereth ... thou wast upon the holy mountain of God; thou hast walked up and down in the midst of the stones of fire" (v.14), the Lord continues: "By the multitude of thy merchandise they have filled the midst of thee with violence, and thou hast sinned: therefore I will cast thee as profane out of the mountain of God: and I will destroy thee, O covering cherub, from the midst of the stones of fire. Thine heart was lifted up because of thy beauty, thou hast corrupted thy wisdom by reason of thy brightness: I will cast thee to the ground, I will lay thee before kings, that they may behold thee" (vv.16-17).

CHAPTER 28:1-19

- On the other hand, the opening and closing words ("By the multitude of thy merchandise they have filled the midst of thee with violence, and thou hast sinned ... I will lay thee before kings, that they may behold thee") evidently refer to the human ruler of Tyre, and verses 18-19 must also be interpreted in this way.

The answer to this dilemma for the expositor may lie in the fact that "the prince of Tyrus" had said, "I am a God, I sit in the seat of God, in the midst of the seas; yet thou art a man, and not God, though thou set thine heart as the heart of God: Behold, thou art wiser than Daniel; there is no secret that they can hide from thee" (vv.2-3). Bearing in mind this proud boast, the Lord pronounces judgment on the human ruler of Tyre in terms of the judgment pronounced on his dark master. In the words of H.A.Ironside, "Verse 16 links the supernatural ruler very closely with the prince who sat on the throne; but God goes on to speak directly of the covering cherub in the following verse, and gives us the secret of his fall ... The closing verses ... link this great being so intimately with the literal Tyrean ruler that one can hardly be distinguished from the other".

But there is another connection. The concept of an earthly prince subject to the power of an unseen superior occurs at a point in the prophecy which emphasises trade and commerce. As we have seen, Tyre was historically the market of the Middle East, and of the world. It was the centre of commerce and trade, and this made it a fitting occasion for God to reveal that this thriving commercial paradise was controlled by Satan, reminding us that behind this godless world, with its commerce and trade, its boasting and vaunting, its professed security through trade - is Satan himself.

As C.J.H.Wright observes, "these chapters force us to reflect soberly on the transience of even the most powerful economic empires, including that which dominates the contemporary world". At the end-time, 'Babylon' will be "the centre of a world-dominating trade empire, which causes catastrophic alarm when it is finally destroyed. Ezekiel's legacy of human megalomania and divine sovereignty lives on, and is still powerfully relevant today".

The "transience" of Tyre is described: "I will cast thee to the ground, I will lay thee before kings, that they may behold thee. Thou hast defiled thy sanctuaries by the multitude of thine iniquities, by the iniquity of thy traffic; therefore will I bring forth a fire from the midst of thee, it shall devour thee and I will bring thee to ashes upon the earth in the sight of all them that behold thee, All they that know thee among the people shall be astonished at thee: thou shalt be a terror, and never shalt thou be any more" (vv.17-19). According to C.L.Feinberg, "Tyre boasted numerous sanctuaries, and the temples of Tyre were the reason it was called the Holy Island by the ancients. These temples were profaned because the king's sin was the occasion of their destruction. His own sin was the fire which ultimately consumed him". John B.Taylor rightly observes here that "The seeds of a nation's destruction are usually to be found within herself". As noted in connection with Chapter 27 verse 36, the words, "thou shalt be a terror", refer to the effect that Tyre's downfall would have on her trading partners: they would be terrified. Compare Chapter 26 verse 21.

Postscript

Following the final conquest of island Tyre by Alexander the Great in 332 BC, "the Romans decided to make it (the mainland city?) the capital of their Phoenician province, and it was a flourishing town in the time of our Lord (Matt. 15: 21; Acts 12: 20) ... The town was in Saracen hands from AD 636-1125. Saladin could not capture it in AD 1189, but in AD 1291 it fell into Egyptian hands. Gradually its strongholds were reduced and it became an obscure site. Present Sur had no ethnic connection with the prosperous Phoenician city of antiquity. The site of the mainland city is uninhabited, as is most of the area of the island city. A few thousand people live on land adjacent to the ancient metropolis" (C.L.Feinberg).

EZEKIEL CHAPTER 28: 20-26

As we have already observed, this section of the prophecy (chs.25-32) comprises seven oracles: against *(i)* Ammon; *(ii)* Moab; *(iii)* Edom; *(iv)* Philistia; *(v)* Tyre; *(vi)* Zidon; *(vii)* Egypt. We have also noted that the heart of the section lies in Chapter 28 verses 24-26: "And there shall be no more a pricking briar unto the house of Israel ... Thus saith the Lord GOD: When I shall have gathered the house of Israel from the people among whom they are scattered, and shall be sanctified in them in the sight of the heathen, then shall they dwell in their land that I have given to my servant Jacob ..." It has also been pointed out that this central passage is preceded by ninety-seven verses of predictions against Ammon, Moab, Edom, Philistia, Tyre and Zidon (25: 1 - 28: 23), and succeeded by ninety-seven verses of predictions against Egypt (29: 1 - 32: 32). As we have said, this speaks for itself. As always, Israel lies at the centre of God's purpose for the world.

These verses fall clearly into two sections: *(1)* God's judgment on Zidon (vv.20-23); *(2)* God's blessing on Israel (vv.24-26).

1) GOD'S JUDGMENT ON ZIDON, vv.20-23

The origin of Zidon, or Sidon, can be traced to the division in the human race following the Flood: "And Canaan begat Sidon his firstborn ... And the border of the Canaanites was from Sidon, as thou comest to Gerar, unto Gaza" (Gen. 10: 15-19). Sidon was originally of greater importance than Tyre, which lay twenty-five miles to the south. (One commentator says twenty miles, another twenty-three, and yet another twenty-five!) But the more strategic situation of Tyre, and the more adventurous spirit of its inhabitants, ultimately resulted in the southern city's pre-eminence (F.A.Tatford). The Sidonians were a seafaring people and, at one time, they divided the trade of the Mediterranean area with Tyre, although, as noted above, the latter assumed supremacy. They were the first to discover the pole star, and were the first mariners to sail by night. Sidon was a walled city, built on a promontory and a small island, and was at one time strongly fortified. It had an excellent harbour, and acquired its wealth very largely from maritime trading, although it also engaged in manufacturing glassware, pottery and other goods, including artistic metal work and woven work. They also conducted a trade in slaves (F.A.Tatford).

Patrick Fairbairn (*An Exposition of Ezekiel*) points out that although Sidonian seamen manned Tyrian vessels (Ezek. 27: 8), and Sidon was virtually an integral part of the great maritime power centred on Tyre, the city "possessed a religious connection with the covenant-people, which does not appear to have extended to Tyre, and which furnished a historical reason for the separate mention of Sidon". Patrick Fairbairn continues, and his comments are well-worth quoting in full: "Whether it arose from Sidon being the elder city, or from her citizens having more frequent intercourse with the Israelites, or, finally, from the character of the religion prevalent in Sidon being of a more seductive and infectious character, the fact is certain that a corrupting influence flowed in upon Israel from Sidon such as is never mentioned in connection with Tyre. So as early as the time of the Judges, the gods of Sidon are named among the false deities that had acquired an ascendancy over the children of Israel (Judges 10: 6). (Judges 10: 12 refers to Israel's deliverance from the Zidonians, although the occasion cannot be identified.) In the days of Solomon, the worship of Ashtaroth, the goddess of the Sidonians, was again openly practised (1 Kings 11: 33). To this we may add that Ahab "took to wife Jezebel the daughter of Ethbaal king of the Zidonians, and went and served Baal, and worshipped him" (1 Kings 16: 31). In this way, Sidon had a disastrous effect upon the northern kingdom of Israel.

It is also worth noting that although Sidon lay within territory allocated to the tribe of Asher at the division of the land of Canaan (Josh. 19: 28), it was never actually occupied by the tribe (Judges 1: 31). Past failures have a 'knock-on effect'. "The city is now known as Saida, a city of no great importance, but a small seaport" (C.L.Feinberg).

No reason is given here for the predicted judgment in Sidon, but it seems likely that her 'corrupting influence' (Patrick Fairbairn, above), like that of Babylon, had come "in remembrance before God, to give unto her the cup of the wine of the fierceness of his wrath" (Rev. 16: 19). Judgment is pronounced on Sidon as follows: "Thus saith the Lord GOD; Behold, I am against thee, O Zidon; and I will be glorified in the midst of thee: and they shall know that I am the LORD, when I shall have executed judgment in her, and shall be sanctified in her. For I will send into her pestilence, and blood into her streets; and the wounded shall be judged in the midst of her by the sword upon her on every side; and they shall know that I am the LORD" (vv.22-23). Attention is drawn to the following:

i)   That God will hold to account those who corrupt his people. This does not mean for one moment that God's people themselves are exonerated from blame in accepting false teaching, in this case idolatry and all its associated evils. God's condemnation of His people because of their idolatry is everywhere in the Old Testament. But all who cause God's people to sin will not escape divine wrath.

The New Testament emphasises the responsibility of God's people in accepting false teaching together with the solemn responsibility of those who propagate error: "I marvel that ye are so soon removed ('removing', RV: with the meaning 'removing yourselves') from ***him that called you*** into the grace of Christ (so, 'removing ourselves' from sound doctrine means 'removing ourselves' from God Himself) unto another gospel: which is not another; but there be some that trouble you, and would pervert the gospel of Christ. But though we, or an angel from heaven, preach any other gospel unto you than that which we have preached unto you, let him be accursed. As we said before, so say I now again, If any man preach any other gospel unto you than that ye have received, let him be accursed" (Gal. 1: 6-9).

ii)   That God is no tribal deity. He is not only the God of Israel. He is "the Judge of all the earth" (Gen. 18: 25). See also Psalm 58 verses 10-11 ("The righteous shall rejoice when he seeth the vengeance: he shall wash his feet in the blood of the wicked. So that a man shall say, Verily there is a reward for the righteous: verily he is a God that judgeth in the earth"); Psalm 94 verses 1-2 ("O LORD God, to whom vengeance belongeth; O God, to whom vengeance belongeth, shew thyself. Lift up thyself, thou judge of the earth: render a reward to the proud"). All men are accountable to Him. He will judge all nations. He is the "God of the earth" (Rev. 11: 4). He is "the Lord of all the earth" (Zech. 6: 5) and "the Lord of the whole earth" (Psalm 97: 5; Micah 4: 13; Zech. 4: 14). His universal sovereignty is everywhere in Scripture.

iii)   That God inflicts judgment through such disasters as plague and war. "I will send into her pestilence, and blood into her streets; and the wounded shall be judged in the midst of her by the sword upon her on every side" (v.23). Revelation 6 verses 1-8 should be read in this connection. While "the precise pestilence to be suffered was not stated, it was made clear that the irresistible tides of war would sweep through the streets of the city. Attacked on every side, Sidon would be unable to defend herself, and the invader's forces would pour through the city, butchering everyone in sight. The Sidonians would fall by the sword in the midst of the city" (F.A.Tatford).

iv) ***That God will be glorified in the judgment He delivers***. "I will be glorified in the midst of thee: and *they shall know that I am the LORD*, when I shall have executed judgment in her, and shall be sanctified in her" (v.22). This does not mean that men and women lift their voices to God in praise, but rather that they recognise His hand in the calamities falling upon them. This is repeated: "For I will send into her pestilence, and blood into her streets; and the wounded shall be judged in the midst of her by the sword upon her on every side; and *they shall know that I am the LORD"* (v.23). It has been pointed out before in these studies that these oft-repeated words (they occur some fifty-four times in the prophecy) emphasise, not so much His existence, but His character. His judgment on Sidon would make His righteousness plain to that nation.

According to F.A.Tatford, the prediction of Sidon's fall was fulfilled at the hand of Babylon following the rebellion against Nebuchadnezzar described in Jeremiah 27 verses 1-11. "Sidon quickly submitted because of the devastating pestilence precisely as Ezekiel had predicted."

2) GOD'S BLESSING ON ISRAEL, vv24-26

As John B.Taylor observes, "When this and all God's other acts are completed, the house of Israel will be able to live free of harm from their neighbour-states". Having dealt with the immediate enemies of Israel, "the prophet anticipated the day when every other foe would be quelled and Israel would dwell at peace. He made no reference to the many events which would take place before that blissful state was achieved but, as so often happens in prophecy, swept over the interim period to look at the ultimate days of blessing" (F.A.Tatford).

While this is perfectly true, we might have expected the prophecy to have immediately continued with the series of oracles concerning Egypt, leaving reference to Israel's millennial blessing to the end of the entire section. However, for good reason already noted, God's blessing on His people lies at the centre of the section, and H.L.Ellison explains the existing structure most satisfactorily: "Though Egypt was technically the neighbour of Israel, the sand-sea between them was a very effective barrier. Since the invasion of Shishak (1 Kings 14: 25f.) and Zerah (2 Chron. 14: 9-15), Egypt had played little part in Judah's history beyond using her as a catspaw to protect herself against Assyria and Babylon. Both Isaiah (Isa. 30: 7) and the Rabshakeh (2 Kings 18: 21) had mocked her ineffective show of strength. So before turning to the old crocodile on the Nile, Ezekiel here sums up God's condemnation of Israel's true neighbours, big and little, that had harmed her. He indicates clearly that all are covered, whether they have been mentioned by name or not. This short oracle is a preparation for Chapters.33-39". Hence we read, "And there shall be no more a pricking brier unto the house of Israel, nor any grieving thorn of all that are round about them, that despised them; and they shall know that I am the Lord GOD" (v.24). We should notice:

a) The current situation, v.24

At the time of writing, not to mention the present time, Israel was surrounded by 'pricking briers', and 'grieving thorns', all of whom "despised them". Briers tear, wound and infect, and Israel had certainly been infected by the idolatrous practices of Zidon. It is not without significance that failure to dispossess the original inhabitants of Canaan, would leave Israel with 'pricking briers', and 'grieving thorns' in their own land: "But if ye will not drive out the inhabitants of the land from before you; then it shall come to pass that those which ye let remain of them shall be pricks in your eyes, and thorns in your sides, and shall vex you in the land wherein ye dwell" (Num. 33: 55).

On a practical note, we must take steps, if necessary, to ensure that we do not become 'pricking briers', and 'grieving thorns' in the assembly. Solomon observed that "As coals are to burning coals, and wood to fire; so is a contentious man to kindle strife" (Prov. 26: 21). Paul warns against, "foolish questions, and genealogies, and contentions, and strivings about the law; for they are unprofitable and vain" (Titus 3: 9).

b) The future situation, vv.25-26

In the future, Israel will enjoy complete immunity from harm and danger. In the words of Micah, "they shall sit every man under his vine and under his fig tree; and none shall make them afraid: for the mouth of the LORD of hosts hath spoken it" (Micah 4: 4). At the time of Ezekiel's prophecy here, Israel had not been scattered and dispersed, although the time was not far hence. But when that time came it did not signal the end of national life. God had said through Jeremiah, "For I am with thee, saith the LORD, to save thee: though I make a full end of all nations whither I have scattered thee, yet will I not make a full end of thee" (Jer. 30: 11; 46: 28). At the endtime, "the LORD shall set his hand again the second time to recover the remnant of his people, which shall be left, from Assyria, and from Egypt, and from Pathros, and from Cush, and from Elam, and from Shinar. And from Hamath, and from the islands of the sea. And he shall set up an ensign for the nations, and shall assemble the outcasts of Israel, and gather together the dispersed of Judah from the four corners of the earth" (Isaiah 11: 11-12). The Lord Jesus described this regathering as follows: "they shall see the Son of man coming in the clouds of heaven with power and great glory. And he shall send his angels with a great sound of a trumpet, and they shall gather together his elect from the four winds, from one end of heaven to the other" (Matt. 24: 30-31).

Now, in Ezekiel's words: "Thus saith the Lord GOD; When I have gathered the house of Israel from the people among whom they are scattered, and shall be sanctified in them in the sight of the heathen, they shall dwell in their land that I have given to my servant Jacob. And they shall dwell safely therein, and shall build houses, and plant vineyards; yea, they shall dwell with confidence, when I have executed judgments upon all those that despise them round about them; and they shall know that I am the LORD their God". We should notice the following:

i) **Their regathering will be divinely accomplished.** "When *I have* gathered the house of Israel from the people among whom they are scattered." It will not be accomplished by military might or by political initiative. As noted above, it will be by divine power.

Moreover, the nation will be reconsecrated. The Lord will be "sanctified in them in the sight of the heathen". This goes further than regathering. The nations of the world will recognise that God is dwelling amongst His people, and they "shall be named the Priests of the LORD: men shall call you the Ministers of our God" (Isaiah 61: 6). We must note the contrast between the words, "I ... shall be sanctified in her (Sidon)" (v.22) and "I shall ... be sanctified in them (Israel) in the sight of the heathen" (v.25). In the first case, it refers to judgment, and in the second to blessing.

CHAPTER 28:20-26

ii) ***Their resettlement will be divinely appointed***. "They shall **dwell** in their land that ***I have given*** to my servant Jacob. And they shall **dwell** safely therein, and shall build houses, and plant vineyards; yea, they shall **dwell** with confidence". (Note the three occurrences of "dwell"). It will be "***their*** land". The matter will be placed beyond doubt. No Arab or Palestinian will object or protest then. Hamas will no longer bombard Israel with missiles. The Lord will honour His promises to the patriarchs, and here, His promise to Jacob in particular: "And he dreamed, and behold a ladder set up on the earth, and the top of it reached to heaven ... And, behold, the LORD stood above it, and said, I am the LORD God of Abraham thy father, and the God of Isaac: the land whereon thou liest, to thee will I give it, and to thy seed" (Gen. 28: 12-13).

In this connection, C.L.Feinberg notes the following: Isaiah 65 verse 21 ("And they shall build houses, and inhabit them; and they shall plant vineyards, and eat the fruit of them"); Jeremiah 23 verse 6 ("In his days Judah shall be saved, and Israel shall dwell safely: and this is the name whereby he shall be called, THE LORD OUR RIGHTEOUSNESS"); Ezekiel 34 verse 27 ("And the tree of the field shall yield her fruit, and the earth shall yield her increase, and they shall be safe in their land, and shall know that I am the LORD, when I have broken the bands of their yoke, and delivered them out of the hand of those that served themselves of them"); Ezekiel 38 verse 8 ("After many days thou shalt be visited: in the latter years thou shalt come back into the land that is brought back from the sword, and is gathered out of many people, against the mountains of Israel, which have been always waste: but it is brought back out of the nations, and they shall dwell safely all of them"); Ezekiel 39 verse 26 ("After that they have borne their shame, and all their trespasses whereby they have trespassed against me, when they dwelt safely in their land, and none made them afraid"); Amos 9 verses 14-15 ("And I will bring again the captivity of my people Israel, and they shall build the waste cities, and inhabit them; and they shall plant vineyards, and drink the wine thereof; they shall also make gardens, and eat the fruit of them. And I will plant them upon their land, and they shall no more be pulled up out of their land which I have given them, saith the LORD thy God"). Having noted these passages, C.L.Feinberg continues: "It is utterly false and wicked to claim, as some erroneously do, that the land does not belong to Israel, for this is to impugn the clear statements of God".

We should note the categorical statements, "they **shall** dwell safely therein ... yea, they **shall** dwell with confidence". There will be none of Israel's present problems then! Constant vigilance against attack from all quarters will no longer be necessary!

iii) Their restoration will be after divine judgment. "They shall dwell with confidence, when *I have* executed judgments upon all those that *despise them* round about them; and they shall know that I am the LORD their God". This links the passage with the six nations named in Chapters.25-28, of which it is said, "And there shall be no more a pricking brier unto the house of Israel, nor any grieving thorn of all that are round about them, *that despised them*; and they shall know that I am the Lord GOD" (v.24).

If the nations will know "that I am the Lord GOD" (v.24), then Israel will also know "that I am the Lord *their* GOD" (v.26). What a difference! What a contrast! In the first case, Gentile nations will know that He is "the Lord GOD" in *judgment*, but in the second, Israel will know that He is "the Lord GOD in *blessing*".

EZEKIEL CHAPTER 29

The 'foreign nations' section of the book of Ezekiel (chapters 25-32) concludes with a series of messages against Egypt. These are recorded in Chapters 29-32, and it will be readily noted that much more attention is given to Egypt than any other of the nations in the section.

While the extensive treatment of Egypt in this way can be attributable to her on-going hostility towards Israel, beginning in patriarchal times and continuing thereafter except for a short time in Solomon's reign, it is more likely that Egypt's condemnation in these chapters is related to her recent failure to help Judah against Nebuchadnezzar. This is mentioned early in the section. See Chapter 29 verses 6-8, "And all the inhabitants of Israel shall know that I am the LORD, because they have been a staff of reed to the house of Israel. When they took hold of thee by thy hand, thou didst break, and rend all their shoulder: and when they leaned upon thee, thou brakest, and madest all their loins to be at a stand. Therefore thus saith the Lord GOD: Behold, I will bring a sword upon thee, and cut off man and beast out of thee". But even before that, attention is drawn to the immense pride of Pharaoh (29: 1-3), and it is not without significance that "a proud look" is the first of seven things that the Lord hates (Prov. 6: 16-17).

Ezekiel 29-32 comprise seven oracles, of which six are dated. Each oracle is introduced with the words, "the word of the LORD came unto me, saying …" They are:

i) **Chapter 29: 1-16**, dated "the tenth year, in the tenth month, in the twelfth day of the month". That is, "the tenth year" of the captivity.

ii) **Chapter 29: 17-21**, dated "the seven and twentieth year, in the first month, in the first day of the month".

iii) **Chapter 30: 1-19**. Undated

iv) **Chapter 30: 20-26**, dated "the eleventh year, in the first month, in the seventh day of the month".

v) **Chapter 31: 1-18**, dated "the eleventh year, in the third month, in the first day of the month".

vi) **Chapter 32: 1-16**, dated "the twelfth year, in the twelfth month, in the first day of the month".

vii) **Chapter 32: 17-32**, dated "the twelfth year, in the fifteenth day of the month".

The reference to "the seven and twentieth year" (29: 17) looks totally out of place, but it is nothing of the sort! As H.L.Ellison rightly points out, "its position is explained by its being in some measure an explanation of Chapter 29 verses 1-16". The reason for its inclusion at this point in the sequence points to the deliberate arrangement of these oracles. Leaving this particular oracle aside, the messages were all delivered to Ezekiel within three years.

As noted above, the first two oracles (vv.1-16 and vv.17-21) are closely connected and, taken together, may be analysed as follows: *(a)* the charges against Egypt (vv.1-7); *(b)* the captivity of Egypt (vv.8-16): "And I will bring again the *captivity* of Egypt" (v.14); *(c)* the conqueror (or conquest) of Egypt (vv.17-21). Alternatively, the three sections of the chapter could be summarised thus: *(a) why* judgment would fall on Egypt (vv.1-7); *(b) what* judgment would fall on Egypt (vv.8-16); *(c) when* judgment would fall on Egypt (vv.17-21).

It should be noted that "the house of Israel" is mentioned in each of the three sections: *(i)* "And all the inhabitants of Egypt shall know that I am the LORD, because they have been a staff of reed to **the house of Israel**" (v.6); *(ii)* "And it (Egypt) shall be no more the confidence of **the house of Israel**" (v.16); *(iii)* "In that day will I cause the horn of **the house of Israel** to bud forth" (v.21). All seven oracles against the "foreign nations" major on the connection with Israel. We should also note the use of "Behold" in each section (vv.3, 8 with 10, 19).

It should also be noted that each of the three sections have a common pattern. In each case the message is delivered firstly as it affects Egypt, and secondly as it affects Israel. This will be pointed out as we proceed. Both

Egypt and Israel would know "that I am the LORD". For Egypt, see verses 6 and 9: for Israel, see verses 16 and 21.

1) THE FIRST ORACLE, vv.1-16

The oracle is introduced as follows: "In the tenth year, in the tenth month, in the twelfth day of the month, the word of the LORD came unto me, saying, Son of man, set thy face against Pharaoh king of Egypt, and prophesy against him, and against all Egypt" (vv.1-2). As C.L.Feinberg points out, "The date given in verse 1 is explicit. It was a year and two days after Nebuchadnezzar had laid siege Jerusalem (Ezek 24: 1-2; 2 Kings 25: 1).

According to C.L.Feinberg, the Pharaoh at this time "was Hophra, the Greek Apries (reigned 588-569 BC); he was the grandson of Pharaoh Necho who conquered godly king Josiah at Megiddo (2 Chron. 35: 20-27)". Zedekiah, king of Judah, was looking for help from Pharaoh-Hophra against Nebuchadnezzar, and while the Egyptians did cause the Babylonians to lift the siege of Jerusalem (Jer. 37: 5-7), they later withdrew leaving Zedekiah at the mercy of Nebuchadnezzar (Jer. 44: 30). According to Jeremiah, Pharaoh-Hophra would find himself at the mercy of Nebuchadnezzar (Jer. 44: 30; 46: 25-26). Ezekiel tells us more in this very chapter about the circumstances in which this would happen (see.vv.17-20).

As noted above, this message contains *(A)* the charges against Egypt (vv.1-7); *(B)* the captivity of Egypt (vv.8-16).

A) THE CHARGES AGAINST EGYPT, vv.1-7

As noted above the section divides into two paragraphs: *(a)* the charge as it affects Egypt (vv.3-5); *(b)* the charge as it affects Israel (vv.6-7). In the first case, following the order of the introduction, the message is addressed to Pharaoh (vv.3-5), and in the second to the inhabitants of Egypt ("all Egypt") (vv.6-7). The reason is not easily explained.

a) The charge as it affects Egypt, vv.3-5

Pharaoh is charged with inordinate pride. "Thus saith the Lord GOD; Behold I am against thee, Pharaoh king of Egypt, the great dragon that lieth in the midst of his rivers, which hath said, My river is mine own, and I have made it for myself" (v.3). Nebuchadnezzar was of the same ilk: "Is not this great Babylon, that I have built for the house of the kingdom, by the might of my power and for the honour of my majesty?" (Dan. 4: 30).

Pharaoh is likened to a "great monster" (JND). The word *tannin* occurs in several passages in the Old Testament and is variously translated: "whale" (Job 7: 12; Ezek. 32: 2); "sea monster" (Lam. 4: 3); "dragon" (e.g. Isaiah 27: 1; 51: 9; Jer. 51: 34); "serpent" (Exodus 7: 9-12). Commentators are unanimous in concluding that the "great monster" here is "the crocodile, which was worshipped by the Egyptians, and was a symbol on late Egyptian coins" (C.L.Feinberg). The Nile is still infested with crocodiles. As Christopher Wright observes, "Pharaoh is portrayed as a grand crocodile basking in the Nile, imagining that the river itself is owned and indeed created by him himself".

> *She sailed away on a lovely summer day*
> *On the back of a crocodile.*
>
> *"You see", said she, "he's as tame as tame could be,*
> *I'll ride him down the Nile".*
>
> *The croc winked his eye as she waved her friends goodbye,*
> *Wearing a happy smile.*
>
> *At the end of the ride, the lady was inside*
> *And the smile on the crocodile.*

The annual inundation of the land by the Nile, whose source was not, of course, in Egypt, brought Egypt immense benefits. Without the floods the country would have been a desert. Egypt was dependent on the Nile for her prosperity. (Canaan was so different! See Deuteronomy 11: 10-12.) We are told that Pharaoh-Hophra's dynasty had carried out improvements to the river and stimulated trade with Egypt's neighbours, and it may be on this account that he said, "My river is mine own, and I have made it for myself". But the means of Egypt's prosperity was divinely-provided. The annual inundation of the land was God-given, but Pharaoh had inflated his status to that of Creator, failing to acknowledge the river made Egypt, not Egypt the river. We must never forget that "Every good gift and every perfect gift is from above, and cometh down from the Father of lights, with whom there is no variableness, neither shadow of turning" (James 1: 17).

The lesson for us is clear. It is a warning against self-sufficiency and pride. None of us is a self-made man or woman. Pharaoh could be described as a self-made man. But it was the Lord's provision (the annual flooding of the Nile) that made Egypt, and that made him. Moses reminded Israel that they were to "Beware that thou forget not the LORD thy God ... and that thou say in thine heart, My power and the might of my mine hand hath gotten me this wealth. But thou shalt remember the LORD thy God: for it is he that giveth thee power to get wealth" (Deut. 8: 11, 17, 18). In New Testament language: "what hast thou that thou didst not receive? Now if thou didst receive it, why dost thou glory, as if thou hadst not received it?" (1 Cor. 4: 7).

But "Pride goeth before destruction, and a haughty spirit before a fall" (Prov. 16: 18), and "Ezekiel prophesies that the basking lord of the Nile will be dragged out, along with masses of fish (Egypt's people), and left to die and rot in the desert (vv.4-5). Then the true Maker and Owner of the Nile will be recognised". Thus: "And all the inhabitants of Egypt shall know that I am the LORD (v.6)" (Christopher Wright).

In Ezekiel's own words, "But I will put hooks in thy jaws, and I will cause the fish of ***thy*** rivers to stick unto thy scales, and I will bring thee up out of the midst of ***thy*** rivers, and all the fish of ***thy*** rivers shall stick unto thy scales. And I will leave thee thrown into the wilderness, thee and all the fish of ***thy*** rivers: thou shalt fall upon the open fields: thou shalt not be brought together, nor gathered: for I have given thee for meat to the beasts of the field and to the fowls of the heaven" (vv.4-5). As F.A.Tatford observes, "Taken out of their element, fish and crocodile were virtually condemned to death, just as the Egyptians would be destroyed if separated from the Nile".

b) The charge as it affects Israel, vv.6-7

Egypt is charged with an unfulfilled pledge. "And all the inhabitants of Egypt shall know that I am the LORD, ***because*** they have been a staff of reed to the house of Israel. When they took hold of thee by thy hand, thou didst break, and rend all their shoulder: and when they leaned upon thee, thou brakest, and madest all their loins to be a stand ('didst make all their loins to tremble', JND)".

In Christopher Wright's words, "The second picture of Egypt was also a familiar local reality - the famous reeds from which papyrus was (and is still) made, and among which baby Moses was hidden. Useful for many purposes, reeds were useless as a staff or crutch. They were not only apt to shatter under stress, but the jagged edges could lacerate hands or armpits and the fall would injure your back". The words "and the fall would injure your back" refer to the NIV translation. We get the impression that Egypt was known for failing people who relied upon her. Approximately one hundred and thirty years before, Rab-shakeh, Sennacherib's envoy had said: "Now, behold, thou trusteth upon the staff of this bruised reed, even upon Egypt, on which if a man lean, it will go into his hand, and pierce it: so is Pharaoh king of Egypt unto all that trust on him" (2 Kings 18: 21). See also Isaiah 36 verse 6. As John P. Taylor suggests, "The Rabshakeh's words to Hezekiah ... suggest that the description was almost proverbial". He adds, "It does not take many instances to establish a reputation for unreliability".

The words, "When they took hold of thee by the hand, thou didst break" evidently refer, as noted above, to an appeal for help by Zedekiah against the Chaldean invaders, but the arrival of the Egyptian army was soon followed by their departure as predicted by Jeremiah: "Behold, Pharaoh's army, which is come forth to help you, shall return to Egypt into their own land" (Jer. 37: 5-7). All of which reminds us that "It is better to trust in the LORD than to put confidence in man. It is better to trust in the LORD than to put confidence in princes" (Psalm 118: 8-9). There are other lessons here. For example:

i) Are **we** people in whom confidence can be placed - or do **we** let people down, just like "a staff of reed"? And damage them in the process. Can it be said of us, "When they took hold of thee by the hand, ***thou didst break***, and rend all their shoulder: and when they leaned upon thee, ***thou brakest***, and madest all their loins to be a stand"? Are we people of our word? Solomon said that "Confidence in an unfaithful man in time of trouble is like a broken tooth, and a foot out of joint" (Prov. 25: 19).

ii) Are we people who look in the wrong direction for help? That is, to the world - instead of to the Lord. In the Lord's words, "Cursed be the man that trusteth in man, and maketh the flesh his arm, and whose heart departeth from the LORD" (Jer. 17: 5). David described a far better "staff" than Egypt: "Yea, though I walk through the valley of the shadow of death, I will fear no evil: for thou art with me; thy rod and thy staff they comfort me" (Psalm 23: 4). We must esteem "the reproach of Christ greater riches than the treasures in Egypt" (Heb. 11: 26).

B) THE CAPTIVITY OF EGYPT, vv.8-16

As noted above, this section also divides into two paragraphs: *(a)* the captivity as it affects Egypt (vv.8-15); *(b)* the captivity as it affects Israel (v.16).

a) The captivity as it affects Egypt, vv.8-15

Following the chapter's own alliteration, we should notice that Egypt would be desolated (vv.8-12a); dispersed (vv.12b-14a); diminished (vv.14b-15).

i) ***Egypt would be desolated.*** "Therefore thus saith the Lord GOD; Behold, I will bring a sword upon thee, and cut off man and beast out of thee. And the land of Egypt shall be *desolate* and waste; and they shall know that I am the LORD: because he hath said, The river is mine, and I have made it. Behold, therefore I am against thee, and against thy rivers, and I will make the land of Egypt utterly waste and *desolate*, from the tower of Syene even unto the border of Ethiopia. No foot of man shall pass through it, nor foot of beast shall pass through it, neither shall it be inhabited forty years, And I will make the land of Egypt *desolate* in the midst of the countries that are desolate, and her cities among the cities that are laid waste shall be *desolate* forty years" (vv.8-12a). The desolation of Egypt is further described in Chapter 30 verses 12-19.

We must notice the *extent* of her desolation (v.10), and the *duration* of her desolation (vv.11-13).

- **As to the extent of her desolation**, "I will make the land of Egypt utterly waste and *desolate*, from the tower of Syene even unto the border of Ethiopia" or "from Migdol to Syene, even unto the border of Ethiopia" (JND). F.A.Tatford identifies this as "from Migdol, the frontier fortress in the north (Exodus 14: 2; Jer. 44: 1) to Syene or Aswan in the south on the frontier of Ethiopia".

- **As to the duration of her desolation**, "No foot of man shall pass through it, nor foot of beast shall pass through it, neither shall it be inhabited forty years ... her cities among the cities that are laid waste shall be *desolate* forty years" (vv.11-12). We must listen here to C.L.Feinberg: "Because no such forty-year period is known in Egyptian history, some claim that a literal fulfilment of the prophecy was never intended, and that it is to be taken as hyperbole. But there is nothing in the context that would indicate a shift from the literal to the figurative …. The period between Nebuchadnezzar's conquest of Egypt and Cyrus' victory was about forty years, so the forty years are understood as the period when Babylon was supreme over Egypt".

ii) Egypt would be dispersed. "I will scatter the Egyptians among the nations, and will ***disperse*** them through the countries. Yet thus saith the Lord GOD; At the end of forty years will I gather the Egyptians from the people whither they were scattered: and I will bring again the captivity of Egypt, and will cause them to return into the land of Pathros, into the land of their habitation" (vv.12b-14a). "The land of Pathros" is what we know as 'Upper Egypt'. (Just to be difficult, 'Upper Egypt' is the south of the country!) The restoration of Egypt would "fit well with the known lenient policy of the Persians toward subject peoples" (C.L.Feinberg). See, for example, Ezra 1 verses 1-4.

iii) Egypt would be diminished. "They shall be there a base kingdom. It shall be the basest of the kingdoms: neither shall it exalt itself any more above the nations: for I will ***diminish*** them, that they shall no more rule over the nations" (vv.14b-15). We should notice the words, "they shall be a ***base kingdom***. ***It shall be the basest of the kingdoms*** neither shall it exalt itself any more above the nations". The word "base" means 'low'. Egypt would "become only a lowly or mean kingdom, small in size and humble in status, and consequently incapable of exalting themselves above any other country. God purposed to make her so mean that she would never again rule over other countries" (F.A.Tatford). But this is not the end of the story: see Isaiah 19 verses 19-25, "In that day shall there be an altar to the LORD in the midst of the land of Egypt ... In that day shall Israel be the third with Egypt and with Assyria, even a blessing in the midst of the land: whom the LORD of hosts shall bless, saying, Blessed be Egypt my people ..."

b) The captivity as it affects Israel, v.16

"And it shall be no more the confidence of the house of Israel, which bringeth their iniquity to remembrance, when they shall look after them: but they shall know that I am the Lord GOD" or "And it shall be no more the confidence of the house of Israel, bringing iniquity to remembrance when they turn after them" (JND). The reduction of Egypt's status among world nations would deter Israel from ever placing confidence in her again, reminding us that the character of the world in which we live should deter us from aligning ourselves with its economic, political and religious systems. (Do ***we*** learn the lessons of the past?) In New Testament language, "Be ye not unequally yoked together with unbelievers: for what fellowship hath righteousness with unrighteousness? And what communion hath light with darkness? and what concord hath Christ with Belial? or what part hath he that believeth with an infidel? and what agreement hath the temple of God with idols?" (2 Cor. 6: 14-16); "Ye adulterers and adulteresses, know ye not that the friendship of the world is enmity against God? Whosoever therefore will be the friend of the world is the enemy of God" (James 4: 4). This brings us to:

2) *THE SECOND ORACLE, vv.17-21*

Having considered *(a)* the charges against Egypt (vv.1-7), and *(b)* the captivity of Egypt (vv.8-16), we must now give attention to:

C) THE CONQUEROR OF EGYPT, vv.17-21

We have already suggested the reason for the insertion of this oracle at this point in the section. In chronological terms it is completely out of order. Although it was delivered to Ezekiel some seventeen years after the first oracle, it precedes the remaining five which were all delivered within two years or so of the first oracle above. It is included at this point in the section to show *how* Egypt would become desolate for forty years (cf. vv.11-13).

As on previous occasions, God would use Nebuchadnezzar, king of Babylon, to accomplish His purposes for Egypt: "And it came to pass in the seven and twentieth year, in the first month, in the first day of the month, the word of the LORD came unto me, saying, Son of man, Nebuchadrezzar king of Babylon caused his army *to serve a great service against Tyrus*: every head was made bald, and every shoulder was peeled: yet had he no wages, nor his army, for Tyrus, *for the service that he had served against it*: therefore thus saith the Lord GOD; Behold, I will give the land of Egypt unto Nebuchadrezzar king of Babylon; and he shall take her multitude, and take her spoil, and take her prey; and it shall be the wages for his army. I have given him the land of Egypt for his labour wherewith *he served against it, because they wrought for me*, saith the Lord GOD" (vv.17-20). The words, "every head was made bald, and every shoulder was peeled", refer to the effect that the siege had on the army: "In their labour to capture the city, their heads had been made bald by the chafing of their helmets and their shoulders had been rubbed bare by the loads of stone and timber they had been compelled to carry" (F.A.Tatford). All this reminds us that we too serve the Lord, sometimes at personal discomfort: "And whatsoever ye do, do it heartily, as to the Lord, and not unto men; knowing that of the Lord ye shall receive the reward of the inheritance: for ye serve the Lord Christ" (Col. 3: 23-24).

For the third time, as noted above, the section comprises two paragraphs: *(a)* the conquest as it affects Egypt (vv.17-20); *(b)* the conquest as it affects Israel (v.21).

a) The conquest as it affects Egypt, vv.17-20

The prophecy ("in the seven and twentieth year") was probably uttered at the end of the thirteen-year siege of Tyre by Nebuchadnezzar. In studying the oracles against Tyre, we noticed that after the fall of Jerusalem (586 BC), Nebuchadnezzar and the Babylonians marched against Tyre and laid siege to the city for thirteen years (586-573 BC). The length of the siege was due to the fact that the Tyrians obtained their supplies by sea. Despite contrary views, Nebuchadnezzar evidently took the mainland fortress (this is clear from Ezekiel 29: 18) as predicted in Ezekiel 26 verses 7-11, only to find that 'the cupboard was bare' and that after thirteen years hard graft there was no booty. But God always pays His workmen, and Nebuchadnezzar received the wealth of Egypt in lieu of the expected wealth of Tyre (vv. 19-21).

As the next chapter indicates, having already broken one of Pharaoh's arms, possibly referring to Nebuchadnezzar's victory over Pharaoh-Necho at Carchemish, the king of Babylon would descend on Egypt and break both arms, in this case the arms of Ahmose 11, or Amasis. (See 30: 21-22. See also 30: 10-11, 24-25.)

b) The conquest as it affects Israel, v.21

"In that day will I cause the horn of the house of Israel to bud forth, and I will give thee the opening of the mouth in the midst of them; and they shall know that I am the LORD." This is not easily explained. While the words "in that day" and "horn" (cp. Psalm 132: 17; Luke 1: 69) have strong Messianic connections, it is difficult to interpret the verse as a direct prophecy of end-time events, since that would demand an abrupt change from the subject of the previous verses, and create difficulty in explaining the role of Ezekiel himself who, it is clearly stated, would be given the ability to speak at the time of Egypt's conquest by Nebuchadnezzar ("in that day").

CHAPTER 29

The word "horn" is used in the Old Testament as the symbol of strength (1 Sam. 2: 1; 1 Kings 22: 11; Jer. 48: 25; Amos 6: 13), and it is therefore suggested that the downfall of Egypt will be accompanied by "hope of the return to Judah and re-establishment of the nation" (M.F.Unger). Having seen the conquest of Egypt in fulfilment of his prophecy, Ezekiel would be enabled to speak of the "the grace of God in final restoration for Kingdom blessing". This he does in Chapters 40-48. The vision in these chapters was given to Ezekiel in "the five and twentieth year of our captivity" (40: 1). That is, "on 28th April, 573 BC" (M.F.Unger). The siege of Tyre ended in 573 BC (M.F.Unger). Without attempting to be more precise, which would be difficult (for a start, this particular prophecy is dated April 571 BC), it is at least arguable that the downfall of Egypt became the occasion of the glorious prophecy in Chapters 40-48, and that this could explain the statement, "In that day will I cause the horn of the house of Israel to bud forth (hope for the future), and I will give thee the opening of the mouth in the midst of them (Ezekiel's prophecy); and they shall know that I am the LORD". If this supposition is correct, then further work is required in connection with the relevant dates.

EZEKIEL CHAPTER 30

This chapter enlarges on Chapter 29. It develops the subject of Egypt's desolation, detailing her downfall, together with the downfall of the judgment of allied nations and peoples: "Ethiopia, and Libya, and Lydia, and all the mingled people, and Chub, and the men of the land that is in league" (v.5). It is worth pointing out that the reason for such detail in describing the downfall of Egypt in a Hebrew book is to disabuse the exiles of any hope or expectation of help from Egypt. In Christopher J.H.Wright's words, "The siege of Jerusalem went on. Did the exiles still think that Pharaoh could try again to relieve Jerusalem? Not a chance, says Ezekiel".

The chapter comprises two oracles (vv.1-19; vv.20-26), both introduced by similar wording: "The word of the LORD came again unto me, saying ..." (v.1); "the word of the LORD came unto me, saying ..." (v.20). The first oracle is undated, but it is generally thought that it was given at the time of the siege of Jerusalem, which was temporarily lifted with the arrival of the Egyptian army (Jer. 37: 5-7). The second oracle was delivered to Ezekiel "in the eleventh year, in the first month, in the seventh day of the month" (v.20), that is, approximately three months after the first oracle (29: 1). Jerusalem fell in eleventh year and fourth month of the Babylonian captivity (Jer. 52: 5-7).

Taken together, the two oracles comprise five paragraphs: *(1)* the imminence of Egypt's judgment (vv.1-5); *(2)* the impotence of Egypt's allies (vv.6-9); *(3)* the instrument of Egypt's destruction (vv.10-12); *(4)* the idolatry of Egypt's cities (vv.13-19); *(5)* the immobilisation of Egypt's strength (vv.20-26). The four paragraphs which comprise the first of the two oracles in the chapter are all introduced with either "Thus saith the Lord GOD" (vv.2, 10, 13), or "Thus saith the LORD ... saith the Lord GOD" (v.6).

1) THE IMMINENCE OF EGYPT'S JUDGMENT, vv.1-5

"The word of the LORD came again unto me, saying, Son of man, prophesy and say, Thus saith the Lord GOD; Howl ye, Woe worth the day!" (vv.1-2) or "Howl ye, alas for the day!" (JND). We should notice that Ezekiel was to make it clear that he was not conveying his own message: "Son of man, prophesy and say, ***Thus saith the Lord GOD***", reminding us that we have the same mandate: "Go ye therefore, and teach all nations ('make disciples of all nations'), baptizing them in the name of the Father, and of the Son, and of the Holy Ghost: teaching them to observe all things whatsoever *I have commanded you*" (Matt 28: 18-19). Before commencing his ministry, Ezekiel was told "thou shalt speak *my words* unto them, whether they will hear, or whether they will forbear" (Ezek. 2: 7), and this still holds good for every servant of God. Attention is drawn to the following:

i) **The nearness of judgment**: "the day is *near*, even the day of the LORD is *near*, a cloudy day; it shall be the time of the heathen" (v.3). In an earlier passage, Ezekiel predicted the imminence of divine judgment on Judah: "thus saith the Lord GOD; an evil, an only evil, behold, is come. An end is come, the end is come: it watcheth for thee; behold, it is come" (Ezek. 7: 5-6). If the prophecies against Jerusalem were in course of fulfillment at the time that Ezekiel prophesied against Egypt, then those against Egypt herself would soon follow suit. God does not pronounce judgment in vain. As C.L.Feinberg observes, "The human heart is ever prone to put off the judgment of God, easily finding solace in the unfounded thought that if God's visitation be postponed long enough, it may never occur at all". This is certainly the view of the "scoffers" described by Peter: "Where is the promise of his coming? for since the fathers fell asleep, all things continue as they were from the beginning of the creation". Having discussed their 'willing ignorance' in this way, Peter adds, "But the day of the Lord will come" (2 Pet. 3: 3-10). This brings us to:

ii) **The name of the day**: "the day is near, even the ***day of the LORD*** is near, a cloudy day; it shall be the time of the heathen" (v.3). Peter uses the expression "the day of the Lord" in connection with the end-time, and so does Paul (1 Thess. 5: 2), not to mention the Old Testament prophets. See, for example Zechariah 14 verse 1. Although commentators tend to wriggle a little over this, it is nevertheless difficult to avoid the conclusion that Ezekiel is using the expression in relation to the invasion and desolation of Egypt which took place within a few years after its prediction. It therefore seems that the expression must be understood in two ways: with reference to *imminent* judgment, as here and, for example, in Zephaniah 1 verses 7 and 14, and, more generally, in describing divine intervention in human affairs

EZEKIEL

at *the end-time.* Students of prophecy often say that 'coming events cast their shadow before them'. In other words, what happened in the past is a picture of what lies in the future. The invasion of Egypt by Nebuchadnezzar is "an adumbration (meaning, 'a shadowy representation') of the true day of the Lord" *(The Scofield Reference Bible).*

iii) The nations involved. "And the sword shall come upon Egypt, and great pain shall be in Ethiopia, when the slain shall fall in Egypt, and they shall take away her multitude, and her foundations shall be broken down. Ethiopia, and Libya, and Lydia, and all the mingled people, and Chub, and the men of the land that is in league, shall fall with them by the sword" (vv.4-5). The sword (v.4) is the emblem of judgment. Compare Romans 13 verse 4. The sword here (v.4) is later identified as the Lord's sword in the hand of the king of Babylon (v.24). Like the "the staff" in the Assyrian's hand (Isaiah 10: 5), "the sword" in Nebuchadnezzar's hand was God's instrument of judgment.

Judgment would therefore fall on Egypt and upon her allies. According to F.Gardiner *(Ellicott's Commentary),* Ethiopia and Egypt were closely connected, and during much of their history were often under one government. Ethiopian soldiers served in great numbers in the Egyptian armies. "Libya" and "Lydia" are a substitute for the original names, Phut and Lud, which are preserved in Ezekiel 27 verse 10. Phut probably refers to Cyrenaica, but F.A.Tatford points out that some opt for western Egypt or Libya. Lud evidently refers to Lydia in Asia Minor, although some opt for a location further east. These countries are known to have supplied mercenaries to the Egyptian army (F.Gardiner). See Jeremiah 46 verse 9. The "mingled people" are unidentified. See also Jeremiah 25 verse 20. It has been suggested that they were "people who were living in Egypt without having acquired citizenship, colonists, or traders, or hired soldiers" (T.Laetsch). F.Gardiner opts for "foreign mercenaries from various quarters in the Egyptian armies". Chub is unidentified, and "the men of the land that is in league", which can be rendered 'the children of the land of the covenant', could refer to the Jews who had sought refuge from Nechadnezzar in Egypt after the murder of Gedaiah. On the other hand, it could be a reference to the entire confederation - "the men of the land that is in league". However, in short, Egypt with all her confederates would perish.

It is worth pointing out that at the end-time, another confederation of nations will emerge: "The kings of the earth set themselves, and the rulers take counsel together, against the LORD, and against his anointed, saying, Let us break their bands asunder, and cast away their cords from us" (Psalm 2: 2-3). That, too, will be destroyed. Christ will "break them with a rod of iron; thou shalt dash them in pieces like a potter's vessel" (Psalm 2: 9).

2) THE IMPOTENCE OF EGYPT'S ALLIES, vv.6-9

The continuity is clear: the words, "the men of the land that is *in league*, shall *fall* with them by the sword" (v.5), lead to, "Thus saith the LORD: They also that *uphold* Egypt shall *fall*; and the pride of her power shall come down: from the tower of Syene shall they fall in it by the sword, saith the Lord GOD. And they shall be desolate in the midst of the countries that are desolate, and her cities shall be in the midst of the cities that are wasted. And they shall know that I am the LORD, when I have set a fire in Egypt, and when all her *helpers* shall be *destroyed*" (vv.6-8). For the second time reference is made to the north and south of the land: "from Migdol to Syene shall they fall in her, by the sword saith the Lord Jehovah" (v.6, JND). As previously noted (see 29: 10), F.A.Tatford identifies this as "from Migdol, the frontier fortress in the north (Exodus 14: 2; Num. 33: 7; Jer. 44: 1) to Syene or Aswan in the south on the frontier of Ethiopia". The words, "her cities shall be in the midst of the cities that are wasted" (v.7) are also found in Chapter 29 verse 12.

The news of Egypt's conquest would reach the first-named ally, Ethiopia (v.5), through fleeing Egyptians ascending the waterways of the Nile seeking refuge from the Babylonian invader: "In that day shall messengers go forth *from me* in ships to make the careless Ethiopians afraid". Isaiah calls these waterways "the rivers of Ethiopia" (Is. 18: 1). Just as Nebchadnezzar is called "my servant" (Jer. 43: 10), so the fleeing Egyptians would be, unwittingly, God's servants in bringing fear to "careless Ethiopians". The Ethiopians are probably described in this way because they "dwelt securely in the lee of their powerful neighbour" (John B. Taylor). The words, "great pain shall come upon them, as in the day of Egypt" is "a reference to a past event, and can only mean, as in the day of judgment upon Egypt at the Exodus" (F.Gardiner).

Egypt's supporters would be unavailing, but where do *we* look for help? David points us in the right direction: "Some trust in chariots, and some in horses: but *we* will remember the name of the LORD our God" (Psalm 20: 7). Another psalmist puts it like this: "I will lift up mine eyes unto the hills, from whence cometh my help. My help cometh from the LORD, which made heaven and earth" (Psalm 121: 1-2). Egypt's allies would fail her, reminding us to

EZEKIEL

Stand up! Stand up for Jesus!
Stand in His strength alone;
The arm of flesh will fail you;
Ye dare not trust you own.

While the arrival of the Chaldean armies must have brought immeasurable fear and disquiet to Egypt, Paul could write to the Corinthians saying, "Moreover I call God for a record upon my soul, that to spare you I came not as yet unto Corinth. Not for that we have dominion over your faith, but are helpers of your joy" (2 Cor. 1: 24). It wasn't like that in Egypt! This brings us to:

3) *THE INSTRUMENT OF EGYPT'S DESTRUCTION, vv.10-12*

"Thus saith the Lord GOD; *I will* also make the multitude of Egypt to cease **by the hand of Nebuchadrezzar** king of Babylon. He and his people with him, the terrible of the nations, shall be brought to destroy the land: and they shall draw their swords against Egypt, and fill the land with the slain" (vv.10-11). See also verse 25. Once again, the passage emphasises that the Lord is in absolute control of history: "He and his people with him, the terrible of the nations, shall **be brought** to destroy the land" (v.11).

The destruction of the land is now described: "And I will make the rivers dry, and sell the land into the hand of the wicked: and I will make the land waste, and all that is therein, by the hand of strangers: I the LORD have spoken it" (v.12). As C.L.Feinberg points out, "The threat to dry up the rivers of Egypt (referring to the branches of the Nile in the Delta) was not a figurative expression, but a grim possibility (cf. Isaiah 19: 4-6). Apart from the Nile, Egypt was nothing more than a barren wilderness. The worst calamity that could have befallen Egypt would be the dessication of her river, for her life depended on the annual inundation of the land by the Nile". Lamar E. Cooper adds, "Destruction of the canal system of irrigation would hasten the desolation of Egypt. This canal system was the only way to irrigate the limited, but fertile, arable land. The land would fall to evil men who would exploit it and its people". As F.A.Tatford points out, "The primary reference was, of course, to the Babylonians, but others have also played their part in the chequered history of the country".

Nebuchadnezzar (the normal spelling) and his armies are called: "the terrible of the nations" (v.11). See also 31: 12. They are similarly described in the book of Habakkuk: "Lo, I raise up the Chaldeans, that bitter and hasty nation, which shall march through the breadth of the land, to possess the dwelling-places that are not theirs. They are terrible and dreadful: their judgment and their dignity shall proceed of themselves. Their horses are swifter than the leopards, and are more fierce than the evening wolves: and their horsemen shall spread themselves, and their horsemen shall come from far: they shall fly as the eagle that hasteth to eat. They shall come all for violence: their faces shall sup up as the east wind, and they shall gather the captivity as the sand" (Hab. 1: 6-9).

4) THE IDOLATRY OF EGYPT'S CITIES, vv.13-19

"Thus saith the Lord GOD; I will also destroy the idols, and I will cause their images to cease out of Noph; and there shall be no more a prince of the land of Egypt: and I will put a fear in the land of Egypt" (v.13). The passage develops what would happen after the "seven and twentieth year" (29: 17): "I will give the land of Egypt unto Nebuchadrezzar king of Babylon" (29: 19-20). There would be no gods to help, and no prince to rule (v.13).

a) No gods to help, v.13

"I will also destroy the idols, and I will cause their images to cease out of Noph". Noph," a contraction of Menoph, refers to Memphis, the capital of Lower Egypt, situated in the region of the Pyramids. It lay on the left bank of the Nile, sixteen miles south of Cairo. It was the seat of several Egyptian dynasties and one of the chief centres of Egyptian idolatry, containing, *inter alia*, the temples of Ptah and Apis.

b) No prince to rule, v.13

"And there shall be no more a prince of the land of Egypt: and I will put a fear in the land of Egypt." F.A.Tatford suggests that "at the same time the royal household came under punishment, and the prophecy declared that there would no longer be a prince of the land of Egypt: no native ruler would rise up to take control". F.Gardiner looks at it slightly differently in saying that this is to be understood, in accordance with the rest of the prophecy, not absolutely, but relatively: there shall be no more a native prince possessing the power of former kings".

The cities of Egypt are detailed in verses 14-18. Judgment would be comprehensive. As F.Gardiner observes, "The mention of these various cities is to make emphatic the universality of the judgment upon the whole land". It also emphasises God's perfect knowledge of every city, reminding us that "the eyes of the LORD are in every place, beholding the evil and the good" (Prov. 15: 3).

- **Pathros:** "And I will make Pathros desolate" (v.14). As already noted (see 29: 14), Pathros is what we know as 'Upper Egypt'. It was "the capital of Upper Egypt, and also the name given to the whole of the region extending to Aswan in the south" (F.A.Tatford). Remember, 'Upper Egypt' is the southern or lower part of the country!

- **Zoan:** "and will set fire in Zoan" (v.14). See also Isaiah 19 verse 11. This is "the Greek Tanis in the eastern delta (sometimes identified with the Raamses of Exodus 1: 11) ... a strongly fortified commercial city" (F.A.Tatford).

- **No:** and I "will execute judgments in No" (v.14). No, mentioned again in verse 15, is No-Amon (see also Nahum 3: 8) is the "celebrated Thebes (its Greek name) of Upper Egypt, still famous for its ruins at Luxor and Karnac" (F.Gardiner). "Thebes was formerly the capital of the whole of Egypt and the cultic centre of the sun-god, Amon" (F.A.Tatford). The city was said to have a hundred gates. It was situated on the Nile, and protected by canals.

- **Sin:** "And I will pour my fury upon Sin, the strength of Egypt; and I will cut off the multitude of No. And I will set fire in Egypt: Sin shall have great pain, and No shall be rent asunder, and Noph shall have distresses daily ('enemies in open day', JND)" (vv.15-16). Sin is otherwise known as Pelusium, so called from the marshes around it, and lay on the easternmost branch of the Nile, only two and a half miles from the sea. Its modern name is Tel Farama, on the Mediterranean coast, not far from Port Said. It was the frontier city, strongly fortified, and considered rightly as the key of Egypt, and hence called in the text its "strength" (F.Gardiner). These verses describe divine judgment in graphic language. Having said, "And they shall know that I am the LORD, when I have set a fire in Egypt" (v.8), He now describes the effects of the inferno. "Pelusium (Sin) would be in great agony - like a living thing writhing in the torment of the flames. Just as intense heat would cause walls to crack, so would the fortress of Thebes (No) be rent asunder, its walls breached by the invading army. Military attacks were normally made under shadow of night, but so great was the power of the Babylonian assailants that their onslaught was made in broad daylight, and Memphis (Noph) suffered continual distresses in the daytime" (F.A.Tatford).

- **Aven and Pibeseth:** "The young men of Aven and of Pi-beseth shall fall by the sword: and these cities shall go into captivity" (v.17). C.L.Feinberg explains that Aven (meaning 'wickedness'), seven miles north-east of Cairo, is otherwise known as Beth-Shemesh (Jer. 43: 13) or Heliopolis, where sun worship flourished, and that Pi-beseth was otherwise known as Bubastis, where sacred cats were mummified. He continues: "The cat-headed goddess was Ubastet. Herodotus claims that annual festivals there witnessed gatherings of about 700,000 people". Aven, or On, was one of the oldest cities in Egypt, and Poti-pherah, Joseph's father-in law, was evidently high priest there (Gen. 41: 45).

- **Tehaphnehes:** "At Tehaphnehes also the day shall be darkened, when I shall break there the yokes of Egypt: and the pomp of her strength shall cease in her: as for her, a cloud shall cover her, and her daughters shall go into captivity" (v.18). Tehaphnehes (see Jer. 2: 16) is otherwise known as Daphne (its Greek name). It was named after the Egyptian queen, Tahpenes, and was a residence of the Pharaohs (Jer. 43: 7, 9). It is also known as Hanes (Is. 30: 4). According to Jeremiah 43 verses 9-10, Nebuchadnezzar would establish his throne at Tahpanhes, which was a strongly fortified frontier town near Pelusium. Its modern name is Tel Defenneh, ten miles west of Quantara on the Suez Canal.

As C.L.Feinberg suggests, "a cloud of distress and calamity would descend upon the once favoured city". The "yokes of Egypt" refers to the tyranny which Egypt exercised over others. The "daughters" of Tehaphnehes could refer to her surrounding towns, but it is more likely, in view of the reference to the young men of Aven and Pi-beseth (v.17), that literal daughters are intended.

In summary: "Thus will I execute judgments in Egypt: and they shall know that I am the LORD" (v.19). In the words of F.A.Tatford, "His ultimate object was that the nations might know and recognise Jehovah as the true God, and His dominion as universal".

5) THE IMMOBILISATION OF EGYPT'S STRENGTH, vv.20-26

"And it came to pass in the eleventh year, in the first month, in the seventh day of the month, that the word of the LORD came unto me saying ..." (v.20).

We should notice that the passage contains six references to "arm"/"arms". The figure stands for strength. See, for example Luke 1 verse 51 and numerous O.T. references. Attention is draw to the *past* tense (v.21), where the *singular* "arm" is used, and to the *future* tense (vv.22-26), where the *plural* "arms" is used.

a) Intervention against Egypt in the past, v.21

"Son of man, *I have broken* the *arm* of Pharaoh king of Egypt; and, lo, it shall not be bound up to be healed, to put a roller to bind it, to make it strong to hold the sword." Reference is made to what *had* happened, and to the singular - "the arm". Most commentators suggest that this refers to the alleged repulse in 588 BC of Pharaoh-Hophra's army, which had been sent to Jerusalem following Zedekiah's plea for help against the besieging Chaldeans. However, there seems to be an equally good, if not better case, for arguing that the passage refers to Pharaoh's defeat by the Babylonians at Carchemish in 605 BC as the result of which "the king of Egypt came not again any more out of his land: for the king of Babylon had taken from the river of Egypt unto the river Euphrates all that pertained to the king of Egypt" (2 Kings 24.7).

It is worth mentioning that when the passage refers to Pharaoh, it is not necessarily the same man. The title refers to the king of Egypt at any given time.

b) Intervention against Egypt in the future, vv.22-26

We should notice two related things here: *(i)* the defeat of Egypt (v.22); *(ii)* the dispersal of Egypt (v.23).

i) **The defeat of Egypt.** "Therefore thus saith the Lord GOD; Behold, I am against Pharaoh king of Egypt, and *will break* his *arms*, the strong, and that which was broken, and I *will* cause the sword to fall out of his hand" (v.22). Reference is made to what *would* happen, and to the plural - *both* arms. This implies final defeat, which would take place when Nebuchadnezzar invaded Egypt. See Chapter 29 verses 17-20. The defeat at Carchemish was a foretaste of what was to come for Egypt! Notice that the passage begins "I *have broken* the arm of Pharaoh", but continues "I ... *will break* his arms, the strong and that which was broken", meaning that the severe blow already inflicted upon Egypt would be followed by complete destruction. The result follows:

ii) ***The dispersal of Egypt***. "And I will scatter the Egyptians among the nations, and will disperse them through the countries" (v.23). Compare the earlier statement to this effect: "I will make the land of Egypt desolate in the midst of the countries that are desolate, and her cities among the cities that are laid waste shall be desolate forty years: and I will scatter the Egyptians among the nations, and will disperse them through the countries" (29: 12).

This is repeated, presumably for emphasis: *(i)* the defeat of Egypt (vv.24-25); *(ii)* the dispersal of Egypt (v.26).

i) ***The defeat of Egypt***. "And I will strengthen the arms of the king of Babylon, and put *my sword* in his hand: but I will break Pharaoh's arms, and he shall groan before him with the groanings of a deadly wounded man. But I will strengthen the arms of the king of Babylon, and the arms of Pharaoh shall fall down; and they shall know that I am the LORD, when I shall put my sword into the hand of the king of Babylon, and he shall stretch it out upon the land of Egypt" (vv.24-25). The contrast is unmistakable:

- ***The increased strength of Nebuchadnezzar***. "I will **strengthen the arms** of the king of Babylon ... I will **strengthen the arms** of the king of Babylon."

- ***The impaired strength of Pharaoh***. "I will **break Pharaoh's arms** ... the **arms of Pharaoh shall fall down**".

Note, as well, the contrast between, "I have broken the arm of Pharaoh king of Egypt; and, lo, it shall not be bound up to be healed, to put a roller (a bandage) to bind it, **to make it strong to hold the sword"** (v.21*)* and, "And I will strengthen the arms of the king of Babylon, and will put *my sword* in his hand ... and they shall know that I am the LORD, when I shall put *my sword* into the hand of the king of Babylon".

How glad we are that we do not rest in the strength of either the arms of Pharaoh or the arms of Nebuchadnezzar! "The eternal God is thy refuge, and underneath are the everlasting arms" (Deut. 33: 27). The Old Testament has a great deal to say about "the arm (singular) of the Lord", usually in connection with His ability to deliver His people and to destroy their enemies. But here Moses refers to the "everlasting arms" (plural) of the Lord, emphasising that His support is completely reliable at all times and in every way. His strength is complete. Unlike ourselves, the strength of

His arms can never diminish or be diminished: "for the arms of the wicked shall be broken: but the Lord upholdeth the righteous" (Psalm 37: 17). His "everlasting arms" are employed in tender ministry: "he shall gather the lambs with his arm, and carry them in his bosom" (Isaiah 40: 11). He did this when here on earth: "Suffer the little children to come unto me ... And he took them up in his arms, put his hands upon them, and blessed them" (Mark 10: 14-16).

ii) **The dispersal of Egypt**. "And I will scatter the Egyptians among the nations, and disperse them among the countries; and they shall know that I am the LORD" (v.26). To repeat the words of F.A.Tatford, "His ultimate object was that the nations might know and recognise Jehovah as the true God, and His dominion as universal".

EZEKIEL CHAPTER 31

The oracles against Egypt (Chs.29-32) commenced with the condemnation of Pharaoh's inordinate pride: "Thus saith the Lord GOD; Behold I am against thee, Pharaoh king of Egypt, the great dragon that lieth in the midst of his rivers, which hath said, My river is mine own, and I have made it for myself" (29: 3). The subject is touched upon again in Chapter 30: "They also that uphold Egypt shall fall; and the pride of her power shall come down" (30: 6).

The condemnation and consequences of Egypt's pride are emphasised particularly in Chapter 31: "Son of man, speak unto Pharaoh king of Egypt, and to his multitude; Whom art thou like in thy greatness?", and then, having demonstrated from the history of Assyria that "Pride goeth before destruction, and an haughty spirit before a fall" (Prov. 16: 18), the Lord says to Pharaoh, "To whom art thou thus like in thy glory and in greatness among the trees of Eden? Yet shalt thou be brought down with the trees of Eden unto the nether parts of the earth ... This is Pharaoh, and all his multitude, saith the Lord GOD" (v.18). The lesson is unmistakeable: "Let him that thinketh he standeth take heed lest he fall" (1 Cor. 10: 12). How necessary for us all to "walk humbly with ... God" (Micah 6: 8).

The larger part of the chapter (vv.3-17), whilst addressed to Pharaoh, describes the pride, exaltation and downfall of Assyria as a lesson to Egypt. However, some commentators adopt the view that *Asshur* (v.3) should read *te'asshur* meaning 'pine tree' but this involves changing the text to make it easier for the commentator to understand! John B. Taylor goes as far as to say, "The reference to Assyria (v.3 AV, RV) is clearly a mistake, because that nation has no place in an allegory addressed to Pharaoh". This is a dreadful admission, and even F.A.Tatford inclines in that direction. Quite clearly, the authorised Version faithfully reproduces the unamended Hebew text.

C.L.Feinberg, who asserts the integrity of the Hebrew text, puts it nicely: "God was in effect saying to Pharaoh and his people, 'If you are inclined to pride yourself on your glory as a mighty empire, just consider what happened to Assyria, described under the figure of a cedar'". The lesson of the chapter may be expressed in the words of Daniel to Belshazzar: "O thou king, the most high God gave Nebuchadnezzar thy father a kingdom, and majesty, and glory, and honour…but when his heart was lifted up, and his mind hardened in pride, he was deposed from his kingly throne, and they took his glory from him … And thou his son, O Belshazzar, **hast not humbled thine heart, though thou knewest all this**" (Dan. 5: 17-23).

A note to this effect is given in the Amplified Version: "The effectiveness of this comparison (of Egypt with Assyria) becomes plain when it is remembered that Assyria had conquered and held Egypt in vassalage and had then, herself been conquered and annihilated only thirty-seven years before the date of this prophecy, and that by the same Chaldean power (then controlled by the father of Nebuchadnezzar) which is now foretold as about to execute judgment upon Egypt. Egypt could not expect to resist the conqueror of her conqueror". (This piece was originally written by F.Gardiner in *Ellicott's Commentary*.)

The chapter may be divided in the following way: *(1)* accusation (vv.1-2); *(2)* exaltation (vv.3-9); *(3)* visitation (vv.10-13); *(4)* education (v.14); *(5)* reverberation (vv.15-17); *(6)* application (v.18).

1) ACCUSATION, vv.1-2

"And it came to pass in the eleventh year, in the third month, in the first day of the month, that the word of the LORD came unto me saying, Son of man, speak unto Pharaoh king of Egypt, and to his multitude, Whom art thou like in thy greatness?"

The message, which was delivered approximately two months after the previous oracle (30: 20) and about two months before the capture of Jerusalem (F.A.Tatford), begins and ends with similar questions addressed to Pharaoh in all his pride: "Whom art thou like in thy greatness?" (v.2); "To whom art thou thus like in glory, and in greatness among the trees of Eden?" (v.18). Pride is the first of seven things that the Lord hates and regards as an "abomination" (Prov. 6: 16-19). Believers must beware of pride. "A man's pride shall bring him low: but honour shall uphold the humble in spirit" (Prov. 29: 23). The New Testament reminds us that "God resisteth the proud, and giveth grace to the humble" (1 Pet. 5: 5). See also James 4 verse 6.

CHAPTER 31

Pride can have some nice aspects. We talk about 'taking pride in our work', and about a 'proud father' or a 'proud mother'. But just listen to Haman talking to his wife and friends: "And Haman told them of the glory of his riches, and the multitude of his children, and all the things wherewith the king had promoted him, and how he had advanced him above the princes and servants of the king" (Esther 5: 11). Here is boastful pride.

- ***He was proud of his possessions.*** "And Haman told them of the glory of his riches ..." (v.11). He was soon to learn that "a man's life consisteth not in the abundance of things which he possesseth" (Luke 12: 15).

- ***He was proud of his posterity.*** "And the multitude of his children." Well, Psalm 127 tells us that "children are an heritage of *the LORD*: and the fruit of the womb is his reward" (v.3).

- ***He was proud of his promotion.*** "And all the things wherein the king had promoted him." Listen to this: "Lift not up your horn on high: speak not with a stiff neck. For promotion cometh neither from the east, not from the west, nor from the south; But God is the judge, he putteth down one, and setteth up another" (Psalm 75: 5-7).

- ***He was proud of his privileges.*** Listen to Haman as he continues: "Yea, Esther the queen did let no man come in with the king unto the banquet which she had prepared, but myself; and tomorrow am I invited unto her also with the king" (Est. 5: 12). Apart from the king, he was the sole guest.

It is all summed up in Jeremiah 9 verses 23-24: "Let not the wise man glory in his wisdom, neither let the mighty man glory in his might, let not the rich man glory in his riches: But let him that glorieth glory in this, that he understandeth and knoweth me, that I am the LORD which exercise lovingkindness, judgment, and righteousness, in the earth: for in these things I delight, saith the LORD".

2) EXALTATION, vv.3-9

The exaltation of Assyria is described here. This is a very descriptive allegorical passage. We should note the following: *(a)* the grandeur of Assyria (v.3); *(b)* the source of Assyria's strength (vv.4-5); *(c)* the protection given by Assyria (v.6); *(d)* the distinctiveness of Assyria (vv.7-9).

a) The grandeur of Assyria, v.3

"Behold, the Assyrian was a cedar in Lebanon with fair branches, and with a shadowing shroud, and of an high stature; and his top was among the thick boughs." Similar symbolism has been used before in the book: see Chapter 17 verses 1-10. In that case, however, the "cedar" represented Jerusalem.

C.L.Feinberg is worth quoting here at length. "Because the cedars were as much as eighty feet in height and beautifully symmetrical, the Assyrian was likened to a cedar in Lebanon. Lebanon was mentioned because it was the region noted for cedars. As to literal fact neither Assyria nor Egypt was in Lebanon. By virtue of the thickly interwoven branches, the cedar afforded a forest-like shade. The top of the tree was covered with thick boughs ... All was meant to convey the idea of majesty and loftiness in nature, to be carried over into the realm of the political and governmental". The figure of a great tree is also used in the Old Testament to depict the strength and grandeur of Nebuchadnezzar. (See Daniel 4: 10-12; 20-22.)

b) The source of Assyria's strength, vv.4-5

"The waters made him great, the deep set him up on high with her rivers running round about his plants, and sent out her little rivers unto all the trees of the field. Therefore his height was exalted above all the trees of the field, and his boughs were multiplied, and his branches became long because of the multitude of the waters, when he shot forth."

Once again, C.L.Feinberg is well worth quoting at length: "Moreover, the cedar tree grew to such an unusual height because it was so profusely watered. The waters and rivers referred to the Tigris river with its branches. But figuratively Ezekiel meant that the surrounding and lesser nations contributed to Assyria's prosperity, which in turn was channelled out to the people in her sphere of influence who were on friendly terms with her. With such factors contributing to her growth and increase it was small wonder that the Assyrian Empire flourished, expanded, outstripped all of its neighbours, and was unusually magnificent". F.Gardiner concurs: "The thought is that the various surrounding and subordinate nations were nourished from the great stream of prosperity which swelled the power and wealth of Assyria".

c) The protection given by Assyria, v.6

"All the fowls of heaven made their nests in his boughs, and under his branches did all the beasts of the field bring forth their young, and under his shadow dwelt all great nations." "All the nations that surrounded Assyria in the day of her glory were granted her protection and support in some measure" (C.L.Feinberg). It will be readily noted that these words combine "the historical with the figurative" and are one of "the occasional intermixes of the real with the figurative" (Patrick Fairbairn) in the passage.

d) The distinctiveness of Assyria, vv.7-9

"Thus was he fair in his greatness, in the length of his branches: for his root was by great waters. The cedars in the garden of God could not hide him: the fir trees (generally understood to be cypresses) were not like his boughs, and the chestnut trees (generally understood to be plane-trees) were not like his branches; not any tree in the garden of God was like unto him in his beauty. I have made him fair by the multitude of his branches: so that all the trees of Eden, that were in the garden of God envied him." Attention is drawn to the following:

i) Assyria's greatness was unrivalled among the nations. In this connection we should note the references to the "garden of Eden". While the "king of Tyre" was "in Eden the garden of God" (Ezek. 28: 13) which, in all probability, refers to the heavenly paradise, Assyria was clearly located on earth. Some commentators, including Lamar E. Cooper, suggest that the expression refers to "the whole world order as initially created by God", and point out that "Assyria was the greatest nation in world history up to the point of its rise as a dominant world power". It is readily granted that this is a "further expression of its greatness by a comparison of the tree representing it with the trees of Paradise", but F.Gardiner continues with the very valid observation that "this comparison may have been suggested by the fact that the traditionary (*sic*) site of Eden was within the bounds of the Assyrian Empire". In this connection, the words "his root was by great waters" might be an allusion to the fact that "a river went out of Eden to water the garden; and from thence it was parted, and became into four heads. The name of the first is Pison ... And the name of second is Gihon ... And the name of the third river is Hiddekel (the ancient name of the Tigris): that is it which goeth toward **the east of Assyria**. And the fourth river is Euphrates" (Gen. 2: 10-14).

ii) Assyria's greatness was bestowed by the Lord. *"I have made him fair by the multitude of his branches: so that all the trees of Eden, that were in the garden of God envied him"* (v.9). We are reminded that "the most High ruleth in the kingdom of men, and giveth it to whomsoever he will" (Dan. 4: 32). The language used to describe the majesty and prowess of Assyria can be interpreted by the language used to describe Nebuchadnezzar: "The tree that thou sawest, which grew, and was strong, whose height reached unto the heaven, and the sight thereof to all the earth; whose leaves were fair, and the fruit thereof much, and in it was meat for all; under which the beasts of the field dwelt, and upon whose branches the fowls of the heaven had their habitation: It is thou, O king, that art grown and become strong: for thy greatness is grown, and reacheth unto heaven, and thy dominion to the end of the earth" (Dan. 4: 20-22). But, like Nebuchadnezzar, Assyria fell through pride. This follows:

3) VISITATION, vv.10-13

We should notice *(a)* the reason for the visitation (v.10); *(b)* the author of the visitation (v.11); *(c)* the means of the visitation (vv.11-12); *(d)* the result of the visitation (v.13).

a) The reason for judgment on Assyria, v.10

"Therefore thus saith the Lord GOD; Because thou hast lifted up thyself in height, and he hath shot up his top among the thick boughs, and his heart is lifted up in his height: I have therefore delivered him into the hand of the mighty one of the heathen; he shall surely deal with him." Once again, we must notice the 'intermix of the real with the figurative'. As we have already noticed, "Assyria's great offence was pride, as it is of so many powers and individuals today. God hates pride because it always robs Him of His rightful glory" (C.L.Feinberg). Because of her pride, God had determined to fell Assyria: over a century previously He had said, "I will punish the fruit of the stout heart of the king of Assyria, and the glory of his high looks ... Shall the axe boast itself against him that heweth therewith? or shall the saw magnify itself against him that shaketh it? As if the rod should shake itself against them that lift it up, or as the staff should lift up itself, as if it were no wood" (Isaiah 10: 12-15).

b) The author of judgment on Assyria, v.11

"***I have therefore delivered*** him into the hand of the mighty one of the heathen; he shall **surely** deal with him: **I have driven him out** for his wickedness."

c) The instrument of judgment on Assyria, vv.11-12

"I have therefore delivered him into **the hand of the mighty one of the heathen**; he shall surely deal with him: I have driven him out for his wickedness. And strangers, **the terrible of the nations** (see 30: 11), have cut him off, and have left him." The "mighty one of the heathen" is clearly Babylon. A century and a quarter before, Isaiah had predicted that the Assyrian would be "cut down ... with iron, and Lebanon shall fall by a mighty one" (Isaiah 10: 34). The proud Assyrian is described as a felled cedar of Lebanon, and it is a botanical fact that a cedar, of the pine genus, does not produce suckers. The ruin of the Assyrian would be irretrievable.

d) The result of judgment on Assyria, vv.12-13

"And strangers, the terrible of the nations, have cut him off, and have left him: upon the mountains and in all the valleys his branches are fallen, and his boughs are broken by all the rivers of the land: and all the people of the earth are gone down from his shadow, and have left him. Upon his ruin shall all the fowls of the heaven remain, and all the beasts of the field shall be upon his branches." The ruin of Assyria is described in terms of a broken shattered tree. As C.L.Feinberg observes, "Ezekiel described the great trunk of the tree as covering the land and filling the watercourses. There is something sad about the felling of a stately and majestic tree; how much more is this true when the reality represented is a mighty nation with its many people ... In spite of their previous dependence upon Assyria, the nations that viewed her fall were ready to take advantage of her ruin. Like vultures upon carrion they were prepared to make the most of the downfall of that very power which had so recently been their mainstay and reliance". F.A.Tatford concurs, although he sees the downfall of Egypt here rather than that of Assyria: "The peoples, who had found a shelter under the spreading forest monarch, naturally deserted it when its protection had gone ... The fallen trunk filled the land, but as it lay helpless, the swarms of birds descended upon it and the wild beasts found a temporary resting-place upon its remains. Birds and beasts had once taken shelter under it but, in the day of its ignominy, they contemptuously devoured it for food. Similarly, the smaller nations which had benefited from her strength and power in the day of he supremacy, took advantage of her fall to secure all they could derive from her calamity".

4) EDUCATION, v.14

The fall of Assyria was to have an educational value for the nations: "To the end that none of all the trees by the waters exalt themselves for their height, neither shoot up their top among the thick boughs, neither their trees stand up in their height, all that drink water (a poetical expression for the trees)". God's hatred of pride is seen again here: "To the end that none of all the trees by the waters exalt themselves for their height". It is the principal lesson of the oracle.

The same lesson is delivered in Zephaniah 3 verses 6-7. God's judgment on other nations should have spoken to God's people: "I have cut off the nations: their towers are desolate; I made their streets waste, that none passeth by: their cities are destroyed, so that there is no man, that there is none inhabitant. I said, Surely thou wilt fear me, thou wilt receive instruction; so their dwelling should not be cut off, howsoever I punished them: but they rose early, and corrupted all their doings". Sadly, the lesson was lost on them. We too need to learn from God's dealings with others. See Revelation 2 & 3, where the words, "He that hath an ear, let him hear what the Spirit saith unto the churches", make it clear that the address to *each* of the seven churches was to be heeded by *all* of them.

The reason why the nations should heed the lesson follows: "for they are all delivered unto death, to the nether parts of the earth, in the midst of the children of men, with them that go down to the pit". As F.A.Tatford observes, "Nations, like human beings, are mortal and have one common end, and when ... they are given over to metaphorical death, they must also - continuing the figure - descend into Sheol or the nether world".

5) REVERBERATION, vv.15-17

"Thus saith the Lord GOD; In the day when he went down to the grave I caused a mourning: I covered the deep for him, and I restrained the floods thereof, and the great waters were stayed: and I caused Lebanon to mourn for him, and all the trees of the field fainted for him. I made the nations to shake at the sound of his fall, when I cast him down to hell with them that descend into the pit: and all the trees of Eden, the choice and best of Lebanon, all that drink water, shall be comforted in the nether parts of the earth. They also went down into hell with him unto them that be slain with the sword; and they that were his arm, that dwelt under his shadow in the midst of the heathen."

All we can say is that it is better to dwell "under the shadow of the Almighty!" (Psalm 91: 1) than to dwell under the shadow of Assyria!

As C.L.Feinberg observes, "The prophet Ezekiel not only described the condition and activities of Assyria during its power and earthly existence, but he also followed the ruined power after death". The fall of Assyria reverberated around the living nations, and at the same time there was a response among the nations in Sheol.

a) The reverberation around the nations, vv.15-16

"Thus saith the Lord GOD; In the day when he went down to the grave (*sheol*) I caused a mourning: I covered the deep for him, and I restrained the floods thereof, and the great waters were stayed: and I caused Lebanon to mourn for him, and all the trees of the field fainted for him. I made the nations to shake at the sound of his fall, when I cast him down to hell with them that descend into the pit (*bar*)."

The reference to the restraint of "the floods" and drying up of "the great waters" depicts the drying up of the streams, or sources, of Assyria's prosperity. The language of earlier verses is repeated here: "the deep" is the same word as in verse 4; "floods" is the same word as "rivers" in verse 4; "great waters" is the same as "multitude of waters" in verse 5. C.L.Feinberg points out the "subtle play on words in making Lebanon, which is literally 'the white mountain', to mourn or to be made black, for such is the meaning of the Hebrew original for the verb 'mourn'". The repercussions of Assyria's fall are described in verse 16: "all the trees of the field fainted for him. I made the nations to shake at the sound of his fall". F.A.Tatford comments as follows: "Some were evidently paralysed by the event ("I restrained the floods thereof, and the great waters were stayed"), and the nations in general were overcome with fear for their own safety. If such a mighty world-power was overthrown, what hope was there for smaller countries? They were warned, as Keil says, 'of the perishable nature of all earthly greatness and of their own destruction'".

b) The repercussions in Sheol, vv.16-17

"And all the trees of Eden, the choice and best of Lebanon, all that drink water, shall be comforted in the nether parts of the earth. They also went down into hell with him unto them that be slain with the sword; and they that were his arm, that dwelt under his shadow in the midst of the heathen."

The references to "hell" (vv.16-17) should be noted. The word "hell" translates the Hebrew *sheol*. The Greek equivalent is *hades*. Both words refer to the temporary destiny of the doomed, although *sheol* is often said to mean 'the unseen state' (*Young's Concordance*).

The noblest kingdoms ("all the trees of Eden, the choice and best of Lebanon") were comforted by the fact that the fate of Assyria and her dependents (who "also went down into hell with him unto them that be slain with the sword; and they that were his arm, that dwelt under his shadow in the midst of the heathen") was "no different from their own ... There was no difference in the future of any of them" (F.A.Tatford). As C.L.Feinberg points out, the allies and confederates of Assyria in the days of her prosperity could not render any assistance in the hour of her calamity and disaster. Those "who were her support in her tyranny and were protected by her, were utterly useless in the hour of need, for they underwent the same fate".

6) APPLICATION, v.18

The lesson of Assyria's fall is now applied to Pharaoh: "To whom art thou like in glory and greatness among the trees of Eden? Yet thou shalt be thus brought down with the trees of Eden unto the nether parts of the earth: thou shalt lie in the midst of the uncircumcised with them that be slain with the sword. This is Pharaoh and all his multitude, saith the Lord GOD."

According to C.L.Feinberg, the reference to the "uncircumcised" is especially forceful because the Egyptians did practice circumcision, and were amazingly meticulous, as the pyramids show, about proper burial, so this placing of them on the level of those mentioned was the deepest disgrace possible to them. To the Egyptians those in this condition were outside the range of the civilised world". F.A.Tatford concurs, adding that "those killed in warfare and buried indiscriminately without funeral rites were regarded as uncircumcised and, therefore, permanently excluded from blessing. Despite her former eminence, Egypt was to lie in Sheol by the side of the lowliest, the dishonoured, the ostracised and the criminal. There was no distinction in death. The Egyptians paid scrupulous attention to burial, but they were to be submitted to utter disgrace".

How thankful we are that whereas God "cast him (the Assyrian) down to hell with them that descend into the pit" (v.16), the Lord's people today can say, "For we know that if our earthly house of this tabernacle were dissolved, we have a building of God, an house not made with hands, eternal in the heavens", and that "we are confident ... and willing rather to be absent from the body, and to be present with the Lord" (2 Cor. 5: 1, 8). The bodies of believers who 'fall asleep' before the return of the Lord Jesus are "sown in corruption" but they will be "raised in incorruption": they are "sown in dishonour" but they will be "raised in glory": they are "sown in weakness", but they will be "raised in power" (1 Cor. 15: 42-43). Believers have been predestinated "to be conformed to the image of his Son, that he might be the firstborn among many brethren" (Rom. 8: 29). As preachers sometimes say:

'God is going to fill heaven with people like His Son!'

EZEKIEL CHAPTER 32

This chapter contains the sixth and seventh oracles against Egypt, and concludes the 'foreign nations' section of the prophecy. The first of the two oracles (vv.1-16) was delivered to Ezekiel "in the twelfth year, in the twelfth month, in the first day of the month (said to be March 585 BC)" (v.1), and the second (vv.17-32) "in the twelfth year, in the fifteenth day of the month", so there was a fortnight's interval between them.

Both oracles take the form of a lamentation, and we should remember that the fall of our fellow-men is not the cause for exultation. The first of the two oracles here commences, "Son of man, take up a lamentation for Pharaoh king of Egypt", and concludes, "This is the lamentation wherewith they shall lament her: the daughters of the nations shall lament her: they shall lament for her, even for Egypt, and for all her multitude, saith the Lord GOD" (vv.2, 16). The second oracle commences, "Son of man, wail for the multitude of Egypt", and concludes, "he (Pharaoh) shall be laid in the midst of the uncircumcised with them that are slain with the sword, even Pharaoh and all his multitude, saith the Lord GOD" (vv.17-18, 32).

The two oracles may be entitled: **(1) the visible downfall of Egypt** (vv.1-16): "I will therefore spread out my net over thee with a company of many people; and they shall bring thee up in my net ... and I will fill the beasts of the whole earth with thee" (vv.3-4)"; **(2) the unseen downfall of Egypt** (vv.17-32): "Son of man, wail for the multitude of Egypt, and cast them down, even her, and the daughters of the famous nations, unto the nether parts of the earth, with them that go down into the pit" (v.18).

1) THE VISIBLE DOWNFALL OF EGYPT, vv.1-16

"And it came to pass in the twelfth year, in the twelfth month, in the first day of the month, that the word of the LORD came unto me, saying, Son of man, take up a lamentation for Pharaoh king of Egypt" (vv.1-2). As noted above, the oracle concludes as it commences: "they shall lament for her, even for Egypt, and for all her multitude, saith the Lord GOD" (v.16).

These verses are easily divided: *(a) the destruction of Egypt* (vv.1-10); *(b) the destroyer of Egypt* (vv.11-16).

a) The destruction of Egypt, vv.1-10

We should notice the following in these verses: *(i)* the dominance of Egypt (v.2)*; (ii)* the downfall of Egypt (vv.3-6); *(iii)* the darkness in Egypt (vv.7-8); *(iv)* the dismay over Egypt (vv.9-10).

i) **The dominance of Egypt, v.2.** "Thou art like a young lion of the nations, and thou art as a whale in the seas: and thou camest forth with thy rivers, and troublest the waters with thy feet, and fouledst their rivers." Pharaoh is addressed in two ways:

- "Thou art like a young lion of the nations." On land, Pharaoh was like a lion. It has been noted that the Egyptian sphinx was a lion-bodied creature.

- "Thou art as a whale in the sea." In the sea, Pharaoh was like a sea-monster (*tannin*). F.Gardiner suggests that the 'sea-monster' (or crocodile) is contrasted here with the lion. He translates: "Thou wast compared to a young lion of the nations" (i.e. their leader and glory); "but thou wast (really) like a crocodile in the seas" stirring up and fouling the rivers, the sources of their prosperity.

As noted when considering Chapter 29, the word *tannin* occurs in several passages in the Old Testament and is variously translated: "whale" (Job 7: 12); "sea monster" (Lam. 4: 3): 1); "dragon" (e.g. Isaiah 27: 1; 51: 9; Jer. 51: 34); "serpent" (Exodus 7: 9-12). Commentators are unanimous in concluding that the "great monster" here is the crocodile, which "was worshipped by the Egyptians, and was a symbol on late Egyptian coins" (C.L.Feinberg). The words "and thou camest forth with thy rivers, and troublest the waters with thy feet, and fouledst their rivers" are said to refer to "the manner of the crocodile to plunge suddenly into a stream and stir up the mud", illustrating the way in which "the Egyptian king disturbed the even tenor of the life stream of the nations around him" (C.L.Feinberg). Although some commentators think otherwise - even to extent of suggesting a reference to mythology - it seems better to stay with the crocodile in interpreting the verses which follow. So:

ii) **The downfall of Egypt, vv.3-6.** "Thus saith the Lord GOD; I will therefore spread out *my net* over thee with a company of many people; and they shall bring thee up in *my net*. Then will I leave thee upon the land. I will cast thee forth upon the open field, and will cause all the fowls of the heaven to remain upon thee, and I will fill the beasts of the whole earth with thee. And I will lay thy flesh upon the mountains, and fill the valleys with thy height. I will also water with thy blood the land wherein thou swimmest, even to the mountains; and the rivers shall be full of thee." We should notice at least four things here:

- **Caught in the net:** "*they* shall bring thee up in *my* net" (v.3). It has been suggested that lions are caught in nets, and sea-creatures with hooks, but the words "bring thee up in my net" ('haul you up in my dragnet', F.A.Tatford) seem to rule out a lion. We'll stay with a crocodile!

- **Cast on to the land:** "Then will *I* leave thee upon the land." Leaving any sea-monster on land would render it powerless. Egypt would be ensnared by its enemies, and become nothing more than a carcase (v.4a).

- **Consumed by predators:** "*I* ... will cause all the fowls of the heaven to remain upon thee, and *I* will fill the beasts of the whole earth with thee" (v4b). As John B.Taylor observes, "he ('the king of Egypt', v.2) is going to be ensnared and hauled out on to dry ground, where his carcase will be a prey for the scavengers of the earth and sky".

- **Comprehensively destroyed**. "And *I* will lay thy flesh upon the mountains, and fill the valleys with thy height. *I* will also water with thy blood the land wherein thou swimmest, even to the mountains; and the rivers shall be full of thee" (vv.5-6). Egypt's "mountains ... valleys ... rivers" would all see divine judgment. The prediction, "I will also water with thy blood the land wherein thou swimmest, even to the mountains; and the rivers shall be full of thee", might well allude to the first plague on Egypt when "the waters that were in the river ... were turned to blood" (Ex. 7: 20-21). F.Gardiner suggests that watering "with thy blood the land wherein thou swimmest" refers to "the land of the inundations of the Nile, now to be watered with blood".

iii) **The darkness in Egypt, vv.7-8.** "And when *I* shall put thee out ('extinguish', margin), *I* will cover the heaven, and make the stars thereof dark; *I* will cover the sun with a cloud, and the moon shall not give her light. All the bright lights of heaven will *I* make dark over thee, and set darkness upon thy land, saith the Lord God". (Compare Isaiah 13: 10). This might well allude to the plague of darkness centuries before: "And Moses stretched forth his hand toward heaven; and there was a thick darkness in all the land of Egypt three days" (Ex. 10: 22). Another day will dawn in world history when "the sun" will "be darkened, and the moon shall not give her light, and the stars shall fall from heaven, and powers of the heavens shall be shaken" (Matt. 24: 29). Men will then "see the Son of man coming in the clouds of heaven with power and great glory" (Matt 24: 30). (See also Joel 2: 10.)

iv) The dismay over Egypt, vv.9-10. "*My* net" (v.3) is followed by "*my* sword" (v.10): "*I* will also vex the hearts of many people, when *I* shall bring thy destruction among the nations, into the countries which thou hast not known. Yea, *I* will make many people amazed at thee, and their kings shall be horribly afraid for thee, when *I* shall brandish *my* sword before them, and they shall tremble at every moment, every man for his own life, in the day of thy fall". The meaning is clear: "the combination of captivity and the sword is enough to make the nations fear for their own lives in case they are the next victims due for judgment" (John B. Taylor). As F.A. Tatford observes, "If Babylon could thus destroy such a mighty power, what hope had they if the enemy's forces suddenly swung against them?"

The "sword of the king of Babylon" (v.11) is, at the same time, God's sword (v.10). The phrase "I will" is frequently repeated, showing again that God accomplishes His purposes through men. This brings us to:

b) The destroyer of Egypt, vv.11-16

In these verses we should notice *(i)* the identification of the destroyer (v.11); *(ii)* the implementation of destruction (vv.12-16).

i) The identification of the destroyer, v.11. "For thus saith the Lord GOD: The sword of the king of Babylon shall come upon thee."

ii) The implementation of destruction, vv.12-16. "By the swords of the mighty will I cause the multitude to fall, the terrible of the nations, all of them: and they shall spoil the pomp of Egypt, and all the multitude thereof shall be destroyed." Note the expressions: "the swords of the mighty" and "the terrible of the nations". For the words, "terrible of the nations", see Chapter 31 verse 12: "And strangers, the terrible of the nations, have cut him (Pharaoh) off". We should notice the following

- "I will ***destroy***", verse 13. "I will destroy all the beasts thereof from beside the great waters; neither shall the foot of man trouble them any more, nor the hoofs of beasts trouble them". So great will be the slaughter and devastation that "the waters will be unruffled by the foot of man or the hoof of beast" (J.B.Taylor)

- "I will make their waters ***deep***", verse 14. "Then will I make their waters deep ('clear', JND), and cause their rivers to run like oil, saith the Lord GOD". According to C.L.Feinberg, the words "I make their waters clear" are, literally, 'make their waters to settle'. That is, with the settling of the mud the water would clear, alluding to verse 2: "thou camest forth with thy rivers, and troublest the waters with thy feet, and fouledst their rivers". In this context, the words, "cause thy rivers to run like oil" evidently mean that Egypt would no longer stir up trouble and strife as it had done in the past.

- "I shall make the land of Egypt ***desolate***", verse 15. "When I shall make the land of Egypt desolate ... when I shall smite all them that dwell therein, then shall they know that I am the LORD". That is, they will know that "God is the Ruler of history, and history is the vindication of His character" (quoted by F.Cundick).

- "The country shall be ***destitute***", verse 15. "When ... the country shall be destitute of that whereof it was full, when I shall smite all them that dwell therein, then shall they know that I am the LORD". See above.

As already noted, the oracle ends as it begins: "This is the lamentation, wherewith they shall lament her: the daughters of the nations shall lament: they shall lament for her, even for Egypt, and for all her multitude, saith the Lord GOD" (v.16). We should notice the reference to the professional 'wailing women'. (See Jeremiah 9: 17-18.)

2) *THE UNSEEN DOWNFALL OF EGYPT, vv.17-32*

"It came to pass also in the twelfth year, in the fifteenth day of the month. That the word of the LORD came unto me ..." (v.17). No actual month is given, but, presumably, the oracle was also delivered to Ezekiel in the twelfth month (see v.1).

The second oracle describes the spiritual end of Egypt. Destruction with the sword (vv.1-16) is followed by consignment to Sheol. We must listen carefully to C.L.Feinberg on the subject of Sheol. "This portion is a remarkable confirmation that beings have existence and identity after this life. It also proves beyond a shadow of doubt that after death destiny is fixed; there is no opportunity given to reverse decisions made in life". It will be noted that the passage does not deal with the after-life in any detail. It deals solely with nations which had "caused terror in the land of the living" (vv.23, 24, 26)

We should notice: *(a)* Egypt's consignment to Sheol (vv.18-21); *(b)* the nations confined in Sheol (vv.22-30); *(c)* Pharaoh's comfort in Sheol (vv.31-32).

a) Egypt's consignment to Sheol, vv.18-21

"Son of man, wail for the multitude of Egypt, and cast them down, even her, and the daughters of the famous nations, unto the nether ('lower', JND) parts of the earth, with them that go down to the pit. Whom dost thou pass in beauty? Go down, and be thou laid with the uncircumcised" (vv.18-19). The words, "Whom dost thou pass in beauty? Go down, and be thou laid with the uncircumcised" tell us that "whatever excellence Egypt may have imagined herself to possess would be as nothing, for her body would be consigned to the grave with all the rest" (C.L.Feinberg). The words, "daughters of the famous nations", evidently refer to Egypt's satellites. The word "pit" (*bor*) means exactly what it says. It is sometimes rendered "well". The word occurs again in verses 24, 25 and 29 and, additionally, in verse 23 where it is rendered "graves". The language here is striking: Ezekiel was told "cast them down, even her, and the daughters of the famous nations, unto the nether parts of the earth, with them that go down to the pit". The question may well be asked, 'How could Ezekiel possibly "cast them down … unto the nether parts of the earth?"'. The answer must lie in the power of God's word through Ezekiel. What Ezekiel said would happen. In the words of C.L.Feinberg, "God's word is alive with power, so Ezekiel's utterance was said to accomplish what God wills".

Egypt would be defeated and destroyed: "They shall fall in the midst of them that are slain by the sword; she is delivered to the sword; draw her and all her multitudes (meaning, 'draw her away to her deserved judgment'). The strong among the mighty (the other nations in Sheol) shall speak to him (that is, speak to Pharaoh) out of the midst of hell (*sheol*) with them that help him; they are gone down, they lie uncircumcised, slain with the sword" (vv.20-21). F.A.Tatford calls this, "a mocking welcome", and C.L.Feinberg describes it as "taunting him because now he is on the same plane as they".

b) The nations confined in Sheol, vv. 22-30

They are *(i)* Asshur (vv.22-23); *(ii)* Elam (vv.24-25); *(iii)* Meshech and Tubal (vv.26-28); *(iv)* Edom (v.29); *(v)* The princes of the north, and the Zidonians (v.30). Note that these peoples are described as "uncircumcised" (vv.21, 24, 25, 26, 27, 28, 29, 30). See also verse 32. F.Gardiner states that the word is "simply used as the ordinary phrase for the heathen". C.L.Feinberg observes that "Though Semitic peoples generally practiced circumcision, these are described as uncircumcised to bear out the concept of their pollution and defilement". Perhaps, too, to emphasise that they were strangers from the covenants of promise" (Eph. 2: 12). It should be said, that while the passage employs "symbolic imagery and was not intended literally" (F.A.Tatford), there can be no doubt that the symbolism conveys dreadful reality.

i) **Asshur, vv.22-23.** "Asshur is there and all her company: his graves are round about him: all of them slain, fallen by the sword: whose graves are set in the sides of the pit, and her company is round about her grave: all of them slain, fallen by the sword, which caused terror in the land of the living." It is significant that Assyria (Asshur) should be named first. Doubtless this is because she is described so minutely in the previous chapter, and because her fall was still a recent event in world history. The Assyrians certainly "caused terror in the land of the living" (v.23). Their cruelty and mercilessness were well-known, and it is not therefore without significance that they had "fallen by the sword" (divine retribution) and were found "in the sides of the pit", which F.A.Tatford calls "the deepst part of the pit". The terror they caused "in the land of the living" was justly recompensed.

Christopher Wright puts it rather vividly: "When the roll is called down yonder, the most significant name on the list is undoubtedly Assyria. It was still a very fresh memory in Ezekiel's own generation that Assyria *had spread terror in the land of the living*. But that's all it was now – a memory. Assyria was dead and buried. The message was ominously clear: if that was the fate of proud Assyria, nothing better could be expected for Egypt - or any of Assyria's successors".

ii) **Elam, vv.24-25.** "There is Elam and all her multitude round about her grave, all of them slain, fallen by the sword, which are gone down uncircumcised into the nether parts of the earth, which caused their terror in the land of the living: yet have they borne their shame with them that go down to the pit. They have set her bed in the midst of the slain with her multitude: her graves are round about him: all of them uncircumcised, slain by the sword: though their terror was caused in the land of the living, yet have they borne their shame with them that go down to the pit: he is put in the midst of them that be slain." It is to be noted that the Elamites "have ... borne their shame with them that go down to the pit".

Note the repetition: "though their terror was caused in the land of the living" (see v.23). According to C.L.Feinberg, and others, "the repetition of phrases throughout the section emphasises the dirge-like monotony".

Elam, an ancient kingdom (Gen 14.1), lay "two hundred miles east of Babylon and west of the Tigris River" (C.L.Feinberg). It is said to have been co-extensive with the modern Iranian province of Khuzistan. Having been conquered by the Assyrians under Ashurbanipal about 640 BC (Ezra 4: 9-10), Elam regained its independence after his death, and having been later united with Media, and then Persia, contributed to the overthrow of the Babylonian empire in 540 BC. Daniel was at Shushan, which was in the Persian province of Elam.

iii) Meshech and Tubal, vv.26-28. "There is Meshech, Tubal, and all her multitude: her graves are round about him (perhaps referring to Pharaoh): all of them uncircumcised, slain by the sword, though they caused their terror in the land of the living. And they shall not lie with the mighty that are fallen of the uncircumcised, which are gone down to hell (*sheol* - the grave) with their weapons of war: and they have laid their swords under their heads, but their iniquities shall be upon their bones, though they were the terror of the mighty in the land of the living. Yea, *thou* (evidently a direct address to Pharaoh) shalt be broken in the midst of the uncircumcised, and shalt lie with them that are slain with the sword." Note, again, the repetition: "though they caused their terror in the land of the living" (vv.23, 25).

This appears to mean that the fallen warriors of Meschech and Tubal were not accorded full military honours like others (v.27). In the case of other nations, so it appears, men "laid their swords under their heads", but that availed nothing, since God laid "their iniquities ... upon their bones". But not these people. There is no common agreement on the identity of Meschech and Tubal, but it seems best to identify them with the Moschi and Tibareni, who were located between the Black and Caspian seas. They are mentioned in Ezek. 27 verse 13, and will attack Israel at the end-time (Ezek. 38: 2; 39: 1).

*iv) **Edom, v.29.*** "There is Edom, her kings, and all her princes, which with their might are laid by them that were slain by the sword: they shall lie with the uncircumcised, and with them that go down to the pit." Nothing needs to be said here about the Edomites. They were the inveterate enemies of God's people. Edom pursued "his brother with the sword, and did cast off all pity, and his anger did tear perpetually, and he kept his wrath for ever" (Amos 1: 11).

v) ***The princes of the north ... and the Zidonians, v.30****.* "There be the princes of the north, all of them, all of them, and all the Zidonians, which are gone down with the slain; with their terror they are ashamed of their might (note this); and they lie uncircumcised with them that be slain by the sword, and bear their shame with them that go down to the pit", or "ashamed of the terror which they caused through their might ... and bear their confusion with them that go down to the pit" (JND). F.A.Tatford identifies "the princes of the north" as 'the rulers of the north or Syrian states', and explains that "the Zidonians" (or Sidonians) was a generic term for the Phoenicians".

The section concludes as it commences (cp. v.18): the above peoples will be joined by Pharaoh and all his multitude (v.31). This brings us to:

c) Pharaoh's comfort in Sheol, vv.31-32

"Pharaoh shall see them, and shall be comforted over all his multitude, even Pharaoh and all his army slain by the sword, saith the Lord GOD. For I have caused my terror in the land of the living: and he shall be laid in the midst of the uncircumcised with them that are slain with he sword, even Pharaoh and all his multitude, saith the Lord GOD."

C.L.Feinberg explains this as follows: "When Pharaoh would see the great army of departed ones in Sheol, he would be comforted over his own multitude, his strange comfort coming from seeing that he was not alone in his misery and doom. His would be the dismal comfort of knowing that others were companions in his misery".

The last word in this study must belong to Christopher Wright: "Finally, as we leave Pharaoh in his dismal new residence, we may notice how climactic it is that this whole section of oracles against the nations leads to this picture of death and descent into the grave and the awful world of the dead. It provides a stark and vivid memory to carry forward into the next section of the book, which will lead our imagination through various scenes of restoration and renewal, climaxing in the glorious picture of resurrection as Ezekiel witnesses the bones of an army long dead coming back to life (37: 1-14). Israel will be restored from the grave of exile to their own land, the land of the living".

It also reminds us that "if our earthly house of this tabernacle were dissolved, we have a building of God, an house not made with hands, eternal in the heavens (2 Cor. 5: 1). We are assured that should we die before the Lord's return, our body will be 'sown' rather than buried (1 Cor. 15: 37, 42-44). Just as a dry seed produces a lovely flower, so our tired worn bodies will re-emerge as bodies of glory. We will certainly recognise one another on resurrection morning, but we will be marvelously different! The Lord Jesus will "transform our body of humiliation into conformity with his body of glory" (Phil. 3: 21, JND).

EZEKIEL CHAPTER 33

We have noted on numerous occasions during these studies that the prophecy of Ezekiel comprises four major sections: *(i)* the ruin of Judah and Jerusalem (chs.1-24); *(ii)* the retribution on surrounding nations (chs.25-32); *(iii)* the restoration of Israel (chs.33-39); *(iv)* the return of the glory of the Lord (chs.40-48).

Lamar E. Cooper is therefore correct in saying that "Chapter 33 is a turning point in the book of Ezekiel". As Patrick Fairbairn points out, Ezekiel "was not to open his mouth to Israel again till the escaped from Jerusalem's desolations came to him, as a witness that the work of judgment was completed, that **the false foundations were thoroughly swept away**". This opened the way for national restoration.

Bearing this in mind, we might have expected the chapter to have commenced with a new date, but we have to wait a short while (twenty verses) before Ezekiel writes: "And it came to pass in the twelfth year of our captivity, in the tenth month, in the fifth day of the month, that one that had escaped out of Jerusalem came unto me, saying, The city is smitten. Now the hand of the LORD was upon me in the evening, afore him that was escaped came: and had opened my mouth, until he came to me in the morning; and my mouth was opened, and I was no more dumb" (vv.21-22). This strongly suggests that it is *at this point* that the new section of the prophecy actually commences, and that the preceding verses (vv.1-20), referring to his role as a watchman, are preparatory. Perhaps, therefore, verses 1-20 are part of the message commencing with Chapter 20 verse 1, and that Chapters.24-32 are therefore a kind of parenthesis.

This was certainly the case at the beginning of Ezekiel's ministry. The prophet was told, "Son of man, I have made thee a watchman unto the house of Israel: therefore hear the word at my mouth, and give them warning from me" (3: 17-21). He was then instructed to "Arise, go forth into the plain, and

I will there talk with thee", and his ministry commenced with a further vision of "the glory of the LORD" (3: 22-23). Although his subsequent preaching was disregarded, he had faithfully warned Judah and Jerusalem of coming judgment, and it could therefore be said of him, "thou hast delivered thy soul" (3: 19, 21).

Now, at the beginning of a new phase in his ministry, Ezekiel is recommissioned as a watchman on similar terms. But his warnings would now carry added weight. Ezekiel had been faithful in his first assignment, and his warnings had become reality. Jerusalem had fallen. Now he warns again (vv.23-29). In view of the accuracy of his past warnings, would they now hear? Whatever the answer, the servant of God must be faithful. As Patrick Fairbairn points out, "But now that the worst has come, is there nothing more to be done? Has the office of heaven's watchman ceased when the cloud of heaven's vengeance has burst on the guilty? Has he no commission to speak to those who are sinking under the stroke of judgment ... Yes: and it is here that a new sphere of labour presents itself to the prophet, and that a new call comes to him to enter into it". Ezekiel 33 emphasises the responsibility entrusted to Ezekiel, and the way in which he discharged his duty as a watchman.

But there is more. "Israel and especially Judah had been victimised by the messages of the false prophets (13: 1 - 14: 23), who had predicted an imminent return to peace and glory that never came. Out of the despair of the exile (v.10), Ezekiel had the opportunity to introduce the truth about the coming Messiah, who would be a servant-shepherd, and set up a glorious new kingdom" (Lamar E. Cooper). This lies ahead in our studies.

The chapter may be divided as follows: *(1) the responsibility he carried* (vv.1-20): "O son of man, I have set thee a watchman unto the house of Israel" (v.7); *(2) the resumption of his preaching* (vv.21-29): "my mouth was opened, and I was no more dumb" (v.22); *(3) the rejection of his message* (vv.30-33): "they hear thy words, but they do them not" (v.32).

1) THE RESPONSIBILITY HE CARRIED, vv.1-20

This section of the chapter comprises two major paragraphs: *(a)* the watchman's responsibility to warn the people (vv.1-9); *(b)* the people's responsibility to heed the watchman (vv.10-20).

a) The watchman's responsibility to warn the people, vv.1-9

In these verses, the Lord reminds Ezekiel of the duties of a watchman generally (vv.1-6), and then of his duties particularly (vv.7-9).

i) A watchman's duties generally, vv.1-6. "Son of man, speak to the children of thy people, and say unto them, When I bring a sword upon the land, if the people of the land take a man of their coasts, and set him for their watchman: if when he seeth the sword come, he blow the trumpet, and warn the people; then whosoever heareth the sound of the trumpet, and taketh not warning; if the sword come, and take him away, his blood shall be upon his own head. He heard the sound of the trumpet, and took not warning; his blood shall be upon him. But he that taketh warning shall deliver his soul. But if the watchman seeth sword come, and blow not the trumpet, and the people be not warned; if the sword come, and take away any person from among them, he is taken away in his iniquity; but his blood will I require at the watchman's hand."

We have already noted (see 3: 17) that "a watchman was a city employee appointed to be a look-out from some high vantage point such as a tower or the city wall. Such an office was extremely important because the safety of the entire population rested with the watchman. If a watchman failed in his duty to warn inhabitants of the town of impending attack, he was held personally responsible for any loss" (Lamar E. Cooper). For examples, see 2 Samuel 18 verses 24-27; 2 Kings 9 verses 17-20.

We should notice the words, "When *I bring the sword* upon a land" (v.2). This refers to *any* land, not necessarily Israel. Compare Ezekiel 14 verses 12-13, "Son of man, when the land ('a land', JND) sinneth against me by trespassing grievously, then I will stretch out mine hand upon it, and will break the staff of the bread thereof, and will send famine upon it, and will cut off man and beast from it". Amongst other things, these verses indicate that God is in control of the affairs of all men, Jew and Gentile. But Ezekiel is made to feel his personal responsibility. We come therefore to:

ii) Ezekiel's duties particularly, vv.7-9. "So thou, O son of man, I have *set* thee a watchman unto the house of Israel; therefore *thou* shalt hear the word at my mouth, and warn them from me ..." F.Cundick (*The Book of Ezekiel*) puts it succinctly: "To fulfil the responsibility of this post it is

CHAPTER 33

imperative to have a good vision (like Paul and his colleagues, 1 Thess. 3: 4), a good trumpet, and a good conscience. The application to the prophet of God is clear. He who sees far into the spiritual nature and issues of affairs is alone competent to give warning. The warning note is to be no 'uncertain sound' that will mislead. Upon his soul rests a burden of responsibility which prevents his sleeping at his post, or neglecting to give the appropriate signal to save those for whom he watches".

In the words of W.H.Burnett, "God made Ezekiel a watchman to his people. As such God held him accountable to faithfully convey His word. Similarly, a great responsibility has been placed upon us, to faithfully present the Gospel, knowing that a day of accountability lies ahead. Let us heed the warning words to Ezekiel, and take our responsibility seriously, and get back to preaching an unadulterated, soul-searching Gospel, wherever and whenever possible" (*Choice Gleanings, 9th August, 2011*).

Paul, as a true watchman, was "pure from the blood of all men", and his explanation follows: "For I have not shunned to declare unto you all the counsel of God" (Acts 20: 26-27). He made it clear to the Ephesian elders that part of their work was to act as watchmen: "For I know this, that after my departing shall grievous wolves enter in among you, not sparing the flock. Also of your own selves shall men arise, speaking perverse things, to draw away disciples after them. Therefore **watch**, and remember ..." (Acts 20: 29-31). Elders are men that "watch (*agrupneo*: to be sleepless) for your souls, as they that must give account" (Heb .13: 17).

At the same time there is a sense in which we are **all** to be watchmen. Hence the injunctions, "**Watch** ye, stand fast in the faith, quit you like men, be strong" (1 Cor. 16: 13); "Therefore let us not sleep, as do others; but let us **watch** and be sober" (1 Thess. 5: 6.) (In both cases, the word "watch" translates *gregoreo*). Sadly, the watchmen in Isaiah's day were "all dumb dogs, they cannot bark; sleeping, lying down, loving to slumber" (Is. 56: 10).

Ezekiel's work as a watchman here was to warn the wicked. We should notice that unlike his first commission as a watchman, the righteous are not mentioned in this passage (compare 3: 20-21). This may be because the righteous remnant had listened, leaving only the unrighteous. "When I say unto the wicked, O wicked man, thou shalt surely die: if thou dost not speak to warn the wicked from his way, that wicked man shall die in his iniquity; but his blood will I require at thine hand. Nevertheless, if thou warn the wicked of his way to turn from it; if he do not turn from his way, he shall die in his iniquity; but thou hast delivered thy soul" (vv.8-9).

Lamar E. Cooper points out that "the responsibility of a believer in Christ is no less awesome. Once the message of salvation is entrusted to us, we are responsible and accountable to share it with those that are lost". Paul recognised this: "I am debtor both to the Greeks, and to the Barbarians; both to the wise, and the unwise" (Rom.1: 14). Paul had a deep sense of obligation. Proclaiming the Gospel to others was the discharge of a debt. He felt this deeply: "Necessity is laid upon me; yea, woe is unto me, if I preach not the gospel!" (1 Cor. 9: 16).

b) The people's responsibility to heed the watchman, vv.10-20

In these verses, the Lord deals with two complaints by His people. In the first place, they complained that salvation was unavailable (vv.10-16); in the second place, they complained that God's treatment was unequal (vv.17-20). In both cases the Lord quotes their complaint. See verses 10, 17.

i) They complained that salvation was unavailable, vv.10-16. "Thus

ye speak, saying, If our transgressions and our sins be upon us, and we pine away in them, how should we then live?" (v.10). God's people were complaining that they were pining away (literally, according to C.L.Feinberg, 'rotting') under the judgment due to their transgressions and sins, and their case was hopeless. They believed that "their doom was sealed and complete destruction awaited them" (C.L.Feinberg).

But their case was not hopeless: repentance would bring mercy: "Say unto them, As I live, saith the Lord GOD, I have no pleasure in the death of the wicked; but that the wicked turn from his way and live: turn ye, turn ye from your evil ways; for why will ye die, O house of Israel?" (v.11). The Lord had made a similar appeal before: see Chapter 18 verses 30-32: "Repent, and turn yourselves from all your transgressions; so iniquity shall not be your ruin. Cast away from you all your transgressions, whereby ye have transgressed; and make you a new heart and a new spirit: for why will ye die, O house of Israel? For I have no pleasure in the death of him that dieth, saith the Lord GOD: wherefore turn yourselves, and live ye".

CHAPTER 33

Having said "turn ye, turn ye from your evil ways; for why will ye die, O house of Israel?" (v.11), the Lord continues with a message mingling hope and warning: "The righteousness of the righteous shall not deliver him in the day of his transgression: as for the wickedness of the wicked, he shall not fall thereby in the day that he turneth from his wickedness; neither shall the righteous be able to live for his righteousness in the day that he sinneth. When I say to the righteous, that he shall surely live; if he trust to his own righteousness, and commit iniquity, all his righteousnesses shall not be remembered; but for his iniquity that he hath committed, he shall die for it. Again, when I say unto the wicked, Thou shalt surely die; if he turn from his sin, and do that which is lawful and right: if the wicked restore the pledge, give again that he had robbed, walk in the statutes of life, without committing iniquity; he shall surely live, he shall not die. None of his sins that he hath committed shall be mentioned unto him: he hath done that which is lawful and right; he shall surely live" (vv.12-16). This should be compared with Chapter 18 verses 19-32. In the words of Patrick Fairbairn, "A yearning tenderness here manifests itself, still seeking ... the return of those who survived to the way of peace. But with that tenderness, what a stern and unflinching holiness! There can be no relaxation of abatement mentioned in respect of this, not even amidst the moanings of pain and cries of distress which arose from the people"

It should be pointed out that although there are points of similarity, these verses are not concerned with the eternal salvation of the soul. This chapter cannot be used to support the suggestion that a person can be saved and then lost. In the words of C.L.Feinberg, "it is imperative to stress" that the Lord is "speaking of a judgment on this side of the grave, and not of judgment in an eschatological or final sense". The words "live" and "die" are used literally, and refer to this life. It should also be said that "God's law requires continued, not sporadic, obedience to its precepts" (C.L.Feinberg). This is clear from verses 15-16 where the expression "walk in the statutes of life" refers to Leviticus 18 verse 5: "Ye shall therefore keep my statutes, and my judgments: which if a man do, he shall live in them". Turning now to the words, "all his righteousnesses shall not be remembered; but for his iniquity that he hath committed, he shall die for it" (v.13), it is worth remembering that "the reference is not to a temporary lapse, but to a persistent choice of evil which changes the course of a man's life" (John P.Taylor, commenting on 18: 21-29).

- **Manasseh** furnishes us with an example of a man who began wickedly, but turned from his wickedness: "And when he was in affliction, he besought the Lord his God, and humbled himself greatly before the God of his fathers, and prayed unto him: and he was intreated of him, and heard his supplication, and brought him again to Jerusalem into his kingdom. Then Manasseh knew that the Lord he was God. Now after this he built a wall without the city of David ... And he took away the strange gods ... and all the altars that he had built ... And he repaired the altar of the Lord" (2 Chron. 33:11-16).

- **Joash and Uzziah** furnish us with examples of men who began righteously, but turned from their righteousness. Joash "did that which was right in the sight of the LORD all the days of Jehoiada the priest", but having hearkened to his apostate princes he became idolatrous and was eventually assassinated by his own servants (read 2 Chron. 24). Uzziah "was marvellously helped, till he was strong. But when he was strong, his heart was lifted up to his destruction: for he transgressed against the LORD his God" (read 2 Chron. 26).

While the arguments in verses 11-16 fully answer the complaint that God's people were in a hopeless position, this was not the case - they were not in a hopeless position - for repentance would bring mercy. The passage also answers the second complaint:

ii) **They complained that God's treatment was unequal, vv.17-20**. "Yet the children of thy people say, The way of the Lord is not equal ... Yet ye say, The way of the Lord is not equal" (vv.17, 20). C.L.Feinberg, as usual, is most helpful here: "Because many in Israel did not comprehend God's principles of operation, they blamed Him for the calamities that had overtaken them, complaining that His moral dealings were not equitable". Feinberg continues: "How often we hear unthinking men accuse God of unfairness. Actually, they were being judged for their own sins. As in every case where the Lord's justice was questioned, Ezekiel was quick to vindicate God's dealings. When sinful man sits in judgment upon God, there is immediate evidence of the partiality and unfairness of his own actions".

There was nothing 'unequal' about God's dealings with Israel: "When the righteous turneth from his righteousness, and committeth iniquity, he shall even die thereby. But if the wicked turn from his wickedness, and do that which is lawful and right. He shall live thereby. Yet ye say, The way of the Lord is not equal. O ye house of Israel, I will judge you every one after his ways" (vv.18-20). There is nothing 'unequal' about that! God's mercy towards the repentant sinner, and judgment upon those who turned from righteousness, proclaimed His righteousness and equity. It disproved their accusation that "The way of the Lord is not equal". He was both righteous and merciful: they were totally unrighteous: their ways were "unequal" (18: 29).

2) THE RESUMPTION OF HIS PREACHING, vv.21-29

In these verses we should notice: *(a)* Ezekiel's mouth (vv.21-22); *(b)* Ezekiel's message (vv.23-29).

a) Ezekiel's mouth, vv.21-22

Having reminded Ezekiel of his responsibilities as a watchman, the new phase in his ministry commences: "And it came to pass in the twelfth year of our captivity, in the tenth month, in the fifth day of the month, that one that had escaped out of Jerusalem came unto me, saying, The city is smitten. Now the hand of the Lord was upon me in the evening, afore he that was escaped came; and had opened my mouth, until he came to me in the morning ('against his coming to me in the morning', JND): and my mouth was opened, and I was no more dumb" (vv.21-22). The sword (v.2) had been unsheathed. God had made His last appeal to the city, and judgment had now fallen. Two matters arise: *(i)* the dating involved *(ii)* the dumbness involved.

i) **The dating involved.** Jerusalem fell "in the eleventh year of our captivity, in the fourth month, the ninth day of the month" (Jer. 39: 2; 52: 5-7; 2 Kings 25: 2-4), but the messenger (or messengers if the words "one that had escaped" are collective) did not arrive at Tel-abib until "the twelfth year of our captivity, in the tenth month, in the fifth day of the month", that is, around eighteen months later. This seems a long time for a five hundred mile journey, especially as it only took Ezra and his party four months to complete (Ezra 7: 9), and has been variously explained. As noted in connection with Chapter 24 verses 25-27, "the Syriac version and some Hebrew manuscripts read eleventh instead of twelfth year, which would allow six months rather than a year and a half for the news of Jerusalem's fall to reach the exiles, and many accept this date" (C.L.Feinberg) But explanations of this type are not completely satisfactory, and F.Gardiner reasons that approximately a year and half could well have passed before Ezekiel received "full and circumstantial details", not from a man who has 'escaped to tell the tale' in the usual sense, but from one of the men who had arrived as a captive from Jerusalem in the group of slow-moving exiles described in Jeremiah 52 verse 15. It has also been suggested that while the fall of Jerusalem is dated by the Spring New Year (Abib), the arrival of the escapee in Tel-Abib is dated by the Hebrew New Year, which began with Tishri, the seventh month on the 'Abib' calendar. While the calculation (after a scribbling on pieces of paper) does give a period for the journey of around six months, it all looks rather suspect, even though F.A.Tatford calls it "more feasible" than the other suggestions!

ii) **The dumbness involved**. Ezekiel had been told "shall it not be in the day when I take from them their strength, the joy of their glory, the desire of their eyes ... that he that escapeth in that day shall come unto thee, to cause thee to hear it with thine ears? In that day shall thy mouth be opened to him which is escaped, and thou shalt speak, and be no more dumb" (24: 25-27). This dumbness had been imposed upon him at the beginning of his ministry: "I will make thy tongue cleave to the roof of thy mouth, that thou shalt be dumb, and shalt not be to them a reprover: for they are a rebellious house. But when I speak with thee, I will open thy mouth, and thou shalt say unto them, Thus saith the Lord God ..." (3: 26-27).

In this connection, it is worth remembering that while it could be said that although the voice of Ezekiel was silent, his actions were louder than words, this is evidently *not* the explanation. Ezekiel was *not* completely dumb. (See, for example, 11: 16, 17; 14: 4; 17: 2, 12; 20: 3.) It is therefore better to understand the prophet's silence with reference to the command, "thou ... shalt *not* be to them as a *reprover*". The word "reprover" means, literally, 'a man of litigation' (C.J.H.Wright). He would not act as an arbitrator or a mediator: his ministry would be purely judicial, that is, until his mouth was opened as recorded here.

b) Ezekiel's message, vv.23-29

We should notice that verses 23-29 refer to the survivors of the downfall of Jerusalem, and reveal what was happening in Judaea, whereas verses 30-33 refer to the exiles in Tel-abib, and tell us what was happening among the exiles there.

CHAPTER 33

As noted above, verses 23-29 are addressed to those who survived the downfall of Jerusalem. We should notice: *(i)* the claim asserted (v.24); *(ii)* the claim examined (vv.25-26); *(iii)* the claim answered (vv.27-29).

i) **Their claim asserted, v.24.** "Son of man, they that inhabit the wastes of the land of Israel speak, saying, Abraham was one, and he inherited the land: but we are many; the land is given us for inheritance." It is saddening to note that even after the final capture of Jerusalem, with all the attendant horrors, God's word was still unheeded. There was still no repentance. The people left in Judah (see Jeremiah chs.40-42) wanted the blessings of Abraham without the faith of Abraham. As F.Cundick observes, "Their conduct was inspired by a religious infatuation which distorted the meaning of both the origin and title-deeds of the children of Israel. They infer that God could re-people the land through them, despite the smallness of their numbers, and so repeat the miracle that He had performed with Abraham and his barren consort. See Isaiah 51 verse 2. They reason that they have a right to the land, and mean to keep it!" ... At the time when claim was made to these "rights", these men were guilty of the breach of ceremonial, civil and moral laws (see vv.25-26). To them the words of our Lord may be applied: If ye were Abraham's children, ye would do the works of Abraham, (John 8: 39). F.Cundick continues: "No form of enthusiasm will avail us if we bypass the obedience required by God".

ii) **Their claim examined, vv.25-26.** The examination discloses their moral unsuitability to inherit the land, and ends with the question, "and shall ye possess the land?" (v.26). Examination revealed the following: "Ye eat with the blood, and lift up your eyes toward your idols, and shed blood: and shall ye possess the land? Ye stand upon your sword, ye work abomination, and ye defile every one his neighbour's wife: and shall ye possess the land?"

The law required that the blood of animals slaughtered for food should be drained away completely. (See, for example, Lev. 17: 10-14; 19: 26; Deut. 12: 23.) The lessons of the blood were so distinctive that it was *always* to be connected in their thoughts with *atonement.* Idolatry persisted - even in Egypt (see Jer. 44: 24-25). They certainly "shed blood": see Jeremiah 41 verses 1-3. According to F.Cundick, the words "Ye stand upon your sword" probably mean "that they resorted to guerilla tactics to live and avenge themselves of the enemy". All this, plus their immorality, led to the self-answering question, "and shall ye possess the land?" The faith and obedience of Abraham (v.24) were conspicuously absent. But not for ever. See Chapter 36 verses 16-38.

iii) ***Their claim answered, vv.27-29.*** Their claim would be answered with judgment. "Thus saith the Lord GOD; As I live, surely they that are in the wastes shall fall by the sword, and him that is in the open field will I give to the beasts to be devoured, and they that be in the forts and in the caves shall die of the pestilence. For I will lay the land most desolate, and the pomp of her strength shall cease; and the mountains of Israel shall be desolate, that none shall pass through. Then shall they know that I am the LORD, when I have laid the land most desolate because of all their abominations which they have committed." This refers, not to the fall of Jerusalem, which had already taken place, but to the final desolation of the land by the Chaldeans. "All must be reduced to the condition of a howling wilderness, as it really was, that the new hope for Israel might spring from another and better root, and that the people might know how impossible it was to attain to blessing from God without first separating from sin" (Patrick Fairbairn). Judgment would be comprehensive: none will escape whether found "in the wastes ... in the open field ... in the forts and caves". The mountains of Israel would be "desolate", but not for ever. See Chapter 36 verses 1-15.

3) THE REJECTION OF HIS MESSAGE, vv.30-33

As noted above, these verses refer to the exiles in Tel-abib, amongst whom Ezekiel lived. There had been a sea-change in their attitude (at least, externally). Whereas, formerly, Ezekiel knew what it was like to live amongst "briers and thorns", not to mention "scorpions" (1: 6), he had suddenly attained popularity. F.A.Tatford puts it like this: "The fate of Jerusalem had at last impressed the exiles with the fact that Ezekiel's predictions were not mere nothings. Their prejudice against him had melted. Their interest and curiosity had been awakened, and they discussed the matter between themselves. They congregated in small groups in the shadow of the walls or in the alleys of the city, and in the doorways of their houses. There was no evidence of contrition or deep desire to know the divine will. Rather were they curious to know what else the prophet had to say. They encouraged each other to go and hear what further message he had". The Lord made sure that Ezekiel was not carried away by his popularity!! As F.Cundick observes, "Persecution brings its sorrows, but popularity has its subtle ensnarement". But not in this case!

CHAPTER 33

So we read: "Also, thou son of man, the children of thy people still are talking against thee ('keep talking of thee', JND) by the walls and in the doors of the houses, and speak one to another, every one to his brother, saying, Come, I pray you, and hear what is the word that cometh forth from the LORD. And they come unto thee as the people cometh ('as a people cometh' JND), and they sit before thee as my people, and they hear thy words, **but they will not do them**: for with their mouth they shew much love, but their heart goeth after their covetousness" (vv.30-31). We should note the discrepancy between hearing and doing ("they **hear** thy words, but they will not **do** them") and the discrepancy between their mouths and their hearts ("with their **mouth** they shew much love, but their **heart** goeth after their covetousness"). It all reminds us that "the LORD seeth not as man seeth; for man looketh on the outward appearance, but the LORD looketh on the heart" (1 Sam. 16: 7). God knew their hearts.

Very clearly, the exiles in Tel-abib were just not taking the prophet seriously. It seems more than likely that "all they saw in events was the possibility of greater scope in commerce" (F.Cundick). See verse 31, "their heart goeth after their covetousness". In the meantime, Ezekiel was merely an object of curiosity: "And, lo, thou art unto them as a very lovely song of one that hath a pleasant voice, and can play well on an instrument: for they hear thy words, **but they do them not**" (v.32). They listened respectfully - "they sit before thee as my people, and they hear thy words" - but without conviction. They had no sense of sin, and no awakened conscience. In the words of F.A.Tatford, "They spoke respectfully and admiringly of the prophet, and showed apparent esteem. Yet their minds were primarily occupied with their possessions and the conduct of their business affairs. They were complimentary about Ezekiel's discourse and diction, and about the beauty of his language. They listened to him as one would listen to an entertainer, more obsessed by the music of his voice than with the content of his message. While they sub-consciously heard what he had to say, they had no intention of putting it into effect in their lives". James would have approved. See James 1 verses 22-25.

It could be well said of the exiles, as it had been said of the nation generally, "this people draw near me with their mouth, and with their lips do honour me, but have removed their heart far from me" (Isaiah 29: 13). Nothing changed in seven hundred years. See Matthew 15 verses 7-8. The words of the Lord Jesus can certainly be applied to these people, "Not every one that saith unto me, Lord, Lord, shall enter into the kingdom of heaven; but he that doeth the will of my Father which is in heaven" (Matt. 7: 21). The exiles, who "come ... sit ... and hear thy words, but they do them not" have their counterpart in the foolish builder described by the Lord Jesus: "And every one that heareth these sayings of mine, and doeth them not, shall be likened unto a foolish man, which built his house upon the sand; and the rain descended, and the floods came, and the winds blew, and beat upon that house; and it fell: and great was the fall of it" (Matt. 7: 26-27).

The 'foolish man' was faced with his folly when the test came, and the Jewish exiles would be faced with their folly when Ezekiel's preaching was fulfilled: "And when this cometh to pass (lo, it will come), then shall they know that a prophet hath been among them" (v.33). In context, this refers to the final desolation of Judaea. See verses 27-29. Whatever the response of the people at the time, Ezekiel could be sure that God would vindicate his faithful preaching: "then shall they know that a prophet hath been among them". Ezekiel was told this at the beginning of his ministry: see Chapter 2 verse 5. The false prophets had no such assurance. The accuracy of God's word, faithfully proclaimed, by His servants will be demonstrated for all to see. God's word cannot fail: "lo, it will come".

EZEKIEL CHAPTER 34

As already noted, Chapter 33 introduces the third section of the prophecy, in which the ruin of Judah and Jerusalem (chs.1-24) and the retribution on surrounding nations (chs.25-32) give place to the restoration of Israel (chs.33-39).

It is significant that the prophecies in Chapters 34-39 were not uttered until judgment had fallen and "*the false foundations were thoroughly swept away*" (Patrick Fairbairn). But even this did not quite complete the work of divine judgment. The survivors in Judah laboured under the delusion that they had been left to repopulate the land, only to learn that all they could expect was the complete desolation of Judah (33: 23-29). Their moral condition did not correspond in the slightest to the faith and obedience of their forefather Abraham. The exiles in Chaldea were no better (33: 30-33). They paid lip-service to Ezekiel's preaching, but "their heart goeth after their covetousness" (33: 31). The final desolation of Judah would be proof "that a prophet hath been among them" (33: 33). This would open the way for national restoration.

But the restoration of Israel has still not taken place. The reason is clear: the nation is *still* in this position. A remnant did return from Chaldea, and the land was repopulated, but only under the heel of foreign powers. The nation is now in part-possession of the land, but "Jerusalem shall be trodden down of the Gentiles, until the times of the Gentiles be fulfilled" (Luke 21: 24). The final phase of this period is yet to be fulfilled (Zech.14: 1-3), and then will commence the glorious era described in the final chapters of this prophecy. In a very real sense, we are still poised at the end of Ezekiel 33. But the following chapters will be shortly fulfilled. When God deals finally with His people in judgment (see Jer. 30: 7-9), the 'golden age' for Israel will commence. The millennial kingdom will be established.

The foundation of such marvellous improvement in the affairs of God's people will be their cleansing and repentance, and, in Patrick Fairbairn's words, "that position being laid down as the first preliminary to a better future, the way now opened itself for the promise of another - the appointment of a good shepherd, one who should be emphatically the good shepherd, to rule over and feed them, in the room of the false ones, who had but sought their own interests and oppressed and ruined the flock".

But there is more. Since the past "shepherds of Israel" (v.2) were their kings, restored Israel must have a king - a shepherd-king. This is dealt with here. But restored Israel must be free from fear of occupation by her neighbours, and this is dealt with in Chapter 35. Restored Israel must also have a land, and this is dealt with in Chapter 36. Restored Israel must also be acceptable to God, and this is also dealt with in Chapter 36. Restored Israel must also have national life and national unity, and this is dealt with in Chapter 37. We can go further. Restored Israel must have security, and this is dealt with in Chapters 38-39. Then restored Israel must have a temple, and this is dealt with, together with other related matters, in Chapters 40-48.

Patrick Fairbairn rightly observes that "the chapter falls naturally into two parts; in the first of which the misrule of the false shepherds is described, with the fatal results to which it had led; and in the second, the gracious interposition of God, to undo the evils that had arisen from the presidency under which the people had been placed, and set over them one whose benign and careful superintendence would ensure the best and most lasting good". It has been said that God, like a master jeweller, sets His brightest gems against a dark background. Ezekiel brings before us the perfect Shepherd (vv.11-16, 23-31) against the background of imperfect shepherds (vv.1-10). As C.L.Feinberg points out, "The passage presents a vivid contrast between Israel's shepherds in the past and the Shepherd of Israel of the future, with the history of the nation and their bright future given under the allegory of a shepherd and a flock". It should be said at this juncture that a parallel passage is found in Jeremiah 23 verses 1-8.

There can be no doubt that a great deal of New Testament ministry on the subject of caring for the flock of God flows from this very chapter. The passage contains salutary lessons for all who have pastoral responsibilities.

Having noted the two major sections of the chapter, the passage may be further divided as follows: *(1)* the condemnation of Israel's shepherds (vv.1-10): "Woe be to the shepherds of Israel that do feed themselves! Should not the shepherds feed the flocks?" (v.2); **(2)** the care of the divine shepherd (vv.11-16): "I will feed my flock, and will cause them to lie down, saith the Lord GOD" (v.15); **(3)** the conflict within the flock (vv.17-22): "ye have thrust with the side and with shoulder, and pushed all the diseased with your horns, till ye have scattered them abroad" (v.21); **(4)** the covenant of peace with the flock (vv.23-31): "I will make with them a covenant of peace, and will cause the evil beasts to cease out of the land: and they shall dwell safely in the wilderness, and sleep in the woods" (v.25).

1) THE CONDEMNATION OF ISRAEL'S SHEPHERDS, vv.1-10

"And the word of the LORD came unto me, saying, Son of man, prophesy against the shepherds of Israel prophesy, and say unto them, Thus saith the Lord GOD unto the shepherds; Woe be to the shepherds of Israel that do feed themselves! Should not the shepherds feed the flocks?" (vv.1-2). We should notice the expressions, "*my* sheep ... *my* flock" (vv.6, 8, 10, 11, 12, 15): compare John 21 verses 15-17, 1 Peter 5 verse 2.

In the words of J.B.Nicholson: "The shepherds, the spiritual leaders, of Israel in the days of Ezekiel had a solemn five-fold indictment levelled against them: they fleeced the flock for their own comfort (v.3); they fed not the flock because of laziness (v.8); they fed on the flock (v.10); they failed to guard the flock (v.8); they felt no responsibility to care for the flock (v.4). In a word, it was loveless neglect they showed" (*What the Bible Teaches - 1 Peter*, page 113).

i) **The flock had not been fed, vv.2-3.** "Thus saith the Lord GOD unto the shepherds; Woe be to the shepherds of Israel that do feed themselves! Should not the shepherds feed the flocks? Ye eat the fat, and ye clothe you with the wool, ye kill them that are fed: but ye feed not the flock." The shepherds were feeding themselves: living off the flock - but not feeding the flock.

Shepherd work today, in the hands of local elders, is to "feed (*poimaino*) the flock of God which is among you, taking the oversight thereof, not by constraint, but willingly; not for filthy lucre, but of a ready mind" (1 Pet. 5: 1-2). The words, "Should not the shepherds feed the flocks?" are relevant today. It is sadly possible to regard 'being on the oversight' as a prestigious position, rather than a demanding task. It is sadly possible to neglect the welfare of a small local assembly in favour of large conventions elsewhere. It is sadly possible to pursue business interests to the exclusion of the welfare of "the flock of God".

ii) The flock had not been tended, v.4. "The diseased (*chala*) have ye not strengthened, neither have ye healed that which was sick (*chalah*), neither have ye bound up that which was broken." Three categories are mentioned:

- ***The "diseased"***, perhaps referring to those who were chronically sick as a result of past mistakes, or temperament. If no cure is available, then they should be strengthened: "wherefore lift up the hands that hang down" (Heb. 12: 12).

- ***The "sick"***, perhaps referring to those with temporary spiritual problems. The work here is to heal: that is, to help them over the problem.

- ***The "broken"***, reminding us that the Lord's people can be injured by the problems and trials of life. The word "broken" (*shabar*) means 'to be shivered, shattered' (Young's *Concordance*).

iii) The flock had not been gathered, v.4. "Neither have ye brought again that which was driven away, neither have ye sought that which was lost." Two categories are mentioned here:

- ***Those who had been "driven away"***. It is not unknown for believers to be "driven away" by "force" and "cruelty" (v.4). Diotrephes is a New Testament example: "prating against us with malicious words: and not content therewith, neither doth he himself receive the brethren, and forbiddeth them that would, and casteth them out of the church" (3 John v.10)

- ***Those who had wandered away***: "that which was lost". The national shepherds were quite unlike the shepherd described by the Lord Jesus: "What man of you, having an hundred sheep, if he lose one of them, doth not leave the ninety and nine in the wilderness, and go after that which is lost, until he find it?" (Luke 15: 4). But there is a great deal of truth in the old saying, 'Better a fence at the top of the cliff than an ambulance station at the bottom".

iv) The flock had not been loved, v.4. "But with force and with cruelty have ye ruled them." Compare 1 Peter 5 verse 3, "Neither as lords over

God's heritage, but being ensamples to the flock". None the less, shepherds are to rule!

As the result of all this, "they were scattered, because there is no shepherd: and they became meat to all the beasts of the field, when they were scattered. My sheep wandered through all the mountains, and upon every high hill: yea, my flock was scattered upon all the face of the earth (referring, undoubtedly, to Israel's dispersion among the nations), and none did search or seek after them" (vv.5-6). The expressions "my sheep" and "my flock" should be noted. They occur with regularity in later verses, reminding us that the Lord Jesus said, "Feed my lambs ... Feed my sheep" (John 21: 15-17, and that the assembly is "the flock of God" (1 Pet. 5: 2). We should also notice:

- **That the sheep were without protection, v.5**. The words, "meat to all the beasts of the field", remind us that "the field is the world" (Matt. 13: 38), and that scattered sheep are vulnerable to a predatory world without the fellowship and security afforded by shepherd care.

- **That the sheep were without direction, v.6a**. "My sheep **wandered** through all the mountains, and upon every high hill."

- **That the sheep were without fellowship, v.6b**: "my flock was **scattered** upon all the face of the earth."

The Divine Shepherd will reverse the results of such appalling misrule: see verses 11-16. But we must take time to note the way in which David describes His work. The shepherd-king said, "The LORD is my shepherd; I shall not want" (Psalm 23: 1).

- The national shepherds **had not fed the flock** (vv.2-3), but David said that the Lord "maketh me to lie down in green pastures".

- The national shepherds **had not tended the flock** (v.4), but David said that the Lord "anointest my head with oil".

- The national shepherds **had not gathered the flock** (v.4), but David said that the Lord "restoreth my soul".

- The national shepherds **had not loved the flock** (v.4), but David said that the Lord would bestow "goodness and mercy" upon him "all the days" of his life.

Moreover, David was **not without protection**: "Yea, though I walk through the valley of the shadow of death, I will fear no evil: for thou art with me … thou preparest a table before me in the presence of mine enemies". Further, David was **not without direction**: "he leadeth me in the paths of righteousness for his name's sake". Then David was **not without fellowship**: he said "thou art with me" in this life, and "I will dwell in the house of the LORD for ever" in the next life!

Finally, we should notice that the national shepherds would be appropriately recompensed for their utter failure: "Therefore, O ye shepherds, hear the word of the LORD: Thus saith the Lord GOD; Behold, I am against the shepherds; and I will require my flock at their hand, and cause them to cease from feeding the flock; neither shall the shepherds feed themselves any more; for I will deliver my flock from their mouth, that they be not meat for them" (vv.9-10). But the New Testament shepherd who faithfully and diligently undertakes his responsibilities will receive "a crown of glory that fadeth not away" (1 Pet. 5: 4).

2) THE CARE OF THE DIVINE SHEPHERD, vv.11-16

Since the national shepherds had so lamentably failed, the Lord himself will undertake the duties of a shepherd. We cannot fail to notice the divine resolution and divine certainty here. For example, "*I will* bring them out from the people" (v.13); "*I will* feed them" (v.14); "*I will* cause them to lie down" (v.15); "*I will* seek that which was lost" (v.16). The Lord would *(a)* recover them (vv.11-13); *(b)* feed them (vv.13-15); *(c)* tend them (v.16).

a) He will recover them, vv.11-13

"For thus saith the Lord GOD; Behold, I, even I, will both search my sheep, and seek them out. As a shepherd seeketh out his flock in the day that he is among his sheep that are scattered; so will I seek out my sheep, and will deliver them out of all places where they have been scattered in the cloudy and dark day (see Joel 2: 2; Zephaniah 1: 15, both referring to "the day of the LORD"). And I will bring them out from the people ('peoples', JND), and gather them from the countries, and will bring them to their own land." As John B.Taylor rightly observes, "The picture of the shepherd searching out the wanderer ... is a remarkable foreshadowing of the parable of the lost sheep (Luke 15: 4ff), which our Lord doubtless based on this passage in Ezekiel". "Scattering is the work of an enemy; shepherd-love brings the sheep together" (F.Cundick).

The Lord Jesus referred to the regathering of Israel in His 'Olivet Discourse'. "And he shall send his angels with a great sound of a trumpet, and they shall gather together his elect from the four winds, from one end of heaven to the other" (Matt. 24: 31). This is the last of three references in the discourse to the elect Jew; see verses 23-24. They constitute the "all Israel" of Romans 11 verse 26. The Messiah will come "with strong hand, and his arm shall rule for him", but He will also "feed his flock like a shepherd: he shall gather the lambs with his arm" (Isaiah 40: 10-11).

The fact that "he shall send his angels with a great **sound of a trumpet**" is foretold in the Old Testament: "And it shall come to pass in that day, that the LORD shall beat off (the land will become a threshing-floor) from the channel of the river (referring to the Euphrates) unto the stream of Egypt (the extent of the land promised to Abraham), and ye shall be gathered one by one, O ye children of Israel. And it shall come to pass in that day, that **the great trumpet shall be blown**, and they shall come which were ready to perish in the land of Assyria, and the outcasts in the land of Egypt, and shall worship the LORD in the holy mount at **Jerusalem**" (Isaiah 27: 12-13).

The Old Testament refers to the elect Jews as follows: "And I will bring forth a seed out of Jacob, and out of Judah an inheritor of my mountains; and mine **elect** shall inherit it, and my servants shall dwell there .... mine **elect** shall long enjoy the work of their hands" (Isaiah 65: 9, 22); "And at that time thy people shall be **delivered**, every one that shall be found written in the book (the 'elect')" (Dan. 12: 1). While the gathering of the Jewish 'elect' will certainly be accomplished by divine power, it will not involve transportation through the air (a rapture). This is confirmed by such passages as Isaiah 49 verses 18-23: "Lift up thine eyes round about, and behold: all these gather themselves together, and come to thee ... **I will lift up mine hand** to the Gentiles, and **set up my standard** to the people: and **they** shall bring thy sons in **their** arms, and thy daughters shall be carried upon **their** shoulders. And kings shall be thy nursing fathers, and their queens thy nursing mothers". This is **not** at variance with Matthew 24 verse 31, "And he shall send **his angels** with a great sound of a trumpet, and **they** shall gather together his elect from the four winds, from one end of heaven to the other". The exiles will be gathered by angelic power, but **Gentiles** will be the vehicle through which it will be accomplished.

The Jewish 'elect' will be gathered "from **the four winds, from one end of heaven to the other".** The Lord Jesus refers here to passages in Deuteronomy and Nehemiah. Having been told that if they disobeyed the Lord, the nation would be scattered "from the one end of the earth even unto the other" (Deut. 28: 64), Moses went on to say that following repentance the Lord would "return and gather thee from all the nations, whither the LORD thy God had scattered thee" and "If any of thine be driven out unto the outmost parts of heaven ('the farthest parts under heaven', NKJV), from thence will the LORD thy God gather thee, and from thence will he fetch thee" (Deut. 30: 2-4). Nehemiah quoted this in prayer: "Remember, I beseech thee, the word that thou commandest thy servant Moses, saying, If ye transgress, I will scatter you abroad among the nations: but if ye turn unto me ... though there were of you cast out unto the uttermost part of the heaven, yet will I gather them from thence, and will bring them unto the place that I have chosen to set my name there" (Neh. 1: 8-9). According to Isaiah 11 verses 11-12, "the LORD ... shall set up an ensign for the nations, and shall assemble the outcasts of Israel, and gather together the dispersed of Judah from the four corners ('wings') of the earth". Andrew Wilson (*Matthew's Messiah*) helpfully points out that Jeremiah 49 verses 32 and 36 prove that the words "four winds" refer to the four compass points.

b) *He will feed them, vv.13-15*

"And I will ... feed them upon the mountains of Israel by the rivers, and in all the inhabited places of the country. I will feed them in a ***good*** pasture, and upon the high mountains of Israel shall their fold be: there shall they lie in a ***good*** fold, and in a fat pasture shall they feed upon the mountains of Israel. I will feed my flock, and I will cause them to lie down, saith the Lord GOD". The shepherd-care will be of the highest quality: "good pasture" and a "good fold". The "good shepherd" provides "good pasture" and "a good fold" today. He said, "I am the door: by me if any man enter in, he shall be saved (so it is 'a good fold'), and shall go in and out, and find pasture" (John 10: 9).

c) *He will tend them, v.16*

"I will seek that which was lost, and bring again that which was driven away, and will bind up that which was broken, and will strengthen that which was sick." The Lord Jesus came, amongst other things, to "bind up the brokenhearted" (Is. 61: 1), and the way in which He continues to do this has been beautifully described by J.Vaughan: "I once heard the prayer of a rough ploughman in a village school-room, and this was his prayer: 'Dear Lord, if there be any poor stricken one in this room tonight, come and bind him up, and bind Thyself, Lord, into the binding'" (Quoted by James Hastings). But as Christopher Wright points out, "The picture is not all one of tender loving care. The flock still needed to be governed. The words, "I will destroy the fat and the strong; I will feed them with judgment" (v.16), point "to the necessary work of justice and protection of the weak that needed to go on". This is developed in the next paragraph. The "fat and the strong" have been defined as "the oppressive nobles or the bullying merchant-classes" (J.B.Taylor). Support for this can certainly be found in Amos 5 verses 11-13. So:

3) THE CONFLICT WITHIN THE FLOCK, vv.17-22

Whereas, thus far, attention has been given to the failure of the national shepherds, relationships within the flock itself are now highlighted. "And as for you, O my flock, thus saith the Lord GOD; Behold, I judge between cattle and cattle, between the rams and the he goats" (v.17) or "between sheep and sheep, between the rams and the he-goats" (JND). This emphasises the fractured relationships between members of the flock: between "sheep and sheep" and between "the rams and the he goats". Bearing in mind that "the flock in biblical times, as today in the Middle East, regularly consisted of a mixture of sheep and goats" (J.B.Taylor), it is not a question of labelling some 'sheep' and others 'goats', but of distinguishing between the fat and strong and the weak and helpless. The way in which "the fat and the strong" (v.16) had treated "the lean" (v.20) is described: "Seemeth it a small thing unto you to have eaten up the good pasture, but ye must tread down with your feet the residue of your pastures? And to have drunk of the deep waters, but ye must foul the residue with your feet? And as for my flock, they eat that which ye have trodden with your feet; and they drink that which ye have fouled with your feet" (vv.18-19). These verses condemn selfishness: a desire for more, and lack of consideration for others. The "fat" and the "strong" wanted everything ("the residue") for themselves.

Hence, "Behold, I, even I, will judge between the fat cattle and between the lean cattle" (v.20). A further reason follows: "Because ye have thrust with side and with shoulder, and pushed all the diseased with your horns, till ye have scattered abroad; therefore will I save my flock, and they shall no more be a prey: and I will judge between cattle and cattle ('sheep and sheep', JND)" (vv.21-22). As J.B.Taylor observes, "The flock will in fact be purified, not only of its bad leadership but also of its bad members".

4) THE COVENANT OF PEACE, vv.23-31

Bad shepherding, better, non-existent shepherding, together with inequity amongst the flock, will give place to shepherd-care of an entirely different order. If past kings had failed to exercise proper shepherd-care, then a new era lay ahead. These verses have been called "the future prospects of the kingdom" (F.Cundick). This beautiful passage may be considered as follows: *(a)* the ruler over them (vv.23-24); *(b)* the covenant with them (vv.25-28); *(c)* the provision for them (v.29); *(d)* the description of them (vv.30-31).

a) The ruler over them, vv.23-24

"I will set up one shepherd **over them**, and he shall feed them, even my servant David; he shall feed them, and he shall be their shepherd. And I the LORD will be their God, and my servant David a prince among them; I the LORD have spoken it." As F.Cundick rightly points out, "the unity of the nation is implied by the term 'one shepherd'. The divisions of the kingdom will be healed when he comes".

Commentators usually understand "David" here either as "the ideal ruler" (F.Cundick) or "one from the line of David" (L.A.Cooper), or as Messiah himself, "David's greater Son, the Lord Jesus Christ" (C.L.Feinberg). John B.Taylor states, "He is not, as some would believe, the historical David resurrected, nor is he a human king of the Davidic line". Without in any way disparaging these views, it seems clear enough that it *is* David himself. The passage is quite explicit, and so are others: "And David my servant shall be king over them; and they shall all have one shepherd ... And they shall dwell in the land that I have given unto Jacob my servant, wherein your fathers have dwelt; and they shall dwell therein, even they, and their children, and their children's children for ever: and my servant David shall be their prince for ever" (Ezek. 37: 24-25); "they shall serve the LORD their God, and David their king, whom I will raise up unto them" (Jer. 30: 9); "afterward shall the children of Israel return, and seek the LORD their God, and David their king: and shall fear the LORD and his goodness in the latter days" (Hos. 3: 5).

b) The covenant with them, vv.25-28

These verses stress the safety and security of the flock. "And I will make **with them** a covenant of peace, and will cause the evil beasts to cease out of the land: and they shall dwell safely in the wilderness, and sleep in the woods. And I will make them and the places round about my hill a blessing: and I will cause the shower to come down in his season; there shall be showers of blessing. And the tree of the field shall yield her fruit, and the earth shall yield her increase, and they shall be safe in their land, and shall know that I am the LORD, when I have broken the bands of their yoke (compare Micah 2: 13), and delivered them out of the hand of those that served themselves of them. And they shall no more be a prey to the heathen, neither shall the beast of the land devour them; but they shall dwell safely, and none shall make them afraid." What a covenant! It will be, indeed, "a covenant of peace". The references to "the evil beasts" and to "the beast of the land" can be taken quite literally. Compare Isaiah 11 verses 6-9. God's "hill" is, of course, Zion. Mount Zion, "the city of the great King" (Psalm 48: 2), lies at the centre of divine blessing for the land, and beyond. The Lord will restore the former and latter rains (v.26). Compare Psalm 72 verse 6. See also Hosea 6 verse 3. "The former rain falls in the Holy Land in October or November; the latter rain from the middle of December to March" (C.L.Feinberg). Feinberg makes the important observation here that "The physical elements presuppose in Israel the indispensable spiritual foundation".

c) The provision for them, v.29

"And I will raise up **for them** a plant of renown" ('a planting of crops for renown' Amp.V.), and they shall be no more consumed with hunger in the land, neither bear the shame of the heathen any more." While some understand the "plant of renown" ('planting' or 'plantation', JND margin) as a reference to the Messiah, because the verb "raise up" is used of Him (Is. 11: 1; Jer. 23: 5), the "context suggests the fruitfulness of the period, and there appears to be a reference to the fruit that will be famous. There will be great fertility and growth of vegetation. It is the truth of Amos 9 verse 13" (C.L.Feinberg).

d) The description of them, vv.30-31

"Thus shall they know that I the LORD their God am with them, and that they, even the house of Israel, are my people, saith the Lord GOD. And ye **my flock**, the **flock of my pasture,** are men, and I am your God, saith the Lord God."

EZEKIEL CHAPTER 35

"Moreover the word of the LORD came unto me, saying, Son of man, set thy face against mount Seir, and prophesy against it" (vv.1-2).

According to Gesenius, Seir means 'hairy' or 'rough', and could be translated 'the rough mountain', because it was "clothed, and, as it were, bristled with trees and thick woods". If this were the case then it was most appropriate that having left Canaan, Esau (meaning 'hairy') should make his home there: "And Esau took his wives, and his sons, and his daughters, and all the persons of his house, and all his cattle, and all his beasts, and all his substance, which he had got in the land of Canaan; and went into the country from the face of his brother Jacob. For their riches were more than that they might dwell together; and the land wherein they were strangers could not bear them because of their cattle. Thus dwelt Esau in mount Seir: Esau is Edom. And these are the generations of Esau the father of the Edomites in mount Seir …" (Gen. 36: 6-9). See also Genesis 32 verse 3. Edom is also known in the Old and New Testaments as Idumea (Isa. 34: 5-6; Ezek. 35: 15; 36: 5; Mark 3: 8). Idumea is the Greek form of Edom.

Seir, or Edom, lay south of Judah, and extended from the Dead Sea to the Gulf of Aqaba. It includes the ruins of its main cities Petra and Teman, and is bounded on the north by Moab.

Since Edom was one the first four nations named in the 'foreign nations' section of the prophecy (chs. 25-32), we have to ascertain, if possible, why Ezekiel is now told to proclaim against her a second time. In this connection it should be noted:

- That while the ***people*** (Edom) are addressed on four occasions in Chapter 25 verses 12-14, with no mention of 'mount Seir', the ***area***, or territory, ('mount Seir') is addressed four times in Chapter 35 (vv.2, 3, 7, 15) with one reference to 'Idumea' (v.15).

CHAPTER 35

- That while in Chapter 25, emphasis is placed on the demonstration of Edom's bitter hatred for Judah at the fall of Jerusalem, Chapter 35 also refers to her desire to permanently acquire the territory of Judah (vv.10, 12).

This puts the chapter into context. In Chapter 34, the Lord gave Ezekiel a glowing picture of Israel's restoration: "I will ... feed them upon the mountains of Israel ... and upon the high mountains of Israel shall their fold be" (34: 13-14); "And they shall no more be a prey to the heathen ... they shall dwell safely, and none shall make them afraid" (34: 28). But all this was seemingly threatened by the territorial greed of the people inhabiting mount Seir who laid claim to "the mountains of Israel, saying, They are laid desolate, they are given to *us* to consume" (v.12). But God's designs on "the mountains of Israel" would not be thwarted by the people living in the mountains south of Judah! C.L.Feinberg concurs with this conclusion: "It may appear at first as though the present prophecy belongs to the oracles against foreign nations, but it is probably here as a point of contrast to Chapter 36, that is, wrath for Mount Seir contrasted with blessing for the mountains of Israel".

But this is not all. The opening section of Chapter 36 (vv.1-15) is addressed to "the mountains of Israel" with the Lord's assurance that He had "spoken against the residue of the heathen, and against all Idumea, which have appointed my land into their possession with the joy of all their heart, with despiteful minds, to cast it out for a prey" (v.5).

This raises the absorbing question of timing. Quite clearly, this section of Ezekiel (chs.33-48) deals with Israel's glorious future, and it could be argued that there is, surely, little point in referring to the territorial ambitions of people in the area around 2,600 years ago! But this very chapter clearly indicates that there will be enemies in the same area at the time of Israel's restoration, of whom the Lord says, "When the *whole earth* rejoiceth, I will make *thee* desolate" (v.14). The Edomite nation was wiped out centuries ago, but their territory will evidently be the stronghold of enemy activity at the end-time. See Isaah 34 verse 5; Chapter 63: 1 verses 4. The passage therefore has a prophetic significance as well as practical lessons.

Ezekiel 35 describes the desolation of "mount Seir" (vv.2, 3, 7, 15). The words "desolate", "perpetual desolations" and "most desolate" punctuate the passage (vv.3, 4, 7, 9, 14, 15). Edom had "sown the wind." The nation had joined in the desolation of Israel (vv.12, 15). Now Edom would "reap the whirlwind" (Hos. 8: 7).

The chapter may be divided into two major sections: *(1)* Edom's desolation announced (vv.1-4); *(2)* Edom's desolation explained (vv.5-15).

1) EDOM'S DESOLATION ANNOUNCED, vv.1-4

"Moreover the word of the LORD came unto me, saying, Son of man, set thy face against mount Seir, and prophesy against it, and say unto it, Thus saith the Lord GOD; Behold, O mount Seir, I am against thee, and will stretch out my hand against thee, and I will make thee most desolate. I will lay thy cities waste, and thou shalt be desolate, and thou shalt know that I am the LORD."

The prediction has been literally fulfilled. "Edom was first subjugated by Babylon, then Medo-Persia, and then in 126 BC by John Hyrcanus the Hasmonean, who compelled them to become Jews. There is no trace of the Edomites now, although their desolate cities can still be identified as predicted by Obadiah (v.18) and Jeremiah (49: 13)" (C.L.Feinberg).

Attention is drawn to the "word of the LORD" (v.1); to the hand of the Lord: "I am against thee, and will stretch out my hand against thee" (v.3); and to the character of the Lord: "thou shalt know that I am the LORD" (v.4). The divine title, "Lord GOD" (*Adonahy Jehovah*) stamps Ezekiel's ministry. *Adonahy* (plural) means 'Sovereign-Lord, or Master' (Thomas Newberry). The words, "and thou shalt know that I am the LORD", also stamp Ezekiel's ministry. As previously noted, they convey, not so much **who** He is, but **what** He is. In the words quoted by F. Cundick, they show that "God is the Ruler of history, and history is the vindication of His character". Or, in the words of the Psalmist, "The LORD is known by the judgment which he executeth: the wicked is snared in the work of his own hands. Higgaion. Selah" (Psalm 9: 16).

2) EDOM'S DESOLATION EXPLAINED, vv.5-15

The reasons for the judgment of Mount Seir are now given. This reminds us that God does not deal with nations in a purely arbitrary fashion, but advances adequate reasons for the severity of His judgments upon them. He pronounces His sentences with a full explanation in each case, and this is particularly clear in Amos 1-2 where the eight pronouncements of judgment are each introduced with the words, "Thus saith the LORD: for three transgressions ... and for four" (Amos 1: 3, 6, 9, 11, 13; 2: 1, 4, 6). Edom is one of the eight cases here: "Thus saith the LORD; for three transgressions of Edom, and for four, I will not turn away the punishment thereof; because he did pursue his brother with the sword, and did cast off all pity, and his anger did tear perpetually, and he kept his wrath for ever. But I will send fire upon Teman, which shall devour the palaces of Bozrah" (Amos 1: 11-12).

Two reasons are given for the coming desolation of their territory: *(a)* their perpetual hatred (vv.5-9): "Because thou hast had a perpetual hatred ..." (v.5); *(b)* their territorial ambitions (vv.10-15): "Because thou hast said, These two nations, and these two countries shall be mine" (v.10). Both sections, like the introductory verses (vv.1-4), conclude in the same way: "ye shall know that I am the LORD" (v.9); "they shall know that I am the LORD" (v.15). See also verse 12.

a) Edom's perpetual hatred, vv.5-9

The section commences with Edom's "perpetual hatred" (v.5), and concludes with Edom's "perpetual desolations" (v.9).

i) *"Perpetual hatred", v.5.* Here is the *reason* for Edom's desolation. "Because thou hast had a perpetual hatred, and hast shed the blood of the children of Israel by the force of the sword in the time of their calamity, in the time that their iniquity had an end." This emphasises two aspects of Edom's hatred for Israel: it was perpetually displayed, and it was particularly displayed.

- It was perpetually displayed. As noted above, Amos also emphasised this aspect of Edom's hatred: "Thus saith the Lord; For three transgressions, and for four, I will not turn away the punishment thereof; because he did pursue his brother with the sword, and did cast off all pity, and his anger did tear *perpetually*, and he kept his wrath for ever" (Amos 1: 11-12).

Edom's hatred had early beginnings. Whilst reference is made to Edom in Exodus 15 verse 15, Deuteronomy 2 verses 4-5 and 23 verse 7, the first historical reference after Genesis 36, is in Numbers 20, where Moses requested permission from the king of Edom to pass through his territory: "And Moses sent messengers from Kadesh unto the king of Edom, Thus saith *thy brother* Israel ... Let us pass, I pray thee, through thy country:

we will not pass through the fields, or through the vineyards, neither will we drink of the water of the wells: we will go by the king's highway, we will not turn to the right hand nor to the left, until we have passed thy borders" (Num. 20: 14-17). He received a curt reply: "And Edom said unto him, Thou shalt not pass by me lest I come out against thee with the sword". A second request was met by more than words: "And Edom came out against him with much people, and with a strong hand" (Num. 20: 18-21). (The river at Petra is called the Wadi-Musa, the 'river of Moses'.)

The same animosity persisted down the centuries until the smouldering fire burst into flame at the destruction of Jerusalem. During the intervening period, Israel gained the ascendancy over Edom. Saul "fought against all his enemies on every side", including Edom (1 Sam. 14: 47). Their animosity therefore persisted until his reign. Significantly, it was Doeg the Edomite who slew Ahimelech and eighty-four other priests, and virtually annihilated the population of Nob. See 1 Samuel 21-22. David totally subjugated Edom (2 Sam. 8: 14; 1 Kings 11: 15-16; 1 Chron.18: 11-13). Jehoshaphat, Jehoram and Amaziah all defeated the Edomites (2 Chron. chs. 20, 21, 22). But Jehoram failed to quell the Edomite rebellion, and Amaziah worshipped their gods! But Edom's hatred for Israel was particularly displayed at the destruction of Jerusalem. So:

- ***It was particularly displayed.*** "Because thou ... hast shed the blood of the children of Israel by the force of the sword in the time of their calamity, in the time that their iniquity had an end." A similar statement is made in Ezekiel 25 verses 12-13, "Because that Edom hath dealt against the house of Judah by taking vengeance, and hath greatly offended, and revenged himself upon them; therefore ... I will also stretch out mine hand upon Edom".

The "vengeance" of Edom was rooted in bitter hatred for God's people. The fall of Jerusalem gave them an opportunity to 'get their own back', to settle old grudges. The Psalmist refers to this: "Remember, O LORD, the children of Edom in the day of Jerusalem; who said, Rase it, rase it, even to the foundation thereof" (Psalm 137: 7). Obadiah refers to this in more detail in a passage (vv.10-14) beginning with the words: "For thy violence against ***thy brother*** Jacob, shame shall cover thee, and thou shalt be cut off for ever". Their burning hatred and bitter animosity over the years, culminated in the atrocities committed at the destruction of Jerusalem. The words, "in the time that their iniquity had an end" or "in the time of the iniquity ('punishment', margin) of the end" (RV), refer to their betrayal of God's people "at the time of their calamity (Obad. 10-14), when they were under the punitive hand of God" (F.A.Tatford).

Israel was expressly forbidden to act towards Edom in this way: "Thou shalt not abhor an Edomite; for he is **thy brother:** thou shalt not abhor an Egyptian; because thou wast a stranger in his land" (Deut. 23: 7), reminding us that the exact opposite of Edom's animosity should mark God's people. See Colossians 3 verses 12-14, "Put on therefore, as the elect of God, holy and beloved, bowels of mercies, kindness, humbleness of mind, meekness, longsuffering, forbearing one another, if any man have a quarrel against any: even as Christ forgave you, even so do ye". The New Testament describes "violence against thy brother": see, for example, Galatians 5 verses 13-15, "But if ye bite and devour one another, take heed that ye be not consumed one of another". See also Ephesians 4 verse 31, "Let all bitterness, and wrath, and anger, and clamour, and evil speaking, be put away from you, with all malice". We are to "love as brethren, be pitiful, be courteous" (1 Pet. 3: 8). We must never forget the Lord's teaching in John 13 verses 34-35.

ii) **"Perpetual desolations", vv.6-9.** Here is the **retribution** incurred by Edom. "Therefore, as I live, saith the Lord GOD, I will prepare thee unto blood, and blood shall pursue thee: sith (an old English word meaning 'seeing that') thou hast not hated blood, even blood shall pursue thee. Thus will I make mount Seir most desolate, and cut off from it him that passeth out and him that returneth. And I will fill his mountains with his slain men: in thy hills, and in thy valleys, and in all thy rivers, shall they fall that are slain with the sword. I will make thee perpetual desolations, and thy cities shall not return: and ye shall know that I am the LORD."

As C.L.Feinberg points out, this is "retribution in kind". He explains that when "the Lord warned Edom that He would prepare them unto blood, the meaning was that He would give them over to universal slaughter. Edom had not hated blood, for to hate blood is to have a dread of murder". Edom had stood "in the crossway, to **cut off** those of his (his Judaean brethren) that did escape (from Jerusalem)" (Obad. v.14), and the Lord would "cut off from it (mount Seir) him that passeth out and him that returneth" (v.7). C.L.Feinberg suggests that this applied to all groups, especially the caravans, for Edom's tribes were the channel of commerce between India, the East and Egypt. This was the source of Edom's wealth".

C.L.Feinberg continues: "the height of indignity in the Orient was not to be properly buried. The slain of Egypt would be found in the mountains, hills, valleys and watercourses, all without benefit of burial. God's sole and final answer to perpetual enmity was perpetual desolation".

b) Edom's territorial ambitions, vv.10-15

Once again, we should notice the *reason* for Edom's desolation (vv.10-13) and the *retribution* incurred by Edom (vv.14-15).

i) **The reason for Edom's desolation, vv.10-13.** "Because thou hast said, These two nations and these two countries shall be mine, and we will possess it; whereas the LORD was there. Therefore, as I live, saith the Lord GOD. I will even do according to thine anger, and according to thine envy which thou hast used out of thy hatred against them; and I will make myself known among them, when I have judged thee. And thou shalt know that I am the LORD, and that I have heard all thy blasphemies which thou hast spoken against the mountains of Israel, saying, They are laid desolate, they are given to us to consume. Thus with your mouth ye have boasted against me, and have multiplied your words against me: I have heard them." These verses have a great deal to tell us, and we should note the following:

- *That God's rights will be asserted.* "Because thou hast said, These two nations and these two countries shall be mine, and we will possess it; whereas **the LORD was there**" (v.10). In their haste to annex the territory of Israel and Judah ("these two nations and these two countries"), Edom totally forgot the Owner of the land! The Assyrians made the same mistake years before, whereupon the Owner of the land plagued them with lions! (2 Kings 17: 24-28). Ezekiel later describes the way in which the Owner of the land will deal with a vast invasion of His territory. See Chapters 38-39. Canaan is Emmanuel's land! (Isaiah 8: 8). In the Millennium, the name of Jerusalem will be *Jehovah-Shammah* – "***the Lord is there!***" (Ezek. 48: 35). Any design on the Lord's people is a design on the Lord himself: "he that toucheth you toucheth the apple of his eye" (Zech. 2: 8). The Lord therefore "hoists a large 'Trespassers will be prosecuted' sign over His land" (Christopher J.H.Wright).

- *That God will proportionately recompense evil.* "Therefore, as I live, saith the Lord GOD. I will even do according to **thine anger**, and according to **thine envy** which thou hast used out of thy hatred against

CHAPTER 35

them" (v.11). This is another case of 'retribution in kind'. "Edom would receive from the hand of the Lord in direct proportion to her anger, envy and hatred against Israel. She could not expect mercy who had shown none to others" (C.L.Feinberg).

- *That God has always in mind the blessing of His people*: "I will make myself known among them (His people), when I have judged thee (Edom)" (v.11).

- *That God is thoroughly aware of mankind's animosity towards His people and towards Him*: "I have heard all thy blasphemies which thou hast spoken against the mountains of Israel, saying, They are laid desolate, they are given to us to consume. Thus with your mouth ye have boasted against me, and have multiplied your words against me: I have heard them" (vv.12-13). He is equally aware of the conversation of those that fear Him. See Malachi 3 verse 16.

ii) The retribution incurred by Edom, vv.14-15. "Thus saith the Lord GOD; When the whole earth rejoiceth, I will make thee desolate. As thou didst rejoice at the inheritance of the house of Israel, because it was desolate, so will I do unto thee: thou shalt be desolate, O mount Seir, and all Idumaea, even all of it: and they shall know that I am the LORD."

Very clearly, the oracle concludes on a prophetic note. We are taken to the millennial age - "when the whole earth rejoiceth" - but when Edom will be excluded from blessing. The picture is enlarged in Isaiah 34 verses 5-17 where Edom is called Idumea. The territory is now part of Jordan and is therefore Islamic. "The controversy of Zion" (Is. 34: 6) will reach its height at the end-time, and divine judgment on Edom implies its participation in the coming invasion of Israel. This is confirmed in Psalm 83 where Edom (v.6) is included with the nations which will say, "Come, and let us cut them off from being a nation; that the name of Israel may be no more in remembrance" (v.4), with this result: "And the streams thereof shall be turned into pitch, and the dust thereof into brimstone, and the land thereof shall become burning pitch. It shall not be quenched night nor day; the smoke thereof shall go up for ever: from generation to generation it shall lie waste; none shall pass through it for ever and ever". While, then, the millennial age will display the beneficence and goodness of God, it will also bear eloquent testimony to the severity of God.

The lesson of the chapter is restated in Chapter 36 where, having referred to Edom's "blasphemies which thou hast spoken against the mountains of Israel, saying, They art laid desolate, they are given us to consume" (35: 12), the Lord continues: "Because the enemy hath said against you ("Ye mountains of Israel"), Aha, even the ancient high places are ours in possession ... Surely in the fire of my jealousy have I spoken against the residue of the heathen, and against all Idumea, which have appointed my land into their possession with the joy of all their heart, with despiteful minds, to cast it out for a prey" (36: 2, 5). As F.A. Tatford so rightly says, "When this occurred, there would be recognition of the supreme authority of Jehovah. No one dare impugn His authority or attack His possession".

EZEKIEL CHAPTER 36:1-15

As already noted, Chapter 33 introduces the third and final section of the prophecy, in which the ruin of Judah and Jerusalem (chs.1-24) and the retribution on surrounding nations (chs.25-32) give place to the restoration of Israel (chs.33-48).

We have also noted that the prophecies dealing with the restoration of Israel were not uttered until judgment had fallen on Judah and Jerusalem, and the "false foundations" had been "thoroughly swept away" (Patrick Fairbairn). Jerusalem had fallen (33: 21), but even this did not quite complete the work of divine judgment. The survivors in Judah laboured under the delusion that they had been left to repopulate the land, only to learn that all they could expect was the complete desolation of Judah (33: 23-29). Their moral condition did not correspond in the slightest to the faith and obedience of their forefather Abraham. The exiles in Chaldea were no better (33: 30-33). They paid lip-service to Ezekiel's preaching, but "their heart goeth after their covetousness" (33: 31). The final desolation of Judah would be proof "that a prophet hath been among them" (33: 33). This would open the way for national restoration.

The remaining chapters of Ezekiel, which set out features of the millennial kingdom, may be summarised as follows:

1) **The restoration of the monarchy, 34: 1 - 35: 15.** This section comprises *(i)* past failure of the kings (34: 1-10); *(ii)* prospective blessing for Israel (34: 11-31); *(iii)* perpetual desolation of Edom (35: 1-15). Israel will enjoy the reign and care of a shepherd-king, and be totally free from the threat of occupation by her neighbours.

2) **The rejuvenation of the land, 36: 1-15.** "But ye, O mountains of Israel, ye shall shoot forth your branches, and yield your fruit to my people of Israel; for they are at hand to come" (36: 8).

3) ***The restoration of the people, 36: 16-38.*** This section comprises *(i)* the restoration of the people to ***the land*** (vv.16-24); *(ii)* the regeneration of the people by ***the Lord*** (vv.25-38).

4) ***The restoration of national life, 37: 1-14.*** "Behold, O my people, I will open your graves ... and bring you into the land of Israel. And ye shall know that I am the LORD, when I have opened your graves, O my people, and brought you up out of your graves, and shall put my Spirit in you, and ye shall live, and I shall place you in your own land: then shall ye know that I the LORD have spoken it, and performed it, saith the LORD" (37: 12-14).

5) ***The restoration of national unity, 37: 15-28.*** "Thus saith the Lord GOD; Behold, I will take the stick of Joseph, which is in the hand of Ephraim, and the tribes of Israel his fellows, and will put them with him, even with the stick of Judah, and make them one stick, and they shall be one in mine hand" (37: 19).

6) ***The restoration of national security, 38: 1 - 39: 29.*** The book of Ezekiel commences with a successful invasion: God did not deliver His people from the Babylonian armies. But in these chapters, a colossal invasion from "the north parts" (38: 15; 39: 2) is summarily judged on "the mountains of Israel" (39: 4).

To this we must add the fourth and final section of the prophecy -

7) ***The restoration of the Lord's presence, 40: 1 - 48: 35.*** The glory of the Lord, last seen standing "upon the mountain which is on the east side of the city" (11: 23), returns "from the way of the east ... came into the house by the way of the gate whose prospect is toward the east ... and, behold, the glory of the LORD filled the house" (43: 1-5). The book closes with, "and the name of the city from that day shall be, The LORD is there" (48: 35).

Having briefly outlined the content of the third and fourth sections of the book (chs. 33-48), we can now proceed with the current chapter. The certainty attaching to the restoration of the land and the people is emphasised throughout the passage. We should note the frequently-repeated words, "Thus saith the Lord GOD" (vv.2, 3, 4, 5, 6, 7, 13, 22, 33, 37), together with the words "saith the Lord GOD" (vv.14, 15, 23, 32) and "I the LORD have spoken it, and will do it" (v.36). It should also be noted that verses 1-15 are addressed to "the mountains of Israel" (vv.1, twice; 4, 8), whereas verses 16-48 are addressed to, or refer to, "the house of Israel" (vv.17, 22 twice; 32).

As noted above, Ezekiel 36 may be divided as follows: **(1) the rejuvenation of the land, vv.1-15:** "But ye, O mountains of Israel, ye shall shoot forth your branches, and yield your fruit to my people of Israel; for they are at hand to come. For, behold, I am for you, and I will turn unto you, and ye shall be tilled and sown ... and I will settle you after your old estates, and will do better unto you than at your beginnings: and ye shall know that I am the LORD" (vv.8-11); **(2) the restoration of the people to the land (vv.16-24):** "I will take you from among the heathen, and gather you out of all countries, and will bring you into your own land" (v.24); **(3) the regeneration of the people by the Lord (vv.25-38):** "A new heart also will I give you, and a new spirit will I put within you ... And I will put my Spirit within you, and cause you to walk in my statutes, and ye shall keep my judgments and do them. And ye shall dwell in the land that I gave to your fathers; and ye shall be my people, and I will be your God" (vv.26-28).

1) THE REJUVENATION OF THE LAND, vv.1-15

As noted above, this section of the chapter is addressed to "the mountains of Israel": "Also, thou son of man, prophesy unto the mountains of Israel, and say, Ye mountains of Israel, hear the word of the LORD" (v.1). The prophecy describes divine blessing, and reverses an earlier prophecy against the mountains of Israel: "Son of man, set thy face toward the mountains of Israel, and prophesy against them, and say, Ye mountains of Israel, hear the word of the Lord GOD; Thus saith the Lord GOD to the mountains, and to the hills, to the rivers, and to the valleys; Behold, I, even I, will bring a sword upon you, and will destroy your high places ..." (Ezek. 6: 1-3). Now the same "mountains ... hills ... rivers ... valleys" are addressed again, but with what a difference! (vv.4-15). The literality of the passage is clear. C.L.Feinberg almost understates the matter in saying that "those who suggest the passage may be expounded in a typical or figurative fashion do not make a convincing case".

It might be helpful to say that the expression "the mountains of Israel" refers to the land in general. As H.L.Ellison observes, "we can legitimately consider the plains of Palestine to be included in the language of the chapter. Whether one stands in the Coastal Plain or in Esdraelon, one is more conscious of the hills than of the plain; it is they that set the predominant note, hence the description in Deuteronomy 11 verse 11 ('But the land, whither ye go to possess it, is a land of hills and valleys, and drinketh the water of the rain of heaven')".

The Lord had said that He would bring His scattered sheep "out from the people, and gather them from the countries, and will bring them to their own land, and feed them upon the mountains of Israel by the rivers, and in all the inhabited places of the country" (34: 13), and that the territorial ambitions of the neighbouring Edomites (the inhabitants of mount Seir) would utterly fail: "I have heard all thy blasphemies which thou hast spoken against the mountains of Israel, saying, They are laid desolate, they are given to us to consume" (35: 12). Edom (Idumea) is now specifically named amongst "the heathen" who will "bear their shame" when the Lord speaks in 'the fire of his jealousy' against those who "have appointed my land into their possession with the joy of all their heart, with despiteful minds, to cast it out for a prey" (36: 5). The links between Chapters 34-36 are therefore clear.

We must now note the following: *(a)* the possession of the land (vv.2-3); *(b)* the proprietor of the land (vv.4-7); *(c)* the productivity of the land (vv.8-9); *(d)* the population of the land (vv.10-12); *(e)* the peace of the land (vv.13-15).

It might be helpful to note that the word "therefore" occurs five times in verses 1-7. John B.Taylor calls this "a mark of heightened emotion, as the prophet blazes out his indignation".

a) *The possession of the land, vv.2-3*

As already noted, the passage (vv.1-15) concerns the mountains of Israel, of which Edom had said gloatingly, "They are laid desolate, they are given us to consume" (35: 12). However, the language suggests not only the threat of occupation, but actual possession of the land by Israel's enemies, not only by Edom, but by other nations as well: "Also, thou son of man, prophesy unto the mountains of Israel, and say, Ye mountains of Israel, hear the word of the LORD: Thus saith the Lord GOD; because the enemy hath said against you, Aha, even the ancient high places are ours in possession: Therefore prophesy and say, Thus saith the Lord GOD; because they have made you desolate, and swallowed you up ('panted after you', JND margin) on every side, that ye might be a *possession* unto the residue of the heathen, and ye are taken up in the lips of talkers, and are an infamy of the people: Therefore, ye mountains of Israel, hear the word of the Lord GOD" (vv.3-4).

CHAPTER 36:1-15

We should emphasise at this point that *our spiritual enemies are just like the Edomites and the rest of the "heathen" (v.5)*. They desire to control us and to rob us of the enjoyment of our possessions. It can be expressed in the words, "thou shalt come to the hill of God, where is the garrison of the Philistines" (1 Sam. 10: 5). How about that! No wonder the hymn-writer says:

> *Principalities and powers,*
> *Mustering their unseen array,*
> *Wait for thine unguarded hours;*
> *'Watch and pray'.*

We should notice the following:

i) Their desire for the land: "the enemy hath said against you, Aha, even the ancient high places are ours in possession". This refers, not to the idolatrous sites, but to the enemy's boast that he was in full control of the land. For "high places" in this sense, see Micah 3 verse 12.

ii) Their desolation of the land: "they have made you desolate, and swallowed you up on every side, that ye might be a possession unto the residue of the heathen".

iii) Their derision for the land: "ye are taken up in the lips of talkers, and are an infamy of the people". The derisory place which the land occupied in the estimate of the surrounding nations is summed up in the words, "ye have borne the shame of the heathen" (v.6). The Lord would repay them in kind: "Therefore thus saith the Lord God: I have lifted up mine hand, surely the heathen that are about you, they shall bear their shame" (v.7).

This highlights the need for the Lord's people to always act in a way which honours Him. We will be derided anyway, but we must not give people just cause to do so. David was told, "thou hast given great occasion to the enemies of the LORD to blaspheme" (2 Sam. 12: 14). In New Testament language, we must give "none occasion to the adversary to speak reproachfully" (1 Tim. 5: 14).

The derision of the heathen had been foretold in Deuteronomy 28 verse 37 ("And thou shalt become an astonishment, a proverb, and a by-word, among all nations whither the LORD shall lead thee"); Jeremiah 24 verse 9 ("And I will deliver them to be removed into all the kingdoms of the earth for their hurt, to be a reproach and a proverb, a taunt and a curse, in all places whither I shall drive them").

b) The proprietor of the land, vv.4-7

"Therefore, ye mountains of Israel, hear the word of the Lord GOD; Thus saith the Lord GOD to the mountains, and to the hills, to the rivers ('ravines', JND margin), and to the valleys, to the desolate wastes, and to the cities that are forsaken, which became a prey and a derision to the residue of the heathen that are round about; therefore thus saith the Lord GOD; Surely in the fire of my jealousy have I spoken against the residue of the heathen, and against all Idumea, which have appointed *my land* into their possession with the joy of all their heart, with despiteful minds, to cast it out for a prey. Prophesy therefore concerning the land of Israel, and say unto the mountains, and to the hills, to the rivers, and to the valleys, Thus saith the Lord GOD; Behold I have spoken in my jealousy and in my fury, because ye have borne the shame of the heathen: therefore thus saith the Lord GOD; I have lifted up mine hand. Surely the heathen that are about you, they shall bear their shame." Israel is called "my land". Compare Isaiah 8 verse 8, where the Assyrian would "fill the breadth of *thy land, O Immanuel*".

Amongst other things, this reminds us that *we belong to Christ.* In Paul's words, "ye are not your own, for ye are bought with a price: therefore glorify God in your body, and in your spirit, which are God's" (1 Cor. 6: 19-20).

We should notice the following:

i)   The jealousy of the owner. "Surely in the fire of *my jealousy* have I spoken against the residue of the heathen, and against all Idumea, which have appointed my land into their possession with the joy of all their heart, with despiteful minds, to cast it out for a prey ... Thus saith the Lord GOD; Behold I have spoken in *my jealousy* and in my fury, because ye have borne the shame of the heathen" (vv.5-6). God is not only "a jealous God" (Ex. 20: 5) in His jealousy for His own glory ("I will not give my glory unto another", Isa. 48: 11), He is jealous of the affections of His people ("thou shalt worship no other god: for the LORD, whose name is Jealous, is a jealous God", Exodus 34: 14) and jealous for the welfare of His people: He is "jealous for Jerusalem and for Zion with a great jealousy" (Zech. 1: 14). See also Zechariah 8 verse 2. See, as well, Joel 2 verse 18, "Then will the LORD be jealous for his land, and pity his people".

CHAPTER 36:1-15

ii) **The fury of the owner.** "Behold I have spoken in my jealousy and in *my fury*, because ye have borne the shame of the heathen" (v.6).

iii) **The hand of the owner.** "I have lifted up *mine hand* (see also 20: 5). Surely the heathen that are about you, they shall bear their shame" (v.7). To lift up the hand "was the gesture of swearing or taking an oath", in this case "that the nations would certainly be recompensed" (F.A.Tatford). Compare Revelation 10 verses 5-6.

c) The productivity of the land, vv.8-9

"But ye (note the contrast with what has gone before), O mountains of Israel, ye shall shoot forth your branches, and yield your fruit to my people of Israel; for they are at hand to come. For, behold, I am for you, and I will turn unto you, and ye shall be tilled and sown." As C.L.Feinberg observes,"These prophecies, especially those in verses 12-15, could not have been fulfilled in the return from Babylon. The promise of productivity was addressed directly to the mountains of Israel themselves. The present great reforestation projects in the State of Israel, amazing as they are, are only harbingers of the reality to come. The conditions depicted here are clearly millennial". According to F.A.Tatford, "During the Ottoman regime from A.D.1517 to A.D.1917, the mountains were stripped of trees and the soil naturally eroded, leaving the hillsides stark and bare. The land itself was gradually covered with a mantle of sand, carried by the wind from the Sahara Desert. Since the return of Israel, the sand has been removed, trees and crops have been planted and a comprehensive reafforestation scheme put into effect. What Ezekiel predicted is beginning to be manifested already. But the complete realisation of the blessings he foretold must, of course, await the coming of the Messiah".

Attention is drawn to the words, "Ye ... shall yield your fruit to my people Israel; *for they are at hand to come*" (v.8). John B.Taylor notes that the AV rendering "takes the subject, not as Israel, but as the blessings which have been promised" and continues, "This is perfectly possible, but the context seems to favor the RSV translation ('for they will soon come home')".

The picture here can be elaborated from other prophetic scriptures. See, for example: "There shall be an handful of corn in the earth upon the top of the mountains: the fruit thereof shall shake like Lebanon" (Psalm 72: 16); "The wilderness and the solitary place shall be glad for them; and the desert shall rejoice, and blossom as the rose" (Isa. 35: 1); "Behold, the days come, saith the LORD, that the plowman shall overtake the reaper, and the treader of grapes him that soweth seed; and the mountains shall drop sweet wine, and all the hills shall melt" (Amos 9: 13).

The Lord's people today are to be fruitful. Paul prayed that the Colossian believers would be "fruitful in every good work, and increasing in the knowledge of God" (Col. 1: 10). He reminded his Galatian readers that "the fruit of the Spirit is love, joy, peace, longsuffering, gentleness, goodness, faith, meekness, temperance ..." (Gal. 5: 22-23).

d) The population of the land, vv.10-12

"And I will multiply upon you man and beast; and they shall increase and bring fruit: and I will settle you after your old estates, and will do better unto you than at your beginnings: and ye shall know that I am the LORD. Yea, I will cause men to walk upon you, even my people Israel; and they shall possess thee and thou shalt be their inheritance, and thou shalt no more henceforth bereave them of men."

As C.L.Feinberg points out, "the productivity of the land would be useless unless there were men to enjoy and use it, so Ezekiel foretold the great increase in population and even of the animals of the land". Feinberg continues: "There will then be an approximation in the land of those conditions which existed in the days of Israel's prosperity, in fact, they will be better than in the halcyon days of Solomon". Zechariah refers to the 'population explosion' here: "I will bring them into the land of Gilead (presently, part of Jordan) and Lebanon (yes, Lebanon!); and place shall not be found for them" (Zech. 10: 10). That is, they will run out of space, requiring territorial enlargement.

The Lord's people today are to be concerned about growth and expansion. We must "grow in grace, and in the knowledge of our Lord and Saviour Jesus Christ" (2 Pet. 3: 18). But we ought also to be concerned with numerical expansion. Jabez prayed, "Oh that thou wouldest bless me indeed, and enlarge my coast" (1 Chron. 4: 10), and so should we!

e) The peace of the land, vv.13-15

"Thus saith the Lord GOD: Because they say unto you, Thou land devourest up men, and hast bereaved thy nations; therefore thou shalt devour men no more, neither bereave thy nations any more, saith the Lord GOD. Neither will I cause men to hear in thee the shame of the heathen any more, neither shalt thou bear the reproach of the people ('peoples', JND) any more, neither shalt thou cause thy nations ('thy nation', JND) to fall any more, saith the Lord GOD."

The land will be source of permanent and peaceful blessing. This was not so in the past. "The land was called a devourer of men because of the many wars that repeatedly decimated the population in times past ... It is possible that the reference was to famine (see v.30). In a sense the land was a bereaver of the nation, for it was subject, through the chastisement of God, to droughts (Jer. 14: 1; Amos 4: 7), to blasting and mildew (Amos 4: 9), locust (Joel 1: 4), and famine (Hag. 1: 10-11; 2: 17)" (C.L.Feinberg). Interestingly enough the twelve spies described Canaan as "a land that eateth up the inhabitants thereof" (Num. 13: 32). A similar passage is found in Leviticus 18 verses 26-28 where Israel is warned against sinful practices "that the land spue not you out also, when ye defile it, as it spued out the nations that were before you".

The section ends with a five-fold statement ("no more ... any more ... any more ... any more ... any more", vv.14-15) to the effect "that the land will no more experience the shame of the nations because of occupation of their land by enemies, as well as the accompanying destitution" (C.L.Feinberg). The land would be the permanent and peaceful inheritance of God's people (v.12).

Christopher J. H. Wright sums up nicely: "What possible status among the nations could be held by a decimated remnant of landless refugees? ... To the question, 'Will Jehovah abandon His land and His people forever?', the answer is a resounding 'No!' ... The shattered exiles were given prophetic words that matched so many of the psalms they initially found it impossible to sing: their enemies would not triumph over them for ever; they would not be put to shame for ever; their God would one day lift up their heads again in the sight of the nations. It must have been hard to believe in BC 587. But it was terribly important that it was said and remembered".

EZEKIEL CHAPTER 36:16-38

We have already noted that Ezekiel 36 may be divided as follows: **(1) the rejuvenation of the land (vv.1-15):** "But ye, O mountains of Israel, ye shall shoot forth your branches, and yield your fruit to my people of Israel; for they are at hand to come. For, behold, I am for you, and I will turn unto you, and ye shall be tilled and sown ... and I will settle you after your old estates, and will do better unto you than at your beginnings: and ye shall know that I am the LORD" (vv.8-11); **(2) the restoration of the people to the land (vv.16-24):** "I will take you from among the heathen, and gather you out of all countries, and will bring you into your own land" (v.24); **(3) the regeneration of the people by the Lord (vv.25-38):** "A new heart also will I give you, and a new spirit will I put within you ... And I will put my Spirit within you, and cause you to walk in my statutes, and ye shall keep my judgments and do them. And ye shall dwell in the land that I gave to your fathers; and ye shall be my people, and I will be your God" (vv.26-28).

1) THE REJUVENATION OF THE LAND, vv.1-15

As noted above, this section of the chapter is addressed to "the mountains of Israel": "Also, thou son of man, prophesy unto the mountains of Israel, and say, Ye mountains of Israel, hear the word of the LORD" (v.1). The prophecy describes divine blessing, and reverses an earlier prophecy against the mountains of Israel: "Son of man, set thy face toward the mountains of Israel, and prophesy against them, and say, Ye mountains of Israel, hear the word of the Lord GOD; Thus saith Lord GOD to the mountains, and to the hills, to the rivers, and to the valleys; Behold, I, even I, will bring a sword upon you, and will destroy your high places ..." (Ezek. 6: 1-3). Now the same "mountains ... hills ... rivers ... valleys" are addressed again, but with what a difference! (vv.4-15).

2) THE RESTORATION OF THE PEOPLE TO THE LAND, vv.16-24

The remaining verses of the chapter may divided as follows: **(i)** God's word

about the house of Israel (vv.16-21); *(ii)* God's word ***to*** the house of Israel (vv.22-38). However, following our initial analysis, we will consider these verses with reference to the restoration of the people to the land (vv.16-24) and the regeneration of the people by the Lord (vv.25-38). The first of these (vv.16-24) clearly falls into two parts: *(a)* the scattering of the house of Israel (vv.16-20): "I scattered them among the heathen" (v.19); *(b)* the regathering of the house of Israel" (vv.21-24): "I will take you from among the heathen, and gather you out of all countries" (v.24).

a) The scattering of the house of Israel, vv.16-20

We should notice *(i)* their conduct in the land (vv.17-19); *(ii)* their testimony in exile (v.20). The people were consistently evil. It has been said that "Israel was guilty of two great sins, the first of which was ***polluting God's land*** (vv.16-19)" and the second "that of ***profaning God's name before the Gentiles*** (vv.20-23)". John P.Taylor calls these verses a "historical retrospect" and continues, "Once again Ezekiel repeats his assertion that Israel's sins deserved God's punishment". Their restoration therefore cannot be attributable to them, but solely to the vindication of the Lord's name (vv.21, 22, 32). The basis of Israel's coming restoration lies in God's jealousy for His Name.

Their conduct *in the land* reminds us of the importance of godly conduct *in the assembly*. See, for example, 1 Corinthians 3 verses 16-17, "Know ye not that ye are the temple of God, and that the Spirit of God dwelleth in you? If any man defile the temple of God, him shall God destroy; for the temple of God is holy, which temple ye are". (See also 1 Tim. 3: 15.)

i) **Their conduct in the land, vv.17-19.** They **polluted the land**. "Son of man, when the house of Israel dwelt in their own land, they defiled it by their own way and by their doings: their way was before me as the uncleanness of a removed woman ('as the uncleanness of a woman in her separation', JND). Wherefore I poured out my fury upon them for the blood that they had shed in the land, and for their idols wherewith they had polluted it: and I scattered them among the heathen, and they were dispersed through the countries: according to their way and according to their doings I judged them." The people "had defiled the land and made it unclean, like the uncleanness of a menstruous woman" (John P. Taylor). C.L.Feinberg points out that in Israel "a woman was not permitted to enter the sanctuary until her purification (cf. Lev. 15: 19; Isa. 64: 6)".

ii)   Their testimony in exile, v.20. They **profaned God's name**. "And when they entered unto the heathen, whither they went, they profaned my holy name, when they said to them ('of them'), These are the people of the LORD, and are gone forth out of his land." While, at first glance, it might seem that it was the heathen who profaned the Lord's name, the words which follow (v.21) make it clear that Israel was responsible: "I had pity for mine holy name, which **the house of Israel had profaned among the heathen** whither they went". The NIV makes this clear: "And wherever they went among the nations they profaned my holy name, for it was said of them, 'These are the Lord's people, and yet they had to leave his land'". The conduct of God's people had profaned His name by causing the heathen to be "astonished that such a fate should happen to the people of the Lord, and it caused them to think lightly of a God who allowed His people to be treated so" (John P. Taylor). The heathen had said, "These are the people of the LORD, and are gone forth out of his land".

C.L.Feinberg has a very telling piece here: "Israel's exile itself was a profanation of God's sacred name ... It is well for us as believers today to realise that God is concerned how He is represented before the unbelieving world by our words and actions. Do we properly represent Him, or misrepresent Him? Do our lives manifest the grace that saved us, or are they a disgrace to the grace that redeemed us? And God has a supreme concern for His manifested excellence. His chief consideration is for the glory of His name, then for the welfare of the people upon whom His name has been placed".

As C.L.Feinberg points out, their conduct *in exile* reminds us of the importance of godly conduct *in the world.* Nathan made it clear that the world was obviously aware of David's misconduct: "thou hast given great occasion to the enemies of the LORD to blaspheme" (2 Sam. 12: 14), just as Paul made it clear that the Gentile nations were aware of Jewish misconduct: "the name of God is blasphemed among the Gentiles through you" (Rom. 2: 24)

b) The regathering of the house of Israel, vv.20-24

This will take place, not on the basis of their merit, but on the basis of the glory of His name: "I had pity for mine holy name, which the house of Israel had profaned among the heathen, whither they went. Therefore say unto the house of Israel, Thus saith the Lord GOD; I do not this for your sakes,

O house of Israel, but for mine holy name's sake, which ye have profaned among the heathen, whither ye went. And I will sanctify my great name, which was profaned among the heathen, which ye have profaned in the midst of them; and the heathen shall know that I am the LORD, saith the Lord GOD, when I shall be sanctified in you before their eyes. For I will take you from among the heathen, and gather you out of all countries, and will bring you into your own land". (Compare Deuteronomy 9 verses 4-6 where Moses said something similar in connection with their original possession of Canaan.) We should notice:

i)   The purpose of the regathering. Not, primarily, for the good of Israel, but for the glory of God. The Lord will not allow His "holy name" (v.20, 22) and "great name" (v.23) to "be profaned in any sense among the nations because of Israel's sin and punishment" (C.L.Feinberg). He will therefore sanctify His name in the very people who had profaned it by restoring them to their land, and accomplishing their regeneration: "And I will sanctify my great name, which was profaned among the heathen, which **ye have profaned** in the midst of them; and the heathen shall know that I am the LORD, saith the Lord GOD, when I shall be **sanctified in you** before their eyes. For I will take you from among the heathen, and gather you out of all countries, and will bring you into your own land". Paul reflected on God's dealings with Israel, albeit from a different standpoint, and saw nothing but His glory: "For God hath concluded them all in unbelief, that he might have mercy upon all. O the depth of the riches both of the wisdom and knowledge of God! How unsearchable are his judgments, and his ways past finding out! ... For of him, and through him, and to him, are all things: to whom be glory for ever. Amen" (Rom. 11: 32-36).

F.A.Tatford makes the very important point that "in restoring Israel to her land, moreover, He also made it clear that their removal from the land had not been caused by His weakness or inability to protect them, but by His deliberate judgment upon them for their sins". In this way, the profanation of His name would be fully answered. "Then shall they know that I am the LORD their God, which caused them ('in that I caused them', JND) to be led into captivity among the heathen" (Ezek. 39: 28).

ii)   The power of the regathering. "***I will take you*** from among the heathen, and gather you out of all countries, and will bring you into your own land." The scriptures abound with relevant passages! See, for example, Matthew 24 verses 30-31. As C.L.Feinberg rightly observes, "It is difficult to see a near reference here in view of the comprehensiveness of the terms, and the lasting nature of the transactions under consideration, namely, eternal issues".

3) THE REGENERATION OF THE PEOPLE BY THE LORD, vv.25-38

C.L.Feinberg places these verses "among the most glorious of the entire range of revealed truth on the subject of Israel's restoration to the Lord and national conversion". Attention is drawn to the following: *(a)* the regeneration of Israel (vv.25-31); *(b)* the reason for her regeneration (v.32); *(c)* the results of her regeneration (vv.33-38).

a) The regeneration of Israel, vv.25-31

F.Cundick rightly introduces his excellent summary of these verses by saying: "The new covenant replaces the old which was 'weak through the flesh'" (Rom. 8: 3), and that "The perfect plumbline of the law will never straighten out the irregular wall of man's heart. Therefore a new work is required". While the word "covenant" does not actually occur in the passage, the correspondence with Jeremiah 31 verses 31-34, which specifically refers to the "new covenant with the house of Israel, and with the house of Judah", is abundantly clear. Both passages refer to the future covenant which the Lord "will make with the house of Israel" (Jer. 31: 33). F.Cundick continues: "Since they were cast out as an unclean people, it would be a compromise of justice were they allowed to return and remain in the land in their former state" The blessings of the new covenant are now enumerated and F.Cundick's summary can hardly be bettered:

i)　**A new state, v.25.** "Then will I sprinkle clean water upon you, and **ye shall be clean**: from all your filthiness, and from all your idols, will I cleanse you." This refers to external cleansing. The word of God, called here "clean water", will be applied to national life. **Such cleansing is to be expected in the lives of regenerate people:** compare 1 Corinthians 6 verse 11. But more was needed, and this follows:

ii)　**A new nature, v.26.** "**A new heart** also will I give you, and a new spirit will I put within you: and I will take away the stony heart out of your flesh, and I will give you an heart of flesh." External cleansing "would not remove their evil propensities" (F.A.Tatford). Tatford continues: "Metaphorically, their former obdurate heart of stone was to be replaced by a warm new heart of flesh capable of responding to Him". **Such a change is to be expected in the lives of regenerate people.**

iii) **A new desire, v.26**. "A new heart also will I give you, and *a new spirit* will I put within you." F.A.Tatford observes that "the spirit of man actuates and regulates him: this also needed replacement if the nation was to be regenerated. So a new spirit would be placed within them. Their whole disposition was to be transformed, and a new will was to be imparted to them". **Such a change is to be expected in the lives of regenerated people.** For example, the law said, "Thou shalt not steal" (Ex. 20: 15), but regenerate people go further: "Let him that stole *steal no more* but rather let him labour, working with his hands the thing that is good, that he may have *to give* to him the needeth" (Eph. 4: 28). It has been observed that while the law said, for example, "thou shalt not bear false witness" as a commandment, the very same words can be said to saved men and women as a statement of fact: they are people who will not "bear false witness!"

iv) **A new power, v.27.** "And I will put *my Spirit* within you, and cause you to walk in my statutes, and ye shall keep my judgments, and do them." "They were to be endowed with the Holy Spirit, enabling them to do the divine will, to walk in His statutes and to obey His laws" (F.A.Tatford). **This is true in the lives of regenerated people today:** "For what the law could not do in that it was weak through the flesh, God sending his own Son in the likeness of sinful flesh, and for sin, condemned sin in the flesh: that the righteousness of the law might be fulfilled in us, who walk not after the flesh, but after the Spirit" (Rom. 8: 3-4).

There can be no doubt that the Lord Jesus was referring to this passage in His conversation with Nicodemus. Having said, "Except a man be born of water and of the Spirit, he cannot enter into the kingdom of God" and "Marvel not that I said unto you, Ye must be born again", Nicodemus replied, "How can these things be?" The Lord's answer takes us back to Ezekiel 36: "Art thou a master of Israel ('the teacher of Israel', JND), and knowest not these things? ... If I have told you earthly things, and ye believe not, how shall ye believe, if I tell you of heavenly things" (John 3: 5-12).

v) **A new behaviour, v.27**. "And I will put my spirit within you, and cause you to walk in my statutes, and ye shall keep my judgments, and do them." Such a change is to be expected in the lives of regenerate people.

vi)   A new fellowship, v.28-30. "And ye shall dwell in the land that I gave to your fathers: and ***ye shall be my people, and I will be your God***" (v.28). That fellowship will not be marred by sin ("I will also save you from all your uncleannesses", v.29), and will be attended by rich blessings ("I will call for the corn, and will increase it, and lay no famine upon you. And I will multiply the fruit of the tree, and the increase of the field, that ye shall receive no more reproach of famine among the heathen",vv.29-30). L.E.Cooper points out that that the word "dwell" ("ye shall dwell in the land", v.28) means to dwell as a permanent resident. ***John refers to our relationship with God as follows:*** "truly our fellowship is with the Father, and with his Son Jesus Christ" (1 John 1: 3).

vii)   A new evaluation, v.31. "Then shall ye remember your own evil ways, and your doings that were not good, and ***shall loathe yourselves in your own sight*** for your iniquities and for your abominations."

Since the above describes what is effectively a 'born again' people', it is perfectly legitimate to re-visit the text and use it to illustrate the life and conduct of those who are today "born again, not of corruptible seed, but of incorruptible, by the word of God, which liveth and abideth for ever" (1 Pet. 1: 23), people who can say, "he saved us, by the washing of regeneration, and renewing of the Holy Ghost" (Titus 3: 5). Examples are given above.

b) The reason for her regeneration, v.32

"Not for your sakes do I this, saith the Lord GOD, be it known unto you: be ashamed and confounded for your own ways, O house of Israel." (See, again, Deuteronomy 9: 4-6.) As we have already noted, Israel will be blessed in this way, not on the basis of personal merit, but on the basis of God's glory. Israel's millennial blessing flows out of God's intention to vindicate His name before the nations of the world. "For from the rising of the sun even unto the going down of the same, my name shall be great among the Gentiles: and in every place incense shall be offered unto my name, and a pure offering: for my name shall be great among the heathen, saith the LORD of hosts" (Mal. 1: 11).

This should create a deep sense of unworthiness in the hearts of God's people. In the words of F.A.Tatford, "Fittingly, therefore, there followed the admonition to the people to blush with shame (cf. Ezra 9: 6) at the remembrance of their character and conduct in the past".

c) The results of her regeneration, vv.33-38

In this connection, we should notice the introductory words, "Thus saith the Lord GOD; In the day that I shall have cleansed you from all your iniquities I will ..." (v.33). Four things follow: *(i)* the rejoicing in her inheritance (vv.33-35); *(ii)* the recognition by the nations (v.36); *(iii)* the response to her requests (v.37); *(iv)* the rise in population (vv.37-38). These verses are largely self-explanatory:

i) **The rejoicing in her inheritance, vv.33-35.** "I will also cause you to dwell in the cities and the wastes shall be builded. And the desolate land shall be tilled, whereas it lay desolate in the sight of all that passed by. And they shall say, This land that was desolate is become like the garden of Eden; and the waste and desolate and ruined cities are become fenced, and are inhabited." This largely restates verses 8-10. We should notice the words: "This land that was desolate is become like **the garden of Eden**" (v.35). This could be said to be an advance on verse 11, "I will settle you after your old estates, and will do better unto you than at your beginnings". C.L.Feinberg calls this, "the ultimate comparison".

ii) **The recognition by the nations, v.36.** "Then the heathen that are left (note this: compare v.3, "the residue of the heathen") round about you shall know that I the LORD build the ruined places, and plant that that was desolate: I the LORD have spoken it, and I will do it." This restates and amplifies verse 23. The nations will say, in effect, "the LORD hath done great things for them" (Psalm 126: 2). Men will call God's people, "the planting of the LORD, that he might be glorified" (Isa. 61: 3).

Simon Sherwin (*Present Truth*, April/May 2019) summarises it nicely: "They will .... be a testimony, or a showcase to the nations, as they see what the Lord has done for His people (v.36), cf. Ephesians 2 verse 7".

iii) **The response to her requests, v.37.** "Thus saith the Lord GOD; I will yet for this be enquired of by the house of Israel, to do it for them." As C.L.Feinberg points out, "There had been a day when the Lord refused to be enquired of by His disobedient people (14: 4; 20: 3), but now the Lord would be accessible for their turning to Him in genuine repentance, and would grant their requests ... The implication is that they would be heard by the Lord".

iv) The rise in population, vv.37-38. "I will increase them with men like a flock. As the holy flock, as the flock of Jerusalem in her solemn feasts; so shall the waste cities be filled with flocks of men: and they shall know that I am the LORD." This restates verses 10-12. What happened at Jerusalem "three times in a year" (Deut. 16: 16), when the city teemed with men, would mark the former "waste cities" of the land. Nehemiah lamented that the Jerusalem was large and its population extremely small (Neh. 7: 4). This will not be so in the millennial age. It is noteworthy that the word "flock" and "flocks" occurs four times in verses 37-38, reminding us of the earlier statement: "And ye my flock, the flock of my pasture, are men, and I am your God, saith the Lord GOD" (34: 31). In that day, Israel's shepherd-king will "feed his flock like a shepherd: he shall gather the lambs with his arm, and carry them in his bosom, and shall gently lead those that are with young" (Isa. 40: 11). In that day, "David my servant shall be king over them; and they all shall have one shepherd: they shall also walk in my judgments, and observe my statutes, and do them" (Ezek. 37: 24).

Other relevant passages are found in Isaiah 49 verse 20 ("The children which thou shalt have, after thou hast lost the other, shall say again in thine ears, The place is too strait for me: give place to me that I may dwell"); Zechariah 10 verse 10 ("I will bring them again also out of the land of Egypt. And gather them out of Assyria; and I will bring them into the land of Gilead and Lebanon; and place shall not be found for them").

EZEKIEL CHAPTER 37

Past chapters have painted a glorious future for Israel. God had promised that He would regather His scattered sheep and "set up one shepherd over them, and he shall feed them, even my servant David ... And I the LORD will be their God, and my servant David a prince among them; I the LORD have spoken it ... And I will make them and the places round about my hill a blessing; and I will cause the shower to come down in his season; there shall be showers of blessing" (34: 23-26). Restored leadership would be accompanied by a restored land with rebuilt cities: "I will settle you after your old estates, and will do better unto you than at your beginnings ... And the desolate land shall be tilled ... And they shall say, This land that was desolate is become like the garden of Eden; and the waste and desolate and ruined cities are become fenced, and are inhabited" (36: 11, 34-35).

But all this would not be a case of putting the same sinful people in a new environment. Israel will be cleansed and regenerated: "I will take you from among the heathen, and gather you out of all countries, and will bring you into your own land. Then will I sprinkle clean water upon you, and ye shall be clean: from all your filthiness, and from all your idols, will I cleanse you. A new heart also will I give you, and a new spirit will I put within you: and I will take away the stony heart out of your flesh, and I will give you an heart of flesh. And I will put my Spirit within you, and cause you to walk in my statutes, and ye shall keep my judgments, and do them" (36: 24-27).

Rather than 'music in the ears' of the exiles in Babylonia, all this was evidently received with scepticism: "behold, they say, Our bones are dried, and our hope is lost: we are cut off for our parts" (37: 11). Had they been asked the same question as Ezekiel, "Can these bones live?", the answer, it seems, would have been unmistakably 'No'. Even Ezekiel seems a little guarded in answering the question (v.3).

Ezekiel 37 demonstrates that the glowing promises in preceding chapters will be fulfilled, even though Israel's situation at the time seemed utterly hopeless. As J.P.Taylor points out, "If God's purpose was to restore Israel, He would do it by however great a miracle. Both the vision and the oracle of the two sticks conveyed the message". The despondent exiles are therefore assured, not only that Israel would be restored to life (vv.1-14), but that the old divisions between Israel and Judah would disappear (vv.15-28). "The new nation will unite the remnants of both peoples in one land under one king, and without their traditional animosity" (J.P.Taylor). In the Lord's own words, "I will make them one nation in the land upon the mountains of Israel; and one king shall be king to them all: and they shall be no more two nations, neither shall they be divided into two kingdoms any more at all" (v.22).

With this in mind, the chapter may be divided as follows: *(1)* national resurrection (vv.1-14); *(2)* national reunification (vv.15-28).

1) NATIONAL RESURRECTION, vv.1-14

This section of the chapter falls into two clear parts: *(a)* the vision (vv.1-10); *(b)* the explanation (vv.11-14).

a) The vision, vv.1-10

We should notice at least four things here: *(i)* the problem (vv.1-2); *(ii)* the possibility (v.3); *(iii)* the promise (vv.4-6); *(iv)* the power (vv.7-10).

i) **The problem, vv.1-2**. "The hand of the LORD was upon me, and carried me out in the Spirit of the LORD, and set me down in the midst of the valley which was full of bones, and caused me to pass by them round about: and, behold, there were very many in the open valley; and, lo, they were very dry." Ezekiel describes the situation of the bones and the state of the bones:

- **The situation of the bones**. They were located in a "valley" (vv.1,2). The same word (*biqah*) is translated "plain" in Ezekiel 3 verses 22 and 23; Chapter 8 verse 4. It was there that the prophet saw "the glory of the LORD ... as the glory which I saw by the river of Chebar" (3: 23). While it cannot be said with any certainty that the two locations are one and the same, it can be said that there are places now filled with "bones" which were once filled with "the glory of the LORD". To put it in other language: "How is the gold become dim! how is the most fine gold changed! The stones of the sanctuary are poured out in the top of every street. The precious sons of Zion, comparable to fine gold, how are they esteemed as earthen pitchers, the work of the hands of the potter!" (Lam. 4: 1-2).

Of every assembly it ought to be said, "It was noised that he was in the house" (Mark 2: 1). But, alas, in many cases spiritual life has gone. The lampstand has been removed (Rev. 2: 5). The building may remain, and the people may remain, but, like Samson, they "wist not that the LORD was departed from him" (Judges 16: 20).

- ***The state of the bones.*** Having been given a tour of the area ("he caused me to pass by them round about"), Ezekiel concludes that there were "very many" and "very dry" (v.2). We know from the explanation that the bones represent the exiled Israelites, and J.P.Taylor points out that they had been in exile "for more than ten years now, and what glimmerings of hope they had when they first arrived have now been altogether extinguished. Their hope was lost: as bones, they were very dry". As already noted, this was what they themselves were saying: "behold, they say, Our bones are dried, and our hope is lost: we are cut off for our parts" (v.11).

While assembly testimony in some parts of the world is evidently flourishing, "dry bones" is not altogether an inappropriate description of assembly testimony in many places in the U.K. Not a few of the Lord's people are disheartened and discouraged over the demise of a large number of assemblies, and the reduction of others to small numbers. Some assemblies have 'the smell of death' about them, not necessarily because of reduced numbers, but because spiritual life is at such a low level. All seems irretrievably lost. The question put to Ezekiel, "can these bones live?" (v.3) is very pertinent today.

ii) ***The possibility, v.3***. "And he said unto me, Son of man, can these bones live? And I answered, O Lord GOD, thou knowest." John the Baptist evidently believed that God was able to raise up children to Abraham from stones (Matt. 3: 9). Ezekiel certainly gives a guarded answer, but we might well feel that J.P.Taylor describes us all in suggesting that the prophet "had the knowledge not to deny God's ability, but ... lacked the faith to believe in it". How do ***we*** see the future? Is there any possibility of revival in local assemblies, let alone revival on a broader basis? It has been said, humorously, yet not so humorously, "Blessed is he that expecteth nothing, for he shall receive the same!" Perhaps the Lord is asking us in *our* local circumstances, "Can these bones live?"

iii)   The promise, vv.4-6. "Again he said unto me, Prophesy upon these bones, and say unto them, O ye dry bones, hear the word of the LORD. Thus saith the Lord GOD unto these bones; Behold, I will cause breath to enter into you *and ye shall live*: and I will lay sinews upon you, and will bring up flesh upon you, and cover you with skin, and put breath in you, *and ye shall live*; and ye shall know that I am the LORD." There is some encouragement here - for Ezekiel, and for us!

iv)   The power, vv.7-10. The operative power in accomplishing Israel's promised revival lay in the word of God (vv.7-8) and the Spirit of God (vv.9-10).

- *The word of God*: "So I prophesied as I was commanded: and as I prophesied, there was a noise, and behold a shaking (*raash*: elsewhere translated 'earthquake', 1 Kings 19: 11-12; Isa. 29: 6; Amos 1: 1; Zech. 14: 5), and the bones came together, bone to his bone, And when I beheld, lo, the sinews and the flesh came up upon them, and the skin covered them above: but there was no breath in them" (vv.7-8). As a result of speaking to the bones, **the skeletons became corpses, but they were still just as dead!** The point here is that "the bones did not come together by their own action, but by the earthquake shaking following the prophetic word" (H.L.Ellison).

- *The Spirit of God*: "Then said he unto me, Prophesy unto the wind, prophesy, son of man, and say to the wind, Thus saith the Lord GOD; Come from the four winds, O breath, and breathe upon these slain, that they that may live. So I prophesied as he commanded me, and the breath came into them, and they lived, and stood upon their feet, an exceeding great army" (vv.9-10). In this connection it should be noted that the Hebrew word *ruah* (*ruach*) is translated **"Spirit"** in verses 1 and 14; **"breath"** in verses 5, 6, 8, 9 and 10; and **"wind"** or **"winds"** in verse 9. In the New Testament the equivalent Greek word *pneuma* is similarly translated: "The **wind** (*pneuma*) bloweth where it listeth, and thou hearest the sound thereof, but canst not tell whence it cometh, and whither it goeth: so is every one that is born of the **Spirit** (*pneuma*)" (John 3: 8). We must now notice the following details:

CHAPTER 37

As a result of speaking to the Spirit ("Come ... O breath"), **the corpses became living people!** The "four winds" represent the entire world. See Revelation 7 verse 1, "I saw four angels standing on the four corners of the earth, holding the four winds of the earth ..." See also Matthew 24 verse 31, "And he shall send his angels ... and they shall gather together his elect from the four winds, from one end of heaven to the other".

The two stages above are certainly significant. In the first place, we have **national resurrection**, but **that is all**. In the second, the nation possesses a **"spiritual life, and not merely a national existence"** (F.A. Tatford). This is true today, and will be the order of events at the end time. The possession of true spiritual life will follow the return to the land: note the order in verses 12-14 and in Chapter 36 verses 24-28.

The two stages have their counterpart today in the proclamation of the Gospel and its results.

- **In the first case,** Ezekiel is commanded to prophesy "to the bones, telling them to hear" (J.B. Taylor). Taylor continues: This "must have seemed to Ezekiel very much like his professional occupation, exhorting lifeless people to listen to God's word. The effect was limited: true, something remarkable happened, but the hearers were still dead men". Hearing the word of God alone did not give them new life, anymore than men and women who are "dead in trespasses and sins", having heard the Gospel, immediately become regenerate. But "faith cometh by hearing, and hearing, by the word of God" (Rom. 10: 17). It is through hearing and receiving the word of God that men and women experience "the washing of regeneration and renewing of the Holy Ghost" (Titus 3: 5).

- **In the second case**, Ezekiel is commanded to prophesy "to the wind (*ruah*) and to appeal to it to come and breathe upon those slain, that they may live" (J.B. Taylor). Taylor continues: "The second action was tantamount to praying, as Ezekiel besought the Spirit of God to effect the miracle of re-creation, to breathe into man's nostrils the breath of life (Gen. 2: 7). This time the effect is devastating. What preaching itself failed to achieve, prayer made a reality". While this is true, it might be better to say 'What preaching in itself could not achieve, **the Spirit of God made a reality**'.

It is worth pointing out the role of **the servant of God** in both cases. So far as the word of God is concerned, Ezekiel, having been instructed to "Prophesy upon these bones" (v.4), obeyed: "So I prophesied as I was commanded" (v.7). So far as the Spirit of God is concerned, having been instructed to "Prophesy unto the wind" (v.9), he obeyed again, "So I prophesied as he commanded me" (v.10). In this way, Ezekiel emphasises that the work of revival is God's work from start to finish. If man plays any part in it himself, it is only in obedience to God's direction. The same can be said of man's contribution to any spiritual revival" (John B.Taylor).

b) *The explanation, vv.11-14*

"Then he said unto me, Son of man, these bones are the whole house of Israel: "behold, they say, Our bones are dried, and our hope is lost: we are cut off for our parts. Therefore prophesy and say unto them, Behold, O my people, I will open your graves, and cause you to come out of your graves, and bring you into the land of Israel (compare 36: 24). And ye shall know that I am the LORD, when I have opened your graves, O my people, and brought you up out of your graves, and shall put my Spirit in you, and ye shall live (compare 36: 27), and I shall place you in your own land: then shall ye know that I the LORD have spoken it, and performed it, saith the LORD." The change of metaphor should be noted. From a valley full of unburied dry bones, the passage turns to the resurrection from the grave. This is not inconsistent. It serves to emphasise in two ways God's intention to revive His dispirited people.

Here is the Lord's answer to His own question, "Son of man, can these bones live?" (v.3) and to the despondency of the exiles in Babylonia, "Our bones are dried, and our hope is lost: we are cut off for our parts" (v.11). These very words make it clear that the prophecy does not refer to the resurrection of individuals (as in Isaiah 26: 19; Dan. 12: 2), but rather to **the resurrection or revival of the nation as a whole.** A similar passage is found in Hosea 6 verse 2, "**After two days will he revive us: in the third day he will raise us up, and we shall live in his sight".** As C.L.Feinberg points out, "The chapter points up the spiritual condition of Israel during the many centuries of her dispersion throughout the world". To which we add, 'and points to the restoration of national life'. Israel will no longer be 'scattered bones': "I will ...bring you into the land of Israel" (v.12); "I shall place you in your own land" (v.14).

2) *NATIONAL REUNIFICATION, vv.15-28*

In the second section of the chapter, the prophet himself is instructed to demonstrate God's intention to reunite His people, reversing the centuries-old cleavage between Judah and Israel dating back to the secession of the ten tribes (1 Kings 12: 16-17) after the death of Solomon. These verses take the form, not of a vision, but of an acted parable. In the vision given to Ezekiel the "dry bones" represent "the *whole* house of Israel", and the parable of the 'two sticks' (representing the southern and northern kingdoms - Judah and Israel) demonstrates that it will indeed be a unified nation in the future.

As before, this part of the chapter falls into two clear parts: *(a)* the parable (vv.15-17); *(b)* the explanation (vv.18-28).

a) The parable, vv.15-17

"The word of the LORD came again unto me, saying, Moreover, thou son of man, take thee one stick, and write upon it, For Judah, and for the children of Israel his companions: then take another stick, and write upon it, For Joseph, the stick of Ephraim (Jeroboam was evidently an Ephraimite, 1 Kings 11: 26) and for all the house of Israel his companions: and join them one to another into one stick; and they shall become one in thine hand."

The first stick was to be inscribed, "For Judah, and for the children of Israel his companions". Judah's "companions" are "the greater part of Benjamin and Simeon, the tribe of Levi, and godly Israelites who had come at different times from the northern kingdom, with its idolatry and false priesthood, into the kingdom of Judah (cf. 2 Chron. 11: 12; 15: 9; 30: 11, 18; 31: 1)" (C.L.Feinberg). The second stick was to be inscribed, "For Joseph, the stick of Ephraim, and for all the house of Israel his companions". This does not require explanation. Neither do the words, "and they shall become one in thine hand". David would have been delighted to hear this. See Psalm 133 verse 1, "Behold, how good and how pleasant it is for brethren to *dwell together in unity*!" We might go further and say that David (vv.24, 25) will be delighted to see this. After all, he saw the nation re-united during his past lifetime (2 Samuel 5: 1-5) and will evidently see it happen again, never to be reversed.

b) The explanation, vv.18-28

Ezekiel was to expect enquiries. People would say, "Wilt thou not shew us what thou meanest by these" (v.18) and, like the prophet, *we* are to be "ready always to give an answer to every man that asketh you a reason of the hope that is in you with meekness and fear" (1 Pet. 3: 15).

God's servant did not have to rack his brains for an explanation: "*Say unto them*, Thus saith the Lord GOD; Behold, I will take the stick of Joseph, which is in the hand of Ephraim, and the tribes of Israel his fellows, and will put them with him, even with the stick of Judah, and make them one stick, and they shall be *one in mind hand.* And the sticks whereon thou writest shall be in thine hand before their eyes. And say unto them, Thus saith the Lord GOD; Behold, I will take the children of Israel from among the heathen, whither they be gone, and will gather them on every side, and bring them into their own land; and I will make them *one nation* in the land upon the mountains of Israel; and *one king* shall be king to them all: and they shall be no more two nations, neither shall they be divided into two kingdoms any more at all" (vv.19-22). For further reading on the subject, see Isaiah 11 verses 12-13; Jeremiah 3 verse 18 and Hosea 1 verse 11.

We should notice that these verses describe different features of the coming unity of God's people which, when taken together, make an excellent object lesson for every assembly of God's people today.

i) **They would be one nation**. As noted, "they shall be *one in mine hand"* (v.19); "I will make them *one nation* in the land" (v.22). None will be left elsewhere. See Chapter 39 verse 28.

The Lord Jesus prayed that His people "all may be one; as thou, Father, art in me, and I in thee, that they also may be one in us" (John 17: 21). Paul therefore urged the Ephesian believers "to keep the unity of the Spirit in the bond of peace" (Eph. 4: 3), reminding them that "There is one body, and one Spirit, even as ye are called in one hope of your calling; one Lord, one faith, one baptism, one God and Father of all, who is above all, and through all, and in you all" (Eph. 4: 4-6). The "unity of the Spirit" was divinely accomplished. Believers cannot 'make' it, but they are to "keep" it.

The unity and fellowship of God's people was a matter of great concern to Paul when he wrote to the Philippians. It is no accident that he frequently uses the word "all" in his introduction: see verse 1 ("to *all* the saints in Chrst Jesus"); verse 4 ("Always in every prayer of mine for you *all*"); verse 7 ("Even as it is meet for me to think this of you *all*, because ... ye *all* are partakers of my grace"); verse 8 ("For God is my record, how greatly I long after you *all* in the bowels of Jesus Christ"). The reason for this emphasis lies in Phillipians 4 verse 2 (two sisters in the assembly were evidently not talking to each together: they could not say with Paul, "I long after you *all* in the bowels of Jesus Christ", 1: 8), and it also explains Chapter 1 verse 27, "Stand fast in *one* spirit, with *one* mind, striving together for the faith of the gospel". It also explains Chapter 2 verse 2, "Fulfil ye my joy, that ye be *likeminde*d, having the *same love*, being of *one accord,* of *one mind*". See also Acts 2 verse 1: "they were all with *one accord* in one place".

It is sad to notice the progress of disunity at Corinth. *(i)* "Contentions *among you*" (1 Cor. 1: 11). The word "contentions" means 'strife … quarrels … wrangling'. *(ii)* "Divisions *among you*" (1 Cor. 11: 18). The word "divisions" is translated "rent" in Matthew 9 verse 16. *(iii)* "Heresies *among you*" (1 Cor. 11: 19). The word "heresies" means 'sects'. This just proves how necessary it is to deal with problems in their infancy. The English proverb that "tall oaks from little acorns grow" applies here as much as anywhere! Notice what James says about this: "But if ye have bitter envy and strife in your hearts, glory not, and lie not against the truth. This wisdom descendeth not from above, but is earthly, sensual, devilish. For where envy and strife is, there is confusion and every evil work" (James 3: 14-16).

ii) **They would recognise one authority.** "*One king* shall be king to them all" (v.22). The king is identified: "David my servant shall be king over them … my servant David shall be their prince for ever" (vv.24, 25). When the division took place, after the death of Solomon, there were two kings: Rehoboam presided over Judah, and Jeroboam presided over Israel. It was a case of divided loyalties. This will not be the case in the millennium. "The sceptre shall not depart from Judah, nor a lawgiver from between his feet, until Shiloh come; and *unto him* shall the gathering of the people be" (Gen. 49: 10).

Believers today should be undivided in recognising that "Jesus Christ is Lord" (Phil. 2: 11). While He is not called 'king of the church', rather "King of Israel" (John 1: 49) and "King of nations" (Rev. 15: 3, JND), He is nevertheless Lord and Head of the church. His will is therefore binding: "If any man think himself to be a prophet or spiritual, let him acknowledge that the things that I write unto you are the commandments of the Lord" (1 Cor. 14: 37).

iii) **They would worship one God**. In the past they had worshipped false gods. "Neither shall they defile themselves any more with their idols, nor with their detestable things, nor with any of their transgressions: but I will save them out of all their dwellingplaces, wherein they have sinned, and will cleanse them: so shall they be my people, and *I* will be their God" (v.23). Comparable words are found in the previous chapter: "Then will I sprinkle clean water upon you, and ye shall be clean: from all your filthiness, and from all your idols, will I cleanse you ... ye shall be my people, and *I* will be your God" (36: 25, 28).

Believers today are to be undivided in heart: "he is thy Lord ... worship thou him" (Psalm 45: 11). Thomas exclaimed, "My Lord and my God (John 20: 28). Believers are told to "keep yourselves from idols" (1 John 5: 21). In the millennium, God's people will be suited to worship Him, something that He has already done for every one of His children today: He has "made us meet to be partakers of the inheritance of the saints in light" (Col. 1: 12).

iv) ***They would follow one shepherd***. "And David my servant shall be king over them; and they all shall have ***one shepherd***: they shall also walk in my judgments, and observe my statutes, and do them" (v.24). This re-introduces the theme of Chapter 34: "And I will set up one shepherd over them, and he shall feed them, even my servant David; he shall feed them, and he shall be their shepherd. And I the LORD will be their God, and my servant David a prince among them" (34: 23-24). Chapter 34 names David as the coming shepherd (v.23) as well as prince (v.24), and this double description is repeated here: see verses 24-25.

The Lord Jesus is today the Shepherd of His people. We "were as sheep going astray; but are now returned unto the Shepherd and Bishop of your souls" (1 Pet. 2: 25). He is the "chief Shepherd" (1 Pet. 5: 4). His shepherd-care takes many forms, including the work of 'under shepherds' who feed ('tend') the church of God" (Acts 20: 28). It follows that they should act as one. Woe to the assembly with a divided oversight! The Shepherd who "leadeth ... in the paths of righteousness for his name's sake" will ensure through His servant David that Israel will "walk in my judgments, and observe my statutes, and do them", reminding us that part of the ministry of New Testament shepherds is to ensure that the assembly is subject at all times to the word of God. In the case of Israel, the ability to do this will be wonderfully provided: "And I will put my Spirit within you, and cause you to walk in my statutes, and ye shall keep my judgments, and do them" (Ezek. 36: 27). The same ability has been given to us through the indwelling of the same Holy Spirit.

CHAPTER 37

v) ***They would enjoy one inheritance.*** Permanent possession of their inheritance is assured since the nation will live under the reign of God's appointed monarch: "And they shall dwell ***in the land*** that I have given unto Jacob my servant, wherein your fathers have dwelt; and they shall dwell therein, even they, and their children, and their children's children ***for ever***: and my servant David shall be their prince ***for ever***" (v.25). No conditions, with appropriate warnings, are made; for the simple reason that then they will be unnecessary!

The Lord's people today have a current inheritance and a future inheritance. As to the former, see Ephesians 1 verse 11. "In whom (Christ) we have obtained an inheritance": as to the latter, see 1 Peter 1 verse 4, "an inheritance incorruptible, and undefiled, and that fadeth not away, reserved in heaven for you". Happy is the assembly where all the believers are enjoying their inheritance now, and gladly anticipating the future!

vi) ***They would gather around one place.*** It is called "my sanctuary". "Moreover I will make a covenant of peace with them; it shall be an everlasting covenant with them: and I will place them, and multiply them (see also 36: 37-38), and will set ***my sanctuary*** in ***the midst*** of them for evermore. ***My tabernacle*** also ***shall be with them***: yea, I will be their God, and they shall be my people (see also 37: 23; 36: 28). And the heathen shall know that I the LORD do sanctify Israel, when ***my sanctuary*** shall be in ***the midst*** of them for evermore" (vv.26-28). The covenant will be "***everlasting***" (v.26), and the "sanctuary" will be in the midst of them for ***evermore***" (vv.26, 28). We should also notice the following:

- "***I will make a covenant of peace with them***" (v.26). The implications of this "covenant of peace" will become clear in Chapters 38-39.

- "***The heathen*** shall know that I the LORD to sanctify Israel" (v.28). This is developed in the next two chapters: see Chapter 38 verse 23 and Chapter 39 verses 21-29. Micah 5 verse 5 is relevant here: "And this man shall be the peace, when the Assyrian shall come into our land: and when he shall tread in our palaces, then shall we raise against him seven shepherds, and eight principal men".

- "***I will ... set my sanctuary in the midst of them for evermore"*** (v.26). This is developed in great detail in chs.40-48. See particularly Chapter 48 verse 8, "the sanctuary shall be in the midst of it (the land)".

EZEKIEL

The world is yet to see the purpose of God for Israel completely and gloriously achieved; and once attained, it will never be rescinded and never be overthrown.

EZEKIEL CHAPTER 38

As we have gladly noted, Chapters 34-48 anticipate, in glowing terms, the restoration of the nation, of which God says, "I ... will do better unto you than at your beginnings" (36: 11) In this connection, we suggested the following summary:

i) **The restoration of the monarchy, 34: 1 - 35: 15.** This section comprises *(i)* the past failure of the kings (34: 1-10); *(ii)* the prospective blessing for Israel (34: 11-31); *(iii)* the perpetual desolation of Edom (35: 1-15). Israel will enjoy the reign and care of a shepherd-king, and be totally free from the threat of occupation by her neighbours.

ii) **The restoration of the land, 36: 1-15.** "But ye, O mountains of Israel, ye shall shoot forth your branches, and yield your fruit to my people of Israel; for they are at hand to come" (36: 8).

iii) **The restoration of the people, 36: 16-38.** This section comprises *(i)* the restoration of the people to **the land** (vv.16-24); *(ii)* the regeneration of the people by **the Lord** (vv.25-38).

iv) **The restoration of national life, 37: 1-14.** "Behold, O my people, I will open your graves, and bring you into the land of Israel. And ye shall know that I am the LORD, when I have opened your graves, O my people, and brought you up out of your graves, and shall put my Spirit in you, and ye shall live, and I shall place you in your own land: then shall ye know that I the LORD have spoken it, and performed it, saith the LORD" (37: 12-14).

v) **The restoration of national unity, 37: 15-28.** "Thus saith the Lord GOD; Behold, I will take the stick of Joseph, which is in the hand of Ephraim, and the tribes of Israel his fellows, and will put them with him, even with the stick of Judah, and make them one stick, and they shall be one in mine hand" (37: 19).

*vii) **The restoration of national security, 38: 1 - 39: 29.*** The book of Ezekiel commences with a successful invasion: God did not deliver His people from the Babylonian armies. But in these chapters, a colossal invasion from "the north parts" (38: 15; 39: 2) is summarily judged on "the mountains of Israel" (39: 4).

*viii) **The restoration of the Lord's presence, 40: 1 - 48: 35***. The glory of the Lord, last seen standing "upon the mountain which is on the east side of the city" (11: 23), returns "from the way of the east" and "came into the house by the way of the gate whose prospect is toward the east ... and, behold, the glory of the LORD filled the house" (43: 1-5). The book closes with, "and the name of the city from that day shall be, The LORD is there" (48: 35).

This brings us to Chapters 38-39, which C.I.Scofield calls 'The prophecy against Gog'. Both chapters, which describe a colossal invasion of Israel from the north (see 38: 15; 39: 2), commence similarly: "Son of man, set thy face against Gog, the land of Magog, the chief prince of Meshech and Tubal, and prophesy against him" (38: 1); "Therefore, thou son of man, prophesy against Gog, and say, Thus saith the Lord GOD; Behold, I am against thee, O Gog, the chief prince of Meshech and Tubal" (39: 1). In broad terms, Chapter 38 describes the arrival of the invader, and Chapter 39 describes the burial of the invader.

If the oracle of the 'dry bones' and 'two sticks' was given to counteract the despondency of the people ("Our bones are dried, and our hope is lost: we are cut off for our parts". 37: 11) then we may conclude that this oracle was given to counteract the argument that "if the present catastrophe (Israel's captivity) were overcome, the predominance of the nations would still remain, and Israel could sink under yet another attack into permanent ruin. Against reasoning of this sort, the prophet offers the comfort of the complete glorious victory of God over all their enemies" (F.Cundick, *The Book of Ezekiel*).

The certainty of these future events is emphasised by the words, "Thus saith the Lord GOD" (vv.3, 10, 14, 17), together with the introduction, "And the word of the LORD came unto me, saying ..." (v.1). There is no need to say anything further! God's word is "for ever ... settled in heaven" (Psalm 119: 89).

Ezekiel ch.38 may be divided as follows: ***(1)*** the identity of the invader (vv.2-7): *(2)* the time of the invasion (vv.8-9); *(3)* the intent of the invasion (vv.10-13); *(4)* the initiative behind the invasion (vv.14-16); *(5)* the intervention against the invasion (vv.17-23).

1) THE IDENTITY OF THE INVADER, vv.2-7

"Son of man, set thy face against Gog, the land of Magog, the chief prince of Meshech and Tubal, and prophesy against him, and say, Thus saith the Lord GOD; Behold, I am against thee, O Gog, the chief prince of Meshech and Tubal: and I will turn thee back, and put hooks into thy jaws, and I will bring thee forth, and all thine army, horses and horsemen, all of them clothed with all sorts of armour, even a great company with bucklers and shields, all of them handling swords: Persia, Ethiopia, and Libya with them; all of them with shield and helmet: Gomer, and all his bands; the house of Togarmah of the north quarters, and all his bands: and many people with thee. Be thou prepared, and prepare for thyself, thou, and all thy company that are assembled unto thee, and be thou a guard unto them."

We should notice the following *(a)* the commander of the army (vv.2-3); *(b)* the capability of the army (v.4); *(c)* the constitution of the army (vv.5-7).

a) The commander of the army, vv.2-3

The commander of the army is Gog, and Ezekiel is commanded to do two things: *(i)* to set his "face against Gog", and *(ii)* to "prophesy against him" (v.2).

- "Son of man, **set thy face against Gog**, the land of Magog, the chief prince of Meshech and Tubal" or "Set your face toward Gog, of the land of Magog, the prince (or 'chief prince', margin) of Rosh, Meshech and Tubal" (RV). The enemy then is Gog, and the prophesy is repeatedly addressed to him (vv.2, 3, 14, 16, 18). As F.Cundick points out, "Whether Gog is a proper noun or not, it does appear that in the context an individual is addressed (38: 3; 39: 1). It is difficult to conceive such a vast host moving without a head or chief. 'Be thou a commander over them' (38: 7. RV/JND margin) may mean this".

Gog's territory is fourfold. First, **Magog.** This is not a person, but a country, hence, "Set your face toward Gog, *of the land of Magog* (RV)". Magog was a descendent of Japheth (Gen. 10: 2). Past historians (Josephus and Jerome) "associated the name with numerous Scythian tribes in the area of the Black Sea. There could, therefore, be some connection here with southern Russia" (Malcolm C. Davis, *Living with the Glory of the Lord*). It has also been said that the land of Magog was originally an area north of the Caspian Sea. As Malcolm Davis sensibly points out, "it is very tempting to link the name **Rosh** (RV: 'chief prince', AV) with the land of Russia, although there is little linguistic support for this identification. Again the names of **Meshech** and **Tubal** appear to be somewhat similar to Moscow and Tobolsk, but proof is lacking". F.A.Tatford goes further in saying "This is quite fallacious. Those towns are actually named after the rivers on which they stand". Meshech and Tubal appear to have been the Muskai and Tuplai (or Mushki and Tabali) of Assyrian inscriptions: the Moschi and Tibareni of the Greeks. It is said that they lived in the neighbourhood of Magog near to the Black Sea, but later migrated north, some say to the Caucasus Mountains.

While Malcolm Davis states that a "strong case can be made, therefore, for including Russia within the scope of this prophecy, and even for maintaining that she will be the chief instigator of the invasion of Israel", C.L.Feinberg is rather more cautious in saying that Ezekiel describes "a coming confederacy of nations about the Black and Caspian seas with Persia and North Africa, who will invade the promised land after Israel's restoration to it". Malcolm Davis is certainly correct in saying that at the present time, "Russia is still the only very large country to the far north of Israel likely to mount such a hostile attack on God's people, since she has links and sympathies even now with other peoples who will be involved in the invasion" and that "some of the countries named by Ezekiel here were probably located within what is part of the Russian confederation of states".

To this we must add that the territories to which Ezekiel refers were either within, or in some cases close to, the ancient Assyrian Empire, to which the Lord evidently refers in verse 17: "Art thou he *of whom I have spoken in old time*, by my servants the prophets of Israel, which prophesied in those days many years that I would bring thee against them?" One of "the prophets" involved must certainly be Micah through whom God said, "And *this man* (Christ) shall be the peace, when *the Assyrian* shall come into our land ..." (Micah 5: 5). Gog and his hordes are described as 'the latter-day Assyrian'.

- "Son of man ... *prophesy against him*, and say, Thus saith the Lord

CHAPTER 38

GOD; Behold, I am against thee, O Gog, the chief prince of Meshech and Tubal". Having read, "my servant David shall be their prince for ever" (37: 25), we now encounter another "prince", but he will most certainly *not* be "prince for ever!"

b) The capability of the army, v.4

"And I will turn thee back, and put hooks into thy jaws, and I will bring thee forth, and all thine army, horses and horsemen, all of them clothed with all sorts of armour, even a great company with bucklers and shields, all of them handling swords." While the invasion is doomed before it begins, we should notice that it will be a massive armed force. This is confirmed later: "And thou shalt come from thy place out of the north parts, thou, and many people with thee, all of them riding upon horses, a great company, and a mighty army" (v.15). As F.A.Tatford observes, "Fully armed and ready for the fray, the great hosts will prepare for the invasion of Israel. But the prophet indicated that, while Gog may make His plans, Jehovah was in supreme control and His intention was to frustrate the invader's machinations and to put hooks in his jaws to drag him and his forces into the land to deal with him there". C.L.Feinberg observes that "some have found great difficulty in the references to armour, buckler, shield, sword and helmet", but continues by saying that "even in our day of advanced weapons of warfare it is interesting to learn that in some parts of the world conflict is going on with primitive weapons", adding, "And how else could an ancient writer have described warfare? He knew nothing of guns and planes". Discussion on the subject sometimes leads to speculation on warfare without fossil fuels, with the suggestion that horses are far more manoeuvrable in the desert than tanks without fuel! It used to be said that most world armies maintained cavalry divisions – but we must beware: speculation about future events can be as wonderful as political hindsight.

c) The constitution of the army, vv.5-7

Other countries are named as Gog's allies: "Persia (modern Iran), Ethiopia, and Libya with them; all of them with shield and helmet". Persia of course borders on ex-Soviet territory (Uzbekistan, Kazakhstan, Azerbaijan). Ethiopia and Libya suggest North African allies. According to Malcolm Davis, all these countries have sympathies with Russia even today. Ancient Ethiopia included what is now Sudan, and "It is quite understandable that all these countries will one day unite under the leadership of Russia to invade Israel. Most of them are also now Islamic, and therefore hostile towards Israel for that reason" (Malcolm Davis).

Then we have "Gomer, and all his bands; the house of Togarmah of the north quarters (see also v.15), and all his bands: and many people with thee. Be thou prepared, and prepare for thyself, thou, and all thy company that are assembled unto thee, and be thou a guard unto them". Gomer is said to be the progenitor of the Cimmerians whose territory lay north of the Black Sea. Some equate this with Crimea, now again under Soviet control. Others suggest that Germany is a derivation of Gomer, but this suggestion is based on the Talmudic reading of Germania (the Kerman of south Persia). See F.A.Tatford. Togarmah is Armenia.

All the above will be under the command of Gog: "and be *thou* (Gog) a guard unto them", or "be thou chief or commander over them" (38: 7, JND margin).

2) THE TIME OF THE INVASION, vv.8-9

In addition to the time of the invasion, clear reference is made to the territory which will suffer invasion. We should notice, first of all, that the section commences with. "After many days thou (Gog) shalt be visited" (v.8). C.L.Feinberg draws attention to the following. *First,* that the attack would not take place for a long time: "After *many days* thou shalt be visited". Feinberg continues, "The events here predicted were not to be expected in the lifetime of Ezekiel or his contemporaries". Second, that the invasion would commence as the result of divine compulsion: "After many days *thou shalt be visited*". While some translate 'thou shalt be mustered', C.L.Feinberg points out that "the verb is the usual one for visitation either in blessing or in punishment". See, for example, Isaiah 29 verse 6. With this in mind, it is possible that the words, "After many days thou shalt be visited", refer to the divine judgment which will fall on the invasion by Gog and his associates.

a) The time of the invasion.

There can be little doubt that the invasion follows chronologically the restoration described in Chapters 36-37. The invasion will take place "in the latter years" when "thou (Gog) shalt come into the land that is brought back from the sword, and is gathered out of many people, against the

CHAPTER 38

mountains of Israel, which have been waste always: but is brought forth out of the nations, and they shall dwell safely all of them" (v.8). Very clearly the invasion will take place *after* the regathering and restoration of Israel. This poses difficulties for most commentators, but the similarity, better, the indentity, of the language here with preceding passages points clearly in this direction. See, for example, Chapter 34 verse 13 ("I will bring them out from the people, and gather them from the countries, and will bring them to their own land, and feed them upon the mountains of Israel by the rivers, and in all the inhabited places of the country"); Chapter 36 verse 24 ("I will take you from among the heathen, and gather you out of all countries, and will bring you into your own land"); Chapter 37 verse 21 ("I will take the children of Israel from among the heathen, whither they be gone, and will gather them on every side, and bring them into their own land"). Ezekiel is a very 'chronological book' and the order of events and language used to describe them leaves little, if any, doubt that this invasion will take place either at the beginning or during the millennium. In the words of F.A.Tatford (*Dead Bones Live*), "The date of the invasion was not stated, but the implication was that it was in the remote future *after* the advent of Messiah ... Since the attack was to come *after* the restoration of Israel in peace to their own land, it must clearly be assigned to *some time during the millennium* ... The days described still lie, of course, in the future, and there is little doubt that *the period in question is actually during the millennium*". C.L.Feinberg states that "The invasion will take place after Israel has been restored to their land".

The words, "in *the latter years* thou shalt come into the land that is brought back from the sword" (v8) and "thou shalt come up against my people of Israel as a cloud to cover the land; it shall be in the *latter days*" (v.16), are "frequently used of the closing period of God's dealing with Israel" (F.Cundick) (see 5), see, for example, Jeremiah 49: 39; Daniel 2: 28; 10: 14; Hosea. 3: 5), whereas the rebellion described in Revelation 20 verse 7 will occur "when the thousand years are expired" or "after the thousand years are finished" (Newberry).

One thing is clear, while the names of Gog and Magog reappear at the end of the millennium, the circumstances are entirely different. As Malcolm Davis points out, the burial of the dead over a period of seven months (Ezek 39: 12-13) and the destruction of weapons over a period of seven years (Ezek. 39: 9-10) could hardly take place at the end of the millennium when the resurrection of the wicked dead and the dawn of the eternal state immediately follows the final rebellion against God. It is generally pointed out that while the enemies of God's people in Ezekiel 38-39 are said to come from "the uttermost north" (Ezek. 39: 2, JND), with some associated nations rather nearer, the enemies in Revelation 20 come from "the four quarters of the earth" (Rev. 20: 8).

While the names "Gog and Magog" in Revelation 20 could "well be symbolic names for God's enemies at the end of the Millennium" (Malcolm Davis), the connection with the "Gog and Magog" in Ezekiel 38-39 certainly highlights the fact that one thousand years will not diminish hatred for God and His people. As Malcolm Davis puts it, "As soon as Satan is released from the abyss at the end of the Millennial Kingdom he will incite the unbelieving nations to revive the old hatred he has for God and Hs people, and had previously manifested in the attack described in Ezekiel Chapters 38-39". Perhaps the attack will be master-minded by someone in "the uttermost north"

"After **many days** thou shalt be visited: in the **latter years** ('latter days', v.16) thou shalt come into the land that is brought back from the sword, and is gathered out of many people, against the mountains of Israel, which have always been waste: but it is brought forth out of the nations, and they shall dwell safely all of them. Thou shalt ascend and come like a storm, thou shalt be like a cloud to cover the land (see also v.16), thou and all thy bands, and many people with thee." F.A.Tatford must be right in saying, "The vast armies, evidently moving extremely rapidly, would plainly drive all before them. It was a terrifying picture for a land which had enjoyed peace and prosperity and freedom from all military disturbance or invasion, and which was evidently totally unprepared for such an attack".

b) *The territory invaded, vv.8-9*

Gog will invade "the land that is **brought back** from the sword, and is **gathered** out of many people, against the **mountains of Israel**, which have always been waste: but it is **brought forth** out of the nations, and they shall dwell safely all of them". This could hardly apply to any period prior to the millennium. The suggestion that the passage refers to the period just before the termination of the covenant made with Antichrist at the mid-point of the Tribulation, thus terminating any sense of security enjoyed by Israel, seems completely untenable.

CHAPTER 38

3) THE INTENT OF THE INVASION, vv.10-13

The section commences, as noted above, with the words, "Thus saith the Lord GOD" (v.10), and continues, "It shall also come to pass, that at the same time (see also v.18) shall things come into thy mind, and thou shalt think an evil thought: and thou shalt say, I will go up to the land of unwalled villages; I will go to them that are at rest, that dwell safely (see also v.14), all of them dwelling without walls, and having neither bars nor gates (see also v.11), to **take a spoil**, and to **take a prey**; to turn thine hand upon the desolate places that are now inhabited, and upon the people that are gathered out of the nations, which have gotten cattle and goods, that dwell in the midst of the land. Sheba, and Dedan, and the merchants of Tarshish, with all the young lions thereof, shall say unto thee, Art thou come **to take a spoil?** hast thou gathered thy company to **take a prey?** to carry away silver and gold, to take away cattle and goods, to **take a great spoil?**"

While the vast mineral wealth of the Dead Sea area has been suggested as the goal of the invasion, there seems no doubt that its object was to completely "overwhelm Israel, destroy their rebuilt cities and carry off illimitable boot ('booty')" (F.A.Tatford).

The words "that dwell in the midst of the land" (v.12) are most interesting. Literally, they read, 'that dwell in the navel of the earth'. According to F.A.Tatford, commenting on the word in Ezekiel 5 verse 5, "Many of the Rabbis referred to Jerusalem as geographically the navel of the world". While the words, "I have set it in the midst of the nations and countries that are round about her" (Ezek. 5: 5), are understood by some commentators with reference to "her place theologically as the centrepiece of God's favour in the world" (J.B.Taylor), it does seem more than likely that this is linked with her geographical position: "When the Most High divided to the nations their inheritance, when he separated the sons of Adam, he set the bounds of their habitation according to the number of the children of Israel" (Deut. 32: 8).

The merchants in the area, Sheba (in south Arabia) and Dedan (in north Arabia), together with Tarshish (either in Spain or North Africa), appear either to be looking for trading opportunities, or expressing concern that they too might fall prey to the cupidity of the invaders. John B. Taylor opts for the first suggestion: "The force of verse 13 seems to be that Gog's enterprise has roused the greed of other nations to join in the plunder, or to traffic in the stolen goods. They are typical of those who will not initiate wrong-doing, but are eager to cash in on the proceeds of it".

4) THE INITIATIVE BEHIND THE INVASION, vv.14-16

The section commences, as noted above, with the words, "Thus saith the Lord GOD" (v.14), and continues: "In that day when my people of Israel dwelleth safely, shalt not thou know it? And thou shalt come from thy place out of the north parts, thou, and many people with thee, all of them riding upon horses, a great company, and a mighty army: and thou shalt come up against my people of Israel, as a cloud to cover the land; it shall be in the latter days, and I will bring thee against my land, that the heathen may know me, when I shall be sanctified in thee, O Gog, before their eyes".

The initiative behind the invasion belongs to God. We should notice the following: *(a)* He is aware that His people's welfare is involved; *(b)* He is aware of the enemy's movements; *(c)* He directs the enemy's movements; *(d)* He will be glorified through the enemy's defeat.

a) He is aware that His people's welfare is involved

"In that day when **my people of Israel** dwelleth safely" (v.14); "thou shalt come up against **my people of Israel**" (v.16). More than that, His people are dwelling in His land: "I will bring thee against **my land**" (v.16).

b) He is aware of the enemy's movements

i) **He is aware of the time of the invasion:** "In **that day** when my people Israel dwelleth safely" (v.14); "it shall be in **the latter days**" (v.16).

ii) **He is aware of the direction of the invasion:** "thou shalt come from thy place out of **the north parts**" (v.15). Compare Chapter 1 verse 4. The chariot throne came from the north for the simple reason that it overshadowed the Babylonian invasion from the north.

iii) **He is aware of the strength of the invasion:** "a great company, and a mighty army" (v.15); "as a cloud to cover the land" (v.16). He knew that the enemy would "come like a storm … like a cloud to cover the land" (v.9).

c) He directs the enemy's movements

While God says "***thou shalt com***e from thy place out of the north parts ... and ***thou shalt come up*** against my people of Israel" (vv.15-16), the enemy was unconsciously acting under divine compulsion: "***I will bring thee*** against my land" (v.16).

d) He will be glorified through the enemy's defeat

God is in complete control: He uses the invasion: "I will bring thee against my land, that ***the heathen may know me***, when I shall be sanctified in thee, O Gog, before their eyes" (v.16).

5) THE INTERVENTION AGAINST THE INVADER, vv.17-23

The section commences, as noted above, with the words, "Thus saith the Lord GOD" (v.17), and continues: "Art thou he of whom I have spoken in old time by my servants the prophets of Israel, which prophesied in those days many years that I would bring thee against them? And it shall come to pass at the same time (see also v.10) when Gog shall come against the land of Israel, saith the Lord GOD, that my fury shall come up in my face. For in my jealousy and in the fire of my wrath have I spoken, Surely in that day there shall be a great shaking in the land of Israel; so that the fishes of the sea, and the fowls of the heaven, and the beasts of the field, and all creeping things that creep upon the earth, and all the men that are upon the face of the earth, shall shake at my presence, and the mountains shall be thrown down, and the steep places shall fall, and every wall shall fall to the ground. And I will call for a sword against him throughout all my mountains, saith the Lord GOD: every man's sword shall be against his brother. And I will plead against him with pestilence and with blood; and I will rain upon him, and upon his bands, and upon the many people that are with him, an overflowing rain, and great hailstones, fire, and brimstone. Thus will I magnify myself, and sanctify myself; and I will be known in the eyes of many nations, and they shall know that I am the LORD".

We should notice the following: *(a)* the Lord's foreknowledge (v.17); *(b)* the Lord's fury (vv.18-20); *(c)* the Lord's faithful word (vv.21-23).

a) The Lord's foreknowledge, v.17

"Art thou he of whom I have spoken in old time by my servants the prophets of Israel, which prophesied in those days many years that I would bring thee against them?" We have already suggested that "he of whom I have spoken in old time by my servants the prophets of Israel" are the Assyrians (see, again, Micah 5: 5).

b) The Lord's fury, vv.18-20

He refers to "my fury" (v.18); "my jealousy" (v.19); "my wrath" (v.19). The whole of creation (in Israel), animate (beast and man) and inanimate (mountains, steep places, and walls: divinely created or humanly-created), will be affected. God's jealousy for His Name will not permit His regathered people to be trampled under foot by this gigantic enemy from the north.

c) The Lord's faithful word, vv.21-23

There is no doubt about the outcome: "And *I will* call for a sword against him throughout all my mountains, saith the Lord GOD: every man's sword shall be against his brother. And *I will* plead against him with pestilence and with blood; and *I will* rain upon him, and upon his bands, and upon the many people that are with him, an overflowing rain, and great hailstones, fire, and brimstone. Thus *will I* ('I will', JND) magnify myself, and sanctify myself; and *I will* be known in the eyes of many nations, and they shall know that I am the LORD".

The whole world will feel the impact of divine intervention on the mountains of Israel. The forces of Gog will perish by war amongst themselves, and by visitation from heaven.

No earthly power, however great, can bring disrepute upon the God of Israel: "Thus will I magnify myself, and sanctify myself; and I will be known in the eyes of many nations, and they shall know that I am the LORD" (v.23).

EZEKIEL CHAPTER 39

As noted in the outline of the book the prophecy of Ezekiel commences with a successful invasion (Chapters 4 and 5). God did not deliver His people from the Babylonian armies. But in Chapters 38-39, a colossal invasion from "the north parts" (38: 15; 39: 2) is summarily judged on "the mountains of Israel" (39: 4).

The two invasions have this in common: both come from the north, and both are under divine control.

- **In the case of the Babylonian invasion**, Jeremiah was told, "Out of **the north** an evil shall break forth upon all the inhabitants of the land. For, lo, I will call all the families of the kingdoms of the north, saith the LORD, and they shall come ..." (Jer. 1: 14-15). Jeremiah records the fulfilment of this prophecy in Chapter.39, where "all the princes of the king of Babylon came in, and sat in the middle gate" (v.3). The Babylonian invasion was certainly under divine control. This is clear from the fact that the Lord's chariot throne came "out of **the north**" (Ezek 1: 4). The Babylonian army marched under the direction and compulsion of God's throne!

- **In the case of Gog's invasion**, God says, "thou shalt come from thy place out of **the north parts**" (Ezek 38: 15); "I ... will cause thee to come up from **the north parts**" (Ezek. 39: 2). Gog and his hordes will also march under the command and compulsion of God's throne: "*I* will bring thee forth, and all thine army" (Ezek. 38: 4).

We suggested in dealing with Chapter 38 that, in broad terms, Chapter 38 describes the descent of the invader on Israel like "a cloud to cover the land" (v.9), and that Chapter 39 describes the destruction of the invader "upon the mountains of Israel" (v.4).

Ezekiel 39 comprises three main paragraphs which may be entitled as follows: **(1) the end of the invasion (vv.1-8)**, and we should notice the expressions, "I will turn thee back ... I will smite thy bow out of thy left hand .... I will give thee unto the ravenous birds ... I will send a fire on Magog" (vv.2, 3, 4, 6); **(2) the enlargement of the details (vv.9-24)** where we should notice that the burning of the weapons, the burial of the dead, the banquet of the scavengers and the enlightenment of Jew and Gentile, amplify information given in verses 1-8; **(3) the explanation of the purpose (vv.25-29)**: "Then shall they know that I am the LORD their God, which caused them to be led into captivity among the heathen, but I have gathered them unto their own land, and have left none of them any more there" (v.28).

1) THE END OF THE INVASION, vv.1-8

The first paragraph may be divided as follows: **(a)** the determining control of the Lord, (vv.1-2); **(b)** the defeat of the enemy (vv.3-5); **(c)** the devastation of enemy countries (v.6); **(d)** the decisive outcome (vv.7-8). We should notice how the section ends: "Behold, it is come, and it is done, saith the Lord GOD. This is the day whereof I have spoken" (v.8).

a) The determining control of the Lord, vv.1-2

"Therefore, thou son of man, prophesy against Gog, and say, Thus saith the Lord GOD; Behold, I am against thee, O Gog, the chief prince of Meshech and Tubal: and **I will turn thee back** ('turn thee about', RV) and leave but a sixth part of thee, and **will cause thee to come up** from the north parts, **and will** bring thee upon the mountains of Israel" or "And I will turn you about, and will lead thee on, and will cause you to come up from the uttermost parts of the north, and will lead you against the mountains of Israel" (Amplified Version). J.N.Darby has, "I will turn thee back, and *lead* thee ..." with a marginal note, "A word of uncertain meaning. Some translate, 'I will divide thee into six parts'". Other translations are, "I will strike thee with six plagues" or "draw thee back with an hook of six teeth" (AV margin). F.A.Tatford observes that the words "leave but a sixth part of thee" (AV) "have little support, and, in fact run counter to the tenor of the passage. On the contrary, God ruthlessly exterminated the whole army". The words "turn thee about" (RV) suggest divine compulsion. While the Lord had said to Gog on one level, "be thou a guard (commander) unto them, on another level, the Lord himself was actually in command! Nebuchadnezzar discovered that God "doeth according to his will in the army of heaven, and among the inhabitants of earth: and none can stay his hand, or say unto him, What doest thou?" (Dan. 4: 35).

The words, "Behold, I am against thee, O Gog, the chief prince of Meshech and Tubal" remind us that no power can resist God. In another setting, the psalmist said "If it had not been the LORD who was on our side, now may Israel say; if it had not been the LORD who was on our side, when men rose up against us: then they had swallowed us up quick, when their wrath was kindled against us ..." (Psalm 124: 1-3). At first glance, Israel seemed doomed, but God was 'on their side', reminding us that "If God be for us, who can be against us? He that spared not his Son, but delivered him up for us all, how shall he not with him also freely give us all things?" (Rom. 8: 31-32).

b) The defeat of the enemy, vv.3-5

"And I will smite thy bow out of thy left hand, and will cause thine arrows to fall out of thy right hand. and thou shalt fall upon the mountains of Israel, thou, and all thy bands, and the people that is with thee: I will give thee unto the ravenous birds of every sort, and to the beasts of the field to be devoured. Thou shalt fall upon the open field: for I have spoken it, saith the Lord GOD."

We have already noticed that it seems likely that the same invasion is described by Micah: "And this man ("whose goings forth have been from of old, from everlasting", and who will be "great unto the ends of the earth") shall be the peace, when the Assyrian shall come into our land ... thus shall he deliver us from the Assyrian, when he cometh into our land ..." (Mic. 5: 2-6). The "Lord GOD" specifically states that Gog is "he of whom I have spoken in old time by my servants the prophets of Israel, which prophesied in those days many years that I would bring thee against them" (Ezek. 38: 17). Isaiah 30 (particularly vv.30-33) should also read in this connection. Prophetic students speak about 'the last Assyrian'.

We should notice that when "the Lord GOD" smites the invader, weapons will fall, and the warriors will fall.

i)   The weapons will fall. "I ... will cause thine arrows to ***fall*** out of thy right hand" (v.3). The weapons will be struck from the invaders' hands before they have opportunity to use them! It has been pointed out that this will make the vast invasion easy prey for Israel. The enemy will have no weapons!

(Not that Israel will be required to do much fighting, if any!) Ezekiel tells us in the next paragraph (vv.9-10) what will happen to the weapons, including the length of time it will take to destroy them.

ii)   The warriors will fall. "Thou shalt *fall* upon the mountains of Israel ... Thou shalt *fall* upon the open field" (vv.4, 5). The gigantic force from the north will fall on the mountains of Israel (v.4), and in the field (v.5). Ezekiel tells us in the next paragraph what will happen to the bodies before they are buried (vv.17-20) and where the remains will be buried, together with how long it will take (vv.11-16). We will meet the "ravenous birds of every sort, and ... beasts of the field" again in verses 17-20. The defeat of the beast and false prophet with their armies will be followed by a similar banquet for the birds: "And I saw an angel standing in the sun; and he cried with a loud voice, saying to all the fowls that fly in the midst of heaven, Come and gather yourselves together unto the supper of the great God; that ye may eat the flesh of kings, and the flesh of captains, and the flesh of mighty men, and the flesh of horses, and of them that sit on them, and the flesh of all men, both free and bond, both small and great" (Rev. 19: 17-18).

c) The devastation of enemy countries, v.6

Gog's defeat in the land will be followed by visitation on the lands from which the invader comes: "I will send a fire on Magog, and among them that dwell carelessly ('at ease', JND) in the isles: and they shall know that I am the LORD" (v.6). We should notice that reference is made to:

i)   "Magog". As noted in our previous study, Magog is not a person, but a country, hence "Set your face toward Gog, *of the land of Magog*" (38: 2, RV). Magog was a descendent of Japheth (Gen. 10: 2). Past historians (Josephus and Jerome) "associated the name with numerous Scythian tribes in the area of the Black Sea. There could, therefore, be some connection here with southern Russia" (Malcolm C. Davis, *Living with the Glory of the Lord*). It has also been said that the land of Magog was originally an area north of the Caspian Sea.

ii)   "The isles". According to C.L.Feinberg, "The isles referred to are the coastland and islands of the Mediterranean. Though the judgment on the enemies will occur in Israel, the catastrophe will extend far out to the ends of the earth to accomplish the purpose of God". However, the expression, "the isles", is amplified in Genesis 10 verse 5, "By these were the isles of the Gentiles divided in their lands, every one after his tongue, after their families, in their nations". The expression, "Surely the isles shall wait for me" (Isaiah 60: 9), indicates "that the far off nations of the world will act under God's decree and direction, and Gentile activity will be exercised in these matters, not by way merely of a political scheme, but with the definite objective of honouring the Lord" (W.E.Vine). At the end-time, "men shall worship him, every one from his place, even all the isles of the heathen" (Zeph. 2: 11).

d) The decisive outcome, vv.7-8

"So will I make my holy name known in the midst of my people Israel; and I will not let them pollute my holy name any more: and the heathen shall know that I am the LORD, the Holy One in Israel. Behold, it is come, and it is done, saith the Lord GOD. This is the day whereof I have spoken." We should notice here the outcome for Israel, for the heathen, and for the integrity of God's word:

i) **For Israel:** "So will I make my holy name known in the midst of my people Israel; and I will not let them pollute my holy name any more" (v.7). Sadly, God's people had an unenviable track record when it came to their conduct. Instead of bringing honour to God, they profaned His name, not only in their own land, but by the way in which they behaved in exile: "And when they entered unto the heathen, whither they went, they profaned my holy name, when they said to them ('of them'), These are the people of the LORD, and are gone forth out of his land" (Ezek. 36: 20).

This is a clear warning to us. David was told that he had "given great occasion to the enemies of the LORD to blaspheme" (2 Sam. 12: 14) and in referring to the Jews, Paul had to say, "the name of God is blasphemed among the Gentiles through you ..." (Rom. 2: 24). While Paul is referring in the first place to bondservants, we must all act in a way that ensures "that the name of God and (his) doctrine be not blasphemed" (1 Tim. 6: 1). Similarly, while Paul is addressing young women, we must all behave to ensure "that the word of God be not blasphemed" (Titus 2: 5).

In intervening against Gog and his hordes, the Lord Himself will do what Israel had failed to do: in His own words, "So will I make my holy name known in the midst of my people Israel". Moreover, they will never lapse into their old ways: "and I will not let them pollute my holy name any more".

He will do this, not for Israel's sake, but "for mine holy name's sake, which ye have profaned among the heathen, whither ye went" (Ezek. 36: 22).

ii) **For the heathen**: "and the heathen shall know that I am the LORD, the Holy One in Israel" (v.7). God will not only be glorified amongst His own people, He will be glorified in the eyes of the whole world. As F.A.Tatford points out, "The sins of Israel had led to the nation's dispersion among the heathen, but the Divine chastisement of them was interpreted by the heathen as an indication of God's inability to protect His people. His holy name was therefore profaned: it was a detraction from His majesty and authority. The attack by Gog upon His land was a further attempt to profane His name. But now His presence was to be known in the midst of Israel and the holiness of His name would be evident there". The Lord vindicated His name amongst the Philistines without any help from Israel (see 1 Samuel 5). He will do so again when Gog invades His land.

iii) **For the integrity of God's word**: "Behold, it is come, and it is done (or 'it cometh, and it shall be done', RV/JND), saith the Lord GOD. This is the day whereof I have spoken" (v.8). As C.L.Feinberg observes, to people who think otherwise, "the word comes that there is no escape from what has been predicted, for it is as good as done". God's people today are similarly assured, not now of coming judgment upon them, but of divine blessing: "whom he did predestinate, then he also called: and whom he called, them he also justified: and whom he justified, **them he also glorified**" (Rom. 8: 30). It is as good as done".

This reminds us that while on the cross, the Lord Jesus cried, "**It is finished**" (John 19: 30), and that He will cry "**It is done**" when completing divine judgment upon earth prior to His public return (Rev. 16: 17). Whether in redemption or in judgment, the Lord Jesus will bring every matter to completion. We may therefore confidently expect that just as He secured redemption for us at Calvary, so will He make all His enemies His footstool, and bring the entire rebellious world to its knees in confession of His sovereignty, to the glory of the Father. The victor of Calvary - "It is finished" - will be the victorious Judge of the wicked world - "It is done". His victory over every enemy, including Gog, is certain: "Behold, it is come, and it is done"

The prophecy now moves on, and the aftermath of the invasion is described. As we noted in introducing the chapter, information given in verses 1-8 is now amplified. So:

CHAPTER 39

2) THE ENLARGEMENT OF THE DETAILS, vv.9-24

It looks something like this: *(a)* the burning of the weapons (vv.9-10): this amplifies verse 3; *(b)* the burial of the dead (vv.11-16): this amplifies verses 4-5; *(c)* the banquet for the scavengers (vv.17-20): this amplifies verse 4; *(d)* the enlightenment of Jew and Gentile (vv.21-24): this amplifies verses 6-8.

a) The burning of the weapons, vv.9-10

In verse 3, we noticed that the "Lord GOD" will, in His own words, "smite thy bow out of thy left hand, and will cause thine arrows to fall out of thy right hand". Now we are told what will happen to Gog's weaponry: "And they that dwell in the cities of Israel shall go forth, and shall set on fire and burn the weapons. Both the shields and the bucklers, the bows and the arrows, and the handstaves, and the spears, and they shall burn them with fire seven years: so that they shall take no wood out of the field, neither cut down any out of the forests; for they shall burn the weapons with fire: and they shall spoil those that spoiled them, and rob those that robbed them, saith the Lord GOD".

This is quite self-explanatory, unless we wish to question the materials involved. As we have already noticed, C.L.Feinberg observes that "some have found great difficulty in the references to armour, buckler, shield, sword and helmet", but continues by saying that "even in our day of advanced weapons of warfare it is interesting to learn that in some parts of the world conflict is going on with primitive weapons", adding, "And how else could an ancient writer have described warfare? He knew nothing of guns and planes". There *may*, however, be another answer to the problem. **See the addendum.**

b) The burial of the dead, vv.11-16

In verses 4-5, we noticed that Gog and his hordes will "**fall upon the mountains of Israel**, thou, and all thy bands, and the people that is with thee ... Thou **shalt fall upon the open field**: for I have spoken it, saith the Lord GOD". Now we are told about the disposal of the bodies. We should notice the following:

i) The place of burial v.11. "And it shall come to pass in that day, that I will give unto Gog a place there of graves in Israel, the valley of the passengers ('passers-by', JND) on the east of the sea: and it shall stop the noses of the passengers ('it shall stop them that pass through', RV, or 'it shall stop [the way] of the passers-by', JND): and there shall they bury Gog and all his multitude: and they shall call it the valley of Hamon-gog." In the words of F.A.Tatford, "So numerous will be the graves which fill the valley that it will be blocked as a thoroughfare. The valley is to be renamed 'the valley of Hamon-Gog', that is, 'the valley of the multitude of Gog'".

The appointed burial place will be "the valley of the passers-by to the east of the sea" (v.11, JND) or "the valley of those who pass through on the east side in front of the Dead Sea (the highway between Syria, Petra and Egypt)" (Amplified Version). In the words of Malcolm Davis, "Gog's army will be buried in a valley east of the Dead Sea in the region of Moab, or modern Jordan. The valley will become so clogged with corpses that it will be impassable to all travellers". It has been suggested (F.A.Tatford) that "the valley of the passengers" should read "the valley of Abarim (meaning 'passenger'), a valley so named after the Abarim mountains, the northwest part of the highlands of Moab".

ii) The period of burying, v.12. "And seven months shall the house of Israel be in burying of them, that they may cleanse the land." This, with the burning of the weapons, emphasises the colossal size of the invasion.

There is an emphasis on 'cleansing the land' (vv.12, 14, 16), and while commentators cite Numbers 35 verses 33-34 in this connection, this does not appear to be relevant here. Malcolm Davis must be correct in saying that these verses "describe the burial of the slain warriors to purify the land from corruption and disease". Deuteronomy 21 verse 23 should now be consulted.

iii) The people involved in burying, vv.13-14. "Yea, all the people of the land shall bury them; and it shall be to them a renown, the day that I shall be glorified ('it will redound to their honour on the day that I glorify myself', F.A.Tatford), saith the Lord GOD." It has been suggested that in burying the dead, the nation will "attract credit to themselves among the nations (that is, for the respect paid to the dead)" (F.A.Tatford).

While, initially, the whole nation will be involved in burying the dead, after seven months the people will hire workers to bury the remaining bodies: "And they shall sever out men of continual employment, passing through the land to bury with the passengers (passers-by) those that remain on the face of the earth, to cleanse it: after seven months shall they search" or "And they shall sever out men of continual employment to go through the land, who, with the passers-by, shall bury those that remain upon the face of the land to cleanse it: at the end of seven months they shall make a search" (JND). This evidently means that after the seven months have ended, workers will be hired to search the land carefully to ensure that no bodies remain.

iv) **The provision for late burials, vv.15-16.** "And the passengers ('the passers-by', JND) that pass through the land, when any seeth a man's bone, then shall he set up a sign by it, till the buriers have buried it in the valley of Hamon-gog. And also the name of the city shall be Hamonah. Thus shall they cleanse the land." Any remains discovered after the seven-month period will be marked for burial in the appointed place. "The name of the city established there will be 'Hamonah', meaning 'the multitude'. Thus the judgment of the Lord's enemies will never be forgotten" (Malcolm Davis).

c) The banquet for the scavengers, vv.17-20

In verse 4, we noticed that the Lord said, "I will give thee unto the ravenous birds of every sort, and to the beasts of the field to be devoured". Now we have further details. Quite clearly, these verses take us back to the fall of Gog and his hordes on the mountains of Israel. As F.A.Tatford observes, Ezekiel reverts "to the slaughter which necessitated the interment arrangements". A similar passage is found in Revelation 19 verses 17-18. While the similarity between the two passages is clear, it does seem that they describe different battles, although the word 'battle' is hardly appropriate. However, some commentators feel that the two passages do describe the same battle. We should note the following:

i) **The Lord controls the natural world.** "And, thou son of man, thus saith the Lord GOD; Speak unto every feathered fowl, and to every beast of the field, Assemble yourselves, and come; gather yourselves on every side to my sacrifice that I do sacrifice for you, even a great sacrifice upon the mountains of Israel, that ye may eat flesh and drink blood" (v.17). The Lord who commanded one cock to crow at a given time (Matt. 26: 74) will command "every feathered fowl" ('carrion birds', F.A.Tatford) to obey His will. The Lord who sat on a docile yet untamed colt (Mark 11: 2) will command "every beast of the field" ('wild beasts', F.A.Tatford) to fulfil His word.

ii) **The Lord is superior to the greatest of men.** "Ye shall eat the flesh of the mighty, and drink the blood of the princes of the earth, of rams, of lambs, and of goats, of bullocks, all of them fatlings of Bashan, and ye shall eat fat till ye be full, and drink blood till ye be drunken, of my sacrifice which have sacrificed for you" (vv.18-19). From the literal ("the flesh of the mighty ... the blood of the princes of the earth"), the Lord turns to the figurative (the "fatlings of Bashan"). Bashan was famous for its fine pastures and well-fed cattle. (See Num. 32: 1-4; Deut. 32: 14; Psalm 22: 12; Amos 4: 1.) The "fatlings of Bashan" stand for strong healthy men. Men at their best. For "my sacrifice", see Isaiah 34 verse 6; Jeremiah 46 verse 10.

iii) **The Lord shares His victory with others.** "Thus shall ye be filled at my table with horses and chariots ('charioteers', JND: 'riders', F.A.Tatford)), with mighty men, and with all men of war, saith the Lord GOD" (v.20). The Lord's table in both Old and New Testaments is a place of fellowship, with particular reference to the peace offering (1 Cor. 10: 16). In Ezekiel 39, the Lord is 'dividing the spoils' (Luke 11: 22). In this case He is dividing them amongst birds and beasts.

d) The enlightenment of Jew and Gentile, vv.21-24

These verses amplify verses 6-8, where the defeat of Gog and the devastation of his land, Magog (v.6), will serve to glorify the Lord: "So will I make my holy name known in the midst of my people; and I will not let them pollute my holy name any more: and the heathen shall know that I am the LORD" (v.7). Now we read further about the effect of Gog's defeat on "the heathen" (vv.21, 23, 24) and on "the house of Israel" (v.22).

i) **"The heathen."** "And I will set my glory among the heathen, and all the heathen shall see my judgment that I have executed, and my hand that I have laid upon them" (v.21). In that day, the Gentiles will "fear the name of the LORD from the west, and his glory from the rising of the sun" (Isa. 59: 19).

ii) **"The house of Israel."** "So the house of Israel shall know that I am the LORD their God from that day and forward" (v.22). Amongst other things, this means that they will never again resort to idolatry. As the Lord had already said, "So will I make my holy name known in the midst of my people; and I will not let them pollute my holy name any more" (v.7).

Moreover the nations will recognise the righteousness of God in inflicting defeat upon Israel and sending them into captivity. Far from inability to deliver His people, their defeat and exile was nothing less than divine judgment because of their sin: "the heathen shall know that the house of Israel went into captivity for their iniquity: because they trespassed against me, therefore I hid my face from them, and gave them into the hand of their enemies: so fell they all by the sword. According to their uncleanness and according to their transgressions have I done unto them, and hid my face from them" (vv.23-24). Compare Chapter 36 verses 16-20.

We should notice the expressions, "So the house of Israel **shall know** ... And the heathen **shall know**" (vv.22, 23). In fact, the "the earth shall be **filled** with the **knowledge** of the glory of the LORD, as the waters cover the sea" (Hab. 2: 14). This brings us to:

3) THE EXPLANATION OF THE PURPOSE, vv.25-29

The chapter closes with a review of God's dealings with Israel. It appears to be a summary of preceding chapters, perhaps of the whole prophecy thus far. Attention is drawn to: *(a)* the return from captivity (vv.25-26); *(b)* the recognition of God's work (vv.27-28); *(c)* the regeneration of the nation (v.29).

a) The return from captivity, vv.25-26

"Therefore thus saith the Lord GOD; Now will I bring again the captivity of Jacob, and have mercy upon the whole house of Israel, and will be jealous for my holy name; after that they have borne their shame, and all their trespasses whereby they have trespassed against me, when they dwelt safely in their land, and none made them afraid", or "Therefore thus saith the Lord GOD: Now will I bring again the captivity of Jacob, and have mercy upon the whole house of Israel; and I will be jealous for my holy name. And they **shall bear** their shame, and all their trespasses whereby they have trespassed against me, when they **shall dwell** securely in their land, and none **shall make** them afraid" (RV, supported by JND).

The meaning of the words (RV), "And they shall bear their shame, and all their trespasses whereby they have trespassed against me, when they shall dwell securely in their land", is best understood with reference to Chapter 36 verses 30 and 31, "ye shall receive no more reproach of famine among the heathen. Then shall ye remember your own evil ways, and your doings that were not good, and shall lothe yourselves in your own sight for your iniquities and for your abominations". Some versions (Amp. Version, RSV, NEB) have "shall *forget* their shame" instead of "shall *bear* their shame" (RV), but this seems to be an interpretation rather than a translation. Amongst other things, we should notice the reference to God's jealousy "I ...will be jealous for my holy name" (v.25). See our comments on Ezekiel 36 verse 5.

b) The recognition of God's work, vv.27-28

Israel's captivity and dispersion will be understood for what it really represented, not the failure of God to keep His people, but His people's failure to obey Him. Israel's distress demonstrated the reality of Israel's God. But the reality of Israel's God will also be demonstrated in Israel's restoration. "*When* I have brought them again from the people ('peoples', JND) and gathered them out of their enemies' lands, and am sanctified in them in the sight of many nations; *then* shall they know that I am the LORD their God, *which caused them to be led into captivity* among the heathen, but I have *gathered them unto their own land*, and have left none of them any more there".

Amongst other things, we should notice the words, "and have left none of them any more there" (v.28). This is reminiscent of Israel's deliverance from Egypt, of which Moses said "there shall not an hoof be left behind" (Exod. 10: 26), and when the time came, "all the hosts of the LORD went out from the land of Egypt" (Exod. 12: 41). So will it be again!

c) The regeneration of the nation, v.29

"Neither will I *hide my face* any more from them: for I have poured out my Spirit upon the house of Israel, saith the Lord GOD." We should notice the contrast with verse 23, "because they trespassed against me, therefore *I hid my face* from them". God's face was previously hidden from His people because of their sin: but now, because His people will walk in His statutes and keep His judgments through the Holy Spirit ("I will put my Spirit within you, and cause you to walk in my statutes and ye shall keep my judgments, and do them", 36: 27), His face will be toward them for ever. (See also 37: 14; 11: 17-20.)

In our next studies, we will see what these conditions make possible: "my

CHAPTER 39

tabernacle also shall be with them ... my sanctuary shall be in the midst of them for evermore" (37: 27-28). We now come to the *grand finale* of the prophecy in Chapters 40-48.

Addendum

MILITARY WEAPONS

By John Speed-Andrews

(Extracted from the November 1970 issue of the Advent Testimony magazine)

"Some years ago I was talking to the late John Weston, who was a great preacher of Second Advent truth, on the subject of the burning of the weapons of war spoken of in Ezekiel 39 verses 9 and 10. He said that he had had some interesting light thrown on the subject while on a visit to Holland. While preaching on this passage, and confessing to some uncertainty as to its meaning, a gentleman had passed to him a message to the effect that at the gas works in Delft a new material, invented, and produced in Holland, was being used to replace steel for the springs in the giant coke-breakers. At a later meeting in England another gentleman told him that he knew this material, as they used it for making the cogwheels in part of the machinery of lorries constructed by his firm. He added that it was being used in Russia in munitions. The material was called *lignostone.* He said that it was remarkably good stuff, and they used to give him a few sacks of off-cuts and bits and pieces to burn, as it was better than coal as fuel.

The Hebrew of the passage in question makes it clear that it is not just a matter of burning the weapons to get rid of them, but that their material will furnish all the fuel needed for seven years. Literally "they will make fire with the weapons". After discussion with Mr. Weston I wrote to the research service of Encyclopaedia Britannica to see if they knew of this material. I was later supplied with the name of a firm in Manchester connected to the firm in Ter Appel in Holland, and producing it in this country. They sent me some literature about it, and I was impressed by their slogan, "For use where wood is insufficient and steel inefficient". They also sent me some samples. It bears all the appearance of wood, one piece being laminated and the other a solid piece. Each is about five inches long by about 1" x ½" in section. It seems that it is, or was, wood, and would have been very much larger before treatment. The treatment appears to be a combination of heat, resin and extreme pressures. The result is something that will not float, as wood would do, and which needs a hacksaw to cut it as would steel. It is tremendously strong, and very free of any friction, so that little lubrication is required. Is it not wonderful how up to date our Bible is?"

F.A.Tatford

(Extracted from 'Dead Bones Live')

"It has often been argued that the modern military weapons, which will be used at the time referred to, are all non-combustible. Some writers have attempted to defend the Biblical statement by assuming that weapons will one day be constructed of lignostone, which is a densified beech wood, compressed to a required density by presses of 1000 tons minimum capacity and usually impregnated with resin. It is used widely in the electrical industry and often in laminates, and is an extremely tough, hard-wearing material. Since this material is employed in place of metal, it does provide a *possible* interpretation."

EZEKIEL CHAPTER 40:1-4

Chapters 40-48 bring us to the *grand finale* of the book. These chapters are so distinct that they certainly deserve a category of their own. Having considered: *(1)* the ruin of Judah and Jerusalem (chs.1-24), *(2)* the retribution on surrounding nations (chs.25-32) and *(3)* the restoration of Israel (chs.33-39), we must now give attention to *(4)* the return of the glory of the Lord (chs.40-48).

What a marvelous conclusion to the prophecy! The publishers (John Ritchie Ltd) of Macolm Davis' excellent book, *Living with the glory of the Lord,* rightly say that "Ezekiel's awe-inspiring prophecy is full of remarkable visions of God's glory, parables of Israel's history, and the prophet's symbolical actions concerning the judgment which befell Jerusalem in 586 BC. But it also predicts that Israel will be wonderfully restored to the LORD in their Promised Land during the coming Millennial Kingdom of Christ. Here are truths nowhere else revealed in Scripture with such clarity". While, as noted, Chapters 33-39 most certainly describe Israel's wonderful restoration 'to the Lord in their Promised Land', Chapters 40-48 go even further in saying, "and the name of the city from that day shall be, The LORD is there (*Jehovah Shammah*)" (48: 35).

Before exploring the detail in Chapter 40, we should notice the general introduction to the vision (vv.1-4), and then the overall structure of the vision, together with the literality of the prophecy. This involves a general survey of the chapters. Having done this, we will then join Ezekiel in visiting the outer and inner courts of the temple with their various gates, and much more.

1) THE INTRODUCTION TO THE VISION

Very clearly, the vision is introduced in the opening verses of Chapter 40, and we should notice the following:

EZEKIEL

a) The date. "In the five and twentieth year of our captivity, in the beginning of the year, in the tenth day of the month, in the fourteenth year after that the city was smitten, in the selfsame day the hand of the LORD was upon me, and brought me thither" (v.1). At the time of the vision, the land of Israel languished under the heel of a Gentile conqueror. Jerusalem had been captured and the temple, the "excellency" of their strength and the "desire" of their eyes" (24: 21), had been destroyed. But this was not the end. When Ezekiel was brought "in the visions of God ... into the land of Israel", he saw "the frame of a city on the south" (40: 2), and was taken on a guided tour of a new temple there, of which it was said prophetically, "the glory of this latter house shall be greater than of the former, saith the LORD of hosts" (Hag. 2: 9).

As C.L.Feinberg points out, "these chapters are a fitting sequel to the series in Chapters 33-39. Though they contrast greatly with Ezekiel's earlier prophecies, they are explained on the ground that he was a priest as well as a prophet". See Chapter 1 verse 3, "the word of the Lord came expressly unto Ezekiel the priest". The words "in the beginning of the year, in the tenth day of the month" could well point to Passover ("This month shall be unto you the beginning of months: it shall be the first month of the year to you ... In the tenth day of this month they shall take to them every man a lamb", Ex.12:1-3.) The Passover is mentioned in Chapter 45 verses 21-24. In the words of F.Cundick, "The festival that commemorates past deliverance quickens hope of yet another. The God who delivered His people of old will do so again". On the other hand, some argue that the word "year" here refers to the civil year, in which case, it is said, the tenth day refers to 'the year of jubilee' (Lev. 25: 9) which took place on the day of atonement (Lev. 23: 27). But the Old Testament does not appear to mention the 'civil year'!

Perhaps we should look at the date from another point of view. Solomon's temple was built when wars had ceased, and the Lord had given "rest on every side". Here is the quotation in full: "Thou (Hiram, king of Tyre) knowest how that David my father could not build an house unto the name of the LORD his God for the wars which were about him on every side ... But now the LORD my God hath given me rest on every side, so that there is neither adversary nor evil occurrent. And, behold, I purpose to build a house unto the name of the LORD my God ..." (1 Kings 5: 3-5). Solomon's kingdom was a picture of the millennial kingdom when "a greater than Solomon" will reign, and when, again, there will be "neither adversary nor evil occurrent". Like Solomon's temple, the millennial temple will be built when war has given place to peace.

CHAPTER 40:1-4

b) The location: "in the selfsame day the hand of the LORD was upon me, and brought me thither. In the visions of God brought he me into the land of Israel" (vv.1-2). Ezekiel had been there before: "And he (the Lord Jesus: the rider in the chariot, 1: 26-27) put forth the form of an hand, and took me by a lock of mine head; and the Spirit lifted me up ... and brought me in the visions of God to Jerusalem" (8: 3). What he saw was appalling! "Go in, and behold the wicked abominations that they do here" (8: 9). Just reread Chapters 8-11. But Ezekiel now sees something infinitely and wonderfully better! At the end of his previous visit to Jerusalem "in the visions of God" (8: 3; 11: 24), he saw the departure of "the glory of the LORD" (11: 22-23). But on this visit, as we shall see, he saw the return of the "glory of the LORD" (43: 1-5).

c) The viewpoint: "he ... set me upon a very high mountain, by which was as the frame of a city ('as the building of a city', JND) on the south" (v.2). The mountain is unidentified, but most commentators assume that it is Mount Zion (Isa. 2: 2; Micah 4: 1; Ezek. 20: 40; Zech. 14: 10) which, at present, can hardly be called "a very high mountain!". However, we must remember that there are going to be some immense topographical changes when the Lord returns to earth.

F.A.Tatford understands the words, "as the frame ('building') of a city" to mean a "structure like a city", and states that "the pre-exilic temple occupied the southern slope of the mountain" and that "the complex of buildings on which he (Ezekiel) gazed apparently represented a new temple". It is worth remembering that both Moses and John needed to get above earth's low level in order to contemplate future events (Deut. 34: 1; Rev. 21: 10). Peter, James and John were required to ascend "an high mountain apart" in order to see the Lord's glory (Matt. 17: 1). See also Matthew 28 verse 16. The lesson for ourselves is clear- we need to leave 'ground level' and look at things from a higher perspective, praying, in the hymn-writer's words, "Lord, plant my feet on higher ground".

It is worth pointing out that nothing is said about the actual construction of the temple. Its chief glory will not be its architecture or its 'fixtures and fittings', but the fact that the Lord is there! This is not to say that it "fell down from heaven" (Acts 19: 35, JND) in the same way, so they said at Ephesus, as the image of Diana! As F. Cundick observes, "No builder is seen. Everything is viewed as 'God's workmanship'". It is worth mentioning at this point that when information we would like is withheld, God is telling us to look in another direction for the point He wishes us to grasp.

We should also note "that unlike the Tabernacle or Solomon's Temple, the temple for the Millennium is a relatively plain building. We are not told the material of which the walls will be made. It seems likely that they will be built of stone. But nothing is said to suggest that the stonework is elaborate or ornate. There is no mention of a golden altar or of a brass laver or sockets of silver. No jewels are mentioned and there is no reference to the varied colours, blue, purple, scarlet, used in the Tabernacle ... This is consistent with the spirit of the New Covenant that will be in operation in its fullness during the Millennial age. It is a covenant that in contrast with the Old Covenant does not dwell on the external or superficial but on the internal and spiritual. The chief glory of the Temple will not be its fillings and fixtures, but the fact that the Lord is there" (Alan Summers, *Assembly Testimony*, November/December 2009).

From his elevated view point, Ezekiel was taken to the buildings in question ("And he brought me thither", v.3), where he met the guide who will take him on a conducted tour of the temple.

d) The guide: "behold, there was a man, whose appearance was like the appearance of brass, with a line of flax in his hand, and a measuring reed; and he stood in the gate" (v.3). The "man is likened to "the appearance of brass", indicating "purity and righteousness" (F.Cundick).

There is some mileage in the suggestion that the "man" may be the interpreting angel of Zechariah (see, for example, Zech. 1: 9, 12; 2: 1, 3) and Revelation (see, for example, Rev. 21: 9, 15; 22: 8-9). While this seems impossible to determine with certainty, it does seem that he is an angel. See Chapter 43 verses 5-6, "So the spirit ('Spirit', JND) took me up, and brought me into the inner court; and, behold, the glory of the LORD filled the house. And I heard *him* speaking unto me out of the house: and *the man* stood by me". It is also significant that from this point onwards, we do not read anything further about the "man", at least not until Chapter 47 verse 3: "And when ***the man that had the line in his hand*** went forth eastward, he measured a thousand cubits ..." This explains Ezekiel 44 verses 2 and 5 ("Then said the LORD unto me ... and the LORD said unto me".) In other words, it all changes when the "glory of the LORD" fills the house. Up to that point the "man" does the speaking, but after that point the Lord is the speaker!

The does not in any way depreciate the role of the guide. He informs Ezekiel about a whole range of associated subjects. For example: *(i)* how Ezekiel was to **approach** his task: "the man said unto me ..." (40: 4); *(ii)* how the priests were to be **accommodated** (Ezekiel was a priest): "he said unto me ..." (40: 45); *(iii)* how the "most holy place" would be **accessed**: he said unto me ..." (41: 4); *(iv)* the size and construction of the **altar**, which is called "the table that is before the LORD": "and he said unto me" (41: 22); *(v)* the food and **activity** of the priests: "Then said he unto me ..." (42: 13); *(vi)* how he was to **admonish** the house of Israel (43: 10): the section begins (43: 7), "And he said unto me ..." The servants of God, angels or men, have important work to do! We should notice that he carries "a line of flax in his hand, and a measuring reed" (v.3). According to C.L.Feinberg, "The line of flax was for the longer measurements; the reed was for the shorter".

Talking of "measurements", C.L.Feinberg tells us that "A cubit is about eighteen inches long ..." Some suggest that a longer cubit was used (said to be the 'Babylonian cubit'), but there appears to be no proof either way. The handbreadth varies because it was derived from parts of the human body ('according to the variations of the human hand', Malcolm Davies).

If the Hebrew cubit was some eighteen inches long, and the handbreadth about three and a half inches then, in imperial measurements (feet and inches) the reed, or rod, (measuring "six cubits and a hand-breadth long", v.5) would have measured, speaking cautiously, approximately 9 ¼ feet. Should we opt for the 'Babylonian cubit', said to be twenty-one inches long, then the reed would have been, it seems, approximately 10 ¾ feet. We will have occasion to make some calculations in terms of imperial measurements as Ezekiel's 'tour of inspection' proceeds, and for this purpose perhaps we ought to stay with an eighteen-inch cubit. To vary the cubit from passage to passage would certainly add confusion to what is already difficult to understand in some places!

e) The instructions. "And the man said unto me, Son of man, behold with thine eyes, and hear with thine ears, and set thine heart upon all that I shall shew thee; for to the intent that I might shew them unto thee art thou brought hither; declare all that thou seest to the house of Israel" (v.4). F. Cundick puts it like this: "Son of man, behold with thine eyes (revelation), and hear with thine ears (communication), and set thine heart upon all that I shall shew thee (affection and understanding)". C.L.Feinberg adds, "What was to be disclosed would require the concentration of Ezekiel's every faculty. Surely no less is required of us in order to comprehend the vast themes set forth in the ensuing chapters". But there is more: Ezekiel was to communicate what he saw and heard to "the house of Israel". This was the purpose of it all. This is exactly what the apostles did: "That which we have seen and heard declare we unto you, that ye also may have fellowship with us" (1 John 1: 3). This is exactly what **we** must do, whether in Gospel testimony or in teaching the Lord's people. This brings us to:

2) *THE STRUCTURE OF THE VISION*

As noted in the Outline of the Book (see our Chapter 1), these chapters deal with three aspects of the millennial kingdom: *(a)* the millennial temple (40: 1 - 42: 20); *(b)* the millennial worship (43: 1 - 46: 24); *(c)* the millennial land (47: 1 - 48: 35).

This *aide-mémoire* (referring again to the introductory outline) continues as follows:

a) *The millennial temple, 40: 1 - 42: 20*

This speaks for itself. Ezekiel was told, "Son of man, behold with thine eyes, and hear with thine ears, and set thine heart upon all that I shall shew thee; for to the intent that I might shew them unto thee art thou brought hither: declare all that thou seest to the house of Israel" (40: 4).

These chapters cover: *(i)* temple courts and entrances (40: 5-47); *(ii)* the temple and its buildings (40: 48 - 41: 26); *(iii)* the priests' quarters (42: 1-14); *(iv)* the encircling wall (42: 15-20).

b) *The millennial worship; 43: 1 - 46: 24*

Ezekiel, the artist, draws a magnificent picture: "Behold, the glory of the God of Israel came from the way of the east: and his voice was like a noise of many waters; and the earth shined with his glory ... And the glory of the LORD came into the house by the way of the gate whose prospect is toward the east" (vv.2, 4).

These chapters deal with the following: *(i)* the advent of the glory of the Lord (43: 1-12); *(ii)* altar of worship (43: 13-27); *(iii)* the approach to God (44: 1-31); *(iv)* the allocation of land, (45: 1-8); *(v)* the application at the time (45: 9-12); *(vi)* the appointed offerings (45: 13 - 46: 24).

c) The millennial land, 47: 1 - 48: 35

These chapters may be summarised as follows: *(i)* Israel's millennial river (47: 1-12); *(ii)* Israel's national borders (47: 13-23); *(iii)* Israel's northern sub-divisions (48: 1-7); *(iv)* Israel's holy central area (48: 8-22); *(v)* Israel's southern sub-divisions (48: 23-29); *(vi)* Israel's millennial city (48: 30-35).

3) THE LITERALITY OF THE DETAILS

It ought to be said at this juncture that the proliferation of detail, with exact measurements, surely points to a literal building. As Malcolm Davis observes, "The chief question to be decided is whether this temple is intended to be understood as a literal temple, or only a figurative representation of spiritual truth found elsewhere in Scripture. Some Bible students have held the view that it is only an ideal temple that never was built, or else a rebuilding of Solomon's temple. But the detailed measurements of this temple do not fit those of Solomon's temple".

Malcolm Davis continues. "Also, it is very doubtful that the Lord would ever reveal nine chapters about a temple that never was built, nor ever will be built ... Again, many Bible students who hold the Amillennial view of Bible prophecy believe that this temple in Ezekiel is a figurative representation of the Church ... They read back New Testament truth into every part of the Old Testament ... but this view is based on an inconsistent principle of interpreting Scripture as a whole. On the one hand, Amillennial students understand all Ezekiel's earlier prophecies concerning the fall of Jerusalem, which have been fulfilled to the letter, quite literally. But, on the other hand, they understand the present prophecy of a rebuilt temple as only figurative and non-literal".

In this connection it should be said, with great respect to H.A.Ironside, that we should tread carefully when reading his comments on Ezekiel 40. He does say, for example, that "it seems to me, that we are not to take Ezekiel's vision too literally, but just as the vision of the heavenly Jerusalem is very largely symbolic, so is the vision of the earthly Jerusalem given in these chapters". His remarks in connection with the millennial sacrifices also call for great caution.

Malcolm Davis continues further: "It is therefore consistent with all that has gone before to accept that these chapters describe a literal temple which is yet to be built in a restored Israel and in a rebuilt city of Jerusalem. If we accept Scripture at face value, in simple faith in God's power to accomplish the seemingly impossible, then we shall find this view by far the most satisfactory one of all those which we have considered".

We come now to the commencement of Ezekiel's conducted tour of the millennial temple. This commences with reference to the wall encircling the temple precincts (40: 5) and to the east gate (40: 6). In the verses which follow, we will accompany Ezekiel as he accompanies the waiting guide (40: 3) in inspecting "the house" (40: 5) and its environs.

EZEKIEL CHAPTER 40:5-16

Having given consideration to *(1)* the general introduction to the vision, *(2)* the structure of the vision and *(3)* the literality of the details (40: 1-4), we now come to the commencement of Ezekiel's conducted tour of the millennial temple.

We have already noted that, in its entirety, the vision describes *(1)* the millennial temple (40: 1 - 42: 20); *(2)* the millennial worship (43: 1 - 46: 24); *(3)* the millennial land (47: 1 - 48: 35).

The description of the millennial temple commences with the temple courts and entrances (40: 5-37), where our attention is drawn, first of all, to *(a)* the wall encircling the temple precincts (40: 5); *(b)* the east gate (40: 6-16); *(c)* the outer court (40: 17-19); *(d)* the northern gate (40: 20-23); *(e)* the southern gate (40: 24-27); *(f)* the gates of the inner court (40: 28-37). The balance of Chapter 40 describes *(g)* the sacrifice preparation rooms (vv.38-43); *(h)* the priest's quarters (vv.44-47).

In Chapter 40 verse 48 to Chapter 41 verse 26, our attention is drawn to the temple itself, with its "altar of wood" (v.22), which commentators generally submit is the equivalent of the altar of incense in the tabernacle.

In Chapter 42, our attention is drawn to what we will call the priests' dining rooms (vv.1-14), and to the encircling wall (vv.15-20). While some suggest that this is in fact the outer wall described in Chapter 40 (the "wall on the outside of the house round about", v.5), there is evidently a strong case for suggesting that it is an overall encircling wall of vastly greater length than the wall seen by Ezekiel at the commencement of his conducted tour.

We now come, therefore, to:

a) The outer wall, v.5

"And, behold, a wall on the outside of the house round about, and in the man's hand a measuring reed of six cubit's long by the cubit, and an hand breadth: so he measured the breadth of the building (that is, the wall of the building), one reed; and the height one Reed." This is evidently the only place where a height is actually given. On the basis that a reed was six (ordinary) cubits and a hand-breadth long (6 x 18 inches plus 3 1/2 inches), the outer wall was therefore approximately 9 1/4 feet wide and 9 1/4 feet high. (Commentators who opt for the longer cubit will, presumably, make the wall 10 ½ feet in width and height.)

It can be easily proved from internal measurements that the wall measured 500 cubits square. This can be calculated from the north to south measurements: the length of the north gateway (50 cubits, see 40: 21), plus the breadth of the outer court (100 cubits, see 40: 23), plus the length of north inner gateway (50 cubits, see 40: 36), plus the distance across inner court (100 cubits, see 40: 47), plus the southern inner gateway (50 cubits, as for the northern inner gate), plus the outer court (100 cubits, as before), plus the south outward gateway (50 cubits as before), totalling 500 cubits. On this basis, using an eighteen-inch cubit, the temple stood within a wall measuring 250 yards square (18" x 500).

It has to be said that commentators who substitute cubits for reeds (AV) in Chapter 42 15-20, do not need the internal measurements above to prove that the wall measured 250 yards square!

The temple precincts (the outer court) will therefore be a perfect square, just as the inner court, lying exactly in the middle of the outer court, will also be a perfectly square (see 40: 47). The altar, evidently lying at the centre of the inner court, will also be "foursquare" (43: 16-17).

We cannot leave this without noting at least three important lessons which emerge from the description of the outer wall.

i) The wall existed "to make a separation between the sanctuary and the profane place" (42: 20). In the words of F. Cundick, "The sanctuary is a place separate from ordinary use. At once we perceive the meaning of the wall. The presence of God is to be regarded with the highest *reverence*". In New Testament language, "What fellowship hath righteousness with unrighteousness

..." (2 Cor. 6: 14-18). It is most significant that Paul uses a series of words here ("fellowship ... communion ... concord ... part ... agreement") which indicate, not so much 'no contact', but 'no contract' with evil.

ii) The fact that the surrounding wall is "foursquare", stresses universality (see, for example, "the four winds of earth"; "the four quarters of the earth" (Rev. 7: 1; 20: 8), and indicates that the millennial temple will be "called an house of prayer for all people ('all the peoples', JND)" (Isa. 56: 7). Compare Isaiah 2 verses 2-4, "And it shall come to pass in the last days, that the mountain of the LORD's house shall be established in the top of the mountains, and shall be exalted above the hills; and all nations ('and all the nations', JND) shall flow unto it. And many people ('peoples', JND) shall go and say, Come ye, and let us go up to the mountain of the LORD, to the house of the God of Jacob ...".

See also Isaiah 25 verses 6-7, "And in this mountain shall the LORD of hosts make unto all people ('peoples', JND) a feast of fat things, a feast of wines on the lees, of fat things full of marrow, of wines on the lees well refined And he will destroy ('swallow up', JND margin) in this mountain the face of the covering cast over all people ('peoples', JND), and the vail that is spread over all nations".

iii) The fact that the square altar lies at the very centre of the temple precincts means that "Every line of approach from the east, north and south converges upon this sacred spot. The centrality of the cross will not be lost in the day of His glory!" (F.Cundick). The altar will remind future millennial nations, as it it reminds us, that the death of the Lord Jesus Christ lies at the very centre of God's provision for men and women.

b) The eastern gate, vv.6-16

Ezekiel now passes through "the gate which looked toward the east" (v.6). (Compare 42: 15). Having passed through the gate with its six "little chambers" (vv.7, 10, 12), and the "porch of the inner gate" (vv.9, 15), he entered "the outward court" (v.17) which was enclosed, as we have already noted, by the outer wall (v.5).

It is not without significance that the the east gate is mentioned first. Details of the north gate (vv.20-22) and the south gate (vv.28-31) follow. Malcolm Davis explains: "This is the most significant outer gate, both because it lies in direct line to the temple proper, and because it is the way by which the glory of the Lord will return from the east to the inner sanctuary at the beginning of the Millennial Kingdom".

These verses deal with two connected places: the gate itself and the porch (or vestibule) to which the gate led. It should be noted that the broad details are given in verses 6-9, are then amplified verses 10-16.

i) The broad details, vv.6-9

We should notice:

- The "gate", which, at the point of entry ("the threshold of the gate", v.6) measured "one reed broad" (approximately nine feet, like the width and height of the wall). The "other threshold of the gate", at the point of exit (v.6), was also "one reed broad". In the words of F.A.Tatford, "The gateway was actually a passage, evidently with three 'guard-rooms' recessed into the wall on each side, each room being one reed (9 ¼ feet) square" (v.7). He continues: "These rooms were virtually sentry boxes for the use of the temple officers responsible for keeping watch on the gate and those who entered it".

The 'temple officers, in this case, were probably the porters (see Nehemiah 11: 19). After the death of Athaliah, Jehoiada "set the porters at the gates of the house of the LORD, that none which was **unclean in any thing should enter in**" (2 Chron. 23: 19). The need for spiritual "porters" remains: "For I know this, that after my departing shall grievous wolves enter in among you, not sparing the flock ... Therefore watch and remember, that by the space of three years I ceased not to warn every one of you night and day with tears" (Acts 20: 29-31). The need is stressed by such passages as, "false brethren unawares brought in" (Gal. 2: 4); "there shall be false teachers among you, who privily shall bring in damnable heresies" (2 Pet. 2: 1); "For there are certain men crept in unawares" (Jude v.4).

We are reminded here that care is required in connection with reception to "the house of God" (1 Tim. 3: 15). See, for example Acts 9 verses 26-28, Revelation 2 verse 2.

Since there were five cubits (7'6") between the 'guard rooms' (F.A.Tatford) or "little chambers" (v.7), to which, presumably, something must be added for the spaces between the first and last "little chambers" adjoining the two thresholds, the "gate" or passage way must have been something like 40 cubits (60 feet) long. It should be noted that the three inner gates (40: 28-29, 32-33, 35-36) will also have the same "little chambers".

The "gate" led to:

- **The "porch"** of "the inner gate". The "porch" measured eight cubits plus two cubits for the doorposts (v.9), giving a total measurement (obviously) of ten cubits.

We are told that the total measurement (length) of the "gate" plus "porch" was fifty cubits (v.15), that is forty cubits (as estimated above) for the "gate" plus ten cubits for the "porch". Ezekiel confirms the calculation: "And from the face of the gate of the entrance unto the face of the porch of the inner gate were fifty cubits" (v.15) or "From the front of the gate at the entrance to the end of the inner vestibule of the gate was fifty cubits (75 feet)" (RSV).

The outer court of the temple was therefore reached, in this case, via the "gate" which involved passing three side rooms on either side placed in line toward the outer court, and then passing through the "porch" or 'inner vestibule' or 'exit chamber'. As noted, the total distance from the front of the outer gate to the end of the inner vestibule or 'exit chamber' was fifty cubits, a measurement which includes the depth of the outer gate, the size of the side rooms with the distance between them, and the door jambs ("the posts", v.9).

ii) Further details, vv.10-16

We should notice:

- **The width of the passage through the gate, v.11.** That is, the passage within the gateway or gate-house. This was ten cubits, which narrowed to eight cubits when passing the 'side rooms' (v.12). The "space before the little chambers" is said to be a barrier or wall of one cubit high, although this is not actually stated. Presumably this was where people stood when seeking entry to the outer court. A measurement of thirteen cubits is also given (v.11). This evidently refers to part of the structure of the gate from east to west ("the length of the gate"), but it is difficult to ascertain its actual significance.

- ***The breadth of the gate, from north to south***. That is, "the measurement from one external side chamber wall to the opposite external side chamber wall" (L.E.Cooper). This was twenty-five cubits (v.13), or approximately 37 feet, made up of the depth of two side rooms opposite each other (two reeds, 18 ½ feet), plus the width of the passage (ten cubits, or 15 feet, including the barrier), plus a further unidentified measurement, perhaps the thickness of the walls of the gate, which protruded into the outer court. After all, it is the measurement of "the roof". The words "door against door" or "entry opposite entry" (JND) are not easily understood, but might refer to the position of the three rooms on each side of the passage being opposite each other. Alternatively, the phrase "'from door to door' (RSV) suggests that a door led from each of the side rooms to the outer court, a reasonable probability to allow the Levitical door-keepers to get to their stations to control the crowds who would throng through the gateways at festival time" (John B.Taylor).

- ***The "posts of threescore cubits" (v.14)*** is elsewhere rendered, "He measured along the faces of the projecting walls all around the inside of the gateway – sixty cubits" (NIV). According to L.A.Cooper, this means "distance around the walls of the inner porch", but exactly how this is calculated is not easily explained or, better, simply not explained! J.W.Schmitt and J. Carl Laney (*Messiah's Coming Temple*) suggest that this refers to the height of the 'tower' associated with the gate (a feature, they say of the eastern and other temple gates), and add that "the only detail that Ezekiel provides concerning these towers is their height". This may or may not be correct. John B.Taylor says that the text here is "hopelessly corrupt", meaning, perhaps, that he doesn't understand it! We do need to be careful when it comes to statements like this.

- ***The windows (v.16)***: "And there were narrow windows to the little chambers, and to their posts within the gate round about, and likewise to the arches; and windows were round about inward: and upon each post were palm trees", or "And there were closed windows (or, 'latticed', or 'with fixed frame', JND) to the chambers, and to their posts within the gate round about, and likewise to the "projections" (JND, who observes, in a marginal note, that "the meaning of the Hebrew word is not clearly ascertained"). However, it does seem that the word "projections" (JND) refers to that part of the gateway which protruded into the outer court.

It is interesting to observe that the only adornment to the gate is palm trees (v.16). This was the case in Solomon's temple, and H.A.Ironside (*Ezekiel*)

CHAPTER 40:5-16

helps us here in saying that "The ornamentation of palm trees suggests victory over every evil force (see Rev. 7: 9-10), for the vision looks on to the time when Jehovah will be supreme throughout all the earth, and all the world will recognise His matchless power".

Although we have not yet reached the relevant verses, we will take the opportunity to note that there is *a constant mention of ascent* in this chapter. The worshippers move to 'higher ground' as they draw near to God.

The worshipper ascends by seven steps from ground level to reach the outer court via the outer gate (40: 22). He then gains access to the inner court by eight steps (40: 31), and then access to the house itself by ten steps (40: 49, RV/JND). "Thus the successive terraces are traceable. The knowledge of God and fellowship with Him is *ascent*. The worshipper approaches by varying but increasing ascents. The ten steps coming at the last, yet nearest to the house, serves to teach us that intensity of effort is accentuated by progress. But effort does bring us to the heart of things! In the language of the holy Scriptures, it means 'from strength to strength', 'from glory to glory', or 'more and more'" (F.Cundick). With this in mind, we can justifiably sing:

> *My heart has no desire to stay*
> *Where doubts arise and fears dismay;*
> *Though some may dwell where these abound,*
> *My prayer, my aim is higher ground.*

How glad we are that "for us, the gates declare plainly that *access* to the divine presence has been made. In dependence upon the sacrifice (the slaughtering tables); under the scrutiny of God (the guard chambers); in the light of understanding (the windows); and in overcoming grace (the palms), we can approach God" (F.Cundick).

At this point Ezekiel exited the east gate with its porch, and entered the outer court. "Then brought he me into the outward court ..." (v.17).

In our next study, we will consider the remaining sections of Chapter 40: *(c)* the outer court (vv.17-19); *(d)* the northern gate (vv.20-23); *(e)* the southern gate (vv.24-27); *(f)* the gates of the inner court (vv.28-37); *(g)* the sacrifice preparation rooms (vv.38-43); *(h)* the priest's quarters (vv.44-47); *(i)* the temple portico (vv.48-49).

EZEKIEL CHAPTER 40:17-47

We have noted that the description of the millennial temple commences with the temple courts and entrances (40: 5-37), where our attention is drawn, first of all, to *(a)* the wall encircling the temple precincts (40: 5), *(b)* the east gate (40: 6-16) and then, to *(c)* the outer court (40: 17-19), *(d)* the northern gate (40: 20-23), *(e)* the southern gate (40: 24-27), and *(f)* the gates of the inner court (40: 28-37), *(g)* the sacrifice preparation rooms (vv.38-43), and *(h)* the priest's quarters (vv.44-47).

Since verses 48-49 describe the temple portico, we will include them in addressing the description of the temple itself.

Having considered *(a)* the wall encircling the temple precincts (40: 5) together with *(b)* the east gate (40: 6-16), we come now to -

c) The outer court, vv.17-19

Having negotiated the entrance, Ezekiel was now in the outer court (v.17). That is, the court surrounded by the square wall measuring 500 cubits (250 yards) on all four sides. The outer court contained thirty chambers which were evidently built against the inside of the outer wall, facing inwards to the court, and standing on a pavement (v.18). F.A.Tatford describes the pavement as lying on the "outer margin of the court" and "paved with stone". This is called the "lower pavement" as opposed to the 'upper pavement' of the inner court (42: 3). It is thought that the thirty chambers were "probably arranged in three groups of ten against the north, east and south walls, with the gateways dividing the ten into two groups of five" (John B. Taylor). The absence of a western gate leads to the conclusion that, presumably, there were no chambers against the western wall.

The use of the "thirty chambers is not described, but they would, almost certainly, be either for worshippers or for the Levites who were on duty in the temple" (John B. Taylor). He continues: "see Jeremiah 35 verse 2

CHAPTER 40:17-47

for a possible use made of them". This, of course, refers to the chambers in Solomon's temple (1 Kings 6: 5-6), but perhaps their use then will be replicated in the millennial temple. One thing seems relatively clear, namely that God ensured that His house made practical provision for His people, perhaps, in this case, for their rest and refreshment.

The measurement of 100 cubits or 50 yards (v.19) represents the distance between the innermost part of the outer gateway and the threshold of the corresponding gateway to the inner court.

Before Ezekiel's guide took him to the gates leading from the outer court to the inner court (see vv.28-37), he led him to the two other gates (or gateways) leading to the outer court, that is, to *(d)* the northern gate (vv.20-23); *(e)* the southern gate (vv.24-27). So –

d) The northern gate, vv.20-23

There is little to say here. The northern gateway measured exactly as the east gate (see vv.6-16). It is here that we learn that all three gates were accessed by seven steps (v.22). The word "arches" (v.22), or "projections" (JND), evidently refers to that part of the gateway which protruded into the outer court. Should there be any difficulty about the wording, "And the gate of the inner court was over against the gate toward the north *and toward the east*" (v.23), help is at hand: "And opposite the gate on the north, as on the east, was a gate the inner court ...." (RSV). As in the case of the eastern gate, the distance between the northern gate and the corresponding gate into the inner court was also exactly the same (100 cubits).

e) The southern gate, vv.24-27

There is nothing further to say here either. Again, the RSV helps us to understand the meaning of the words, "And there were windows in it and the arches thereof round about *like those windows*" (v.25). The RSV simply reads, "like the windows of the others". Note the same seven steps (v.26). As in the case of the eastern gate, the distance between the southern gate and the corresponding gate into the inner court was also exactly the same (100 cubits).

As John B. Taylor observes in connection with the seven steps (all three sets of them), "this indicates that the temple area is thought of as a huge raised area, built up above the level of the surrounding land". For the second time in our studies we ought to break into song: "Lord, plant my feet on higher ground!". If the outer wall separated between the holy and the profane (42: 20), then, very clearly and in every sense - physically and spiritually - holy ground is higher than profane ground!

We might wish to consider why there were three, not four, gates or gateways into the outer court. L.E.Cooper suggests the following: "The identical physical structure and appearance of these gates suggests their equality in form and function. This idea also is consistent with concepts related to the Trinity, which considers God as three coequal manifestations of the one divine being (see John: 10: 22-30)". Perhaps this should be considered in the light of Ephesians 2 verse 18, "For through *him* (the Lord Jesus) we both (Jew and Gentile) have access by one *Spirit* unto the *Father*". In which case, the "seven steps" might well emphasise the perfection and completeness of access to God. Very clearly, there was no 'back entrance' to the temple precincts. There was no western gate. Worshippers must approach God in the divinely-appointed way and that involved, as noted above, three gates. Solomon's throne had six steps, and it is specifically stated that "there was not the like made in any kingdom" (1 Kings 10: 20). His throne reflected human ability at its best (*six* steps), but God is approached by *seven* steps - utter perfection!

f) The gates of the inner court, vv.28-37

In these verses, Ezekiel is conducted into the inner court via the inner south gate (vv.28-31), after which he is taken to the inner east gate (vv.32-34), and the inner north gate (vv.35-37). As we know, the inner court, measuring 100 cubits square (50 yards), lay at the centre of the outward court, but since no reference is made to a dividing wall between the two, it is *possible* that the inner court was simply an elevated area (eight steps high) reached by three gates or gateways leading from the outer court. These three gates, identical in measurement to the outer gates, were exactly opposite the outer gates with an intervening distance of 100 cubits (50 yards). The three inner gates were approached by eight steps, and the northern inner gate was evidently the place where the sacrificial animals were washed (v.38) and killed (v.39).

With this in mind, we must now notice what is said about the three inner gates.

i)   The inner south gate, vv.28-31. This gate measured exactly the same as the outer south gate vv.13, 15), that is "fifty cubits long (25 yards) and five and twenty cubits broad (12 ½ yards)" (v.29). There is one clear difference between the two gates. As noted, the outer gate was approached via seven steps (v.26), and the inner gate by eight steps (v.31). If 'seven' in Scripture is the number of completeness, then 'eight' indicates a new departure outside of, but connected with, creation-order. Hence circumcision was on the eighth day; eight souls were saved in ark to commence a new world; the new form of the last world empire will be 'the eighth'. The Lord's resurrection took place on the "eighth day", that is on "the morrow after the sabbath" (*Morrish's Bible Dictionary*).

We should also notice that verse 30 seems to indicate a difference in detail of the inner south gate: the arches, or vestibules, lay toward the outer court, that is, at the point of entering the gate (vv.30-31), whereas in the case of the outer south gate, this part of the gateway lay at the point of exit (vv.8-9). That is, entering the inner court.

ii)   The inner east gate, vv.32-34. This gate also measured exactly the same as the outer east gate, that is "fifty cubits long (25 yards) and five and twenty cubits broad (12 ½ yards)" (v.29). There is the same clear difference between the two gates. The outer gate was approached via seven steps (v.22), and the inner gate by eight steps (vv.34). There is also the same second difference between the two gates as noted above in connection with the inner south gate.

iii)   The inner north gate, vv.35-37. This gate also measured exactly the same as the outer east gate, that is "fifty cubits long (25 yards) and five and twenty cubits broad (12 ½ yards)" (v.36). There is the same clear difference between the two gates. The outer gate was approached via seven steps (v.22), and the inner gate by eight steps (v.37). There is also the same second difference between the two gates as noted above in connection with the inner south gate.

The striking similarity between all six gates (with just the difference between the number of steps involved and the position of the vestibule) reminds us of divine consistency. There was no confusion about the approach to God. The worshipper was always on familiar ground, whichever gate he was passing through. Having said that, there was a third difference between the inner north gate and the inner south and east gates. This brings us to:

EZEKIEL

g) *The equipment for sacrifice, vv.38-43*

Our word 'equipment' covers the various tables (vv.39, 40, 41, 42, 43) and instruments (v.42), together with the hooks on which the carcases were hung (v.43).

The section commences as follows: "And the chambers, and the entries thereof, were by the posts of the gates, where they washed the burnt offering" (v.38). The plural here ("the chambers, and the entries thereof ... by the posts of the gates") gives the impression that reference is made here to all three gates, and this appears to be supported by alternative translations: "And there was a cell and its entry by the posts of the gates (plural)" (JND): "And a chamber with the door thereof as by the posts at the gates (plural)" (RV). Not all commentators agree, particularly F.A.Tatford: "In the porch of the north gate and in close proximity to the inner court where the sacrifices were offered upon the altar, was a chamber, set apart primarily for the washing of the burnt offering. As Leviticus 1 verse 11 indicates, the burnt offering was slain on the north side of the altar, and the intestines and legs had to be washed before the sacrifice was placed on the altar (Lev. 1: 9)".

It should be noted, however, that the following verses revert to the singular: "the porch of the gate" (v.39); "as one goeth up to entry of the north gate" (v.40): "by the side of the gate" (v.41). According to verse 43, "*within* were hooks, an hand broad, fastened round about, and upon the tables was the flesh of the offering", and it appears that the word "within" refers to the "chambers" in verse 38. In summary, despite the problem arising from the use of the plural in verse 38, F.A.Tatford does seem correct in saying that "It seems reasonably clear, that the gate referred to was the northern gate to the inner court".

Leaving now the washing of the burnt offering (v.38), we must notice the position of the tables used in connection with the slaughter of the burnt, sin and trespass offerings (v.39).

It does appear that the slaughter and preparation of the animals took place at the approach to the northern inner gate. In connection with the slaughter of the animals, we are told that the tables on which this took place were located two on either side of the porch at the entrance, and two on either side of the eight steps leading up to the entrance of the gate, that is, eight tables in all (v.41). L.E.Cooper makes the pertinent observation that "The use of sets of eight tables for sacrifice also may have messianic overtones".

See our note on the 'eight steps' above (page 6). The four tables, two on either side of the eight steps leading up to the entrance of the gate were of "hewn stone (not brick: stone is a divinely-provided material) for the burnt offering, of a cubit and a half long (27 inches), and a cubit and a half broad (27 inches), and one cubit high (18 inches): whereupon also they laid the instruments wherewith they slew the burnt offering and the sacrifice" (v.42). This speaks for itself. In the words of F.A.Tatford, "They (the four tables) were obviously too small to be used for slaying the animal, but they were provided for the instruments of slaughter .... to be laid upon".

The details given here remind us of the great care that was to be taken in preparing the sacrifices. These were to be prepared and offered in a manner acceptable to God. The fact that the burnt offering was to be washed (v.38) reminds us, not, of course, that the Lord Jesus needed cleansing (the very suggestion is abhorrent to every child of God), but that He "offered himself without spot to God" in all His perfect purity.

We must take the opportunity to ask, 'Are we offering God the 'second best' in our worship?' His people were severely censured for doing this. See Malachi 1 verses 7-14. They were not only to bring the very best animals for sacrifice, but those sacrifices were to be offered with great care. Should we do less?

Before we leave these verses we ought to comment on the fact that the sacrifices here are connected with the **north** inner gate. As noted above, the burnt offering was slain on the north side of the altar (Lev. 1: 11). As Martin Hayward (*The Burnt Offering*) points out, "All of the points of the compass have certain associations ... the north seems to be the place of exposure to danger. It was from the north that danger threatened Israel so often ... The underlying thought behind these references to the north is of fore-boding, of terribleness, of exposure to danger, of judgment. Couple with this the fact that the north side of the altar would necessarily be in the shadows, and we have a picture built up of a place of ominous portent".

h) The priest's quarters, vv.44-47

Ezekiel now observed further details in connection with the inner court. His attention is drawn to two chambers: "And without the inner gate were the chambers of the singers in the inner court, which was at the side of the north gate; and their prospect was toward the south: one at the side of the east gate, having the prospect toward the north" (v.44). According to J.N.Darby (margin) this follows "the present Hebrew text". However, J.N.Darby's New Translation reads, "And outside the inner gate were two cells in the inner court, one at the side of the north gate, and its front towards the south; the other was at the side of the south gate, the front towards the north". The RV margin concurs. This translation is based on the Septuagint Version, and has the logic, as L.E.Cooper points out, that the north gate would open toward the south, and the south toward the north. All we can say is that we wait for further help on this point! It does seem, however, that this translation maintains the symmetry of the overall plan.

Both chambers, or "cells" (JND), are said to be "for the singers" (AV and RV), although the RV margin omits reference to them as does JND. This may be correct since the passage proceeds to assign both chambers to the priests: "This chamber, whose prospect is toward the south, is for the priests, the keepers of the charge of the house. And the chamber whose prospect is toward the north is for the priests, the keepers of the charge of the altar: these are the sons of Zadok, among the sons of Levi, which come near to the LORD to minister unto him" (vv.45-46). However, whatever the merits or demerits of the translations, it remains that "singing was a priestly function in Old Testament worship. See, for example, 1 Chronicles 16 verses 4-6; Chapter 23 verse 5 and 2 Chronicles 29 verses 26-29" (quoted by L.E.Cooper). We should note the words, "And when the burnt offering began, the song of the LORD began also …" (2 Chron 29: 27). It should be noted that although the singers came from the ranks of the Levites, they were not necessarily priests.

Attention is drawn to the fact that "The only priests who could minister at the altar were the descendents of Zadok, the priest who remained loyal to David during the insurrection of Absalom (2 Sam. 15: 24-29), and whose descendents remained loyal to the Lord through the course of Israel's growing idolatry (Ezek.44: 15)" (Lamar E. Cooper). We must not leave this without noticing: *(i)* that loyalty to God will be rewarded, and *(ii)* that the function of the priests was to "minister" unto the Lord: they "come near to the LORD to minister unto him". This reminds that it was as the church at Antioch "***ministered to the Lord***, and fasted" that "the Holy Ghost said, Separate me Barnabas and Saul for the work whereunto I have called them" (Acts 13: 2). Like "the priests … the sons of Zadok" (v.46), we are to "draw near …" (Heb. 10: 22).

The section concludes with the measurements of the inner court - one hundred cubits square (v.47), that is, fifty yards square. The altar stood at the centre of the inner court, before the temple which itself stood at the west side of the inner court, hence the absence of a west gate. While we have already noted this, Malcolm Davies puts it beautifully in saying, "Since this altar reminds us of Christ's work on the cross of Calvary, it indicates that His finished work will be the very centre of all God's purposes and plans for both the Millennial Kingdom and eternity. Calvary will never be forgotten, but continually remembered with intense gratitude by all mankind as well as all heaven". We will have more to say about the millennial sacrifices in due course.

In Chapter 40 verses 48-49, we commence to enter the temple itself.

EZEKIEL CHAPTER 40:48 - 41:26

Having considered the temple courts and entrances (40: 5-47), we come now to the temple itself. We may divide the passage as follows: *(1)* the porch (40: 48-49); *(2)* the temple building (41: 1-4); *(3)* the side rooms (41: 5-11); *(4)* the west building (41: 12); *(5)* the external dimensions (41: 13-15); *(6)* the panelling (41: 16-20); (7*)* the altar (41: 21-22); *(8)* the doors (41: 23-26).

1) THE PORCH, 40: 48-49

Ezekiel now ascends the steps leading to the temple, which stood on the west side of the inner court, then passes through the porch or vestibule (40: 48-49) into the holy place (41: 1-2) and from there into the "most holy place" (41: 3-4).

"And he brought me to the porch of the house, and measured each post of the porch ... and he brought me by the steps whereby they went up to it: and there were pillars by the posts, one on this side, and another on that side." While the AV reads, simply, "the steps", the RV and JND marginal notes refer to "ten steps". It is well worth saying again, that in approaching God, the worshippers were constantly ascending: seven steps leading to the outer gates, eight steps leading to the inner gates, and ten steps leading to the temple itself. No wonder, then, that in preparation for the Passover, Peter and John were shown "a large upper room" (Luke 22: 12). W.E.Vine defines this as "a chamber, often over a porch, or connected with a roof, where meals were taken and privacy obtained". The words "upper room" (*anagaion* or *anōgeon*) mean 'above ground'. As N.Crawford observes, "It is tragic when a local testimony comes down to the level of the world". It happened at Corinth, "For ye are yet carnal: for whereas there is among you envying, and strife, and divisions, are ye not carnal, and **walk as men?**" (1 Cor. 3: 3).

We have already offered explanations in connection with the seven steps and the eight steps. Now we ought to say something about the ten steps!

It has to be said that there is not an easy explanation. Ten in Scripture is the number which coveys the 'complete ground of human responsibility', hence, for example, Pharaoh was visited by ten plagues, there were ten commandments, and there were ten servants to whom the pounds were entrusted (*Morrish's Bible Dictionary*). Bearing in mind that the Passover lamb was taken on "the tenth day", indicating that after men had been tested and found wanting God made provision for them, perhaps the ten steps leading to the temple teach us the same lesson, namely, that in approaching God we are reminded of our own failure, but that, in His grace and mercy, we can nevertheless approach Him in worship.

Coming now to the porch itself, it appears that verse 48 refers to the gate of the porch, and verse 49 to the porch itself. These verses pose difficulties to the expositor!

- *The gate of the porch, v.48.* It does seem, from F.A.Tatford's calculation of the total length of the temple (41: 13) that "the posts" of five cubits each refer to the thickness of the walls either side of the gate. Commentators tell us that "the breadth of the gate" was fourteen cubits. This figure is the result of assuming that the porch was twenty cubits wide and deducting six cubits ("three cubits on this side, and three cubits on that side") to arrive at fourteen cubits.

- *The porch itself, v.49.* Ezekiel then moved into the porch itself, knowing nothing of the problems arising in the minds of modern commentators! We are told that "The length of the porch was twenty cubits, and the breadth eleven cubits on that side". This seems clear enough. But to make F.A.Tatford's calculation of the total length of the temple (41: 13) work out, the length of the porch (20 cubits) has to be regarded as 20 cubits north to south, not east to west (in other words, the length becomes the ***breadth)***, which makes its ***length*** (which we would have regarded as the breadth) 12 cubits (18 feet). That is, following the Septuagint version which has twelve cubits here, not eleven. No doubt Ezekiel would have sighed over our ignorance!

2) THE TEMPLE BUILDING, 41: 1-4

Our attention is drawn to *(a)* the holy place (vv.1-2); *(b)* the "most holy place" (vv.3-4).

a) The holy place, 41: 1-2

Some diagrams entitle this 'the nave'. We must notice the measurements of the doorway, from the porch into the holy place (vv.1-2a), and then the measurements of the holy place itself (v.2a).

i) The door of the holy place, vv.1-2a. Verse 2 is clear enough: "And the breadth of the door was ten cubits; and the sides of the door were five cubits on the one side, and five cubits on the other side", totalling, of course, twenty cubits - "the breadth, twenty cubits" (v.2a). But how "the posts" fit into this overall measurement ("six cubits broad on the one side, and six cubits broad on the other side") is not altogether clear. It does seem however, as before, from F.A.Tatford's calculation of the total length of the temple (41: 13) that "the posts" refers to the thickness of the walls. The words, "which was the breadth of the tabernacle" might mean "which resembled the tabernacle" (C.F.Keil quoted by F.A.Tatford).

ii) The holy place itself, v.2a. This is all perfectly clear: "and he measured the length thereof, forty cubits: and the breadth, twenty cubits". In imperial measurements, 60 feet long and 30 feet wide.

b) The "most holy place", 41: 3-4

Our attention is drawn to the measurements of the doorway from the holy place into the "most holy place" (v.3), and then the measurements of the "most holy place itself" (v.4). Whereas in the tabernacle, the 'holiest of all' was entered via the veil, here it is entered via a door. *Perhaps* this is all part of the general absence of reference to "the varied colours, blue, purple, scarlet used in the Tabernacle", which is consistent with the spirit of the New Covenant that will be in operation in its fullness during the Millennial age. It is a covenant that, in contrast with the Old Covenant, does not dwell on the external or superficial, but on the internal and spiritual" (Alan Summers).

We should notice the following:

- **The door of the most holy place, v.3.** This is clear enough: "the door, six cubits; and the breadth of the door, seven cubits". In the words of F.A.Tatford, "The jambs at the entrance he measured as two cubits, but the actual entrance as six cubits wide, and the sidewalls on each side as seven cubits, making an overall breadth of twenty cubits". For the third time, the "post of the door" appears to refer to the thickness of the wall. If this is not the case, then F.A.Tatford has some explaining to do!

- **The most holy place itself, v.4.** This is all perfectly clear: "So he measured the length thereof, twenty cubits: and the breadth, twenty cubits". In imperial measurements, 30 feet long and 30 feet wide. The meaning of the words, "So he measured the length thereof, twenty cubits: and the breadth, twenty cubits, *before the temple*", is not apparent: The RSV has "twenty cubits, and its breadth, twenty cubits, *beyond the nave*", which *may* suggest that the "most holy place" brought the combined length of the holy places to sixty cubits: the holy place or 'nave', (v.2, RSV) was forty cubits in length.

Before proceeding further, we really ought to stop and note at least two lessons which emerge from all the detail.

- **That the worshippers move to 'higher ground' as they draw near to God**. Yes, we've said this before, but it really is an important lesson. So the worshipper ascends from ground level to reach the outer court via the outer gate: seven steps. Then he ascends from the outer court to the inner court: eight steps. Finally, he ascends from the inner court to the entrance of the temple itself: ten steps.

- **That the entrances** "*gradually diminished in width as the approach became closer to the innermost shrine.* The porch was **fourteen** cubits wide (40: 48 RSV), the entrance to the nave or holy place, **ten** cubits (41: 2), and the entrance to the holy of holies, **six** cubits (41: 3)" (F.A.Tatford). As Malcolm Davies points out, "This suggests the truth of the greater holiness required in those who desire greater nearness to God".

- **That Ezekiel himself did not enter "the most holy place".** The angelic guide evidently entered alone to complete the temple measurements. F.A.Tatford reminds us that "under the Levitical economy the holy of holies was reserved for the high priest and he might enter only once a year, on the day of atonement (Lev. 16: 1-9). Ezekiel, therefore, made no attempt to enter here". How wonderful to know that the Lord's people today may "come boldly to the throne of grace ..." (Heb. 4: 16) and, through the Lord Jesus, "have access by one Spirit unto the Father" (Eph. 2: 18).

- **That the measurements of the temple correspond with the measurements of Solomon's temple.** The length of the porch (20 cubits), plus the length of the holy place (20 cubits), plus the length of the most holy place (20 cubits), totalling 60 cubits (splendid arithmetic here!) mean that this temple will be the same length as Solomon's temple. And so will its width (20 cubits). See 1 Kings 6 verse 2. While the height of Solomon's temple is given, we are not given the height of the millennial temple.

The tabernacle was only half this size. It was ten cubits in breadth (15 feet) and thirty cubits in length (45 feet), and this was divided into ten cubits (15 feet) for the holy of holies and twenty cubits (30 feet) for the holy place. The 'holy of holies' in the tabernacle, in Solomon's temple and in the millennial temple, are all cubes (10 x 10 cubits, 20 x 20 cubits and 20 x 20 cubits respectively. As Malcolm Davis observes, the "vast eternal city of New Jerusalem in Revelation Chapter 21" will also have cuboid shape. The consistency in these measurements, particularly in connection with their cuboid shape, indicates that God is perfectly consistent in all that He is, and in all that he says and does.

- *That no reference is made to most of the tabernacle furniture and fittings.* Malcolm Davis puts it nicely: "No veil is mentioned ... nor the ark of the covenant, for Christ, who is the fulfillment of the meaning of both these articles, will be personally reigning in this future temple. Also, there is no mention made of the tables of the law, nor of any high priest, since Christ will then combine the two offices of priest and king, reigning as a Priest upon His throne". In this connection, it has been pointed out that in the millennium, Israel "shall say no more, The ark of the covenant of the LORD: neither shall it come to mind: neither shall they remember it; neither shall they visit it; neither shall that be done any more. At that time they shall call Jerusalem the throne of the LORD; and all the nations shall be gathered unto it, to the name of the LORD, to Jerusalem" (Jer. 3: 16-17). In this coming age, the absence of the ark of the covenant will not be regretted because the true Ark will be there! God in Christ will rule in person, with Jerusalem, rather than the ark, as His throne. Similarly, the Lord's supper will be no longer necessary when the Lord Jesus returns for His people.

Then in worship purer, sweeter,
Thee Thy people shall adore,
Tasting of enjoyment greater
Far than thought conceived before –
Full enjoyment,
Full, unmixed, and evermore.

3) THE SIDE ROOMS, 41: 5-11

Verses 5-11 describe the side chambers. Quite clearly, these were located on the exterior of the main temple building with its porch, holy place and most holy place. We should note *(a)* the location of the chambers (vv.5-6): *(b)* the differing dimensions of the chambers (v.7); *(c)* the general dimensions of the area (vv.8-10); *(d)* the entrance to the chambers (v.11).

a) The location of the chambers, vv.5-6

"After he measured the wall of the house, six cubits; and the breadth of every side chamber, four cubits, round about the house on every side. And the side chambers were three, one over the other, and thirty in order; and they entered into the wall which was of the house for the side chambers round about, that they might have hold, but they had not hold in the wall of the house." Compare the details given in 1 Kings 6 verses 5-10, which describe the chambers in Solomon's temple.

The chambers (each four cubits, or 6 feet, wide) were arranged around the north, south and west walls of the temple, which were six cubits (9 feet) thick. While the side chambers were "round about the house on every side", this did not, evidently, include the east wall since it was there that the entrance to the temple was located. There were evidently thirty chambers on each floor – ninety chambers in total. As F.A.Tatford points out, "The whole of the side chambers was virtually a separate building although adjacent to the temple". The beams supporting the stories were supported by the walls of the temple but not inserted in them, and this is best explained by the way in which the side chambers of Solomon's temple were supported by the main building: "without in the wall of the house he made narrowed rests round about, that the beams should not be fastened in the walls of the house" (1 Kings 6: 6).

This raises some questions: first of all, obviously, what was the purpose of these side chambers? F.A.Tatford answers for most commentators in saying, "They were probably designed for storerooms". John B.Taylor agrees, adding "probably store-rooms for the tithes and offerings". Perhaps, however, they *might* have been used to accommodate the priests, although they do seem rather small for this purpose. A second question arises in connection with the way in which the adjacent building, with its ninety chambers, was attached to the temple building. F.A.Tatford answers: "they (the supporting beams) did not pierce the walls of the temple and thereby violate the holiness of the sacred building". This reminds us of the sanctity of the local assembly. See 1 Corinthians 3 verses 16-17.

b) The differing dimensions of the chambers, v.7

"And there was an enlarging, and a winding about still upward to the side chambers: for the winding about of the house went still upward round about the house: therefore the breadth of the house was still upward, and so increased from the lowest chamber to the highest by the midst."

At first glance, this ("a winding about") suggests that Ezekiel is describing some kind of stairway, which must have existed of course. There was certainly one in Solomon's temple (1 Kings 6: 8). But verse 7 does not directly refer to a staircase. The verse appears to mean that the higher you went (moving up the storeys) the bigger the chambers. The New Translation makes this a little (just 'a little') clearer: "And for the side chambers there was an enlarging, and it went round about [the house] increasing; for the surrounding of the house increased upward round about the house; therefore the house had width upward, and so ascended [from] the lower [storey] to the upper, by the middle one" (JND). Solomon's temple had the same arrangement. See 1 Kings 6 verse 6, where the chambers, working upwards, were five, six and seven cubits broad respectively. This, in both cases - the millennial temple and Solomon's temple - was achieved (we are told) by reducing the thickness of the outer wall of the side chambers.

While the details do call for a cool head (bring on the ice-pack), the emerging lesson is clear: that in spiritual life and in the enjoyment of God's Word, things get bigger and bigger the higher you go. We all need to leave 'ground level' and 'set our mind on things above' (Col. 3: 2, JND). This brings us to:

c) The general dimensions of the area, vv.8-10

These cover the raised platform on which the side chambers were built, the foundation on which they were built, the thickness of the wall of the building containing the side chambers, and the free space round the entire complex, that is, on its east north and south sides. We should notice:

i) The raised platform on which they were built.
"I saw also the height of the house round about" (v.8), or "And I saw that the house had an elevation

round about" (JND). F.A.Tatford renders this: "I saw also that the house had a raised platform all around". This raised platform presumably brought the floor of the ground floor chambers to the level of the temple floor which was, of course, elevated from the level of the inner court by the height of ten steps.

ii) ***The foundation on which they were built***. "The foundations of the side chambers were a full reed of six great cubits (9 feet)" (v.8), or "the foundations of the side chambers, a full reed, six cubits to the joint" (JND). Mercifully, J.N.Darby explains himself in saying, "to the level place where the side chambers began" (margin).

iii) ***The thickness of the wall of the building containing the side chambers***: "The thickness of the wall, which was for the side chamber (side-chambers', JND) without, was five cubits (7 ½ feet)" (v.9).

iv) ***The unused space round the entire complex***. That is, the temple plus side-chambers.

The meaning of the words, "and that which was left was the place of the side chambers that were within" (v.9) becomes clear in the New Translation: "The thickness of the wall, which was for the side-chambers without, was five cubits, **as also** *what was left free along the building of the side-chambers that pertained to the house*". So if you wanted to walk round the outside of the complex, there was a walkway 7 ½ feet wide between the wall enclosing the side-chambers and the edge of the raised platform on which the complex was built.

In the final piece of information at this juncture, we are told, "And between the chambers was the wideness of twenty cubits (30 feet) round about the house on every side". This evidently refers to the distance between the raised platform on which the temple and side-chambers were built and the surrounding buildings, such as the priests' chambers (42: 3-14). The RSV calls this space "the temple yard". So there was what F.A.Tatford calls "a free space of this width (20 cubits or 30 feet) running round the platform". But not, of course on the east side since this faced the inner court. Commentators point out that this "free space" would enable daylight to penetrate the 'side chambers'.

d) The entrance to the chambers, v.11

"And the doors of the side chambers were toward the place that was left, one door toward the north, and another door toward the south: and the breadth of the place that was left was five cubits round about." So if you wanted to access the side-chambers, you walked round the outside of the building, along the path measuring 7 ½ feet wide (v.9), and entered either through the north-facing door or the south-facing door. Presumably, there must have been some internal way of accessing the chambers on the west side of the building.

4) THE WEST BUILDING, 41: 12

The title belongs to F.A.Tatford, and he says all that is necessary, namely that there's not much that can be said about the building! "To the west of the temple, and divided from it by 'the separate place' or free space of twenty cubits ('the temple yard', RSV, v.12), was a large building seventy cubits broad (105 feet) and ninety cubits long (135 feet) and with a wall five cubits (7 ½ feet) deep". We are not told the purpose of this building. John B. Taylor says, simply, "presumably ... used for storage purposes". F.A.Tatford goes a little further in quoting Kliefoth (not known) who states that it was "for the reception of all refuse, sweepings, all kind of rubbish - in brief, of everything that was separated or rejected when holy service was performed in the temple - and that this is the reason why it received the name of 'the separate place'".

5) EXTERNAL DIMENSIONS, 41: 13-15

If we rightly understand the measurements, they fall into two parts. The first gives us the measurements of the temple itself, and the second the measurements of the "separate "place" which includes the "west building" above.

While it is not easy to calculate how Ezekiel arrives at the total figures, it is clear that both areas are one hundred cubits (150 feet or 50 yards) square. So we read:

- **The temple itself:** "an hundred cubits long" (v.13a): and "the breadth of the face of the house (v.14a) ... an hundred cubits". According to F.A.Tatford, the length of the temple (100 cubits), with its side chambers against the western wall, is made up as follows: "5 cubits for the wall of the porch (40: 48), 11 for the porch (40: 49), 6 for the wall of the holy place (41: 1), 40 for the holy place (41: 2), 2 for the wall of the holy of holies (41: 3), 20 for the holy of holies (41: 4), 6 for the wall of the temple (41: 5), 4 for the side chambers (41: 5), and 5 for the wall of the side chambers (41: 9), making a total of 100 cubits".

The "breadth of the face of the house" (the east front of the temple), 100 cubits, comprises: 20 cubits for the breadth of the house, 12 for the thickness of the two side walls (6 cubits each), 8 for the two side chambers (4 cubits each), 10 for the walls of the side chambers (5 cubits each), 10 for the remainder of the raised area (5 cubits each) and forty for the separate places or 'temple yard' (20 cubits each), making a total of 100 cubits (F.A.Tatford).

- The "separate place: "an hundred cubits long" (v.13b) and "the breadth" of "the separate place toward the east (we might have expected 'toward the west' here), an hundred cubits" (v.14b). The breadth is simply calculated: the 'west building', north to south, was 90 cubits long and its two walls 5 cubits each. Easy! The length (or depth) of the "separate place" (east to west), was also 100 cubits comprising the width (depth) of the 'west building' (70 cubits), plus its two walls of 5 each and, apparently, the depth of the temple yard (20 cubits), which, at this point, ran between the side chambers against the western wall of the temple and the 'west building'. It appears that in verse 15, Ezekiel confirms the north/south length of the building (the 'west building', v.12). In NIV language: "Then he measured the length of the building facing the courtyard at the rear of the temple, including its galleries on each side; it was a hundred cubits". The "galleries" are unidentified: "a word the sense of which is uncertain" (JND margin).

So, when Ezekiel entered the outer east gate, passed into the outer court, and then went through the inner east gate, he was confronted with three squares, one directly behind the other. Each measured one hundred cubits square. Firstly, the inner court, secondly the temple area, thirdly, the area containing the 'west building'.

Having considered all this, John B.Taylor nicely observes that "Only a man like Ezekiel could have found such pleasure in this kind of symmetrical precision. To him it meant that everything about the temple was a perfect fit: nothing was out of place". No doubt the apostle Paul would have said

'Amen' to this and then said of the local assembly, "Let all things be done decently and in order" (1 Cor. 14: 40).

6) THE PANELLING, 41: 15-20

Commentators divide verse 15, making part of the verse refer to the external measurements, and the rest refer to the panelling. These verses deal *(a)* with the panelling itself (vv15-17) and *(b)* with the decoration of the panelling (vv. 18-20).

a) The panelling itself, vv.15-17

F.A.Tatford really says it all: "The prophet now commenced to describe the interior of the temple. He noted that throughout it was panelled with wood; the holy place, the holy of holies and the porches of the court (perhaps referring to the inner court) were all panelled. Each also had windows with recessed frames. The walls were wainscotted (lined with boards) from the floor to above the windows. It had been previously stated that the windows had been closed (40: 16), but it was now disclosed that they were covered: it can hardly be implied that the panelling covered the windows as it reached above them, but the meaning is not clear. (As Malcolm Davies observes, with a smile on his face, 'We await 'further light' on this matter!'). On all the walls of the interior there was wood panelling".

In this connection, we cannot fail to notice, with Malcolm Davis, that "the wood will not be overlaid with gold, nor even silver, as was frequently the case in the tabernacle and Solomon's temple". In this connection it is well worth listening, again, to Alan Summers on the subject: "Unlike the Tabernacle or Solomon's Temple, the temple for the Millennium is a relatively plain building. We are not told the material of which the walls will be made. It seems likely that they will be built of stone. But nothing is said to suggest that the stonework is elaborate or ornate. There is no mention of a golden altar or of a brass laver or sockets of silver. No jewels are mentioned and there is no reference to the varied colours, blue, purple, scarlet used in the Tabernacle ... This is consistent with the spirit of the New Covenant that will be in operation in its fullness during the Millennial age. It is a covenant that in contrast with the Old Covenant does not dwell on the external or superficial but on the internal and spiritual. **The chief glory of the Temple will not be its fittings and fixtures, but the fact that the Lord is there**".

b) The decoration of the panelling, vv.18-20

Malcolm Davis explains most helpfully. Having noted that the wood panelling was decorated with alternating patterns of cherubim and palm trees, he continues: "Palm trees speak of righteousness, fruitfulness, salvation, victory, and beauty, while cherubim speak of God's holiness and executive judgment, all of which qualities will characterise the whole of the Millennial Kingdom. (Ezekiel's first vision - see chapter 1 - involved cherubim in just the setting suggested here.) But the cherubim have only two faces each, not four as in their earlier appearances in the visions of the prophecy, namely, the face of a man and the face of a lion. The face of a lion will illustrate Christ's kingly majesty then, while the face of a man will illustrate His true and perfect humanity. The face of the ox will be gone, because Christ will in His exaltation no longer be the Suffering and Lowly Servant of the LORD. The face of the eagle will also be gone, because the eternal Son of God has deigned to come down to earth as the Messianic Son of Man to rule the world for God His Father. The Lamb slain from before the foundation of the world has at last become the Lion of the tribe of Judah, ruling on the throne of His father David".

7) THE ALTAR, 41: 21-22

Before examining the altar, we should notice that Ezekiel tells us that "As for the temple, the doorposts were squared; and the front of the sanctuary had the same appearance' (v.21, JND). This, surely, together with the three squares noted above (the inner court, the temple area, and the area containing the 'west building') plus the overall square plan of the temple precincts (500 cubits or 250), reminds us again that in the Millennium, God's "house shall be called an house of prayer for all people" (Isa. 56: 7).

We must let Malcolm Davis give us yet another splendid piece in connection with the "altar of wood" (v.22). This was three cubits (4 ½ feet) high and two cubits (3 feet) square. Having noted that the majority of commentators agree that this altar is the equivalent of the altar of incense in the tabernacle, although some suggest that, since it is described as "the table that is before the LORD", it refers to a new table of showbread, Malcolm Davis continues: "It may be called a table because it speaks of fellowship with God in prayer, worship and praise ... The LORD always wanted His Temple to be 'a house of prayer for all nations' and this will be realised in the Millennial Kingdom. This identification is confirmed by the fact that the altar of wood is placed in front of the Holy Place, therefore on the direct line from the main altar of sacrifice in the inner court (see 43: 13-17) to the Most Holy Place, just as was the altar of incense in the tabernacle". Very clearly, the fact that this altar was made entirely of wood, indicates that it was not meant for sacrifice. The fact that it is made of wood, not of "shittim wood" overlaid "with pure gold" (Ex. 30: 1-3), emphasises that the millennial temple will not be known for its rich and costly adornment, but for the glory of the Lord's presence.

The 'altar of incense' in assembly life should be in regular use. The Lord Jesus said, "this do in remembrance of me" (Luke 22: 19). It should also be in regular use in our personal lives: "By him therefore let us offer the sacrifice of praise to God continually, that is, the fruit of our lips giving thanks to his name" (Heb .13: 15).

8) THE DOORS, 41: 23-26

The section commences by telling us that "the temple and the sanctuary had two doors" (v.23). The first of these was the door leading from the porch to the holy place (41: 1-2) and the second the door leading from the 'holy place' to "the most holy place" (41: 3-4). Reference is made to: *(a)* the doors themselves (vv.23-25); *(b)* the "thick planks" (v.25); *(c)* the windows (v.26).

a) The doors themselves, vv.23-25

"Both were double doors with two folding leaves apiece, on which were carved cherubim and palm trees" (Malcolm Davis), that is, "each of the leaves was divided into two leaves, so that each door consisted of four leaves" (F.A.Tatford). In Ezekiel's words, "And the doors had two leaves apiece, to turning leaves; two leaves for the one door, and two leaves for the other door. And there were made on them, on the doors of the temple, cherubims and palm trees, like as were made upon the walls" (vv.24-25). It has been pointed out that this means that it would be possible for a door to be opened only a quarter of the full width of the entrance, and that this would be all that was needed for a man to enter (John B.Taylor).

b) The "thick planks", v.25

Sounds familiar doesn't it? ('As thick as two short planks!'). According to John B.Taylor, the word rendered "planks" represent an unknown Hebrew word (see also 1 Kings 7: 6), but commentators seem generally agreed that it refers to a wooden canopy in front of the porch outside the temple building, perhaps over the entrance steps.

c) The windows, v.26

To quote F.A.Tatford, "Recessed windows were found in the sidewalls of the porch, and both sides of these walls, the side-rooms (presumably referring to the "side chambers", (vv.5-11) and the canopy, were decorated with palm trees".

EZEKIEL CHAPTER 42

Having considered the temple courts and entrances (40: 5-47) together with the temple and its buildings (40: 48 – 41: 26), we come now *(1)* to the priests' quarters (42: 1-14), and *(2)* to the encircling wall (42: 15-20).

1) THE PRIESTS' QUARTERS, 42: 1-14

Ezekiel now inspects the priests' chambers. But before we begin, we really ought to remind ourselves that while the Old Testament priesthood was selective, **every** believer in the Lord Jesus has been born into God's priestly family. We learn this from:

i)   *1 Peter 2.* "Ye also, as lively stones. are built up a spiritual house, an holy **priesthood**" (v.5); "But ye are a chosen generation, a royal **priesthood**" (v.9). But to whom is Peter writing? Chapters 1 & 2 make it clear that he is not writing to a select few, but to **all believers.**

-   **In Chapter 1**, Peter refers to: "The strangers scattered throughout Pontus, Galatia, Cappadocia, Asia, and Bythinia" (v.1); to those "elect according to the foreknowledge of God the Father" (v.2); to those "begotten … again unto a lively hope by the resurrection of Jesus Christ from among the dead" (v.3).

-   **In Chapter 2,** Peter refers to "newborn babes" (v.2); to those who have "tasted that the Lord is gracious" (v.3); to those "which believe" (v.7).

ii)   *Hebrews 10.* "Having therefore, brethren, boldness to enter into the holiest by the blood of Jesus, by a new and living way, which he hath consecrated for us, through the veil, that is to say, his flesh; and having an high priest over the house of God; let us draw near with a true heart in full assurance of faith, having our hearts sprinkled from an evil conscience, and our bodies washed with pure water" (vv.19-21). The words, "hearts sprinkled from an evil conscience, and our bodies washed with pure water", refer to the consecration of the priests in Exodus 29 verses 4 and 21. The epistle is addressed to "holy brethren, partakers of the heavenly calling" (Heb. 3: 1). It is therefore addressed to **all believers.**

The purpose of our priesthood is "to offer up **spiritual sacrifices**, acceptable to God by Jesus Christ" (1 Pet. 2: 5); "By him therefore let us offer the **sacrifice of praise** to God continually, that is, the fruit of our lips, giving thanks to his name" (Heb. 13: 15).

But there is another way in which we exercise our priesthood. The best way in which we can help each other is to **pray for each other.** Let's watch a priest at work: "Epaphras, who is one of you, a servant of Christ saluteth you, always labouring fervently for you in prayers, that ye may stand perfect and complete in all the will of God" (Col. 4: 12). Epaphras was the man who first evangelised the district. He was now in prison (see Philemon 23), but he was still on very active service! Very energetic active service too. The words "labouring fervently" translate the Greek word *agōnizomai,* and you don't have to be very clever to work out its meaning. Just think of our English word, 'agony'. It means 'to strive' or 'to wrestle'. There was nothing casual or 'laid back' about the prayers of Epaphras. He was in earnest. He was also most intelligent in his prayers for the assembly at Colosse. It wasn't just a case of 'Lord, bless the saints at Colosse'. He was quite specific: "that ye may stand perfect and complete in all the will of God". He knew all about the problems and pressures described by Paul in Colossians 2 verses 8-23, and prayed for their spiritual preservation.

After our 'diversion' above, we must continue Ezekiel's tour of inspection: "Then he brought me forth into the utter court, the way toward the north: and he brought me into the chamber that was over against the separate place (see 41: 10: the 'temple yard'), and which was before the building toward the north" (v.1). We must notice *(a)* the location of their quarters (vv.1-2); *(b)* the description of their quarters (vv.3-12); *(c)* the purpose of their quarters (vv.13-14). These chambers were evidently not provided as general living accommodation.

a) The location of their quarters, vv.1-2

To reach the priests' chambers, Ezekiel was conducted from the temple area itself, via the outer court ("utter court"), to the chambers opposite the temple yard on the north side of the temple. Perhaps it is worth mentioning that "utter" means 'outer', not 'inner'. This seems rather obvious (!), but some commentators (it would be churlish to mention their names!) do say "the inner court", perhaps because this seems more logical.

To get to the outer court, Ezekiel must have been taken along the northern edge of the inner court, out through the inner north gate, down the seven steps, and into the outer court. Once through the inner north gate and down the steps into the outer court, he would have turned left, and if our plan is correct, the priests' quarters would have been something like fifty yards along on the left. The entrance to the priests' quarters was evidently on the north side of the complex (i.e. facing the outer court): hence the route from the temple. Otherwise, Ezekiel could have come down the ten steps of the temple, turned left then left again into the 'temple yard' (the space twenty cubits wide between the raised platform on which the temple with its side-chambers was built, and the surrounding buildings, including the priests' chambers: see 41: 10), and entered by the back door - if there was one. But there wasn't! Hence the walk round to the front of the building.

The priests' quarters were located in two buildings, the first of which was one hundred cubits in length and fifty in breadth, that is, in length it was identical to the temple area - lying on the whole length of its northern boundary. Between this building and the northern inner gate lay one of the two chambers described in Chapter 40 verses 44-45: "And outside the inner gate were two cells in the inner court, one at the side of the north gate (here), and its front toward the south, that is, looking towards the two altars (41: 22; 43: 13-27) in the inner court before the temple building. The other was at the side of the south gate, with its front towards the north (also looking towards the two altars above)" (JND). Both chambers ('cells', JND) were places were the priests worked.

Very clearly then, the priests' quarters were located within a short distance of their work. In the first place, their quarters faced south, that is, "over against the separate place, and which was before the building toward the north" (v.1). To enter the temple, the priests had only to take the same route as Ezekiel but in the reverse direction, probably not much more that a couple of hundred yards. And if they were functioning in the chambers described in Chapter 40 verses 44-45, it was just a case of going next door!

Moreover it was exactly the same on the other side of the temple. See verses

10-12. Half the priests were accommodated north of the temple, and half south of the temple.

All this is most interesting. Abraham "pitched his tent ... and there he built an altar unto the LORD" (Gen. 12: 8). See also Genesis 13 verses 3-4. The Levites pitched their tents "round about the tabernacle of testimony" (Num. 1: 53), with Moses, and Aaron and his sons "toward the east, even before the tabernacle of the congregation" (Num. 3: 38). They lived near their spiritual centre!

It isn't always possible to reside in the shadow of the assembly hall, but like David, our hearts should be there: "Lord, I have loved the habitation of thy house, and the place where thine honour dwelleth" (Psalm 26: 8). We may not live 'on top' of the building where the assembly meets, but how close are we to it in spiritual terms?

b) The description of their quarters, vv.3-12

Malcolm Davis is certainly not wrong in saying that verses 1-12 are "somewhat difficult to understand in detail". These verses (vv.3-9) indicate that there were two parallel accommodation blocks on each of the two sites, that is on the site north of the temple and on the south of the temple. In each case there was evidently a walkway between the two blocks, each of which was three stories high, with one block 50 cubits long and the other 100 cubits long, both being entered from the eastern end.

i)   The number of accommodation blocks. "Over against the twenty cubits which were for the inner court, and over against the pavement which was for the utter (outer) court, was gallery against gallery in three storeys" (v.3). This appears to mean that the two 'galleries', referring to the accommodation blocks, faced the temple in one direction, and the outer wall in the other. It was exactly the same on the other side of the temple (vv.10-12).

ii)   The walkway between the accommodation blocks. "And before the chambers was a walk of ten cubits (15 feet) breadth inward, a way of one cubit (100 cubits, JND); and their doors toward the north" (v.4). In other words the pathway between the two blocks was 10 cubits wide (15 feet) and 100 cubits long (150 feet). So it ran the whole length of the longer accommodation block. Both blocks were entered from the outer court: "their doors (were) toward the north".

iii)   The height of the accommodation blocks. "Gallery against gallery in three storeys ... Now the upper chambers were shorter: for the galleries were higher than these, than the lower, and than the middlemost of the building. For they were in three storeys, but had not pillars as the pillars of the court: therefore the building was straitened more than the lowest and the middlemost from the ground" (vv.3, 5-6). The New Translation is helpful: "And the upper cells, because the galleries encroached upon them, were shorter than the lower, and the middlemost of the building. For they were in three [storeys], but had no pillars as the pillars of the courts; therefore [the third storey] was straitened more than the lowest and middlemost from the ground".

Like the side chambers of the temple, this building was three-storeyed, and each row of chambers was faced with a gallery. The chambers and galleries were not directly over one another, but were arranged in tiers, so that the size of the chambers on the third storey was obviously smaller than those beneath it. This is the exact opposite of the way in which the side-chambers of the temple were arranged!

iv)   The wall in front of the accommodation blocks. "And the wall that was without over against the chambers toward the utter (outer) court on the forepart of the chambers, the length thereof was fifty cubits. For the length of the chambers that were in the utter court was fifty cubits" (vv.7-8). Malcolm Davis explains this nicely: "The 50 cubit long wall built outside parallel to these chambers on the side of the outer court will probably serve the purpose of a screen wall to screen the windows while the serving priests are changing their clothes inside. There will be every provision for the maintenance of due decorum".

v)   The length of the accommodation blocks. "For the length of the chambers that were in the utter court was fifty cubits: and, lo, before the temple were an hundred cubits" (v.8). So, whether north or south of the temple, there were two accommodation blocks: the block fronting the outer court was 50 cubits (75 feet) long, and block fronting the temple was 100 cubits (150 feet) long. The chambers were entered from the east: "And from under these chambers was the entry on the east side, as one goeth into them from the utter (outward) court" (v.9). It seems that the general entrance to the northern block was on the north side of the complex (i.e. facing the outer court: see v.2), but once you were in, the actual entry into the two blocks was from the east. The words "from *under* these chambers" seems to indicate that entrance involved ascending from a lower level, perhaps referring to the level of the outer court.

vi) ***The parallel accommodation blocks.*** While Malcolm Davis is undoubtedly correct in saying that "verses 10-12 describe an identical building (buildings) on the south side of the inner court", the wording of verse 10 is difficult to understand. J.N.Darby makes it a little clearer: "In the breadth of the wall of the court toward the south (not 'east', AV) before the separate place, and before the building, were cells ('chambers', AV)". Thereafter (vv.11-12) it is clear that Ezekiel is describing identical buildings to the south of the temple: "And the way (passage or walkway) before them (the chambers) was like the appearance of the chambers which were toward the north, as long as they, and as broad as they ..."

c) *The purpose of their quarters, vv.13-14*

The purpose of these chambers, lying north and south of the temple itself, is stated in verses 13-14. F.A.Tatford puts it succinctly: "The chambers on both sides were regarded as holy and they had two purposes. Part of the meal (or cereal) offering was presented to God on the altar, but the remainder was eaten by the priests (Lev. 2: 3, 10; 7: 10; 12, 13). Part of the flesh of the sin and trespass offerings also belonged to the priests (Lev. 7: 6). These were holy and could be eaten only in the specified places, and it was for this that some of these chambers were provided. Secondly, the priests were not allowed to mix with the people while still wearing their priestly garments. They must first deposit these in the chambers provided and don their ordinary clothes before going out into the outer court to intermingle with the ordinary people. These chambers were in effect, their vestries".

We should note the emphasis on holiness here: "holy chambers" (v.13); "most holy things" (v.13); 'holy garments' (v.14). Turning for a moment to the detail, we should notice:

i) That in the first case (v.13) - the priests eating part of the sacrifices - they ate part of what had been offered to God. In the case of the peace offering particularly, they enjoyed what God enjoyed. No wonder we are told that there they "shall eat the most holy things". We do exactly the same in our worshipful remembrance of the Lord Jesus.

ii) That in the second case (v.14), the removal of the 'holy garments' before leaving the 'holy place' was to ensure that they were not ceremonially defiled by the outside world. The same principle underlies Haggai 2 verses 12-13, namely, that while holiness, or purity, is ***not*** transmissible, impurity *is* transmissible. It is so important to 'keep our garments' (our character) clean in this world and that we do not become soiled by its evil influences.

The millennial temple will certainly be a place of priestly activity. Interestingly enough, the Lord Jesus did say, "In my Father's house are many mansions (abiding places)" (John 14: 2) and, possibly, He may have been alluding to the side chambers of Solomon's temple and of the millennial temple, both of which are called "the house". In the case of the two temples, there is a finite number of "chambers", but in the "Father's house" there are **many** 'abiding places'. However, we have already noted that the priests' chambers were not provided as general living accommodation, whereas the "Father's house" **will** be our home for ever!

2) THE ENCIRCLING WALL, 42: 15-20

Most commentators seem to follow the Septuagint Version which has 'cubits' in verse 17 as opposed to "reeds" (AV), which follows the Hebrew text here and in Chapter 45 verse 2. If the measurement is in cubits then the wall here is obviously the same wall, with its four gates each reached by seven steps, described by Ezekiel at the commencement of his temple tour. See Chapter 40 verse 5. On this basis, using an eighteen-inch cubit, the temple will stand within a square wall having a circumference of 1000 yards (2000 cubits of 18 inches).

If, however, we follow the Hebrew text (where each side measures 500 **reeds**), the temple site will stand within a square wall having a circumference of 6,167 yards. This calculation is based on a "reed" measuring "six cubits long by the cubit and an hand breadth" (40: 5), that is, 2,000 reeds of 111 inches (18 inches x 6 plus 3 inches).

In passing, attention is drawn to the measurement of the "holy portion of the land" (45: 1), which includes the temple site (45: 2). This will measure 25,000 reeds long ('reeds' is italicized in the A.V.) and the unit of measurement of the breadth is unspecified. This indicates, on the above basis, and on the assumption that the unit of measurement is 'reeds', that the area is approximately 44 miles long and 18 miles wide. In acknowledging the cubit/ reed problem, Malcolm Davis does say, "The Hebrew says (in 42:15-20) that it was in reeds, definitely *qanim*, whereas the Septuagint changes this to cubits, a much shorter measurement".

CHAPTER 42

It should be said that the argument that the measurements are actually in cubits, not reeds, because the temple and its environs must "fit into the borders of present day Israel", must be set against the fact that "Israel in the Millennium will be a very different place from the Israel we know today. Isaiah and Zechariah speak of a physical rearrangement of the landscape of Israel. The landscape is levelled into a great plain (Zech. 14. 10), the Mount of Olives is cloven in two (Zech. 14. 4), and the temple stands on a mountain top (Isa. 2: 2; Mic. 4: 1, 2)" (Alan Summers). Malcolm Davis points out that "even if we adopt the reading 'cubits' for 'reeds' throughout these passages, the area of the Millennial Temple complex will be far greater than the area currently available on Mount Moriah in present-day Jerusalem ... We sometimes underestimate the almighty power of God to accomplish His purposes in the world in the future!!"

Although, seemingly, a 'minority view', it seems quite clear that there are **two walls**: the first wall (measured in cubits) encircling the temple precincts, and the second wall (measured in reeds) some undefined distance away (but see below), and encircling the first wall, which will ensure that there is a complete separation between "the sanctuary of the LORD" (48: 10) and the "profane place for the city" (48: 15) where the word "profane" simply means that it will not have the sanctity of the temple, frequented only by the priests. We are specifically told in Chapter 42 that the purpose of what we have described as 'a second wall', was "to make a separation between the sanctuary and the profane place" (v.20).

In this connection, we should note that the temple complex will be surrounded by "suburbs" (an 'open space', RV) measuring 50 cubits wide (25 yards) on all sides. John B.Taylor calls this "a kind of 'green belt' between the sacred and the profane". Alan Summers (*Assembly Testimony*, January/February, 2010) calls it a *cordon sanitaire.* As Malcolm Davis pertinently observes, "The presence of sin in the world even during Christ's Millennial Kingdom will make this necessary".

EZEKIEL CHAPTER 43

"The glory of the LORD" is a key phrase in the book of Ezekiel (see 1: 28; 3: 12, 23; 8: 4; 9: 3; 10: 4, 18, 19; 11: 22, 23; 43: 2, 4, 5; 44: 4), and having witnessed its departure from "the threshold of the house" (Ezek. 10: 18), we now witness its return: "And, behold, the glory of the God of Israel came from the way of the east ... and the visions were like the vision that I saw by the river Chebar; and I fell on my face ... And the glory of the LORD came into the house ... and, behold, the glory of the LORD filled the house" (43: 2-5). The "glory of the LORD" left the temple by the east gate (10: 19), and returns by the east gate (43: 4).

Having fallen on his face at his first sight of "the glory of the LORD" (1: 28), Ezekiel does so again at its return (43: 3).

This reminds us that "the Lord of glory" (1 Cor. 2: 8; James 2: 1) came into the world, but like "the glory of the LORD" which left the house (Ezek. 10: 18) and was last seen standing "upon the mountain which is on the east side of the city" (Ezek. 11: 23), He too left the temple *en route* for the Mount of Olives (Matt.24: 1-3), saying, "Ye shall not see me henceforth, till ye shall say, t Blessed is he that cometh in the name of the Lord" (Matt. 23: 39). He will come back to the Mount of Olives (Zech. 14: 4), and return to the temple. Israel *will* see Him again, and do so, as He said, with the language of Psalm 118 verse 26 on their lips: "Blessed be he that cometh in the name of the LORD".

When the ark of the covenant fell into Philistine hands, a dying mother gave birth, and named the child "Ichabod, saying, The glory is departed from Israel: because the ark of God was taken, and because of her father in law and her husband. And she said, The glory is departed from Israel: for the ark of God is taken" (1 Sam. 4: 19-22). But the ark returned to Beth-Shemesh ('the house of the sun'), and "the Levites took down the ark of the LORD ... and the men of Beth-shemesh offered burnt-offerings and sacrificed sacrifices the same day unto the LORD" (1 Sam. 6: 15), reminding us that "the Sun of righteousness" will "rise with healing in his wings" and God's people will "go forth, and grow up as calves of the stall" (Mal. 4: 2). The words "grow up" mean 'leap' or 'frisk', leading to the translation, "And ye shall go forth and leap like fatted calves" (JND), that is, like calves coming out into the sunlight. The remnant will rejoice that righteousness has at last triumphed. It will indeed be a "morning without clouds" for them! The nation will be rejuvenated.

As noted in our Outline of the book and on subsequent occasions, Ezekiel Chapters 40-48 may be summarised in the following way: *(a)* the millennial temple (40: 1 – 42: 20); the millennial worship (43: 1 - 46: 24); *(c)* the millennial land (47: 1 - 48: 35).

The chapters dealing with the millennial worship cover the following: *(a)* the advent of the glory of the Lord (43: 1-12); *(b)* the altar of worship (43: 13-27); *(c)* the approach to God (44: 1-31); *(d)* the allocation of land, 45: 1-8; *(e)* the application at the time (45: 9-12); *(f)* the appointed offerings (45: 13 - 46: 24).

1) THE ADVENT OF THE GLORY OF THE LORD, 43: 1-12

Ezekiel saw this marvellous event take place from two vantage points: from "the gate that looketh toward the east" (v.1) and from the "inner court" of the temple (v.5). We may call this the *entrance* of the glory of the Lord: "And the glory of the LORD came into the house" (v.4), and the *enthronement* of the glory of the Lord: "the glory of the LORD filled the house" (v.5). As we shall see, the millennial temple will be the place of His throne (v.7). His glorious advent is accompanied by the *existence of* holiness (vv.6-12).

a) The entrance of the glory of the Lord, vv.1-4

"Afterward he brought me to the gate, even to the gate that looketh toward the east. And, behold, the glory of the God of Israel came from the way of the east, and his voice was like the noise of many waters: and the earth was shined with his glory. And it was according to ... the vision that I saw when I came to destroy the city: and the visions were like the vision that I saw by the river Chebar, and I fell upon my face. And the glory of the LORD came into the house by the way of the gate whose prospect is toward the east." The Lord who left the original temple through its east gate (Ezek. 10: 19-20) now returns through the east gate of the millennial temple.

EZEKIEL

The details of Ezekiel's description of the return of the glory of the Lord are absorbing, not merely from a technical point of view, but in their spiritual lessons. But before continuing, it is perhaps worth repeating that, unlike the image of "the great goddess Diana" which, they said, "fell down from Jupiter" (Acts 19: 35), and unlike the new Jerusalem which will descend "out of heaven from God" (Rev. 21: 10), it hardly seems likely that the millennial temple, or its environs for that matter, will descend from heaven. The millennial temple will not be constructed before the Lord returns to earth, but at some point after that event, when He will then take up occupancy. Zechariah 6 verses 12-13 and 15 make most significant reading on the subject.

It might be helpful to notice that the passage refers to the arrival of "the glory of the God of Israel" (v.2) and "the glory of the LORD" (vv.4, 5). Quite obviously we cannot separate the Lord from His glory. We might therefore say that the passage describes the return of the Lord in glory to the temple, and this is supported by the words, "and the earth shined with his glory" (v.2). On the threshold of his ministry Ezekiel saw "upon the likeness of the throne ... the likeness of the appearance of a man above upon it", and summed up the vision by saying, "This was the likeness of the appearance of the glory of the LORD" (1: 26, 28). So it is not simply a case of *what* he saw but rather *who* he saw. He saw a *man* on the throne! He saw the Lord Jesus in His glory! And now he saw Him again: "the visions were like the vision that I saw by the river Chebar" (v.3). So we will not say 'it', but 'Him'.

Looking now at the details, we ought to consider the following: *(i)* the glory He bore: He is "the glory of the God of Israel" (v.2) *(ii)* the direction from which He came: He came from "the east" (vv.1, 2, 4); *(iii)* the sound of His voice: it was "like a noise of many waters" (v.2); *(iv)* the effect of His coming: "the earth shined with his glory" (v.2) *(v)* the consistency of His glory: nothing had altered, "it was according to the appearance" of past visions (v.3); *(vi)* the purpose of His coming: "And the glory of the LORD came into the house" (v.4).

i) **The glory He bore**. It was the "glory of the God of Israel". We are reminded that Isaiah said, "In the year that king Uzziah died I saw also the LORD sitting upon a throne, high and lifted up, and his train filled the temple" and continued "mine eyes have seen the King, the LORD of hosts ..." (Isa. 6: 1, 5). Well, who did Isaiah see? The New Testament answers: "These things saith Esaias, when he saw his glory, and spake of *him* ..." (John 12: 41). That is, of course, the Lord Jesus. In His prayer, He said, "O Father, glorify thou me with thine own self with the glory which I had with thee before the world was" (John 17: 5). But, more specifically, in context, here it was "the glory of the God of Israel" and this takes us to a galaxy of references. See for example: "And the glory of the LORD abode upon mount Sinai … And the sight of the glory of the LORD was like devouring fire on the top of the mount in the eyes of the children of Israel" (Ex. 24: 16-17).

When He came to earth two thousand years ago, He was "despised and rejected of men; a man of sorrows and acquainted with grief: and we hid as it were our faces from him; he was despised, and we esteemed him not" (Isa. 53: 3). John tells us that "he came unto his own, and his own received him not" (John 1: 11). When He returns to earth, it will be "in the glory of his Father with the holy angels" (Mark 8: 38), and here He enters the millennial temple in "the glory of the God of Israel". It is a statement of His deity. God had said, "I am the LORD: that is my name: and my glory will I not give to another" (Isa. 42: 8) and therefore the Lord Jesus must be "of the full deity possessed, eternally divine". He comes in "the glory of the God of Israel".

ii)   The direction from which He came. He came from "the east" (vv.1, 2, 4), which F.Cundick calls "the way of light".

The "east" is the place of sun-rising. Japan is called 'the land of the rising sun' and this was (perhaps it is still the case) enshrined in the names of the vessels in her merchant fleet. The sun-rising marks the beginning of a new day and therefore points to the return of Christ. Just as sunrise marks the beginning of a new day, so the return of Christ will mark the beginning of a new era on earth. As previously noted, in a different connection, God said through Malachi, "But unto you that fear my name shall the Sun of righteousness arise with healing in his wings" (Mal. 4: 2) with evident blessing for God's people at the time. It is often said that the great hope of the church is the "morning star" which appears before day-break and requires observers to look up into the sky. It is a heavenly hope, whereas the hope of Israel is connected with the rising sun, and to see the sun rise you are required to look at the circumference of the earth. It is an earthly hope. Not all agree with this difference, but for our present purpose, the fact that "the glory of the God of Israel came from the way of the east" signals the beginning of a new 'day' in world history. Wise men once came "from the east" to Jerusalem (Matt. 2: 1), now the very "King of the Jews" that they had come to worship, comes Himself from the east.

iii) **The sound of His voice**. It was "like a noise of many waters" (v.2). Compare Chapter 1 verse 24, "And when they went (the cherubim), I heard the noise of their wings, like the noise of great waters, as the voice of the Almighty, the voice of speech, as the noise of a host ..." See also Psalm 93 verse 4: "The LORD on high is mightier than the noise of many waters, yea, than the mighty waves of the sea", and Revelation 1: 13-15, "And in the midst of the seven candlesticks one like unto the Son of man ... and his feet like unto fine brass, as if they burned in a furnace; and his voice as the sound of many waters." (Revelation 1 verses 13-15) It is a picture of tremendous, irresistible power. It has been said that "To stand near many waters, as in a waterfall, is to be overwhelmed by the sheer power of the sound as it covers the whole range of audible frequencies. It is impossible to speak above it, or against it. The voice of the Son of man is overwhelming: it drowns all others. When He speaks, He is the unanswerable One" (J.Allen, *What the Bible Teaches - Revelation*).

iv) **The effect of His coming.** "The earth shined (Hebrew, *or*) with his glory" (v.2). Compare Deuteronomy 33 verse 2; Isaiah 60 verse 3; Habakkuk 3 verse 3.

Nebuchadnezzar was told that "Thou , O king, art a king of kings (not **the** 'King of kings'); for the God of heaven hath given thee a kingdom, power, and strength, and glory. And wheresoever the children of men dwell, the beasts of the field and the fowls of the heaven hath he given into thine hand, and hath made thee ruler over them all. Thou art this head of gold" (Dan. 2: 37-38). The "times of the Gentiles" (Luke 21: 24) began with such a king. And what did he do? "He made an image of gold" and commanded "all the people, the nations, and the languages" to fall down and worship the image (Dan. 3: 1, 7). The "times of the Gentiles will end similarly: "and power was given him ('the beast': the final satanically-inspired world ruler) over all kindreds, and tongues, and nations" (Rev. 13: 7). He too will be represented by an image (Rev. 13: 14-15).

But in the millennial age, the world will not shine with the glory of Nebuchadnezzar, nor with the glory of the beast, but with the glory of Christ. "The earth shined with *his* glory". In the words of Psalm 72: 11, "all kings shall fall down before him: all nations shall serve him ... His name shall endure for ever (not so Nebuchadnezzar: not so the beast): his name shall be continued as long as the sun: and men shall be blessed in him: all nations shall call him blessed. Blessed be the LORD God, the **God of Israel**, who only doeth wondrous things. And blessed be his glorious name for ever: and let the whole earth be filled with his glory; Amen, and Amen" (vv. 11, 17-19). David prayed in times of difficulty, "Make thy face to shine (Heb. *or*) upon thy servant" (Ps. 31: 16), and another psalmist cried, "God be merciful unto us, and bless us; and cause his face to shine (Heb. *or*) upon us" in order that God's "way may be known upon earth, thy saving health among all nations" (Ps. 67: 1-2). But now the whole earth will shine "with his glory".

v) *The consistency of His glory*. Nothing had altered. What Ezekiel saw "was according to the appearance of the vision which I saw, even according to the vision that I saw when I came to destroy the city: and the visions were like the vision that I saw by the river Chebar" (v.3). In the first place, the prophet refers to Chapter 10 verses 1-22, and in the second to Chapter 1 verses 4-28. If the dates at the top of the Scofield Bible are correct, there was an interval of approximately twenty years between the two visions mentioned in this verse and the current vision of the returning glory of "the God of Israel". There had been no alteration in the character of God. He said, "I am the LORD, I change not" (Mal. 3: 6) and the Lord Jesus is "the same yesterday, and to day, and for ever" (Heb. 13: 8).

vi) *The purpose of His coming*. "And the glory of the LORD came into the house" (v.4). The millennial temple will not be an empty shell. It will be the dwelling place of God: "the place of my throne, and the place of the soles of my feet, where I will dwell in the midst of the children of Israel" (v.7). It was always God's purpose to dwell amongst His people. This was one reason for constructing the tabernacle: "let them make me a sanctuary; that I may dwell among them" (Ex. 25: 8). The previous chapter (Exodus 24) describes His glory: "And the sight of the glory of the LORD was like devouring fire on the top of the mount in the eyes of the children of Israel" (vv. 16-17). This is the God who desires to dwell amongst His people! The word "sanctuary" means a place set apart for God, a place of holiness. It must have been an awesome experience to enter the tabernacle. Just think of the reverence required and the preparation needed! We draw near to the **same God** in worship and prayer, individually and collectively, and should do so with godly fear. Once completed, "a cloud covered the tent of the congregation, and the glory of the LORD filled the tabernacle" (Ex. 40: 34-35).

The tabernacle was followed by the temple to which Solomon referred in saying, "I have surely built thee an house to dwell in, a settled place for thee to abide in for ever" (1 Kings 8: 13). This too was filled with the glory of the Lord: "the glory of the LORD filled the house" (2 Chron. 7: 1-2). See also 1

Kings 8 verses 10-11, "the glory of the Lord filled the house of the LORD". As David observed in Psalm 29, "The voice of the LORD maketh the hinds to calve, and discovereth the forests: and in his temple doth every one speak of his glory" (v.9) or "and in his temple doth every one say, Glory!" with the footnote, "perhaps – 'everything saith'". Others say, "every whit utters his glory" (quoted by Harold St.John). Whatever the exact rendering, one thing is clear: a temple is a place in which God is glorified.

This should be true of the *local assembly*: "If any man defile the **temple** of God, him shall God destroy; for the **temple** of God is holy, which **temple** ye are" (1 Cor. 3: 17). The local assembly should be a place where the glory of God and the glory the Lord Jesus are fully upheld. "In all things" He must have "the preeminence" (Col. 1: 18). This brings us to:

b) The enthronement of the glory of the Lord, v.5

"So the spirit ('Spirit', JND) took me up, and brought me into the inner court; and, behold, the glory of the LORD filled the house." It should be noted that Ezekiel was not taken to the inner court by the angel guide, but in the power of the Holy Spirit. The words, "So the Spirit took me up" or "the Spirit *lifted me up*" (JND) occur elsewhere. The four chapters describing Ezekiel's vision of the fearful idolatry in the temple (chs.8-11) commence and conclude in the same way: "and the the Spirit *lifted me up* ... and brought me in the visions of God to Jerusalem" (8: 3, JND); "And the Spirit *lifted me up*, and brought me in the vision by the Spirit of God into Chaldea, to them of the captivity; and the vision that I had seen went up from me" (11: 24, JND).

We can certainly say that in his ministry Ezekiel was directed by the Spirit of God, and that is this particular case (He "brought me into the inner court; and, behold, the glory of the LORD filled the house") we come to the mainstream of the Holy Spirit's ministry, which is to occupy God's people with the Lord Jesus. See John 15 verse 26; 16 verses 13-14. We have an example in Stephen: "But he, being full of the Holy Ghost, looked up stedfastly unto heaven, and saw the *glory of God*, and Jesus standing on the right hand of God" (Acts 7: 55).

The temple is called "the house" in three consecutive verses: "the glory of the LORD came *into the house*" (v.4); "the glory of the LORD *filled the house*" (v.5); "I heard him speaking unto me *out of the house*" (v.6). This serves to remind us that in the New Testament, the local church is described, not only as "the temple of God" (1 Cor. 3: 17), but as "the house of God" (1 Tim. 3: 15). Like the local assembly (the "house of God"), the "house" here is also "the pillar and ground of the truth". We must now listen to "the law of the house" (v.12).

This brings us to:

(c) The existence of holiness, vv.6-12

Ezekiel now listens to the voice of the Lord Himself: "I heard him ('I heard one', JND) speaking unto me out of the house …" In fact, as we noticed in introducing this final section of the book (see our comments on 40: 3), the remainder of the prophecy is God speaking directly to Ezekiel. "So the spirit ('Spirit', JND) took me up, and brought me into the inner court; and, behold, the glory of the LORD filled the house. And I heard *him* ('I heard one') speaking unto me out of the house: and *the man* stood by me." It is significant that from this point onwards, we do not read anything further about the "man", at least not until Chapter 47 verse 3: "And when *the man that had the line in his hand* went forth eastward, he measured a thousand cubits …" This explains Ezekiel 44 verses 2 and 5 ("Then said the LORD unto me … and the LORD said unto me"). In other words, it all changes when the "glory of the LORD" fills the house. Up to that point the "man" does the speaking, but after that point the Lord is the speaker!

It has been said that the business of the prophets was to address the present in the light of the future, and that is exactly what Ezekiel is now called upon to do. These verses deal with his current ministry to "the house of Israel." We should notice the following: *(i)* the millennial temple will be holy (v.7); *(ii)* Solomon's temple had become unholy (v.8); *(iii)* God's people were to cease their unholy practices (v.9); *(iv)* the holiness of the temple was to be a lesson to the people (v.10); *(v)* desires after holiness would be accompanied by further teaching (v.11); *(vi)* holiness will pervade the whole temple site (v.12).

i) The millennial temple will be holy, v.7

The nation will finally cease to defile the dwelling place of God and the name of God. "And he said unto me, Son of man, the place of my throne, and the place of the soles of my feet, where I will dwell in the midst of the children of Israel, and my holy name, shall the house of Israel no more defile, neither they, nor their kings, by their whoredom, nor by the carcases of their kings in their high places." The reference to "the carcases of their kings in their high places" is perhaps best explained by the translation, "the lifeless idols of their kings" (NIV). Their idols were no better than lifeless carcases.

David was told that he had "given great occasion to the enemies of the LORD to blaspheme" (2 Sam. 12: 14), and the nation had followed suit: "the name of God is blasphemed among the Gentiles through you" (Rom. 2: 24). But no more.

The temple is called "the place of my throne, and the place of the soles of my feet". This may well suggest that while the temple will be the centre of divine rule (He will be "a priest upon his throne", Zech. 6: 13), it will be but "the place of the soles of my feet". That is, He is infinitely greater than the temple, which will be His footstool (Psalm 99: 5; 132: 7; Isaiah 66: 1), reminding us that the Lord dwells in heaven, and the temple is simply His earthly habitation (John B.Taylor). It has been pointed out that the words here are an echo of Solomon's prayer in 1 Kings 8 verses 12, 13 and 27 (John B.Taylor)

ii) Solomon's temple had become unholy, v.8

Israel had failed, lamentably, to recognise the holiness of God: "In their setting of their thresholds, and their posts by my posts, and the wall between me and them, they have even defiled my holy name by their abominations that they have committed; wherefore I have consumed them in mine anger ..." See, for example Ezekiel 8 verses 1-18. Hence the temple site will have "a wall ... to make a separation between the sanctuary and the profane place" (42: 20). It has often been said that there is a great difference between a ship in the sea, and the sea in a ship! In the case of Israel, it was 'the sea in the ship'. It is so today - so much so that a leading Anglican cleric bemoaned the fact that the church had not kept pace with the world. 2 Corinthians 6 verse 14 to 7 verse 1 now becomes compulsory reading.

iii) God's people were to cease their unholy practices, v.9

"Now let them put away their whoredom (harlotry), and the carcases of their kings (their idolatry), far from me, and I will dwell in the midst of them for ever." In Paul's words above, "Wherefore come out from among them (idolaters at Corinth), and be ye separate saith the Lord, and touch not the unclean thing; and I will receive you, and will be a Father unto you, and ye shall be my sons and daughters, saith the Lord Almighty" (2 Cor. 6: 17-18).

iv) The holiness of the temple was to be a lesson to the people, v.10

"Thou son of man, shew the house to the house of Israel, that they may be ashamed of their iniquities: and let them measure the pattern." The absolute holiness of God, demonstrated by the pattern of the house, was intended to create a sense of shame over past and present unholiness. This was certainly the lesson in Paul's teaching: "Know ye not that ye are the temple of God, and that the Spirit of God dwelleth in you? If any man defile (mar) the temple of God, him shall God destroy (mar); for the temple of God is holy, which temple ye are" (1 Cor. 3: 16-17). Malcolm Davis looks at verses 10-11 slightly differently, but most helpfully: "A long and considered look at the Lord's future plans for them would convince them how much they had forfeited by their sins. The ultimate objective was to secure their full obedience to His laws and statutes again".

v) Desires after holiness would be accompanied by further teaching, v.11

"And if they be ashamed of all that they have done, shew them the form of the house, and the fashion thereof, and the goings out thereof, and all the forms thereof, and all the laws thereof: and write it in their sight, that they may keep the whole form thereof. And all the ordinances thereof ... and do them." A complete description of the temple, and its ordinances, was to be made available if the children of Israel were willing to display true humility and shame at their past history. In words which were frequently heard in years gone by, 'If we live in the light of what we already know, God will give us more light'.

vi) Holiness will pervade the whole temple site, v.12

"This is the law of the house; Upon the top of the mountain the whole limit thereof round about shall be most holy. Behold, this is the law of the house." In the millennium once-dangerous animals and reptiles will no longer be a threat: "They shall not hurt nor destroy in all my **holy mountain**: for the earth will be full of the knowledge of the LORD, as the waters cover the sea" (Isa. 11: 9).

2) THE ALTAR OF WORSHIP, vv.13-27

As noted above, we now learn that millennial worship will be offered in connection with an altar and the sacrifices offered upon it.

This is not at all surprising. Everything must begin with an altar. In this chapter we are told about the construction of the altar (vv.13-17) and the consecration of the altar (vv.18-27).

a) The construction of the altar, vv.13-17

The first, and perhaps the most important, point to notice is that it will be foursquare: "And the altar shall be twelve cubits long, twelve broad, square in the four squares thereof. And the settle shall be fourteen cubits long and fourteen broad in the four squares thereof" (vv.16-17). Once again, universality is stressed. As we have already noted, God's "house shall be called an house of prayer for *all* people" (Isa. 56: 7). We must not forget that the millennial temple will be a place to which the whole world will come, and that the millennial earth will not be filled with a conglomeration of religion. It will be a world converted to the worship of the Lord.

Isaiah 60 now becomes compulsory reading! The chapter begins by saying, "Arise, shine; for thy light is come, and the glory of the LORD is risen upon thee ... And the Gentiles shall come to thy light, and kings to the brightness of thy rising ... the forces ('wealth') of the Gentiles shall come unto thee. The multitude of camels shall cover thee, the dromedaries of Midian and Ephah; all they from Sheba shall come: they shall bring gold and incense; and they shall show forth the praises of the LORD. All the flocks of Kedar shall be gathered together unto thee, the rams of Nabaioth shall minister unto thee: **they shall come up with acceptance upon mine altar, and I will glorify the house of my glory**" (vv.1-7). (The best commentary on the Bible is the Bible itself!)

Malcolm Davis draws attention to the facts that its measurements are "in long cubits, for verse 13 explains that the cubit used here was actually a cubit plus an hand-breadth, or about 21 inches. The altar was built in square sections. Each section downwards being two cubits wider than the one above". The description, however, starts at the base of the altar, and works upward.

CHAPTER 43

i)   The base of the altar, v.13. "The bottom was a cubit [in height] and the breadth a cubit, and its border on the edge thereof round about, one span: and this was the base of the altar" (JND). F.A.Tatford explains: "A foundation was sunk in the ground and the altar proper rested upon this. The size of the foundation was not indicated except that it was a cubit high (or deep) and projected beyond the next stage by one cubit on each side ("one cubit broad", RSV) and had a rim (a border or moulding) of a span (3 inches). Bearing in mind the known size of the 'altar hearth' and the 'upper settle' (vv.16-17), and the references to "one cubit" (vv.13, 14), it is not difficult to calculate that the foundation was almost certainly eighteen cubits square (31 feet 6 inches). Then, working upwards:

ii)   The lower settle, v.14. "And from the bottom on the ground to the lower settle was two cubits (3 feet 6 inches), and the breadth one cubit" (JND). So the next part of the altar, resting on the foundation, was two cubits deep (3 feet 6 inches). Bearing in mind that the "lower settle" rested on the foundation with one cubit to spare all round, this would mean, extending the above calculation, that it was sixteen cubits square (28 feet). Then, working upwards:

iii)   The upper settle, v.14. "And from the small settle to the great settle, four cubits and the breadth a cubit" (JND). So the next part of the altar, the 'great settle', resting on the 'lower settle', was four cubits deep (7 feet). Bearing in mind that the 'great settle' rested on the 'lower settle' with one cubit to spare all round, this would mean that it was fourteen cubits square (24 feet 6 inches). This is confirmed in verse 17. Then working upwards:

iv)   The altar hearth, vv.15-16. "And the upper altar was four cubits (7 feet); and from the hearth of God and upward were four horns, And the hearth of God was twelve [cubits] long, by twelve broad, square in the four sides thereof" (JND). So the top of the altar was 12 cubits square (21 feet), and 4 cubits (7 feet) in depth (v.15). Malcolm Davis notes that in verse 15, two unusual words are used in the Hebrew to describe the 'altar hearth', that is, the top of the altar or the "upper altar". One means 'the mountain of God', (JND) while the other is a variant spelling of Ariel in Isaiah 29 verse 1, literally 'lion of God', and has been translated 'hearth of God'. This altar top had four horns projecting upward at its four corners.

The millennial altar will therefore stand some 10 long cubits high (2 plus 4 plus 4 cubits working upwards), i.e. 17 feet 6 inches above the ground. It will be higher than the altar in Solomon's temple, which measured about 15 feet high, bearing in mind that the ordinary cubit was used there as the standard of measurement. "The Millennial altar, unlike the Tabernacle altar, will have steps up to its top, but on the east side only. It will thus be the largest of all Israel's sacrificial altars, and stand in the very centre of the new temple complex. Again, we emphasise that this will prove the eternal centrality and importance of Christ's sacrifice on Calvary's cross for the accomplishment of all God's purposes of grace and redemption" (Malcolm Davis).

b) The consecration of the altar, vv.18-27

The altar was 'cleansed' and 'purged', not because it was in any way contaminated, but to emphasise the purity of its function. As John B.Taylor observes, "basic to the action described here is the aim of setting the altar apart for its holy function and cleansing it from every taint of the secular". In this respect we should notice the following, together with appropriate extracts from *The Book of Ezekiel,* by F.Cundick:

i) **On the first day**, a bullock for a **sin-offering** was sacrificed on the altar (vv.19-21). This "points to Christ the perfect, energetic Servant of God, who came to do His will in making expiation for sins upon the cross".

ii) **On the second day**, a "kid of the goats" for a **sin-offering** was sacrificed (v.22). Here, "The kid of the goats ... points to Christ, who was sent in the likeness of sinful flesh to die a substitutionary death"..

iii) **Thereafter**, that is, after cleansing the altar, "thou shalt offer a young bullock without blemish, and a ram out of the flock without blemish". These were to be offered "for a **burnt offering** unto the LORD" (vv.23-24). Now, "the ram for a burnt-offering ... typifies Christ the fully consecrated one, wholly acceptable to God". In this case "the priests shall cast salt upon them" (v.24). The order is important: first sin is dealt with (sin-offerings), to be followed by worship (burnt offerings).

All these offerings picture in different ways the death of the Lord Jesus, and the application of salt reminds us that He is incorruptible: "The salt ... denotes the preservative power of holiness, and the sign of a covenant which will never suffer failure" .

The "seven days of ceremony (v.26), according to numerical significance, draw attention to the perfection of the work of Christ". Once the altar was

CHAPTER 43

purged in this way, the way opens for God's people to offer their worshipful sacrifices: "And when these days are expired, it shall be, that upon the eighth day, and so forward, the priests shall make your burnt offerings upon the altar, and your peace offerings; and I will accept you, saith the Lord GOD" (v.27). Compare Exodus 29: verse 37 and 2 Chronicles 7 verses 8-9.

Malcolm Davis draws attention to the fact that "only the Levitical priests of the line of Zadok will be allowed to officiate at the altar, because they alone remained faithful to the Lord at the time of Absalom's rebellion". See Ezekiel 44 verses 15-16, referring to 2 Samuel 15 verses 24-29, and 1 Kings 1 verse 8. Malcolm Davis continues: "The fact that here in this vision Ezekiel was instructed to take certain priestly actions himself ("thou shalt take ... thou shalt offer") may indicate that he was of the Zadokite Levitical line".

EZEKIEL CHAPTER 44

We have noted that the chapters dealing with millennial worship (Chs.43-46) cover the following: *(a)* the advent of the glory of the Lord (43: 1-12); *(b)* the altar of worship (43: 13-27); *(c)* the approach to God (44: 1-31); *(d)* the allocation of land, 45: 1-8; *(e)* the application at the time (45: 9-12); *(f)* the appointed offerings (45: 13 - 46: 24).

Having considered the advent of the glory of the Lord (43: 1-12) and the altar of worship (43: 13-27), we come now to:

3) THE APPROACH TO GOD, 44: 1-31

In this connection, reference is made *(A)* to "the prince" (vv.1-3), *(B)* to the people (vv.4-9), and *(C)* to the priests (vv.10-31).

A) The prince, vv.1-3

"Then he brought me back the way of the gate of the outward sanctuary which looketh toward the east; and it was shut. Then said the LORD unto me; This gate shall be shut, it shall not be opened, and no man shall enter in by it; because the LORD, the God of Israel hath entered in by it, therefore it shall be shut. It is for the prince; the prince he shall sit in it to eat bread before the LORD; he shall enter in by way of the porch of that gate, and shall go out by the way of the same." We must now consider *(a)* the identity of "the prince"; *(b)* the presence of "the prince"; *(c)* the identity of the gate.

a) The identity of "the prince"

Very clearly "the prince" cannot be the Lord Jesus. If this were the case, why does "the prince" offer a sin-offering for himself? (45: 22); why does he worship? (46: 2). After all, at the time of the Lord's second advent it will be said, "Let all the angels of God worship him" (Heb. 1: 6). Then, how are we

CHAPTER 44

going to explain the fact that "the prince" has a literal family to whom he can give part of his own inheritance? (16: 5). Finally, "the prince" will not be a priest, whereas the Lord Jesus will be "a priest upon his throne" (Zech. 6: 13).

In view of the fact that "this prince is not our Lord Jesus Christ, then who can he be?" asks John Stubbs (writing in the *Believer's Magazine*, date unrecorded). He continues, "Some have wondered if he is none other than David, the king of Israel". Although not all agree, there seems little doubt that David will be raised, as other Old Testament saints, to share in the millennial kingdom of Christ, and will very likely (some would say, most certainly) be the Lord's vice-regent on the earth at that time. He is certainly called a "prince" in Ezekiel 34 verse 24 and Chapter 37 verse 25, and both passages relate to Israel's glorious future in the millennium. It is perfectly true that while "the prince" of Ezekiel 37 is also called a ***"king"*** (v.24), there is no indication in Ezekiel 45 and 46 that "the prince" mentioned there is a royal personage, although the land allocated to him (Ezek 45: 7-8) strongly implies someone of great importance. John Stubbs therefore submits that the prince in Ezekiel 34 and 37 is a ***royal*** prince, whereas the prince of Chapters 45 and 46 is rather a ***religious*** prince. He also notes that "the prince of Chapters 34 and 37 is named, but not the prince in Chapters 45 and 46. Moreover the prince of the earlier chapters seems to be ***over*** the people, but the prince of the later chapters seems to be ***among*** the people. It has to be said, however, that these differences hardly justify the conclusion that there will be two princes in Jerusalem during the millennium.

A more serious objection to the suggestion that David is "the prince" in all the relevant passages is the fact that "the prince" in Ezekiel has a literal family to whom he can give part of his own inheritance (16: 5). After all, as John Stubbs, and others, rightly observe, no one saved and raised from the dead will marry and bear children (Luke 20: 35). Quite clearly, David is excluded on this basis.

But against this, it may be well worth maintaining that "the prince" here ***is*** David and that while agreeing absolutely that "his sons" (46: 16) could not possibly be children begotten in resurrection, they could be sons begotten when previously on earth, now also raised from the dead, including, for example, Solomon. (Just think how appropriate it would be if Solomon was associated with the millennial temple!) It could be argued that the passage does not mean, ***all*** David's sons. After all, it is hardly likely that Absalom would be included here! Again, the expression "his sons" might include his royal descendants on earth such as Hezekiah and Josiah, but, again, certainly *not* all of them. In this connection, it is quite clear that Zerubbabel will have an honoured place in the millennial kingdom (Hag. 2: 20-23). He was, of course, descended from David (Matt. 1: 12). While it might be imprudent to speak with certainty, we could be forgiven for strongly inclining in this direction.

It is clear, whatever the answer may be, that "the prince" here will represent the people in bringing their offerings before the priests (45: 17, 22), and while he will not be allowed to enter into the inner court of the future Temple, he will be able to draw nearer than the people, possibly having a full view of the operations of the new priesthood, the sons of Zadok (46: 1-3). As John Stubbs observes, "One of the great changes to be observed in Israel's religious service in the future is the person and ministry of this prince. No such office was held in the Levitical economy. The work of the prince is something entirely new and a break with the past". He adds, nicely, "What a contrast this is to this age of grace when believers are now privileged to draw near to God right into the holiest! May we never cease to thank God for this and ever make use of this privilege".

b) *The presence of "the prince"*

The tabernacle had a single entrance on the east (Exod. 27: 13). As we have noticed, the millennial temple will have three external gates, to the north, south and east. The east gate in the millennial temple however is unusual in that it is reserved for the use of two persons, one Divine and one human. It is the gate through which the Lord returns to the temple (Ezek. 43: 1, 2, 4; 44: 2) and the gate in which "the prince" sits to "eat bread before the LORD" (44: 3). It has been well suggested that "Closing the gate was a way of providing an affirming sign of the Lord's intention to remain in permanent residence" (quoted by L.E.Cooper, *Ezekiel*). To 'sit in the gate' is an expression which suggests administrative responsibility. See, for example, Ruth 4 verses 1-2, Proverbs. 31 verse 23, not to mention Genesis 19 verses 1 and 9. L.E.Cooper puts it like this: "The prince of Ezekiel's temple is a godly representative of the messianic King. He will sit in the gate, commune with God, and serve as a guarantor of mercy, justice and righteousness. He will be the perfect spiritual-administrative leader of the new kingdom".

The external eastern gate must not be confused with the inner eastern gate through which "the prince" passes on sabbath days and new moons. See

CHAPTER 44

Ezeiel 46 verses 1-3, "Thus saith the Lord GOD; The gate of the inner court that looketh toward the east shall be shut the six working days; but on the sabbath it shall be opened, and in the day of the new moon it shall be opened. And the prince shall enter by the way of the porch of that gate without, and shall stand by the post of the gate, and the priests shall prepare his burnt offering and his peace offerings, and he shall worship at the threshold of the gate: then he shall go forth; but the gate shall not be shut until the evening. Likewise the people of the land shall worship at the door of this gate before the LORD in the sabbaths and in the new moons".

In keeping with this, Ezekiel is brought in by the north gate: "Then brought he me the way of the north gate before the house: and I looked, and, behold, the glory of the LORD filled the house of the LORD; and I fell on my face" (v.4).

c) The identity of the gate

This has no direct reference to the passage, but as Alan Summers observes, "It is sometimes said that the East Gate in Jerusalem will be re-opened for the Messiah when, as prophesied by Ezekiel, He returns in glory. The East Gate through which the Lord will pass according to Ezekiel however is *not* the East Gate of *Jerusalem* but the East Gate of *the temple*. In the Millennial kingdom the temple and the city are separated from one another (45: 6-7). Today the Temple Mount lies within the walls of Jerusalem. In the vision seen by Ezekiel, Jerusalem lies to the south of the mountain on which the temple stands (Ezek.40.2; 48.15, 19, 30-35). Around the temple is a cordon sanitaire to separate it from the land associated with "the prince", the Levites and the city (45: 2). If therefore the East Gate in Jerusalem will one day be re-opened it will *not* be as a result of the fulfilment of this prophecy" (*Assembly Testimony, January/February, 2010)*. This brings us to:

B) The people, vv.4-9

"Then brought he me the way of the north gate before the house", that is, by the inner northern gate leading to the inner court facing the temple itself which was now filled with the "glory of the LORD": "I looked, and, behold, the glory of the LORD filled the house of the LORD: and I fell upon my face" (v.4). As L.E.Cooper observes, "Ezekiel's reaction was predictable. He fell on his face at the sight of the glory of God out of fear and reverence (cf. 1: 28; 43: 1-5)". L.E.Cooper then quotes another commentator (J.G.McConville) in saying, "The new reference to the glory of God simply makes clear that it is the return of God to the temple that serves as a basis for the regulations to follow". The presence of the Lord in His temple was to have an effect on Ezekiel's current ministry, reminding us again that the business of the Old Testament prophet was to address the present in the light of the future. It was to have an effect on him personally (v.5) and then on his message to "the house of Israel" (vv.6-9).

a) Its effect on Ezekiel personally, v.5

"And the LORD said unto me (compare 43: 6), Son of man, mark well, and behold with thine eyes, and hear with thine ears all that I say unto thee concerning all the ordinances of the house of the LORD, and all the laws thereof; and mark well the entering in of the house, with every going forth of the sanctuary." We should note the crisp instructions: "mark well ... behold with thine eyes ... hear with thine ears". Paul gave similar instructions to Timothy: "Study to shew thyself approved unto God, a workman that needeth not to be ashamed, rightly dividing (or 'handling aright', RV) the word of truth" (2 Tim. 2: 15). The word "study" really means to 'strive diligently' (JND). "It signifies to hasten to do a thing, to exert oneself, endeavour, give diligence" (W.E.Vine). Paul refers here to quality work: "rightly dividing (*orthotomeo*: from *orthos*, straight, and *temno*, to cut: hence 'cutting in a straight line', JND) the word of truth". It has been suggested that Paul is alluding here to his trade as a tentmaker, which would involve cutting along a straight line. The expression was used in other ways: for example, ploughing a straight furrow, making a road, cutting and squaring stones. Whatever the metaphor, one thing is very clear: we cannot expect divine approval if we misinterpret, mishandle, or misapply the Word of God. It is the "word of truth", as opposed to "words to no profit" (2 Tim. 2: 14), and as opposed to the "word" of Hymenaeus and Philetus; who "concerning the truth have erred" (2 Tim. 2: 17-18). The expression, "the word of truth", emphasises its total accuracy and reliability.

Moreover, Ezekiel was to be diligent in connection with "***all*** the ordinances of the house of the Lord ... ***all*** the laws thereof ... "***every*** going forth of the sanctuary". It was a case of "diminish not a word" (Jer.26: 2) and declaring "all the counsel of God" (Acts 20: 27).

The words "mark well the entering in of the house, with every going forth of the sanctuary" are elsewhere rendered "mark well those who may be admitted to the temple and all those who are to be excluded from the sanctuary" (RSV). This agrees with what follows:

b) Its effect on his message to "the house of Israel", vv.6-9

These verses are addressed to "the rebellious, even to the house of Israel" (v.6). As to the past, they had utterly failed to recognise that a holy God could only find pleasure in a holy people. His sanctuary had been polluted by people completely unsuited and unqualified to be there - "ye have brought into my sanctuary strangers, uncircumcised in heart, and uncircumcised in flesh, to be in my sanctuary, to pollute it ... and ye have not kept the charge of mine holy things but ye have set keepers of my charge in my sanctuary for yourselves" (vv.7-8). The future would be so different: "No stranger, uncircumcised in heart (inwardly), nor uncircumcised in flesh (outwardly), shall enter into my sanctuary, of any stranger that is among the children of Israel" (v.9). For "uncircumcised in heart, and uncircumcised in flesh", see Deuteronomy 30 verse 6 which refers to the reverse: when the nation returns to the land after age-long dispersion, "the LORD thy God will circumcise thine heart, and the heart of thy seed, to love the LORD thy God with all thine heart, and with all thy soul, that thou mayest live". Notice what Paul says about circumcision and uncircumcision in Romans 2 verses 28-29.

In New Testament terms, the local assembly, described "the temple of God", is "holy, which temple ye are" (1 Cor. 3: 17). It can be adversely affected by the "leaven" of immorality (1 Cor. 5: 6) and by the "leaven" of erroneous teaching (Gal. 5: 9). So far as the latter is concerned, Galatians 2 verse 4, 2 Peter 2 verse 1 and Jude 4 become compulsory reading. This leads to:

C) The priests, vv.10-31

Ezekiel's message sharply divides the priesthood into two categories: those who "are gone away far from me, when Israel went astray" (vv.10-14) and "the priests the Levites, the sons of Zadok, that kept the charge of my sanctuary when the children of Israel went astray from me" (vv.15-31). We could simplify this and say, simply, the unfaithful priests (vv.10-14) and the faithful priests (vv15-31). In the first case, the priests "shall *not* come near unto me, to do the office of a priest unto me, nor to come near to any of my holy things, in the most holy place" (v.13) and, in the second, the priests "*shall* come near to me to minister unto me, and they shall stand before me to offer unto me the fat and the blood, saith the Lord GOD" (v.15).

a) The unfaithful priests, vv.10-14

Severe censure is passed on the Levites for past participation in idolatry. We have to decide whether the words, "And the Levites that are gone away from me", mean exactly that (i.e. the sons of Kohath, Gershon and Merari), or mean, "the priests the Levites" (as in v.15), who were of course a select family in the tribe of Kohath. If the former is meant then L.E.Cooper is correct in saying, "they were confirmed in their subordinate status that they are given in Numbers". But if the latter is meant, then Malcolm Davis is correct in saying that they "will be downgraded from the full priesthood to the role of temple servants as a punishment for the sins of their forebears". A place is given them in the sanctuary, but only in connection with the people, for example as gate keepers, and in preparing the burnt-offerings. As noted above, they will not be permitted to "come near unto me, to do the office of a priest unto me, not to come near to any of my holy things in the most holy place". Three times the expression occurs "they shall bear their iniquity ... shame" (vv.10, 12, 13). As we have already noted, the unfaithfulness in question evidently includes the period of Absalom's rebellion together with Adonijah's attempt to usurp the throne. In both cases the sons of Zadok were faithful to David. It might refer also to unfaithfulness in tolerating admission to the temple of the people described in verses 6-7. Although it is not an exact parallel, they would 'receive (receive back) the things done in the body ... whether it be good or (in this case) bad' (2 Cor. 5: 10). Or, again in New Testament terms, "If any man's work shall be burned, he shall suffer loss: but he himself shall be saved ..." (1 Cor. 3: 15). Malcolm Davis puts it nicely: "A measure of grace will be shown towards them, however; for they will be allowed to slaughter the animals for sacrifice in the outer court, and to have charge of the gates". All this carries a warning for believers today. Spiritual failure will deprive us of future reward. See 1 Corinthians 3 verse 15.

b) The faithful priests, vv.15-31

"But the priest the Levites, the sons of Zadok, that kept the charge of my sanctuary when the children of Israel went astray from me, they shall come near to me to minister unto me, and they shall stand before me to offer unto me the fat and the blood, saith the Lord GOD: they shall enter into my sanctuary, and they shall come near to my table, to minister unto me, and they shall keep my charge" (vv.15-16). Quite clearly the faithfulness of the Zadokite priests had been demonstrated in circumstances other than

CHAPTER 44

those arising during the rebellion of Absalom and the attempted usurpation of Adonijah.

It is well worth noticing that Zadok was a descendant of Phinehas. See 1 Chronicles 6 verses 4-8. Following his intervention at Shittim, God gave to Phinehas His "covenant of peace", saying, "he shall have it, and his seed after him, even the covenant of an everlasting priesthood; because he was zealous for his God, and made an atonement for the children of Israel" (Num. 25: 12, 13). See also Malachi 2 verses 4-5. Now, in the Millennium, God honours His ancient promise, and we are not in the least surprised! Our God "cannot lie (Titus 1: 2).

We should notice the emphasis on nearness to the Lord: "they shall **come near** to me ... they shall **stand before me** .... they shall **come near** to my table (that is, to the altar)". All of which reminds us that we may "draw near with a true heart, in full assurance of faith, having our hearts sprinkled from an evil conscience, and our bodies washed with pure water" (Heb. 10: 22), referring to the consecration of the priests (Exod. 29: 4, 20-21). It was while the assembly at Antioch "ministered to the Lord, and fasted" that the "Holy Ghost said, Separate me Barnabas and Saul for the work whereunto I have called them" (Acts 13: 1-2). The word "ministered" (*leitourgeo*) is used in the New Testament for priestly ministry. See, for example, Hebrews 8 verse 2 where the Lord Jesus is described as "A minister of the sanctuary, and of the true tabernacle, which the Lord pitched, and not man"; Hebrews 8 verse 6, "But now hath he obtained a more excellent ministry"; Hebrews 10 verse 11, "And every priest standeth daily ministering and offering oftentimes the same sacrifices, which can never take away sins". We 'minister' to the unsaved when we preach the Gospel to them. We 'minister' to each other in our fellowship and service. But we also 'minister to the **Lord**' in our devotion and worship. So the church at Antioch was a place where the Lord Jesus was honoured and adored. This involves the priesthood of all believers. See 1 Peter 2 verses 1-10; Hebrews 10 verses 19-22. The word priest (*hiereus*) means 'a person who offers sacrifices', and every believer should therefore be offering "the sacrifice of praise to God continually, that is, the fruit of our lips, giving thanks to his name" (Heb. 13: 15).

But priests, with all their privileges, were not to do as they liked. The sanctity of their ministry was to pervade every aspect of their lives and, if the date at the top of the Scofield Bible is correct, nothing has changed in 2,590 years. We should notice the following:

EZEKIEL

- ***They were to be clothed in linen garments (vv.17-19).*** No wool was to be worn or "any thing that causeth sweat" (v.18). When they had completed their ministry at the altar in the inner court, they were to leave their priestly garments in "holy chambers" as described in Chapter 42 verse 14. For "woollen and linen" together, see Deuteronomy 22 verse 11. According to an authority quoted by Jamieson, Fausset & Brown, the "researches of modern science have proved that wool when combined with linen ... brings on malignant fevers, and exhausts the strength" in hot climates. It does seem, therefore, that in this case, as before, there is good practical reason for this prohibition. According to L.E.Cooper, "Linen was a symbol of purity in contrast to wool, which was an animal by-product and therefore unclean. The priests were to wear linen turbans and linen undergarments. They were to avoid any weight of cloth of any kind that would cause excessive perspiration". "Sweat" was classed as uncleanness (C..L.Feinberg)

- ***The growth of the hair was to be regulated (v.20).*** "Neither shall they shave (*galach*, to shave: the word used of Abalom's annual haircuts) their heads, nor suffer their locks to grow long; they shall only poll (*kasam*, to 'poll' or 'shear') their heads." It was not to be too short, and not too long! Let's leave the last word to Malcolm Davis, "A 'short back and sides' will be the order of the day". (This is what Absalom should have had!)

- ***Their senses were not to be clouded by wine in the course of their ministry (v.21).*** There used to be an advertisement on the London tube-trains which read, 'Total abstention from intoxicating liquor promotes accuracy in skilled movements'. The priests were not to be drunk on duty (or, for that matter,on any other occasion). Compare Leviticus 10 verse 9. Were Nadab and Abihu intoxicated on duty?

- ***They were to be careful in selecting their wives (v.22).*** Priests were to marry "maidens of the seed of the house of Israel, or a widow that had a priest before". Need we say more? Well, just to say that since all believers are priests, men and women, both need to look for suitable partners in life. A sister needs good spiritually-minded husband, and a brother needs a good spiritually-minded wife.

- ***They were to instruct the nation (v.23).*** "And they shall teach my people the difference between the holy and profane, and cause them to discern between the unclean and the clean." Bearing in mind the preceding verses, we could say without fear of contradiction, that the teaching was to be by example as well as by precept. As L.E.Cooper observes, "The priests were to provide the kind of unblemished example that would encourage Israel to worship God and attract unbelieving nations to serve Him". Malachi tells us that "the priest's lips should keep knowledge and they should seek the law at his mouth: for he is the messenger of the LORD of hosts" (Mal. 2: 7). Bible teachers should be priestly men.

- **They were to act as adjudicators in matters of controversy (v.24).** Compare Deuteronomy 17 verses 8-13. These verses deal with the procedure in cases of matters too difficult for local settlement. In which case, the matter was to be resolved by men in the presence of God. "Then shalt thou arise, and get thee up into the place which the Lord thy God shall choose; and thou shalt come unto the priests the Levites, and unto the judge that shall be in those days, and enquire; and they shall shew thee the sentence of judgment." So the men concerned were in touch with the word of God, and in touch with God Himself, so much so that the adjudicator is described as "the priest that standeth to minister there before the LORD".

The answer to the problems of the day lay in recourse to God. This reminds us that elders should be priestly men, and that difficult problems can only be met by waiting on God and considering His holy Word. This cannot be over-emphasised. All too often, decisions are made, sometimes hastily, without spending time in earnest prayer for divine guidance through the Word of God. God makes it clear through Ezekiel that matters were to be resolved by the priests with reference to His "standards": "And in controversy, they shall stand in judgment; and they shall judge it according to my judgments: and they shall keep my laws and my statutes in all mine assemblies; and they shall hallow my sabbaths".

- **They must abstain from any defilement by contact with a dead person, vv.25-27.** "The priests of that day will need to avoid contact with dead bodies of mankind, since that is ceremonially defiling. But they will be allowed to contract defilement for a very close relative. Even so, they will have to count seven days after they have become unclean, then to offer a sin offering as they go into the Holy Place again to resume their appointed service" (Malcolm Davis). Compare Leviticus 21 verses 1-3.

- **The provision for the priests, vv.28-31.** Malcolm Davis says it all: "As under Mosaic Law, the Lord will be their inheritance, and they will have no special possession in the land of Israel (v.28). Their food will be the regular offerings of the people and devoted things. The people will be responsible to give them the firstfruits of all their harvests, and even the best of their dough, for nothing less than the best will do for God (vv.29-30). If the people follow these rules, then they will experience the Lord's blessing on them and their households (v.30). In much the same way those servants of God who live 'of the gospel' today are entitled to be supported by the Lord's people in material things. The principle will still apply in the millennial age, as it did in Old Testament days".

Malcolm Davis continues: "There is then an added stipulation that the priests will not be allowed to eat anything, bird or animal, which has died a natural death, or even a violent death. Ceremonial cleanness must be maintained in every way, and violence will have no place in Christ's Millennial Kingdom of peace and righteousness". Priests were to be careful what they ate, and we must take care over our spiritual diet.

What do we feed on?

EZEKIEL CHAPTER 45

We have noted that the chapters dealing with millennial worship (Chs.43-46) cover the following: *(a)* the advent of the glory of the Lord (43: 1-12); *(b)* the altar of worship (43: 13-27); *(c)* the approach to God (44: 1-31); *(d)* the allocation of land, 45: 1-8; *(e)* the application at the time (45: 9-12); *(f)* the appointed offerings (45: 13 - 46: 24). Very clearly, the millennial temple and its environs will not be a museum – far from it! It will be a functional temple. God will be worshipped there.

Having considered the advent of the glory of the Lord (43: 1-12), the altar of worship (43: 13-27) and the approach to God (44: 1-31), we come now to:

4) THE ALLOCATION OF LAND, 45: 1-8

The passage deals with provision made *(a)* for the priests and Levites (vv.1-5): "The holy portion of the land shall be for the priests the ministers of the sanctuary ... also the Levites, the ministers of the house (shall) have for themselves, for a possession for twenty chambers" (vv.4, 5); *(b)* for the people (v.6): "it shall be for the whole house of Israel"; *(c)* for "the prince"(vv.7-8).

"Moreover, when ye shall divide by lot the land for inheritance, ye shall offer an oblation unto the LORD, an holy portion of the land" (v.1). These verses deal principally with the central part of the land, with a brief reference to the entire land at the end of the section: "and the ***rest of the land*** shall they give to the house of Israel according to their tribes" (v.8). This is expanded in Chapter 47 verses 13 to Chapter 48 verse 35, which includes a certain repetition of the details given in Chapter 45. See Chapter 48 verses 8-22. As John B.Taylor points out, "The sacred district is called 'an oblation', the word normally translated a 'heave-offering' (*terumah*) in the AV". The heave-offering was part of the peace-offering when it was offered "for a thanksgiving" (Lev. 7: 11-14, 32-34). In this case, the "oblation" or "heave-offering", the designated part of the land, is offered in "grateful recognition

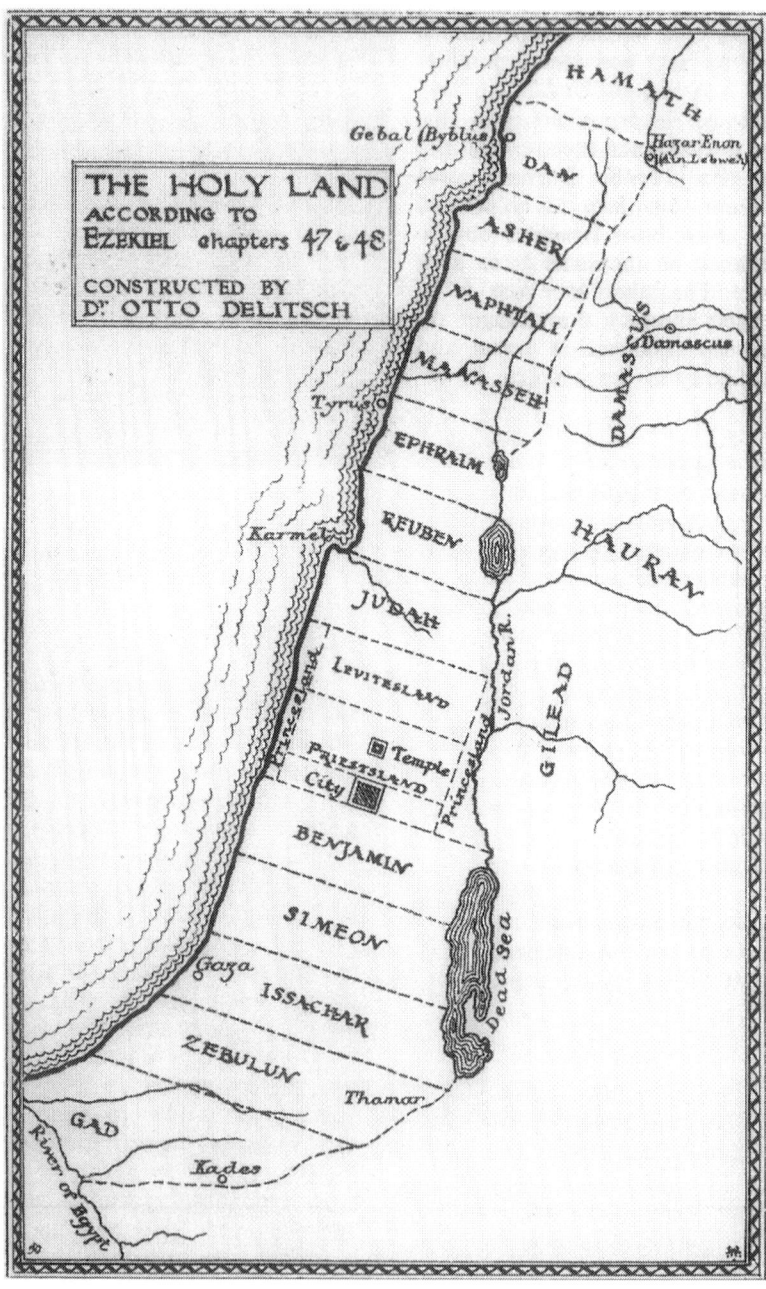

by the restored people of Jehovah's grace to them" (F.Cundick). While, as John B.Taylor observes, "This was the Lord's rightful claim on a part of what was all His land", it was to be given to Him with joyful willingness.

We should remember that the land belonged to the Lord. It is called "thy land, O Immanuel" (Isa 8: 8). In the millennium Israel will give to the Lord what rightly belongs to Him in the first place. David recognised the principle in saying, "All things come of thee, and of thine own have we given thee ...all this store that we have prepared to build thee an house for thine holy name cometh of thine hand and is all thine own" (1 Chron. 29: 14, 16). In New Testament language, "Upon the first day of the week let every one of you lay by him in store, as God hath prospered him ..." (1 Cor. 16: 2).

Naught that I have mine own I call,
I hold it for the Giver;
My heart, my strength, my life, my all,
Are His, and His for ever.

It might be helpful if we set out the details of the "oblation" which, as we have noted, refers to the central part of the land: *(a)* the area allocated to the priests (vv.1-4); *(b)* the area allocated to the Levites (v.5); *(c)* the area allocated to the city (v.6); *(d)* the area allocated to the prince (vv.7-8). Plus *(e)* the area allocated to the tribes (v.8).

a) The area allocated to the priests, vv.1-4

This is called "an holy portion of the land" which will be "for the priests (Zadokite priests, 48: 11) the ministers of the sanctuary" (vv.1, 4). "The length shall be the length of five and twenty thousand reeds, and the breadth shall be ten thousand. This shall be holy in all the borders thereof round about" (v.1). The expositor has, again, to face the question of the unit of measurement here. Is it the cubit or the reed? As Malcolm Davis points out, "no unit of measurement is expressly given in connection with the 25,000 units of its length or the 10,000 units of its breadth, nor throughout the remainder of the measurements given in this whole section. The Authorised Version supplies the word 'reeds' in italics here, whereas most other translations change this to 'cubits' in view of the vast difference in overall size made by the two units of measurement, and the fact that the word 'cubits' is clearly expressed in verse 2 in connection with the breadth of the suburbs around the Holy Portion". Malcolm Davis continues by pointing out, as already noted, that the Hebrew text definitely has the word *qanim* (reeds) in Chapter 42 verse 16 as the unit of measurement for the whole temple sanctuary complex, giving a very large area indeed (said to be some 60 by 24 miles in size) as opposed to something like 8.3 by 3.3 miles if the unit of measurement is the 'cubit'.

But, as already pointed out, the argument that the unit of measurement cannot be the 'reed in view of the fact that there would not be room for such a huge area', can be effectively answered by the altered topography in the millennium.

With all the complications arising from the unit of measurement, we must not forget the overall lesson: "The length shall be the length of five and twenty thousand reeds, and the breadth shall be ten thousand. ***This shall be holy in all the borders thereof round about***" (v.1). We are not likely to get the answer to the 'reed'/ 'cubit' problem until we see the site ourselves in the millennium, but 'holiness unto the Lord' is a daily requirement ***now!***

This large area contains *(i)* the temple complex (vv.2-3) and *(ii)* the living accommodation of the priests (v.4).

*i) **The temple complex, vv.2-3.*** "Of this (the above area) there shall be for the sanctuary five hundred in length, with five hundred in breadth, square round about, and fifty cubits round about for the suburbs thereof" (v.2). We are told two things here. The first is already familiar to us, but the second makes new reading.

- ***The temple complex*** will be 500 cubits square and lie at the centre of the area described above (25,000 x 10,000 reeds/cubits). We have discussed the square design on several occasions during our studies, noting that the temple area, with the altar at its very centre will be called "an house of prayer for ***all*** people" (Isa. 56: 7).

- ***The temple complex will be surrounded by "suburbs"*** (an 'open space', RV) measuring 50 cubits wide (25 yards) on all sides. John B. Taylor calls this "a kind of 'green belt' between the sacred and the profane". Alan Summers (*Assembly Testimony*, January/February, 2010) calls it a *cordon sanitaire.*

*ii) **The living accommodation of the priests, v.4.*** Having pointed out that the temple complex lay at the centre of the overall area (25,000 x 10,000 'reeds'/'cubits'), the Lord informed Ezekiel that the "holy portion of the land shall be for the priests the ministers of the sanctuary, which shall come near to minister unto the LORD: it shall be a place for their houses and an holy place for the sanctuary".

It is therefore noteworthy that "the holy portion of the land", as this area is called (1, 4), includes the temple and the houses of the priests. The same standard applies to both. The whole area "shall be holy in all the borders thereof round about" (v.1). It was not a question of distinguishing between the holy and the profane. Both were holy. The priests did not have one standard of behaviour when they entered the temple, and another when they got home! Zacharias, a "priest ... of the course of Abia", with Elisabeth, "of the daughters of Aaron" is a case in point: "they were both righteous before God, walking in all the commandments and ordinances of the Lord blameless" (Luke 1: 5-6).

b) *The area allocated to the Levites, v.5*

This is of the same size as the area described in verse 1: "And the five and twenty thousand of length, and the ten thousand of breadth, shall also the Levites, the ministers of the house, have for themselves, for a possession of twenty chambers (or 'have for themselves, for a possession, for their habitations', JND)". See also Chapter 48 verse 13, "And over against the border of the priests the Levites shall have five and twenty thousand in length, and ten thousand in breadth". So the second major area lay to the north of the area occupied by the priests. The expression "twenty chambers" could be rendered 'lodging places' (see Young's *Concordance*) or, according to the Malayalam Bible, 'villages'.

So the Lord made provision for all His servants, whether the priests or the Levites. The Levites were not confined to a small area. He made adequate provision for priests and Levites alike. There was no preferential treatment, reminding us that God has "given unto us (without distinction) all things that pertain to life and godliness" (2 Pet. 1: 3). We should notice, of course, that the priests' accommodation was located nearer to their work. Priestly men need to be near to the Lord! But the Lord had in mind the welfare of all His servants.

Thus far we have *(i)* a rectangle of 25,000 'reeds'/'cubits' east to west by 10,000 'reeds'/ 'cubits' north to south, in the middle of which lies the temple complex (vv.1-4), and *(ii)* a similar rectangle on its immediate north which will be given to the serving Levites (v.5).

But we have not finished. We must now transfer our attention from the two northern rectangles (housing the priests and Levites respectively), to a southern rectangle, viz:

c) The area allocated to the city, v.6

"And ye shall appoint the possession of the city five thousand broad, and five and twenty thousand long, over against the oblation of the holy portion (so it lies south of the temple complex): it shall be for the whole house of Israel." Of the 25,000 units long (east to west), it appears that the city area will be subdivided into the city proper at the centre, with grazing land and farmland on its east and west (48: 15-18). We must remember that "the name of the city from that day shall be, The LORD is there" (48: 35). It will not be a case of a holy temple and a 'grotty' city! "In that day shall there be upon the bells of the horses, HOLINESS UNTO THE LORD; and the pots in the **LORD'S house** shall be like the bowls before the altar Yea, every pot *in Jerusalem* and in Judah shall be *holiness unto the LORD of hosts*" (Zech. 14: 20-21). There will be no double-standards anywhere then!

Putting all three areas together, we have a total area of 25,000 'reeds'/'cubits' long and 25,000 'reeds'/'cubits' broad. See Chapter 48 verse 20. Another square! A universal temple and a universal city: "And it shall come to pass in the last days, that the mountain of the **LORD'S house** shall be established in the top of the mountains, and shall be exalted above the hills; and all nations shall flow unto it. And many people shall go and say, Come ye, and let us go up to the mountain of the LORD, to *the house* of the God of Jacob; and he will teach us of his ways, and we will walk in his paths: for out of *Zion* shall go forth the law, and the word of the LORD from *Jerusalem*" (Isa 2: 2-3).

But we still haven't finished! The section ends by giving details of the land assigned to "the prince":

d) The area allocated to the prince, vv.7-8

This will lie either side of the central 'square' comprising the area occupied by the priests (the sons of Zadok), with the temple area at its centre, the area occupied by the Levites, and the area occupied by the city. "And a portion shall be for the prince (*nasi*) on the one side and on the other side of the oblation of the holy portion, and of the possession of the city, before the oblation of the holy portion, and before the possession of the city, from the west side westward, and from the east side eastward: and the length shall be over against one of the portions, from the west border unto the east border" (v.7). Very clearly, "the prince" is a most important person, and while he is not called a "king" in these chapters, we cannot but wonder if he is not 'Christ's vice-regent on earth' of whom it is said, "And David my servant shall be king over them" (Ezek. 37: 24); "And I will set up one shepherd over them, and he shall feed them, even my servant David; he shall feed them, and he shall be their shepherd. And I the LORD will be their God, and my servant David a prince (*nasi*) among them" (Ezek. 34: 23-24). This brings us, finally to:

e) The area allocated to the tribes, v.8

"In the land shall be his possession in Israel: and my princes shall no more oppress my people; and **the rest of the land** shall they give to the house of Israel according to their tribes."

5) THE APPLICATION AT THE TIME, 45: 9-12

Having said, "my princes shall no more oppress my people" (v.8), the Lord now addresses the princes at the time of writing: "Let it suffice you, O princes of Israel: remove violence and spoil, and execute judgment and justice, take away your exactions from my people, saith the Lord GOD" (v.9).

These verses appear to be a parenthesis in which God censures the princes at the time of writing for their infamous conduct in failing to rule justly and equitably, reminding them that they were to act righteously at all times. This is another case of the prophet 'addressing the present in the light of the future'.

We should remember that the kings and princes, the rulers of the nation, were "the shepherds of Israel" (Ezek. 34: 2), and it was to these very people that the Lord said, "Where is the flock that was given thee, thy beautiful flock?" (Jer. 13: 20). The opposite of shepherds are wolves! "Her princes in the midst thereof are like wolves ravening the prey, to shed blood, and to destroy souls, to get dishonest gain" (Ezek. 22: 27). Paul knew all about this: "Take heed therefore unto yourselves, and to all the flock, over the which the Holy Ghost hath made you overseers, to feed (*poimainō*), to tend as a shepherd) the church of God, which he hath purchased with his own blood. For I know this, that after my departing shall grievous wolves enter in among you, not sparing the flock" (Acts 20: 28-29). Diotrephes had this character: "I will remember his deeds which he doeth, prating against us with malicious words: and not content therewith, neither doth he himself receive the brethren, and forbiddeth them that would, and casteth them out of the church" (3 John 9-10). Peter warns elders against misconduct: "Feed the flock of God which is among you, taking the oversight thereof, not by constraint, but willingly; not for filthy lucre, but of a ready mind; neither as lords over God's heritage, but being ensamples to the flock" (1 Pet. 5: 2-3). We should pray for "elders that rule well" (1 Tim. 5: 17), and that those **who do so** will continue in the same way.

One most important feature of 'ruling well' is integity in character and leadership. This means that elders do not 'bend the rules' to suit themselves, or to suit their families and friends. It means that they are to be 'straight up and down'. The insistence on scrupulous business transactions (vv.10-12) exhibits a principle applicable to all aspects of leadership. "Ye shall have just balances, and a just ephah, and a just bath ..." (v.10). These verses remind us that "A just weight and balance are the LORD'S: all the weights of the bag are his work" (Prov.16: 11). (See also Proverbs 11: 1; Leviticus 19: 35-36.) This didn't always happen in Israel: see Amos 8 verse 5, "When will the new moon be gone, that we may sell corn? And the sabbath, that we may set forth wheat, making the ephah small, and the shekel great, and falsifying the balances by deceit?" For the record, we are told that the ephah was a dry measure equal to about one bushel, and that a bath was a liquid measure equal to about nine gallons (C.L.Feinberg). That will have to do! Other definitions exist!

6) *THE APPOINTED OFFERINGS, 45: 13-25*

This continues in Chapter 46, where even a cursory reading will show that the sacrifices of "the prince" predominate (see vv.1-15), but not, by any means, to the exclusion of the common people. Reference is then made to the procedure should "the prince" wish to give a gift to his sons or to his servants. He was only to give what belonged to him: he was not to take somebody else's inheritance for the purpose (46:6-18). Finally, Ezekiel was given a conducted tour of the temple kitchens where the priests 'boiled' the sacrifices of the people (vv.19-24).

Having rebuked the contemporary leaders of Israel for their use of unjust

CHAPTER 45

weights and measures, the Lord returns to discussing the millennial kingdom, in which just weights will be used in receiving and offering gifts to God (Malcolm Davis). There will be no malpractice then.

In the first place we are told what "the prince" was to receive (vv.13-16), and in the second what he was to give (vv.17-25). His privilege in receiving the "oblation" from the "people of the land" (v.16) was matched by his responsibility to act on behalf of "all the people of the land" (v.22) by providing and offering sacrifices on their behalf.

a) What the prince was to receive, vv.13-16

"This is the oblation that ye shall offer; the sixth part of an ephah of an homer of wheat, and ye shall give the sixth part of an ephah of an homer of barley: concerning the ordinance of oil, the bath of oil, ye shall offer the tenth part of a bath out of the cor, which is an homer of ten baths; for ten baths are a homer: and one lamb out of the flock, out of two hundred, out the fat pastures of Israel (compare Ezek 34: 14); for a meat offering, and for a burnt-offering, and for peace-offerings, to make reconciliation for them, saith the Lord GOD. All the people of the land shall give this oblation for the prince of Israel."

Very clearly, this "oblation", covering grain, oil and lambs, was not for the prince personally, but to put him in a position to act on their behalf. It should be noted, again, that the use of *terumah* ("oblation" or 'heave-offering', v.13) indicates something offered with joyful gratitude and willingness.

b) What the prince was to do, vv.17-25

In the words of Malcolm Davis, "From the dues paid to him by the people, the prince is to provide the sacrifices for public worship". It is not a case of, "If any man of you bring an offering unto the LORD ... And when any will offer a meat-offering unto the LORD ... If a soul shall sin through ignorance against any of the commandments of the LORD .... If a soul sin, and commit a trespass against the LORD ..." (Lev. 1: 2; 2: 1; 4: 2; 6: 2). The passage refers to national occasions on which "the prince" has a leading role, not in offering the sacrifices, but in preparing them. It is, strikingly, a case of "Let all things be done decently and in order" (1 Cor. 14: 40). The nation will speak with one voice on these occasions.

The prince will function in this way "in the feasts, and in the new moons, and in the sabbaths, in all solemnities of the house of Israel" (v.17). We should notice that this involves (in order of mention), "burnt-offerings ... meat-offerings ... drink-offerings ... the sin-offering ... the meat-offering ... the burnt-offering ... the peace offerings". All of which brings to the inevitable question, 'Why, in view of Christ's finished work, will sacrifices be required in millennial worship?

We must let Malcolm Davis answer on behalf of us all. This is **the** definitive answer: "The object of these sacrifices is said several times to be to make reconciliation, or, more accurately, atonement, for the people. The word *kaphar*, which means 'to cover (sin)', is used, as in the Pentateuch. It is an Old Testament concept, which is never found in the New Testament after Calvary had taken place. These sacrifices will only be efficacious as they look back to Christ's one offering of Himself at Calvary. No other sacrifice has ever, before or since, been able to put away sin fully and finally, as Christ's one sacrifice did for all time. The Millennial sacrifices will, at the most, give assurance to Israel that Christ's sacrifice is still effective for them and move them to grateful worship of the Lord. The Prince will offer burnt offerings, meal offerings, drink offerings, peace offerings, and sin offerings on the feast days, the new moons, and the sabbath days; a very full range of offerings, on many occasions, speaking of Christ and His sacrifice". It should be remembered that just as the Old Testament sacrifices had no intrinsic value, so also the sacrifices in the millennial age. The Old Testament sacrifices looked forward to the final sacrifice made by the Lord Jesus, and the millennial sacrifices will look back to that same unique and unparalleled event.

The balance of Chapter 45 deals with the offerings to be made on the occasion of certain annual ceremonies and feasts.

i)   **At the new year, v.18-20.** That is "in the first month, in the first day of the month" and to the cleansing of the sanctuary with the blood of a young bullock "without blemish", as a sin offering. The blood of the bullock was to be applied to "the posts of the house ... the four corners of the settle of the altar ... the posts of the gate of the inner court" (vv.18-19). All of which reminds us that we have "boldness to **enter into the holiest** by the blood of Jesus" (Heb. 10: 19). Israel will be reminded of this as well.

As Malcolm Davis nicely observes, "Gracious provision will be made on

CHAPTER 45

the seventh day for the simple among the people who fail to celebrate it correctly" (v.20).

In this connection, F. Cundick observes "how appropriate that *affliction of soul* is omitted at the opening of the seventh month (Lev. 23: 27). The usual two goats used on the day of atonement are omitted (Lev.23: 27). The year opens with an already accomplished cleansing!"

ii)   At Passover, vv.21-24. That is, "In the first month, in the fourteenth day of the month".

As throughout Scripture, Old and New Testaments, the feasts of passover and unleavened bread are inseparable (v.21) for very good reasons. Redeemed people are to be holy people. The prince was to prepare a "bullock for a sin offering" for himself and for all the people of the land, on passover day (v.22) and prepare for the seven days of unleavened bread, "seven bullocks and seven rams without blemish daily" as a burnt offering, and "a kid of the goats as a sin offering", together with appropriate meal and oil offerings (vv.23-24). No reference is made to "a lamb for an house" (Ex. 12: 3) but rather to "a bullock for a sin-offering" (v.22) indicating that then, with "a bullock" replacing a lamb, "appreciation of Messiah's grace will reach a high level in the nation" (F.Cundick). The other offerings mentioned are those required in connection with the associated feast of unleavened bread. See Numbers 28 verses 16-19. Israel will then say, in effect, as we do today, "Christ our Passover is sacrificed for us: therefore let us keep the feast (that is, the feast of unleavened bread)" (1 Cor. 5: 7-8).

It has been suggested that "the prince" cannot possibly be David since, risen from the dead, he will have no sin by then. This is certainly true, but surely David will be only too pleased to offer a sin offering, reminding him, let alone everybody else, including, surely, resurrected Israelites, that he is there on the basis of the work accomplished by the Lamb of God!

No reference is made to the Feast of Firstfruits, to the Feast of Weeks, to the Feast of Trumpets or to the Day of Atonement. As F. Cundick explains, there will be "No wave sheaf offering, for the resurrection of Christ will be evident. No feast of weeks, for the gift of the Spirit will be known. No blowing of trumpets, for the gathering of Israel will have taken place. No evening sacrifice (see 46: 13-15), for the sun of Israel will no more go down". We have already noted the reason for omitting reference to the Day of Atonement.

This brings us to the third occasion on which offerings will be made during the year:

iii) At the feast of tabernacles, v.25. That is, "In the seventh month, in the fifteenth day of the month" (Lev. 23: 39). This is, of course, "the autumn harvest festival of ingathering, and speaks of the joy and triumph of Christ in His millennial kingdom" (Malcolm Davis). The sacrifices evidently to be offered on every day of the feast will be the same as those to be offered during Passover. Zechariah 14 verses 16-21 tell us more about the celebration of the Feast of Tabernacles during the millennium.

EZEKIEL CHAPTER 46

We come now to the final part of the section in the prophecy describing the 'Millennial Worship' (Chs. 43-46) which will follow the return of the glory of the Lord (43: 1-5). All worship flows from the contemplation of His glory.

As noted previously on several occasions, the section may be divided as follows: *(a)* the advent of the glory of the Lord (43: 1-12); *(b)* the altar of worship (43: 13-27); *(c)* the approach to God (44: 1-31); *(d)* the allocation of land, (45: 1-8); *(e)* the application at the time (45: 9-12); *(f)* the appointed offerings (45: 13 - 46: 24).

Ezekiel 46 continues the subject with which Chapter 45 concludes (the appointed offerings), and draws our attention to the following: *(a)* provision for access (vv.1-3); *(b)* presenting the sacrifices (vv.4-7); *(c)* procedure for movement (vv.8-10); *(d)* preparing the sacrifices (vv.11-15); *(e)* providing an inheritance (vv.16-18); *(f)* producing food from the sacrifices (vv.19-24).

a) Provision for access, vv.1-3

"Thus saith the LORD God; The gate of the inner court that looketh toward the east shall be shut six working days; but on the sabbath it shall be opened, and in the day of the new moon it shall be opened" (v.1).

We can be forgiven for asking, 'Why only on "the sabbath ... and on the day of the new moon?" Malcolm Davis (*Living with the Glory of the Lord*) answers most helpfully: "The Sabbath was a type of the coming rest for the people of Israel during the Millennium, the seventh dispensation; for they will have been regathered from their wanderings all over the world, and will find their promised rest in the Promised Land at last. Therefore the Sabbath is mentioned here in connection with their grateful worship. Likewise, the celebration of the New Moon is very Jewish, since the Jewish calendar was lunar, not solar. The Jewish nation, like the moon, has waned and almost disappeared, but in the Millennial Kingdom will shine again like the new moon after she is re-established in her own land".

Chapter 44 commences with reference to the closure of the *outer* east gate: "This gate shall be shut, it shall not be opened, and no man shall enter in by it; because the LORD, the God of Israel, hath entered in by it, therefore it shall be shut. It is for the prince; the prince he shall sit in it to eat bread before the LORD; he shall enter by way of the porch of that gate, and shall go out by the way of the same" (44: 2-3).

It is worth remembering that while the tabernacle had a single entrance on the east (Ex. 27: 13), the millennial temple will have three external gates, to the north, south and east. The east gate in the millennial temple however is unusual in that it is reserved for the use of two persons, one Divine and one human. It is the gate through which the Lord returns to the temple (Ezek. 43: 1, 2, 4; 44: 2) and the gate in which "the prince" sits to "eat bread before the LORD" (44: 2). As already noted, it has been well suggested that "Closing the gate was a way of providing an affirming sign of His intention to remain in permanent residence" (quoted by L.E.Cooper, *Ezekiel*). To 'sit in the gate' is an expression which suggests administrative responsibility. See, for example, Ruth 4 verses 1-2, Proverbs. 31 verse 23, not to mention Genesis 19 verses 1, 9. L.E.Cooper puts it like this: "The prince of Ezekiel's temple is a godly representative of the messianic King. He will sit in the gate, commune with God, and serve as a guarantor of mercy, justice and righteousness. He will be the perfect spiritual-administrative leader of the new kingdom".

But we are now facing the *inner* eastern gate through which "the prince" passes on sabbath days and new moons. "Thus saith the Lord GOD; The gate of the inner court that looketh toward the east shall be shut the six working days; but on the sabbath it shall be opened, and in the day of the new moon it shall be opened. And the prince shall enter by the way of the porch of that gate without, and shall stand by the post of the gate, and the priests shall prepare his burnt offering and his peace offerings, and he shall worship at the threshold of the gate: then he shall go forth; but the gate shall not be shut until the evening. Likewise the people of the land shall worship at the door of this gate before the LORD in the sabbaths and in the new moons" (vv.1-3).

This gate, the *inner* eastern gate, with one further exception mentioned later (v.12), was only to be opened on the sabbath, and in the day of the new moon - and on these occasions both prince and people could worship here: "he shall worship at the threshold of the gate ... likewise the people of the land shall worship at the door of this gate before the Lord in the sabbaths and new moons" (vv.2-3). But there does seem to be a slight difference here: "The prince remains inside the east gate of the inner court .... while the people are just outside the gate, in the outer court" (L.E.Cooper). So while the *"prince"* will enter by this gate, he will not proceed further. He will "worship at the threshold of the gate", and then retire by the way in which he entered. Even "the prince" was restricted in this way. It has been pointed out that although "the prince" was not permitted to set foot within the inner court, he would have a full view of what was happening at the central altar.

We are more privileged. "Having therefore, brethren, boldness to enter the holiest by the blood of Jesus ... Let us draw near with a true heart in full assurance of faith, having our hearts sprinkled from an evil conscience, and our bodies washed with pure water" (Heb. 10: 19-22).

Is this only possible for us on sabbath days and new moons? The question does not require an answer! At all times we may "come boldly unto the throne of grace ..." (Heb. 4: 16). On "working days" as well! (v.1). We should say, however, that the Lord's people then and the Lord's people now do have at least one thing in common. In the millennium all, "the prince" (v.2) and "the people of the land", will be able to worship in the temple, and that marvellous privilege belongs to *every child of God* today. Even a cursory glance at the chapter will show that the sacrifices of "the prince" predominate in verses 1-18, but not to the exclusion of the common people.

But do notice the difference. The priests will prepare the prince's offerings (v.2), which he offers on behalf of himself and the people (45: 17, 22). But every believer today is a priest, having the privilege to "offer up spiritual sacrifices, acceptable to God by Jesus Christ" (1 Pet. 2: 5).

b) Presentation by the prince, vv.4-7

"And the burnt-offering that the prince shall offer unto the LORD in the sabbath day shall be six lambs without blemish, and a ram without blemish, and the meat offering shall be an ephah for a ram, and the meat offering for the lambs as he shall be able to give, and an hin of oil to an ephah. And in the day of the new moon it shall be a young bullock without blemish, and six lambs, and a ram: they shall be without blemish and he shall prepare a meat offering, an ephah for a bullock, and an ephah for a ram, and for the lambs according as his hand shall attain unto, and an hin of oil to an ephah."

This is not the time to launch a study of the Levitical offerings, but it will perhaps be helpful to bear in mind that the burnt offering prefigures the utter and complete devotion of the Lord Jesus to His Father, a strength of devotion which brought Him "unto death, even the death of the cross" (Phil. 2: 8). The "meat offering" (or 'meal offering') prefigures His perfect life and the accompanying oil prefigures His enjoyment of the power and presence of the Holy Spirit. As L.E.Cooper points out, "Every aspect of worship is to be a celebration of the redemptive work that God has done in Jesus the Messiah".

We should notice the expression in connection with the meal offering accompanying the lambs, "as he shall be able to give ... according as his hand shall attain unto ...." (vv. 5, 7). Notice, too, that previously (Numbers 28: 9), two "lambs of the first year without spot" were to be offered, presumably meaning, following Numbers 28 verses 3-8, two lambs in the morning and two in the evening. In Ezekiel 46, it is "six lambs" in the morning. In the past it was "two tenth deals of flour for a meat offering" whereas, here, it is "as he shall be able to give" or "what he was able to give" (F.A.Tatford). In the Millennial Kingdom, the evening sacrifice will be omitted.

c) *Practising crowd control, vv.8-10*

Instructions follow for entering and exiting the temple. The "prince" would enter and leave by the inner east gate after offering **personally** (v.8), but the people who "come before the Lord in **the solemn feasts**", including "the prince" (vv.9-10), were to do so from two directions: if entering from the north outer gate, then exiting by the south outer gate, and *vice versa*. "And the prince in the midst of them, when they go in shall go in, and when they go forth, shall go forth" (v.10). As C.L.Feinberg observes, "It is heartening to witness the prince worshipping in the midst of the people ... He thus sets a godly example of worship by his presence". It reminds us of Peter's words, "The elders which are **among you** I exhort ...." (1 Pet. 5: 1).

This is a case of good crowd control! As F.A.Tatford observes, "At the festival times, ever male had to appear before Jehovah and the number attending could, therefore, be quite large. The two orderly streams of people would facilitate the traffic", or, in the words of Malcolm Davis, this "will encourage and facilitate order and decorum, and avoid congestion". All of this reminds us that "God is not the author of confusion, but of peace as in all churches of the saints" and Let all things be done decently and in order" (1 Cor. 14: 33, 40).

d) Preparing the sacrifices, vv.11-15

On these occasions, "the solemn feasts", the prince ("as *he* is able to give") will offer the sacrifices specified in verse 11: "And in the feasts and in the solemnities the meat-offering shall be an ephah to a bullock, and an ephah to a ram, and to the lambs as he is able to give and an hin of oil to an ephah" (v.11). Once again we encounter the expression "as he is able to give" or 'as much as he is able to give', in connection with the meal offering accompanying the lambs.

How much are we able to give? What about our capacity?

The word "prepare" occurs in these verses four times (vv.12, 13, 14, 15). The passage covers both individual and collective offerings.

i) Individually: voluntary offerings made by "the prince", v.12. In addition to the offerings in connection with the sabbath and new moon (vv.4-7) and in connection with "the feasts and "solemnities" (v.11), provision will be made for "the prince" to offer "a voluntary burnt-offering or peace-offerings ... unto the LORD". These will evidently be the same as those to be offered on the sabbath day (vv.2, 4).

Such occasions would provide an exception to the regulations described in verses 1-3. The inner east gate will be opened to allow him to make similar preparation as for the sabbath day and the new moons. As before (v.8) "the prince" will exit by the way he entered.

In the case of a voluntary burnt or peace offering, the east gate was to be opened for the prince, but after the offering it was to be closed, whereas on the sabbath and new moons, it remained open until the evening.

ii) Nationally, by the people, vv.13-15. Having noted the sacrifices to be offered by an individual (vv.4-7; 11-12), the passage continues by describing the "daily ... burnt-offering unto the LORD" which, with a "meat-offering", will be offered every morning (vv.13-15).

The burnt offering was to be "a lamb of the first year without blemish": the meal offering, "the sixth part of an ephah, and the third part of a hin of oil, to temper with the fine flour" (vv.13-14).

As already noted, while the Old Testament required a lamb both morning and evening, here, in the Millennial Kingdom, only a morning sacrifice will be required. Malcolm Davis suggests that "The reason for this probably is that, once the Millennial day has come, and all suffering for Israel has ceased, the night will be gone for ever, and so the evening sacrifice of a lamb will no longer be relevant, either for Israel, or for the rest of the world. The dark night of Gentile rule will have gone, and Israel's glorious morning of rule under Christ will never again be darkened by apostasy". A case of Psalm 30 verse 5!

e) Providing an inheritance, vv.16-18

Reference is then made to procedure should "the prince" wish to give a gift to his sons or to his servants. He was only to give what belonged to him: he was not to take somebody else's inheritance for the purpose. "If the prince give a gift unto any of his sons, the inheritance thereof shall be his sons'; it shall be their possession by inheritance. But if he give a gift of his inheritance to one of his servants, then it shall be his to the year of liberty; after it shall return to the prince: but his inheritance shall be his sons' for them (or 'to his sons alone shall his inheritance remain', JND). "Moreover the prince shall not take of the people's inheritance by oppression, to thrust them out of their possession; but he shall give his sons inheritance out of his own possession: that my people be not scattered every man from his possession." In summary:

i) He could give a gift to his sons (v.16). It would remain their inheritance, and must be given out of his own possession (v.18).

ii) He could give a gift to his servants, but it would only remain theirs unto the year of liberty, the Year of Jubilee (see Leviticus ch.25). In other words, it would be leased to them. There will be twenty such Years of Jubilee during the Millennial Kingdom, since they will be celebrated every fifty years.

iii) He must not dispossess any of the people - "that my people be not scattered every man from his possession". This was the sin committed by Ahab and Jezebel against Naboth (1 Kings ch.21). F.A.Tatford points out that "the dispossession of property owners by ruthless and covetous landlords had been a curse in the past, as other prophets had indicated (Amos 5: 11; Micah 2: 2), but this was not to recur in the new age which Ezekiel was describing". This reminds us of at least three things:

- **We have been given an inheritance**: it is "an inheritance incorruptible, and undefiled, and that fadeth not away, reserved in heaven for you" (1 Pet. 1: 4).

- **We have not been given an inheritance as servants**: the Lord Jesus said, "Henceforth I call you **not** servants: for the servant knoweth not what his lord doeth: **but** I have called you friends ..." (John 15: 15). But more than "friends": "The Spirit itself beareth witness with our spirit, that we are the children of God: and if children, then heirs; heirs of God, and joint-heirs with Christ" (Rom 8: 16-17). "And because ye are sons, God hath sent forth the Spirit of his Son into your hearts, crying, Abba, Father. Wherefore thou art no more a servant, but a son; and if a son, then an heir of God through Christ" (Gal. 4: 6-7).

- **We must remember that "materialism is always a barrier to effective worship"** (L.E.Cooper). The context in which these instructions are given points clearly to this lesson.

f) Producing food from the sacrifices, vv.19-24

Finally, Ezekiel was given a conducted tour of the temple kitchens where the priests (v.20) and Levites (v.24) 'boiled' the sacrifices. This was done in two locations:

i) **For the purpose of preparing food for the priests (vv.19-20)**, this will be done at the west end of **the priests' chambers**, which were located in parallel to the north and south of the temple building.

"After he brought me through the entry, which was at the side of the gate, into the holy chambers of the priests, which looked toward the north: and, behold, there was a place on the two sides westward. Then said he unto me, This is the place where the priests shall boil the trespass offering and the sin-offering, where they shall bake the meat offering; that they bear them not out into the utter (outer) court, to sanctify the people" (vv.19-20). In the words of F.A.Tatford, "Here he saw the kitchens where the priests boiled the trespass and sin offerings and baked the meal offerings. These were to be eaten only by the priests (see Lev. 6: 26, 29; 7: 6-10) and were not brought out into the outer court (see Lev. 6: 26; 7: 6), to ensure that holiness was not communicated by them to the people in the outer court". Malcolm Davis puts it the other way round in saying that the offerings were prepared "in a place separate from the ordinary citizens outside in the outer court, lest they bring the latter into physical contact with things that were sanctified for the Lord's use alone, and thus cause them to become ceremonially unclean". Compare Chapter 44 verse 19, "And when they go forth into the utter court … they shall put on other garments; and they shall not sanctify the people with their garments".

ii) ***For the purpose of preparing food for the people (vv.21-24)*** four 'kitchens' were provided, one in each corner of ***the outer court***. These took the form of a small court measuring "forty cubits long and thirty broad". Here the "ministers of the house shall boil the sacrifice of the people" which F.A.Tatford helpfully explains as "the kitchens used for cooking the sacrificial meals (e.g. the flesh of the peace offerings) which were eaten by the people". He continues, these "were the kitchens where the Levites boiled that part of the sacrifices which was eaten by the offerers". See Leviticus 7 verses 15-21. Perhaps the words, "boil the sacrifice ***of the people***" points in his direction. It should be remembered that in the case of the peace offering, the Lord, the priest and the offerer each had his portion.

F.A.Tatford continues by helpfully explaining that "Each enclosure had a row of masonry, under which were recesses in which were hearths. Fire was placed within the stones which formed the hearth, and pots were set upon the stones to cook the sacrifices". In Bible language, "And here was a row of building round about in them, round about them four, and it was made with boiling places under the rows round about" (v.23, AV).

In this connection, John B.Taylor makes the pertinent observation that the temple will be "a place for sacrificing, cooking and eating, as well as for prayer and so-called 'spiritual' activities" He continues, "The Christian church has been the poorer when it has drawn a firm dividing-line between spiritual life and social activities. In Ezekiel's temple, at any rate, there was envisaged a healthy fusion of the two elements …" While we would not wish to 'go over the top' here, there is none the less a great deal of 'mileage' in his observation. Problems sometimes arise in assembly life because believers just don't know each other well enough, and L.E.Cooper must be right in saying that while, here, "God provided for fellowship between Himself

CHAPTER 46

and human beings", He also "provided for interaction between humans and incorporated it as a vital part of worship .... The temple service in the Millennium will allow one to eat the good things of God and share in a time of fellowship as well as worship".

Our final studies in the book of Ezekiel will be devoted, obviously, to Chapters 47 & 48 where, having considered the millennial temple (chs 40-42) and the millennial worship (chs.43-46), we will consider the millennial land.

EZEKIEL CHAPTER 47

Having considered *(1)* the millennial temple (Chs. 40-42) and *(2)* the millennial worship (Chs. 43-46), we come now, finally, to:

3) THE MILLENNIAL LAND, Chs. 47-48

These chapters may be summarised as follows: *(A)* Israel's millennial river (47: 1-12); *(B)* Israel's national borders (47: 13-23); *(C)* Israel's northern sub-divisions (48: 1-8); *(D)* Israel's holy central area (48: 9-22); *(E)* Israel's southern sub-divisions (48: 23-29); *(F)* Israel's millennial city (48: 30-35).

A) Israel's millennial river, 47: 1-12

Three prophets, Ezekiel, Joel and Zechariah, all refer, in different ways, to the Millennial River.

- **Ezekiel.** "Afterward he brought me again unto the door of the house; and, behold, waters issued out from under the threshold of the house eastward: for the forefront of the house stood toward the east, and the waters came down from under, from the right side of the house, at the south side of the altar" (47: 1). According to Ezekiel, the waters of the river "issue out toward the east country, and go down into the desert, and go into the sea: which being brought forth into the sea, the waters shall be healed" (47: 8).

- **Joel.** According to Arnold G. Fruchtenbaum (writing in the *Prophetic Witness,* September 2013), "The entire Ezekiel passage is summarised in Joel 3 verse 18". Here is the complete passage: "And it shall come to pass in that day, that the mountains shall drop down new wine, and the hills shall flow with milk, and all the rivers ('water-courses', JND) of Judah shall flow with waters; and a fountain shall come forth from the house of the LORD, and shall water the valley of Shittim".

The fact that, according to Joel, "a fountain shall come forth of **the house of the LORD**, and shall water the valley of Shittim", strongly suggests that this is the same river described by Ezekiel, which will "issue out from under the threshold of the house eastward". According to James Hastings' *Dictionary of the Bible*, "the Valley of Shittim' must refer to some valley leading from Jerusalem to the Dead Sea".

- Zechariah. "And it shall be in that day, that living waters shall go out from Jerusalem; half of them toward the former sea ('eastern sea', JND), and half of them toward the hinder sea ('western sea', JND margin against Joel 2: 20): in summer and in winter shall it be" (Zech.14: 8). This implies that the river will not flow directly from the Temple to the Dead Sea, but will first flow to Jerusalem.

Zechariah plainly states that the "living waters" will flow, half towards the Dead Sea ("the former sea") and half towards the Mediterranean Sea ("the hinder sea"), with which, of course, Ezekiel agrees: "And it shall come to pass, that every thing that liveth, whithersoever the *rivers* (plural) shall come, shall live" (47: 9) or "And it shall come to pass, that every living thing which moveth, whithersoever **the double river** shall come, shall live" (JND).

In the words of Arnold Fruchtenbaum: "While the river will begin in the Temple and initially flow eastward, it is clear from this passage that it will flow southward to the City of Jerusalem, where it will be divided into **two branches**. The western branch will flow down the mountain and empty into the Mediterranean Sea. The eastern branch will flow into the Dead Sea. The branching out of these waters toward the areas designated for growing food on both sides of Jerusalem will provide the necessary water for the growth of crops". Compare Isaiah 33 verse 21.

We must now draw particular attention to the details. These verses describe the river issuing from the temple itself, and flowing to the Dead Sea. Ezekiel draws our attention to *(a)* the source of the river (v.1-2); *(b)* the depth of the river (vv.3-6); *(c)* the effect of the river (vv.7-12).

a) The source of the river, vv.1-2

"Afterward he brought me again unto the door of the house; and, behold, waters issued out from under the threshold of the house eastward: for the forefront of the house stood toward the east, and the waters came down from under, from the right side of the house, at the south side of the altar" (v.1). We should notice:

i) ***Its source*** - the temple itself: "Behold, waters issued out from under the threshold of the house eastward ..." The river evidently rises within the temple of which the Lord said, "Son of man, the place of my throne, and the place of the soles of my feet, where I will dwell in the midst of the children of Israel for ever, and my holy name, shall the house of Israel no more defile ..." (43: 7). All this reminds us of the source of our salvation, with all its many blessings. They flow, not from an earthly throne, however glorious, but from the heavenly throne, from God himself.

ii) ***Its route*** - via the altar: "the waters came down from under the right side of the house, at the south side of the altar ..." Philip Harding (writing in the *Believer's Magazine* under the title *The Waters from the Sanctuary*) nicely observes that "the Lord Jesus Christ has been to the altar and from the altar has passed to His place at the right hand of God. There He has been eternally glorified, as a result of which the stream of spiritual life and power began to flow in the coming of the gracious Spirit of God (John 7: 37-39)".

The basis on which God has so blessed us and provided for us, is the death of the Lord Jesus. In Paul's words, we are "justified freely by his grace through the redemption that is in Christ Jesus: whom God hath set forth to be a propitiation, through faith, in his blood ..." (Rom. 3: 24-25).

iii) ***Its direction*** - eastward: "Then brought he me out by the way of the gate northward, and led me about the way without unto the utter (outer) gate by the way of the gate that looketh ***eastward*** ('and led me round outside unto the outer gate towards [the gate] that looketh eastward', JND); and, behold, there ran out waters on the right side." Ezekiel was not allowed to pass through the outer eastern gate. See Chapter 44 verses 1-3. The Bible does not countenance inconsistencies!

This is emphasised in verses 1-2: the "waters issued out from under the threshold of the house ***eastward*** ... the forefront of the house stood toward the ***east*** ... the utter gate by the way that looketh ***eastward*** ..." It was, of course, from the east that the "glory of the God of Israel" returned to the temple (43: 2). This reminds us that the river of divine blessing, which we enjoy today, leads to eternal glory.

b) The depth of the river, vv.3-6

As Philip Harding helpfully observes, "A thousand cubits were measured indicating advancement, then Ezekiel was brought through, indicating practical experience. Every thousand cubits measured became the practical possession of Ezekiel who was led forward, ever advancing, making constant progress, his experience deepening all the time. Such is the mind of God for our spiritual experience today. It is not His mind that we become stationary and our experience becomes static and stagnant. God desires that we advance, make progress, and know more and still more of the spiritual power of our life eternal. He desires that we have a richer and fuller practical experience and appreciation of His ways and a deepening enjoyment of communion with Himself".

While the river here speaks primarily of divine blessing, in all its fullness, for the land of Israel and the people of Israel in the Millennium kingdom, the increasing depth of the river has valuable lessons for us today. Without, for one moment, forgetting the literality of the river, we must remember that "whatsoever things were written aforetime were written for our learning" (Rom.15: 4).

i) **"The waters were to the ancles", v.3.** Here is the complete quotation: "And when the man that had the line in his hand went forth eastward, he measured a thousand cubits, and he brought me through the waters; the waters were to the ancles (AV spelling)".

Over this verse we can write **'Walking in the Spirit'**. The connection between rivers and the Holy Spirit is made clear by the Lord Jesus: "he that believeth on me, as the scripture hath said, out of his belly shall flow rivers of living water. (But this spake he of the Spirit which they that believe on him should receive: for the Holy Ghost was not yet given; because that Jesus was not yet glorified)" (John 7: 38-39). Ankles are certainly connected with walking: the man "lame from his mother's womb" was enabled to walk when his "feet and ancle bones received strength" (Acts 3: 7).

When we trust in the Lord Jesus, having been "without strength" (Rom. 5: 6), one of the first commandments given is "Rise, take up thy bed, and walk" (John 5: 8). The believer's "walk" simply means the believer's manner of life, before God and men. Paul refers to this in various ways, particularly in Ephesians, which can be broadly summarised as the wealth, walk and warfare of the Christian. So: "I therefore, the prisoner of the Lord, beseech you that ye **walk** worthy of the vocation wherewith ye are called" (4: 1); "This I say therefore, and testify in the Lord, that ye henceforth **walk** not as other Gentiles walk, in the vanity of their mind" (4: 17); "Be ye therefore followers of God, as dear children, and **walk** in love, as Christ also hath loved us, and hath given himself for us ..." (5: 1-2); "For ye were once sometimes darkness, but now are ye light in the Lord: **walk** as children of light" (5: 8); "See then that ye **walk** circumspectly, not as fools, but as wise" (5: 15).

Over the above, we can write Paul's words elsewhere on the subject: "If we live in the Spirit, let us also **walk** in the Spirit" (Gal. 5: 25).

What about **our** 'walk' or 'manner of life'? This means living according to the instruction and guidance of the Spirit of God. He only guides by means of the Word of God, of which He is Himself the author. The 'leading of the Spirit' has to do with our whole manner of life. See Romans 8 verse 14 ("For as many as are led by Spirit of God, they are the sons of God"); Galatians 5 verse 18 ("If ye be led of the Spirit ye are not under the law").

ii) **"The waters were to the knees", v.4**. Here is the complete quotation: "Again he measured a thousand, and brought me through the waters; the waters were to the knees".

Over these words we can write **'Praying in the Spirit'.** Daniel "kneeled upon his knees three tines a day, and prayed" (Dan. 6: 10.) Paul told the Ephesians that "For this cause I bow my **knees** unto the Father of our Lord Jesus Christ ..." (Eph. 3: 14). Later in the same epistle he urged them to continue "praying always with all prayer and supplication **in the Spirit** ..." (Eph. 6: 18). Philip Harding refers here to "The power and ministry of the Spirit influencing the believer in a life of prayer and sweet communion with God", reminding us that "Likewise **the Spirit** also helpeth our infirmities: for we know not what we should pray for as we ought: but **the Spirit** itself maketh intercession for us with groanings that cannot be uttered. And he that searcheth the hearts knoweth what is the mind of **the Spirit**, because he maketh intercession for the saints according to the will of God" (Rom. 8: 26-27). Philip Harding continues: "Prayer in the Spirit will be effective, for the Holy Spirit is thus bringing our desires into harmony with the will of God that we might will what He wills". Notice too Jude's contribution to the subject: "But ye, beloved, building up yourselves on your most holy faith, praying in **the Holy Ghost** ..." (Jude 20).

CHAPTER 47

iii) "The waters were to the loins", v.4. Here is the complete quotation: "Again he measured a thousand, and brought me through; the waters were to the loins".

In this connection, we can follow two lines of enquiry: *'Fruit in the Spirit'* and *'Strength in the Spirit:*

- **Fruit in the Spirit.** See, for example, Acts 2 verse 30, "Therefore being a prophet, and knowing that God had sworn with an oath to him (David), that of the ***fruit of his loins***, according to the flesh, he would raise up Christ to sit on his throne ..."

- **Strength in the Spirit.** See, for example, Proverbs 31 verse 17, "She girdeth her loins with strength". According to *Morrish's New & Concise Bible Dictionary*, "loins" refer to "the part of man that is used to prefigure the seat of strength". Paul prayed that The Ephesian believers might be "strengthened with might by ***his Spirit*** in the inner man: that Christ may dwell in your hearts by faith" (Eph. 3: 16-17), meaning "strengthened by the gracious Spirit of God to enthrone Christ as absolute Lord of one's life, that He might hold the reins of government and thus rule in every sphere. Only when Christ is enthroned in the heart are we able, by the power of the Holy Spirit, to press on with patience (under pressure), without succumbing to the circumstances of life, and to do it joyfully (Col. 1:11)" (Philip Harding).

iv) "Waters to swim in", v.5. Here is the complete quotation: "Afterward he measured a thousand; and it was a river that I could not pass over: for the waters were risen, waters to swim in, a river that could not be passed over". So after about a mile and a half, with no tributaries added, the river had grown from a trickle to a flow, and from a flow to a flood. According to Lamar E. Cooper the word underlying "ran out" (v.2) means, literally, 'to trickle'.

Over this verse we can write *'Enjoying the fulness of the Spirit'*. Notice how Paul continues in the passage above (Ephesians 3: 16-19). "That he would grant you, according to the riches of his grace, to be strengthened with might by ***his Spirit*** in the inner man: that Christ may dwell in your hearts by faith ... that ye might be filled with all the fulness of God".

Philip Harding calls this "The depth and richness of spiritual life that is eternal" and refers, again, to Ephesians 3 verse 19, "That ye might be filled with all the fulness of God", adding that this refers to "the quality and character of the life imparted to us (eternal life), giving us the capacity to know more and more of God, and to have a deepening appreciation of Christ for ever and ever, as well as greater desires now to enjoy communion with God in the Sanctuary (John 17: 3)". "Waters to swim in" reminds us of the necessity for "increasing in the knowledge (full knowledge) of God" (Col. 1: 10).

The section ends with a question, "Son of man, hast thou seen this? Then he brought me, and caused me to return to the brink ('bank, JND) of the river". Of course Ezekiel had seen it, but that isn't the point of the question. The question emphasises the amazing sight: "abundance of water in a desert which was known for its drought" (F.A.Tatford).

c) The effect of the river, vv.7-12

"Now when I had returned, behold, at the bank of the river were very many trees on the one side and on the other. Then said he unto me, These waters issue out toward the east country, and go down into the desert ('plain', JND: 'Arabah', JND margin), and go into the sea: which being brought forth into the sea, the waters shall be healed. And it shall come to pass, that every thing that liveth, which moveth, whithersoever the rivers shall come, shall live: and there shall be a very great multitude of fish, because the waters shall come thither: for they shall be healed; and everything shall live whither the river cometh. And it shall come to pass, that the fishers shall stand upon it: from En-gedi even unto En-eglaim (so this not an allegory: literal places are named): they shall be a place to spreads forth nets; their fish shall be according to their kinds as the fish of the great sea, exceeding many."

To quote Arnold Fruchtenbaum, "Since the eastern branch empties into the Dead Sea, the character of the Dead Sea wilt change. It will begin swarming with life". We should notice that the effect of this river on the Dead Sea will be such that it will contain as many varieties of fish as the Mediterranean (v.10).

Philip Harding nicely summarises the overall lesson as follows: "If we know practically what it means to have personal experience of the waters flowing from the Sanctuary, then these influences will be felt by those with whom we come in contact". In a word, we will be able to communicate life to others in telling them of the Saviour, of whom John wrote saying, "He that hath the Son, hath life" (1 John 5:12).

But, equally, "he that hath not the Son, hath not life", and this solemn fact is also illustrated: "But the miry places thereof and the marishes ('marshes', JND) thereof shall not be healed; they shall be given to salt" (v.11). Thinking now in terms of believers, Philip Harding observes that there are places that will not be healed or influenced for good, which remind us of the flesh which will never change but will be eradicated at the coming of Christ. Thus we are told, "make not provision for the flesh" (Rom. 13: 14), and to "have no confidence in the flesh" (Phil. 3: 3), but to yield ourselves to the Spirit's influence (Eph. 5: 18) and to "Walk in the Spirit", not fulfilling "the lust of the flesh" (Gal. 5: 16).

The river will be lined by fruit trees of unprecedented vigour, whose leaves will have medicinal value. "And by the river upon the bank thereof, on this side and on that side, shall grow all trees for meat, whose leaf shall not fade, neither shall the fruit thereof be consumed: it shall bring forth new fruit according to his months, **because their waters they issued out of the sanctuary**; and the fruit thereof shall be for meat, and the leaf thereof for medicine" (v.12). Compare Revelation 22 verse 2, though this evidently refers to the eternal state, not the millennium as here.

We should remember that the godly man is likened to "a tree planted by the rivers of waters, that bringeth forth his fruit in his season; his leaf also shall not wither and whatsoever he doeth shall prosper" (Psalm 1: 3).

Philip Harding puts it nicely in saying, "Wherever the waters flow, they carry with them life that produces food, fruit, fragrance and beauty. It is the gracious Spirit of God who provides food for every believer, producing fruit in the life that is fragrant to God and thus beautifying that believer with Christ-likeness. The food is the Word of God, being the product of the Spirit (1 Cor. 2: 13; 2 Tim. 3: 16; 1 Pet. 1: 11; 2 Pet. 1: 21), which produces the fruit of the Spirit (Gal. 5: 22-23) in the believer, developing the moral features of Christ for the pleasure and glory of God. The willing submission of believers to the work of the Spirit will result, not only in spiritual enrichment, but, in spiritual power and holiness which will have its influence upon all who are brought into touch with them".

B) Israel's national borders, 47: 13-23

"Thus saith the Lord GOD, This shall be the border whereby ye shall inherit the land" (v.13). All we need do at this juncture is to notice the four borders.

We ought, as well, to compare the boundaries here with those given in Numbers 34 verses 3-12. C.L.Feinberg observes that they are practically the same. The two and a half Transjordanian tribes will be relocated!

i) *"The north side ... And this is the north side" (vv.15-17).* The northern border of Israel in the Millennium appears to lie well north of Damascus.

ii) *"The east side ... And this is the east side" (v.18).* The eastern border will run from the region of Damascus to the Jordan, including Gilead, with the Dead Sea at the extreme south.

iii) *"The south side ... And this is the south side southward (v.19).* The southern border will extend from the south of the Dead Sea across to the river of Egypt, not the Nile, but a stream (the Wadi-el-Arish) entering the Mediterranean just south of Gaza.

iv) *"The west side ... This is the west side (v.20).* The western border is, of course, the Mediterranean.

Ezekiel 47 therefore concludes by anticipating the next and final chapter. The land, its borders now enumerated, will be divided amongst the tribes. However, before we leave the chapter, we should notice three matters of interest:

i) "Joseph shall have **two portions**" (v.13). Compare 1 Chronicles 5 verses 1-2, "Now the sons of Reuben the firstborn of Israel (for he was the firstborn; but, forasmuch as he defiled his father's bed, his birthright was given unto the sons of Joseph the son of Israel: and the genealogy is not to be reckoned after the birthright. For Judah prevailed above his brethren, and of him came the chief ruler; but the birthright was Joseph's)". The 'double portion' is carefully maintained in the Old Testament - Ephraim and Manasseh. See, for example Ezekiel 48 verses 4-6. But not in Ezekiel 48 verse 32. The 'double portion' is also maintained in the New Testament: "Manasses ... Joseph" (Rev. 7: 6, 8).

ii) "And ye shall inherit it, one as well as another; concerning the which **I lifted up mine hand** to give it unto your fathers; and this land shall fall unto you for inheritance" (v.14). Compare Revelation 10 verses 5-6: "And the angel which I saw stand upon the sea and upon the earth lifted up his hand to heaven, and sware by him that liveth for ever and ever ... that there should be time ('delay', JND) no longer". There will be no doubt about the matter: "this land **shall** fall unto you for inheritance".

iii) "And it shall come to pass, that ye shall divide it by lot (that is each tribal inheritance will, in itself, be divided by lot) for an inheritance unto you, and to **the strangers that sojourn among you**, which shall beget children among you; and they shall be unto you as born in the country among the children of Israel: they shall have inheritance with you among the tribes of Israel. And it shall come to pass, that in what tribe the stranger sojourneth, there shall ye give him his inheritance, saith the Lord God" (vv.22-23). What a lovely note on which to conclude the chapter. Provision for the stranger! Had Ruth possessed a copy of Ezekiel, she would have heartily approved! "Why have I found grace in thine eyes, that thou shouldest take knowledge of me, seeing I am a stranger?" (Ruth 2:10).

EZEKIEL CHAPTER 48

As already noted, having considered *(1)* the millennial temple (Chs. 40-42) and *(2)* the millennial worship (Chs. 43-46), we have come, finally, to *(3)* the millennial land (Chs. 47-48), and with it, to *(A)* Israel's millennial river (47: 1-12); *(B)* Israel's national borders (47: 13-23); *(C)* Israel's northern sub-divisions (48: 1-8); *(D)* Israel's holy central area (48: 9-22); *(E)* Israel's southern sub-divisions (48: 23-28, with a summary covering all the sub-divisions in v.29); *(F)* Israel's millennial city (48: 30-35).

Having already listened to Ezekiel's description of Israel's millennial river and Israel's national borders, we come to -

C) Israel's northern sub-divisions, 48: 1-7

This is the northern part of the area described as "the rest of the land" that was to be given "to the house of Israel according to their tribes" (45: 8). Details of the southern counterpart are given in Chapter 48 verses 23-28.

As Lamar E. Cooper and others point out, "The order for the allotments to the seven tribes located north of the sacred district (vv.8-22) does not follow any pattern found elsewhere in the Old Testament. While the allotments will be of equal size: ('And ye shall inherit it, one as well as another' see 47: 14), exact dimensions are not given". We should also notice that each tribal allotment extends across the breadth of the land from east to west, and each tribal boundary will be parallel to the one to its north and/or south.

The seven tribes are, north to south, Dan, Asher, Naphtali, Manasseh, Ephraim, Reuben and Judah. Dan is therefore farthest away from what Malcolm Davis rightly calls the 'Holy Portion' (see, again, vv.8-22), and it is generally said that this is the result of the tribe's heavy involvement in idolatry (Judges 18: 30-31; 1 Kings 12: 28-30). In this connection, it is worth mentioning that Dan is completely omitted, together with Ephraim, from the list of tribes given in Revelation ch.7, which details the 144,000

Jewish evangelists sealed by God for service during the period leading to the Lord's return as "KING OF KINGS, AND LORD OF LORDS" (Rev. 19: 16). But in His grace, the Lord will include these two tribes in the millennial apportionment of the land.

We are therefore reminded that although all believers are children of God, unfaithfulness will make them unfit to serve Him now, and have an adverse effect on their future reward. This lesson is clearly taught in the New Testament. See, for example, 2 Peter 1 verses 5-11: "And beside this, giving all diligence, add to your faith virtue ... knowledge ... temperance ...patience ... godliness ... brotherly kindness ... charity ... Wherefore the rather, brethren, give diligence to make your calling and election sure: for if ye do these things, ye shall never fall: for so an entrance shall be ministered unto you abundantly into the everlasting kingdom of our Lord and Saviour Jesus Christ". All believers will enter the kingdom, but an 'abundant entrance' depends on their spiritual track record.

In this connection, it is noticeable that the tribes descended from Leah (Reuben, Simeon, Judah, Issachar and Zebulun) and Rachel (Joseph, represented by Ephraim and Manasseh, and Benjamin) are placed nearest the temple, while the tribes descended from Bilhah (Dan and Naphtali) and Zilpah (Gad and Asher), Jacob's two concubines, are placed farthest away from it. However, it is perhaps more significant that Judah and Benjamin, the two tribes which remained loyal to David, are allocated territory immediately north and south respectively of the "holy oblation" (vv.8-22), presumably as a reward for their faithfulness. While Lamar E. Cooper is right in saying that the territory to be occupied by Dan, Asher, Naphtali and Gad *may* reflect their descent from Jacob's two concubines, there can be little doubt that the territory to be occupied by Judah and Benjamin reflects their faithfulness to 'the man after God's own heart' (1 Sam. 13: 14). The lesson for us will not go unnoticed.

D) Israel's holy central area, 48: 8-22

The northern perimeter of the area adjoins the territory of Judah which, as noted above, and in common with each tribal allocation, extends across the breadth of the land from east to west. In Bible language, "And by the border of Judah, from the east side unto the west side, shall be the offering which ye shall offer ..." (v.8) or, "Bordering the territory of Judah from east to west will be the portion you are to present as a special gift ..." (NIV).

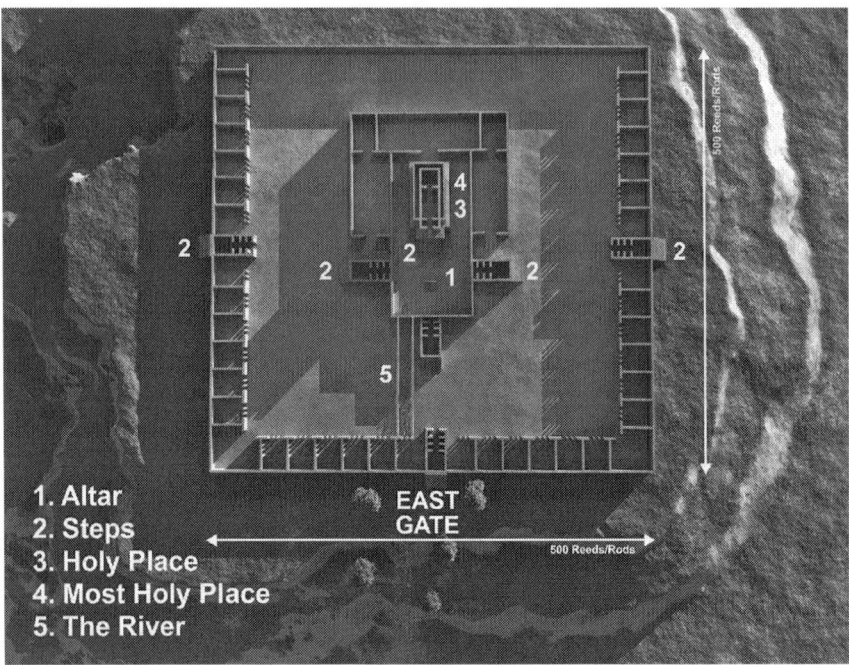

1. Altar
2. Steps
3. Holy Place
4. Most Holy Place
5. The River

It might be helpful if we commenced our study of these verses by noting the size of the whole area, the centre of the area, and the description of the area, all in verse 8.

- **The size of the area:** "And by the border of Judah, from the east side unto the west side, shall be the offering which ye shall offer of five and twenty thousand *reeds* in breadth, and in length as one of the other parts, from the east side unto the west side". While the Authorised Version reads "five and twenty thousand *reeds* in breadth", the word "reeds" is italicised, indicating that no unit of measurement is expressly given in the original text. It is generally thought that it would have been more appropriate to insert 'cubits' instead of 'reeds', and with this in mind, F.A. Tatford writes: "The holy portion dedicated to Jehovah adjoined that of Judah and was in the centre of the country. It was 25,000 cubits (approximately 7 miles) broad from north to south, and equal to the tribal portions from east to west" in breadth and length.

However, if "reeds" is correct, then the area will measure approximately 44 miles in breadth and length.

CHAPTER 48

- **The centre of the area:** "and the sanctuary shall be in the midst of it". C.L.Feinberg draws attention to this in saying, "A certain area in the heart of the land will be set aside for the sanctuary, pointing up its central importance in the life of the redeemed nation". This reminds us that the Lord's supper, of which He said, "this do in remembrance of me" (Luke 22: 19), is central to the life of every assembly.

- **The description of the area:** "And by the border of Judah, from the east side unto the west side, shall be *the offering* which ye shall offer ..." The word "offering" here *(terumah)* is normally translated 'heave-offering' in the Authorised Version. It is rendered "oblation" in verses 9-10. The heave-offering was part of the peace-offering when it was offered "for a thanksgiving" (Lev. 7: 11-14, 32-34). In this case, the "oblation" or "heave-offering", the designated part of the land, is offered in "grateful recognition by the restored people of Jehovah's grace to them" (F.Cundick). While, as John B.Taylor observes, "This was the Lord's rightful claim on a part of what was all His land", it was to be given to Him with joyful willingness.

As we noted when dealing with the parallel passage (45: 1-8), we should remember that the land belonged to the Lord. It is called "thy land, O Immanuel" (Isa 8: 8). In the millennium Israel will give to the Lord what rightly belongs to Him in the first place. David recognised the principle in saying, "All things come of thee, and of thine own have we given thee ... all this store that we have prepared to build thee an house for thine holy name cometh of thine hand, and is all thine own" (1 Chron. 29: 14, 16). In New Testament language, "Upon the first day of the week let every one of you lay by him in store, as God hath prospered him ..." (1 Cor. 16: 2).

Having been given the overall size of this central area, Ezekiel is given details of *(i)* the area allocated to the priests (vv.9-12); *(ii)* the area allocated to the Levites (vv.13-14); *(iii)* the area allocated to the city with its "suburbs" (vv.15-17); *(iv)* the area allocated for food-production (vv.18-19).

Putting all four areas together, we have a total area of 25,000 'reeds' (or 'cubits', if this is preferred) in length (east-west), and 25,000 'reeds'/'cubits' in breadth (north-south). See v.20). As we said when studying the parallel passage (45:1-8) - another square!

But we haven't quite finished. Having given details of the central "square" (called "the holy oblation"), Ezekiel takes us either side of the square "holy oblation" and shows us the area "for the prince" (vv.21, 22). We must now look at these five areas in a little more detail.

i) *The area allocated to the priests, vv.9-12*

"The oblation that ye shall offer unto the LORD shall be of five and twenty thousand in length, (that is, east – west. Notice, again, no unit of measurement is specified), and of ten thousand in breadth, (this is north – south: see plan below). And for them, even for **the priests**, shall be this holy oblation; toward the north five and twenty thousand in length, and toward the west ten thousand in breadth, and toward the east ten thousand in breadth, and toward the south five and twenty thousand in length" (vv.9-10).

As we said before, with the complications arising from the unit of measurement, we must not forget the overall lesson: "And for them, even for the priests, shall be this **holy oblation**". To repeat ourselves yet again, we said in connection with the parallel passage that while we are not likely to get the answer to the 'reed'/ 'cubit' problem until we see the site ourselves in the millennium, 'holiness unto the Lord' is a daily requirement **now!** This is stressed again in verse 12, "And this oblation of the land that is offered shall be unto them a thing **most holy** by the border of the Levites".

While the parallel passage in Chapter 45 gives details in connection with the temple complex and its surrounding "suburbs" (or 'open space', RV margin), together with details of the living accommodation of the priests (vv.2-4), all we are told here is that "the sanctuary of the LORD shall be in the midst thereof" (v.10). But that is quite enough! It reminds that the house of God today - the local assembly (see 1 Tim. 3: 15) - should lie at the centre of our time and interest.

But there is an additional piece of information here: "It shall be for the priests that are sanctified of the sons of Zadok, which have kept my charge, which went not astray when the children of Israel went astray, as the Levites went astray" (v.11). In passing, Solomon dismissed Abiathar (descended from Ithamar through Eli) and gave the high priesthood to Zadok (descended from Eleazar), "that he might fulfil the word of the LORD, which he spake concerning the house of Eli in Shiloh". See 1 Kings 2 verses 26-27, 35.

C.L.Feinberg draws attention to the fact that verse 11 repeats the distinction made in Chapter 44 verses 9-16, and continues by saying, "how God delights to dwell at length on the fidelity and faithfulness of His servants. Evidently Levites were more involved in apostasy and idolatry than the priests, which is confirmed by the fact that at the time of the return from Babylonian exile there were less than four hundred Levites and an equal number of Nethinim who returned (see Ezra 2: 40-58; Neh. 7: 43-60). At the same time there were 4,289 priests".

ii) The area allocated to the Levites, vv.13-14

However, the Lord will be gracious to the Levites, and their portion of the land will be located to the north of the area given to the priests. In fact, it will be exactly the same size as the priests' portion, although the priests' portion will be smaller in living space since it will include the temple area. "And over against the border of the priests the Levites shall have five and twenty thousand in length, and ten thousand of breadth: all the length shall be five and twenty thousand, and the breadth ten thousand" (v.13).

Unlike the parallel passage, no mention is made here of the possession of twenty chambers (or 'a possession, for their habitations', JND)". See Chapter 45 verse 5.

But there is an additional piece of information. It takes the form of an instruction: "they shall not sell of it, neither exchange, not alienate the firstfruits of the land: for it is holy unto the LORD" (v.14). Commentators say that this refers to both priests and Levites, but the prohibition on trading the land and its produce is significant. They were not allowed to do this, because it wasn't theirs in the first place! It belonged to the Lord! We too have a rich spiritual inheritance, and it is incumbent upon us all to "Buy the truth, and sell it not; also wisdom, and instruction, and understanding" (Prov. 23: 23). Esau sold his birthright "for one morsel of meat", and bitterly regretted it (Heb. 12: 16-17). Christians sometimes trade their enjoyment of their rich inheritance for the pleasures of this passing world. Divine truth is not ours to compromise or deny. We must not 'play fast and loose' with the Word of God.

Thus far we have a rectangle of 25,000 'units' ('reeds'/'cubits') east to west by 20,000 'units' (ditto) north to south, (detailing the equal areas allocated to the priests and Levites respectively), to the south of which lies the temple complex (45:1-4), and a further rectangle of 25,000 units east to west and 5,000 units north to south. This brings us to:

iii) The area allocated to the city, vv.15-17

To summarise thus far, since the whole of the 'Holy Portion' will be 25,000 'units' ('cubits'/'reeds') square, within which the sections allocated to the priests and Levites will total 25,000 'units' long (east to west) and 20,000 'units' broad (north to south), "this leaves a tract of land 25,000 'units' long and 5,000 'units' broad in which the millennial city of Jerusalem will be built, including dwelling places for its inhabitants and some open country" (Malcolm Davis). So we read, "And the five thousand (unspecified units) that are left in the breadth over against the five and twenty thousand (ditto), shall be a profane place for the city, for dwelling and for suburbs: and the city shall be in the midst thereof" (v.15).

Of the 25,000 units long (east to west), the city area of 4,500 units square (v.16) will be surrounded by suburbs on all sides measuring 250 units, so the whole area becomes 4,750 units square (vv.16-17), which seems to leave a further 250 units on all four sides of the city for which we are not given details. As noted above, Malcolm Davis calls this "open country", and who among us can dispute his conclusion?! Whether these "suburbs" are those described in Chapter 45 verse 2 is not easily ascertained. According to Young's *Concordance*, the word *migrash* means 'a place for driving cattle'.

But will the city be a second-rate place? After all, it is described as a "profane place" (v.15). This will not be the case at all. The word "profane" here simply means that it will not have the sanctity of the temple, frequented only by the priests. The city will in fact be called *Jehovah-shammah*, "The LORD is there" (48: 35). As we have said before, it will not be a case of a holy temple and a 'grotty' city! "In that day shall there be upon the bells of the horses, HOLINESS UNTO THE LORD; and the pots in the **LORD'S house** shall be like the bowls before the altar Yea, every pot *in Jerusalem* and in Judah shall be **holiness unto the LORD of hosts"** (Zech. 14: 20-21).

But is that all? If so what about the balance of the 25,000 units on the southern periphery? Thus far, we have only accounted for 5,000 units. The answer follows:

iv) The area allocated for food-production, vv.18-19

Two areas of land each measuring 10,000 units long (east-west) and 5,000 units broad (north-south), will lie either side of the city with its suburbs. "And the residue in length over against the oblation of the holy portion shall be ten thousand eastward, and ten thousand westward ... and the increase thereof shall be for food unto them that serve the city. And they that serve the city shall serve it out of all the tribes of Israel". F.A.Tatford comments on this as follows: "This space was to be cultivated by the city workers and was to provide food for the workers. Since the city belonged to the whole nation, its inhabitants included members from all the tribes of Israel, and they had, therefore, to work for the common good".

Putting all four areas together, we have a total area of 25,000 'units' ('reeds'/'cubits') east-west and 25,000 'units' north-south. See, again, Chapter 48 verse 20. The universal temple (it will be 100 cubits long and 100 cubits wide, 41: 13-14) with its universal altar (it will be "twelve cubits long, twelve broad, square in the four squares thereof", 43: 16-17), will be associated with a universal city (each side, including suburbs) measuring 4,750 units (48: 16-17) in a universal setting (48: 20). "And it shall come to pass in the last days, that the mountain of the **LORD'S house** shall be established in the top of the mountains, and shall be exalted above the hills; and all nations shall flow unto it. And many people shall go and say, Come ye, and let us go up to the mountain of the LORD, to *the house* of the God of Jacob; and he will teach us of his ways, and we will walk in his paths: for out of **Zion** shall go forth the law, and the word of the LORD from **Jerusalem**" (Isa 2: 2-3).

But we still haven't finished! The section ends by giving details of the land assigned to "the prince":

v) *The area allocated to the prince, vv.21-22*

"And the residue shall be for the prince (*nasi*), on the one side and on the other of the holy oblation, and of the possession of the city, over against the five and twenty thousand (unspecified) of the oblation toward the east border, and westward over against the five and twenty thousand (unspecified) toward the west border" (v.21) The balance of these two verses is not easily understood. However, Merril F.Unger (*Commentary on the Old Testament*) sums it up as follows: "the prince's portion ... will consist of the area remaining on both sides of the sacred area, westward toward the Mediterranean and eastward toward the Dead Sea, between the border of Judah on the north and Benjamin on the south", adding that the "allotment will be arranged so that the property of the Levites as well as that of the city will be situated in the centre of the area belonging to the prince". That is, we presume, between the western and eastern parts of his portion.

As we said in connection with the details given in Chapter 45 verses 1-8, it is very clear that "the prince" is a most important person, and while he is not called a 'king' in these chapters, we cannot but wonder if he is not 'Christ's vice-regent on earth' of whom it is said "And David my servant shall be king over them" (Ezek. 37: 24); "And I will set up one shepherd over them, and he shall feed them, even my servant David; he shall feed them, and he shall be their shepherd. And I the LORD will be their God, and my servant David a prince (*nasi*) among them" (Ezek. 34: 23-24). This brings to:

E) *Israel's southern sub-divisions, 48: 23-29*

This is perfectly straight forward. The five remaining tribes are, north to south, Benjamin, Simon, Issachar, Zebulun, and Gad. The southern boundary, given in Chapter 47 verse 19, is repeated in verse 28, "the border shall be even from Tamar unto the waters of strife in Kadesh (Meribah-Kadesh', JND), and to the river toward the great sea". The "river" (or 'brook', F.A.Tatford) in question is the Wadi el Arish. As already noted, the entire nation will be united west of the Jordan.

It does seem sad that the last geographical reference in Ezekiel recalls "strife". This took place in Exodus 17 verses 1-7 and in Numbers 20 verses 2-13. On the first occasion, Moses "called the name of the place Massah and Meribah, because of the chiding of the children of Israel, and because they tempted the LORD, saying, Is the LORD among us, or not?" (Exodus 17: 7), and on the second occasion it was said, "This is the water of Meribah; because the children of Israel strove with the LORD, and he was sanctified in them".

The section ends with a summary: "This is the land which ye shall divide by lot unto the tribes of Israel for inheritance, and these are their portions, saith the Lord GOD" (v.29). The division of the land "by lot" follows the practice used in the original division of the land: see Joshua 13 verse 6. However, we must not think of division by lot as some kind of 'lucky dip!' Solomon would be appalled at the suggestion, and direct us to his words on the subject, "The lot is cast into the lap; but the whole disposing thereof is of the LORD" (Prov.16: 33).

CHAPTER 48

F) Israel's millennial city, 48: 30-35

In the words of M.F.Unger, "In the Kingdom age the resplendent city of Jerusalem will be the capital of the earth and its religious and governmental centre". The city will have twelve gates named after the twelve tribes: three gates on the north - Reuben, Judah, and Levi; three on the east - Joseph, Benjamin, and Dan; three on the south – Simeon, Issachar, and Zebulun; three on the west – Gad, Asher, and Naphtali (vv.30-34).

M.F.Unger continues: "At last the nation, so long divided and scattered, will be united in blessed harmony and in fellowship with the Lord. Ancient rivalries and jealousies will have vanished, and harmonious unity will prevail. The dimensions of the city are given, but the unit (commonly taken as the cubit) is not specified. If the cubit is assumed, the city's circumference will be somewhat less than six miles, compared to the Jerusalem of Josephus' day, which was about four miles (*Antiquities. 5. 4.3*). The prophet evidently glimpsed 'a city that is compact together; to which the tribes go up' (Psalm 122: 3-4, NASB), the common centre of the whole nation and the religious and governmental mecca of the earth".

The 'new Jerusalem', in the new earth, will also have twelve gates "and at the gates twelve angels, and names written thereon, which are the names of the twelve tribes of the children of Israel" (Rev. 21: 12).

The book ends on a magnificent note: "and the name of the city from that day shall be, the LORD is there", translating *Jehovah-shammah*. The book therefore commences and concludes with the glory of the Lord. Ezekiel watched its departure "from off the threshold of the house" (10: 18) and from the city (11: 22-23), and saw its return to the house (43: 1-5) and to the city (48: 35). As M.C.Unger observes, "The manifested presence of God, revealed in Christ's redemptive work, will enable the infinitely holy God to restore and dwell amongst His people, who had so grievously sinned that His manifested presence had to be withdrawn from them, and He had to order the destruction of His temple and city. To keep His promises of grace, He will return to the restored temple and reunited people in such blessing that the shout of the millennial earth will be: 'Great is the LORD, and greatly to be praised in the city of our God, in the mountain of his holiness. Beautiful for situation is Mount Zion .... the city of the great King' (Psalm 48: 1-2). 'The LORD is there!'".

When the Lord Jesus was here, some two thousand years ago, "it was noised that he was in the house" (Mark 2: 1). This will certainly be the case in millennial Jerusalem, and it ought to be true in the case of every assembly today. On another occasion the Lord Jesus "entered into an house ... but he could not be hid" (Mark 7: 24), What better testimony could any assembly have than that?

Amongst other things, Paul earnestly desired that people visiting the assembly at Corinth, having seen its godly order, would be led to "worship God, and report that God is in you of a truth" (1 Cor. 14: 25) or, in Ezekiel's language, be able to say "The LORD is there".

EZEKIEL

EZEKIEL

EZEKIEL

EZEKIEL